PLURALITY AND DIVERSITY IN LAW

Ius Comparatum – Global Studies in Comparative Law

Founding Editors

Jürgen Basedow, Max Planck Institute for Comparative and International Private Law, Hamburg, Germany

George A. Bermann, Columbia University, New York, USA

Former Series Editors

Katharina Boele-Woelki, Bucerius Law School, Hamburg, Germany

Diego P. Fernández Arroyo, Institut d'Études Politiques de Paris (Sciences Po), Paris, France

Series Editors

Giuditta Cordero-Moss, University of Oslo, Oslo, Norway

Gary Bell, National University of Singapore, Singapore

Series Assistant Editor

Alexandre Senegacnik, IACL, Paris, France

Editorial Board Members

Ewa Baginska, Gdansk University, Gdansk, Poland

Vivian Curran, University of Pittsburgh, Pittsburgh, PA, USA

Nicolás Etcheverry, Universidad de Montevideo, Montevideo, Uruguay

Makane Moise Mbengue, Université de Genève, Geneva, Switzerland

Marilda Rosado de S. Ribeiro, Universidade do Estado do Rio de Janeiro, Rio de Janeiro, Brazil

Marilyne Sadowsky, Université Paris 1 Panthéon-Sorbonne, Paris, France

Dan Wei, University of Macau, Macau, China

PLURALITY AND DIVERSITY IN LAW

Family Forms and Family's Functions

Edited by
Jacqueline Heaton
Aida Kemelmajer

Cambridge – Antwerp – Chicago

Intersentia Ltd
8 Wellington Mews
Wellington Street | Cambridge
CB1 1HW | United Kingdom
Tel: +44 1223 736 170
Email: mail@intersentia.co.uk
www.intersentia.com | www.intersentia.co.uk

Distribution for the UK and
Rest of the World (incl. Eastern Europe)
NBN International
1 Deltic Avenue, Rooksley
Milton Keynes MK13 8LD
United Kingdom
Tel: +44 1752 202 301 | Fax: +44 1752 202 331
Email: orders@nbninternational.com

Distribution for Europe
Lefebvre Sarrut Belgium NV
Hoogstraat 139/6
1000 Brussels
Belgium
Tel: +32 (0)2 548 07 13
Email: mail@intersentia.be

Distribution for the USA and Canada
Independent Publishers Group
Order Department
814 North Franklin Street
Chicago, IL 60610
USA
Tel: +1 800 888 4741 (toll free) | Fax: +1 312 337 5985
Email: orders@ipgbook.com

Plurality and Diversity in Law. Family Forms and Family's Functions
© The editors and contributors severally 2023

The editors and contributors have asserted the right under the Copyright, Designs and Patents Act 1988, to be identified as authors of this work.

No part of this book may be reproduced, stored in a retrieval system, or transmitted, in any form, or by any means, without prior written permission from Intersentia, or as expressly permitted by law or under the terms agreed with the appropriate reprographic rights organisation. Enquiries concerning reproduction which may not be covered by the above should be addressed to Intersentia at the address above.

Artwork on cover: pluie_r / Shutterstock

ISBN 978-1-83970-305-8
ISSN 2214-6881
D/2023/7849/6
NUR 822

British Library Cataloguing in Publication Data. A catalogue record for this book is available from the British Library.

PREFACE

Legal rules play an important role in recognising, protecting, and supporting the family. As the notion of a 'family' is constantly changing, the law sometimes lags behind and fails to afford recognition, protection, or support to the diverse forms of the family present in society. So too, the law sometimes fails to afford proper recognition to the diverse functions a family fulfils. The rise in step-families, parenthood outside marriage and the use of assisted reproduction, including surrogacy, has re-shaped the notion of 'family' and the issue of how many parents a child can legally have. The functions of the family have, likewise, changed inter alia as a result of women's increased participation in paid labour, greater emphasis on personal responsibility for one's own financial welfare, and the movement away from the welfare state in some jurisdictions. In this book, we seek to ascertain whether, and if so how, family law recognises multiple parents in the various family forms that occur in modern society. We also investigate which functions of the family the law recognises and whether the presence of children changes the recognition that is afforded to these functions.

The subject matter of the book coincides with one of the main topics of the Fourth Thematic Congress of the International Academy of Comparative Law which was held in Pretoria, South Africa from 6 to 8 October 2021. The title of that congress was 'Plurality and Diversity in the Law' and the session on family law was titled 'Diversity and Plurality in the Law: Family Forms and Family's Functions'. The book consists of special national reports and a general report on the family law topic.

Twenty special national reports were received. Two of the reports (Estonia and Portugal) were not revised for publication in this book, and appear online only. The remainder of the reports are published in this book as well as online. Fourteen of the published reports are in English. They concern jurisdictions from Africa (South Africa), Asia (Japan and Vietnam), Europe (Austria, Croatia, Denmark, Germany, Greece, Poland, and the Netherlands), Oceania (Australia), South America (Argentina), the Middle East (Turkey), and the United Kingdom (England and Wales). Four reports are in French. Three of them pertain to jurisdictions in Europe (Belgium, Italy, and Luxembourg) and one pertains to North America (Quebec, Canada). The general report (in English and in French) discusses and draws conclusions from the research presented in the special national reports.

The special national reports are based on answers to a questionnaire which was prepared by the general rapporteurs, who are also the editors of this book.

The questionnaire (in English and in French) is an Appendix to this book. The first objective of the questionnaire was to determine whether, and if so how, family law in the jurisdictions surveyed recognises that a child can have multiple parents in the case of step-families where children from one or both spouses/partners are raised in the same household; families where children are raised in more than one household, for example because their parents jointly exercise custody after separation or have never shared a household but share parenting responsibilities; polygamous families where children are raised in a household where one party has more than one spouse/partner; families where children have been adopted but maintain links (legal or de facto) with their biological families; families where children are cared for in terms of a *kafala* arrangement; families where a child was born as a result of donor-assisted reproductive technology using one male and one female gamete; families where a child was born as a result of 'three-parent' medical technology; and families where a child was born as a result of surrogacy. The second objective of the questionnaire was to determine whether the law recognises multiple functions of the family, which functions the law favours, and whether the presence of children in the family makes a difference in regard to the functions that are protected and favoured by the law.

We wish to express our sincere gratitude to the special rapporteurs for their insightful reports and their commitment to this book project. Thanks also go to the President of the International Academy of Comparative Law, Professor Katharina Boele-Woelki, the Secretary-General, Professor Diego Fernández Arroyo, and the Deputy Secretary-General, Doctor Alexandre Senegacnik for their enthusiasm for the family law topic. We also thank the editorial staff at Intersentia for their skill and tireless work. Special thanks go to Mr Ahmed Hegazi, who is the publisher at Intersentia, Ms Ella Brice-Jeffreys, who is overseeing the publication of this book and Ms Rebecca Bryan, who is the copy editor of the book.

Jacqueline Heaton and Aida Kemelmajer
Pretoria, South Africa and Mendoza, Argentina
November 2022

PRÉFACE

Les règles juridiques jouent un rôle important dans la reconnaissance, la protection et le soutien de la famille. Comme la notion de « famille » est en constante évolution, la loi est parfois à la traîne et ne permet pas de reconnaître, de protéger et de soutenir les diverses formes de famille présentes dans la société. De même, quelquefois la loi ne reconnaît pas correctement les diverses fonctions qu'une famille remplit. L'accroissement du nombre de familles recomposées, la parentalité en dehors du mariage et le recours à la procréation assistée, y compris la gestation pour autrui, ont remodelé la notion de « famille » et la question du nombre de parents qu'un enfant peut légalement avoir. De même, les fonctions de la famille ont changé, entre autres, en raison de la participation généralisée des femmes au travail rémunéré, de l'importance accrue accordée à la responsabilité personnelle de leur propre bien-être financier et de l'éloignement de l'État-providence dans certaines juridictions. Dans ce livre, nous cherchons à déterminer si, et si oui, comment le droit de la famille reconnaît la multiplicité des parents sous diverses formes familiales qui se manifestent dans la société moderne. Nous analysons également quelles sont les fonctions de la famille que la loi reconnaît et si la présence d'enfants change la reconnaissance accordée à ces fonctions.

Le sujet du livre coïncide avec l'un des principaux thèmes du Quatrième Congrès Thématique de l'Académie Internationale de Droit Comparé qui s'est tenu à Pretoria, en Afrique du Sud, du 6 au 8 octobre 2021. Le titre de ce congrès était « Pluralité et diversité en droit » et la session sur le droit de la famille s'intitulait « Diversité et pluralité dans le droit : formes familiales et fonctions de la famille ». Le livre se compose de rapports nationaux spéciaux et du rapport général sur le sujet du droit de la famille.

Vingt rapports nationaux spéciaux ont été reçus. Deux des rapports (Estonie et Portugal) n'ont pas été révisés pour la publication dans ce livre et ne sont disponibles qu'en ligne. Le reste des rapports est publié dans ce livre ainsi qu'en ligne. Quatorze des rapports publiés sont en anglais. Elles concernent des juridictions d'Afrique (Afrique du Sud), d'Asie (Japon et Vietnam), d'Europe (Autriche, Croatie, Danemark, Allemagne, Grèce, Pologne et Pays-Bas), d'Océanie (Australie), d'Amérique du Sud (Argentine), du Moyen-Orient (Turquie) et du Royaume-Uni (Angleterre et Pays de Galles). Quatre rapports sont en français. Trois d'entre eux concernent des juridictions en Europe (Belgique, Italie et Luxembourg) et une concerne l'Amérique du Nord (Québec, Canada). Le rapport général (en anglais et en français) examine et tire des conclusions des recherches présentées dans les rapports nationaux spéciaux.

Les rapports nationaux spéciaux ont été construits sur les réponses à un questionnaire qui a été préparé par les rapporteurs généraux, qui sont également les éditeurs de ce livre. Le questionnaire (en anglais et en français) est une annexe de ce livre.

Le premier objectif du questionnaire était de déterminer si, et dans l'affirmative, comment, le droit de la famille dans les juridictions étudiées reconnaît qu'un enfant peut avoir plusieurs parents dans le cas de familles recomposées où les enfants d'un ou des deux conjoints/partenaires sont élevés dans le même ménage; les familles où les enfants sont élevés dans plus d'un ménage, par exemple, parce que leurs parents exercent conjointement la garde après la séparation ou n'ont jamais partagé un ménage mais partagent les responsabilités parentales; les familles polygames où les enfants sont élevés dans un ménage où l'une des parties a plus d'un conjoint/partenaire; les familles dont les enfants ont été adoptés mais entretiennent des liens (légaux ou de facto) avec leur famille biologique; les familles où les enfants sont pris en charge dans le cadre d'un arrangement de *kafala* ; les familles où un enfant est né à la suite d'une technologie de procréation assistée par donneur utilisant un gamète mâle et un gamète femelle; les familles où un enfant est né à la suite d'une technologie médicale dite « à trois parents »; et les familles où un enfant est né à la suite d'une gestation pour autrui.

Le deuxième objectif du questionnaire était de déterminer si la loi reconnaît des fonctions multiples de la famille, quelles sont les fonctions que la loi favorise, et si la présence d'enfants dans la famille fait une différence en ce qui concerne la fonction qui est protégée et favorisée par la loi.

Nous tenons à exprimer notre sincère gratitude aux rapporteurs spéciaux pour leurs rapports éclairants et pour leur engagement dans le projet de publication de ce livre. Merci également à la Présidente de l'Académie internationale de Droit Comparé, la professeure Katharina Boele-Woelki, au Secrétaire général, le Professeur Diego Fernández Arroyo, et au Secrétaire général adjoint Alexandre Senegacnik pour leur enthousiasme pour le droit de la famille. Nous remercions également la rédaction d'Intersentia pour sa compétence et son travail infatigable. Nous remercions tout particulièrement l'éditeur de Intersentia, M. Ahmed Hegazi, Mme Ella Brice-Jeffreys, qui supervise la publication de ce livre et Mme Rebecca Bryan, qui est la rédactrice en chef du livre.

Jacqueline Heaton et Aida Kemelmajer
Pretoria, South Africa et Mendoza, Argentina
Novembre 2022

CONTENTS

Preface v
Préface vii
List of Rapporteurs... xv

General Report: Family Forms and Family's Functions – A Comparative Perspective
    Jacqueline HEATON and Aida KEMELMAJER 1

1. Introduction 2
2. Part A. Diversity and Plurality of Family Forms 4
3. Part B. Diversity and Plurality of Family's Functions ... 35
4. Conclusion... 41

Rapport General: Formes et fonctions familiales – Une perspective comparative
    Jacqueline HEATON et Aida KEMELMAJER........................... 45

1. Introduction 46
2. Partie A. Diversité et pluralité des formes familiales... 47
3. Partie B. Diversité et pluralité des fonctions de la famille............... 81
4. Conclusion... 87

Argentina
    Graciela MEDINA.. 91

1. Overview of the Legal System............................. 92
2. Step-Family 93
3. Adoption 104
4. Filiation by Assisted Procreation 106
5. Multi-Parenthood 106
6. Parenthood of the Surrogate 108
7. Branches of Law where the Family Receives Special Protection 109
8. Family Functions which are Predominantly Favoured by Argentine Law 111
9. Conclusion.. 112

Australia
Henry KHA 113

1. Introduction 113
2. Step-Parenting in Australia 114
3. The Scope of Legal Parenthood. 116
4. Trends in Australian Adoption Law 119
5. Family Formation and Assisted Reproductive Technology 122
6. The Privatisation of Australian Family Law 126
7. The Normative Model of Family. 129
8. The Function of Family in a Eudemonistic Liberal Society 130
9. Conclusion. 132

Austria
Elmar BUCHSTÄTTER and Marianne ROTH 135

1. Introduction 136
2. The Concept of Family. 136
3. Diversity and Plurality of Family Forms 140
4. Conclusion. 159

Belgique
Nicole GALLUS, Yves-Henri LELEU, Géraldine MATHIEU
et Frederik SWENNEN. 161

1. Diversité et pluralité des formes familiales 161
2. Diversité et pluralité des fonctions de la famille. 172

Canada
Michelle GIROUX et Louise LANGEVIN 189

1. Le traitement des différentes formes familiales 191
2. L'établissement de la parenté dans le contexte de la procréation assistée
   et de la maternité de substitution 200
3. Conclusion 208

Croatia
Branka REŠETAR and Nataša LUCIĆ 211

1. Introduction 211
2. Part A. Diversity and Plurality of Family Forms 212
3. Part B. Diversity and Plurality of Family's Functions 221
4. Conclusion. 225

Denmark
Ingrid LUND-ANDERSEN and Frank H. PEDERSEN 227

1. Introduction 227
2. Step-Parents 228
3. Parentage of a Child Born as a Result of Donated Gametes 235
4. Parentage of a Child Born through Surrogacy 238
5. Various Functions of the Family 242
6. Closing Considerations 248

England and Wales
Claire FENTON-GLYNN and Jens M. SCHERPE 251

1. Introduction 252
2. Legal Parenthood in England and Wales: There can Only be Two 252
3. Parental Responsibility in England and Wales: Accommodating Multiple Parental Relationships and 'Non-Traditional' Families? 259
4. Recognising Adult Relationships and Family Functions 261
5. Conclusion 267

Germany
Anne SANDERS 269

1. Introduction 269
2. Family Functions in Germany 271
3. Diversity and Plurality of Family Forms 275
4. Conclusions 288

Greece
Eleni ZERVOGIANNI 291

1. Introduction: General Remarks on the Notion of Family in Greek Law 291
2. Diversity and Plurality of Family Forms 294
3. Diversity and Plurality of Family's Functions 309
4. Conclusions 315

Italie
Roberta ALUFFI 317

1. Diversité et pluralité des formes familiales 317
2. Diversité et pluralité des fonctions de la famille 339

Japan
Maia ROOTS 343

1. Introduction 344
2. Part A. Diversity and Plurality of Family Forms 344
3. Part B. Diversity and Plurality of Family Functions. 366

Luxembourg
Françoise HILGER 371

1. Multiplicité de la parentalité 371
2. Diversité et pluralité des fonctions de la famille...................... 374

Poland
Błażej BUGAJSKI and Anna WYSOCKA-BAR. 377

1. Introduction 377
2. Legal Responsibilities and Rights of a Step-Parent 378
3. Parenthood and the Use of Assisted Reproductive Technology 387
4. Diversity and Plurality of Family Functions 392
5. Conclusion... 394

South Africa
Anne LOUW 395

1. Introduction 395
2. Part A. Diversity and Plurality of Family Forms 396
3. Part B. Diversity and Plurality of Family's Functions 413

The Netherlands
Wendy SCHRAMA 417

1. Introduction 417
2. Part A. Diversity and Plurality of Family Forms 418
3. Part B. Diversity and Plurality of Family's Functions 430
4. Conclusion... 433

Turkey
Meliha Sermin PAKSOY 435

1. Introduction 435
2. Multiplicity of Parenthood in the Context of Step-Families............. 436
3. Multiplicity of Parenthood if a Child is Raised in More than
   One Household... 440

4.	Prohibition of Polygamy and De Facto Polygamous Families	441
5.	Multiplicity of Parenthood in the Case of an Open Adoption	442
6.	Multiplicity of Parenthood in the Case of Foster Families	444
7.	'Parenthood of the Birth Mother' Rule and Donor-Assisted Reproductive Technologies	445
8.	Parenthood in a Same-Sex Relationship	446
9.	Family's Functions	447
10.	Conclusion	450

Vietnam
Thi Anh VAN NGO 451

1.	Introduction	452
2.	Diversity and Plurality of Family Forms	452
3.	Diversity and Plurality of Family's Functions	466

Appendix: Questionnaire 471
Index 481

LIST OF RAPPORTEURS

Roberta Aluffi
Associate Professor of Comparative Law, Università degli Studi di Torino, Italy

Elmar Buchstätter
University Assistant at the Department of Private Law, Paris Lodron University Salzburg, Austria

Błażej Bugajski
Senior Lecturer, Cracow University of Economics, Poland

Claire Fenton-Glynn
Professor of Child and Family Law, University of Cambridge, England

Nicole Gallus
Professeure, Université Libre de Bruxelles et avocate, Belgique

Michelle Giroux
Professeure titulaire, Faculté de droit, Université d'Ottawa, Ottawa, Canada

Jacqueline Heaton
Professor, University of South Africa

Françoise Hilger
Chargée de cours, Université du Luxembourg

Aida Kemelmajer
Professor, University of Cuyo, Argentina

Henry Kha
Senior Lecturer, Macquarie Law School, Macquarie University, Australia

Louise Langevin
Professeure titulaire, Faculté de droit, Université Laval, Québec, Canada

Yves-Henri Leleu
Professeur ordinaire et Doyen de la Faculté de Droit, Université de Liège, Belgique, et avocat

Anne Louw
Associate Professor, University of Pretoria, South Africa

Nataša Lucić
Associate Professor, Faculty of Law, J.J. Strossmayer University of Osijek, Croatia

Ingrid Lund-Andersen
Professor, University of Copenhagen, Denmark

Géraldine Mathieu
Professeure, Faculté de droit, Université de Namur, Belgique

Graciela Medina
Professor, University of Buenos Aires, Argentina

Meliha Sermin Paksoy
Assistant Professor, Altinbas University Faculty of Law, Turkey

Frank Høgholm Pedersen
Associate Professor, University of Copenhagen, Denmark

Branka Rešetar
Full Professor, Faculty of Law, J.J. Strossmayer University of Osijek, Croatia

Maia Roots
Associate Professor, Tohoku University Graduate School of Law, Japan

Marianne Roth
Professor of Civil Law, Civil Procedure and Comparative Law, Paris Lodron University Salzburg, Austria

Anne Sanders
Professor, University of Bielefeld, Germany; Professor II University of Bergen, Norway

Jens M. Scherpe
Professor of Comparative Law, Aalborg University, Denmark; Director, Nordic Centre for Comparative and International Family Law; Emeritus Fellow, Gonville and Caius College, University of Cambridge, England

Wendy Schrama
Professor of Family Law and Comparative Law, Utrecht University, the Netherlands; Director of the Utrecht Centre for European Research into Family Law, the Netherlands

Frederik Swennen
Professeur ordinaire et Doyen de la Faculté de Droit, Université d'Anvers, Belgique, et avocat

Thi Anh Van Ngo
Lecturer, Ho Chi Minh City University of Law, Vietnam

Anna Wysocka-Bar
Senior Lecturer, Jagiellonian University, Cracow, Poland

Eleni Zervogianni
Associate Professor of Civil Law, Aristotle University of Thessaloniki, Greece

GENERAL REPORT

Family Forms and Family's Functions – A Comparative Perspective

Jacqueline HEATON and Aida KEMELMAJER

1. Introduction 2
2. Part A. Diversity and Plurality of Family Forms 4
   2.1. Recognition of Multiple Parents in the Context
        of Step-Families 4
   2.2. Recognition of Multiple Parents if a Child is Raised in
        More than One Household 12
   2.3. Recognition of Multiple Parents if a Child is Raised in
        a Polygamous Family 15
   2.4. Recognition of Multiple Parents in the Case of Open
        Adoption 17
   2.5. Recognition of Multiple Parents in the Case of *Kafala* 21
   2.6. Recognition of Multiple Parents in the Case of Donor-Assisted
        Reproduction (Without Surrogacy). 22
   2.7. Recognition of Multiple Parents in the Case of a
        'Three-Parent Child'. 28
   2.8. Recognition of Multiple Parents in the Case of Surrogacy. 29
   2.9. General Recognition of Multi-Parenthood 34
3. Part B. Diversity and Plurality of Family's Functions 35
   3.1. Legal Recognition of Various Functions of the Family 35
   3.2. The Functions which are Predominantly Favoured. 39
   3.3. The Role of Children in the Legal View on the Functions
        of the Family 40
4. Conclusion. 41

Abstract

This report discusses and draws conclusions from the findings presented in the special national reports on the theme 'Diversity and Plurality in the Law: Family

Forms and Family's Functions'. Two main issues are investigated. The first is whether, and if so, how, family law in the jurisdictions surveyed recognises that a child can have multiple parents. The focus falls on step-families where children from one or both spouses/partners are raised in the same household; families where children are raised in more than one household, for example because their parents jointly exercise custody after separation or have never shared a household but share parenting responsibilities; polygamous families where children are raised in a household where one party has more than one wife/husband/partner; families where children have been adopted but maintain links (legal or de facto) with their biological families; families where children are cared for in terms of a *kafala* arrangement; families where a child was born as a result of donor-assisted reproductive technology using one male and one female gamete; families where a child was born as a result of 'three-parent' medical technology; and families where a child was born as a result of surrogacy. The second main issue that is investigated in the report is which family functions are recognised and favoured by the law, and whether the presence of children in the family makes a difference in this regard.

1. INTRODUCTION

This report gives an overview of the findings from the special national reports on the theme 'Diversity and Plurality in the Law: Family Forms and Family's Functions'. The findings are based on the answers to a questionnaire relating to this topic. The full text of the questionnaire, in English and French, is appended to this general report.

The questionnaire had two main objectives. The first was to determine whether, and if so, how, family law in the jurisdictions surveyed recognises that a child can have multiple parents. For the sake of comparability, multiple-parent families were limited to:

- step-families where children from one or both spouses/partners are raised in the same household;
- families where children are raised in more than one household, for example because their parents are jointly exercising custody/care after separation or have never shared a household but share parenting responsibilities;
- polygamous families where children are raised in a household where one party has more than one wife/husband/partner;
- open-adoption families, that is families where children have been adopted but maintain links (legal or de facto) with their biological families;

- families where children have not been adopted but live in a household in terms of a *kafala* arrangement;[1]
- families where a child was born as a result of donor-assisted reproductive technology using one male and one female gamete (i.e. sperm and an egg/ovum);
- families where a child was born as a result of so-called 'three-parent' medical technology;[2]
- families where a child was born as a result of surrogacy.

The second main objective of the questionnaire was to determine which functions of the family the law recognises and favours, and whether the presence of children in the family makes a difference in this regard.

As multicultural challenges in family law were the focus of the 20th Congress of the International Academy, which took place in Fukuoka, Japan in 2018, the questionnaire did not consider the multiplicity/plurality of civil, cultural, indigenous and religious unions. Furthermore, the special rapporteurs were specifically instructed not to elaborate on private international law and medical law, and on cultural, indigenous and religious rights and legal pluralism.

Twenty special national reports were submitted – 16 in English[3] and four in French.[4] Below we highlight some of the points from the reports.

---

[1] See the Appendix for an explanation of *kafala*.
[2] See the Appendix for an explanation of 'three-parent' technology.
[3] Argentina: Prof. Graciela Medina, University of Buenos Aires; Australia: Dr Henry Kha, Macquarie University; Austria: Mr Elmar Buchstätter and Prof. Marianne Roth, Paris Lodron University Salzburg; Croatia: Profs Branka Rešetar and Nataša Lucić, J.J. Strossmayer University of Osijek; Denmark: Prof. Ingrid Lund-Andersen and Associate Prof. Frank Høgholm Pedersen, University of Copenhagen; England and Wales: Prof. Claire Fenton-Glynn, University of Cambridge and Prof. Jens M. Scherpe, Aalborg University; Estonia: Prof. Irene Kull and Dr Maarja Torga, University of Tartu (Online Report, i.e. answers to questionnaire, dated 10.04.2020); Germany: Prof. Anne Sanders, University of Bielefeld; Greece: Associate Prof. Eleni Zervogianni, Aristotle University of Thessaloniki; Japan: Prof. Maia Roots, Tohoku University; Poland: Dr Błażej Bugajski, Cracow University of Economics and Dr Anna Wysocka-Bar, Jagiellonian University in Cracow; Portugal: Prof. Paula Távora Vítor and Ms Rosa Cândido Martins, University of Coimbra (Online Report, i.e. answers to questionnaire, dated 07.09.2021); South Africa: Prof. Anne Louw, University of Pretoria; the Netherlands: Prof. Wendy Schrama, University of Utrecht; Turkey: Assistant Prof. Meliha Sermin Paksoy, Altinbas University; Vietnam: Ms Thi Anh Van Ngo, Ho Chi Minh City University of Law.
[4] Belgium: Prof. Nicole Gallus, Université Libre de Bruxelles, Prof. Yves-Henri Leleu, Université de Liège, Prof. Géraldine Mathieu, Université de Namur and Prof. Frederik Swennen, Université d'Anvers; Italy: Associate Prof. Roberta Aluffi, University of Turin; Luxembourg: Prof. Françoise Hilger, Université du Luxembourg; Quebec, Canada: Prof. Michelle Giroux, Université d'Ottawa and Prof. Louise Langevin, Université Laval, Québec.

2. PART A. DIVERSITY AND PLURALITY OF FAMILY FORMS

2.1. RECOGNITION OF MULTIPLE PARENTS IN THE CONTEXT OF STEP-FAMILIES

At the outset, it should be mentioned that some jurisdictions, like Argentina,[5] prefer to use the term 'blended families' and 'parents related by marriage', rather than 'step-families' and 'step-parents', because of the negative connotations attached to being a step-parent. For purposes of this report, however, we use the terminology that was used in the questionnaire, that is, 'step-families' and 'step-parents'.

Most of the jurisdictions on which reports were submitted do not recognise that a step-parent is an additional legal parent to a step-child, and the step-parent does not automatically acquire responsibilities and rights in respect of the step-child. A step-parent can, however, become a legal parent of his or her step-child by adopting the step-child. Once an adoption order has been granted, the step-parent has the same legal responsibilities and rights as the parent with whom the step-parent shares a household. In some jurisdictions, such as England and Wales and the Netherlands, step-parent adoption completely terminates the legal relationship between the child and the other parent, that is, the parent with whom the step-parent does not share a household.[6] In these jurisdictions, the law does not recognise multiple parents after the adoption because, after the adoption, the law still recognises only two parents. In other jurisdictions, such as Argentina, Belgium and Italy, step-parent adoption by way of 'simple adoption' does not terminate the child's legal relationship with his or her parents[7] and can therefore be said to result in the child having multiple parents after the adoption.

If a step-parent does not adopt his or her step-child, he or she can acquire responsibilities and rights in respect of the child if the child's legal parent delegates them to him or her, gives him or her a mandate to perform responsibilities and rights, or enters into an agreement conferring responsibilities and rights on the step-parent. Depending on the scope of the responsibilities and rights the step-parent obtains in this way and the source from which they arise, the step-parent can legally become an additional parent to the step-child, with the result that the child has multiple parents. If, for instance, all parental responsibilities and rights are conferred on the step-parent by way of an agreement between the

---

[5] Medina Report.
[6] England and Wales: Fenton-Glynn and Scherpe Report; the Netherlands: Schrama Report.
[7] Argentina: Medina Report; Belgium: Gallus, Leleu, Mathieu and Swennen Report; Italy: Aluffi Report.

step-parent and the child's parent, this means that the step-parent is added as a holder of parental responsibilities and rights and the child has multiple parents. This can occur in, for example, South Africa, as is explained below. If the step-parent acquires very limited responsibilities and rights, it is doubtful whether this qualifies as recognition of multiple parents. Where the step-parent's authority to exercise responsibilities and rights arises from delegation by the child's parent, there is no recognition of multiple parents, as the step-parent is merely fulfilling the parent's responsibilities and rights on behalf of the parent. In South Africa, the child's parent may enter into an agreement with the step-parent conferring any or all parental responsibilities and rights on the step-parent[8] and the parent may authorise the step-parent to exercise parental responsibilities and rights on his or her behalf. However, such authorisation does not divest the parent of his or her responsibilities and rights or absolve him or her from fulfilling his or her responsibilities.[9] In England and Wales, too, the step-parent may obtain parental responsibilities and rights if the child's parent consents to this.[10] In Luxembourg, the child's parent may give the step-parent a mandate regarding the child's day-to-day education.[11] Portuguese law allows a step-parent to exercise responsibilities and rights regarding his or her step-child if he or she is living with the child's parent in a de facto union and the child's parent delegates responsibilities and rights in respect of daily matters to the step-parent.[12] In Argentina, too, a parent may delegate parental responsibilities and rights to the step-parent if the parent is not fully able to exercise the responsibilities and rights because he or she is travelling, is ill or suffers from a temporary inability or it is not possible or convenient for the child's other parent to exercise the responsibilities and rights.[13] Unless both parents consent to the delegation, the court must approve the delegation.[14] As the step-parent's power to exercise responsibilities and rights arises from delegation, no multiplicity of parenthood arises in these instances.

A court can also confer responsibilities and rights on a step-parent. This is the case in, for instance, England and Wales,[15] the Netherlands[16] and

---

[8] S. 22 of the Children's Act 38 of 2005.
[9] S. 30(3) and (4) of the Children's Act 38 of 2005.
[10] S. 4A of the Children Act 1989.
[11] This is a relatively new dispensation, which came into operation on 27.06.2018: Hilger Report.
[12] Vítor and Martins Online Report.
[13] S. 674 of the Argentine Civil and Commercial Code.
[14] Medina Report.
[15] S. 4A of the Children Act 1989. If the relationship between the step-parent and the child's parent is not formalised as a marriage or a civil partnership, the step-parent can obtain parental responsibility by means of a child arrangements order: ss 8, 12(2) and 12(2A) of the Children Act 1989.
[16] Art. 1:253t of the Dutch Civil Code.

South Africa.[17] Depending on the scope of the responsibilities and rights conferred on the step-parent and depending on whether the court order terminates or limits the responsibilities and rights of one of the child's parents, the order may result in the child having multiple parents.

Some jurisdictions automatically impose a duty of support/maintenance on a step-parent even if he or she does not adopt the step-child. Thus, Estonian law imposes a duty of support on a step-parent who is married to the step-child's parent.[18] In the Netherlands, too, a step-parent who is the spouse or registered partner of the child's parent has a duty to support the child.[19] In Argentina, a step-parent has a subsidiary duty to support his or her step-child while the child is a minor or if the child is disabled. As a rule, this duty exists only while the step-parent shares a household with the step-child's parent.[20] In addition to the subsidiary duty of support, the step-parent and the parent to whom the step-parent is married are jointly and severally liable for obligations relating to the ordinary needs of the household or the support and education of the children in the household.[21] Polish law also holds a step-parent liable for a step-child's support, but in that country the duty arises only if it is justified by so-called 'principles of community life'.[22] These principles refer to circumstances where the imposition of the duty reflects a common sense of fairness based on moral rules and good societal practices.[23] In Poland, the duty of support is reciprocal in the sense that the step-parent may claim maintenance from the step-child if the step-parent contributed to the upbringing and financial support of the child and the claim is in conformity with the principles of community life.[24] In Japan, a step-parent is liable for a step-child's support if the court finds that there are 'special circumstances' for imposing a duty of support on the step-parent.[25] In Quebec, the *in loco parentis* doctrine can be used to compel a step-parent who acts as a parent to the child to support his or her step-child

---

[17] S. 23 of the Children's Act 38 of 2005. The High Court may also award any or all parental responsibilities and rights to the step-parent in terms of the common law.
[18] Kull and Torga Online Report.
[19] Art. 1:395 of the Dutch Civil Code.
[20] S. 676 of the Argentine Civil and Commercial Code. However, the step-parent must support his or her step-child after the cessation of cohabitation with the child's parent if the changed situation may cause serious harm to the step-child and the step-parent undertook a duty of support towards the child while living with the child's parent: Medina Report.
[21] S. 461 of the Argentine Civil and Commercial Code.
[22] Art. 144 §1 of the Family and Guardianship Code.
[23] Judgment of Supreme Court of 04.04.1968, III CZP 27/68, OSNC 1969, no. 1, item 6; A. Zbiegień-Turzańska, 'Comment on Art. 5 of the Polish Civil Code' in K. Osajda (ed.), *Kodeks cywilny. Komentarz*, 27th ed., Legalis Online Database 2020, item 55.
[24] Art. 144 §2 of the Family and Guardianship Code.
[25] Roots Report.

even after he or she divorces the child's parent.[26] In Croatia, a step-parent has the duty to maintain his or her step-child after the death of the child's parent if the child's surviving parent does not have the means to support the child and does not exercise parental responsibilities in respect of the child.[27] In South Africa, two court judgments have stated that a stepfather can be held liable for his step-child's maintenance.[28] In Turkey, a step-parent also has a duty to contribute to a step-child's maintenance, because the step-parent must contribute to family expenses.[29] Some Turkish authors adopt the view that the duty which the Turkish Civil Code imposes on 'parents' to cover expenses relating to the care, protection and education of their children[30] extends to step-children and that the status of step-parenthood by itself obliges the step-parent to support the step-child.[31] In Belgium, spouses and persons who are in legal cohabitation (i.e. persons who are what is called 'registered partners' or 'civil/domestic partners' in some jurisdictions) are obliged to contribute to the domestic expenses and are jointly liable for debts for needs for the household and the upbringing of children in the common household.[32] Therefore, a step-parent who is married to the step-child's parent or is the step-parent's partner indirectly fulfils a duty of support towards his or her step-child. If the parent dies, the step-parent must maintain and educate the child from the assets he or she inherited from the predeceased parent and from the benefits the step-parent received in terms of the marriage contract or cohabitation agreement or by donation.[33] It is doubted whether the imposition of a direct or indirect duty of support on a step-parent, through whatever legal mechanism, on its own amounts to recognition of multiplicity of parenthood.

In Poland, a step-child[34] who shares a household with his or her parent and step-parent at the time when the step-parent dies may not be excluded from living in the house and using the household appliances. This right operates

---

[26] S. 2(2) of the Divorce Act, which applies federally. The step-parent will be *in loco parentis* if he or she has acted as a genuine replacement parent to the child. The step-parent must demonstrate his or her willingness to assume, on an ongoing and permanent basis, the responsibilities that the law normally assigns to the parents: s. 15.1(1) of the Divorce Act; *Chartier c. Chartier* [1999] 1 SCR 242.
[27] Art. 288 para. 3 of the Family Act 2015.
[28] *Heystek v. Heystek* 2002 (2) SA 754 (T); *MB v. NB* 2010 (3) SA 220 (GSJ).
[29] Paksoy Report.
[30] Art. 327 of the Turkish Civil Code.
[31] Paksoy Report. Most commentators argue that obligations of the step-parent are secondary and complementary to the parents' obligations: ibid.
[32] Art. 1477 of the Belgian Civil Code.
[33] Arts 203 §3 and 1477 §5 of the Belgian Civil Code.
[34] The Polish Civil Code does not expressly refer to 'a child', but, according to the rapporteurs for Poland, 'it is obvious that a child should be perceived as "another close one" of the deceased within the meaning of Art. 923 §1 of the CC': Bugajski and Wysocka-Bar Report, section 2.1 n. 3.

for three months from the date on which the step-parent's estate opens for succession.[35] Clearly, this right does not constitute recognition of parenthood on the part of the step-parent and therefore does not relate to the child's legally having multiple parents.

Other examples of responsibilities and rights conferred on a step-parent which do not constitute recognition of multiplicity of parenthood are the following: In Turkey, the step-parent, jointly with the parent with whom he or she shares a household, may set up house rules, which the child must follow.[36] Furthermore, each spouse must give the other reasonable support in exercising parental responsibilities and rights over the latter's children and must represent the other spouse (i.e. the child's parent) if the parent cannot represent the child and the circumstances require representation.[37] As these examples relate to the position as between the parent and step-parent, they do not confer parenthood on the step-parent and do not amount to recognition of multiple parents. Austrian law also compels a step-parent to support the child's parent in exercising non-essential parental responsibility.[38] The duty operates, not only in a marriage, but also in a registered partnership,[39] and an informal partnership.[40] It is important to note that the step-parent incurs the duty as against the child's parent, not against the step-child. Consequently, the duty does not confer parental responsibilities and rights on the step-parent and does not result in his or her acquisition of parenthood.[41] Furthermore, the duty exists only to the extent that it is required by the parent's absence or incapacity due to illness.[42] If the child's parents have joint parental responsibilities and rights, the step-parent only has the duty and right to represent the child's parent if and when both of the child's parents are incapacitated or absent.[43] Thus, there is no multiplicity of parenthood in this context. In Croatia, a step-parent who lives in the same household as the child may make decisions with respect to daily matters if the child's parent agrees to this.[44] In urgent cases, the step-parent may act alone, but he or she must inform the child's parent of the act without undue delay.[45] In these circumstances, too, the step-parent does not legally become an additional parent to the child. Similarly, in Argentina, the step-parent and the child's parent must cooperate in respect of the upbringing and education of the child; the step-parent may make

---

[35] Bugajski and Wysocka-Bar Report.
[36] Art. 339 II of the Turkish Civil Code.
[37] Paksoy Report.
[38] S. 90(3) of the Austrian General Civil Code.
[39] S. 8(2) of the Registered Partnership Act.
[40] S. 139(2) of the General Civil Code.
[41] Buchstätter and Roth Report.
[42] Ibid.
[43] Ibid.
[44] Rešetar and Lucić Report.
[45] Ibid.

decisions relating to the child in emergency situations; and the step-parent must perform daily acts in the domestic sphere relating to the child.[46]

Interestingly, in Poland, step-parenthood has consequences for court proceedings and proceedings in front of public administration authorities. As Polish law confers few responsibilities and rights on step-parents,[47] it is doubted whether these consequences amount to recognition of multiple parents. They probably relate to justice being seen to be done where family members are involved in proceedings. In terms of civil, penal (i.e. criminal) and judicial administrative procedure, a judge may not hear a case concerning, inter alia, his or her relation by affinity in the straight line, which includes his or her step-child. The exclusion also applies to a step-child's hearing a case in which his or her step-parent is a party, and to presiding in administrative proceedings, including tax proceedings, in which his or her step-parent is a party. A step-child further has the right to refuse to testify in civil, penal and administrative (including tax) proceedings if a party to the proceedings is his or her step-parent, and a step-parent may refuse to testify in proceedings in which his or her step-child is a party. A step-parent may not be an expert witness in civil, penal or administrative (including tax) proceedings if the case concerns his or her step-child and a step-child may not be an expert witness in proceedings concerning his or her step-parent.[48]

In Japan, a step-parent and step-child have a reciprocal duty to 'help each other … as relatives who live together' if the step-parent is married to the child's parent.[49]

In some jurisdictions, if the relationship between the child's parent and the step-parent ends, the step-parent has or may acquire a right to maintain contact/visitation/personal relations with the child. Thus, in Croatia, the step-parent has a right to have contact with the child if this is in the best interests of the child.[50] In Belgium, the Civil Code entitles the step-parent to maintain contact with the child if he or she and the child have a special bond of affection and contact is not contrary to the child's best interests.[51] In Germany, the step-parent can ask for visitation rights if this will benefit the child.[52] In Denmark, the step-parent can apply for contact rights if he or she is considered to be the child's closest family member.[53] In Quebec, the *in loco parentis* doctrine entitles the step-parent to claim contact with the child. The step-parent may even claim custody, but this will only entitle the step-parent to make routine decisions

---

[46] S. 673 of the Argentine Civil and Commercial Code.
[47] Bugajski and Wysocka-Bar Report.
[48] Ibid.
[49] Roots Report.
[50] Art. 120 para. 2 of the Family Act 2015.
[51] Art. 375*bis*, al. 2 of the Belgian Civil Code.
[52] S. 1685 of the German Civil Code.
[53] S. 20(1) and (2) of the Parental Responsibility Act (Consolidation Act No. 1768 of 30.11.2020).

about the child's life; it will not confer parental authority and legal guardianship on the step-parent.[54] The *in loco parentis* doctrine applies only if the step-parent is married to the child's parent; it does not assist a step-parent who is or was not married to the parent's child.[55] Regardless of the role he or she has played during the life together, the unmarried step-parent is in the same position as any other third party.[56] In Italy, a step-parent may obtain a right of contact if he or she has established a meaningful and lasting family relationship with the child and therefore is the child's social parent (*genitore sociale*).[57]

Allowing the step-parent to have contact with the step-child after the termination of the step-parent's relationship with the child's parent may be said to recognise the step-parent's position as an additional parent to the step-child and may, in this sense, constitute recognition of multiplicity of parenthood.

Vietnam stands out as an exception in respect of step-parents' legal position, as it confers extensive responsibilities and rights on a step-parent. However, the step-parent does not replace either of the child's parents or acquire all the responsibilities and rights the child's parents have. In terms of the Marriage and Family Law 2014, a stepfather or stepmother is included as a family member, and a step-parent must, inter alia, look after and raise the step-child, protect the lawful rights and interests of the step-child, and respect the step-child's rights to select a career.[58] Step-parents may not discriminate against their step-children due to their gender or the marital status of the child's biological parents, abuse their minor step-children's labour, or incite or force the step-children to act against the law or social ethics. Step-parents are encouraged to create conditions for step-children to live in a harmonious family environment, and must closely collaborate with schools in educating the step-children. In addition to the responsibilities described above, a step-parent who cares for and raises his or her step-child as if he or she was biologically related to the child may inherit from the step-child, and vice versa. It is important to note that the rights of step-parents and step-children are not automatically established, but

---

[54] LRC 1985, ch. 3 (2nd suppl.) (Divorce Act).

[55] Bill C-78 (An Act to amend the Divorce Act), which came into force in July 2020, allows the court to assign adjudicative responsibilities in respect of the child not only to spouses and parents, but also to a person who 'shall take its place or intend to take its place' (free translation). The Act thus codifies the principles of the judgment in *TVF and DF v. GC* [1987] 2 SCR 244.

[56] *TVF and DF v. GC* [1987] 2 SCR 244.

[57] Two approaches have been considered to ensure the maintenance of the family relationship between the child and the social parent: application of art. 337 *ter* of the Civil Code, which regulates the right of the child to continuity of the relationship with both parents, ascendants and relatives, in the context of procedures for the award of custody of a child born in or out of wedlock; and secondly, the application of art. 333 of the Civil Code, which allows the judge to adopt appropriate measures in matters of parental responsibility, when the parent harms the child. All the same, it is considered a right of the child and not of the step-parent.

[58] Van Ngo Report.

are dependent on consideration of evidence of living together or caring for and nurturing each other. Even when step-parents live with step-children, they do not incur all the obligations that parents do. For instance, step-parents do not have responsibilities and rights in respect of compensation for damages caused by step-children, managing step-children's assets, or disposing of property of step-children. Furthermore, there is no financial duty of support between step-parent and step-child.[59] The conclusion one can draw from the above is that, in Vietnam, there is recognition of multiple parents in the context of step-parenthood, but that this recognition does not extend to all legal aspects of being a parent.

In those jurisdictions where a step-parent has no parental responsibilities and rights by virtue of his or her step-parenthood, a conflict cannot arise between the exercising of parental responsibilities and rights by a step-parent and a parent of the child.

In jurisdictions where the step-parent may or must assist the parent in exercising parental responsibilities and rights, such as Argentina, Austria, and Croatia, the parent's legal position is stronger than that of the step-parent.[60] In Portugal, a step-parent to whom a parent has delegated responsibilities for daily matters must comply with the instructions and guidelines laid down by the parent with whom the child resides.[61] In Vietnam, the step-parent's rather extensive responsibilities and rights are said not to create a conflict with those of the parent, as their purpose is to 'complement and facilitate better care and nurturing of the children'.[62]

In South Africa, a step-parent who has obtained parental responsibilities and rights alongside the child's parent through an agreement or a court order conferring specific or full parental responsibilities and rights on him or her is on an equal footing with the child's parents. The starting point is that the co-holders of parental responsibilities and rights may act independently when exercising their parental responsibilities and rights.[63] However, they must give due consideration to each other's views and wishes before making any decision which is likely to change significantly or to have a significant adverse effect on a co-holder's exercise of parental responsibilities and rights.[64] If guardianship has been awarded to the step-parent, his or her consent is required, alongside the consent of the child's other guardians, for the child's marriage, adoption, departure or removal from South Africa, or application for a passport, and for

---

[59] Ibid.
[60] Argentina: Medina Report; Austria: Buchstätter and Roth Report; Croatia: Rešetar and Lucić Report.
[61] Vítor and Martins Online Report.
[62] Van Ngo Report, section 2.1.2.
[63] S. 30(2) of the Children's Act 38 of 2005.
[64] S. 31(2) of the Children's Act 38 of 2005.

the alienation or encumbrance of any immovable property of the child.[65] If the step-parent and parent (or any other co-holder of parental responsibilities and rights) are experiencing problems in exercising their responsibilities and rights (e.g. if they cannot agree on when one of them should have contact with the child) they must try to agree on a parenting plan which will regulate the exercising of their responsibilities and rights.[66] If they cannot agree on a parenting plan, if one of them breaches the terms of the plan, or if one of them is of the view that a decision made or an act performed by another co-holder is not in the best interests of the child, the court can be approached to resolve the matter on the basis of the best interests of the child.[67]

2.2. RECOGNITION OF MULTIPLE PARENTS IF A CHILD IS RAISED IN MORE THAN ONE HOUSEHOLD

As recognition of multiple parents in step-families was discussed under the previous heading, the discussion under the present heading focuses on conferring legal responsibilities and rights on people other than step-parents.

As set out in the instructions to the rapporteurs, the multiplicity of parents we have in mind under this heading relates to the situation where children are raised in more than one household, for example because their parents jointly exercise custody after separation or have never shared a household but share parenting responsibilities. These cases include married parents who have divorced and unmarried parents who jointly have parental responsibilities and rights but do not live together.

In general, the jurisdictions surveyed only recognise sharing of parenthood across more than one household in the case of two parents who have separated or have never lived together. In most jurisdictions, the child's parents continue to have parental responsibilities and rights after separation, but the parent who has custody of the child and with whom the child resides may have more responsibilities and rights than the other legal parent. This is the position in, inter alia, Austria,[68] Croatia,[69] Estonia,[70] Greece,[71] South Africa,[72] Turkey,[73] and Vietnam.[74] In Greece, for example, the court divides the responsibilities

---

[65] S. 18(5) read with s. 18(3)(c) of the Children's Act 38 of 2005.
[66] S. 33(2) of the Children's Act 38 of 2005.
[67] The court's power arises from ss 45 and 46 of the Children's Act 38 of 2005 and the common law jurisdiction of the High Court as upper guardian of all minors: Louw Report.
[68] Buchstätter and Roth Report.
[69] Rešetar and Lucić Report.
[70] Kull and Torga Online Report.
[71] Zervogianni Report.
[72] Louw Report.
[73] Paksoy Report.
[74] Van Ngo Report.

and rights between the parents on the ground of what it considers to be the child's best interests. The Greek Civil Code states that, in principle, the child's interests are best served by both parents being involved in the child's upbringing.[75] Parents may, however, agree on deviations from the principle of joint exercise of parental care.[76] If parents are unable jointly to exercise parental care, the court can divide parental care between them.[77] In these circumstances the child will be raised in two households. If one of the parents is awarded the right to have contact with the child, the child will also, to an extent, be raised in two households. In South Africa, parents who have never been married to each other and do not cohabit may enter into an agreement which confers part or all of the aspects of parental responsibilities and rights on the child's father.[78] In such event, the child may be raised in two households and the law will recognise the multiple parents. The position is the same if the court confers parental responsibilities and rights on the unmarried father and the child is raised in both parents' households or if the unmarried father recognises the child, contributes or attempts to contribute to the child's upbringing for a reasonable period, and contributes or attempts to contribute to expenses in connection with the child's maintenance for a reasonable period of time and the child is raised in both parents' households.[79]

The position in Japanese law is strikingly different. If a child's parents divorce or if they are unmarried, only one of them has parental responsibilities and rights.[80] However, there is a legal loophole which the courts have used to separate physical custody from the rest of parental authority and to award physical custody to one of the parents and parental authority minus physical custody to the other parent. This is rarely done. If parents remain married but are separated, physical custody is split from the rest of parental authority more commonly.[81]

Some jurisdictions recognise multiple parents by allowing persons who are not the child's legal parents to acquire full or limited responsibilities and rights towards a child alongside the child's legal parents. In this case, the term 'parenthood' would be used in a loose sense. If the person's responsibilities and rights are limited (e.g. if the person is allowed to have contact with the child and/or to have the child stay with him or her for certain periods of time) this might also be viewed as recognition of multiple parents of a child who is raised in more than one household. The term 'parent' would be used loosely.

---

[75] Art. 1511 para. 2 of the Greek Civil Code as amended by Art. 5 of Law 4800/2021.
[76] Art. 1514 para. 1 of the Greek Civil Code as amended by Art. 8 of Law 4800/2021.
[77] Zervogianni Report.
[78] S. 22 of the Children's Act 38 of 2005.
[79] Ss 21(1)(b) and 23 of the Children's Act 38 of 2005.
[80] Roots Report. The issue of allowing for joint parental authority after divorce is currently being considered by the Legislative Council (Family Law Subcommittee): ibid.
[81] Ibid.

An example is Denmark, where a person who does not live with the child and is not the child's legal parent can apply for the right to have contact with the child if the person qualifies as the child's closest family member. As the person's social relationship with the child is an important factor in this regard, the person is called the child's 'social parent'.[82] The social parent can only acquire contact rights if one or both of the child's parents are dead, if one of the parents is unknown (e.g. because donor sperm was used), or if the child has no or very limited contact with his or her legal parent.[83] If the application for contact rights is based on the absence or limited extent of contact by the child's legal parent, the reason for the absence or limited extent of contact has considerable weight. If the child has had a close relationship with the social parent for several years, the application could succeed despite the legal parent's objection.[84]

Australian and South African law also enable persons who are not the child's legal parents to obtain responsibilities and rights alongside the child's legal parents through an agreement with the parent or a court order.[85] Such persons include a grandparent, an unmarried father who does not have parental responsibilities and rights in respect of his child, and other persons who have an interest in the care, wellbeing or development of the child.[86] Depending on the scope of the responsibilities and rights awarded to such a person, this configuration of shared responsibilities and rights might also be considered legal recognition of multiple parents of a child who is raised in more than one household, with the term 'parents' being used in a loose sense.

In the Netherlands, parenthood and parental responsibilities and rights could be split in some instances, for instance, in the case of intentional multi-parent families where the child is raised from birth by parents who do not share a household. The parties often enter into an agreement about their respective legal positions even before the child is conceived.[87] Whether splitting parenthood and parental responsibilities and rights is possible depends on the factual situation in each case.[88] The birth mother is always the child's legal parent who has parental responsibilities and rights. As Dutch law only recognises two legal parents, the birth mother's legal parenthood means that there can, at most, be one other legal parent, with a non-legal parent who has parental responsibilities and rights being added to the legal parents. The other legal parent could be either the partner of the birth mother or another adult in a second household, but this person will have no parental responsibilities

---

[82] Lund-Andersen and Pedersen Report.
[83] S. 20(1) and (2) of the Parental Responsibility Act.
[84] Lund-Andersen and Pedersen Report.
[85] Australia: Kha Report; South Africa: Louw Report.
[86] Australia: ss 64 and 65C of the Family Law Act 1975; South Africa: ss 22–24 of the Children's Act 38 of 2005.
[87] Schrama Report.
[88] Ibid.

and rights. The third person would not be the child's legal parent but could get parental responsibilities and rights. As the Dutch rapporteur states: '[t]he situation is quite complex'.[89]

If a child is brought up in more than one household and the persons who are the child's legal parents or have parental responsibilities and rights experience conflict in exercising their respective responsibilities and rights, the court may be approached to resolve the dispute in the interests of the child. This is the position in, inter alia, Croatia,[90] England and Wales,[91] Greece,[92] Portugal,[93] and South Africa.[94] However, in Portugal the court will not entertain disputes about decisions regarding daily matters.[95]

In some jurisdictions, the persons who are in conflict must seek counselling or mediation before going to court. For example, in Croatia the parties must initiate counselling at a social welfare centre or try to resolve their dispute using family mediation.[96] In South Africa, co-holders of parental responsibilities and rights who are experiencing problems in exercising their responsibilities and rights must try to agree on a parenting plan which will regulate the exercising of their responsibilities and rights.[97] The parenting plan must be prepared with the assistance of a family advocate, social worker or psychologist or through mediation.[98]

2.3. RECOGNITION OF MULTIPLE PARENTS IF A CHILD IS RAISED IN A POLYGAMOUS FAMILY

Most of the jurisdictions surveyed do not recognise polygamy or multiple parents in the context of a polygamous family.

In Vietnam, polygamy was recognised in the past but, since 1959, is no longer permitted.[99] Polygamous families which were formed before the prohibition came into operation and those which are accepted because families lost contact due to the division of the country in the Vietnam War are, however, still recognised.[100] Although polygamous families are not regulated by the Marriage

---

[89] Schrama Report, section 2.2.1.
[90] Rešetar and Lucić Report.
[91] Fenton-Glynn and Scherpe Report.
[92] Zervogianni Report.
[93] Vítor and Martins Online Report.
[94] The court's power arises from ss 45 and 46 of the Children's Act 38 of 2005 and the common law jurisdiction of the High Court as upper guardian of all minors: Louw Report.
[95] Vitor and Martins Online Report.
[96] Rešetar and Lucić Report.
[97] S. 33(2) of the Children's Act 38 of 2005.
[98] S. 33(5) of the Children's Act 38 of 2005.
[99] Van Ngo Report.
[100] Ibid.

and Family Law 2014, the rapporteur for Vietnam states that every wife is viewed as the stepmother of the children born of the other wives. Therefore, the children have multiple parents. Very few polygamous marriages still exist.[101] The only dispute that has been brought to court is whether the children born of one wife can inherit from the other wives in the polygamous household. The court held that the children inherit only from their birth mother, not from the other wives in the polygamous family.[102]

In South Africa, polygamy is part of the culture and religion of several groups. Polygamous customary marriages are fully recognised,[103] but polygamous religious marriages have received only limited recognition. The Children's Act 38 of 2005 does not automatically confer parental responsibilities and rights on any member of the polygamous family apart from the child's biological father and the woman who gave birth to the child.[104] However, another member of the family can obtain parental responsibilities and rights through an agreement with the child's father or mother or by way of a court order,[105] thus causing the child to have multiple parents. The rapporteur for South Africa states that it is not yet clear whether the rules override 'conflicting designation of parenthood in terms of customary law or any system of religious law'.[106] If a conflict arises between co-holders of parental responsibilities and rights, the conflict must be resolved in the best interests of the child, which, in terms of the Children's Act, means that, inter alia, the child's need to remain in the care of his or her parent, family and extended family, to maintain a connection with his or her family, extended family, culture or tradition, and the child's physical and emotional security and his or her intellectual, emotional, social and cultural development must be taken into consideration.[107] Polygamous families have also received express recognition in the context of South African adoption law, since 'persons sharing a common household and forming a permanent family unit' may jointly adopt a child.[108] This means that if, for instance, a husband in a customary marriage and his multiple wives jointly adopted a child, he and his wives would all share parental responsibilities and rights and the adopted child would have multiple parents.[109]

---

[101] Ibid.
[102] Case No. 20/2009/DS-PT by the Supreme People's Court, dated 12.02.2019.
[103] S. 2 of the Recognition of Customary Marriages Act 120 of 1998.
[104] Ss 19 and 20 of the Children's Act 38 of 2005.
[105] In terms of ss 22, 23 and 24 of the Children's Act 38 of 2005 or the common law jurisdiction of the High Court as upper guardian of all minors.
[106] Louw Report, section 2.3.
[107] S. 7(1) of the Children's Act 38 of 2005.
[108] S. 231(1)(a)(iii) of the Children's Act 38 of 2005.
[109] Louw Report.

2.4. RECOGNITION OF MULTIPLE PARENTS IN THE CASE OF OPEN ADOPTION

Open adoption refers to families where children have been adopted but maintain links (legal or de facto) with their original relatives. If the child is allowed to retain links with his or her family of origin, this might qualify as recognition of multiplicity of parents. If the family of origin (or some members of that family, such as the child's original parents) have contact rights in respect of the child, this might qualify as recognition of multiple parents, but it would probably be going too far to state that multiple parents are recognised if the family of origin only has the right to obtain information about the child.

In some countries, such as Belgium, simple adoption does not sever the parental relationship and therefore creates a potential legal multiplicity of two parents of origin and up to two adoptive parents.[110] Simple adoption occurs, for example, in the case of step-parent adoptions. In the case of a step-parent adoption, the child has three legal parents, because the parent who is married to the step-parent remains the child's legal parent. Such step-parent adoptions do not fall within the ambit of 'open adoption' as envisaged in the questionnaire.

The Polish version of 'open adoption' creates a legal relationship between the adoptive parent and the adopted child, but not between the relatives of the adoptive parent and the adopted child.[111] It means that the child does not legally become a sibling of the adoptive parents' biological children or a grandchild of the adoptive parents' parents.[112] This form of adoption also does not fall within the ambit of open adoption as defined in the questionnaire.

The Argentine version of simple adoption could qualify as open adoption as defined in the questionnaire. In terms of this version of simple adoption, the adoptive parent acquires parental responsibilities and rights in respect of the adopted child but the family of origin has the right to contact the adopted child, unless this is contrary to the child's best interests; the child retains his or her right to claim support from his or her family of origin if the adoptive parent cannot support him or her; the child can combine the surnames of his or her adoptive parent and his or her family of origin; the family of origin does not inherit assets the adoptive parent donated to the child and the adoptive parent does not inherit assets the family of origin donated to the child.[113]

In Austria, a child who is adopted by a single person retains his or her legal relationship with one of his or her biological parents. The adoptive parent legally replaces the biological parent who is of the same sex as the adoptive parent and the child retains his or her legal relationship with the biological parent of the

---

[110] Gallus, Leleu, Mathieu and Swennen Report.
[111] Art. 124 §1 of the Family and Guardianship Code.
[112] Bugajski and Wysocka-Bar Report.
[113] Medina Report.

opposite sex.[114] Thus, for instance, if a child is adopted by a single woman, the child retains his or her legal relationship with his or her biological father, but not with his or her biological mother. This rule ensures that the child has two legal parents; it does not create an additional parent for the child and therefore does not result in the child having multiple parents.

In Greece, an adopted person can retain the bonds with his or her family of origin if he or she is adopted as an adult.[115] Such an adoption is possible only between close relatives by blood or marriage.[116] The adoptive parents are primarily responsible for the adoptee's maintenance,[117] but the adoptee is liable to maintain his or her adoptive parents and his or her biological parents.[118] In this case, there is recognition of multiple parents.

In Japan, open adoption is called 'regular adoption' or, simply, 'adoption'.[119] The adopted person is usually an adult, but a minor can also be adopted via regular adoption. The majority of regular adoptions of minors are step-parent adoptions.[120] The adoptive parents and the child who is to be adopted must consent to the adoption and submit a notice of adoption to the family registration office.[121] If the child is a minor, the family court's permission must be obtained before the notice can be submitted.[122] It is unclear whether regular adoption enables the child's original parents to seek contact with the child, but it is clear that they retain a secondary duty of support towards their child and can inherit from the child if he or she dies without a spouse or descendant.[123] The adopted child inherits from both the adoptive and the original parents.[124]

Australia has rejected the practice of closed adoptions.[125] Thus, for example, the New South Wales Adoption Act 2000 expressly encourages openness in adoption, emphasises the best interests of the child both in childhood and later life, ensures that adoption law and practice assist a child to know and have access to his or her birth family and cultural heritage, recognises the changing nature of practices of adoption, allows access to certain information relating to adoptions, and provides for the giving of post-adoption financial and other assistance to adopted children and their birth and adoptive parents in certain

---

[114] S. 197(3) of the Austrian General Civil Code.
[115] Art. 1584 sentence 2 of the Greek Civil Code.
[116] Art. 1579 of the Greek Civil Code: the adoptive parents and the adopted child must be related to each other by blood or marriage in the fourth degree or less.
[117] Art. 1587 of the Greek Civil Code.
[118] Zervogianni Report.
[119] Roots Report.
[120] Ibid.
[121] Arts 799 and 739 of the Civil Code.
[122] Art. 798 of the Civil Code.
[123] Roots Report.
[124] Art. 887 of the Civil Code.
[125] Kha Report.

circumstances.[126] Adoption plans are used to promote contact between the adopted child and various parties. These plans set out the arrangements for the sharing of the child's information (including the child's medical information and information about important events in the child's life) and the means and nature of contact between the parties and the child.[127] Where there is a dispute between the parties, the views of the adoptive parents prevail, as they are the child's legal parents.[128] Although the adoptive parents' views prevail, this system nevertheless seems to qualify as recognition of multiple parents in the adoption context.

Most of the jurisdictions reported on permit an adopted child's parents of origin and/or other relatives to have contact with him or her or to obtain contact by way of a court order. In Quebec, the civil law system of adoption permits agreements to facilitate the exchange of information and/or interpersonal relationships (i.e. contact/visitation) between the adoptive parent and members of the child's family of origin if this is in the child's best interests.[129] Quebec also recognises indigenous customary adoption, which is governed not by State law, but by the competent authority designated for the indigenous (i.e. First Nation) community or the child's indigenous nation.[130] In terms of this type of adoption, rights and obligations may be retained between the child and his or her family of origin.[131] Whether indigenous customary adoption will continue to apply is unclear, as it may be replaced by additional guardianship (*tutelle suppletive*), which allows a parent to appoint a person who will exercise guardianship and parental authority when it is impossible for the parents or one of them to exercise guardianship and parental authority fully.[132] The child's best interests – which is an unknown concept in indigenous custom – is applicable when the court makes a decision authorising additional guardianship.[133] The current civil law adoption system, which – as indicated above – permits agreements to facilitate the exchange of information or interpersonal relationships between the adoptive parent and members of the child's family of origin, may also reduce the incidences of indigenous customary adoption.[134]

In Denmark, the court can allow contact if the child's biological relatives request this,[135] especially if the child had contact with them before the adoption.[136]

---

[126] S. 7 of the Adoption Act 2000 (NSW).
[127] S. 46(1) of the Adoption Act 2000 (NSW).
[128] S. 95 of the Adoption Act 2000 (NSW).
[129] Art. 579 of the Quebec Civil Code.
[130] Arts 543.1, 152.1, 574.1, and 132.0.1 of the Quebec Civil Code.
[131] Art. 132.0.1 of the Quebec Civil Code.
[132] Giroux and Langevin Report.
[133] Art. 199.3 of the Quebec Civil Code.
[134] Giroux and Langevin Report.
[135] S. 20 a of the Parental Responsibility Act.
[136] Lund-Andersen and Pedersen Report.

England and Wales,[137] Portugal,[138] and South Africa[139] also empower the court to allow contact between the adoptive family and the child's family of origin. In Belgium, the child's family of origin may be granted personal relations with the child even if they have never previously had a relationship with the child or, in the case of grandparents, even if they have never met the child.[140] However, biological parents are rarely granted this right, as the law departs from the premise that mechanisms other than full adoption would be more suitable if it is in the child's best interests to maintain the relationship between him or her and his or her biological parents.[141] In Austria, biological parents can have post-adoption contact with the child, if they qualify as third parties who are entitled to contact in the best interests of the child.[142]

In Turkish law, it is unclear whether biological parents have contact rights after an adoption. The Turkish Civil Code is silent on this issue.[143] The view of some writers and the Turkish Court of Cassation is that, since the lineage/filiation links between the child and his or her biological parents remain intact despite the adoption, the biological parents have contact rights which they cannot give up. Some writers are of the view that biological parents may ask the court to grant them contact rights or may give up their contact rights at the time of adoption. According to another view, the parents necessarily give up their contact rights when they consent to the adoption.[144] In Japan, it is also unclear whether regular adoption enables the child's original parents to seek contact with the child.[145]

In Austria,[146] Belgium,[147] and Japan,[148] biological parents have a secondary/subsidiary duty of support in respect of their child, despite the adoption. Thus, if the adoptive parents are unable to support the child, the biological parents must do so. In Turkey, the position is less clear. Some writers and the Court of Cassation are of the view that the biological parents' duty of support ceases at the time of the adoption, while other writers argue that biological parents retain a secondary duty of support towards the child.[149] It is clear though that the

---

[137] Ss 51A and 51B of the Adoption and Children Act 2002.
[138] Vítor and Martins Online Report.
[139] S. 234 of the Children's Act 38 of 2005.
[140] Art. 375*bis* of the Belgian Civil Code.
[141] Gallus, Leleu, Mathieu and Swennen Report.
[142] S. 188(2) of the Austrian General Civil Code.
[143] Paksoy Report.
[144] Ibid.
[145] Roots Report.
[146] Buchstätter and Roth Report.
[147] Art. 353-14 of the Belgian Civil Code.
[148] This applies in the case of regular (i.e. open) adoption: Roots Report.
[149] Paksoy Report.

adopted child is obliged to support his or her adoptive and biological parents.[150] It is doubted whether the retention of the parental duty of support amounts to recognition of multiple parents.

In Germany, open adoption is not formally recognised by the law but, with the help of the adoption agency, adoptive parents and the child's biological parents sometimes enter into agreements on open adoption.[151] Compliance is solely at the discretion of the adoptive parents.[152] In Vietnam, too, the child's adoptive and original parents can agree to an open adoption, but such agreements rarely occur.[153] The agreement can permit the maintenance of some or all of the rights and obligations of the original parents after the adoption.[154] The scope of the responsibilities and rights the original parents have after the adoption will determine whether the agreement creates a multiplicity of parents.

In Croatia[155] and Estonia,[156] the law does not provide for open adoption at all.

2.5. RECOGNITION OF MULTIPLE PARENTS IN THE CASE OF *KAFALA*

None of the jurisdictions officially recognise *kafala* as a means to afford legal recognition to multiple parents. In Italy, judges have on occasion recognised *kafala* either as simple adoption or as a gracious decision requiring no internal adaptation measures. The Court of Cassation recognised a notarial *kafala*, approved by a Moroccan judge, in view of the interests of the child. However, judges have never faced questions related to possible multi-parenting in the context of *kafala*.[157]

Further, as the rapporteur for the Netherlands points out, *kafala* might entitle the child to live with his or her guardian in an EU Member State. This is so because the EU Court of Justice has ruled that, although *kafala* does not create a parent–child relationship, it might, under specific conditions, have the implication that the child must be granted a right of entry and residence in order to enable the child to live with his or her guardian in the host Member State.[158]

---

[150] Ibid.
[151] Sanders Report.
[152] Ibid.
[153] Van Ngo Report.
[154] Ibid.
[155] Rešetar and Lucić Report.
[156] Kull and Torga Online Report.
[157] Aluffi Report.
[158] Case C-129/18, *SM v. Entry Clearance Officer, UK Visa Section*, 26.03.2019, ECLI:EU:C: 2019:248.

2.6. RECOGNITION OF MULTIPLE PARENTS IN THE CASE OF DONOR-ASSISTED REPRODUCTION (WITHOUT SURROGACY)

The discussion under this heading does not relate to donor-assisted reproduction via surrogacy, because surrogacy is discussed under a separate heading below.[159]

Most of the jurisdictions surveyed regulate and permit donor-assisted reproduction. Luxembourg does not do so,[160] but is in the process of producing legislation to create a legal framework for donor-assisted reproduction and access to information on a child's origins.[161] Germany allows sperm donation, but not the donation of ova.[162] Turkey does not allow donor-assisted reproduction at all.[163]

In Croatia, the law provides that the identity of the donor must be known,[164] because the child who is born as a result of donor-assisted reproduction has the right to know his or her origin.[165] England and Wales also require the identity of gamete donors to be known,[166] as do all states and territories in Australia.[167] Since 1 July 2018, German law has required that the identity of men who donate sperm to official sperm banks must be known.[168] It goes without saying that the mere fact that the donor's identity is known does not mean that the donor is viewed as a parent who has responsibilities and rights. Conversely, it is clear that the law cannot confer responsibilities and rights on an anonymous donor. Several jurisdictions, including Greece,[169] Italy,[170] Quebec,[171] South Africa,[172] and Vietnam,[173] prescribe that donors must be anonymous.[174] Of course, some persons engage in donor-assisted reproduction outside the boundaries of the law. For example, a woman may use the sperm of a friend or acquaintance to fertilise herself at home. In such event, the identity of the donor will be known despite the prohibition on identifying the donor. In these circumstances,

---

[159] See section 2.8, Recognition of Multiplicity of Parenthood in the Case of Surrogacy, below.
[160] Hilger Report.
[161] Bills 6568 and 7674.
[162] Sanders Report.
[163] Paksoy Report.
[164] Rešetar and Lucić Report.
[165] Art. 15 of the Assisted Human Reproduction Act 2012.
[166] Fenton-Glynn and Scherpe Report.
[167] Kha Report.
[168] Sanders Report.
[169] Zervogianni Report.
[170] Art. 9 al. 3, Law no. 40/2004.
[171] Giroux and Langevin Report.
[172] S. 41 of the Children's Act 38 of 2005.
[173] Van Ngo Report.
[174] In Japan, gamete donors are usually anonymous: Roots Report.

the ordinary rules of the law in respect of acquisition of parental status and responsibilities and rights would apply just as they would if the donor's identity was unknown.

In the jurisdictions where donor-assisted reproduction is allowed, the woman who gives birth to a child is the child's legal mother. This rule applies regardless of whether the child was conceived using the gamete of a third-party donor or of the birth mother's spouse or registered/civil partner. It also applies even if a third-party donor's identity may be disclosed. This is the position in, inter alia, Argentina,[175] Australia,[176] Austria,[177] Belgium,[178] Denmark,[179] England and Wales,[180] Estonia,[181] Germany,[182] Greece,[183] Italy,[184] Japan,[185] Poland,[186] Portugal,[187] Quebec,[188] South Africa,[189] the Netherlands,[190] and Vietnam.[191] It would also be the position in Turkey if donor-assisted reproduction were to occur despite the prohibition on gamete and embryo donations.[192] As the birth mother alone is the child's mother, the rule does not create multiple parents for the child.

In many jurisdictions, the birth mother's husband or registered/civil partner is presumed or legally considered to be the child's father/parent to the exclusion of the donor, regardless of whether or not the donor's identity may be disclosed. This is the position in, inter alia, Australia,[193] Belgium,[194] England and Wales,[195]

---

[175] S. 562 of the Argentine Civil and Commercial Code.
[176] Kha Report.
[177] S. 143 of the Austrian General Civil Code.
[178] Arts 27 and 56 of the Bill of 06.07.2007.
[179] S. 30 of the Children's Act (Consolidation Act No. 1250 of 29.11.2019 and Act No. 227 of 15.02.2022).
[180] S. 33 of the Human Fertilisation and Embryology Act 2008.
[181] Kull and Torga Online Report.
[182] S. 1591 of the German Civil Code.
[183] Art. 1463 of the Greek Civil Code.
[184] Art. 269 s. 3 of the Italian Civil Code.
[185] Art. 9 of the Act on the Providing etc. of Assisted Reproductive Technology and the Special Provisions to the Civil Code Regarding Legal Parent-Child Relationships of Children Born Through Such Technology 2020.
[186] Art. 61¹ of the Family and Guardianship Code.
[187] Vítor and Martins Online Report.
[188] Giroux and Langevin Report.
[189] S. 40(1)–(3) of the Children's Act 38 of 2005.
[190] Schrama Report.
[191] Van Ngo Report.
[192] Art. 282 of the Turkish Civil Code.
[193] Kha Report.
[194] Gallus, Leleu, Mathieu and Swennen Report. It should be noted that in Belgium the Constitutional Court has held that impeding the legal establishment of the paternity of the donor disproportionately infringes the child's right to respect for private and family life and the child's right to have his or her interests taken into account: Judgment no. 19/2019 of the Belgian Constitutional Court of 07.02.2019, available at www.const-court.be.
[195] Ss 35 and 42 of the Human Fertilisation and Embryology Act 2008.

Estonia,[196] Greece,[197] Japan,[198] Poland,[199] Portugal,[200] Quebec,[201] South Africa,[202] the Netherlands,[203] and Turkey.[204] In some countries, such as Germany[205] and the Netherlands,[206] the rule applies only to male spouses/partners, thus excluding a birth mother's female spouse or partner from automatically becoming the child's legal parent. This rule, too, does not create multiple parents for the child.

Returning to the position of the father of the child born of assisted reproduction, if the birth mother is unmarried or if the presumption of paternity on the part of the birth mother's husband is rebutted (where this is possible), the sperm donor can, in some jurisdictions, become the child's legal parent by acknowledging the child or getting a court declaration that he is the child's father, but then he alone will be the child's father. Consequently, the rule does not add another parent for the child. This is the position in, inter alia, Belgium,[207] Germany,[208] Greece,[209] Poland,[210] and Turkey.[211] In Japan, the sperm donor can acknowledge the child even without the consent of the birth mother, and the child can bring an action for recognition of the paternity of the sperm donor.[212] However, the Legislative Council of the Ministry of Justice has proposed that statutory rules should be enacted to prohibit the sperm donor from recognising the child and the child from bringing an action for recognition of the sperm donor's paternity.[213] In the Netherlands, a mother's female partner can use the acknowledgement procedure and thereby become the child's legal parent to the exclusion of the donor.[214] Denmark adopts a different approach to the legal parenthood of some sperm donors, but the outcome is also that the child has only one father. In Denmark, a sperm donor can be anonymous, non-anonymous or known. An anonymous donor never becomes the child's legal parent and has no legal relationship with the child. A non-anonymous donor also does not become the child's legal parent, but the child has the right to contact the donor after the

---

[196] Kull and Torga Online Report.
[197] Art. 1465 of the Greek Civil Code; Art. 9 of Law 4356/2015.
[198] Roots Report. The rule applies only to the birth mother's husband, not to her partner: ibid.
[199] Art. 62 §1 of the Family and Guardianship Code.
[200] Vítor and Martins Online Report.
[201] Arts 538 and 539 of the Quebec Civil Code.
[202] S. 40(1) of the Children's Act 38 of 2005.
[203] Art. 1:199 sub a of the Dutch Civil Code.
[204] Art. 285 of the Turkish Civil Code.
[205] Sanders Report.
[206] Schrama Report.
[207] Gallus, Leleu, Mathieu and Swennen Report.
[208] Ss 1592 no. 2 and 1594–98 of the German Civil Code.
[209] Zervogianni Report.
[210] Art. 72 §1 of the Family and Guardianship Code.
[211] Paksoy Report.
[212] Roots Report.
[213] Ibid.
[214] Art. 1:204 of the Dutch Civil Code; Schrama Report.

child turns 18.[215] If the sperm donor is a known donor, he is the legal father if the child's birth mother is single.[216] If spouses or partners use a known donor, they can agree to allow the donor – instead of the birth mother's husband or partner – to be the legal parent, or they can agree that the birth mother's spouse or partner is the child's parent.[217] Choosing the latter option enables the birth mother's spouse or partner to be the child's second parent alongside the birth mother.[218] In the Netherlands, a known sperm donor can also become the child's parent if the parties agree that the mother's partner will not acknowledge the child and that the sperm donor will acknowledge the child.[219] In these cases, too, the donor does not become an additional parent; the child still has only two parents.

In England and Wales, a partner of a woman who is not a party to a marriage or civil partnership can become the child's parent if he or she meets the so-called 'agreed fatherhood conditions'.[220] These conditions apply to males and females who did *not* donate a gamete for the assisted reproduction.[221] The conditions are that the partner and the child's mother must agree that the partner will become a parent, and that they must not be within the prohibited degrees of relationship.[222]

In some jurisdictions, a mother can be the child's only parent if she is single (i.e. she is not a party to a marriage or recognised partnership) and the sperm donor is anonymous. This is the position in, for example, Quebec[223] and South Africa.[224] In Greece,[225] the birth mother is the child's only parent if she does not have a spouse or registered partner and the sperm donor does not acknowledge the child. In principle, the position is the same in Germany.[226] However, the German Federal Court of Justice has held an unmarried man who consented to his partner's insemination with donor sperm liable for the maintenance of the child who was born as a result of the assisted reproduction even though the man refused to acknowledge the child.[227] The court held that the man's consent to

---

[215] Lund-Andersen and Pedersen Report.
[216] S. 27 b and c of the Children's Act (Consolidation Act No. 1250 of 29.11.2019 and Act No. 227 of 15.02.2022).
[217] S. 27 of the Children's Act (Consolidation Act No. 1250 of 29.11.2019 and Act No. 227 of 15.02.2022).
[218] Lund-Andersen and Pedersen Report.
[219] Schrama Report.
[220] S. 36 of the Human Fertilisation and Embryology Act 2008.
[221] Fenton-Glynn and Scherpe Report.
[222] Ss 36, 43 and 44 of the Human Fertilisation and Embryology Act 2008; Marriage (Prohibited Degrees of Relationship) Act 1986.
[223] Art. 538 of the Quebec Civil Code.
[224] S. 40(2) of the Children's Act 38 of 2005 read with ss 22–24 and the High Court's common law power as upper guardian of all minors.
[225] Zervogianni Report.
[226] Sanders Report.
[227] Bundesgerichtshof (BGH, Federal Court of Justice, FCJ), Decision of 23.09.2015 – case XII ZR 99/14, NJW 2015, 68, p. 3434.

the insemination constituted an 'intentional assumption of parenthood' which resulted in his liability for child support.[228] In England and Wales – where donors are not anonymous[229] – the mother is the child's only parent if she is not a party to a marriage or civil partnership and she does not have a partner who meets the 'agreed fatherhood conditions' described above.[230]

In some jurisdictions, donor-assisted reproduction is reserved for single women and heterosexual couples. This is the case in, inter alia, Greece[231] and Poland.[232] Jurisdictions such as Belgium,[233] England and Wales,[234] Estonia,[235] Quebec,[236] and South Africa[237] apply the same rules regarding donor-assisted reproduction and the acquisition of parental responsibilities and rights to heterosexual and same-sex couples. In Austria, only female same-sex partners have the same right to access assisted reproduction as heterosexual persons do.[238] The reason why male same-sex couples are excluded is that a male couple would need to use surrogacy to have a child and surrogacy is prohibited in Austria.[239]

In most jurisdictions, the anonymity or disclosure of the identity of the donor has no influence on the rules as to who becomes a child's parent and this is the position regardless of whether the donor wants to participate in raising the child. Examples of such jurisdictions are Croatia,[240] Germany,[241] Poland,[242] Portugal,[243] and South Africa.[244]

In South Africa, the donor is, in principle, disqualified from being a parent, because the definition of the term 'parent' excludes any person who is biologically related to a child only because he or she donated a gamete for purposes of assisted reproduction.[245] Despite this exclusion, a donor whose identity is known could, potentially, obtain parental responsibilities and rights in terms of a court order if he or she wanted to participate in raising the child and such participation is in the child's best interests.[246] If such an order is made, the donor would become an

---

[228] Sanders Report.
[229] See above under this heading (i.e. section 2.6).
[230] Fenton-Glynn and Scherpe Report.
[231] Zervogianni Report.
[232] Bugajski and Wysocka-Bar Report.
[233] Gallus, Leleu, Mathieu and Swennen Report.
[234] Ss 35 and 42 of the Human Fertilisation and Embryology Act 2008.
[235] Kull and Torga Online Report.
[236] Giroux and Langevin Report.
[237] S. 40 of the Children's Act 38 of 2005 read with s. 13 of the Civil Union Act 17 of 2006.
[238] Buchstätter and Roth Report.
[239] Ibid.
[240] Rešetar and Lucić Report.
[241] Sanders Report.
[242] Bugajski and Wysocka-Bar Report.
[243] Vítor and Martins Online Report.
[244] Louw Report.
[245] S. 1 of the Children's Act 38 of 2005.
[246] Ss 22–24 of the Children's Act 38 of 2005; the common law power of the High Court; Louw Report.

additional holder of parental responsibilities and rights. Thus, the child would get a third parent if he or she already has two married legal parents or a second parent if his or her mother is unmarried. The donor would probably face an uphill battle to convince the court that he or she should obtain full parental responsibilities and rights alongside the child's married parents or unmarried mother,[247] but if the child has formed a bond with the donor, the court might be willing to confer contact rights on the donor.[248] In Belgium,[249] too, a gamete donor can be granted contact rights if this is in the child's interests.

In Argentina, courts have, in some instances, allowed the donor to become a third parent despite the fact that the Argentine Civil and Commercial Code[250] states that a person may not have more than two filial bonds. For instance, in Mar del Plata, Buenos Aires province, a same-sex couple and their child's biological mother were recognised as the child's parents and were allowed jointly to exercise paternal and maternal roles.[251]

In Ontario, Canada, four intended parents can be recognised, if they gave their consent in writing before the embryo was conceived. For example, it can be a gay couple and a lesbian couple who want a child. One of the women carries the child, whose biological father is one of the men. An administrative procedure for the recognition of filiation applies. With the permission of the court, more than four parents may be recognised.[252] Denmark is a notable exception in respect of the position of a known sperm donor. A known sperm donor is the legal father if the child's birth mother is single, and he can be the legal father if spouses or partners agree to allow him to be the legal parent.[253] In the Netherlands, a known sperm donor and the woman to whom he donates his sperm can enter into an agreement which provides whether he can acquire the status of legal parent after the child's birth. If the agreement provides that he will acknowledge the child and thereby become the child's legal parent, the partner of the birth mother cannot also acknowledge the child.[254] Therefore, the child cannot have more than two legal parents.

The High Court of Australia has ruled that a known sperm donor can be declared the legal parent of the child.[255] In this case, the birth mother and the sperm donor were listed as the child's parents on the child's birth certificate and

---

[247] Louw Report.
[248] Ibid.
[249] Art. 375*bis* of the Belgian Civil Code.
[250] S. 558.
[251] Court of Family Matters No. 2 of Mar Del Plata *CMF y otros s/materia a categorizar* (*CMF and others, to be determined*) 24.11.2017. Online appointment: AR/JUR/103023/2017.
[252] See definition in the Children's Law Reform Act, RSO 1990, c.C.12, s. 2 'intended parent': party to a surrogacy agreement excludes the substitute; and Children's Law Reform Act, ss 10(2) and 11.
[253] Lund-Andersen and Pedersen Report.
[254] Schrama Report.
[255] *Masson v. Parsons* [2019] HCA 21.

the sperm donor played an active role in the child's upbringing even though the child lived with the birth mother and her female partner. When the birth mother wanted to move to New Zealand with her partner and the child, the sperm donor sought a parenting order stating that he has equal shared parental responsibility along with the child's mother and stopping the mother from relocating the child. The court unanimously ruled that the sperm donor was a parent according to the natural and ordinary meaning of the word and that he qualified as a parent under the Family Law Act 1975 (Cth). The rapporteur for Australia points out that this case is atypical, as it is unusual to record the sperm donor as one of the parents on the child's birth certificate and to have a sperm donor who intends to play a role in the child's upbringing. The court declined to resolve the issue of whether a sperm donor who did not have the intention of being involved in the child's life could be found to be a legal parent,[256] because the facts of the case did not concern this issue.[257]

In Austria, a person can donate his or her gamete to a specific person (e.g. a family member or friend). The starting point is that the donor does not become the child's legal parent. However, a known sperm donor – but not a known ovum donor – can be acknowledged as the child's father if the mother or the child consents to this and the man who is the child's existing legal father does not object.[258] Alternatively, the donor can become the child's legal father if the child[259] applies for a so-called 'father-swap'.[260] In this case, the child does not have two legal fathers, as one father replaces the other.

2.7. RECOGNITION OF MULTIPLE PARENTS IN THE CASE OF A 'THREE-PARENT CHILD'

The so-called 'three-parent' medical technology is similar to in vitro fertilisation, but uses the genetic material of two females and one male, instead of only one female and one male. As a rule, the DNA of the one female is used to 'correct' the DNA of the other female in order to remove genetic mutations that cause serious hereditary diseases.

Most of the special rapporteurs state that the law of their country does not make provision for three-parent children and that their jurisdictions do not permit such genetic manipulation. Australia is considering the legal viability of allowing mitochondrial donations, but at present it is not legally recognised.[261] The national rapporteur for Turkey indicates that three-parent technology is

---

[256] Ibid., para. 55.
[257] Kha Report.
[258] Ss 146, 147(3) and 148(3) of the Austrian General Civil Code.
[259] Only the child can make the application: Buchstätter and Roth Report.
[260] The father-swap is governed by s. 150 of the Austrian General Civil Code.
[261] Kha Report.

not regulated in that country but some in vitro fertilisation clinics are offering mitochondrial transplantation. The rapporteur is of the view that this is illegal, because surrogacy and donations of gamete cells and embryos are forbidden in Turkey. She predicts that the Turkish legislator will soon explicitly forbid three-parent technology.[262]

Generally, the ordinary rules on determination of parentage/filiation/kinship and the acquisition of the legal status of parent would apply to a three-parent child, were such a child to be born.[263] Therefore, the child would not have three legal parents, but two. Thus, the persons who wished to have the child would be the child's legal parents and the donor of any genetic material would not be legally related to the child and would have no rights or responsibilities in respect of the child.

In South African law, it is uncertain whether mitochondrial transfer is prohibited and whether all three parents can be recognised.[264] The Children's Act 38 of 2005 expressly allows more than one person to hold the same parental responsibilities and rights in respect of the same child[265] and does not set a limit on the number of holders of parental responsibilities and rights. However, the sections of the Act which relate to automatic acquisition of parental responsibilities and rights do not refer to three parents.[266] They refer to a biological mother and father, and to a married person who is artificially fertilised together with her spouse, and excludes any gamete donor.[267]

2.8. RECOGNITION OF MULTIPLE PARENTS IN THE CASE OF SURROGACY

The discussion below is restricted to national surrogacy; it does not extend to cross-border/international surrogacy.

The jurisdictions surveyed adopt four different approaches to surrogacy. The first approach is to prohibit surrogacy altogether. This approach is adopted in Austria,[268] Croatia,[269] Estonia,[270] Germany,[271] Italy,[272]

---

[262] Paksoy Report.
[263] See e.g. Denmark: Lund-Andersen and Pedersen Report; England and Wales: Fenton-Glynn and Scherpe Report; Germany: Sanders Report; Poland: Bugajski and Wysocka-Bar Report.
[264] Louw Report.
[265] S. 30(1) and (2) of the Children's Act 38 of 2005.
[266] Ss 19–21 of the Children's Act 38 of 2005.
[267] S. 40 of the Children's Act 38 of 2005. The definition of 'parent' in s. 1 of the Children's Act 38 of 2005 excludes 'any person who is biologically related to a child by reason only of being a gamete donor for purposes of artificial fertilisation'.
[268] Buchstätter and Roth Report.
[269] Rešetar and Lucić Report.
[270] Kull and Torga Online Report.
[271] Sanders Report.
[272] Act 40/2004, Norme in materia di procreazione medicalmente assistita.

Quebec,[273] and Turkey.[274] In these jurisdictions, the ordinary rules regarding acquisition of the status of legal parent would apply if surrogacy were nevertheless to occur. Thus, the woman who gave birth to the child would be the child's mother. If she is married or a partner in a registered/civil partnership, her husband or partner would generally be the child's other legal parent. The intended parents would have to adopt the child in order to obtain the legal status of parent and the adoption would, generally, substitute the adoptive parents for the child's original parents.[275] Where this is possible, the intended father could recognise the child and acquire parental responsibilities and rights in this way. Thus, for example, in Turkey, if the birth mother is single, the intended father would be able to recognise the child and then become the child's legal father. If the birth mother is married, her husband would be the child's legal father unless he filed a lawsuit called 'rejection of the lineage'.[276] If he did so, the intended father would be able to recognise the child and become the child's legal father.[277] Thus, the child would have only two legal parents. In Italy, the Constitutional Court on 28 January 2021 declared that a child who had, since birth, been cared for by the couple who shared the decision to give birth to him has an interest in being recognised by the law. However, this interest of the child does not automatically take precedence over any other interest. The interests need to be balanced. In this case, the child's interests must be balanced against the interest of the State in discouraging a practice that it considers punishable by criminal sanction. A solution that denies any possibility of the child having his relationship with both members of the couple recognised would not achieve such balance, but any other solution would be compatible with the Constitution. Choosing the solution is primarily a matter for the legislature, which enjoys a wide margin of discretion. At the moment, the court is deferring to the legislature without, however, renouncing the right to declare that the protection which is provided by simple adoption is insufficient.

The second approach is slightly different to the first in that it allows altruistic surrogacy but does not permit a deviation from the ordinary rules regarding legal parenthood. This approach is adopted in Australia. Like the laws of the jurisdictions which prohibit surrogacy, Australian law confers parental status on the surrogate mother because she is the woman who gives birth to the child.[278]

---

[273] Art. 541 of the Quebec Civil Code. The situation is different in the English-speaking parts of Canada, where either the common law or legislation allows multi-parenting. For instance, British Columbia and Ontario have reformed their law.

[274] Paksoy Report.

[275] If the particular jurisdiction permits open adoption, the original parents may retain responsibilities and rights in respect of the child and the adoptive and original parents might be the child's multiple parents: see section 2.4 Recognition of Multiplicity of Parenthood in the Case of Open Adoption above.

[276] Paksoy Report.

[277] Ibid.

[278] S. 69P of the Family Law Act 1975 (Cth).

Her husband/partner is also a legal parent of the child.[279] To obtain the status of legal parents, the intended parents must obtain a parenting order.[280]

The third approach is neither to prohibit nor to allow surrogacy; instead, the law does not deal with it at all. This approach is adopted by Argentina,[281] Belgium,[282] England and Wales,[283] Japan,[284] Luxembourg,[285] Poland,[286] and the Netherlands.[287] Because these jurisdictions do not have specific rules on surrogacy, the ordinary rules regarding acquisition of legal parenthood apply when surrogacy does occur. Like the jurisdictions which prohibit surrogacy, most of the countries that do not regulate surrogacy confer parental status on the woman who gives birth to the child, that is, the surrogate mother. This is also the starting point in Argentina, but in that country, some courts have held that whatever is not prohibited is allowed and have declared the rule that maternity is established by giving birth unconstitutional in surrogacy cases. In these cases, the intended parents have been declared to be the child's legal parents to the exclusion of the surrogate mother.[288] Returning to the position in the majority of jurisdictions that do not regulate surrogacy: the surrogate mother – being the woman who gives birth – is the child's mother. If she has a husband or registered/civil partner, some jurisdictions confer the legal status of parent on the husband or partner to the exclusion of the intended father, while others confer the legal status of parent on the intended father to the exclusion of the mother's husband or partner. In Poland[289] and the Netherlands,[290] the surrogate mother's husband or partner is the child's legal father regardless of whose sperm was used for the fertilisation of the surrogate mother. In the Netherlands, the intended parents must adopt the child regardless of whether either or both of them donated gametes for the fertilisation of the surrogate mother. The intended parents need the consent of the surrogate mother for the adoption. Further, before the adoption can take place, a child protection measure has to be initiated by the Child Care and Protection Board. This Board applies to the court for termination of the parental responsibilities of one or both parents, that is, the birth mother and her spouse or registered partner. The intended parents may, in the interim, be awarded joint guardianship.

---

[279] Ss 69P and 69Q of the Family Law Act 1975 (Cth).
[280] Kha Report.
[281] Medina Report.
[282] Gallus, Leleu, Mathieu and Swennen Report.
[283] Fenton-Glynn and Scherpe Report.
[284] Roots Report.
[285] Hilger Report. A draft law proposes the prohibition of surrogacy in Luxembourg: Draft Law 6568A (previously Draft Law 6568).
[286] Bugajski and Wysocka-Bar Report.
[287] Schrama Report.
[288] Medina Report.
[289] Bugajski and Wysocka-Bar Report.
[290] Schrama Report.

After a year of being a family and taking care of the child, the intended parents may apply to adopt the child. If the surrogate mother is single, one of the intended parents may legally recognise the child if the surrogate mother consents to this. Once the child has been legally recognised, the court can award sole parental responsibilities to the intended parent and the other parent may then apply to adopt the child.[291] In England and Wales, too, an intended parent may obtain parental responsibilities if the surrogate mother is single and consents to the (male or female) intended parent being treated as the legal parent of the child.[292] If the gamete of an intended parent was used, that intended parent is the child's biological parent and can gain the status of legal parent through the common law.[293] Regardless of whether the surrogate mother is a party to a marriage or partnership or is single, legal parenthood can be transferred to the intended parents by way of a parental order.[294]

The final approach is to recognise and regulate surrogacy and confer the status of legal parents on the intended parents to the exclusion of the birth mother and her spouse or registered/civil partner. The three countries in the survey which adopt this approach are Greece, South Africa, and Vietnam. These countries allow altruistic surrogacy but not commercial surrogacy. South African law permits gestational and traditional altruistic surrogacy as long as the child who is to be born of the surrogacy has a genetic link to at least one of the intended parents,[295] while Vietnamese and Greek law allow only gestational altruistic surrogacy.[296] In Vietnam, the intended parents become the child's legal parents from the time of the child's birth, except if both intended parents die or lose their legal capacity before the child is handed over to them.[297] In these exceptional circumstances, the birth mother has the right to nurture the child. If the birth mother refuses to nurture the child, guardianship and support of the child is determined in accordance with the Civil Code and the Marriage and Family Law 2014.[298] South African law recognises the legal parenthood of the intended parents, provided that the surrogate motherhood agreement was approved and confirmed by the High Court before the surrogate mother was artificially fertilised. This rule applies regardless of whether the intended parents are of the opposite or the same sex.[299] If the surrogate mother is genetically related to the child, she may terminate the surrogate agreement during her pregnancy or within 60 days of the child's birth.[300] If she terminates the agreement before

---

[291] Ibid.
[292] Fenton-Glynn and Scherpe Report.
[293] Ibid.
[294] Ss 54 and 54A of the Human Fertilisation and Embryology Act 2008.
[295] S. 294 of the Children's Act 38 of 2005.
[296] Vietnam: Van Ngo Report; Greece: Zervogianni Report.
[297] Van Ngo Report.
[298] Ibid.
[299] Ss 292 and 297 of the Children's Act 38 of 2005.
[300] S. 298(1) of the Children's Act 38 of 2005.

the child's birth, the intended parents do not become the child's parents because the surrogate mother is considered the child's legal parent at birth, together with her spouse or partner. However, if the surrogate mother does not have a spouse or partner, the intended father becomes the child's parent alongside the surrogate mother.[301] If the agreement is terminated after the child's birth, the parental responsibilities and rights acquired by the intended parents are terminated and vest in the surrogate mother and her husband or partner, or in the surrogate mother and the intended father if the surrogate mother does not have a spouse or partner.[302] A surrogate motherhood agreement that does not comply with the requirements stipulated in the Children's Act 38 of 2005 is invalid and the child is for all purposes deemed to be the child of the birth mother.[303] Greece has a similar system of requiring court approval of surrogacy. If the legal requirements for surrogacy have been met and the surrogacy has been authorised by the court, the intended mother is the child's legal mother from the time of the child's birth.[304] If the intended mother is married or has a registered partner, her spouse or registered partner becomes the child's legal father. Another aspect of Greek surrogacy law that is similar to South African surrogacy law is that if the surrogate mother is genetically linked to the child because her ovum was used, she is in a better position to be the child's legal parent than a surrogate mother who is not genetically linked to the child. In Greece, a surrogate mother whose ovum was used for the fertilisation that resulted in the pregnancy can challenge the legal status of the intended mother within six months from the child's birth.[305] If the challenge is successful, the surrogate mother becomes the child's legal mother[306] and her spouse or partner is henceforth presumed to be the child's father.[307] Her spouse or partner may, however, contest fatherhood.[308]

Portugal will probably join the group of jurisdictions that confers parental status on the intended parents. In Portugal, surrogacy used to be recognised in limited circumstances.[309] Because parts of the legal regime of surrogacy were declared unconstitutional, surrogacy is currently unregulated in Portugal. The law that will probably become applicable once the constitutional impediments are overcome states that the intended parents are the legal parents of the child.[310]

---

[301] S. 299(b) of the Children's Act 38 of 2005.
[302] S. 299(a) of the Children's Act 38 of 2005.
[303] S. 297(2) of the Children's Act 38 of 2005.
[304] Art. 1464 para. 1 of the Greek Civil Code.
[305] Art. 1464 para. 2 of the Greek Civil Code.
[306] Art. 1464 para. 3 of the Greek Civil Code.
[307] Art. 1465 para. 1 of the Greek Civil Code and Art. 9 of Law 4356/2015 on registered partnerships.
[308] Art. 1467 of the Greek Civil Code and Art. 9 sentence 3 of Law 4356/2015.
[309] Vítor and Martins Online Report.
[310] Ibid.

Lastly, it should be noted that in some of the jurisdictions that do permit surrogacy or leave it unregulated, surrogacy is available only to heterosexual couples. This is the position in Greece[311] and Vietnam.[312] Portugal is set to allow lesbian couples to use surrogacy to have a child, but not male same-sex couples.[313] It goes without saying that in countries where same-sex marriage and partnership is not allowed (such as Poland),[314] same-sex couples are not legally permitted to use surrogacy to have a child.

2.9. GENERAL RECOGNITION OF MULTI-PARENTHOOD

None of the countries surveyed have a general law that recognises multi-parenthood in a generic, broad manner. In its Consultation Paper on the reform of the law on surrogacy, the Law Commission of England and Wales, in conjunction with the Scottish Law Commission, stated that there could be merit in a future exploration of the possibility of allowing a child to have more than two legal parents, as this 'would enable the legal position to reflect reality where there is genuine co-parenting of a child by three or four people.'[315]

In the Netherlands, a multidisciplinary committee undertook research on multi-parent families. The report of the Committee was published in 2016.[316] One of the revolutionary recommendations was that legal multi-parenthood should be allowed for a maximum of four parents in two households and that multi-parent responsibilities should be introduced.[317] Eventually, the Dutch government decided not to proceed with the reform, mostly because of the complexity of a four-parent system and an anticipated increase in conflicts if the child had multiple parents. Instead of opting for a multi-parenthood system, the government indicated that a system of partial parental responsibilities is the way forward to solve problems experienced by social parents. A draft bill on shared care/custody has since been published for consultation. Unfortunately, the draft bill does not afford full legal recognition to multi-parent families. The draft bill relates to partial parental responsibilities, which does not recognise the status of multi-parent families, and does not really resolve the problems arising from multi-parenthood.[318] The rapporteur for the Netherlands predicts that

---

[311] Zervogianni Report.
[312] Van Ngo Report.
[313] Vítor and Martins Online Report.
[314] Bugajski and Wysocka-Bar Report.
[315] Law Commission of England and Wales and Scottish Law Commission, 'Building Families through Surrogacy: A New Law', June 2019, ss 7.85–7.90.
[316] State Committee on the Reassessment of Parenthood, 'Child and Parents in the 21st Century'.
[317] Schrama Report.
[318] Ibid.

this draft bill will turn out to be no more than a step in the direction of further law reform, which may result in more equality for multi-parent families.[319]

In South Africa, there is no general law recognising multiplicity of parenthood, nor are there plans to enact such a law. It should, however, be noted that the Children's Act 38 of 2005 gives no indication of the maximum number of legal parents a child may have. The Act makes provision for more than one person to acquire and exercise parental responsibilities and rights in respect of the same child, but it is unclear whether all co-holders of parental responsibilities and rights would qualify as the child's parents.[320]

Finally, it is interesting to note that Vietnam does not have a law that recognises multi-parenthood, but its Marriage and Family Law 2014 protects multi-generational families, such as grandparents, parents and children who live together.[321] The Law also regulates the responsibilities and rights of daughters-in-law, sons-in-law and parents-in-law who live in the same household.[322]

3. PART B. DIVERSITY AND PLURALITY OF FAMILY'S FUNCTIONS

3.1. LEGAL RECOGNITION OF VARIOUS FUNCTIONS OF THE FAMILY

Because these issues are closely bound up with local traditions and culture, there is no universal definition or understanding either of the concept of 'family' or of its functions. Consequently, a unit which qualifies as a family for purposes of legal protection in one jurisdiction may not qualify as such in another. The same applies to a particular function of the family. Even within a single jurisdiction, a particular type of family or a particular function of the family may qualify for protection in one area but not in another.[323] It should also be borne in mind that there is a difference between the existence of a particular family function and the legal protection of the function,[324] and that all functions may not be recognised in respect of all units that qualify as a family within a particular jurisdiction. For instance, in Austria,[325] Belgium,[326] and Italy,[327] multiple family functions are

---

[319] Ibid.
[320] Louw Report.
[321] Van Ngo Report.
[322] Ibid.
[323] E.g. in South Africa, not all types of polygamous marriages receive the same recognition. Polygamous customary marriages are fully recognised, but polygamous religious marriages are recognised for limited purposes only: Louw Report.
[324] Gallus, Leleu, Mathieu and Swennen Report.
[325] Buchstätter and Roth Report.
[326] Gallus, Leleu, Mathieu and Swennen Report.
[327] Aluffi Report.

recognised but they do not receive the same level of recognition and protection in all the types of families that occur in each of these countries. Further, the concept of 'family' keeps changing due to, inter alia, social development and medical advancements, for example in the field of assisted reproduction.[328] The functions of the family also change over time.[329]

Some of the rapporteurs stated that it was difficult to identify the various functions of the family and to indicate the extent to which their countries' law recognises these functions, because the functions and the policy with regard to the functions are not spelled out.[330] Consequently, the various functions and the law's recognition of these functions are largely matters of conjecture and personal opinion.[331] Furthermore, family law is not the only field that is relevant in determining the extent of the legal recognition of the various functions of the family. Because fields such as tax law, the law of succession/inheritance, social security law, and criminal law place families or family members in a special position, they must also be considered.[332] Regional and international instruments, too, influence the recognition and protection that is afforded to various types of families and various family functions, because local law is tested against these instruments and must be adapted because of successful court challenges based on these instruments. For example, in Europe, decisions by the European Court of Human Rights have compelled countries to adapt their laws to accommodate new notions of the family and its functions.[333]

Despite the above-mentioned difficulties, most rapporteurs agree that providing economic security and financial support to children and economically weaker family members is an important function of the family and is recognised as such by the law.[334] The issue of whether the State views a family as consisting of individual people or as a unit influences the extent of the legal protection that is afforded to this function. In countries where the State prizes individual responsibility, the premise is that each person must ensure his or her own economic welfare, regardless of whether or not he or she is in a family relationship and has care responsibilities in respect of spouses, partners, children or other

---

[328] See e.g. Buchstätter and Roth Report.
[329] Zervogianni Report.
[330] Fenton-Glynn and Scherpe Report; Sanders Report; Schrama Report; Bugajski and Wysocka-Bar Report.
[331] See e.g. Sanders Report; Schrama Report; Bugajski and Wysocka-Bar Report.
[332] Schrama Report; Bugajski and Wysocka-Bar Report.
[333] Buchstätter and Roth Report; Aluffi Report.
[334] See e.g. Australia: Kha Report; Belgium: Gallus, Leleu, Mathieu and Swennen Report; Denmark: Lund-Andersen and Pedersen Report; England and Wales: Fenton-Glynn and Scherpe Report; Estonia: Kull and Torga Online Report; Germany: Sanders Report; Greece: Zervogianni Report; Japan: Roots Report; Luxembourg: Hilger Report; Portugal: Vítor and Martins Online Report; the Netherlands: Schrama Report; South Africa: Louw Report; Turkey: Paksoy Report; Vietnam: Van Ngo Report.

relatives.[335] For example, in the Netherlands, community of property and post-divorce maintenance have been limited, thus imposing the State's preference for individual responsibility on spouses and partners.[336] In Belgium, too, the premise is that the functions of the family are performed by the individual members of the family for the benefit of individual members of the family.[337] In Germany, entitlement to post-divorce maintenance has also been restricted, but the family is still seen as the main source of economic security.[338]

As the rapporteurs from Quebec indicate, an important consideration in the context of the economic security and financial support function of the family is that vulnerable family members must be protected while the individual freedoms of family members must simultaneously be respected.[339]

Having and raising children are also recognised as functions of the family (or of some families).[340] Some jurisdictions even view having children as the natural function of the family.[341] The absence of children does not mean that there is no 'family'. Some jurisdictions do, however, provide public assistance for assisted reproduction and some extend such access to people who fall outside the ambit of the traditional, heterosexual family. For example, in Denmark, single women, same-sex and heterosexual couples can have free fertility treatment at public clinics.[342] By providing financial aid to parents, the State also recognises that raising children is a function of the family. Such aid is provided, for instance, by way of the Child and Youth Benefit in Denmark[343] and the Child Support Grant in South Africa.[344] Denmark and South Africa set an income threshold for the grants. In South Africa, the grant is restricted to low-income families, while the Danish income threshold is so high that most families with children receive the grant.[345] On top of the grant, single parents in Denmark receive an extra amount from the State.[346] Argentina[347] and Germany[348] also give grants to family members. Obviously, the laws relating to parental responsibilities and rights, legal parenthood, adoption, affiliation and so forth – which formed

---

[335] Schrama Report.
[336] Ibid.
[337] Gallus, Leleu, Mathieu and Swennen Report.
[338] Sanders Report.
[339] Giroux and Langevin Report.
[340] See e.g. Argentina: Medina Report; Australia: Kha Report; Denmark: Lund-Andersen and Pedersen Report; Germany: Sanders Report; Greece: Zervogianni Report; Japan: Roots Report; Poland: Bugajski and Wysocka-Bar Report; Portugal: Vítor and Martins Online Report; South Africa: Louw Report; Turkey: Paksoy Report; Vietnam: Van Ngo Report.
[341] Turkey: Paksoy Report.
[342] Lund-Andersen and Pedersen Report.
[343] Ibid.
[344] The grant is regulated by the Social Assistance Act 13 of 2004.
[345] Lund-Andersen and Pedersen Report.
[346] Ibid.
[347] Medina Report.
[348] Sanders Report.

the subject of section 2 of this report – also afford recognition to the family's function of having and raising children.

Several jurisdictions recognise that the family functions as a place where persons take care of each other.[349] In Australia, the caring role of a spouse or de facto partner is recognised as a non-financial contribution and is one of the factors in determining the division of relationship property.[350] Australian law also protects close personal relationships other than marriages or de facto relationships between two adults who live together if one of the adults provides domestic support and personal care to the other or both adults provide domestic support and personal care to each other.[351] Such relationships can exist between, inter alia, siblings or a grandparent and an adult grandchild, thus giving legal recognition to the function of care within the extended family. In Italy, the burden of taking care of children, the elderly and persons living with disabilities falls predominantly on family members – particularly women – because the State does not provide extensive public services.[352] The position in Quebec is similar, because the welfare state has waned.[353] In Germany, around 71% of all people who need care are cared for by family members at home.[354] The State recognises this burden, not only through the child, spousal and parental support grants referred to above, but also by affording the persons who provide care the right to take time off from work.[355] In Croatia, children's duty to take care of their elderly and infirm parents is stipulated in the Constitution[356] and the Family Act 2015 compels family members to help and respect each other.[357] In Japan, caring for elderly family members is traditionally viewed as the responsibility of the eldest son and his wife.[358] In 2018, the Civil Code was amended to introduce the possibility of compensating a non-relative who cared for an elderly family member. The rapporteur for Japan states that the amendment was primarily intended to benefit a daughter-in-law who cared for her mother-in-law.[359] In terms of the amendment, a relative who is not an heir and has made a special contribution to the deceased's maintenance by, for instance, providing unpaid nursing can claim payment for the contribution from the deceased's heirs.[360] The amendment was controversial. The rapporteur for Japan states that it

---

[349] See e.g. Portugal: Vítor and Martins Online Report; Turkey: Paksoy Report; Vietnam: Van Ngo Report.
[350] Kha Report.
[351] Ibid.
[352] Aluffi Report.
[353] Giroux and Langevin Report.
[354] Sanders Report.
[355] Ibid.
[356] Rešetar and Lucić Report.
[357] Ibid.
[358] Roots Report.
[359] Ibid.
[360] Ibid.

was lauded by some for 'enabling a daughter-in-law to receive some of the inheritance in return for the care that she had provided' while 'others feared that this provision could result in other family members forcing daughters-in-law into caring for elderly family members, since they could now expect a monetary reward' once the family member passes away.[361]

Another function of the family is to provide a special bond, which is legally recognised and protected inter alia by family members being placed in a preferential position to be appointed as a guardian or curator, a right not to testify in criminal proceedings, and a special duty of care. This is the position in, for instance, the Netherlands.[362]

The rapporteur for Greece identifies another function of the family, namely that it is a refuge of love and companionship. She states that this function has been recognised through liberalised divorce laws and the recognition of cohabitation agreements for heterosexual and same-sex couples.[363] This function goes hand in hand with the function of raising children, as children's interests are served best by being raised in a loving environment.[364]

The Belgian report refers to the special family function of allowing the members of the family to flourish towards a sufficient degree of autonomy and happiness, through the love, affection and mutual aid or sharing that normally characterises family life.[365] In this regard, the State and the laws it enacts must be wary of encroaching on or intervening in private life, for fear of unduly limiting the right to self-determination. The Belgian rapporteurs consider their country to be one of the most advanced jurisdictions in the world in respecting self-determination.[366]

3.2. THE FUNCTIONS WHICH ARE PREDOMINANTLY FAVOURED

Some rapporteurs state that it is difficult, or even impossible, to answer the question of which family function predominates in their jurisdiction, because no function is expressly favoured, research on this issue is hard to come by, and the answer depends on how predominance is determined and measured.[367] Some rapporteurs identify the function of having and raising children as the one

---

[361] Roots Report, section 3.1.4.
[362] Schrama Report.
[363] Zervogianni Report.
[364] Ibid.
[365] Gallus, Leleu, Mathieu and Swennen Report.
[366] Ibid.
[367] E.g. Austria: Buchstätter and Roth Report; Estonia: Kull and Torga Online Report; Germany: Sanders Report; Japan: Roots Report; the Netherlands: Schrama Report; Luxembourg: Hilger Report.

that is predominantly favoured in their jurisdiction,[368] while others identify the economic security and financial support function as predominating.[369] Another group of rapporteurs is of the view that both of these functions predominate in their jurisdictions.[370] The Greek rapporteur identifies the family's function of being a refuge of love and companionship as predominating in Greece, but states that the function goes hand in hand with the function of raising children.[371]

3.3. THE ROLE OF CHILDREN IN THE LEGAL VIEW ON THE FUNCTIONS OF THE FAMILY

In general, the law in the countries surveyed does not view the family's functions differently depending on whether children are present in the family.[372] However, if children are present, the function of raising children may be elevated above the other functions of the family.[373] Furthermore, the presence of children plays a role in respect of the scope of the functions of the family in that families with children have to provide economic security and financial support, not only to the adults in the family, but also to the children. Families with children may also receive greater State assistance than families without children, for example by way of free schooling, tax benefits and State grants.[374] Furthermore, as is quite obvious, the caretaking function of the family encompasses more people if there are children in the family. In some jurisdictions, childcare responsibilities may be taken into account in awarding maintenance and/or dividing property on divorce or separation.[375]

Finally, it should be noted that the question whether a child is a step-child, biological child, child born as a result of donor-assisted reproductive technology, 'three-parent' child, or child born as a result of surrogacy plays no role in respect of the functions of the family or the scope of the functions.[376]

---

[368] E.g. Argentina: Medina Report; Poland: Bugajski and Wysocka-Bar Report; Vietnam: Van Ngo Report; Italy: Aluffi Report.
[369] E.g. Australia: Kha Report.
[370] E.g. Estonia: Kull and Torga Online Report; Portugal: Vítor and Martins Online Report.
[371] Zervogianni Report.
[372] E.g. Estonia: Kull and Torga Online Report; Greece: Zervogianni Report; Luxembourg: Hilger Report; Quebec: Giroux and Langevin Report.
[373] E.g. Austria: Buchstätter and Roth Report; Australia: Kha Report; England and Wales: Fenton-Glynn and Scherpe Report; Turkey: Paksoy Report. See also Louw Report.
[374] See e.g. Denmark: Lund-Andersen and Pedersen Report; Germany: Sanders Report.
[375] E.g. the Netherlands: Schrama Report.
[376] E.g. Austria: Buchstätter and Roth Report; Greece: Zervogianni Report; Poland: Bugajski and Wysocka-Bar Report; Portugal: Vítor and Martins Online Report; the Netherlands: Schrama Report; Turkey: Paksoy Report.

4. CONCLUSION

The first objective of the questionnaire on the theme 'Diversity and Plurality in the Law: Family Forms and Family's Functions' was to determine whether, and if so, how, family law in the jurisdictions surveyed recognises that a child can have multiple parents. The information provided by the rapporteurs shows that, in most jurisdictions, the starting point is that family law recognises only two legal parents.

Generally, in countries that do not permit same-sex marriages/partnerships, the two parents who are legally recognised are one male and one female person, that is, one father and one mother. The law in all the jurisdictions consider the woman who gives birth to be the child's mother. Thus, gestation, not a biological (genetic) link, is the determining factor in so far as legal motherhood is concerned. For the father, in contrast, either marriage to (or a legally recognised partnership with) the birth mother or a biological link is the foundation of legal parenthood. If the birth mother has a husband/partner, this person is the child's father (or second parent, if the particular jurisdiction recognises same-sex marriages/partnerships). If the presumption of paternity is rebutted, the biological father (i.e. the person whose sperm merged with the mother's ovum) can, in some jurisdictions, become the child's legal parent by acknowledging the child or getting a court order declaring that he is the child's father, but then he alone will be the child's father. In other words, the biological father does not become an additional parent. However, in some countries, the courts are allowing both the biological father and the mother's husband/partner to be the child's legal parent if this is in the best interests of the child. If the birth mother is unmarried and not a party to a recognised partnership, the law generally adopts one of two approaches: (1) the biological father is the child's second legally recognised parent if he acknowledges the child or gets a court order declaring that he is the child's father; or (2) the mother is the child's only legally recognised parent.

'Three-parent' technology does not alter application of the above-mentioned rules. Assisted reproduction without surrogacy changes the rules, but does so without adding another parent. In the case of assisted reproduction without surrogacy, the husband/partner of the birth mother is the child's second parent regardless of whether his sperm was used for the assisted reproduction; that is, it is irrelevant whether he is the child's biological father. If surrogacy takes place, the jurisdictions generally adopt one of two approaches: (1) the surrogate mother's husband/partner is the legal parent to the exclusion of the intended father; or (2) the intended father is the legal parent to the exclusion of the mother's husband or partner. Here, too, the child has only two legal parents.

If the two legally recognised parents are married or are partners in a recognised partnership and their relationship ends, both of them remain the child's legal parents. They retain all the responsibilities and rights encompassed in legal parenthood unless the court orders otherwise. The same applies if the child's parents were never married and were not partners in a recognised partnership but jointly had parental responsibilities and rights in respect of the child (e.g. because the father recognised the child).

If one of the parents remarries or enters into a new legally recognised partnership, the step-parent usually does not become the child's third legal parent, unless he or she adopts the child. In some jurisdictions, the step-parent adoption does not terminate the child's legal relationship with his or her parents of origin and can therefore be said to result in the child having multiple parents. In other jurisdictions, the adoption terminates the child's legal relationship with the parent who is not married to the step-parent or is not the step-parent's partner. In the latter instance, the step-parent replaces the other parent as legal parent, resulting in the child still having only two legal parents. If the step-parent does not adopt the child, he or she can acquire responsibilities and rights by way of a court order, an agreement, delegation or a mandate or in terms of a specific statutory provision which confers a right or imposes a responsibility on the step-parent. Delegation and a mandate does not have the result that the step-parent legally becomes an additional parent to the child. If the step-parent obtains responsibilities and rights by way of a court order or an agreement, the scope of the responsibilities and rights determine whether the step-parent can be said legally to have become an additional parent to the step-child. Some jurisdictions impose a duty of support on a step-parent. This duty, on its own, does not amount to recognising the step-parent as an additional parent of the step-child. In some jurisdictions, if the relationship between the child's parent and the step-parent ends, the step-parent has or may have or acquire a right to maintain contact with the child. This right to contact may qualify as legal recognition of the step-parent's position as an additional parent to the step-child and may, in this sense, constitute recognition of multiplicity of parenthood.

Subject to exceptions relating to some step-parent adoptions, full adoption normally substitutes the adoptive parents as legal parents for the parents of origin. *Kafala* is not legally recognised in the jurisdictions surveyed and does not result in a similar change of legal parenthood. In some jurisdictions, the child's original parents retain their duty of support after the adoption. It is doubted whether the retention of this duty amounts to recognition of multiple parents. If the family of origin (or some members of that family) have contact rights in respect of the child, this might qualify as recognition of multiple parents after the adoption, albeit in a limited sense. Entitling the family of origin to the right to obtain information about the child does not, however, qualify as recognising multiple parents after the adoption.

None of the jurisdictions have, or plan to introduce, a general law that recognises multi-parenthood in a generic, broad manner.

The second main objective of the questionnaire was to determine which family functions the law recognises and favours, and whether the presence of children in the family makes a difference in this regard. The main functions identified by the rapporteurs are the provision of economic security and financial support to children and economically weaker family members; having and raising children; being a place where persons take care of each other; providing a special bond to the family members; and being a refuge of love and companionship.

The two functions which predominate are the provision of economic security and financial support to children and economically weaker family members, and having and raising children.

Generally, the law in the countries surveyed does not view the family's functions differently depending on whether children are present in the family. However, if children are present, the function of raising children may be elevated above the other functions and, naturally, the scope of the provision of economic security and financial support and of caretaking responsibilities is increased.

The question whether a child is a step-child, biological child, child born as a result of donor-assisted reproductive technology, 'three-parent' child, or child born as a result of surrogacy plays no role in respect of the functions of the family or the scope of the functions.

RAPPORT GENERAL

Formes et fonctions familiales – Une perspective comparative

Jacqueline Heaton et Aida Kemelmajer

1. Introduction 46
2. Partie A. Diversité et pluralité des formes familiales 47
   2.1. Reconnaissance de la multiplicité des responsabilités parentales dans le contexte des familles recomposees 47
   2.2. Reconnaissance de la multiparentalité si un enfant est élevé dans plus d'un ménage 56
   2.3. Reconnaissance de parentalité multiple si un enfant est élevé dans une famille polygame 60
   2.4. Reconnaissance des parents multiples en cas d'adoption ouverte 61
   2.5. Reconnaissance de parentalité multiple dans le cas de *kafala*... 66
   2.6. La reconnaissance de parentalité multiple dans le cas de la procréation assistée par donneur (sans gestation pour autrui) 66
   2.7. Reconnaissance des parents multiples dans le cas d'un « enfant à trois parents » 74
   2.8. Reconnaissance des parents multiples en cas de gestation pour autrui 75
   2.9. Reconnaissance générale de la multiparentalité 80
3. Partie B. Diversité et pluralité des fonctions de la famille 81
   3.1. Reconnaissance juridique des diverses fonctions de la famille 81
   3.2. Les fonctions qui sont principalement favorisées 86
   3.3. Le rôle des enfants dans la vision juridique des fonctions de la famille 86
4. Conclusion 87

Résumé

Ce rapport examine et tire des conclusions des renseignements présentées dans les rapports nationaux spéciaux sur le thème « Diversité et pluralité dans le droit : formes familiales et fonctions de la famille ». Deux questions principales sont étudiées. La première est de savoir si, et si oui, comment, le droit de la famille dans les juridictions étudiées reconnaît qu'un enfant peut avoir plusieurs parents. L'accent est mis sur les familles recomposées où les enfants de l'un ou des deux conjoints/partenaires sont élevés dans le même ménage ; les familles où les enfants sont élevés dans plus d'un ménage, par exemple parce que leurs parents exercent conjointement la garde après la séparation ou n'ont jamais partagé un ménage mais partagent les responsabilités parentales ; les familles polygames où les enfants sont élevés dans un ménage où l'une des parties a plus d'une femme/mari/partenaire ; les familles dont les enfants ont été adoptés mais entretiennent des liens (légaux ou de facto) avec leur famille biologique ; les familles où les enfants sont pris en charge dans le cadre d'un arrangement de *kafala* ; les familles où un enfant est né à la suite d'une technologie de procréation assistée par donneur utilisant un gamète mâle et un gamète femelle ; les familles où un enfant est né à la suite d'une technologie médicale dite « à trois parents » ; et les familles où un enfant est né à la suite d'une gestation pour autrui. La deuxième question principale qui est examinée dans le rapport est de savoir quelles fonctions familiales sont reconnues et favorisées par la loi, et si la présence d'enfants dans la famille fait une différence à cet égard.

1. INTRODUCTION

Ce rapport général donne un aperçu des conclusions des rapports nationaux spéciaux sur le thème « Diversité et pluralité de formes familiales et fonctions familiales ». Le rapport est rédigé sur la base des réponses à un questionnaire préparé spécialement pour ce sujet. Le texte intégral du questionnaire en anglais et en français est joint en annexe au présent rapport général.

Le questionnaire avait deux objectifs principaux. Le premier consistait à déterminer si, et dans l'affirmative, comment, dans les juridictions examinées, le droit de la famille reconnaît qu'un enfant peut avoir plusieurs parents. Par souci de comparabilité, les familles pluriparentales se limitent à :

- des familles recomposées où les enfants d'un ou de deux conjoints/partenaires sont élevés dans le même foyer ;
- des familles où les enfants sont élevés dans plus d'un foyer, par exemple parce que leurs parents exercent conjointement la responsabilité parentale après la séparation ou n'ont jamais partagé un foyer, mais partagent la responsabilité parentale ;

- des familles polygames où les enfants sont élevés dans un foyer où une partie a plus d'une femme/partenaire ;
- des familles d'adoption ouverte, c'est-à-dire des familles où des enfants ont été adoptés, mais ils conservent des liens (légaux ou de facto) avec leurs familles biologiques.
- des familles où les enfants n'ont pas été adoptés, mais vivent dans un foyer en termes de kafala ;[1]
- des familles où un enfant est né à la suite d'une technique de reproduction assistée à l'aide d'un donneur de gamètes, masculin ou féminin (c'est-à-dire, le sperme ou l'œuf/ovule) ;
- des familles où un enfant est né à la suite d'une technologie médicale dite « à trois parents » ;[2]
- des familles où un enfant est né à la suite d'une gestation pour autrui.

Le deuxième objectif principal du questionnaire était de déterminer quelles fonctions familiales la loi reconnaît et favorise, et si la présence d'enfants dans la famille fait une différence à cet égard.

Étant donné que les défis multiculturels en droit de la famille étaient au cœur des sujets et thèmes du 20e Congrès de l'Académie internationale qui s'est tenu à Fukuoka, au Japon, en 2018, le questionnaire ne tenait pas compte de la multiplicité/pluralité des unions civiles, culturelles, autochtones et religieuses. En plus, les rapporteurs spéciaux ont reçu l'instruction spécifique de ne pas s'étendre sur le droit international privé et le droit médical, ni sur les droits culturels, autochtones et religieux et le pluralisme juridique.

Vingt rapports nationaux spéciaux ont été reçus (seize en anglais[3] et quatre en français[4]). Nous soulignons ci-dessous certains des points des rapports :

2. PARTIE A. DIVERSITÉ ET PLURALITÉ DES FORMES FAMILIALES

2.1. RECONNAISSANCE DE LA MULTIPLICITÉ DES RESPONSABILITÉS PARENTALES DANS LE CONTEXTE DES FAMILLES RECOMPOSEES

D'emblée, il faut dire que certaines juridictions, comme l'Argentine, préfèrent utiliser les expressions « familles recomposées » « parents liés par le mariage »,

---

[1] Voir l'annexe pour une explication sur la *kafala*.
[2] Voir l'annexe pour une explication sur la technologie médicale dite « à trois parents ».
[3] Argentine : Mme. Graciela Medina, Université de Buenos Aires ; Australie : Dr Henry Kha, Université Macquarie ; Autriche : M. Elmar Buchstätter et Prof. Marianne Roth, Paris Lodron, Université de Salzbourg ; Croatie : Prof. Branka Rešetar et Nataša Lucić, J.J.Strossmayer Université de Osijek; Danemark : Prof. Ingrid Lund-Andersen et associée Prof. Frank Høgholm

« père ou mère par alliance », en raison des connotations négatives attachées au mot « beau-parent ». Toutefois, aux fins du présent rapport, nous utilisons la terminologie usée dans le questionnaire, c'est-à-dire « familles recomposées » et « beaux-parents ».[5]

La plupart des juridictions examinées ne reconnaissent pas que le conjoint ou le cohabitant de la mère ou du père est un parent légal supplémentaire ni qu'il ou elle prend automatiquement des responsabilités et des droits à l'égard de l'enfant. Toutefois, il ou elle peut devenir un parent légal en adoptant le fils ou la fille du conjoint ou du cohabitant. Une fois qu'une décision d'adoption a été accordée, il ou elle a les mêmes responsabilités et droits juridiques que le parent avec lequel il partage un ménage. Dans certaines juridictions, comme l'Angleterre, le pays de Galles et les Pays-Bas, cette adoption met complètement fin à la relation juridique entre l'enfant et l'autre parent ; c'est-à-dire, le parent avec lequel il ne partage pas un ménage.[6] Dans ces juridictions, il n'y a pas de multiplicité des responsabilités parentales après l'adoption de l'enfant parce que, même après l'adoption, la loi ne reconnait que deux parents. Dans d'autres juridictions, telles que l'Argentine, la Belgique et l'Italie, l'adoption par le beau-parent par voie d'une « adoption simple » ne met pas fin à la relation juridique de l'enfant avec ses parents d'origine et peut donc être considérée comme donnant lieu à une multiplicité de parentalité après l'adoption.[7]

Si le beau-parent n'adopte pas l'enfant du conjoint ou du cohabitant, il ou elle peut acquérir des responsabilités et des droits à l'égard de l'enfant si le parent légal de l'enfant lui délègue, lui donne un mandat d'exercer ses responsabilités et ses droits, ou conclut un accord lui conférant des responsabilités et des droits.

Pedersen, Université de Copenhague ; Angleterre et pays de Galles : Prof. Claire Fenton-Glynn, Université de Cambridge et Prof. Jens M Scherpe, Aalborg University; Estonie : Prof. Irene Kull et Dr Maarja Torga, Université de Tatu (Rapport qui contient les réponses au questionnaire, publié en ligne) ; Allemagne : Prof. Anne Sanders, Université de Bielefeld ; Grèce : Associate Prof. Eleni Zervogianni, Université Aristote de Thessalonique ; Japan : Prof. Maia Roots, Université de Tohoku ; Pologne : Dr Błażej Bugajski, Université d'Économie à Cracovie et Dr Anna Wysocka-Bar, Université Jagoellonian à Cracovie ; Portugal : Prof. Paula Távora Vítor et Mme Rosa Cândido Martins, Université de Coimbra (Rapport qui contient les réponses au questionnaire, publié en ligne ; Afrique du Sud : Prof. Anne Louw, Université de Pretoria ; Pays-Bas : Prof. Wendy Schrama, Université d'Utrecht ; Turquie : Professeur assistant Meliha Sermin Paksoy, Université Altinbas ; Vietnam : Prof. Thi Anh Van Ngo, Université de Droit d'Hô-Chi-Minh-Ville.

[4] Belgique : Prof. Nicole Gallus, Université Libre de Bruxelles, Prof. Yves-Henri Leleu, Université de Liège, Prof. Géraldine Mathieu, Université de Namur et Prof. Frederik Swennen, Université d'Anvers ; Italie : Prof. associée Roberta Aluffi, Université de Turin ; Luxembourg : Prof. Françoise Hilger, Université du Luxembourg ; Québec, Canada : Prof. Michelle Giroux, Université d'Ottawa et Prof. Louise Langevin, Université Laval, Québec.

[5] Rapport Medina.

[6] Angleterre et pays de Galles : Rapport Fenton-Glynn and Scherpe ; Pays-Bas : Rapport Schrama.

[7] Argentine : Rapport Medina ; Belgique : Rapport Gallus, Leleu, Mathieu et Swennen ; Italie : Rapport Aluffi.

Selon l'étendue des responsabilités et des droits que le beau-parent obtient de cette manière et la source d'où ils proviennent, le beau-parent peut devenir un parent supplémentaire pour l'enfant, ce qui entraîne une multiplicité de parents. Si, par exemple, toutes les responsabilités et tous les droits parentaux sont conférés au beau-parent par le biais d'un accord entre le beau-parent et le parent de l'enfant, cela signifie que le beau-parent est ajouté en tant que titulaire des responsabilités et des droits parentaux et que l'enfant a plusieurs parents. Cela peut se produire, par exemple, en Afrique du Sud, comme expliqué ci-dessous. Si le beau-parent acquiert des responsabilités et des droits très limités, il est douteux que cela puisse être considéré comme une reconnaissance de la multiplicité des responsabilités parentales. Lorsque le pouvoir du beau-parent d'exercer ses responsabilités et ses droits découle de la délégation par le parent de l'enfant, il n'y a pas de multiplicité de la parentalité, car le beau-parent ne fait que s'acquitter des responsabilités et des droits du parent au nom du parent. En Afrique du Sud, le parent de l'enfant peut conclure un accord avec le beau-parent conférant tout ou partie des responsabilités et des droits au beau-parent et peut l'autoriser à les exercer en son nom,[8] mais cette autorisation ne prive pas le parent de ses responsabilités et ses droits ni ne le dispense de s'acquitter de ses responsabilités.[9] En Angleterre et au pays de Galles, également, le beau parent peut obtenir des responsabilités et des droits si les parents de l'enfant en consentent.[10] Au Luxembourg, le parent de l'enfant peut confier au beau-parent un mandat concernant l'éducation quotidienne de l'enfant.[11] La loi portugaise permet à un beau-parent d'exercer des responsabilités et des droits à l'égard de l'enfant s'il vit avec le parent de l'enfant dans une union de fait et si le parent de l'enfant délègue au beau-parent des responsabilités et des droits en ce qui concerne les affaires quotidiennes.[12] En Argentine également, un parent peut déléguer des responsabilités et des droits parentaux au beau-parent lorsqu'il n'est pas en mesure d'exercer pleinement la fonction pour des raisons de voyage, de maladie ou d'incapacité temporaire, pourvu que l'autre parent soit dans l'impossibilité de l'exercer, ou qu'il ne soit pas convenable que ce dernier l'exerce. Cette délégation nécessite une autorisation judiciaire, à moins que l'autre parent n'exprime son accord d'une façon effective.[13] Étant donné que le pouvoir du parent d'exercer ses responsabilités et ses droits découle de la délégation, il n'y a pas de multiplicité de la parentalité.[14]

---

[8] Article 22 de la loi de 2005 sur l'enfance.
[9] Article 30(3) et (4) de la loi de 38 de 2005 sur l'enfance.
[10] Article 4A de la loi de 1989 sur l'enfance.
[11] Il s'agit d'une dispense relativement nouvelle, qui est entrée en vigueur le 27.06.2018 : Rapport Hilger.
[12] Rapport en ligne Vítor et Martin.
[13] Article 674 du Code civil et commercial argentin.
[14] Rapport Medina.

Le tribunal peut également conférer des responsabilités et des droits à un beau-parent. C'est le cas, par exemple, en Angleterre[15] et au pays de Galles, aux Pays-Bas[16] et en Afrique du Sud.[17] Selon l'étendue des responsabilités et des droits conférés au beau-parent et selon que l'ordonnance du tribunal met fin ou limite les responsabilités et les droits des parents de l'enfant, la situation peut donner lieu à une multiplicité de parents.

Certaines juridictions imposent automatiquement une obligation alimentaire au beau-parent même s'il n'adopte pas l'enfant. Ainsi, la loi estonienne impose une obligation alimentaire au beau-parent qui est marié au parent de l'enfant.[18] Également, aux Pays-Bas,[19] le conjoint ou le partenaire enregistré du parent de l'enfant a le devoir de soutenir l'enfant. En Argentine, un beau-parent a l'obligation subsidiaire de soutenir son beau-fils pendant que l'enfant est mineur ou si l'enfant est handicapé.[20] En règle générale, cette obligation n'existe que lorsque le beau-parent partage un ménage avec l'autre parent. Outre l'obligation subsidiaire de pension alimentaire, le beau-parent et le parent avec lequel le beau-parent est marié sont solidairement responsables des obligations relatives aux besoins ordinaires du ménage ou au soutien et à l'éducation des enfants du ménage.[21]

La loi polonaise tient également le beau-parent responsable de la pension alimentaire de l'enfant, mais dans ce pays, l'obligation n'est engagée que si elle est justifiée par ce que l'on appelle les « principes de la vie communautaire ».[22] Ces principes font référence aux circonstances dans lesquelles l'imposition de l'obligation reflète un sens commun de l'équité, fondé sur des règles morales et de bonnes pratiques sociétales.[23] En Pologne, l'obligation alimentaire est réciproque, c'est-à-dire que le beau-parent peut réclamer une pension alimentaire à l'enfant de son conjoint si celui-ci a contribué à l'éducation et au soutien financier

---

[15] Article 4A de la loi de 1989 sur les enfants. Si la relation entre le beau parent et le parent de l'enfant n'est pas formalisée comme un mariage ou une union civile, le beau-parent peut obtenir la responsabilité parentale au moyen d'une ordonnance d'arrangements avec l'enfant : articles 8, 12(2) et 12(2A) de la loi de 1989 sur les enfants.

[16] Article 1:253 du Code civil néerlandais.

[17] Article 23 de la loi 38 de 2005 sur l'enfance. La Haute Cour peut également attribuer tout ou partie des responsabilités et droits parentaux au beau-parent en vertu de la *common law*.

[18] Rapport en ligne Kull et Torga.

[19] Article 1:395 du Code civil néerlandais.

[20] Article 676 du Code civil et commercial argentin. Toutefois, le beau-parent doit subvenir aux besoins de son beau-fils après la cessation de la cohabitation avec le parent de l'enfant si la situation modifiée peut causer un préjudice grave a l'enfant et que le beau-parent a assumé un devoir de soutien envers lui tout en vivant avec son parent. Rapport Medina.

[21] Article 461 du Code civil et commercial argentin.

[22] Article 144 §1 du Code de la famille et de la tutelle.

[23] Arrêt de la Cour Suprême du 04.04.1968, III CZP 27/68, OSNC 1969, n° 1, point 1.6 ; A. Zbiegień-Turzańska, 'Comment Art. 5 Polish Civil Code' in K. Osajda (ed.), *Kodeks cywilny. Komentarz*, 27ᵉ ed., Legalis Online Database 2020, point. 55.

de l'enfant et si la demande est conforme aux « principes de la vie communautaire ».[24] Au Japon, un beau-parent est responsable de la pension alimentaire si le tribunal constate qu'il existe des « circonstances spéciales » pour lui imposer une obligation alimentaire.[25]

Au Québec, la doctrine *in loco parentis* peut être utilisée afin d'obliger un beau-parent « qui agit à titre de parent de l'enfant » à soutenir l'enfant même après avoir divorcé du parent de l'enfant.[26]

En Croatie, un beau-parent a le devoir d'entretenir l'enfant après le décès du parent de l'enfant si le survivant n'a pas les moyens de soutenir l'enfant et n'exerce pas ses responsabilités parentales à l'égard de l'enfant.[27]

En Afrique du Sud, deux décisions de justice ont déclaré qu'un beau-père peut être tenu responsable de l'entretien de son beau-fils. En Turquie,[28] un beau-parent a également le devoir de contribuer à l'entretien d'un enfant, car le beau-parent doit contribuer aux dépenses de la famille.[29] Certains auteurs turcs sont de l'avis que l'obligation que le Code civil turc impose aux « parents » de couvrir les dépenses liées aux soins, à la protection et à l'éducation de leurs enfants s'étend aux beaux-enfants[30] et que le statut de belle fille en soi oblige le beau-parent à soutenir le bel-enfant.[31] En Belgique, les conjoints et les personnes qui cohabitent légalement (c'est-à-dire les personnes qui sont ce qu'on appelle des partenaires enregistrés ou des partenaires civils/domestiques dans certaines juridictions) sont tenus de contribuer aux dépenses domestiques et sont solidairement responsables des dettes pour les besoins du ménage et l'éducation des enfants dans le ménage commun.[32] Par conséquent, une personne qui est mariée ou qui est le partenaire du parent de l'enfant remplit indirectement une obligation alimentaire envers l'enfant. Si le parent meurt, le beau-parent doit entretenir et éduquer l'enfant avec des biens qu'il a hérité du parent prédécédé et des avantages que le beau-parent a reçu du contrat de mariage, de l'accord de cohabitation ou par don.[33]

---

[24] Article 144 §2 du Code de la famille et de la tutelle.
[25] Rapport Roots.
[26] Le paragraphe 2(2) de la Loi sur le divorce, qui s'applique au fédéral. Le beau-parent sera *in loco parentis* s'il a agi en tant que véritable parent de remplacement de l'enfant. Il doit démontrer sa volonté d'assumer, de façon continue et permanente, les responsabilités que la loi attribue normalement aux parents : article 15.1(1) de la Loi sur le divorce ; *Chartier c. Chartier* [1999] 1 RCS 242.
[27] Article 288 paragraphe 3, de la loi de 2015 sur la famille.
[28] *Heystek c. Heystek* 2002 (2) SA 754 (T); *MB c NB* 2010 (3) SA 220 (GSJ).
[29] Rapport Paksoy.
[30] Article 327 du Code civil turc.
[31] Rapport Paksoy. La plupart des commentateurs soutiennent que les obligations du beau parent sont secondaires et complémentaires aux droits et obligations des parents.
[32] Article 1477 du Code civil belge.
[33] Article 203, §3 et 1477, §5 du Code civil belge.

Il est douteux que l'imposition d'une obligation alimentaire directe ou indirecte à un beau-parent, par quelque mécanisme juridique que ce soit, équivaut à reconnaître la multiplicité de la parentalité.

En Pologne, un enfant[34] qui partage un ménage avec son parent et son beau-parent, au moment de la mort du beau-parent ne peut être exclu de la maison ni de l'utilisation des appareils ménagers. Ce droit s'applique pendant trois mois à compter de la date d'ouverture de la succession du beau-parent.[35] Bien sûr, ce droit ne constitue pas une reconnaissance de la parentalité de la part du beau-parent et donc, n'implique pas que l'enfant a légalement plusieurs parents. D'autres exemples de responsabilités et de droits conférés à des beaux parents qui ne constituent pas une reconnaissance de la multiplicité des filiations sont les suivants : en Turquie, le beau-parent, conjointement avec le parent avec lequel il partage un ménage, peut établir des règles de la maison que l'enfant doit suivre.[36] En outre, chaque époux doit accorder à l'autre un soutien raisonnable dans l'exercice des responsabilités et des droits parentaux à l'égard des enfants de ce dernier et doit représenter l'autre conjoint (c'est-à-dire le parent de l'enfant) si le parent ne peut pas représenter l'enfant et les circonstances exigent cette représentation.[37]

Ces exemples se rapportent à la situation entre le parent et le beau-parent ; par conséquent, ils ne confèrent pas la parentalité au beau-parent et n'équivalent pas à la reconnaissance de plusieurs parents. La loi autrichienne oblige également un beau-parent à aider le parent de l'enfant à exercer sa responsabilité parentale non essentielle.[38] L'obligation s'applique non seulement dans le cadre d'un mariage, mais aussi dans le cadre d'une cohabitation enregistrée[39] et d'une cohabitation informelle.[40] Il est important de noter que le beau-parent assume l'obligation à l'égard du parent de l'enfant, et non à l'égard de l'enfant. Par conséquent, cette obligation ne confère pas des responsabilités et des droits parentaux au beau-parent et n'entraîne pas l'acquisition de la paternité ou de la maternité.[41] En outre, l'obligation n'existe que dans la mesure où elle est requise par l'absence ou l'incapacité du parent pour cause de maladie.[42] Si les parents de l'enfant ont la responsabilité parentale, le beau-parent a le devoir et le droit de représenter le

---

[34] Le Code civil polonais ne fait pas expressément référence à « un enfant », mais, selon les rapporteurs pour la Pologne, « il est évident qu'un enfant doit être perçu comme « un autre proche » du défunt au sens de l'article 923 §1 du CC » : Rapport Bugajski et Wysocka-Bar.
[35] Bugajski et Wysocka-Bar Rapport.
[36] Article 339 II du Code civil turc.
[37] Rapport Paksoy.
[38] Article 90(3) du Code civil général autrichien.
[39] Le paragraphe 8(2) de la Loi sur les unions civiles enregistrées.
[40] Article 139(2) du Code civil général.
[41] Rapport Buchstätter and Roth.
[42] Ibid.

parent de l'enfant seulement si et quand les deux parents de l'enfant sont inaptes ou absents.[43] Par conséquent, il n'y a pas de multiplicité de parentalité dans ce contexte. En Croatie, un beau-parent qui vit dans le même ménage que l'enfant peut prendre des décisions concernant les affaires quotidiennes si le parent de l'enfant y consent.[44] En cas d'urgence, le beau-parent peut agir seul, mais il doit en informer le parent de l'enfant sans retard injustifié.[45] Dans ces circonstances également, le beau-parent ne devient pas légalement un parent supplémentaire de l'enfant. De même, en Argentine, le beau-parent et le parent de l'enfant doivent coopérer en ce qui concerne l'assistance et l'éducation de l'enfant ; le beau-parent peut prendre des décisions concernant l'enfant dans des situations d'urgence ; par ailleurs, il doit accomplir des actes quotidiens dans la sphère domestique concernant l'enfant.[46]

Il est intéressant de noter qu'en Pologne, la parentalité a des conséquences sur les procédures judiciaires et les procédures devant les autorités de l'administration publique. Étant donné que la législation polonaise confère peu de responsabilités et de droits aux beaux-parents[47] il est douteux que ces conséquences équivalent à la reconnaissance de parents multiples. Cela concerne les affaires lorsque des membres de la famille sont impliqués dans des procédures. En ce qui concerne la procédure civile, pénale et judiciaire administrative, un juge ne peut pas connaître d'une affaire concernant, entre autres, sa relation par affinité, qui comprend son beau-fils ou sa belle-fille. L'exclusion s'applique également lorsqu'il s'agit d'interroger un beau-fils dans une affaire dans laquelle son beau-parent est partie, et à être juge d'une procédure administrative, y compris une procédure fiscale dans laquelle son beau-parent est partie. En outre, un beau-fils ou une belle-fille a le droit de refuser de témoigner dans une procédure civile, pénale et administrative (y compris fiscale) si une partie à la procédure est son beau-parent, et un beau-parent peut refuser de témoigner dans une procédure dans laquelle son beau-fils ou sa belle-fille est partie. Un beau-parent ne peut pas être un expert dans une procédure civile, pénale ou administrative (y compris fiscale) si l'affaire concerne son beau-fils ou une belle-fille et réciproquement.[48] Au Japon, un beau-parent et un enfant ont le devoir réciproque de « s'aider l'un a l'autre ... en tant que parents qui vivent ensemble » si le beau-parent est marié au parent de l'enfant.[49]

Dans certaines juridictions, si la relation entre le parent de l'enfant et le beau-parent prend fin, le beau-parent a ou peut acquérir le droit de maintenir des contacts/ des visites/ des relations personnelles avec l'enfant. Ainsi, en Croatie,

---

[43] Ibid.
[44] Rapport Rešetar et Lucić.
[45] Ibid.
[46] Article 673 du Code civil et commercial argentin.
[47] Rapport Bugajski and Wysocka-Bar.
[48] Ibid.
[49] Rapport Roots.

le beau-parent a le droit d'avoir des contacts avec l'enfant si cela est dans l'intérêt supérieur de l'enfant.[50] En Belgique, le Code civil autorise le beau-parent à maintenir le contact avec l'enfant si lui-même et l'enfant ont un lien d'affection particulier et les contacts ne sont pas contraires à l'intérêt supérieur de l'enfant.[51] En Allemagne, le beau-parent peut demander des droits de visite si cela profite à l'enfant.[52] Au Danemark, le beau-parent peut demander le droit de contact s'il est considéré comme le membre de la famille le plus proche de l'enfant.[53]

Au Québec, la doctrine *in loco parentis* autorise le beau-parent à solliciter le contact avec l'enfant. Le beau-parent peut même demander la garde, mais cela ne lui donnera que le droit de prendre des décisions routinières concernant la vie de l'enfant ; elle ne confère pas l'autorité parentale et la tutelle légale au beau-parent.[54] La doctrine *in loco parentis* ne s'applique que si le beau-parent est marié au parent de l'enfant ; elle n'aide pas un beau-parent qui n'est pas ou n'a pas été marié à l'enfant du parent.[55] Quel que soit le rôle qu'il ait joué au cours de la vie commune, le beau-parent non marié est dans la même position que tout autre tiers.[56]

En Italie, un beau-parent peut obtenir un droit de contact s'il a établi une relation familiale significative et durable avec l'enfant et donc, il est le parent social de l'enfant (*genitore sociale*).[57] Le fait de permettre au beau-parent d'avoir des contacts avec l'enfant après la fin de la relation du beau-parent avec le parent de l'enfant peut être considéré comme reconnaissant la position du beau-parent en tant que parent supplémentaire de l'enfant et peut, en ce sens, constituer une reconnaissance de la multiplicité des parents.

Le Vietnam se distingue comme une exception en ce qui concerne la situation juridique des beaux-parents, car la loi vietnamienne confère des responsabilités et des droits étendus à un beau-parent. Toutefois, le beau-parent ne remplace

---

[50] Article 120, paragraphe 2, de la loi de 2015 sur la famille.
[51] Article 375*bis*, al. 2 du Code civil belge.
[52] S. 1685 du Code civil allemand.
[53] S. 20(1) et (2) de la loi sur la responsabilité parentale (loi de codification n° 1768, 30.11.2020).
[54] LRC 1985, ch. 3 (2e suppl.) (Loi sur le divorce).
[55] Le projet de loi C-78 (Loi modifiant la Loi sur le divorce), entré en vigueur en juillet 2020, permet au tribunal d'attribuer des responsabilités décisionnelles à l'égard de l'enfant non seulement aux conjoints et aux parents, mais aussi à une personne qui « prend sa place ou à l'intention de la remplacer » (traduction libre). La Loi codifie ainsi les principes de l'arrêt *T.V.F. et D.F. c. G.C.* [1987] 2 RCS 244.
[56] *T.V.F. and D.F. v. G.C.* [1987] 2 RCS 244.
[57] Deux approches ont été envisagées pour assurer le maintien de la relation familiale entre l'enfant et le parent social : l'application de l'article 337*ter* du Code civil, qui régit le droit de l'enfant à la continuité de la relation avec ses deux parents, ascendants et proches, dans le cadre des procédures d'attribution de la garde d'un enfant né dans le mariage ou hors mariage ; et deuxièmement, l'application de l'article 333 du Code civil, qui permet au juge d'adopter des mesures appropriées en matière de responsabilité parentale, lorsque le parent fait du mal à l'enfant. Néanmoins, il est considéré comme le droit de l'enfant et non comme un droit du parent.

ni les parents de l'enfant ni n'acquiert toutes les responsabilités et tous les droits dont disposent les parents de l'enfant. En vertu de la loi de 2014 sur le mariage et la famille, un beau-père ou une belle-mère est inclus en tant que membre de la famille et un beau-parent doit, entre autres, s'occuper de l'enfant, élever et protéger les droits et les intérêts légitimes de l'enfant, et doit respecter les droits de l'enfant de choisir une profession.[58] Les beaux-parents ne peuvent pas exercer de discrimination à l'encontre de leurs beaux-enfants en raison de leur sexe ou de l'état matrimonial des parents biologiques de l'enfant, abuser du travail des beaux-enfants, ni inciter ou forcer les enfants à agir contre la loi ou l'éthique sociale.[59] Les beaux-parents sont encouragés à créer les conditions permettant aux enfants de vivre dans un environnement familial harmonieux et doivent collaborer étroitement avec les écoles dans l'éducation des enfants. En plus des responsabilités décrites ci-dessus, un beau-parent qui prend soin de l'enfant et l'élève comme s'il était biologiquement lié peut hériter, et vice versa. Il est important de souligner que ces droits ne sont pas automatiquement établis, mais dépendent de la preuve de la vie ensemble ou des soins et de l'entretien des autres. Même lorsque les beaux-parents vivent avec des beaux-enfants, ils n'encourent pas toutes les obligations des parents. Par exemple, les beaux-parents n'ont pas de responsabilités à cause des faits illicites des beaux-enfants, ils ne gèrent pas les biens des beaux-enfants, ni ont la disposition des biens des enfants. En outre, ils n'ont pas l'obligation de soutien.[60] La conclusion que l'on peut tirer de ce qui précède est que, au Vietnam, il existe une reconnaissance des parents multiples dans le contexte de la belle-parentalité, mais que cette reconnaissance ne s'étend pas à tous les aspects juridiques du fait d'être parent.

Dans les juridictions où un beau-parent n'a pas de responsabilité parentale, un conflit ne peut survenir entre l'exercice de la responsabilité parental par un beau-parent et un parent de l'enfant.

Dans les juridictions où le beau-parent peut ou doit aider le parent à exercer ses responsabilités et ses droits parentaux, comme l'Argentine, l'Autriche et la Croatie, la situation juridique du parent est plus forte que celle du beau-parent.[61] Au Portugal, un beau-parent auquel un parent a délégué des responsabilités pour les affaires quotidiennes doit se conformer aux instructions et directives établies par le parent avec lequel l'enfant réside.[62]

Au Vietnam, les responsabilités et les droits assez étendus du beau-parent ne créeraient pas de conflit avec ceux du parent, car leur but est de « compléter et faciliter de meilleurs soins aux enfants ».[63]

---

[58] Rapport Van Ngo.
[59] Ibid.
[60] Ibid.
[61] Argentina : Rapport Medina ; Autriche : Rapport Buchstätter et Roth ; Croatie : Rapport Rešetar et Lucić.
[62] Rapport en ligne Vítor and Martins.
[63] Rapport Van Ngo.

En Afrique du Sud, un beau-parent qui a obtenu des responsabilités et des droits parentaux aux côtés du parent de l'enfant par le biais d'un accord ou d'une ordonnance du tribunal lui conférant des responsabilités et des droits parentaux spécifiques ou complets est sur un pied d'égalité avec les parents de l'enfant. Le point de départ est que les cotitulaires de la responsabilité parentale peuvent agir de manière indépendante dans l'exercice de leurs responsabilités et droits parentaux.[64] Toutefois, ils doivent tenir dûment compte des points de vue et des souhaits de chacun avant de prendre toute décision susceptible de changer de manière significative ou d'avoir un effet négatif significatif sur l'exercice par un cotitulaire de la responsabilité parentale.[65] Si la garde a été accordée au beau-parent, son consentement est requis pour le mariage, l'adoption, le déplacement de l'enfant hors du pays ou la demande de passeport, et pour la vente ou l'imposition des droits réels sur des immeubles de l'enfant.[66] Si le beau-parent et le parent (ou tout autre cotitulaire de la responsabilité parental) éprouvent des difficultés à exercer leurs responsabilités (par exemple, s'ils ne peuvent pas accorder sur le moment où l'un d'eux devrait avoir des contacts avec l'enfant), ils doivent essayer d'élaborer un plan parental qui réglementera l'exercice de leurs responsabilités.[67]

S'ils ne peuvent pas accorder un plan parental, si l'un d'eux enfreint les modalités du régime ou si l'un d'eux est d'avis qu'une décision prise ou un acte accompli par l'autre n'est pas dans l'intérêt supérieur de l'enfant, le tribunal peut être saisi afin de résoudre la question sur la base de l'intérêt supérieur de l'enfant.[68]

2.2. RECONNAISSANCE DE LA MULTIPARENTALITÉ SI UN ENFANT EST ÉLEVÉ DANS PLUS D'UN MÉNAGE

Étant donné que la reconnaissance des parents multiples dans les familles recomposées a été abordée sous la rubrique précédente, la discussion porte sur l'attribution de responsabilités à des personnes autres que les beaux-parents.

Comme indiqué dans les instructions aux rapporteurs, la multiplicité des parents dont nous tenons compte dans cette section concerne la situation dans laquelle les enfants sont élevés dans plus d'un ménage, par exemple parce que leurs parents exercent conjointement la garde après la séparation ou n'ont jamais partagé un ménage, mais partagent la responsabilité parentale. Ces cas

---

[64] Article 30(2) de la loi 38 de 2005 sur les enfants.
[65] Article 31(2) de la loi 38 de 2005 sur les enfants.
[66] S. 18(5) et 18(3)(c) de la loi 38 de 2005 sur les enfants.
[67] Article 33(2) de la loi 38 de 2005 sur les enfants.
[68] Le pouvoir de la Cour découle des articles 45 et 46 de la loi de 2005 sur les enfants et de la compétence de *common law* de la Haute Cour en tant que tuteur supérieur de tous les mineurs : Rapport Louw.

comprennent les parents mariés divorcés et les parents non mariés qui exercent conjointement la responsabilité parentale, mais ne vivent pas ensemble.

En général, les juridictions examinées autorisent à partager la parentalité seulement aux deux parents qui se sont séparés ou qui n'ont jamais vécu ensemble. Dans la plupart des juridictions, les parents de l'enfant continuent à exercer la responsabilité parentale après la séparation, mais le parent qui a la garde de l'enfant et avec qui l'enfant réside peut avoir plus de responsabilités et de droits que l'autre parent légal. C'est la situation, entre autres, en Autriche,[69] Croatie,[70] Estonie,[71] Grèce,[72] Afrique du Sud,[73] Turquie[74] et au Vietnam.[75]

En Grèce, par exemple, le tribunal peut partager les responsabilités et les droits entre les parents sur la base de ce qu'il considère constituer l'intérêt supérieur de l'enfant. Le Code civil grec stipule qu'en principe, l'intérêt de l'enfant est mieux servi par la participation des deux parents à l'éducation de l'enfant.[76] Toutefois, les parents peuvent convenir de dérogations au principe de l'exercice conjoint des soins parentaux.[77] Si les parents ne sont pas en mesure d'exercer conjointement la garde parentale, le tribunal peut répartir la garde parentale entre eux.[78] Dans ces circonstances, l'enfant sera élevé dans deux ménages. Si l'un des parents obtient le droit d'avoir des contacts avec l'enfant, il sera également, dans une certaine mesure, élevé dans deux ménages. En Afrique du Sud, un père qui n'a jamais été marié à la mère de l'enfant et qui n'a jamais cohabité avec elle peut conclure un accord qui confère une partie ou la totalité des aspects des responsabilités et des droits parentaux au père de l'enfant.[79] Dans ce cas, l'enfant peut être élevé dans deux ménages et la loi reconnaîtra les parents multiples. La situation est la même si le tribunal confère des responsabilités et des droits parentaux au père non marié et que l'enfant est élevé dans le ménage des deux parents ou si le père non marié reconnaît l'enfant, contribue ou tente de contribuer à l'éducation de l'enfant pendant une période raisonnable, et contribue ou tente de contribuer aux dépenses liées à l'entretien de l'enfant pendant une période raisonnable et que l'enfant est élevé chez les deux parents.[80]

La situation en droit japonais est étonnamment différente. Si les parents d'un enfant divorcent ou s'ils ne sont pas mariés, un seul d'entre eux a des

---

[69] Buchstätter et Roth Raport.
[70] Rapport Rešetar et Lucić.
[71] Rapport en ligne Kull et Torga.
[72] Rapport Zervogianni.
[73] Rapport Louw.
[74] Rapport Paksoy.
[75] Rapport Van Ngo.
[76] Article 1511, paragraphe 2, du Code civil grec tel que modifié par l'article 5 de la loi 4800/2021.
[77] Article 1514 al. 1 du Code civil grec tel que modifié par l'article 8 de la loi 4800/2021.
[78] Rapport Zervogianni.
[79] S. 22 de la loi sur l'enfance 38 de 2005.
[80] S. 21(1)b) et 23 de la loi sur les enfants 38 de 2005.

responsabilités et des droits parentaux.[81] Cependant, il existe une lacune juridique que les tribunaux ont utilisée pour séparer la garde physique du reste de l'autorité parentale et pour accorder la garde physique à l'un des parents et l'autorité parentale moins la garde physique à l'autre parent. Cela se fait rarement. Si les parents restent mariés mais sont séparés, la garde physique est plus souvent séparée du reste de l'autorité parentale.[82]

Certaines juridictions reconnaissent les parents multiples en permettant aux personnes qui ne sont pas les parents légaux de l'enfant d'acquérir des responsabilités et des droits complets ou limités envers un enfant aux côtés des parents légaux. Dans ce cas, le terme « parentalité » serait utilisé dans un sens vague. Si les responsabilités et les droits sont limités (par exemple, si la personne est autorisée à entrer en contact avec l'enfant et/ou à ce que l'enfant reste avec elle pendant une certaine période), cela pourrait également être considéré comme une reconnaissance des parents multiples d'un enfant élevé dans plus d'un ménage. Le terme « parent » serait ici aussi utilisé de manière vague. Un exemple est le Danemark, où une personne qui ne vit pas avec l'enfant et qui n'est pas le parent légal de l'enfant peut demander le droit d'avoir des contacts avec l'enfant si cette personne est considérée comme le membre de la famille le plus proche de l'enfant. Comme la relation sociale de la personne avec l'enfant est un facteur important à cet égard, la personne est appelée le parent social de l'enfant.[83] Le parent social ne peut acquérir des droits de contact que si l'un des parents de l'enfant ou les deux sont décédés, si l'un des parents est inconnu (par exemple parce que le sperme d'un donneur a été utilisé) ou si l'enfant n'a aucun contact ou un contact très limité avec son parent légal.[84] Si l'enfant entretient une relation étroite avec le parent social depuis plusieurs années, la demande devrait aboutir malgré l'objection du parent légal.[85] Les lois australienne et sud-africaine permettent également aux personnes qui ne sont pas les parents légaux de l'enfant d'obtenir des responsabilités et des droits aux côtés des parents légaux de l'enfant par le biais d'un accord avec le parent ou d'une ordonnance du tribunal.[86] Ces personnes comprennent un grand-parent, un père célibataire qui n'exerce pas la responsabilité parentale à l'égard de son enfant, et d'autres personnes qui ont un intérêt dans les soins, le bien-être ou le développement de l'enfant.[87] Selon l'étendue des responsabilités et des droits accordés à une telle

---

[81] Rapport Roots. La question de l'autorisation de l'autorité parentale conjointe après le divorce est actuellement examinée par le Conseil législatif (Sous-comité du droit de la famille) : ibid.
[82] Ibid.
[83] Rapport Lund-Andersen et Pedersen.
[84] Article 20, paragraphes 1 et 2, de la loi sur la responsabilité parentale.
[85] Rapport Lund-Andersen et Pedersen.
[86] Australie : Rapport Kha ; Afrique du Sud : Rapport Louw.
[87] Australie : articles 64 et 65C de la loi de 1975 sur le droit de la famille ; Afrique du Sud : articles 22–24 de la loi 38 de 2005.

personne, cette configuration de responsabilités et de droits partagés pourrait également être considérée comme une reconnaissance juridique des parents multiples d'un enfant élevé dans plus d'un ménage, si on utilise le mot « parents » dans un sens vague.

Aux Pays-Bas, la parentalité et les responsabilités et droits parentaux pourraient être divisés dans certains cas, par exemple dans des familles multiparentales intentionnelles où l'enfant est élevé dès la naissance par des parents qui ne partagent pas le ménage. Souvent, les parties concluent un accord sur leurs positions juridiques avant même que l'enfant ne soit conçu.[88] La question de savoir s'il est possible de séparer la parentalité, les responsabilités et des droits parentaux dépend de la situation factuelle.[89] La mère biologique est toujours le parent légal de l'enfant qui exerce la responsabilité parentale. Comme la loi néerlandaise ne reconnaît que deux parents légaux, la parentalité légale de la mère biologique signifie qu'il est possible avoir, au maximum, un autre parent ajouté au parent légal. L'autre parent légal pourrait être le partenaire de la mère biologique ou un autre adulte d'un deuxième ménage, mais cette personne n'aura aucune responsabilité ni aucun droit parental. La troisième personne ne serait pas le parent légal de l'enfant, mais obtiendrait des responsabilités et des droits parentaux. Comme l'indique le rapporteur néerlandais : « La situation est assez complexe ».[90]

Si un enfant est élevé dans plus d'un ménage et si les personnes qui sont ses parents légaux ou qui exercent la responsabilité parentale sont en conflit dans l'exercice de leurs responsabilités et droits respectifs, le tribunal peut résoudre la question sur la base de l'intérêt de l'enfant. Telle est la situation, entre autres, en Croatie,[91] Angleterre et pays de Galles,[92] Grèce,[93] Portugal[94] et au Afrique du Sud.[95] Cependant, au Portugal, le tribunal n'examinera pas les litiges concernant les décisions relatives aux affaires quotidiennes.[96] Dans certaines juridictions, les personnes en conflit doivent demander des conseils ou une médiation avant de s'adresser aux tribunaux. Par exemple, en Croatie, les parties doivent solliciter des conseils dans un centre de protection sociale ou tenter de résoudre leur différend par la médiation familiale.[97] En Afrique du Sud, les cotitulaires

---

[88] Rapport Schrama.
[89] Ibid.
[90] Rapport Schrama, section 2.2.1.
[91] Rapport Rešetar et Lucić.
[92] Rapport Fenton-Glynn et Scherpe.
[93] Rapport Zervogianni.
[94] Rapport en ligne Vítor et Martins.
[95] Le pouvoir de la Cour découle des articles 45 et 46 de la loi de 2005 sur les enfants et de la compétence de *common law* de la Haute Cour en tant que tuteur supérieur de tous les personnes mineures : Rapport Louw.
[96] Ibid.
[97] Rapport Rešetar et Lucić.

de la responsabilité parentale qui éprouvent des difficultés doivent essayer de se mettre d'accord sur un plan parental qui réglementera l'exercice de leurs responsabilités et de leurs droits.[98] Le plan parental doit être préparé avec l'aide d'un défenseur de la famille, d'un travailleur social, d'un psychologue ou encore par une médiation.[99]

2.3. RECONNAISSANCE DE PARENTALITÉ MULTIPLE SI UN ENFANT EST ÉLEVÉ DANS UNE FAMILLE POLYGAME

La plupart des juridictions étudiées ne reconnaissent pas la polygamie ou les parents multiples dans le contexte d'une famille polygame.

Au Vietnam, la polygamie a été reconnue dans le passé, mais, depuis 1959, la polygamie n'est plus autorisée.[100] Les familles polygames formées avant l'entrée en vigueur de l'interdiction et celles qui sont acceptées parce que les familles ont perdu le contact en raison de la division du pays pendant la guerre du Vietnam sont cependant toujours reconnues.[101] Bien que les familles polygames ne soient pas réglementées par la loi de 2014 sur le mariage et la famille, le rapporteur pour le Vietnam déclare que chaque femme est considérée comme la belle-mère des enfants nés des autres épouses. Par conséquent, les enfants ont plusieurs parents. Très peu de mariages polygames existent aujourd'hui encore.[102] La seule question portée devant les tribunaux est de savoir si les enfants nés d'une femme peuvent hériter des autres épouses du ménage polygame. Le tribunal a statué que les enfants n'héritent que de leur mère biologique, et non des autres épouses de la famille polygame.[103] En Afrique du Sud, la polygamie fait partie de la culture et de la religion de plusieurs groupes. Les mariages coutumiers polygames sont pleinement reconnus,[104] mais les mariages religieux polygames n'ont reçu qu'une reconnaissance limitée. La loi 38 de 2005 ne confère pas automatiquement la responsabilité parentale à un membre de la famille polygame, à l'exception du père biologique de l'enfant et de la femme qui a donné naissance à l'enfant,[105] mais un autre membre de la famille peut obtenir des responsabilités et des droits parentaux par le biais d'un accord avec le père ou la mère de l'enfant ou par le biais d'une ordonnance du tribunal,[106] ce qui entraînerait la naissance

---

[98] Article 33(2) de la loi 38 de 2005 sur les enfants.
[99] Article 33(5) de la loi 38 de 2005 sur les enfants.
[100] Rapport Ngo.
[101] Ibid.
[102] Ibid.
[103] Arrêt n° 20/2009/DS-PT de la Cour populaire suprême, daté 12.02.2019.
[104] Article 2 de la loi 120 de 1998 sur la reconnaissance des mariages coutumiers.
[105] Articles 19 et 20 de la loi 38 de 2005 sur les enfants.
[106] Aux termes des articles 22, 23 et 24 de la loi 38 de 2005 sur les enfants ou de la compétence de *common law* de la Haute Cour en tant que tuteur supérieur de tous les mineurs.

de plusieurs parents. Le rapporteur pour l'Afrique du Sud déclare qu'il n'est pas encore clair si les règles l'emportent sur « la désignation contradictoire de la parentalité en termes de droit coutumier ou de tout système de droit religieux ». En cas de conflit entre les cotitulaires de responsabilités et de droits parentaux, le conflit doit être résolu dans l'intérêt supérieur de l'enfant, ce qui, en termes de la loi sur l'enfance, signifie que, entre autres,[107] il faut tenir compte du besoin de l'enfant de rester sous la garde de ses parents, de sa famille et de sa famille élargie, de maintenir un lien avec sa famille, sa famille élargie, sa culture ou sa tradition, ainsi que la sécurité physique et émotionnelle de l'enfant et son développement intellectuel, émotionnel, social et culturel.[108] Les familles polygames ont également reçu une reconnaissance expresse dans le contexte de la loi sud-africaine sur l'adoption, puisque « les personnes qui partagent un ménage commun et forment une unité familiale permanente » peuvent adopter conjointement un enfant.[109] Cela signifie que si, par exemple, un mari dans un mariage coutumier et ses épouses multiples adoptaient conjointement un enfant, lui et ses épouses partageraient tous les responsabilités et les droits parentaux et l'enfant adopté aurait plusieurs parents.[110]

2.4. RECONNAISSANCE DES PARENTS MULTIPLES EN CAS D'ADOPTION OUVERTE

L'adoption ouverte désigne les familles où des enfants ont été adoptés, mais entretiennent des liens (légaux ou de facto) avec leurs parents d'origine. Si l'enfant est autorisé à conserver des liens avec sa famille d'origine, cela pourrait être considéré comme une reconnaissance de la multiplicité des parents. Si la famille d'origine (ou certains membres de cette famille, tels que les parents d'origine de l'enfant) a des droits de communication à l'égard de l'enfant, cela pourrait être considéré comme une reconnaissance des parents multiples, mais il serait probablement exagéré d'affirmer que les parents multiples sont reconnus si la famille d'origine n'a que le droit d'obtenir des informations sur l'enfant.

Dans certains pays, comme la Belgique, l'adoption simple ne rompt pas la relation avec la famille d'origine et crée donc une multiplicité juridique potentielle de deux parents biologiques et jusqu'à deux parents adoptifs. L'adoption simple se produit, par exemple, dans le cas d'adoptions par des beaux-parents.[111] Dans le cas d'une adoption par un beau-parent, l'enfant a trois parents légaux, car le parent qui est marié au beau-parent reste le parent légal de l'enfant.

---

[107] Rapport Louw.
[108] Article 7(1) de la loi 38 de 2005 sur l'enfance.
[109] Article 231(1)(a) (iii) de la loi 38 de 2005 sur les enfants.
[110] Rapport Louw.
[111] Rapport Gallus, Leleu, Mathieu et Swennen.

Ces adoptions par beau-parent n'entrent pas dans le cadre de l'« adoption ouverte » telle qu'envisagée dans le questionnaire.

La version polonaise de « l'adoption ouverte » crée une relation juridique entre le parent adoptif et l'enfant adopté, mais pas entre les parents du parent adoptif et de l'enfant adopté.[112] Cela signifie que l'enfant ne devient pas légalement un frère ou une sœur des enfants biologiques des parents adoptifs ou un petit-enfant des parents des parents adoptifs.[113] Cette forme d'adoption n'entre pas non plus dans le cadre de l'adoption ouverte telle que définie dans le questionnaire.

La variante argentine de l'adoption simple pourrait être considérée comme une adoption ouverte telle que définie dans le questionnaire. Dans ce sens, le parent adoptif par adoption simple a des responsabilités et des droits parentaux à l'égard de l'enfant adopté, mais la famille d'origine a le droit de communiquer avec l'enfant adopté, à moins que cela ne soit contraire à l'intérêt supérieur de l'enfant ; l'enfant conserve son droit de demander une pension alimentaire à sa famille d'origine si le parent adoptif ne peut pas le soutenir ; l'enfant peut combiner les noms de famille de son parent adoptif et de sa famille d'origine.[114]

En Autriche, un enfant adopté par une seule personne conserve ses relations juridiques avec l'un de ses parents biologiques. Le parent adoptif remplace légalement le parent biologique du même sexe que le parent adoptif et l'enfant conserve sa relation juridique avec le parent biologique du sexe opposé. Ainsi, par exemple, si un enfant est adopté par une femme célibataire, l'enfant conserve sa relation juridique avec son père biologique, mais pas avec sa mère biologique. Cette règle garantit que l'enfant a deux parents légaux[115] ; elle ne crée pas de parent supplémentaire pour l'enfant et n'entraîne donc pas que l'enfant ait plusieurs parents.

En Grèce, une personne adoptée peut conserver les liens avec sa famille d'origine si elle est adoptée à l'âge adulte.[116] Une telle adoption n'est possible qu'entre parents proches par le sang ou le mariage.[117] Les parents adoptifs sont principalement responsables de l'assistance matérielle de l'adopté,[118] mais celui-ci est tenu de maintenir ses parents adoptifs et ses parents biologiques.[119] Dans ce cas, il y a reconnaissance de plusieurs parents.

Au Japon, l'adoption ouverte est appelée « adoption régulière » ou, simplement, « adoption ».[120] La personne adoptée est généralement un adulte,

---

[112] Article 124 §1 du Code de la famille et de la tutelle.
[113] Rapport Bugajski et Wysocka-Bar.
[114] Rapport Medina.
[115] Article 197, paragraphe 3, du Code civil général autrichien.
[116] Article 1584 envoyé. 2 du Code civil grec.
[117] Article 1579 du Code civil grec, selon lequel les parents adoptifs et l'adopté doivent être, au moins, des parents au quatrième degré par le sang ou le mariage.
[118] Article 1587 du Code civil grec.
[119] Rapport Zervogianni.
[120] Rapport Roots.

mais un mineur peut également être adopté par adoption régulière. La plus part des adoptions régulières de mineurs sont des adoptions par des beaux-parents.[121] Les parents adoptifs et l'enfant à adopter doivent consentir à l'adoption et soumettre un avis d'adoption au bureau d'enregistrement de la famille.[122] Si l'enfant est mineur, l'autorisation du tribunal de la famille doit être obtenue avant que l'avis puisse être soumis.[123] Il n'est pas clair si l'adoption régulière permet aux parents d'origine de l'enfant de chercher à entrer en contact avec l'enfant, mais il est clair qu'ils conservent une obligation secondaire de subsistance envers leur enfant et peuvent hériter de l'enfant s'il décède sans conjoint ou descendant.[124] L'enfant adopté hérite à la fois des parents adoptifs et des parents d'origine.[125]

L'Australie a rejeté la pratique des adoptions fermées.[126] Ainsi, par exemple, la loi de 2000 sur l'adoption de Nouvelle-Galles du Sud encourage expressément l'adoption ouverte ; elle met l'accent sur l'intérêt supérieur de l'enfant tant dans l'enfance que plus tard dans la vie ; ordonne que la législation et la pratique aident l'enfant à connaître et à avoir accès à sa famille biologique et à son patrimoine culturel ; reconnait la nature changeante des pratiques d'adoption ; permet l'accès à certaines informations relatives aux adoptions ; et prévoit l'octroi d'une aide financière après l'adoption aux enfants adoptés et à leurs parents biologiques et adoptifs dans certaines circonstances.[127] Les programmes d'adoption sont utilisés pour favoriser les contacts entre l'enfant adopté et les diverses parties. Ces programmes prévoient les modalités de partage des renseignements de l'enfant (y compris les renseignements médicaux et sur les événements importants de la vie) ainsi que les moyens et la nature des contacts entre les parties et l'enfant.[128] En cas de dispute entre les parties, les points de vue des parents adoptifs prévalent, car ils sont les parents légaux de l'enfant.[129] Bien que les opinions des parents adoptifs prévalent, ce système semble néanmoins être considéré comme une reconnaissance des parents multiples dans le contexte de l'adoption.

La plupart des juridictions examinées permettent aux parents d'origine d'un enfant adopté et/ou à d'autres membres de la famille d'avoir des contacts avec lui, quelque fois à travers d'une décision judiciaire. Au Québec, le système permet des accords visant à faciliter l'échange de renseignements et/ou les relations interpersonnelles (c'est-à-dire les contacts/communication) entre le parent adoptif et les membres de la famille d'origine de l'enfant si cela est dans l'intérêt

---

[121] Ibid.
[122] Articles 799 et 739 du Code civil.
[123] Article 798 du Code civil.
[124] Rapport Roots.
[125] Article 887 of the Civil Code.
[126] Rapport Kha.
[127] Article 7 de la loi de 2000 sur l'adoption (NSW).
[128] Article 46 de la loi de 2000 sur l'adoption (NSW).
[129] Article 95 de la loi de 2000 sur l'adoption (NSW).

supérieur de l'enfant.[130] Le Québec reconnaît également l'adoption coutumière autochtone, qui est régie, non pas par la loi de l'État, mais par l'autorité compétente désignée pour la communauté autochtone (c'est-à-dire la Première Nation) ou la nation autochtone de l'enfant.[131] En ce qui concerne ce type d'adoption, les droits et obligations peuvent être conservés entre l'enfant et sa famille d'origine. Il n'est pas clair si l'adoption coutumière autochtone continuera à s'appliquer, car elle peut être remplacée par une tutelle supplémentaire[132] (tutelle supplétive), qui permet à un parent de nommer une personne qui exercera la tutelle et l'autorité parentale lorsqu'il est impossible pour les parents ou l'un d'entre eux d'exercer pleinement la tutelle et l'autorité parentale.[133] L'intérêt de l'enfant, notion inconnue dans la coutume autochtone, demeure applicable lorsque le tribunal doit prendre une décision autorisant la tutelle supplétive.[134] Le système d'adoption qui, comme indiqué ci-dessus, permet des accords visant à faciliter l'échange d'informations ou les relations interpersonnelles entre le parent adoptif et les membres de la famille d'origine de l'enfant, peut également réduire l'incidence de l'adoption coutumière autochtone.[135]

Au Danemark, le tribunal peut autoriser les contacts si les parents biologiques de l'enfant en font la demande,[136] en particulier si l'enfant a été en contact avec eux avant l'adoption.[137] L'Angleterre et le pays de Galles,[138] le Portugal[139] et l'Afrique du Sud[140] habilitent également le tribunal à autoriser les contacts entre la famille adoptive et la famille d'origine de l'enfant. En Belgique, la famille d'origine de l'enfant peut se voir accorder des relations personnelles avec l'enfant, même si elle n'a jamais eu de relation avec l'enfant ou, dans le cas des grands-parents, même s'ils n'ont jamais rencontré l'enfant.[141] Cependant, les parents biologiques obtiennent rarement ce droit, car la loi considère que des mécanismes autres que l'adoption plénière seraient plus appropriés s'il est dans l'intérêt supérieur de l'enfant de maintenir la relation entre lui et ses parents d'origine.[142] En Autriche, les parents biologiques peuvent avoir des contacts post-adoption avec l'enfant, s'ils sont qualifiés comme des tiers ayant le droit de contacter l'enfant dans l'intérêt supérieur de l'enfant.[143]

---

[130] Article 579 du Code civil du Québec.
[131] Article 543.1, 152.1, 574.1 et 132.0.1 du Code civil du Québec.
[132] Article 132.0.1 du Code civil du Québec.
[133] Rapport Giroux et Langevin.
[134] Article 199.3 Code civil du Québec.
[135] Rapport Giroux et Langevin.
[136] Article 20 a de la loi sur la responsabilité parentale.
[137] Rapport Lund-Andersen et Pedersen.
[138] Ss 51A et 51B de la loi de 2002 sur l'adoption et les enfants.
[139] Rapport en ligne Vítor et Martins.
[140] Article 234 de la loi 38 de 2005 sur les enfants.
[141] Article 375*bis* du Code civil belge.
[142] Rapport Gallus, Leleu, Mathieu et Swennen.
[143] Article 188, paragraphe 2, du Code civil général autrichien.

En droit turc, il n'est pas clair si les parents biologiques ont des droits de contact après une adoption. Le Code civil turc est muet sur cette question.[144] Certains auteurs et la Cour de cassation turque affirment que, puisque les liens de filiation entre l'enfant et ses parents biologiques sont maintenus intacts malgré l'adoption, les parents biologiques ont des droits de communication qu'ils ne peuvent pas renoncer. D'autres auteurs estiment que les parents biologiques peuvent demander au tribunal de leur accorder des droits de communication ou peuvent renoncer à leurs droits au moment de l'adoption. Selon un autre point de vue, les parents renoncent nécessairement à leurs droits de communication quand ils donnent leur consentement à l'adoption.[145] Au Japon, il n'est pas clair non plus si l'adoption régulière permet aux parents d'origine de l'enfant d'avoir communication avec l'enfant.[146]

En Autriche,[147] en Belgique[148] et au Japon,[149] les parents biologiques ont également une obligation secondaire de soutien à l'égard de leur enfant, malgré l'adoption. Ainsi, si les parents adoptifs ne sont pas en mesure de soutenir l'enfant, les parents biologiques doivent le faire. En Turquie, la position est moins claire.[150] Certains auteurs et la Cour de cassation affirment que le devoir de pension alimentaire des parents biologiques cesse au moment de l'adoption, tandis que d'autres auteurs soutiennent que les parents biologiques conservent une obligation secondaire de soutien envers l'enfant. Il est clair cependant que l'enfant adopté est tenu de soutenir ses parents adoptifs et biologiques.[151] Il est douteux de considérer que l'obligation parentale de payer une pension alimentaire équivaut à la reconnaissance de parents multiples.

En Allemagne, l'adoption ouverte n'est pas formellement reconnue par la loi, mais, avec l'aide de l'agence d'adoption, les parents adoptifs et les parents biologiques de l'enfant concluent parfois des accords sur l'adoption ouverte.[152] Le respect est alors à la seule discrétion des parents adoptifs.[153]

Au Vietnam, aussi, les parents adoptifs et biologiques de l'enfant peuvent accepter une adoption ouverte, mais de tels accords sont rares.[154] L'accord peut permettre le maintien de tout ou partie des droits et des obligations des parents d'origine après l'adoption.[155] L'étendue des responsabilités et des droits

---

[144] Rapport Paksoy.
[145] Ibid.
[146] Rapport Roots.
[147] Rapport Buchstätter et Roth.
[148] Article 353-14 du Code civil belge.
[149] Il s'applique à l'adoption régulier (ouverte) : Rapport Roots.
[150] Rapport Paksoy.
[151] Ibid.
[152] Rapport Sanders.
[153] Ibid.
[154] Rapport Van Ngo.
[155] Ibid.

des parents biologiques après l'adoption déterminera si l'accord a créé une multiplicité de parents.

En Croatie[156] et en Estonie, la loi ne prévoit pas du tout l'adoption ouverte.[157]

2.5. RECONNAISSANCE DE PARENTALITÉ MULTIPLE DANS LE CAS DE *KAFALA*

Aucune des juridictions ne reconnaît officiellement la *kafala* comme un moyen d'accorder une reconnaissance juridique à plusieurs parents. En Italie, les juges ont parfois reconnu la *kafala*, soit comme une simple adoption, soit comme une décision gracieuse ne nécessitant aucune mesure d'adaptation interne. La Cour de cassation a reconnu une *kafala* notariée, approuvée par un juge marocain, compte tenu de l'intérêt de l'enfant. Cependant, les juges n'ont jamais été confrontés à des questions liées à une éventuelle multiparentalité dans le contexte de la *kafala*.[158]

En outre, comme le souligne le rapporteur pour les Pays-Bas, la *kafala* pourrait permettre à l'enfant de vivre avec son tuteur dans un État membre de l'UE. Il en est ainsi parce que la Cour de justice de l'UE a jugé que, bien que la *kafala* ne crée pas une relation parent–enfant, elle pourrait, dans des conditions spécifiques, avoir pour conséquence d'accorder à l'enfant un droit d'entrée et de séjour afin de lui permettre de vivre avec son tuteur dans l'État membre d'accueil.[159]

2.6. LA RECONNAISSANCE DE PARENTALITÉ MULTIPLE DANS LE CAS DE LA PROCRÉATION ASSISTÉE PAR DONNEUR (SANS GESTATION POUR AUTRUI)

La discussion sous cette section ne concerne pas la procréation assistée par gestation pour autrui parce que la gestation pour autrui est discutée sous une section distincte ci-dessous.[160]

La plupart des juridictions examinées réglementent et autorisent la procréation assistée par donneur. Le Luxembourg ne le fait pas,[161] mais est en train d'introduire une législation visant à créer un cadre juridique pour la

---

[156] Rapport Rešetar et Lucić.
[157] Rapport en ligne Kull et Torga.
[158] Rapport Aluffi.
[159] Affaire C-129/18, *SM v. Entry Clearance Officer, UK Visa Section*, 26.03.2019, ECLI:EU:C:2019:248.
[160] Voir ci-dessous la section 2.8 Reconnaissance de la multiplicité de la parentalité dans le cas de gestation pour autrui.
[161] Rapport Hilger.

procréation assistée par donneur et l'accès à l'information sur les origines d'un enfant.[162] L'Allemagne autorise le don de sperme, mais pas le don d'ovules.[163] La Turquie n'autorise pas du tout la procréation assistée par donneur.[164] En Croatie, la loi prévoit que l'identité du donneur doit être connue,[165] parce que l'enfant né à la suite de la procréation assistée par donneur a le droit de connaître son origine.[166] L'Angleterre et le pays de Galles exigent également que l'identité des donneurs de gamètes soit connue,[167] comme le font tous les états et territoires d'Australie.[168] Depuis le 1er juillet 2018, la loi fédérale exige que l'identité des hommes qui donnent du sperme à des banques de sperme officielles soit connue.[169] Il faut dire que le simple fait que l'identité du donneur soit connue ne signifie pas que le donneur est considéré comme un parent. Inversement, il est clair que la loi ne confère pas des responsabilités et de droits à un donneur anonyme.

Plusieurs juridictions, dont la Grèce,[170] l'Italie,[171] le Québec,[172] l'Afrique du Sud[173] et le Vietnam,[174] ordonnent que les donneurs doivent être anonymes.[175] Bien entendu, certaines personnes pratiquent la procréation assistée par donneur en dehors des limites de la loi. Par exemple, une femme peut utiliser le sperme d'un ami ou d'une personne connue pour se féconder à la maison. Dans ce cas, l'identité du donneur sera connue malgré l'interdiction d'identifier le donneur. Dans ces circonstances, les règles ordinaires de la loi en matière d'acquisition du statut parental et des responsabilités et droits s'appliqueraient comme elles le feraient si l'identité du donneur était inconnue.

Dans les juridictions où la procréation assistée par donneur est autorisée, la femme qui donne naissance à un enfant est la mère légale de l'enfant. Cette règle s'applique indépendamment du fait que l'enfant ait été conçu à l'aide du gamète d'un tiers donneur ou du conjoint ou du partenaire enregistré/civil de la mère biologique. Elle s'applique également même si l'identité d'un tiers donateur peut être connue. C'est la situation, entre autres, de l'Argentine,[176] l'Australie,[177]

---

[162] Projets de loi 6568 et 7674.
[163] Rapport Sanders.
[164] Rapport Paksoy.
[165] Rapport Rešetar et Lucić.
[166] Article 15 de la loi de 2012 sur la procréation assistée.
[167] Rapport Fenton-Glynn et Scherpe.
[168] Rapport Kha.
[169] Rapport Sanders.
[170] Rapport Zervogianni.
[171] Article 9 c. 3 de la loi n. 40/2004.
[172] Rapport Giroux et Langevin.
[173] Article 41 de la loi 28 de 2005 sur les enfants.
[174] Rapport Van Ngo.
[175] Au Japon la donation de gamètes est normalement anonyme.
[176] Article 562 du code civil et commercial d'Argentine.
[177] Rapport Kha.

l'Autriche,[178] la Belgique,[179] le Danemark,[180] l'Estonie,[181] l'Allemagne,[182] la Grèce,[183] l'Italie,[184] le Japon,[185] la Pologne,[186] le Portugal,[187] le Québec,[188] les Pays-Bas,[189] l'Afrique du Sud,[190] l'Angleterre et le pays de Galles[191] et le Vietnam.[192] Ce serait également le cas en Turquie si la procréation assistée par donneur devait avoir lieu malgré l'interdiction des dons de gamètes et d'embryons.[193] Comme la seule mère biologique est la mère de l'enfant, la règle ne crée pas plusieurs parents pour l'enfant.

Selon la loi de nombreuses juridictions, le mari ou le partenaire enregistré ou civil de la mère biologique est présumé ou légalement considéré comme le père ou le parent de l'enfant, à l'exclusion du donneur, indépendamment du fait que l'identité du donneur puisse ou non être connue. C'est la situation, entre autres, de l'Australie,[194] la Belgique,[195] l'Angleterre et le pays de Galles,[196] l'Estonie,[197] la Grèce,[198] le Japon,[199] la Pologne,[200] le Portugal,[201] le Québec,[202] les Pays-Bas,[203] la Turquie[204] et l'Afrique du Sud.[205] Dans certains pays, comme l'Allemagne[206] et les

---

[178] Article 143 du Code civil général autrichien.
[179] Articles 27 et 56 du projet de loi du 06.07.2007.
[180] Article 30 de la loi sur les enfants (loi consolidée n° 1250, 29.11.2019 et loi n° 227, 15.02.2022).
[181] Rapport en ligne Kull et Torga.
[182] S. 1591 du Code civil allemand.
[183] Article 1463 du Code civil grec.
[184] Article 269 s. 3 du Code civil italien.
[185] Article 9 de la loi sur les technologies de procréation assistée et dispositions spéciales du Code civil relatives aux relations légales parent–enfant des enfants nés grâce à cette technologie 2020.
[186] Pologne : article 61 du Code de la famille et de la tutelle.
[187] Rapport en ligne Vítor and Martins.
[188] Rapport Giroux et Langevin.
[189] Rapport Schrama.
[190] S. 40(1)–(3) de la loi 38 de 2005 sur les enfants.
[191] Article 33 de la loi de 2008 sur la fécondation humaine et l'embryologie.
[192] Rapport Van Ngo.
[193] Article 282 du Code civil turc.
[194] Rapport Kha.
[195] Rapport Gallus, Leleu, Mathieu et Swennen. Il convient de noter qu'en Belgique, la Cour constitutionnelle a jugé que le fait d'entraver l'établissement légal de la paternité du donneur porte atteinte de manière disproportionnée au droit de l'enfant au respect de la vie privée et familiale et au droit de l'enfant à la prise en compte de ses intérêts : arrêt n° 19/2019 de la Cour constitutionnelle belge du 07.02.2019, disponible sur www.const-court.be.
[196] Les articles 35 et 42 de la loi de 2008 sur la fécondation humaine et l'embryologie.
[197] Rapport en ligne Kull et Torga.
[198] Article 1465 du Code civil grec ; article 9 de la loi 4356/2015.
[199] Rapport Roots. La règle s'applique seulement à l'époux de la mère, pas à l'homme qui n'est pas marié.
[200] Article 62 §1 du Code de la famille et de la tutelle.
[201] Rapport en ligne Vítor et Martins.
[202] Articles 538 et 539 du Code civil du Québec.
[203] Article 1:199 al. a) du Code civil néerlandais.
[204] Article 285 du Code civil turc.
[205] Article 40(1) de la loi 38 de 2005 sur les enfants.
[206] Rapport Sanders.

Pays-Bas,[207] la règle ne s'applique qu'aux conjoints/partenaires de sexe masculin, excluant ainsi le conjoint ou le partenaire féminin d'une mère biologique de devenir automatiquement le parent légal de l'enfant. Cette règle ne crée pas non plus de parents multiples pour l'enfant.

Revenons à la situation du père de l'enfant né de la procréation assistée : si la mère biologique n'est pas mariée ou si la présomption de paternité du mari de la mère biologique est réfutée (lorsque cela est possible), le donneur de sperme peut, dans certaines juridictions, devenir le parent légal de l'enfant en reconnaissant l'enfant ou en obtenant une déclaration judiciaire selon laquelle il est le père de l'enfant, mais alors lui seul sera le père de l'enfant. Par conséquent, la règle n'ajoute pas un autre parent pour l'enfant. C'est la situation, entre autres, en Belgique,[208] Allemagne,[209] Grèce,[210] Pologne[211] et Turquie.[212] Au Japon, le donneur de sperme peut reconnaître l'enfant même sans le consentement de la mère biologique, et l'enfant peut intenter une action en reconnaissance de la paternité du donneur de sperme.[213] Cependant, le Conseil législatif du ministère de la Justice a proposé que des règles légales soient promulguées pour interdire au donneur de sperme de reconnaître l'enfant et à l'enfant d'intenter une action en reconnaissance de la paternité du donneur de sperme.[214]

Aux Pays-Bas, la partenaire féminine d'une mère peut également utiliser la procédure de la reconnaissance et devenir ainsi le parent légal de l'enfant à l'exclusion du donneur.[215] Le Danemark adopte une approche différente de la parentalité légale de certains donneurs de sperme, mais le résultat est également que l'enfant n'a qu'un seul père. Au Danemark, un donneur de sperme peut être anonyme, non anonyme ou connu. Un donneur anonyme ne devient jamais le parent légal de l'enfant et n'a aucune relation juridique avec l'enfant. Un donneur non anonyme ne devient pas non plus le parent légal de l'enfant, mais l'enfant a le droit de contacter le donneur après que l'enfant ait atteint l'âge de 18 ans.[216] Si le donneur de sperme est un donneur connu, il est le père légal si la mère biologique de l'enfant n'est pas mariée.[217] Si les conjoints ou les partenaires utilisent un donneur connu, ils peuvent accepter de permettre au donneur – au lieu du mari ou du partenaire de la mère biologique – d'être le parent légal, ou ils peuvent convenir que le conjoint de la mère biologique ou le partenaire

---

[207] Rapport Schrama.
[208] Rapport Gallus, Leleu, Mathieu et Swennen.
[209] Articles 1592 n° 2 et 1594 du Code civil allemand.
[210] Rapport Zervogianni.
[211] Article 72 §1 du Code de la famille et de la tutelle.
[212] Rapport Paksoy.
[213] Rapport Roots.
[214] Ibid.
[215] Article 1:204 du Code civil néerlandais ; Rapport Schrama.
[216] Rapport Lund-Andersen et Pedersen.
[217] Article 27 b–c de la loi sur les enfants (loi consolidée n° 1250, 29.11.2019 et loi n° 227, 15.02.2022).

enregistré/civil est le parent de l'enfant.[218] Choisissant la dernière option permet au conjoint ou au partenaire hétérosexuel ou de même sexe de la mère biologique d'être le deuxième parent de l'enfant aux côtés de la mère biologique.[219] Aux Pays-Bas, un donneur de sperme connu peut également devenir le parent de l'enfant si les parties conviennent que le partenaire de la mère ne reconnaîtra pas l'enfant et que le donneur de sperme reconnaîtra l'enfant. Dans ces cas également, le donneur ne devient pas un parent supplémentaire ; l'enfant n'a encore que deux parents.[220]

En Angleterre et au pays de Galles, le cohabitant d'une femme qui n'est pas mariée ni est dans une union civile peut devenir le parent de l'enfant s'il remplit les soi-disant « conditions de paternité convenues ».[221] Ces conditions s'appliquent aux hommes et aux femmes qui n'ont pas donné le gamète pour la procréation assistée.[222] Les conditions sont que le partenaire et la mère de l'enfant doivent convenir que le partenaire deviendra le parent et qu'ils n'aient d'empêchement de parenté.[223]

Dans certaines juridictions, une mère peut être la seule titulaire de la responsabilité parentale de l'enfant si elle est célibataire (c'est-à-dire qu'elle n'est pas mariée ou elle n'est pas partie d'une union civile enregistrée) et le donneur de sperme est anonyme. C'est la position, par exemple, au Québec[224] et en Afrique du Sud.[225] En Grèce,[226] la mère biologique est la seule titulaire si elle n'a pas de conjoint ou de partenaire enregistré et le donneur de sperme ne reconnaît pas l'enfant. En principe, la situation est la même en Allemagne.[227] Cependant, la Cour fédérale de justice allemande a déclaré responsable de l'entretien de l'enfant né à la suite de la procréation assistée à un homme célibataire qui a consenti à l'insémination de son partenaire avec du sperme de donneur, même si l'homme a refusé de reconnaître l'enfant.[228] Le tribunal a statué que le consentement de l'homme à l'insémination constituait une « présomption intentionnelle de parentalité » qui entraînait sa responsabilité pour la pension alimentaire de

---

[218] Article 27 de la loi sur les enfants (loi consolidée n° 1250, 29.11.2019 et loi n° 227, 15.02.2022).
[219] Rapport Lund-Andersen et Pedersen.
[220] Rapport Schrama.
[221] Article 36 de la loi de 2008 sur la fécondation humaine et l'embryologie.
[222] Rapport Fenton-Glynn et Scherpe.
[223] Les articles 36, 43 et 44 de la loi de 2008 sur la fécondation humaine et l'embryologie ; Loi de 1986 sur le mariage (degrés de relation interdits).
[224] Article 538 du Code civil du Québec.
[225] Le paragraphe 20 de l'article 40 de la loi 38 de 2005 sur les enfants se lit avec les articles 22–24 et le pouvoir de *common law* de la Haute Cour en tant que tuteur supérieur de tous les mineurs.
[226] Rapport Zervogianni.
[227] Rapport Sanders.
[228] Bundesgerichtshof (BGH, Cour fédérale de justice, FCJ), décision du 23.09.2015 – affaire XII ZR 99/14, *NJW* 2015, 68, p. 3434.

l'enfant.[229] En Angleterre et au pays de Galles – où les donneurs ne sont pas anonymes[230] – la mère est la seule personne responsable de l'enfant si elle n'est pas mariée ou elle n'est pas dans une union enregistrée, et elle n'a pas de partenaire qui remplit les « conditions de paternité convenues » décrites ci-dessus.[231]

Dans certaines juridictions, la procréation assistée par donneur est réservée aux femmes célibataires et aux couples hétérosexuels. C'est le cas, entre autres, de la Grèce[232] et de la Pologne.[233]

Les juridictions telles que la Belgique,[234] l'Angleterre et le pays de Galles,[235] l'Estonie,[236] le Québec[237] et l'Afrique du Sud[238] appliquent les mêmes règles en ce qui concerne la procréation assistée par donneur et l'acquisition de responsabilités et de droits parentaux aux couples hétérosexuels et de même sexe. En Autriche, seules les femmes partenaires de même sexe ont le même droit d'accès à la procréation assistée que les personnes hétérosexuelles.[239] La raison pour laquelle les couples de même sexe masculin sont exclus est qu'un couple d'hommes devrait utiliser la gestation pour autrui pour avoir un enfant et que la gestation pour autrui est interdite en Autriche.[240]

Dans la plupart des juridictions, l'anonymat ou la connaissance de l'identité du donneur n'a aucune influence sur les règles déterminant qui devient le parent d'un enfant, indépendamment du fait de savoir si le donneur veut ou non participer aux soins de l'enfant. Des exemples de telles juridictions sont la Croatie,[241] l'Allemagne,[242] la Pologne,[243] le Portugal[244] et l'Afrique du Sud.[245]

En Afrique du Sud, le donneur est, en principe, disqualifié d'être parent, car la définition du « parent » exclut toute personne biologiquement liée à un enfant uniquement parce qu'elle a fait don d'un gamète à des fins de procréation assistée.[246] Malgré cette exclusion, un donneur dont l'identité est connue pourrait, potentiellement, obtenir des responsabilités et des droits parentaux à

---

[229] Rapport Sanders.
[230] Voir ci-dessus sous cette rubrique.
[231] Rapport Fenton-Glynn et Scherpe.
[232] Rapport Zervogianni.
[233] Rapport Bugajski et Wysocka-Bar.
[234] Rapport Gallus, Leleu, Mathieu et Swennen.
[235] Articles 35 et 42 de la loi de 2008 sur la fécondation humaine et l'embryologie.
[236] Rapport en ligne Kull et Torga.
[237] Rapport Giroux et Langevin.
[238] L'article 40 de la loi 38 de 2005 sur les enfants se lit avec l'article 13 de la loi de 2006 sur l'union civile.
[239] Rapport Buchstätter et Roth.
[240] Ibid.
[241] Rapport Rešetar et Lucić.
[242] Rapport Sanders.
[243] Rapport Bugajski et Wysocka-Bar.
[244] Rapport en ligne Vítor et Martins.
[245] Rapport Louw.
[246] Article 1 de la loi 38 de 2005 sur les enfants.

travers une ordonnance du tribunal s'il veut participer à l'éducation de l'enfant et si cette participation est dans l'intérêt supérieur de l'enfant.[247] Si une telle ordonnance est rendue, le donneur deviendrait un titulaire supplémentaire des responsabilités et des droits parentaux. Ainsi, l'enfant obtiendrait un troisième parent s'il a déjà deux parents légaux mariés ou un deuxième parent si sa mère n'est pas mariée. Le donneur serait probablement confronté à une bataille difficile pour convaincre le tribunal qu'il devrait obtenir toutes les responsabilités et les droits parentaux aux côtés des parents mariés ou de la mère non mariée de l'enfant,[248] mais si l'enfant a formé un lien avec le donneur, le tribunal pourrait lui conférer des droits de communication.[249] En Belgique également, le juge peut accorder des droits de contact au donneur de gamètes si cela est dans l'intérêt de l'enfant.[250]

En Argentine, malgré que le Code civil et commercial argentin dispose[251] que « nul ne peut avoir plus de deux liens de filiation, quelle que soit la nature de la filiation », dans certains cas, les tribunaux ont autorisé le donateur à devenir un troisième parent. Par exemple, à Mar del Plata, dans la province de Buenos Aires, un couple de même sexe et la mère biologique de leur enfant ont été reconnus comme les parents de l'enfant et ont été autorisés à exercer conjointement la responsabilité parentale.[252]

En Ontario, quatre parents d'intention peuvent être reconnus si ceux-ci ont donné leur consentement par écrit avant la conception de l'embryon. Par exemple, il peut s'agir d'un couple gai et d'un couple lesbien qui désirent un enfant. Une des femmes porte l'enfant dont le père biologique est l'un des hommes. Une procédure administrative de reconnaissance de la filiation s'applique. Avec l'autorisation du tribunal, plus de quatre parents peuvent être reconnus.[253]

Le Danemark est une exception notable en ce qui concerne la position d'un donneur de sperme connu. Un donneur de sperme connu est le père légal si la mère biologique de l'enfant n'est pas mariée, et il peut être le père légal si les conjoints ou les partenaires acceptent de lui permettre d'être le parent légal.[254] Aux Pays-Bas, un donneur de sperme connu et la femme à qui il donne son

---

[247] Articles 22–24 de la loi 38 de 2005 sur les enfants ; le pouvoir de *common law* de la Haute Cour ; Rapport Louw.
[248] Rapport Louw.
[249] Ibid.
[250] Article 375*bis* du Code civil belge.
[251] Article 558.
[252] Cour des affaires familiales n° 2 de Mar Del Plata, *CMF y otros s/materia a categorizar* (*CMF et autres, à déterminer*) 24.11.2017 ; en ligne AR/JUR/103023/2017.
[253] Voir définition dans Children's Law Reform Act, RSO 1990, c. C.12, s. 2 « parent d'intention » : la partie à un accord de maternité de gestation pour autrui exclut le substitut ; and Children's Law Reform Act, ss 10(2) and 11.
[254] Rapport Lund-Andersen et Pedersen.

sperme peuvent conclure un accord qui prévoit s'il peut acquérir le statut de parent légal après la naissance de l'enfant. Si l'accord prévoit qu'il reconnaîtra l'enfant et deviendra ainsi le parent légal de l'enfant, le partenaire de la mère biologique ne peut pas non plus reconnaître l'enfant.[255] Par conséquent, l'enfant ne peut pas avoir plus de deux parents légaux.

La Haute Cour d'Australie a statué qu'un donneur de sperme connu peut être déclaré parent légal de l'enfant.[256] Dans ce cas, la mère biologique et le donneur de sperme étaient inscrits comme parents de l'enfant sur le certificat de naissance de l'enfant et le donneur de sperme jouait un rôle actif dans l'éducation de l'enfant même si l'enfant vivait avec la mère biologique et sa partenaire féminine. Lorsque la mère biologique a voulu déménager en Nouvelle-Zélande avec son partenaire et l'enfant, le donneur de sperme a demandé une ordonnance parentale pour empêchait la mère de déménager l'enfant sur la base du fait qu'il partageait la responsabilité parentale avec la mère de l'enfant. Le tribunal a statué à l'unanimité que le donneur de sperme était un parent selon le sens naturel et ordinaire du mot et qu'il était qualifié de parent en vertu de la loi de 1975 sur le droit de la famille. Le rapporteur pour l'Australie souligne que ce cas est atypique, car il est inhabituel d'enregistrer le donneur de sperme comme l'un des parents sur le certificat de naissance de l'enfant et d'avoir un donneur de sperme qui a l'intention de jouer un rôle dans l'éducation de l'enfant. Le tribunal a refusé de résoudre la question de savoir si un donneur de sperme qui n'avait pas l'intention d'être impliqué dans la vie de l'enfant pouvait être considéré comme un parent légal[257] parce que les faits de l'affaire ne concernaient pas cette question.[258]

En Autriche, une personne peut faire don de son gamète à une personne spécifique (par exemple, un membre de sa famille ou un ami). Le point de départ est que le donneur ne devient pas le parent légal de l'enfant. Cependant, un donneur de sperme connu – mais pas une donneuse d'ovules connue – peut être reconnu comme le père de l'enfant si la mère ou l'enfant donne son accord et l'homme qui est le père légal de l'enfant ne s'y oppose pas.[259] Alternativement, le donneur peut devenir le père légal de l'enfant si l'enfant[260] demande un soi-disant « *father swap* ».[261] Dans ce cas, l'enfant n'a pas deux pères légaux, car un père remplace l'autre.

---

[255] Rapport Schrama.
[256] *Masson c. Parsons* [2019] HCA 21.
[257] Ibid., paragraphe 55.
[258] Rapport Kha.
[259] Articles 146, 147(3) et 148(3) du Code civil général autrichien.
[260] Seul l'enfant peut faire la demande. Rapport Buchstätter et Roth.
[261] Le « *father swap* » est réglé par l'article 150 du Code civil général autrichien.

2.7. RECONNAISSANCE DES PARENTS MULTIPLES DANS LE CAS D'UN « ENFANT À TROIS PARENTS »

La technologie médicale dite « à trois parents » est similaire à la fécondation in vitro, mais utilise le matériel génétique de deux femmes et d'un homme, au lieu d'une seule femme et un homme. En règle générale, l'ADN d'une femme est utilisé pour « corriger » l'ADN de l'autre femme afin d'éliminer les mutations génétiques qui causent de graves maladies héréditaires.

La plupart des rapporteurs spéciaux déclarent que la loi de leur pays ne prévoit pas les enfants à trois parents et que leurs juridictions n'autorisent pas une telle manipulation génétique. L'Australie envisage la viabilité juridique de l'autorisation des dons mitochondriaux, mais à l'heure actuelle, elle n'est pas légalement reconnue.[262] Le rapporteur spécial de la Turquie indique que la technologie n'est pas réglementée dans ce pays, mais que certaines cliniques de fécondation in vitro proposent une transplantation mitochondriale. La rapporteuse pense que cette technologie est illégale, car la gestation pour autrui et les dons de cellules gamètes et d'embryons sont interdits en Turquie. Elle prédit que le législateur turc interdira bientôt explicitement la technologie à trois parents.[263]

En générale, les règles ordinaires relatives à la détermination de la filiation ou de la parenté et à l'acquisition du statut juridique de parent s'appliqueraient à un enfant à trois parents si un tel enfant venait à naître.[264] Par conséquent, l'enfant n'aurait pas trois parents légaux, mais deux. Ainsi, les personnes qui souhaiteraient avoir l'enfant seraient les parents légaux de l'enfant et le donneur de tout matériel génétique ne serait pas légalement lié à l'enfant et n'aurait aucun droit ou responsabilité à l'égard de l'enfant.

Dans la loi sud-africaine, il n'est pas certain que le transfert mitochondrial soit interdit et que les trois parents puissent être reconnus.[265] La loi 38 de 2005 sur l'enfance autorise expressément plus d'une personne à assumer les mêmes responsabilités et droits parentaux à l'égard du même enfant[266] et ne fixe pas de limite au nombre de titulaires de responsabilités et de droits parentaux. Toutefois, les articles de la loi qui portent sur l'acquisition automatique des responsabilités et des droits parentaux ne font pas référence à trois parents.[267]

---

[262] Rapport Kha.
[263] Rapport Paksoy.
[264] Voir, par exemple, Danemark : Rapport Lund-Andersen et Pedersen ; Angleterre et pays de Galles Rapport Fenton-Glynn et Scherpe ; Allemagne : Rapport Sanders ; Pologne : Rapport Bugajski et Wysocka-Bar.
[265] Rapport Louw.
[266] Article 30(1) et (2) de la loi 38 de 2005 sur les enfants.
[267] Article 19–21 de la loi 38 de 2005 sur les enfants.

Ils se réfèrent à une mère et à un père biologique, ainsi qu'à une personne mariée qui est fécondée artificiellement avec son conjoint, et excluent tout donneur de gamètes.[268]

2.8. RECONNAISSANCE DES PARENTS MULTIPLES EN CAS DE GESTATION POUR AUTRUI

La discussion ci-dessous est limitée à la gestation pour autrui nationale ; elle ne s'étend pas à la gestation pour autrui transfrontalière/internationale.

Les juridictions examinées adoptent quatre approches différentes de la gestation pour autrui. La première approche consiste à interdire complètement la gestation pour autrui. Cette approche est adoptée en Autriche,[269] Croatie,[270] Estonie,[271] Allemagne,[272] Italie,[273] au Québec[274] et en Turquie.[275] Dans ces juridictions, les règles ordinaires concernant l'acquisition du statut de parent légal s'appliqueraient si la gestation pour autrui devait néanmoins avoir lieu. Ainsi, la femme qui a donné naissance à l'enfant serait la mère de l'enfant. Si elle était mariée ou partenaire d'une union civile enregistrée, son mari ou partenaire serait généralement l'autre parent légal de l'enfant. Les parents d'intention devraient adopter l'enfant afin d'obtenir le statut juridique de parent et l'adoption remplacerait généralement les parents adoptifs par les parents d'origine de l'enfant.[276] Lorsque cela est possible, le père d'intention pourrait reconnaître l'enfant et ainsi acquérir les responsabilités et les droits parentaux. Ainsi, par exemple, en Turquie, si la mère biologique est célibataire, le père d'intention pourrait reconnaître l'enfant et devenir ensuite le père légal de l'enfant. Si la mère biologique est mariée, son mari serait le père légal de l'enfant, à moins qu'il n'intente une action en justice appelée « rejet de la lignée ».[277] S'il le faisait,

---

[268] Article 40 de la loi 38 de 2005 sur les enfants. La définition de « parent » à l'article 1 de la loi 38 de 2005 sur les enfants exclut « toute personne qui est biologiquement liée à un enfant en raison du seul fait qu'elle est un donneur de gamètes à des fins de fécondation artificielle ».
[269] Rapport Buchstätter et Roth.
[270] Rapport Rešetar et Lucić.
[271] Rapport en ligne Kull et Torga.
[272] Rapport Sanders.
[273] Loi 40/2004, Norme in materia di procreazione medicalmente assistita.
[274] Article 541 du Code civil du Québec. La situation est différent dans le Canada anglophone, ou soit le *common law*, soit la loi, autorisent la multiparentalité. Par exemple, la Colombie Britannique et l'Ontario ont modifié leur lois.
[275] Rapport Paksoy.
[276] Si la juridiction particulière autorise l'adoption ouverte, les parents d'origine peuvent conserver des responsabilités et des droits à l'égard de l'enfant et les parents adoptifs et originaux peuvent être les parents multiples de l'enfant : voir ci-dessus 4 Reconnaissance de la multiplicité de la parentalité dans le cas de l'adoption ouverte.
[277] Rapport Paksoy.

le père d'intention serait en la possibilité de reconnaître l'enfant et de devenir le père légal de l'enfant.[278] Ainsi, l'enfant n'aurait que deux parents légaux.

En Italie, la Cour constitutionnelle, le 28 janvier 2021, déclare qu'il est indubitable que l'enfant, pris en charge pendant des années depuis sa la naissance par le couple qui a partagé la décision de le mettre au monde, a intérêt à ce que la réalité des faits soit reconnue par le droit. Mais cet intérêt de l'enfant ne prime pas automatiquement sur tout autre intérêt. La mise en balance des différents intérêts s'impose. Dans ce cas, l'intérêt de l'enfant doit être balancé avec l'intérêt de l'État à décourager une pratique qu'il considère passible de sanction pénale. Une solution qui niait toute possibilité pour l'enfant de voir reconnue sa relation avec les deux membres du couple ne serait pas équilibrée. Mais toute autre solution est compatible avec la constitution. Le choix de la solution incombe en premier lieu au législateur, qui jouit d'une large marge d'appréciation lui permettant de balancer tous les droits et les principes en jeu. Pour l'instant, la Cour cède le pas au législateur, sans pour autant renoncer à dénoncer comme insuffisante la protection assurée à l'intérêt de l'enfant par l'adoption simple.

La deuxième approche est légèrement différente de la première en ce qu'elle permet la gestation pour autrui altruiste, mais ne permet pas de s'écarter des règles ordinaires concernant la parentalité légale. Cette approche est adoptée en Australie. Comme les lois des juridictions qui interdisent la gestation pour autrui, la loi australienne confère le statut parental à la mère porteuse parce qu'elle est la femme qui donne naissance à l'enfant.[279] Son mari/partenaire est également le parent légal de l'enfant.[280] Afin d'obtenir le statut de parents légaux, les parents d'intention doivent obtenir une ordonnance de filiation.[281]

La troisième approche n'est ni d'interdire ni d'autoriser la gestation pour autrui ; au lieu de cela, la loi ne s'en occupe pas du tout. Cette approche est adoptée par l'Argentine,[282] la Belgique,[283] l'Angleterre et le pays de Galles,[284] le Japon,[285] le Luxembourg,[286] la Pologne[287] et les Pays-Bas.[288] Étant donné que ces juridictions n'ont pas de règles spécifiques sur la gestation pour autrui, les règles ordinaires concernant l'acquisition de la parentalité légale s'appliquent lorsque la gestation pour autrui se produit. Comme les juridictions qui interdisent la

---

[278] Ibid.
[279] Article 69P de la loi de 1975 sur le droit de la famille (Cth).
[280] Article 69P et 69Q de la loi de 1975 sur le droit de la famille (Cth).
[281] Rapport Kha.
[282] Rapport Medina.
[283] Rapport Gallus, Leleu, Mathieu et Swennen.
[284] Rapport Fenton-Glynn et Scherpe.
[285] Rapport Roots.
[286] Rapport Hilger. Un projet de loi propose l'interdiction de la gestation pour au nombre de personnes au Luxembourg : Projet de loi 6568A (anciennement Projet de loi 6568).
[287] Rapport Bugajski et Wysocka-Bar.
[288] Rapport Schrama.

gestation pour autrui, tous les pays qui ne réglementent pas la gestation pour autrui confèrent le statut parental à la femme qui donne naissance à l'enfant, c'est-à-dire la mère porteuse. C'est également le point de départ en Argentine, mais certains tribunaux ont pris comme argument que « tout ce qui n'est pas interdit est autorisé » et ont déclaré inconstitutionnelle la règle selon laquelle dans les cas de gestation pour autrui la maternité est établie par l'accouchement. Dans ces cas, les parents d'intention ont été déclarés parents légaux de l'enfant, à l'exclusion de la mère porteuse.[289] Revenons à la situation dans la majorité des juridictions qui ne réglementent pas la maternité de substitution : la femme porteuse – étant la femme qui accouche – est la mère de l'enfant. Si la femme porteuse a un mari ou un partenaire enregistré/civil, certaines juridictions confèrent le statut juridique de parent au mari ou au partenaire à l'exclusion du père d'intention, tandis que d'autres confèrent le statut de parent au père d'intention à l'exclusion du mari ou du partenaire de la mère. En Pologne[290] et aux Pays-Bas,[291] le mari ou le partenaire de la mère porteuse est le père légal de l'enfant, quel que soit le sperme utilisé pour la fécondation de la femme porteuse. Aux Pays-Bas, les parents d'intention doivent adopter l'enfant, soit que l'un d'eux ou les deux aient fait don de gamètes pour la fécondation de la femme porteuse. Les parents d'intention ont besoin du consentement de la femme porteuse pour l'adoption. En outre, avant que l'adoption ne puisse avoir lieu, une mesure de protection de l'enfance doit être prise par le Conseil de la garde et de la protection de l'enfance. Cette commission s'adresse au tribunal pour la résiliation des responsabilités parentales de l'un ou des deux parents, c'est-à-dire la mère biologique et son conjoint ou partenaire enregistré. Les parents d'intention peuvent, pendant la procédure, se voir attribuer une tutelle conjointe. Après d'un an de prise en charge de l'enfant, les parents d'intention peuvent demander l'adoption de l'enfant. Si la mère porteuse est célibataire, l'un des parents d'intention peut légalement reconnaître l'enfant si la mère porteuse y consent. Une fois que l'enfant a été légalement reconnu, le tribunal peut attribuer la responsabilité parentale exclusive au parent d'intention et l'autre parent peut alors demander l'adoption de l'enfant.[292] En Angleterre et au pays de Galles, également, un parent d'intention peut obtenir des responsabilités parentales si la femme porteuse est célibataire et consent à ce que le parent d'intention (homme ou femme) soit traité comme le parent légal de l'enfant.[293] Si le gamète d'un parent d'intention a été utilisé, ce parent d'intention est le parent biologique de l'enfant et peut obtenir le statut de parent légal par le biais de la *common law*.[294]

---

[289] Rapport Medina.
[290] Rapport Bugajski et Wysocka-Bar.
[291] Rapport Schrama.
[292] Ibid.
[293] Rapport Fenton-Glynn et Scherpe.
[294] Ibid.

Indépendamment du fait que la femme porteuse soit mariée ou dans une union civile, ou qu'elle soit célibataire, la parentalité légale peut être transférée aux parents d'intention par le biais d'une ordonnance parentale.[295]

L'approche finale consiste à reconnaître et à réglementer la gestation pour autrui et à conférer le statut de parents légaux aux parents d'intention, à l'exclusion de la mère biologique et de son conjoint ou partenaire enregistré/civil. Les trois pays de l'enquête qui adoptent cette approche sont la Grèce, l'Afrique du Sud et le Vietnam. Ces pays autorisent la gestation pour autrui altruiste, mais pas la gestation pour autrui commerciale. La loi sud-africaine autorise la gestation pour autrui altruiste tant que l'enfant qui doit naître a un lien génétique au moins avec un des parents d'intention,[296] tandis que les lois vietnamienne et grecque n'autorisent que la gestation pour autrui altruiste.[297] Au Vietnam, les parents d'intention deviennent les parents légaux de l'enfant à partir du moment de la naissance de l'enfant, sauf si les deux parents d'intention décèdent ou perdent leur capacité légale d'agir avant que l'enfant ne leur soit confié.[298] Dans ces circonstances exceptionnelles, la femme porteuse a la responsabilité et le droit de nourrir l'enfant. Si la mère refuse de le nourrir, la tutelle et le soutien de l'enfant sont déterminés conformément au Code civil et à la loi de 2014 sur le mariage et la famille.[299] La loi sud-africaine reconnaît la parentalité légale des parents d'intention, à condition que l'accord de gestation pour autrui ait été approuvé et confirmé par le Haute Cour avant la fécondation de la femme porteuse. Cette règle s'applique indépendamment du fait que les parents d'intention soient du sexe opposé ou du même sexe.[300] Si la femme porteuse est génétiquement liée à l'enfant, elle peut résilier l'accord de substitution pendant sa grossesse ou dans les 60 jours suivant la naissance de l'enfant.[301] Si elle résilie l'accord avant la naissance de l'enfant, les parents d'intention ne deviennent pas les parents de l'enfant parce que la mère porteuse est considérée comme le parent légal de l'enfant à la naissance avec son conjoint ou partenaire. Toutefois, si la mère porteuse n'a pas de conjoint ou de partenaire, le père d'intention devient le parent de l'enfant aux côtés de la femme porteuse.[302] Si l'accord est résilié après la naissance de l'enfant, les responsabilités et droits parentaux acquis par les parents d'intention sont résiliés et dévolus à la mère porteuse et à son mari ou partenaire, ou à la mère porteuse et au père d'intention si la mère porteuse n'a pas de conjoint ou de partenaire.[303] Un accord de gestation par substitution

---

[295] Articles 54 et 54A de la loi de 2008 sur la fécondation humaine et l'embryologie.
[296] Article 294 de la loi 38 de 2005 sur les enfants.
[297] Vietnam : Rapport Van Ngo ; Grèce : Rapport Zervogianni.
[298] Rapport Van Ngo.
[299] Ibid.
[300] Ss 292, 297 de la loi 38 de 2005 sur les enfants.
[301] Article 298(1) de la loi 38 de 2005 sur les enfants.
[302] Article 299(b) de la loi 38 de 2005 sur les enfants.
[303] Article 299(a) de la loi de 38 2005 sur les enfants.

qui ne respecte pas les exigences stipulées dans la loi 38 de 2005 sur les enfants est invalide et l'enfant est considéré comme l'enfant de la femme gestante.[304] La Grèce a un système similaire exigeant l'approbation de la gestation pour autrui par un tribunal. Si toutes les conditions légales ont été remplies et la gestation pour autrui a été autorisée par le tribunal, la mère d'intention est la mère légale de l'enfant depuis la naissance de l'enfant.[305] Si la mère d'intention est mariée ou si elle vit avec un partenaire enregistré, son conjoint ou partenaire devient le père légal de l'enfant. Un autre aspect de la loi grecque sur la gestation pour autrui similaire à la loi sud-africaine est que si la femme porteuse est génétiquement liée à l'enfant parce que son ovule a été utilisé, elle est mieux placée pour être le parent légal de l'enfant qu'une femme porteuse qui n'est pas génétiquement liée à l'enfant. En Grèce, une femme porteuse dont l'ovule a été utilisé pour la fécondation et qui a abouti à la grossesse peut contester le statut juridique de la mère d'intention dans les six mois suivant la naissance de l'enfant.[306] Si la contestation réussit, la femme porteuse devient la mère légale de l'enfant[307] et le conjoint ou le partenaire de la mère porteuse est désormais présumé être le père de l'enfant.[308] Ce conjoint ou partenaire peut toutefois contester la paternité.[309]

Il est probable que le Portugal rejoigne le groupe de juridictions qui confèrent le statut parental aux parents d'intention. Au Portugal, la gestation pour autrui était reconnue dans des circonstances limitées.[310] Parce que certaines parties du régime juridique de la gestation pour autrui ont été déclarées inconstitutionnelles, elle n'est pas actuellement réglementée au Portugal. La loi qui deviendra probablement applicable une fois surmontés les obstacles constitutionnels, prévoit que les parents d'intention sont les parents légaux de l'enfant.[311]

Finalement, il convient de noter que dans certaines juridictions qui autorisent la gestation pour autrui ou la laissent non réglementée, elle n'est disponible que pour les couples hétérosexuels. C'est la situation en Grèce[312] et au Vietnam.[313] Le Portugal devrait permettre aux couples de lesbiennes d'utiliser la gestation pour autrui pour avoir un enfant, mais pas aux couples de même sexe masculin.[314] Il va sans dire que dans les pays où le mariage et l'union civile homosexuels ne

---

[304] Article 297(2) de la loi 38 de 2005 sur les enfants.
[305] Article 1464, paragraphe 1, du Code civil grec.
[306] Article 1464, paragraphe 2, du Code civil grec.
[307] Article 1464, paragraphe 3, du Code civil grec.
[308] Article 1465, paragraphe 1, du Code civil grec et article 9 de la loi 4356/2015 sur les union enregistrées.
[309] L'article 1467 du Code civil grec et l'article 9, article 9, envoyé 3, de la loi 4356/2015.
[310] Rapport en ligne Vítor et Martin.
[311] Ibid.
[312] Rapport Zervogianni.
[313] Rapport Van Ngo.
[314] Rapport en ligne Vítor et Martins.

sont pas autorisés (comme la Pologne[315]), les couples de même sexe ne sont pas légalement autorisés à utiliser la gestation pour autrui pour avoir un enfant.

2.9. RECONNAISSANCE GÉNÉRALE DE LA MULTIPARENTALITÉ

Aucun des pays étudiés n'a une loi générale qui reconnaît la multiparentalité de manière générique et large. Dans un document de consultation sur la réforme de la loi sur la gestation pour autrui, la Law Commission of England and Wales, en collaboration avec la Scottish Law Commission, a déclaré qu'il pourrait être utile, à l'avenir, d'explorer la possibilité de permettre à un enfant d'avoir plus de deux parents légaux, car cela « permettrait à la situation juridique de refléter la réalité lorsqu'il y a une véritable coparentalité d'un enfant par trois ou quatre personnes ».[316]

Aux Pays-Bas, un comité multidisciplinaire a entrepris des recherches sur les familles multiparentales. Le rapport du comité a été publié en 2016.[317] L'une des recommandations révolutionnaires était que la multiparentalité légale devrait être autorisée pour un maximum de quatre parents dans deux ménages et que des responsabilités multiparentales devraient être introduites.[318] Finalement, le gouvernement néerlandais a décidé de ne pas poursuivre la réforme, principalement en raison de la complexité d'un système à quatre parents et d'une augmentation prévue des conflits si l'enfant avait plusieurs parents. Au lieu d'opter pour un système multiparental, le gouvernement a indiqué qu'un système de responsabilités parentales partielles est la voie à suivre pour résoudre les problèmes rencontrés par les parents sociaux. Un projet de loi sur les soins et la garde partagés a été publié pour consultation. Malheureusement, l'avant-projet de loi n'accorde pas une pleine reconnaissance juridique aux familles multiparentales. Le projet de loi concerne les responsabilités parentales partielles, qui ne reconnaissent pas le statut des familles multiparentales et ne résolvent pas vraiment les problèmes découlant de la multiparentalité.[319] Le rapporteur pour les Pays-Bas prédit que ce projet de loi sera seulement un pas dans la direction de la poursuite de la réforme législative, qui pourrait se traduire par une plus grande égalité pour les familles multiparentales.[320]

En Afrique du Sud, il n'existe pas de loi générale reconnaissant la multiplicité de la parentalité, et il n'est pas prévu de promulguer une telle loi. Il convient

---

[315] Rapport Bugajski et Wysocka-Bar.
[316] Law Commission of England and Wales et Scottish Law Commission, « Building families through surrogacy: A new law » (juin 2019), ss 7.85–7.90.
[317] Comité d'État sur la réévaluation de la parentalité « L'enfant et les parents au 21ème âge ».
[318] Rapport Schrama.
[319] Ibid.
[320] Ibid.

toutefois de noter que la loi 38 de 2005 sur les enfants ne donne aucune indication sur le nombre maximal de parents légaux qu'un enfant peut avoir. La loi prévoit qu'une seule personne peut acquérir et exercer des responsabilités et des droits parentaux à l'égard du même enfant, mais il n'est pas clair si tous les cotitulaires de responsabilités et de droits parentaux seraient considérés comme les parents de l'enfant.[321]

Finalement, il est intéressant de noter que le Vietnam n'a pas de loi qui reconnaît la multiparentalité, mais sa loi sur le mariage et la famille de 2014 protège les familles multigénérationnelles, telles que les grands-parents, les parents et les enfants qui vivent ensemble.[322] La loi réglemente également les responsabilités et les droits des belles-filles, des gendres et des parents qui vivent dans le même ménage.[323]

3. PARTIE B. DIVERSITÉ ET PLURALITÉ DES FONCTIONS DE LA FAMILLE

3.1. RECONNAISSANCE JURIDIQUE DES DIVERSES FONCTIONS DE LA FAMILLE

Ces questions sont étroitement liées aux traditions et à la culture locale ; ainsi, il n'existe pas de définition ou de compréhension universelle du concept de « famille » ni de ses fonctions. Par conséquent, une unité qui peut être considérée comme une famille aux fins de la protection juridique dans une juridiction peut ne pas être considérée comme telle dans une autre. Il en va de même pour une fonction particulière de la famille. Même au sein d'une même juridiction, un type particulier de famille ou une fonction particulière de la famille peut être protégé dans un domaine, mais pas dans un autre.[324] Il convient également de tenir compte la différence entre *l'existence* d'une fonction familiale particulière et la *protection juridique* de cette fonction,[325] et que toutes les fonctions ne peuvent pas être reconnues pour toutes les unités qui peuvent être considérées comme une famille dans une juridiction particulière. Par exemple, en Autriche,[326] en Belgique[327] et en Italie[328] les multiples fonctions familiales sont reconnues, mais

---

[321] Rapport Louw.
[322] Rapport Van Ngo.
[323] Ibid.
[324] Par exemple, en Afrique du Sud, tous les types de mariages polygames ne reçoivent pas la même reconnaissance. Les mariages coutumiers polygames sont pleinement reconnus, mais les mariages religieux polygames ne sont reconnus qu'à des fins limitées : Rapport Louw.
[325] Rapport Gallus, Leleu, Mathieu et Swennen.
[326] Rapport Buchstätter et Roth.
[327] Rapport Gallus, Leleu, Mathieu et Swennen,
[328] Rapport Aluffi.

elles ne bénéficient pas du même niveau de reconnaissance et de protection dans tous les types de familles qui se présentent dans chacun de ces pays. En outre, le concept de « famille » ne cesse de changer en raison, entre autres, du développement social et des progrès médicaux, par exemple dans le domaine de la procréation assistée.[329] De même, les fonctions de la famille changent avec le temps.[330]

Certains rapporteurs ont déclaré qu'il était difficile d'identifier les différentes fonctions de la famille et d'indiquer dans quelle mesure la législation de leur pays reconnaît ces fonctions, car les fonctions et la politique en ce qui concerne ces fonctions ne sont pas précisées.[331] Par conséquent, les diverses fonctions et la reconnaissance de ces fonctions par la loi sont en grande partie des questions de conjecture et d'opinion personnelle.[332] En outre, le droit de la famille n'est pas le seul domaine pertinent pour déterminer l'étendue de la reconnaissance juridique des diverses fonctions de la famille. Parce que des domaines tels que le droit fiscal, le droit des successions, le droit de la sécurité sociale et le droit pénal placent les familles ou les membres de la famille dans une position particulière, ces derniers doivent également être pris en compte.[333] Les instruments régionaux et internationaux influent également sur la reconnaissance et la protection accordées à divers types de familles et à diverses fonctions familiales, car le droit local est mis à l'épreuve par rapport à ces instruments et doit être adapté en raison des contestations judiciaires réussies fondées sur ces instruments. Par exemple, en Europe, les décisions de la Cour européenne des droits de l'homme ont contraint les pays à adapter leurs lois afin de tenir compte des nouvelles notions de la famille et de ses fonctions.[334]

Malgré les difficultés susmentionnées, la plupart des rapporteurs conviennent que la sécurité économique et le soutien financier aux enfants et aux membres de la famille économiquement plus faibles est une fonction importante de la famille, reconnue comme telle par la loi.[335] La question de savoir si l'État considère une famille comme constituée de personnes individuelles ou comme une unité influence l'étendue de la protection juridique accordée à cette fonction.

---

[329] Voir, par exemple, Rapport Buchstätter et Roth.
[330] Rapport Zervogianni.
[331] Rapport Fenton-Glynn et Scherpe ; Rapport Sanders ; Rapport Schrama ; Rapport Bugajski et Wysocka-Bar.
[332] Voir, par exemple, Rapport Sanders ; Rapport Schrama ; Rapport Bugajski et Wysocka-Bar.
[333] Rapport Schrama ; Rapport Bugajski et Wysocka-Bar.
[334] Rapport Buchstätter et Roth ; Rapport Aluffi.
[335] Voir, par exemple, Australie : Rapport Kha ; Belgique : Rapport Gallus, Leleu, Mathieu et Swennen ; Danemark : Rapport Lund-Andersen et Pedersen ; Angleterre et pays de Galles : Rapport Fenton-Glynn et Scherpe ; Estonie : Rapport en ligne Kull et Torga ; Allemagne : Rapport Sanders ; Grèce : Rapport Zervogianni ; Japon : Rapport Roots ; Portugal : Rapport en ligne Vítor et Martins ; Pays-Bas : Rapport Schrama ; Afrique du Sud : Rapport Louw ; Turquie : Rapport Paksoy ; Vietnam : Rapport Van Ngo.

Dans les pays où l'État accorde une grande importance à la responsabilité individuelle, la prémisse est que chaque personne doit assurer son propre bien-être économique, qu'elle soit ou non dans une relation familiale et qu'elle ait des responsabilités familiales à l'égard de ses conjoints, partenaires, enfants ou autres membres de sa famille.[336] Par exemple, aux Pays-Bas, la communauté de biens et la pension alimentaire postérieure au divorce ont été limitées, imposant ainsi la préférence de l'État pour la responsabilité individuelle aux époux et partenaires.[337] En Belgique également, la prémisse est que les fonctions de la famille sont exercées par les membres individuels de la famille au profit des autres membres individuels de la famille.[338] En Allemagne, également, le droit à une pension alimentaire après le divorce est restreint, mais la famille reste considérée comme la principale source de sécurité économique.[339]

Comme l'indiquent les rapporteurs du Québec, une considération importante dans le contexte de la sécurité économique et de la fonction de soutien financier de la famille est que les membres vulnérables de la famille doivent être protégés tandis que, simultanément, les libertés individuelles des membres de la famille doivent être respectées.[340]

Avoir et élever des enfants est également reconnu comme des fonctions de la famille (ou de certaines familles).[341] Certaines juridictions considèrent même le fait d'avoir des enfants comme la fonction naturelle de la famille.[342] L'absence d'enfants ne signifie pas qu'il n'y a pas de « famille ». Toutefois, certaines administrations offrent une aide publique pour la procréation assistée et d'autres étendent cet accès aux personnes qui ne relèvent pas de la famille hétérosexuelle traditionnelle. Par exemple, au Danemark, les femmes célibataires, les couples de même sexe et les hétérosexuels peuvent bénéficier d'un traitement de fertilité gratuit dans les cliniques publiques.[343] En apportant une aide financière aux parents, l'État reconnaît également que l'éducation des enfants est une fonction de la famille. Cette aide est fournie, par exemple, au moyen de l'allocation pour enfants et jeunes au Danemark[344] et la subvention de pension alimentaire pour enfants en Afrique du Sud.[345] Le Danemark et l'Afrique du Sud fixent un seuil

---

[336] Rapport Schrama.
[337] Ibid.
[338] Rapport Gallus, Leleu, Mathieu et Swennen.
[339] Rapport Sanders.
[340] Rapport Giroux et Langevin.
[341] Voir, par exemple, Argentine, Rapport Medina ; Australie : Rapport Kha ; Danemark : Rapport Lund-Andersen et Pedersen ; Allemagne : Rapport Sanders ; Grèce : Rapport Zervogianni ; Pologne : Rapport Bugajski et Wysocka-Bar ; Portugal : Rapport en ligne Vítor et Martins ; Afrique du Sud : Rapport Louw ; Turquie : Rapport Paksoy ; Vietnam : Rapport Van Ngo.
[342] Turquie : Rapport Paksoy.
[343] Rapport Lund-Andersen et Pedersen.
[344] Ibid.
[345] La subvention est régie par la loi 13 de 2004 sur l'assistance sociale.

de revenu pour les subventions. En Afrique du Sud, la subvention est limitée aux familles à faible revenu, tandis que le seuil de revenu danois est si élevé que la plupart des familles avec enfants reçoivent la subvention.[346] En plus de la subvention, les parents célibataires au Danemark reçoivent un montant supplémentaire de l'État.[347] L'Argentine[348] et l'Allemagne accordent également des subventions aux membres de la famille. Certainement, les lois relatives aux responsabilités et aux droits parentaux, à la parentalité légale, à l'adoption, à l'affiliation, etc. – qui ont fait l'objet de la première partie de ce rapport – reconnaissent également la fonction de la famille d'avoir et d'élever des enfants.

Plusieurs juridictions déclarent que la famille fonctionne comme un lieu où les personnes prennent soin les unes des autres.[349] En Australie, le rôle de soignant d'un conjoint ou d'un partenaire de fait est reconnu comme une contribution non financière et constitue l'un des facteurs déterminant le partage des biens.[350] La loi australienne protège également les relations personnelles étroites autres que les mariages ou les relations de fait entre deux adultes qui vivent ensemble si l'un des adultes fournit un soutien domestique et des soins personnels à l'autre ou si les deux adultes fournissent un soutien domestique et des soins personnels l'un à l'autre.[351] De telles relations peuvent exister, entre autres, entre frères et sœurs ou un grand-parent et un petit-enfant adulte, ce qui confère une reconnaissance juridique à la fonction de prise en charge au sein de la famille élargie. En Italie, la prise en charge des enfants, des personnes âgées et des personnes handicapées incombe principalement aux membres de la famille – en particulier aux femmes – parce que l'État ne fournit pas de services publics étendus.[352] La situation au Québec est similaire, parce que l'État-providence a décliné.[353] En Allemagne, environ 71 % de toutes les personnes qui ont besoin de soins sont prises en charge par des membres de leurs familles dans les maisons.[354] L'État reconnaît cette charge, non seulement par le biais des allocations de pension alimentaire pour des enfants, les couples et les parents mentionnées ci-dessus, mais aussi en accordant aux personnes qui fournissent des soins le droit de compenser des heures du travail.[355] En Croatie, le devoir des enfants de prendre soin de leurs parents âgés et malades est stipulé dans la Constitution[356]

---

[346] Rapport Lund-Andersen et Pedersen.
[347] Ibid.
[348] Rapport Medina.
[349] Voir, par exemple, Portugal : Rapport en ligne Vítor et Martins ; Turquie : Rapport Paksoy ; Vietnam : Rapport Van Ngo.
[350] Rapport Kha.
[351] Ibid.
[352] Rapport Aluffi.
[353] Rapport Giroux et Langevin.
[354] Rapport Sanders.
[355] Ibid.
[356] Rapport Rešetar et Lucić.

et la loi de 2015 sur la famille oblige les membres de la famille à s'entraider et à se respecter mutuellement.[357] Au Japon, les soins aux membres âgés de la famille sont traditionnellement considérés comme la responsabilité du fils aîné et de sa femme.[358] En 2018, le Code civil a été modifié pour introduire la possibilité de compenser un non-parent qui s'occupait d'un membre âgé de la famille. Le rapporteur pour le Japon déclare que l'amendement visait principalement à bénéficier à une belle-fille qui s'occupait de sa belle-mère.[359] En ce qui concerne la modification, un parent qui n'est pas un héritier et qui a versé une contribution spéciale à la pension alimentaire du défunt, par exemple en fournissant des soins infirmiers impayés, peut réclamer le paiement de la contribution des héritiers du défunt.[360] L'amendement a été controversé. Le rapporteur pour le Japon indique qu'il a été salué par certains pour avoir « permis à une belle-fille de recevoir une partie de l'héritage en échange des soins qu'elle avait fournis », tandis que « d'autres craignaient que le résultat de cette disposition soit que d'autres membres de la famille forcent les belles-filles à s'occuper des membres âgés de la famille, puisqu'ils pouvaient maintenant s'attendre à une récompense monétaire une fois que le membre de la famille serait décédé ».[361]

Une autre fonction de la famille est de fournir un lien spécial, qui est légalement reconnu et protégé, entre autres, par le fait que les membres de la famille sont placés dans une position préférentielle pour être nommés tuteurs ou curateurs, par un droit de ne pas témoigner dans le cadre de procédures pénales et par une obligation spéciale de diligence. C'est le cas, par exemple, aux Pays-Bas.[362]

Le rapporteur pour la Grèce identifie une autre fonction de la famille, à savoir qu'elle est un refuge d'amour et de camaraderie. Cette fonction a été reconnue à travers la libéralisation des lois sur le divorce et la reconnaissance des accords de cohabitation pour les couples hétérosexuels et de même sexe.[363] Cette fonction va de pair avec la fonction d'élever des enfants, car les intérêts des enfants sont mieux servis en étant élevés dans un environnement aimant.[364]

Le rapport belge fait référence à la fonction familiale particulière de permettre aux membres de la famille de s'épanouir vers un degré suffisant d'autonomie et de bonheur, à travers l'amour, l'affection et l'entraide ou le partage qui caractérisent normalement la vie familiale.[365] À cet égard, l'État et les lois qu'il promulgue

---

[357] Ibid.
[358] Rapport Roots.
[359] Ibid.
[360] Ibid.
[361] Rapport Roots, section 3.1.4.
[362] Rapport Schrama.
[363] Rapport Zervogianni.
[364] Ibid.
[365] Rapport Gallus, Leleu, Mathieu et Swennen.

doivent éviter d'empiéter sur la vie privée ou d'intervenir dans celle-ci, de peur de limiter indûment le droit à l'autodétermination. Les rapporteurs belges considèrent leur pays comme l'une des juridictions les plus avancées au monde en matière d'autodétermination.[366]

3.2. LES FONCTIONS QUI SONT PRINCIPALEMENT FAVORISÉES

Certains rapporteurs affirment qu'il est difficile, voire impossible, de répondre la question quelle est la fonction prédominante, car aucune fonction n'est expressément favorisée, la recherche sur cette question est difficile à trouver et la réponse dépend de la manière dont la prédominance est déterminée et mesurée.[367] Certains rapporteurs identifient la fonction d'avoir et d'élever des enfants comme étant celle qui est principalement favorisée dans leur juridiction,[368] tandis que d'autres identifient la sécurité économique et la fonction de soutien financier comme prédominantes.[369] Un autre groupe de rapporteurs pensent que ces deux fonctions prédominent dans leurs juridictions.[370] Le rapporteur grec identifie la fonction d'être un refuge d'amour et de compagnie comme prédominante en Grèce, mais affirme que cette fonction va de pair avec la fonction d'élever des enfants.[371]

3.3. LE RÔLE DES ENFANTS DANS LA VISION JURIDIQUE DES FONCTIONS DE LA FAMILLE

En général, la loi des pays examinés ne considère pas les fonctions de la famille différemment selon que les enfants sont présents ou non dans la famille.[372] Cependant, si des enfants sont présents, la fonction d'élever des enfants peut être considérée comme supérieure aux autres fonctions de la famille.[373] En plus, la

---

[366] Ibid.
[367] Par exemple, Autriche : Rapport Buchstätter et Roth ; Estonie : Rapport en ligne Kull et ; Allemagne : Rapport Sanders ; Japon : Rapport Roots ; Pays-Bas : Rapport Schrama ; Luxembourg : Rapport Hilger.
[368] Par exemple, Argentine : Rapport Medina ; Pologne : Rapport Bugajski et Wysocka-Bar ; Vietnam : Rapport Van Ngo ; Italie : Rapport Aluffi.
[369] Par exemple, Australie : Rapport Kha.
[370] Par exemple, Estonie : Rapport en ligne Kull et Torga ; Portugal : Rapport en ligne Vítor et Martins.
[371] Rapport Zervogianni.
[372] Par exemple Estonie : Rapport en ligne Kull et Torga ; Grèce : Rapport Zervogianni ; Luxembourg : Rapport Hilger ; Québec : Rapport Giroux et Langevin.
[373] Par exemple, Autriche : Rapport Buchstätter et Roth ; Australie : Rapport Kha ; Angleterre et pays de Galles : Rapport Fenton-Glynn et Scherpe ; Turquie : Rapport Paksoy. Voir aussi le Rapport Louw.

présence d'enfants joue un rôle en ce qui concerne l'étendue des fonctions de la famille dans la mesure où les familles avec enfants doivent fournir une sécurité économique et un soutien financier, non seulement aux adultes de la famille, mais aussi aux enfants. Les familles avec enfants peuvent également bénéficier d'une aide publique plus importante que les familles sans enfants, par exemple sous la forme d'une scolarité gratuite, d'avantages fiscaux et de subventions de l'État.[374] En outre, comme il est tout à fait évident, la fonction de garde de la famille englobe plus de personnes s'il y a des enfants dans la famille. Dans certaines juridictions, les responsabilités en matière de garde d'enfants peuvent être prises en compte lors de l'octroi d'une pension alimentaire et/ou du partage des biens en cas de divorce ou de séparation.[375] Pour finir, il convient de noter que la question de savoir si un enfant est un beau-fils, un enfant biologique, un enfant né à la suite d'une technologie de procréation assistée par donneur, un enfant « à trois parents » ou un enfant né à la suite d'une gestation pour autrui ne joue aucun rôle en ce qui concerne les fonctions de la famille ou l'étendue des fonctions.[376]

4. CONCLUSION

Le premier objectif du questionnaire sur le thème « Diversité et pluralité en droit : formes familiales et fonctions de la famille » était de déterminer si, et si oui, comment, le droit de la famille dans les juridictions étudiées reconnaît qu'un enfant peut avoir plusieurs parents. Les informations fournies par les rapporteurs montrent que, dans la plupart des juridictions, le point de départ est que le droit de la famille ne reconnaît que deux parents légaux.

Dans les pays qui n'autorisent pas les mariages/partenariats entre personnes de même sexe, généralement, les deux parents légalement reconnus sont un homme et une femme, c'est-à-dire un père et une mère. Dans toutes les juridictions, la loi considère que la femme qui accouche est la mère de l'enfant. Ainsi, la gestation, et non le matériel génétique, est le facteur déterminant en ce qui concerne la maternité légale. En revanche, pour le père, le mariage ou l'union civile enregistrée avec la mère biologique ou le lien génétique avec l'enfant est le fondement de la parentalité légale. Si la mère biologique a un mari/partenaire, cette personne est l'autre parent de l'enfant (ou le deuxième parent, si la juridiction particulière reconnaît les mariages/partenariats de même sexe).

---

[374] Voir, par exemple, Danemark : Rapport Lund-Andersen et Pedersen ; Allemagne : Rapport Sanders.
[375] Par exemple, Pays-Bas : Rapport Schrama.
[376] Par exemple, Autriche : Rapport Buchstätter et Roth ; Grèce : Rapport Zervogianni ; Pologne : Rapport Bugajski et Wysocka-Bar ; Portugal : Rapport en ligne Vítor et Martins ; Pays-Bas : Rapport Schrama ; Turquie : Rapport Paksoy.

Si la présomption de paternité est renversée, le père biologique (c'est-à-dire la personne dont le sperme a fécondé l'ovule de la mère) peut, dans certaines juridictions, devenir le parent légal de l'enfant en reconnaissant l'enfant ou en obtenant une ordonnance du tribunal déclarant qu'il est le père de l'enfant ; mais dans ce cas, il sera le seul père de l'enfant. En d'autres termes, le père biologique ne devient pas un parent supplémentaire. Cependant, dans certains pays, les tribunaux autorisent à la fois le père biologique et le mari/partenaire de la mère à être le parent légal de l'enfant si cela est dans l'intérêt supérieur de l'enfant. Si la mère biologique n'est pas mariée et n'est pas dans une union enregistrée, la loi adopte généralement l'une des deux approches suivantes : (1) le père biologique est le deuxième parent légalement reconnu de l'enfant s'il reconnaît l'enfant ou obtient une décision de justice déclarant qu'il est le père de l'enfant ; ou (2) l'autre est le seul parent légalement reconnu de l'enfant.

La technologie « à trois parents » ne modifie pas l'application des règles susmentionnées. La reproduction assistée sans subrogation change les règles, mais elle le fait sans ajouter un autre parent. Dans le cas de la procréation assistée le mari/partenaire de la mère biologique est le deuxième parent de l'enfant, indépendamment du fait que son sperme ait été utilisé ou non pour la procréation assistée ; c'est-à-dire qu'il n'est pas pertinent qu'il soit génétiquement le père de l'enfant. Si la gestation pour autrui a lieu, les juridictions adoptent généralement l'une des deux approches suivantes : (1) le mari/partenaire de la femme porteuse est le parent légal à l'exclusion du père d'intention ; ou (2) le père d'intention est le parent légal à l'exclusion du mari ou du partenaire de la mère. Ici aussi, l'enfant n'a que deux parents légaux.

Si les deux parents légalement reconnus sont mariés ou sont partenaires dans une union civile reconnue et que leur relation prend fin, ils restent tous deux les parents légaux de l'enfant. Ils conservent toutes les responsabilités et tous les droits englobés dans la parentalité légale, à moins que le tribunal n'en décide autrement. Il en va de même si les parents de l'enfant n'ont jamais été mariés et n'étaient pas partenaires reconnus, mais avaient conjointement des responsabilités et des droits parentaux à l'égard de l'enfant (par exemple, parce que le père a reconnu l'enfant).

Si l'un des parents se remarie ou conclut une nouvelle union civile légalement reconnue, le beau-parent ne devient généralement pas le troisième parent légal de l'enfant, à moins qu'il n'adopte l'enfant. Dans certaines juridictions, l'adoption par le beau-parent ne met pas fin à la relation juridique de l'enfant avec ses parents d'origine et l'enfant peut donc être considéré comme ayant plusieurs parents. Dans d'autres juridictions, l'adoption met fin à la relation juridique de l'enfant avec le parent qui n'est pas marié ou qui n'est pas le cohabitant du beau-parent. Dans ce dernier cas, le beau-parent remplace l'autre parent en tant que parent légal, de sorte que l'enfant n'a toujours que deux parents légaux.

Si le beau-parent n'adopte pas l'enfant, il peut acquérir des responsabilités et des droits par le biais d'une ordonnance du tribunal, d'un accord, d'une délégation ou d'un mandat ou selon les termes d'une disposition légale spécifique qui confère un droit ou impose une responsabilité au beau-parent. La délégation et un mandat n'ont pas pour résultat que le beau-parent devienne légalement un parent supplémentaire pour l'enfant. Si le beau-parent obtient des responsabilités et des droits par le biais d'une ordonnance du tribunal ou d'un accord, l'étendue des responsabilités et des droits détermine si le beau-parent peut être considéré légalement comme un parent supplémentaire. Certaines juridictions imposent une obligation de soutien au beau-parent. Ce devoir, en soi, n'équivaut pas à reconnaître le beau-parent comme un parent supplémentaire. Dans certaines juridictions, si la relation entre le parent de l'enfant et le beau-parent prend fin, le beau-parent a ou peut acquérir le droit de communication avec l'enfant. Ce droit de contact peut être considéré comme une reconnaissance juridique de la position du beau-parent en tant que parent supplémentaire et peut, en ce sens, constituer une reconnaissance de la multiplicité de la parentalité.

Sous réserve d'exceptions relatives à certaines adoptions par des beaux-parents, l'adoption pleine, habituellement, remplace les parents adoptifs en tant que parents légaux aux parents d'origine. La *kafala* n'est pas légalement reconnue dans les juridictions examinées et n'entraîne pas la parenté légale.

Dans certaines juridictions, les parents d'origine de l'enfant conservent leur obligation de pension alimentaire après l'adoption. Il est douteux de considérer que le maintien de ce devoir équivaut à une reconnaissance de parents multiples. Si la famille d'origine (ou certains membres de cette famille) exerce des droits de contact à l'égard de l'enfant, cela pourrait être considéré comme une reconnaissance de plusieurs parents après l'adoption, bien que dans un sens limité. Toutefois, le droit de la famille d'origine d'obtenir des informations sur l'enfant ne constitue pas une reconnaissance des parents multiples après l'adoption.

Aucune des juridictions n'a ou ne prévoit d'introduire une loi générale qui reconnaît la multiparentalité de manière générique et large.

Le deuxième objectif principal du questionnaire était de déterminer quelles fonctions familiales la loi reconnaît et favorise et si la présence d'enfants dans la famille engendre une différence à cet égard. Les principales fonctions identifiées par les rapporteurs sont : la fourniture d'une sécurité économique et d'un soutien financier aux enfants et aux membres de la famille économiquement plus faibles ; le fait d'avoir et d'élever des enfants ; d'être un lieu où les personnes prennent soin les unes des autres ; d'offrir un lien spécial aux membres de la famille ; et d'être un refuge d'amour et de compagnie.

Les deux fonctions qui prédominent sont la fourniture d'une sécurité économique et d'un soutien financier aux enfants et aux membres de la famille économiquement plus faibles, ainsi que le fait d'avoir et d'élever des enfants.

D'une manière générale, les lois examinées n'envisagent pas les fonctions de la famille différemment selon que des enfants soient ou non présents dans la famille. Toutefois, si des enfants sont présents, la fonction d'éducation des enfants peut être considérée comme supérieure aux autres fonctions et, naturellement, la portée de l'obligation de fournir une sécurité économique et un soutien financier et de responsabilités de prise en charge est accrue.

La question de savoir si un enfant est un beau-fils, un enfant biologique, un enfant né à la suite d'une technologie de procréation assistée par donneur, un enfant « à trois parents » ou un enfant né à la suite d'une gestation pour autrui ne joue aucun rôle en ce qui concerne les fonctions de la famille ou l'étendue des fonctions.

NEW FAMILY FORMS AND FAMILY FUNCTIONS IN ARGENTINE LAW

Graciela MEDINA

1. Overview of the Legal System..92
2. Step-Family 93
   2.1. Denomination of Parents Related by Marriage 94
   2.2. Parents Related by Marriage: Legal Regulation 94
   2.3. Number of Parents Related by Marriage 95
   2.4. Duties and Rights of the Parent Related by Marriage.............95
   2.5. Personal Duties...96
   2.6. Delegation of the Exercise of the Parental Responsibility in Favour of the Parent Related by Marriage.......................97
   2.7. The Other Parent is Unable to Exercise the Right 97
   2.8. Economic Duties 98
   2.9. Child Support...98
   2.10. Child Support Duty of the Parent Related by Marriage after Coexistence with the Father or Mother of the Child...............99
   2.11. Responsiblity of the Parent for the Wrongful Acts of Minors who Live with Him or Her 101
   2.12. Parental Responsibility when a Child is Raised in More than One Household..101
3. Adoption 104
   3.1. Full Adoption 104
   3.2. Open Adoption 104
4. Filiation by Assisted Procreation 106
5. Multi-Parenthood 106
6. Parenthood of the Surrogate 108
7. Branches of Law where the Family Receives Special Protection 109
   7.1. Civil Liability..110
   7.2. Compensation for Non-Financial Consequences 110

8. Family Functions which are Predominantly Favoured by
   Argentine Law... 111
9. Conclusion.. 112

1. OVERVIEW OF THE LEGAL SYSTEM

The Argentine Civil Code and Commercial Code were unified in 2015 in the Civil and Commercial Code, which includes all the principles of the human rights treaties to which Argentina has adhered and given constitutional hierarchy to in the 1994 Constitution. This is what Professor Rivera refers to as the 'constitutionalisation of private law'.[1]

The new Code includes family law in its text. This means that, in Argentina, family law is not regulated by a special Family Law Code, but that its rules are part of the Civil and Commercial Code and, therefore, they are inspired by its principles.

The Civil and Commercial Code accepts, respects and regulates different family models. It deals with diversity and plurality in respect of families involving children, specifically families where children have multiple parents, that is:

– step-families where children from one or both spouses/partners are raised in the same household;
– families where children are raised in more than one household, for example because their parents are jointly exercising custody/care after separation or have never shared a household but share parenting responsibilities;
– open-adoption families, that is families where children have been adopted but maintain links (legal or de facto) with their biological families;
– families where a child was born as a result of donor-assisted reproductive technology using one male and one female gamete (i.e. sperm and an egg/ovum);
– families where a child was born as a result of so-called 'three-parent' medical technology;
– families where a child was born as a result of surrogacy.

Below, I explain how the new forms of family are recognised in Argentine private law.

---

[1] J.C. Rivera, *Instituciones de Derecho Civil – Parte General*, 7th ed., Abeledo Perrot, Argentina 2020, p. 293.

2. STEP-FAMILY

The 'step-family' is the 'family structure originated by the marriage or common law marriage of a couple, in which one or both members have children from the previous marriage or de facto relationship'.[2]

This family model was not recognised in the previous Argentine Civil Code. Currently, it is regulated specifically, with the duties and rights of 'parents related by marriage'.

The Argentine Law on family matters was extensively modified in 2015 by the enactment of the Civil and Commercial Code. This set of rules regulates the step-family and grants legal responsibilities and rights to the step-parent who shares the household with the child – both personally and economically.

In the personal sphere, the step-parent has the right to cooperate in the upbringing and education of the other parent's children, to carry out the daily tasks related to the children's training in the domestic sphere and to make decisions in emergency situations. In the economic sphere, the step-parent must contribute to meeting the needs of the child who lives in the household and, in some cases, the step-parent has an obligation to provide support after the cessation of cohabitation if the changed situation may cause serious harm to the child or adolescent and the step-parent undertook a duty of support towards the child while he or she was cohabiting with the child's parent.

The obligations and rights of step-parents are not equal to the parents', nor do they conflict with the obligations and rights of the child's parents. Regarding personal rights, the decision of the father or mother always prevails over the step-parent's.

Regarding economic rights, step-parents have an obligation to provide support only while their step-children are minors or have a disability, for as long as there is cohabitation with the children's parent. In exceptional circumstances, a step-parent has a duty of support when the relationship with the father or mother of the minor ends.[3]

The economic responsibility of biological parents is wider: it exists with or without cohabitation and the duty may extend up to the age of 25 as long as the child is studying. The child support duty of biological parents is also wider than the duty of step-parents because the duty of a parent is not merely a subsidiary duty like that of the step-parent. Parents' child support obligation to their children comprises the satisfaction of the needs of the supported children in terms of maintenance, education, recreation, clothing, medical expenses, and the necessary expenses to acquire a profession or job. Child support is proportional

---

[2] G. Medina and E. Roveda, *Derecho de Familia*, Abeledo Perrot, Argentina 2016, p. 109 (free translation).
[3] Ibid., p. 818.

to the economic capacity of the parents and the needs of the supported child/children.

Another difference between the legal position of parents and step-parents is that the law does not create inheritance rights between them.[4]

2.1. DENOMINATION OF PARENTS RELATED BY MARRIAGE

The Argentine Civil and Commercial Code does not use the terms 'stepfather' and 'stepmother' due to their negative charge and pejorative connotation. Nor has it chosen to call them 'upbringing father/mother', 'heart father/mother', 'affectionate mother/father' or 'supportive father/mother'. The new Argentine Code uses the term 'parent related by marriage' (*padres por afinidad*) for the new spouse or partner who lives with a parent with children. This neutral term already existed in the Argentine Civil Code, which established parenting bonds arising from the marriage and with the spouse's blood relatives. The chosen term seeks to reverse the process of stigmatisation of this type of relationship where society had a negative view of the relationship. It is enough to remember the content of the children's story 'Cinderella' to exemplify this.

2.2. PARENTS RELATED BY MARRIAGE: LEGAL REGULATION

The Argentine legislation specifically grants rights and responsibilities to the parent related by marriage who shares a household with his or her partner's child.

Section 672 of the Argentine Civil and Commercial Code provides that the parent related by marriage is the 'spouse or partner who lives with the person who is in charge of the personal care of the child or adolescent'.[5]

This section covers two cases. The first is that of the spouse of the biological parent; here we can talk about a by-marriage bond, since the celebration of marriage gives rise to this bond between the married person and the relatives of the other spouse.[6]

The second case is that of the 'partner'. In this case, there is in fact no parenting by marriage since this bond arises only from marriage and not from mere cohabitation.

The regulation applies to couples of the same or the opposite sex.

---

[4] G. Medina and G. Rolleri, *Derecho de las Sucesiones*, Abeledo Perrot, Argentina 2017, p. 525.
[5] Free translation.
[6] S. 536 of the Argentine Civil and Commercial Code.

The Argentine Civil and Commercial Code requires coexistence (cohabitation, living together) with the child to confer duties on the parent related by marriage.[7]

2.3. NUMBER OF PARENTS RELATED BY MARRIAGE

Children may have two biological parents and two parents related by marriage, that is to say, it is not possible to have four mothers or fathers.

2.4. DUTIES AND RIGHTS OF THE PARENT RELATED BY MARRIAGE

The parent related by marriage has a set of duties and rights that are not equal to the duties and rights of the legal parents. We may divide these duties into personal and economic duties.

Prior to listing the duties and rights of the parent related by marriage, it is necessary to clarify that they do not replace or diminish, but supplement, the duties and rights of parents. The law grants these functions based on the cooperation taking place in this type of family and always based on the best interests of the child.

This duty and right of cooperation in daily tasks, such as decision-making power in emergency situations, has two basic functions. On the one hand, it constitutes a guiding function in the internal parental relationship; on the other hand, it affects external relations, to the extent that third parties shall respect these powers granted by law.

Lastly, since its role is supplementary and it does not replace the corresponding responsibility of the biological parent, the law states that, in the event of disagreement, the parent's decision shall prevail, because he or she is the person in charge of defining the criteria relating to the education and development of the child.

In the event of disagreement between any of the parents and the parents related by marriage, the parent's opinion shall prevail. The rights and duties granted to parents related by marriage are not to the detriment of the parents, who retain full authority and responsibility in the upbringing and education of their children.[8]

---

[7] A. Kemelmajer de Carlucci, M. Herrera and N. Llovera, *Tratado de Derecho de Familias. T. II: Arts. 509 a 593*, Rubinzal-Culzoni, Argentina 2014, p. 300.

[8] G. Medina and E. Roveda, *Derecho de Familia*, Abeledo Perrot, Argentina 2016, p. 821; M. Córdoba *Tratado de la Familia*, T. II, La Ley, Argentina 2020, p. 269.

A parent related by marriage who intends to make a decision that is different from the opinion of the parents has no cause of action: the Code thus avoids all legal proceedings by stating that the parents have the final say.

2.5. PERSONAL DUTIES

Section 673 of the Argentine Civil and Commercial Code provides:[9]

> The spouse or partner of a parent shall cooperate in the upbringing and education of the other's children, perform all daily acts related to its training in the domestic sphere and make a decision in emergency situations. In case of disagreement between the parent and his/her spouse or partner, the parent's judgment shall prevail. This collaboration does not affect the rights of the holders of parental responsibility.

Therefore, there are three personal duties and rights:

1. cooperate in the child's upbringing and education;
2. perform all daily tasks in the domestic sphere; and
3. make decisions in emergency situations.

The parent related by marriage may not waive this set of duties.[10]

As can be seen, the rule reflects the common duties that parents' new partners usually undertake in relation to the children.

Reality shows that it is normal for the parent related by marriage to cooperate in the upbringing and education of the child, and in performing daily tasks related to the training of the child in the domestic sphere; in this context, the partner 'adds' or 'contributes' to the child's life, taking care of him or her, supporting his or her needs, collaborating with the other parent, and providing an example in life. This is normal and expected behaviour in relation to the children of the person with whom one has a loving relationship.

The 'making decisions in emergency situations' duty is more complex, since the validity of the act performed by the parent related by marriage is determined in view of whether, in the circumstances of the specific case, there was an emergency.

---

[9] Free translation.
[10] G. Medina and E. Roveda, *Derecho de Familia*, Abeledo Perrot, Argentina 2016, p. 818.

2.6. DELEGATION OF THE EXERCISE OF THE PARENTAL RESPONSIBILITY IN FAVOUR OF THE PARENT RELATED BY MARRIAGE

In exceptional circumstances, the parent who is in charge of the child may delegate the exercising of parental responsibility to the parent related by marriage, by virtue of section 674 of the Argentine Civil and Commercial Code. This section provides:[11]

> The parent in charge of the child may delegate to his/her spouse or partner the exercise of parental responsibility when he/she is not in a position to fully fulfil the function due to travel reasons, illness or temporary inability, and whenever it is impossible for the other parent to exercise it or it is not convenient for the other parent to exercise this right. This delegation requires court approval, unless the other partner states his/her agreement in a reliable way.

For the delegation to be effective, the following requirements must be met:

1. the person who delegates must be in charge of his or her child; and
2. the person who delegates must not be in a position to fully fulfil the function.

The rule applies, but is not limited, to cases in which custody may be delegated due to the impossibility of fulfilling parental responsibility functions, or when it is not convenient for the other parent to exercise this right, or in case of travel, illness, temporary inability, etc. I also think that, through advance directives, the parent who is in charge of the child may delegate the exercise of this right.

2.7. THE OTHER PARENT IS UNABLE TO EXERCISE THE RIGHT

If the other parent can assume the sole exercise of the parental responsibilities, delegation is not permissible.[12] The delegation requires court approval, unless both parents agree on delegating the responsibility to the parent related by marriage. Before making its decision, the court must first hear the child.

---

[11] Free translation.
[12] C. Baddo, 'El rol del progenitor afin' (December 2018) *Derecho de Familia y de las Personas* 24.

2.8. ECONOMIC DUTIES

Parents related by marriage must contribute to the support of minor children and children with restricted abilities, or if the other spouse or partner who lives with them has a disability.[13]

The Argentine Civil and Commercial Code states that this duty to contribute creates a joint obligation between spouses and partners. This is important because both in marriage and in common law marriage, the responsibility of the members of the couple is, in theory, separate.

Specifically, section 461 of the Argentine Civil and Commercial Code states:[14]

> Spouses are jointly and severally liable for the obligations contracted by one of them to meet the ordinary needs of the household or the support and education of the children according to what is set forth in section 455. Apart from those cases, and except as otherwise provided in the marriage regime, neither spouse is liable for the obligations of the other. The spouse who does not comply with this obligation may be sued by the other one to do so.

2.9. CHILD SUPPORT

Section 676 of the Argentine Civil and Commercial Code provides:[15]

> The child support duty from the spouse or partner regarding the children of the other is subsidiary. This duty ceases upon dissolution of the marital bond or breakup of coexistence. However, if the change in situation may cause serious harm to the child or adolescent and the spouse or partner undertook to support, during their life together, the other's child, temporary child support may be set to be paid by the parent related by marriage, the duration of which shall be established by the judge according to the earning capacity of the liable party and the needs of the supported child and the length of coexistence.

The child support duty that is imposed on the parent related by marriage is subsidiary to the main obligation, which continues to be borne by the child's parent.

The priority issue is unclear when, between the liable parties, there are also bilateral or unilateral ascendants and siblings. Here, there are two sources of obligations: those on the part of the parent and those on the part of the parent related by marriage.

---

[13] Ss 456 and 520 of the Argentine Civil and Commercial Code.
[14] Free translation.
[15] Free translation.

The placement of this duty of support within parental responsibility would seem to give the obligation of the parent related by marriage prevalence over that of kinship since, in general, the obligations derived from it prevail, especially when the rules contained in the marital property regime and in the common law marriage regime provide that the obligation gives rise to joint and several liability, without making reference to the fact that the duty of support of the parent related by marriage is subsidiary to the duty of the child's blood relatives.

It may also be understood that the child support duty on the part of the parent related by marriage does not prevail over the duty of the natural family. Thus, it could be argued that it is an exception that does not replace the kinship parties, who have the main liability to support the child, and that the liability of the parent related by marriage operates as a last option only if the child's natural family cannot support the child.

I believe that the judge will analyse the issue using flexible criteria and make a decision based on the best interests of the child in each specific case.

Case law has considered the obligation of the parent related by marriage to be subsidiary, that is to say, it applies after the duty of the other relatives. Thus, in a case where a paternal grandmother was sued on the grounds of her maintenance obligation, she opposed, among other exceptions, the duty that in that sense corresponded to the duty of the cohabitant of the mother as a parent related by marriage. The exemption was rejected by the court, based on the subsidiary nature of the maintenance obligation of the parent related by marriage. The presiding officer stated that this duty is of a lower order than the duty of the child's relatives in a straight line, that is, the child's parents and grandparents have the duty in the first place. Thus, the child support duty shall be satisfied in the first instance by the persons who have a blood relationship with the child, and a claim can only be instituted against the parent related by marriage if there are no such relatives, if they do not have the resources to support the child, or their resources are not enough to support the child.[16]

2.10. CHILD SUPPORT DUTY OF THE PARENT RELATED BY MARRIAGE AFTER COEXISTENCE WITH THE FATHER OR MOTHER OF THE CHILD

The parent related by marriage has a limited, particular and temporary child support duty after breaking up with the father or mother of the child. After the breakup of the couple, the child support duty of the parent related by

---

[16] Court in Civil Matters in and for the City of Buenos Aires, Courtroom G, 04.07.2016, *SM y otro c. STA s/alimentos* (*MS and other v. STA, child support proceedings*). Microjuris, cita: MJJ98244.

marriage is an exceptional obligation that is only temporary and arises if two requirements are simultaneously present:[17]

1. the change in situation may cause serious harm to the child or adolescent, and
2. the parent related by marriage has assumed, while coexisting with the child's parent, the support of the parent's child.

The rule uses the conjunctive word 'and', meaning that both requirements must be met at the same time, and that the non-fulfilment of one of them will prevent the progress of the action against the parent related by marriage.

The wording of the rule at this point is not clear since, instead of mentioning issues related to child support, such as the 'child's needs', a 'situation of extreme need' or any similar wording, the phrase used is 'serious harm', which is not related to child support. My view is that the expression will be interpreted as a state of need of the child who cannot be supported by any of the main liable parties.

In these cases, however, it is assumed that if the partner related by marriage contributed economically to the needs of his or her partner's child, the breakup will probably affect the child's quality of life. This in itself does not allow a claim for child support because here the only purpose is to avoid 'serious harm'. For example, a contribution to the payment of rent that allows the minor to continue living in an expensive home may not be requested, but the parent related by marriage may be requested to make a contribution when the parents or relatives do not have the resources to ensure that the child has a decent place to live.[18]

The provision of child support by the parent related by marriage after the coexistence has terminated is supportive, because the parent related by marriage supports the basic needs of the supported children; his or her duty is limited in content and he or she is never obliged to support the children of his or her partner at the same level than when they shared a household.

A court has decided a case where a woman who had lived with a man for one year claimed child support from her former partner for her daughter until she reached adulthood, based on the circumstances of the girl, who did not have a biological father and who was in a bad economic situation. The court only ordered child support for one year because the regulation clearly establishes

---

[17] G. Bedrossian, 'La obligación alimentaria a cargo del progenitor afín' RDF 84, 205 TR LALEY AR/DOC/2995/2018.
[18] G. Bedrossian, 'Obligación alimentaria extendida: múltiples aplicaciones de la figura del progenitor afín' AR/DOC/3313/2019 (December 2019) *Revista Codiglio Civil y Comercial* 88.

that the child support of the parent related by marriage is subsidiary and temporary.[19]

2.11. RESPONSIBILITY OF THE PARENT FOR THE WRONGFUL ACTS OF MINORS WHO LIVE WITH HIM OR HER

The parent related by marriage does not assume objective parental responsibility for damage caused by the minor children of his or her spouse or partner, since his or her duties and rights do not exclude or replace the rights of the parents, unless he or she exercises parental responsibility according to section 675[20] of the Civil and Commercial Code or unless parental responsibility has been delegated to him or her in terms of section 674 of the Civil and Commercial Code.[21] He or she may always be released from responsibility by demonstrating that he or she had no fault, according to what is set forth in section 1756[22] of the Civil and Commercial Code.

2.12. PARENTAL RESPONSIBILITY WHEN A CHILD IS RAISED IN MORE THAN ONE HOUSEHOLD

Parents in families where children are raised in more than one household (e.g. because the children's parents are exercising joint custody/care after

---

[19] Court in Civil, Commercial, Mining and Rural, and Family Matters for Constituencies II to V, Courtroom I, 10.12.2017, *OGN c. RCA s/alimentos* (*OGN v. RCA, child support proceedings*), Rubinzal-Culzoni, RC J 9641/17. Cf. s. 676 Civil and Commercial Code.

[20] S. 675 reads: 'Joint exercise with the parent related by marriage. In case of death, absence or inability of the parent, the other parent may assume this exercise together with his/her spouse or partner. This agreement between the parent and his/her spouse or partner related to the exercise of parental responsibility requires court approval. In case of conflict, the opinion of the parent shall prevail. This exercise ceases with the end of the marriage or common law marriage. It also ceases if the parent who was not exercising the parental responsibilities fully recovers his/her abilities' (free translation).

[21] S. 674 reads: 'Delegation to the parent related by marriage. The parent in charge of the child may delegate to his/her spouse or partner the exercise of parental responsibility when he/she is not in a position to fully fulfil the function due to travel reasons, an illness or temporary inability, and whenever it is impossible for the other parent to exercise it or it is not convenient for the other parent to exercise this right. This delegation requires court approval, unless the other parent states his/her agreement in a reliable way' (free translation).

[22] S. 1756 reads: 'Other persons in charge. Persons to whom the exercise of parental responsibility has been delegated, guardians and conservators are responsible like parents for the damage caused by those they are in charge of. However, they are released if they prove that it was impossible for them to avoid the damage; such impossibility does not result from the mere fact that the circumstance occurred when they were not present. The premises in charge of hospitalised persons are responsible for the negligence in the care of those who, temporarily or permanently, have been placed under its supervision and control' (free translation).

separation or have never shared a household, but they share child-raising responsibilities) have joint parental responsibility.[23]

It is important to highlight that even when parents are separated, both of them have parental responsibility and it is assumed that each of them has the consent of the other to perform any legal act related to the life of the minor, except for cases that require joint approval or where there has been an objection by one of the parents, in which case a court decision is needed by default.

This provision is important for third parties as it gives them an assurance that either parent represents the minor and can act for him or her even when the parents are separated. Thus, for example, principals, physicians and sport centres have certainty that the consent of only one of the parents is valid, even if the parents are divorced or separated or their marriage has been annulled. All third parties must comply with the parent's request unless they receive a clear opposing instruction from the other.

The most important acts for the child's life require the joint consent of both parents. These acts are included in a closed list in section 645:

1. authorisation to get married;
2. authorisation to join religious communities, the armed forces or security services;
3. authorisation to leave the Argentine Republic or to establish a permanent residence abroad;
4. authorisation to be a party to legal proceedings, in cases where the child cannot act on his or her own;

---

[23] S. 641. Parental responsibilities refer both to entitlement and exercise. While the entitlement refers to the set of duties and rights that the law recognises in favour of both parents, the exercise refers to s. 641 which includes parental responsibility and states:

'The exercise of parental responsibility corresponds:

a) in case of coexistence with both parents, to both of them. It is presumed that the acts performed by one have the agreement of the other, except the cases included in section 645 or if the other person expressly opposes;
b) in case of cessation of coexistence, divorce or marriage nullity, to both parents. It is presumed that the acts performed by one have the agreement of the other, except the cases included in the previous subsection. By the will of the parents or by court decision, in the interest of the child, the exercise can be attributed to only one of them, or different modalities can be established;
c) in case of death, absence with presumption of death, deprivation of parental responsibility or suspension of the exercise of one parent, to the other;
d) in case of an out-of-wedlock child with only one filial bond, to the only parent;
e) in case of an out-of-wedlock child, with two filial bonds, if one was established by court decision, to the other parent. In the interest of the child, the parents – by mutual agreement – or the judge may decide the joint exercise or establish different modalities' (free translation).

5. administration of the assets of the child, unless such administration has been delegated in accordance with what has been established in the chapter of the Code dealing with family relations.

In all cases, if one parent does not grant his or her consent or is unable to do so, the judge must decide, taking into account the interests of the family.[24]

When the act involves the adolescent children, that is, children over 13 years old, express consent is needed.[25]

According to section 642 of the Argentine Civil and Commercial Code, in case of disagreement between the parents, either of them may approach the judge with jurisdiction, who shall decide the dispute by way of the shortest procedure established by the local law, after holding a hearing with the parents with the involvement of the Public Ministry.

If the disagreements are repetitive or there is another reason that seriously hinders the exercising of parental responsibility, the judge may confer parental responsibility totally or partially on one parent, or distribute it between the parents, for a period that shall not exceed two years. The judge may also order interdisciplinary intervention measures and submit disputes to mediation.[26] The judge may order an out-of-court mediator to help the parties to resolve their disputes.[27]

In practice, the two major problems with joint custody are recurrent failure of a parent to comply with the regime, and problems deriving from child support. In case law, there has been an instance of serious and repeated opposition by the mother to the exercise by the father of his visitation right and, in this case, the mother was held liable to pay damages to the father.[28] Furthermore, preventing the father from having contact with the child constitutes a criminal offence with a penalty of up to one year in prison.

Regarding child support, both parties have the same obligation regarding the child.

In the case of separated parents, the Civil and Commercial Code established a system of joint legal custody, which has two forms: joint physical custody, where the child spends a similar amount of time in each parents' household; and sole physical custody, where the child spends more time with one of them.[29]

---

[24] G. Medina and E. Roveda, *Derecho de Familia*, Abeledo Perrot, Argentina 2016, p. 768.
[25] Ibid.
[26] Ibid.
[27] S. 642 of the Argentine Civil and Commercial Code.
[28] Court of Appeals in Civil Matters, Courtroom K, 02.12.2019, *F, DE c. D, LV s/daños y perjuicios – ordinario* (*F, DE v. D. LV, damages, ordinary proceedings*), docket 39.782/2010.
[29] S. 650 of the Argentine Civil and Commercial Code.

Section 666 of the Argentine Civil and Commercial Code takes into account this criterion and consequently provides that, if the custody is joint, in any of its forms, what is appropriate is for each parent to contribute to the payment of child support when he or she is in charge of the child and whenever the resources of both are equivalent.

If the parents do not have the same income, the one who has the highest income must pay child support to the child and not to the other parent, so that the child has the same standard of living in both households.[30]

3. ADOPTION

3.1. FULL ADOPTION

In Argentina, there are three types of adoption: full adoption, simple adoption and step-child adoption. In full adoption, in theory, the bonds with the biological family are extinguished, whereas in simple adoption, the bonds with the biological family are maintained, so it could be part of an open adoption.

3.2. OPEN ADOPTION

In simple adoption, the adopted child or adolescent 'maintains a specific family status in relation to his/her biological family, since the kinship bond with the biological family is not completely broken but, on the contrary, there is a new family bond created with the adopter but not with the rest of his/her biological family'.[31]

Simple adoption has the following effects:

1. as a rule, the rights and responsibilities arising from the bond of origin are not extinguished by the adoption; however, the title and exercise of parental responsibility are transferred to the adopters;
2. the family of origin has visitation rights with the adopted child, unless this is contrary to the best interests of the child;
3. the adopted child retains the right to claim child support from his or her family of origin if the adopters are not able to provide support; and
4. the adopters or the adopted child who is of a sufficient age and maturity may request that the child's last name of origin be kept, either by adding it to the last name of the adopters or one of them, or by putting the last name of the adopters or one of them before the child's last name of origin.

---

[30] G. Medina and E. Roveda, *Derecho de Familia*, Abeledo Perrot, Argentina 2016, p. 802.
[31] U. Basset, 'Comentario al Art 627' in *Código Civil y Comercial: tratado exegético*, vol. III, 3rd ed., Thomson Reuters, Argentina 2020 (free translation).

Furthermore, after simple adoption has been agreed upon, the adopted child may start filiation proceedings against his or her biological parents and the adopted child's blood parent can recognise the child. But neither the recognition after the adoption nor the progress of the filiation proceedings changes the effects of the simple adoption.

In Argentina, the judge grants full or simple adoption according to the circumstances and, mainly, taking into consideration the best interests of the child. When it is more convenient for the child or adolescent, upon application by the parties and for valid reasons, the judge may maintain the legal bond between the child and one or more of the child's relatives in the family of origin in full adoption, and create a legal bond with one or more relatives of the family of the adopter in simple adoption. In this case, the legal regime of succession is not modified, nor is parental responsibility or marriage impediments, which are regulated by the Code for each type of adoption.

Parental responsibility is always exercised by the adopter even when there is a visitation right with the adoptive family. All legal responsibilities are exercised by the adopters, who are liable for damages caused by the minor. The adopters are also the adopted child's legal representatives.

Adopted children may claim child support from their biological parents in simple adoption if their adopters are not able to provide support. This obligation is subsidiary and is based on maintaining ties with the biological family.

Regarding inheritance rights, adoptive children, irrespective of the type of adoption, inherit like blood descendants, that is, they are legitimate heirs and have the right to a legitimate portion of three-quarters of the inheritance.[32]

The difference lies in the inheritance rights of the parents in simple adoption. Section 2432 of the Argentine Civil and Commercial Code provides that adopters are considered ascendants. However, in simple adoption, neither do the adopters inherit the assets that the adopted child may have received gratuitously from his or her family of origin, nor does the adopted child's family of origin inherit the assets that the adopted child may have received gratuitously from his or her adoptive family. These exclusions do not operate if, as a consequence, there are vacant assets. In respect of the rest of the assets, the adopters exclude the parents of origin.

This section provides that, as a general principle, in simple adoption, the adopter inherits intestate from the adopted child and is a forced heir under the same conditions as the biological parents, excluding from the heirship the biological parents, with respect to all the assets of the adopted child. As for the adopters, they are considered ascendants of the adoptee.

---

[32] Ibid.

This general principle is subject to an exception regarding parents by simple adoption, who shall not inherit the assets that the adopted child could have received gratuitously from his or her biological family. The exception does not apply if the assets received from the biological family remain vacant; in this case, the adopter by simple adoption inherits.

4. FILIATION BY ASSISTED PROCREATION

The Argentine Civil and Commercial Code regulates three types of filiation: natural filiation, filiation by adoption and filiation by assisted procreation. The latter arises from assisted procreation techniques.

Argentine law does not recognise any type of filial bond between the donor and the child if the child was born as a result of donor-assisted reproductive technology using one male and one female gamete, regardless of whether the donor is anonymous or known.

According to section 562 of the Argentine Civil and Commercial Code, a person who is born via assisted human reproduction is the child of the person who gave birth and of the man or woman who gave his or her prior informed and free consent in accordance with sections 560 and 561, duly registered with the Civil Registry, regardless of who provided the gametes.

In the Argentine Civil and Commercial Code, multi-parenthood is not allowed since there is a rule that expressly states: 'No person may have more than two filial bonds, irrespective of the nature of the filiation'.[33] This rules out the possibility of the existence of multiple fathers or mothers.

Children who were born by this technique have the right to know their origins in a limited way, even though there are legal precedents that have declared the nuclear family unconstitutional and have recognised a child with three parents.

5. MULTI-PARENTHOOD

Argentina does not have legislation to recognise multi-parenthood in a generic, broad manner. However, in several legal precedents before the enactment of the Civil and Commercial Code, there were petitions for multi-parenthood; the cases were resolved in different ways: in some of them, multi-parenthood was upheld, whereas in others it was denied.

The first case in which multi-parenthood was accepted after the reform of the Civil and Commercial Code was in Mar del Plata, Buenos Aires Province. A same-sex couple and the biological mother of a minor filed a petition by

---

[33] S. 558 of the Argentine Civil and Commercial Code.

which they requested the recognition of the triple parenthood that had been denied by the Civil Registry. The judge granted relief, taking into account that the procreational will had always been of the three people, that is to say, the same-sex couple and the mother who jointly exercised paternal and maternal roles.[34]

The second case that accepted multi-parenthood after the reform of the Civil and Commercial Code (which contains a written rule prohibiting it) was resolved by a judge on family matters[35] of original jurisdiction in 2020. It concerned an isolated case in a small rural community in the interior of the Argentine Republic. A nine-year-old girl was living alternately with a person whom she believed to be her biological father and with her legal father (her mother's husband, who had recognised her as his daughter). During the week she lived with her legal father, and on weekends with the alleged biological father; she recognised both men as fathers. The mother did not live with the girl, but with another later partner. When the girl was nine years old, the man who stated that he was the biological father challenged the paternity of the man who had recognised the girl as his daughter. During the proceedings, the girl stated that she wanted to continue to have both parents and to continue to have her legal father's last name.

The judge started her judgment with a quote from the Little Prince: 'The essential is invisible to the eyes'.[36] She stated that what is important is love and that this is so even more than law and public order. The judge did not order any genetic test to determine whether the alleged biological father was actually the child's father; she disregarded that the action had been filed out of term; she declared unconstitutional the rule providing that one can only have one father and one mother; and she ordered the registration of the triple parenthood based on the best interests of the minor and her right to identity.

There was another case where a judge dismissed a petition for multi-parenthood in Buenos Aires in 2019 on the grounds of the constitutionality of section 558 of the Argentine Civil and Commercial Code. In this case, a same-sex couple alleged that they had agreed with a common friend to have a child together. The boy was registered as the child of his biological parents.

---

[34] Court of Family Matters No. 2 of Mar Del Plata, 24.11.2017, *CMF y otros s/materia a categorizar* (*CMF and others, to be determined*), online appointment: AR/JUR/103023/2017.
[35] Civil Court in Family and Successions, Unique Denomination, Monteros, 02.07.2020, *LFF c. SCO s/filiación* (*LFF v. SCO, filiation*), online appointment: AR/JUR/132/2020.
[36] Free translation. In the third paragraph of the first page, the judge stated: 'Before going on to develop each point that I said in the first paragraph – moving away from any rigid and traditional format that judges have to write the rulings, without such forms today deserving so much value – I allow myself to quote a reflection from the book *The Little Prince*, which says: "It only looks good with the heart. The essential is invisible to the eyes ... The eyes are blind. We must seek with our hearts"' (free translation).

Sometime later, due to an alleged hindering of contact with the minor, they requested the registration of the third filiation. The judge dismissed the petition after considering that the procreational will of the three adults had not been proven, that the Civil and Commercial Code established a binary filiation system, which was constitutional, and that the gay husband was a father related by marriage.[37]

The court decided that section 558 of the Civil and Commercial Code, which establishes double filiation for everyone who is born in the country, does not result in discrimination that is repugnant to constitutional guarantees, as it is applicable to all persons equally, without distinguishing between persons on the grounds of gender, sex, age, political opinion, religion or ethnic or cultural origin.

6. PARENTHOOD OF THE SURROGATE

Argentina does not regulate surrogacy in the Civil and Commercial Code and emphatically provides that the mother is the one who gives birth to the child. Specifically, section 565 states that, in natural filiation, maternity is established by proof of birth and the identity of the newborn.

In practice, a search on the Internet suffices to find a variety of offers to hire a woman to carry out a pregnancy on behalf of third parties and ultimately to deliver the child to the applicant couple.

The lack of regulation in Argentina has not solved the problem of surrogacy – quite the contrary. As there is no express prohibition of surrogacy, assisted fertilisation centres carry out the practice, since there are no penalties for performing surrogacy like there are in other countries around the world. When children are born, there are problems with their registration in the name of the principal party, especially in the case of the intended mother since, as I have already stated, filiation is attributed by the fact of childbirth.

This has occurred relatively frequently in recent years and has forced the parties to approach the courts. Generally, the courts have been inclined to point out that section 19 of the Constitution states that everything that is not prohibited is allowed, and, since contracts of gestation carried out by another person are not expressly prohibited, these contracts have been considered to be allowed. Consequently, the section of the Argentine Civil and Commercial Code that states that maternity is established by the fact of childbirth has been declared unconstitutional.

In cases where judges were called upon to decide disputes, it has been held that the parents are those who had the intention to produce the child,

---

[37] Court of Original Jurisdiction in Civil Matters in and for the City of Buenos Aires No. 77, 16.07.2019, *A, NR y otros y otro c. GCBA y otros s/amparo* (*A, NR and others and another v. GCBA and others, without protection*), online appointment: AR/JUR/26167/2019.

irrespective of whether they contributed biological material, and without the need for adoption. That is to say, it has been accepted that gestation carried out by another is a case of filiation by procreational will and the registration of children has been ordered directly in the name of the person(s) who had the intention to cause the child to be born.

This solution has been applauded by progressive voices and criticised by others who consider it to be a general principle that this type of contract is prohibited as being contrary to the public order and good practice and as having as its object the delivery of a child, which is an illegal object. However, the nullity theory does not provide an answer to the conflicts which originate when the contract is made and performed immediately and the nationality or maternal filiation must be determined. These situations have forced courts acting in and for the city of Buenos Aires to issue a decision in the case of alleged agreements entered into and performed in India by Argentine citizens that required the registration of the child as Argentine by virtue of the nationality of the principal parties and also in the case of alleged agreements entered into and performed within the country.

In a few precedents, adoption by the spouse of the child's biological parent has been required as a way to solve the problem.[38]

In no case has multi-parenthood been accepted in the case of surrogacy, that is, the pregnant person (i.e. surrogate mother) has not been recognised as the mother of the child; consequently, she does not have the duties and rights arising from parental responsibility.

7. BRANCHES OF LAW WHERE THE FAMILY RECEIVES SPECIAL PROTECTION

In Argentina the law recognises that the family may have various functions, including producing and raising children, protecting the vulnerable (i.e. women and children), providing economic security, and fulfilling caring functions. This is reflected in different branches of law.

---

[38] Cámara Nacional de Apelaciones en lo Civil y Comercial Federal, sala I, 22.03.2022, *S, ER y otro c. Dirección de Obra Social Servicio Penitenciario Federal s/amparo de salud*, *La Ley* 10.05.2022, 4 with notes by de Silvia Marrama, TR LALEY AR/JUR/32428/2022. S. Marrama, 'Filiación adoptiva y subrogación de vientres' (2020) *Anales. Institutos* 47, available at https://repositorio.uca.edu.ar/handle/123456789/11081; S. Marrama, 'Prácticas abusivas en convenios de maternidad subrogada' in *Temas de Derecho de Familia, Sucesiones y Bioética online*, Erreius, 2020 available at https://repositorio.uca.edu.ar/handle/123456789/11140 (13).

7.1. CIVIL LIABILITY[39]

In the event of the father's or a mother's death, compensation is paid to the child by the perpetrator of the wrongful act resulting in the death of the father as compensation for the loss of the father's support. The compensation consists of the amount necessary for alimony and child support for children up to the age of 21 who have the right to receive it, and for children without capacity or with restricted capacity even if they have not been legally declared as having restricted capacity. This compensation is paid even when another person must provide support to the child. In order to determine the amount of compensation, the judge must take into account the probable lifespan of the victim; his or her personal circumstances and those of the claimants; and the loss of chance of future help as a result of the death of the children.

Anyone who had custody of the deceased minor also has this right to receive compensation. The law requires compensation to be paid to the children and spouse or partner of the deceased because it assumes that the support of its members is the function of the family.

7.2. COMPENSATION FOR NON-FINANCIAL CONSEQUENCES

Section 1741 states: 'The injured party is entitled to claim compensation for non-financial consequences'.[40] If the fact that causes the injury results in the death of a spouse, cohabitant, descendant or parent or if the spouse, cohabitant, descendant or parents suffer serious disability, the ascendants, descendants, spouse and those who lived with the deceased or disabled person may receive, as successors and assigns, compensation according to the circumstances.

In exceptional cases, section 1741 allows claims for non-economic damage by indirectly injured parties who are relatives of the injured party. In doing

---

[39] S. 1745 reads: 'Compensation for death.
In the event of death, compensation must consist of:

(a) the expenses necessary for the victim's attendance and subsequent funeral. The right to repeat them rests with the person who pays them, even if it is due to a legal obligation;
(b) what is necessary for maintenance of the spouse, the cohabitant, children under twenty-one years of age with maintenance rights, children who are incapable or have restricted capacity, even if they have not been declared such judicially; this compensation is due even if another person is required to provide maintenance to the indirect injured party; the judge, in order to determine reparation, must take into account the probable life of the victim, his personal conditions and those of the claimants;
(c) the loss of a chance of future aid as a result of the death of the children; this right also applies to the person who has custody of the deceased child' (free translation).

[40] Free translation.

so, the law presupposes that these persons are responsible for the functions of caring for vulnerable persons, and this is the reason why it permits them to claim for great suffering that they must necessarily feel as a result of being in charge of taking care of the vulnerable person.

The Argentine Civil and Commercial Code permits relatives to claim compensation for personal damage when, due to an illegal act, a member of the family suffers a serious disability, because it recognises that the relatives are the ones who provide care for the disabled person. The compensation relates to the consequences of the violation of personal rights, personal integrity, psychophysical health, legitimate spiritual beliefs, and interference in the person's life project.

8. FAMILY FUNCTIONS WHICH ARE PREDOMINANTLY FAVOURED BY ARGENTINE LAW

The upbringing and education of children is the most favoured function of the family in Argentina and, to support this function, the government grants different types of State benefits, such as universal income support per child, family income support, family adoption allowance, and annual school aid, among others.

The Universal Allowance per Child is an amount of money that the government pays to only one of the parents, prioritising the mother, for each child under 18 years old or without an age limit if the child is disabled. It is only paid for five children. 80 per cent of the allowance is paid monthly, and to receive the remaining 20 per cent and continue receiving the allowance, there is a requirement that the Universal Allowance Records, which prove school attendance and health expenses, must be filled in.

The Family Allowance per Child is an amount paid by the government for workers in an employment relationship, single taxpayers, retirees and pensioners with dependants who are under 18 years old or are disabled.

The Pregnancy Allowance is paid from the twelfth week of gestation until childbirth or termination of pregnancy and is subject to compliance with the medical check-ups included in the programme. 80 per cent of the total amount is paid monthly, and the remaining 20 per cent is paid when the health check-ups and either childbirth or termination of the pregnancy are proven.

The Maternity Allowance is the benefit given to registered workers during their 90 days of maternity leave, and up to 270 days if the child has Down's syndrome.

Annual School Aid is a sum given by the government for each school-age child. It is paid to parents who receive the Universal Allowance per Child. It is paid to only one parent once a year.

The Family Allowance for Birth and Adoption is paid by the government to employed workers in an employment relationship on the birth or adoption of a child. This allowance is paid to only one parent.

The government also provides a prepaid card with money to buy food (Tarjeta Alimentar) to:

- people who receive the Universal Allowance per Child with children up to and including six years of age;
- pregnant women from three months' gestation who receive the Pregnancy Allowance; and
- disabled persons who receive the Universal Allowance per Child, with no limit in respect of age.

9. CONCLUSION

The broad concept of 'family' involves fundamental rights that are related to equality, the free development of personality, freedom of conscience, and human dignity, by guaranteeing that each person can choose with whom he or she shares a life and with whom he or she maintains bonds of affection and solidarity, starting from a primordial postulate, within the framework of a philosophy of understanding and tolerance.

The predicable characteristic of every type of family is found in the elements of love, respect and solidarity on which it is founded, and by virtue of which a unity of life or destiny is built, which intimately links its members and closest relatives.

This liberal vision then defends the principle of autonomy of people: the right of each person to choose and carry out their own life plan. It also demands the neutrality of the State vis-à-vis individual moral perspectives. Each person must then have the widest possibility of sustaining and adhering to different forms of life. This is the basis of the principle of freedom in family law that is enshrined in human rights treaties. However, Argentine law does not recognise polygamy; in the country, a polygamous culture does not exist, and polygamy is contrary to public policy.

The family in Argentina exists regardless of whether there are children in it. Thus, for example, a family can be constituted by a single couple or by two sisters who live together. In these families without children, the most important function is solidarity.

In families with children, the fundamental functions of a family are the development and upbringing of children and in this type of family State assistance is much more important than in families without children, for example by way of Annual School Aid, the Family Allowance per Child, etc.

THE DIVERSIFICATION OF FAMILY FORMS AND FUNCTIONS IN THE LAW OF AUSTRALIA

Henry KHA

1. Introduction 113
2. Step-Parenting in Australia 114
3. The Scope of Legal Parenthood 116
4. Trends in Australian Adoption Law 119
5. Family Formation and Assisted Reproductive Technology 122
6. The Privatisation of Australian Family Law 126
7. The Normative Model of Family 129
8. The Function of Family in a Eudemonistic Liberal Society 130
9. Conclusion 132

1. INTRODUCTION

Australia has experienced significant changes in the legal recognition of different family forms in the recent few decades. The changes in family forms have been driven by greater acceptance of same-sex relationships and advancements in technology. There has been an increase in the diversity of what constitutes a family unit, including the phenomenon of step-parenting, the legalisation of adoption by same-sex couples, and the rise of assisted reproductive technologies. The law has been somewhat belated in representing these changes in social mores, but at present the law has moved forward to recognise a greater diversity of family forms. The function of family in Australian law has increasingly moved towards imposing a model of self-sufficiency on the family unit along with a greater diversification of family formation in the law. The diversification of family forms and functions in the law of Australia can be attributed to the rise of eudemonistic liberalism and the privatisation of family law. The pursuit of happiness in various different types of relationships and families is the main philosophy that has led to the law increasingly recognising the diversification of family forms. At the same time, Australian public policy has moved towards placing obligations on the family unit rather than on the State. This report explores how Australian law has recognised the diversification of family forms and the assumptions that underpin these forms by critically analysing the function of family law.

2. STEP-PARENTING IN AUSTRALIA

Australian law does not formally recognise informal parenthood in the context of step-families. A party is either the legal parent of the child or not. The focus of Australian family law is on biological parents and therefore step-parents are treated in the same way as strangers under the Family Law Act 1975 (Cth).[1] A 'step-parent' is defined as someone who is not a parent of the child, who is currently or previously married or in a de facto partnership with a parent of the child, and who treats the child as a member of the family formed with the parent.[2] Step-parents have the legal right to apply for parenting orders, but this is not unique as 'any other person concerned with the care, welfare or development of the child' may also apply.[3] A step-parent who is granted care of the child under a parenting order is not in the same position as a legal parent. The only way in which a step-parent can become the legal parent is through the formal process of adoption. Therefore, step-parents are not automatically recognised as legal parents, even when acting in the capacity of a legal parent in a parenting order that has been granted in favour of the step-parent. There is an emphasis on legal formalism in the *de jure* recognition of the rights and obligations of step-parents.

Step-parents can formally adopt a child either as a 'prescribed adopting parent' under the Family Law Act 1975 (Cth) or more typically through the adoption law of the state and territory jurisdictions of Australia.[4] Adoption law is generally a matter for states rather than the federal jurisdiction. The Federal Circuit and Family Court of Australia can grant leave for proceedings to be commenced for the adoption of a child by a prescribed adopting parent,[5] but only if it would promote the best interests of the child.[6] This provision has been typically used to allow the spouse or de facto partner of the legal parent to become the prescribed adopting parent in the event of the death of the legal

---

[1] A. Harland, D. Cooper, C. Turnbull and L. Rundle, *Family Law Principles*, 3rd ed., Thomson Reuters, Pyrmont 2021, p. 194.
[2] Family Law Act 1975 (Cth), s. 4(1).
[3] Ibid., s. 65C(c).
[4] Adoption Act 2000 (NSW); Adoption Act 1984 (Vic); Adoption Act 1988 (SA) and the Adoption Regulations 2004 (SA); Adoption Act 1994 (WA); Adoption Act 2009 (QLD) and Adoption of Children Regulation 2009 (QLD); Adoption Act 1988 (Tas); Adoption Act 1993 (ACT); Adoption of Children Act 2016 (NT).
[5] Family Law Act 1975 (Cth), s. 60G(1).
[6] Ibid., s. 60G(2).

parent. However, this federal provision has not been used to the same extent as adoption under state law, because step-families are more likely to arise due to divorce or separation rather than death.[7] Moreover, adoption under state law provides comprehensive adoption orders. The Commonwealth of Australia is vested with jurisdiction over 'divorce and matrimonial causes; and in relation thereto, parental rights, and the custody and guardianship of infants' under section 51(xxii) of the Australian Constitution. The prescribed adopting parent provision only pertains to parental rights in the context of a relationship, whereas adoption under state law covers the entire field of adoption law. Step-parents may also be bound to pay child maintenance in a court order.[8] This indicates the willingness of the State to impose financial obligations on family members rather than on itself. This is a recurring theme of Australian family law and it is consistent with the increasing privatisation of family law.

The Federal Circuit and Family Court of Australia exercises jurisdiction in regard to marriage, divorce and matrimonial causes, and parenting matters.[9] Welfare of children and adoption law is a residual power exercised by the states and territories. I will focus on New South Wales (NSW) adoption law as it is the most populous state and it is illustrative of the main adoption provisions that exist in all states and territories of Australia. The only type of parenthood that is formally recognised in Australia is based on legal parenthood. The Supreme Court of NSW will only grant an adoption order to a step-parent according to section 30 of the Adoption Act 2000 (NSW):

> The Court must not make an adoption order in favour of a step parent of a child unless:
>
> (a) the child is at least 5 years old, and
> (b) the step parent has lived with the child and the child's birth or adoptive parent for a continuous period of not less than 2 years immediately before the application for the adoption order, and
> (c) specific consent to the adoption of the child by the step parent has been given in accordance with this Act by the appropriate persons, and
> (d) the Court is satisfied that the making of the adoption order is clearly preferable in the best interests of the child to any other action that could be taken by law in relation to the child.

It is evident that the adoption law's aim of promoting the best interests of the child is consistent with the paramountcy principle from Article 3 of the United Nations Convention on the Rights of the Child (UNCRC). There are also clear

---

[7] A. Harland, D. Cooper, C. Turnbull and L. Rundle, *Family Law Principles*, 3rd ed., Thomson Reuters, Pyrmont 2021, p. 194.
[8] Family Law Act 1975 (Cth), s. 66M.
[9] Australian Constitution, ss 51(xxi) and 51(xxii).

parameters that attempt to define the best interests of the child in the context of step-parent adoption, particularly that the child is at least at the age of five and there has been a continued relationship involving cohabitation between the child and the step-parent for at least two years. The adoption of children at the age of five or above places the child's age of adoption at Jean Piaget's preoperational age of cognitive development. This is at the stage of development where children have begun to conceptualise ideas, but not beyond the individual self.[10] Public policy has allowed a step-parent to adopt a child from the age of five because this is when the child is no longer an infant and has developed a sense of self-identity. The fixing of the child's age of adoption by a step-parent at five years old suggests that Piaget's theory of cognitive development that children develop at pre-determined stages based on age is an acceptable rationale for adoption law. However, this is arguably too rigid and it ignores the sociocultural context of step-parenting. It could potentially be in the best interests of the child under the age of five to be adopted by the step-parent in affirming the child's identity and sense of belonging in the family.[11]

A step-parent who shares a household with the child's parent for at least two years can obtain legal responsibilities and rights to care for the child by applying for an adoption order.[12] Once an adoption order is granted to the step-parent, he or she exercises the same legal responsibilities and rights as the other legal parent with whom the step-parent shares a household.[13] Once an adoption order has been granted to the step-parent, he or she exercises the same legal responsibilities and rights as the child's other parent even if he or she no longer shares the same household. The statute makes no distinction in parental rights based on cohabitation once an adoption order has already been granted. 45% of known adoptions in Australia in 2012–2013 were granted to step-parents.[14] Therefore, step-parenting makes up a significant proportion of adoptions and demonstrates the prevalence of open adoption in Australia.

3. THE SCOPE OF LEGAL PARENTHOOD

This section focuses on the scope of legal parenthood in the context of naturally born children. Discussion about legal parenthood in the context of assisted reproductive technology is discussed later in this report. Australia recognises that

---

[10] K.B. Aspiranti, 'Preoperational Stage (Piaget)' in S. Goldstein and J.A. Naglieri (eds), *Encyclopedia of Child Behavior and Development*, Springer, Boston 2011, p. 1105.
[11] N. Taylor, 'What Do We Know About Involving Children and Young People in Family Law Decision Making? A Research Update' (2006) 20 *Australian Journal of Family Law* 154, 159.
[12] Adoption Act 2000 (NSW), s. 30.
[13] Ibid., s. 95.
[14] K. O'Halloran, *The Politics of Adoption: Ius Gentium: Comparative Perspectives on Law and Justice*, 3rd ed., Springer, Dordrecht 2015, p. 419.

other parties beyond the biological parents can exercise legal parenthood. This can include grandparents, uncles and aunts, other relatives or foster parents. The Family Law Act 1975 (Cth) expressly states that 'a grandparent of the child'[15] or 'any other person concerned with the care, welfare or development of the child' may apply for a parenting order.[16] Moreover, the Act states that '[a] parenting order in relation to a child may be made in favour of a parent of the child or some other person'.[17] The statute envisages that a party may be exercising the role of a parent without being the biological parent of the child by stating 'some other person.' The broad scope of legal parenthood recognises the diversity of caregivers of children in Australia and aims to promote the best interests of the child by allowing the most suitable person to receive a parenting order to look after the child.

The broad scope of legal parenthood can be seen in case law. In *Mulvany & Lane*, the applicant discovered that he was not the biological father of the child a few months before a parenting trial.[18] The applicant attempted to stop the mother of the child from relocating to Hong Kong with the child. The trial judge allowed the applicant to have standing as any other person concerned with the child. The trial judge placed greater weight in favour of the primary consideration of 'the benefit to the child of having a meaningful relationship with both of the child's parents' by interpreting this to mean preference to the biological mother.[19] The Full Family Court of Australia allowed the applicant's appeal on the basis that the trial judge erred in misinterpreting the Act to *a priori* prioritise the natural parent over all other parties that have performed a parental or caregiving role. The trial judge was seen to have focused too much on the semantics of the term 'parent' rather than making an objective assessment based on the paramountcy principle.[20] The Court stated that the emphasis should be on the best interests of the child and how that is promoted by also considering the additional considerations and the parental or caregiving role played by others.[21] Although Australia does legally recognise multiplicity of parenthood, the legislation prioritises biological parents over all other parties by mentioning only parents in the primary considerations when determining the best interests of the child and the frequent mention of parents throughout the statute.[22] However, it should be noted that 'parent' is not definitively defined in statute, but it is generally assumed to refer to biological parents.

---

[15] Family Law Act 1975 (Cth), s. 65C(ba).
[16] Ibid., s. 65C(c).
[17] Ibid., s. 64C.
[18] [2009] FamCAFC 76.
[19] Family Law Act 1975 (Cth), s. 60CC(2)(a).
[20] *Mulvany & Lane* [2009] FamCAFC 76, [82].
[21] Ibid.
[22] Family Law Act 1975 (Cth), s. 60CC(2).

Nevertheless, the judiciary has consistently refused to axiomatically prioritise biological parents over other parties in a parenting order. In *Donnell v. Dovey*,[23] the Full Family Court of Australia ruled that the trial judge failed to recognise the kinship obligations and child-rearing practices of the child's Aboriginal and Torres Strait Islander cultures.[24] The child was descendant from the Wakka Wakka tribe on his mother's side and the Torres Strait Islands on his father's side. According to Wakka Wakka kinship, it was culturally appropriate for the child to live with his eldest sibling upon the death of his mother. Thus, the child's adult sister was the primary caregiver to the child and she sought a parenting order to give legal effect to their existing living arrangements. The father contested the parenting order by claiming sole parental responsibility for the child and wanting the child to live with him. The case is significant as the Court recognised that it can be in the best interests of the child to be cared for by a non-parent over a biological parent.[25] The Court stated:

> In a particular case, the maintenance of a meaningful relationship with a non-parent may be equally important or more important than the maintenance (or establishment) of such a relationship with a parent. As with the additional considerations, it is not necessary to classify a non-parent as a 'parent' to ensure that clearly relevant matters are given appropriate weight.[26]

In other words, the court will treat both parents and non-parents equally when assessing parenting orders in the best interests of the child. Indigenous Australians are comprised of different Aboriginal groups found across Australia and Torres Strait Islanders who primarily live in northern Queensland. Torres Strait Islanders are considered to be Melanesian and they are culturally distinct from Aboriginal Australians, but they are still considered to be Indigenous Australians. According to Adelaide Titterton, '[h]owever, there is significant scope for the family law system to become more accessible and more culturally safe for Indigenous litigants'.[27] As illustrated in the case of *Donnell v. Dovey*, the Australian family justice system can sometimes struggle to understand Indigenous kinship practices in the care of children. Most Australians are of European background and the family justice system is centred on notions of the nuclear family and the expectation that biological parents should be the primary caregivers of children, even when it may not always be culturally appropriate in

---

[23] [2010] FamCAFC 15.
[24] Family Law Act 1975 (Cth), s. 61F.
[25] A. Titterton, 'Indigenous Access to Family Law in Australia and Caring for Indigenous Children' (2017) 40(1) *UNSW Law Journal* 146, 179.
[26] *Donnell v. Dovey* [2010] FamCAFC 15 [101].
[27] A. Titterton, 'Indigenous Access to Family Law in Australia and Caring for Indigenous Children' (2017) 40(1) *UNSW Law Journal* 146, 185.

the Indigenous cultural context.[28] Although the Australian family justice system has struggled to be culturally sensitive to Indigenous parties in parenting cases, the Family Law Act 1975 (Cth) expressly recognises the right of the child to his or her culture,[29] and the court must have regard to any kinship obligations and child-rearing practices of the child's Aboriginal or Torres Strait Islander culture.[30] Furthermore, specialised Indigenous lists have been created to hear some family law cases in Sydney as part of an initiative by Judge Robyn Sexton.[31] These family law hearings are more informal with the judge sitting on the same level as the parties and with particular attention to Indigenous cultural practices, such as the display of an Aboriginal flag and artworks, an acknowledgement of country and attention to Indigenous customs.[32]

Australian law does not recognise polygamy, as marriage is defined as 'the union of 2 people to the exclusion of all others, voluntarily entered into for life'.[33] However, Australia does recognise a polygamous marriage legally contracted outside of Australia in so far as it is a marriage that is justiciable by the Australian courts.[34] Due to the absence of legal recognition of polygamous relationships, there are no specific or express provisions that outline the legal parenthood responsibilities of a polygamous family in federal, state or territory law. Therefore, a parent in a polygamous marriage would have to claim legal parenthood by either adopting the child as a step-parent as mentioned above or asserting that the party is the biological parent of the child.[35]

4. TRENDS IN AUSTRALIAN ADOPTION LAW

Australian law does recognise a multiplicity of legal parenthood in the case of an open adoption. Prior to the introduction of the Adoption Act 2000 (NSW), the NSW Law Reform Commission recommended the promotion of openness to encompass, inter alia, the following:

- adoptive parents who recognise and are comfortable with the fact that the adoptee is also a member of his or her birth family and are able to discuss the adoptee's loss and other issues surrounding the adoption with the adoptee;
- a simple exchange of information and photographs between the birth parents and the adoptive parents, that may or may not involve the adoptee;

---

[28] A. Parashar and F. Dominello, *The Family in Law*, Cambridge University Press, Cambridge 2017, p. 14.
[29] Family Law Act 1975 (Cth), s. 60CC(3)(h).
[30] Ibid., s. 61F.
[31] J. Southward, 'It Takes a Village' (2018) 45 *Law Society Journal* 28, 30.
[32] Ibid.
[33] Marriage Act 1961 (Cth), s. 5.
[34] Family Law Act 1975 (Cth), s. 6.
[35] Status of Children Act 1996 (NSW), s. 9; Family Law Act 1975 (Cth), s. 4.

- the situation where the birth parents select the adoptive parents from agency profiles and have an initial meeting with them, which may or may not be followed by subsequent exchanges of information and photographs or actual contact;
- informing the birth parents if the child's placement has broken down and involving them in developing a new case plan for the child;
- informing the birth parents if the child dies;
- intermittent contact between birth parents and the adoptee, either ad hoc, depending on requests of the adoptee or the birth parents, or defined, such as on birthdays or at Christmas; and/or
- situations where a close relationship develops between birth family and adoptive family that is somewhat more informal.[36]

The above recommendations have been incorporated in the Adoption Act 2000 (NSW). The Act expressly encourages openness in adoption, emphasises the best interests of the child both in childhood and later life, ensures that adoption law and practice assist a child to know and have access to his or her birth family and cultural heritage, recognises the changing nature of practices of adoption, allows access to certain information relating to adoptions, and provides for the provision of post-adoption financial and other assistance to adopted children and their birth and adoptive parents.[37] Australia has rejected the practice of closed adoptions that reached its zenith in the early 1970s as a matter of public policy.[38] The 'Stolen Generations' refer to the forced removal of thousands of Indigenous children from their families by the Australian authorities, which were part of assimilation policies between 1910 and 1970.[39] The negative stigma associated with these forced adoptions in the Stolen Generations, and the end of social pressure on mothers who gave birth to children out of wedlock to adopt out their children, led to the decline of closed adoption in Australia by the 1970s.[40]

Adoption plans are used in order to promote care and contact of the adopted child with various parties. These plans set out the arrangements for the sharing of the child's information (including the child's medical information and information about important events in the child's life), and the means and

---

[36] New South Wales Law Reform Commission, *Review of the Adoption of Children Act 1965 (NSW)* (Report 81, 1997), para. 7.5.
[37] Adoption Act 2000 (NSW), s. 7.
[38] K. O'Halloran, *The Politics of Adoption: Ius Gentium: Comparative Perspectives on Law and Justice*, 3rd ed., Springer, Dordrecht 2015, p. 409.
[39] Human Rights and Equal Opportunities Commission, *Bringing Them Home: Report of the National Inquiry into the Separation of Aboriginal and Torres Strait Islander Children from their Families* (Report, April 1997), p. 37.
[40] D. Higgins, 'Unfit Mothers ... Unjust Practices? Key Issues from Australian Research on the Impact of Past Adoption Practices' (2011) 87(1) *Family Matters* 56, 56.

nature of contact between the parties and the child.[41] These plans can recognise the multiplicity of parenthood between the biological parents and the adoptive parents. In particular, these plans facilitate contact between the child and the biological parents, even promoting contact between the child and the non-consenting birth parent.[42] However, where there is a dispute between these two parties, the adoptive parents would prevail as they are the legal parents of the child with the rights and responsibilities for promoting the best interests of the child.[43]

Australia does not formally recognise *kafala* parenthood, because adoption severs the legal relationship between the existing parent and the child.[44] Moreover, adoption confers on the adopted child the same legal status that a biological child would enjoy in regard to the law of succession and the rights of the child.[45] Although the law does not formally incorporate *kafala* parenthood, state adoption agencies have recognised the significance of recognising some *kafala* practices in open adoptions. For example, NSW adoption law states in regard to placement of children for adoption that 'the child's given name, identity, language and cultural and religious ties should, as far as possible, be preserved.'[46] Adoption NSW (now part of the NSW Department of Communities and Justice) has engaged with the Muslim community in order to give effect to the aforementioned NSW adoption law by allowing the child's birth identity to be preserved.[47] NSW is generally more innovative when it comes to incorporating different cultural practices in adoption law compared to the other states and territories in Australia.[48] Such incorporation of *kafala* parenthood practices is contingent on the size of the Muslim community, with NSW being particularly more multicultural in comparison to other parts of Australia.

Australia passed same-sex marriage legislation in 2017,[49] and continues to recognise same-sex de facto relationships.[50] Same-sex couples generally have the same right as an opposite-sex married or de facto couple. Since 2010 in NSW, two persons, regardless of gender or sexual orientation, can adopt a child.[51] The campaign for the legalisation of same-sex adoption occurred across Australia since the 2000s on the premise that adopted children would not have

---

[41] Adoption Act 2000 (NSW), s. 46(1).
[42] Ibid., s. 46(2A).
[43] Ibid., s. 95.
[44] Ibid., s. 96.
[45] Ibid., s. 95.
[46] Ibid., s. 32.
[47] K.M. Eddie, 'The Application of Kafala in the West' in N. Hosen (ed.), *Research Handbook on Islamic Law and Society*, Edward Elgar Publishing, Cheltenham 2018, p. 54.
[48] K. O'Halloran, *The Politics of Adoption: Ius Gentium: Comparative Perspectives on Law and Justice*, 3rd ed., Springer, Dordrecht 2015, p. 448.
[49] Marriage Amendment (Definition and Religious Freedoms) Act 2017 (Cth).
[50] Family Law Act 1975 (Cth), s. 4AA.
[51] Adoption Amendment (Same Sex Couples) Act 2010 (NSW); Adoption Act 2000 (NSW), s. 28.

their best interests adversely affected based on the sole fact that they were cared for by a same-sex couple.[52] By 2018, all states and territories of Australia have legalised adoption by same-sex couples.[53] Therefore, same-sex couples have the same rights to adopt children as opposite-sex couples.

Understanding of family is based on the traditional notions of upbringing by biological parents or other types of parenthood that attempt to fit this normative model (e.g. step-parents). The Australian government currently does not have any plans to further recognise multi-parenthood. Either or both of the child's parents, a child, a grandparent of the child or any other person concerned with the care of the child can apply for a parenting order.[54] The understanding of family is based on the traditional notions of upbringing by biological parents or other types of parenthood that attempt to fit this normative model (e.g. step-parents, grandparents).

5. FAMILY FORMATION AND ASSISTED REPRODUCTIVE TECHNOLOGY

The use of assisted reproductive technology has increased in Australia, particularly through in vitro fertilisation and gestational surrogacy. This has raised various ethical issues and has broadened the understanding of the formation of family and parenthood in the law. The anonymous donation of gametes is prohibited in all states and territories of Australia.[55] According to the Australian National Health and Medical Research Council's *Ethical Guidelines on the Use of Reproductive Technology in Clinical Practice and Research*, anonymous donation of gametes is prohibited: 'clinics must ensure that the genetic origin of the person who would be born is certain'.[56] The birth mother and her spouse or partner are presumed to be the legal parents of the child.[57] Only the birth mother and her spouse or partner would be presumed to be the legal parents of the child in a situation where the sperm donor was known and the child was born as a result of artificial conception procedures.[58] Typically the birth mother and her spouse or partner would be listed as the parents on the child's

---

[52] A. Sifris and P. Gerber, 'Jack & Jill or Jack & Bill: The Case for Same-Sex Adoption' (2009) 34(3) *Alternative Law Journal* 168, 170–71.
[53] 'Australia now has Adoption Equality', *Human Rights Law Centre*, 20.04.2018, available at https://www.hrlc.org.au/news/2018/4/20/australia-now-has-adoption-equality, accessed 30.05.2022.
[54] Family Law Act 1975 (Cth), s. 65C.
[55] For example in NSW: Assisted Reproductive Technology Act 2007 (NSW), s. 31.
[56] National Health and Medical Research Council, *Ethical Guidelines on the Use of Reproductive Technology in Clinical Practice and Research* (2017), para. 6.1.2.
[57] Family Law Act 1975 (Cth), s. 69Q; Status of Children Act 1996 (NSW), s. 9.
[58] Family Law Act 1975 (Cth), s. 60H.

birth certificate. Where a single mother has given birth to a child as a result of a known sperm donation, typically the birth mother alone would be recorded as the parent on the child's birth certificate. Information about all sperm donations has to be certain and the identity of the donor must be known.

Australia has had a troubled history of anonymous sperm donations. The practice of anonymous sperm donation can be traced back to the 1940s in Australia.[59] However, it was only in the 1990s that the practice of anonymous sperm donation began to be prohibited.[60] The legal change was attributed to donor-conceived individuals seeking the right to access information about their sperm donors, as they had previously been denied access and experienced a sense of lost identity.[61] Recently, retrospective access to anonymous donor information for donor-conceived children was legalised in Victoria under the Assisted Reproductive Treatment Amendment Act 2016 (Vic). The Act allows donor children to access information about their identity, date of birth, physical characteristics, and genetic information, even if the donor is opposed to the release of his information. Access to information about their biological parents is facilitated through the Victorian Assisted Reproductive Treatment Authority. This has been a positive development as it recognises the importance of promoting the best interests of donor-conceived children by advancing their welfare in learning who they are and allowing them to access important information about family medical history.

Although a sperm donor is not normally considered to be a legal parent, a recent High Court of Australia case has held that it is possible for a known sperm donor to be declared the legal parent of the child. In *Masson v. Parsons*, a child was conceived using Mr Masson's sperm, which was artificially inseminated into the ovum of Ms Parsons.[62] After Ms Parsons gave birth, both she and Mr Masson were listed as the child's parents on her birth certificate. Mr Masson had intended to play a role in the parenting and upbringing of the child. The child lived with Ms Parsons and her female partner. Mr Masson played a continually active role in the development of the child. Ms Parsons wanted to move back to her country of origin, New Zealand, with her partner and the child. Mr Masson filed for a parenting order seeking equal shared parental responsibility for the child with Ms Parsons and to stop the overseas relocation of the child. The Court unanimously ruled that Mr Masson was a parent according to the natural and ordinary meaning of the word for the purposes of qualifying as a parent

---

[59] M. Taylor-Sands, 'Removing Donor Anonymity: What Does It Achieve? Revisiting the Welfare of Donor-Conceived Individuals' (2018) 41(2) *UNSW Law Journal* 555, 557.
[60] For example, the Infertility Treatment Act 1995 (Vic) banned anonymous sperm donations.
[61] F. Kelly, D. Dempsey, J. Power, K. Bourne, K. Hammarberg and L. Johnson, 'From Stranger to Family or Something in Between: Donor Linking in an Era of Retrospective Access to Anonymous Sperm Donor Records in Victoria, Australia' (2019) 33(3) *International Journal of Law, Policy and the Family* 277, 292–93.
[62] [2019] HCA 21.

under the Family Law Act 1975 (Cth). Therefore, the appeal was allowed and Mr Masson could contest the parenting matter and the overseas relocation of the child at trial level.

Although the Court in this case permitted the sperm donor to be declared the legal father, this case is rather atypical as it would be unusual for the sperm donor to be recorded as one of the parents on the child's birth certificate and to intend to play a role in the parenting and upbringing of the child. The Court declined to clearly resolve the issue of whether a sperm donor who has donated his sperm that has resulted in a child being born as a result of an artificial conception procedure without having any intention of being involved in the child's life could be found to be a legal parent.[63] The case did not concern this particular issue and therefore the Court avoided answering this question. The case has been criticised by some academics for failing to properly define legal parenthood, because the High Court has left the definition vague based on the ordinary meaning of the word 'parent'.[64] On the contrary, the broad definition of legal parenthood based on its ordinary and natural meaning can provide greater flexibility and accommodate the increasingly diverse forms of parenthood according to the sociocultural context. The decision indicates that the High Court has opted to recognise legal realism in the formation of family rather than restricting the definition of parenthood based on a narrow definition found in legal formalism. This is a positive development in promoting inclusion of various forms of parenthood and avoids unjustly denying legal recognition of persons who have fulfilled parenting functions. Therefore, parenthood in Australia is viewed as a question of fact rather than law.

Australia is currently considering the legal viability of allowing mitochondrial donations, but at present these are not recognised under the law. Mitochondrial donations are currently banned in Australia, as there is a prohibition on any form of human germline genetic modification under the Prohibition of Human Cloning for Reproduction Act 2002 (Cth). The Act specifically prohibits the creation of a human embryo by fertilisation that contains genetic material provided by more than two persons,[65] altering the genome of a human cell where that alteration is inheritable,[66] and intentionally placing an embryo in the body of a woman.[67] Mitochondrial replacement therapy involves the donation of mitochondrial DNA from a woman unaffected by mitochondrial disease to the intended mother's embryo with nuclear DNA through modification of either

---

[63] Ibid., [55].
[64] F. Kelly and H. Robert, 'Legal Parentage and Assisted Conception following the High Court's Decision in Masson v Parsons' (2019) 33(2) Australian Journal of Family Law 144, 152–54; R. Chisholm, 'Who is a "Parent"? The Need for Review of Australian Laws' (2021) 34(1) Australian Journal of Family Law 7, 28–30.
[65] Prohibition of Human Cloning for Reproduction Act 2002 (Cth), s. 13.
[66] Ibid., s. 15.
[67] Ibid., s. 20.

an oocyte or zygote. Therefore, this medical procedure would be in violation of the aforementioned sections. Another issue for the legalisation of mitochondrial donation is that all state and territory reproductive health laws stipulate that the genetic origins of the resulting child must be certain.[68] This could prohibit the anonymous donation of mitochondrial DNA. The Australian Senate Community Affairs References Committee has recommended further study and exploration of 'the strong potential of mitochondrial donation to address the debilitating effects of inheriting mitochondrial disease'.[69] However, the Committee has stopped short of recommending the legalisation of mitochondrial donations.[70]

Only the birth mother and her husband (or cohabitating male partner)[71] are presumed to be the legal parents of the child in Australia.[72] This follows the Roman law principle of *mater semper certa est* ('the mother is always certain') and Australia's legal position is consistent with New Zealand law.[73] Commercial surrogacy, whether contracted by Australian parties domestically or overseas, is illegal in all states and territories of Australia.[74] In NSW, Queensland and the Australian Capital Territory, commercial surrogacy (including both domestic and overseas arrangements) is also a criminal offence,[75] but no one has so far been prosecuted.[76] Therefore, the intended parents are excluded from the presumption of legal parenthood for a child born through a commercial surrogacy arrangement.[77]

A legal loophole exists where a child born from a commercial surrogacy arrangement (almost always as a result of a gestational surrogacy, but it can also technically be through a traditional surrogacy) can be brought to Australia based on demonstrating that an Australian citizen is the biological father of the child in a DNA test.[78] This raises a significant evidentiary burden on the intended parents.[79] In *Berniers & Dhopal*, the Full Family Court of Australia

---

[68] Australian Senate Community Affairs References Committee, *Science of Mitochondrial Donation and Related Matters* (Report, 2018), p. 92.
[69] Ibid., p. ix.
[70] Ibid., p. 81.
[71] Family Law Act 1975 (Cth), s. 69Q.
[72] Ibid., s. 69P.
[73] H. Kha and K. Rankin, 'Mater Semper Certa Est? Reconceiving New Zealand Surrogacy Law' (2019) 9(12) *New Zealand Family Law Journal* 172, 172–78.
[74] Surrogacy Act 2010 (NSW), s. 8.
[75] P. Parkinson, *Australian Family Law in Context: Commentary and Materials*, 7th ed., Thomson Reuters, Pyrmont 2019, p. 668.
[76] H. Cohen, 'Surrogacy Booming in Australia Despite Legal Issues', *Australian Broadcasting Centre*, 10.02.2017, available at https://www.abc.net.au/news/2017-02-10/surrogacy-booming-in-australia-despite-legal-issues/8255966, accessed 30.05.2022.
[77] Status of Children Act 1996 (NSW), s. 9(1) states: 'A child born to a woman during a marriage to which she is a party is presumed to be a child of the woman and her spouse.'
[78] P. Parkinson, *Australian Family Law in Context: Commentary and Materials*, 7th ed., Thomson Reuters, Pyrmont 2019, p. 668.
[79] *Mason & Mason and Anor* [2013] FamCA 424.

ruled that only state and territory courts can determine the legal parentage of children born as a result of a surrogacy arrangement.[80] The case involved the application of the intended parents for a determination of the legal parenthood of a child born through a commercial gestational surrogacy arrangement. The genetic makeup of the child was derived from sperm donated from the intended father and an anonymously donated ovum. The Court commented:

> There is no question that the father is the child's biological father, but that does not translate into him being a parent for the purposes of the Act. Further, the mother is not even the biological mother, and thus is even less likely to be the 'legal parent'.[81]

This case highlights that intended parents in surrogacy arrangements are not afforded any presumption of legal parenthood, even where one of the intended parents is biologically related to the child. It is necessary for intended parents in a commercial surrogacy arrangement to apply for a parenting order in the same way as intended parents in an altruistic surrogacy arrangement. Altruistic surrogacy is legal in all states and territories of Australia.[82] In NSW a parenting order would have to be sought by the intended parents in order to transfer the parentage of a child of a surrogacy arrangement.[83] In making a parenting order, the Court will consider, inter alia, the best interests of the child,[84] and the age and wishes of the child.[85] The affected parties must consent to the parenting order,[86] and the child must be living with the intended parents.[87]

6. THE PRIVATISATION OF AUSTRALIAN FAMILY LAW

The function of family in Australia includes the facilitation of the birth and upbringing of children, protecting the vulnerable and promoting economic security, and fulfilling caring functions. Providing economic security is the most important function favoured by Australian policy-makers due to the shift towards greater privatisation of family functions. Therefore, there is relatively less expectation that marriages or de facto relationships will likely lead to the birth of children. Although the total fertility rate in Australia has declined from a peak of 3.55 in 1961 to 1.74 in 2017, it is still assumed that most families will

---

[80] [2017] FamCAFC 180.
[81] Ibid., [65].
[82] Surrogacy Act 2010 (NSW), s. 23.
[83] Ibid., s. 18.
[84] Ibid., s. 22.
[85] Ibid., s. 26.
[86] Ibid., s. 31.
[87] Ibid., s. 33.

produce children and this is reflected in the heavy reference to parents in the Family Law Act 1975 (Cth).[88]

Australian family law has recognised that non-normative models of family should be afforded the same legal recognition as a biologically constructed family. The rationale for this is to fulfil Australia's international obligations under the UNCRC by promoting the generally accepted principle in Australia of the best interests of the child.[89] Therefore, the function of family is to promote the best interests of the child by recognising different legal forms of parenthood, such as step-parenting, children born from de facto relationships, children born from surrogacy, and gamete donor arrangements as described in previous sections. The ideal function of family is to allow a child to gain the same legal recognition and upbringing as the normative family formed through conventional biological means.

Fulfilling caring functions in the form of caring relationships rather than caring per se is a hallmark of Australian family law. Federal and state/territory laws confer legal rights on recognised relationships where care is a feature of the relationship rather than someone simply providing care (such as the role of paid caregivers). Recognised relationships under federal law, such as marriages and de facto relationships, are administered under the Family Law Act 1975 (Cth).[90] The caring role of a spouse or de facto partner is recognised as a non-financial contribution and it is one of the factors in determining the division of relationship property.[91] Non-marital and non-de facto relationships are governed by state and territory law. The Property (Relationships) Act 1984 (NSW) is a statute that is concerned with the division of relationship property. The Act has jurisdiction over de facto relationships not covered under the Family Law Act 1975 (Cth),[92] defined as 'a close personal relationship (other than a marriage or a de facto relationship) between two adult persons, whether or not related by family, who are living together, one or each of whom provides the other with domestic support and personal care'.[93] Victoria and Tasmania are the only

---

[88] Australian Institute of Family Studies, 'Births in Australia', 08.12.2021, available at https://www.abs.gov.au/statistics/people/population/births-australia/latest-release, accessed 30.05.2022.

[89] It should be noted that there is not a consensus on this issue by some academics. For example, Jonathan Crowe and Lisa Toohey have argued for a weak interpretation of the paramountcy principle with some deference to the rights of the parents: J. Crowe and L. Toohey, 'From Good Intentions to Ethical Outcomes: The Paramountcy of Children's Interests in the Family Law Act' (2009) 33(2) *Melbourne University Law Review* 391, 413–14.

[90] As a result of the enactment of the Family Law Amendment (De Facto Financial Matters and Other Measures) Act 2008 (Cth), de facto relationships are treated in the same way as marriages in cases of relationship property division.

[91] Family Law Act 1975 (Cth), s. 79(4).

[92] Property (Relationships) Act 1984 (NSW), s. 5(1)(a). If the meaning of de facto relationship is not satisfied under the Family Law Act 1975 (Cth), s. 4AA, then it can be recognised under state or territory law.

[93] Property (Relationships) Act 1984 (NSW), s. 5(1)(b).

states that also have registered caring relationships that allow parties to have their caring relationships formally acknowledged by the State.[94] However, most caring relationships are unregistered and can still be legally recognised.[95] The fact that caring relationships are recognised across all Australian jurisdictions demonstrates the significance of the family functioning as a social unit of care. This suggests that there is an expectation for family and caregivers to provide financial security rather than the State and illustrates the privatisation of Australian family law.

The shift towards the privatisation of family law can be seen in the promotion of alternative dispute resolution. Spousal maintenance is rarely used as a financial remedy for the less financially able party after separation,[96] because of the clean break principle and the difficulties of enforcement.[97] Therefore, parties are strongly encouraged, but are not compelled, to come to their own agreement on how the relationship property should be divided. Parenting disputes must first be resolved through alternative dispute resolution before the case can proceed to court, unless there is the presence of family violence in the relationship.[98] Although at the moment the law does not mandate the use of alternative dispute resolution to resolve a family property dispute, the Australian Law Reform Commission has recommended that alternative dispute resolution be compulsory for family property disputes.[99] Such a proposal would further promote the privatisation of Australian family law.

Another development is the rise of binding financial agreements, which refer to pre-nuptial and post-nuptial financial agreements.[100] The public policy rationale is to encourage parties to consensually resolve their own financial disputes rather than litigating the case in court. However, such binding financial agreements can lead to unfair outcomes because of the disparity in bargaining power within couples.[101] In *Thorne v. Kennedy*,[102] the High Court of Australia has recognised the significance of equity in the promotion of a just and fair outcome as a result of the vitiation of pre-nuptial agreements.[103] The Court set aside a

---

[94] Relationships Act 2008 (Vic), s. 5; Relationships Act 2003 (Tas), s. 11.
[95] G. Douglas, *Obligation and Commitment in Family Law*, Hart, Oxford 2018, pp. 215–16.
[96] P. Parkinson, *Australian Family Law in Context: Commentary and Materials*, 7th ed., Thomson Reuters, Pyrmont 2019, p. 426.
[97] G. Douglas, *Obligation and Commitment in Family Law*, Hart, Oxford 2018, pp. 159–60.
[98] Family Law Act 1975 (Cth), s. 60I; H. Kha, 'Evaluating Collaborative Law in the Australian Context' (2015) 26(3) *Australasian Dispute Resolution Journal* 178, 178–79.
[99] Australia Law Reform Commission, *Family Law for the Future – An Inquiry into the Family Law System* (Report No. 135, 2019), p. 18.
[100] Family Law Act 1975 (Cth), pt VIIIA.
[101] E. Kuiper, '"What's Mine is Mine": A Socialist Feminist Critique of Binding Financial Agreements in Australia' (2021) 34(2) *Australian Journal of Family Law* 129, 136.
[102] (2017) 263 CLR 85.
[103] H. Kha, 'The Vitiation of Pre-Nuptial Agreements in the High Court of Australia' (2018) 2 *International Family Law Journal* 145, 145–47.

pre-nuptial agreement that the fiancée signed 11 days prior to her wedding despite receiving independent legal advice that it was adverse to her personal interests to sign it. The contract was found to have been vitiated and thus voidable due to undue influence and unconscionable conduct. The trend towards privatisation of family law advances the function of family as a self-sufficient economic unit, but also poses challenges in the guise of economic imbalance and exploitation among family members. There is a prevailing belief that parties should privately resolve their financial issues and allocate their income, savings and assets in the relationship property pool rather than involve the State in the provision of government welfare or the use of judicial resources at taxpayers' expense. Hence, there has been a recent development in promoting the economic security of a separating family through alternative dispute resolution and binding financial agreements.

7. THE NORMATIVE MODEL OF FAMILY

Parenting and property issues are treated as distinct issues as a matter of family law. If children are present in the family, then the focus will be on parenting issues. The function of family is to promote the best interests of the child,[104] and this has been interpreted to mean that a legal presumption should exist to recognise the birth mother and her spouse or partner as the legal parents of the child.[105] This is the paramount consideration, regardless of the manner in which the child was born and how the child relates to his or her legal parents. It also means that the reproduction of biological children is generally privileged as fulfilling the normative model of family. Therefore, there is an assumption that it is ideal that family functions as a means for the reproduction of biological children. The family unit is viewed as a unit that provides a sense of economic security and family stability.

Step-families are viewed as a family form that attempts to create a normative family as close as possible to a functional biological family. This is seen in the fact that step-children who are legally adopted are conferred the same rights as a child born to biological parents in a conventional birth. Likewise, the step-parents are legally expected to discharge the same parental rights and responsibilities as any other legal parent would exercise. The aim of adoption is therefore to completely transfer expected family functions from one parent to another parent. It completely severs all previous legal rights and responsibilities exercised by a former parent. However, in the past few decades in Australia, there has been a shift towards open adoption and there is a legal recognition that the

---

[104] Family Law Act 1975 (Cth), s. 60CA.
[105] Ibid., s. 69Q.

function of a step-family is to promote the child's identity.[106] This means that the court 'must take into account the culture, any disability, language and religion of the child and the principle that the child's given name, identity, language and cultural and religious ties should, as far as possible, be preserved'.[107] There is also particular emphasis that Aboriginal identity and kinship should be promoted as far as possible.[108]

Once a parenting order is granted, children born as a result of surrogacy are also given the same legal rights as any other child. Likewise, the intended parents exercise the same legal rights and responsibilities as any other parent. The aim is that surrogate-born children are able to enjoy the same social recognition and legal rights as a normative biological family. The function of this type of family is to enable a single person or couple who cannot biologically produce children to create a family. Therefore, the function of surrogacy is to allow the transfer of parentage from the birth mother to the intended parents. The function of donor-assisted reproductive technologies is to enable a single woman or an infertile couple to have children. Typically, the donor of the gamete is not listed on the birth certificate as a parent of the child. The function of this type of family is to recognise the legal parentage of the birth mother and her spouse or partner as if the child was born through conventional biological means of reproduction.

8. THE FUNCTION OF FAMILY IN A EUDEMONISTIC LIBERAL SOCIETY

Although same-sex marriage was introduced in Australia in 2017, the function of marriage is still predicated based on its Judeo-Christian history that can be traced to its English heritage. Marriage still bears the hallmarks of the legal definition outlined by Wilde J. (later Lord Penzance), albeit no longer exclusively confined to opposite-sex relationships: 'the union of 2 people to the exclusion of all others, voluntarily entered into for life'.[109] In 2017, the Australian government conducted the Australian Marriage Law Postal Survey, which was a voluntary national postal survey that asked Australians: 'should the law be changed to allow same-sex couples to marry?'[110] A total of 12,691,234

---

[106] K. O'Halloran, *The Politics of Adoption: Ius Gentium: Comparative Perspectives on Law and Justice*, 3rd ed., Springer, Dordrecht 2015, p. 424.
[107] Adoption Act 2000 (NSW), s. 32.
[108] Ibid., ss 33–39.
[109] Marriage Act 1961 (Cth), s. 5. Compare *Hyde v. Hyde and Woodmansee* (1866) LR 1 P&D 130, 133, where Sir James Wilde stated: 'I conceive that marriage, as understood in Christendom, may for this purpose be defined as the voluntary union for life of one man and one woman, to the exclusion of all others'.
[110] Australian Bureau of Statistics, 'Australian Marriage Law Postal Survey, 2017', 15.11.2017, available at https://www.abs.gov.au/ausstats/abs@.nsf/mf/1800.0, accessed 30.05.2022.

Australians participated in the survey.[111] 61.6% of participants voted yes and 38.4% voted no to the question.[112] Since a majority of the participants surveyed voted in favour of legal change, the Parliament of Australia legalised same-sex marriage under the Marriage Amendment (Definition and Religious Freedoms) Act 2017 (Cth). The Act amended the definition of marriage under the Marriage Act 1961 (Cth) to omit 'a man and a woman' and to replace it with '2 people'.[113] The legal change has significantly altered the definition of marriage and understandings of recognised forms of kinship in Australia.

Despite the change in the legal definition of marriage, the function of marriage is to legally bind a monogamous couple in a civil contract that has been formed as a result of consent and it is intended to be indissoluble. This was originally intended to promote the procreation of children in wedlock and thereby create a nuclear family unit. However, with the recognition of same-sex marriages, the function of marriage has shifted to promote the goal of eudemonistic liberalism. This is in consonance with the philosophy that the law should value the desire of legally affirming a mutual relationship based on contemporary notions of love and companionship rather than the essentialist view of marriage as the condition precedent for children.[114]

In the same year as the introduction of same-sex marriage, the Full Family Court of Australia allowed children to access Stage 2 gender reassignment treatment without court authorisation in the case of *Re Kelvin*.[115] Stage 1 treatment refers to reversible puberty-blocking treatment, Stage 2 treatment involves gender-affirming hormone treatment, and Stage 3 treatment is the use of surgical interventions to affirm the desired gender.[116] Before this case, it was necessary for children who wanted Stage 2 treatment to apply for court approval,[117] because it was previously perceived that the medical treatment performed on minors was non-therapeutic and thus would need to be considered by the judiciary.[118] In *Re Kelvin*, the Court found that a *Gillick*-competent mature minor could undergo Stage 2 treatment without court authorisation,[119] because of the changes to medical knowledge of gender dysphoria that the therapeutic benefits of the treatment now outweighed the risks.[120]

---

[111] Ibid.
[112] Ibid.
[113] Marriage Amendment (Definition and Religious Freedoms) Act 2017 (Cth), s. 3.
[114] M. Rheinstein, *Marriage Stability, Divorce and the Law*, University of Chicago Press, Chicago 1972, pp. 20–25.
[115] [2017] FamCAFC 258.
[116] Ibid., [8]–[16].
[117] *Re Jamie* [2013] FamCAFC 110.
[118] *Secretary of the Department of Health and Community Services v. JWB and SMB* (1992) 175 CLR 218.
[119] *Gillick v. West Norfolk and Wisbech Area Health Authority* [1986] AC 112.
[120] [2017] FamCAFC 258.

The expansion of the doctrine of the mature minor to allow young persons to access gender reassignment treatment is a reflection that young persons have legal agency to form their identity in increasingly diverse families in Australia. The legal change also reflects the view that the judiciary is basing its decision on the value of eudemonistic liberalism. Parties have increased choice in deciding how they wish to live their lives in the construction of their family form with the function of producing individual happiness. This is a modern manifestation of John Stuart Mill's no-harm principle. Mill states that 'the only purpose for which power can be rightfully exercised over any member of a civilized community, against his will, is to prevent harm to others'.[121] In other words, the Australian law has been willing to accommodate different family forms on the condition that it does not cause objective harm, it promotes individual civil liberties, and it achieves the pursuit of happiness.

9. CONCLUSION

The family forms of Australia have become increasingly diverse in the legal recognition of step-parenting either through adoption as prescribed adopting parent under federal law or adoption under state or territory law, and the expansion of open adoption that allows the child to maintain a relationship with his or her birth parents and to have a legally recognised relationship with the adopted parents. While there has been progress in some areas of legally recognised family forms, other areas could be further expanded. Although Australian Indigenous kinship has been formally recognised in statute law and case law, better awareness among the judiciary of Indigenous kinship is necessary to better assist judges in promoting culturally informed decision-making in parenting orders. The interpretation of legal parenthood based on the ordinary meaning affirms legal realism and promotes justice in the recognition of the increasingly varied forms of parenting. This approach avoids having a rigidly constructed definition of legal parenthood based on legal formalism that may unjustly fail to recognise persons who have taken on the obligation of parenting and protects them from being denied legal recognition according to contrived technicalities. The existence of parenting orders in relation to children born to international commercial surrogacy is designed to ensure that there is an orderly legal process to the recognition of parentage and provides a legal safeguard to ensure all parenting orders are made with the best interests of the child in mind. The debate on the donation of mitochondrial DNA raises

---

[121] J.S. Mill, 'On Liberty' in J. Robson (ed.), *The Collected Works of John Stuart Mill, Volume XVIII – Essays on Politics and Society Part I*, University of Toronto Press, Toronto 1977, p. 223.

serious ethical considerations on the formation of a child with three biological parents. This represents a significant departure from the understanding that a child has two biological parents, even in the context of the donation of human gametes.

The diversification of family forms in Australia has demonstrated three consistent themes on the function of family. The first is the privatisation of family law. The greater recognition of various forms of family allows legal obligations to be placed on more individuals rather than on the State. The second is the promotion of economic security and family stability. The law has transposed the normative model of a nuclear family onto non-normative family forms in an attempt to replicate a standard idealised form of family. The third is to promote eudemonistic liberalism. The recognition of same-sex marriage and the right of mature minors to undergo gender reassignment treatment are examples that demonstrates that the law is expanding the recognition of non-heteronormative relationships based on the philosophy of eudemonistic liberalism. The function of family in Australia is primarily focused on maximising individual liberties and the pursuit of happiness, which is evident in the toleration of different forms of family in Australia. Despite all the visible changes in family forms, the core ideology is still based on the assumption of familism through the increasing transfer of family obligations and responsibilities onto caregivers in the private family context and away from the State.

MODERN FAMILY FORMS AND THEIR IMPACT ON PARENT–CHILD RELATIONSHIPS IN AUSTRIAN LAW

Elmar Buchstätter and Marianne Roth

1. Introduction 136
2. The Concept of Family... 136
   2.1. Family Forms 136
   2.2. Family's Functions 138
   2.3. The Role of Children in the Family 138
3. Diversity and Plurality of Family Forms 140
   3.1. Recognition of Multiple Parents in the Context of
        Step-Families.. 140
        3.1.1. Step-Parents without Parental Responsibilities........ 141
               3.1.1.1. Spouses and Registered Partners 141
               3.1.1.2. Informal Partners............................ 143
        3.1.2. Step-Parents as Foster Parents....................... 145
        3.1.3. Rights and Obligations of a Step-Parent and the
               Biological Parent Towards the Child 147
               3.1.3.1. Joint Parental Responsibilities 148
               3.1.3.2. Sole Parental Responsibilities............... 148
        3.1.4. The Child's Place of Residence 149
   3.2. Recognition of Multiple Parents in the Case of an Adoption....... 150
   3.3. Recognition of Multiple Parents in the Case of Medically
        Assisted Procreation 152
        3.3.1. Introduction to Austrian Reproductive Law............. 152
        3.3.2. Legal Limitations of Medically Assisted Reproduction..... 154
               3.3.2.1. Surrogacy 154
               3.3.2.2. Three-Parent Child 155
        3.3.3. Rights and Obligations of the Anonymous Donor......... 156
        3.3.4. Rights and Obligations of the Known Donor 158
4. Conclusion.. 159

1. INTRODUCTION

The concept of 'family' has changed in recent decades: a multitude of variants has emerged from the traditional understanding of family as 'opposite-sex marriage with biological children'. On the one hand, this is due to demographic change and an increasingly liberal approach to relationship and family forms in politics and society; on the other hand, advances in medically assisted reproduction mean that the desire to have children can be fulfilled even for those who would otherwise be denied it. Today's legislature is challenged by the almost unrestricted access to a variety of life concepts, as those concepts often require separate legal treatment: changes in existing families can add secondary figures who begin to exercise elements of parenthood even though there is no biological link to the child, and conversely there may be others who have no emotional bond but a purely biological one. In addition, there can be legal shifts in rights and obligations towards a child, for example through adoption or foster parenthood. The resulting settings of 'multiple parents' have in common that they can lead to unclear or even contradictory legal positions with regard to care and representation or even contact. The Austrian legislator is called upon to weigh the interests of all parties involved and to find solutions that not only protect the best interests of the child, but also bring long-term legal peace for the entire family. This report aims to identify relevant constellations and provide an insight into those areas of the Austrian legal system that are affected.

2. THE CONCEPT OF FAMILY

2.1. FAMILY FORMS

If one goes strictly by the wording of the General Civil Code (*Allgemeines Bürgerliches Gesetzbuch*, ABGB),[1] Austrian law understands the term 'family' to mean the 'progenitors and all their descendants',[2] with the main roles divided between the 'parents' and the 'children'[3] – the legal basis of it being a marriage contract.[4] These merely programmatic statements, however, do not correspond

---

[1] Judicial Law Gazette (*Justizgesetzsammlung*, JGS) No. 946/1811, in the version dated 09.09.2021, Federal Law Gazette (*Bundesgesetzblatt*, BGBl) I No. 175/2021.

[2] Non-official translation of the General Civil Code by P.A. Eschig and E. Pircher-Eschig, *Das österreichische ABGB – The Austrian Civil Code*, 2nd ed., LexisNexis, Vienna 2021, s. 40 of the General Civil Code.

[3] S. 42 of the General Civil Code: irrespective of the degree of kinship, 'parents' refers to all relatives in the ascending line and 'children' refers to all relatives in the descending line.

[4] S. 44 of the General Civil Code.

with today's much broader understanding of family. The qualification of legal entities is already limited by the law itself and adapted to the facts of the respective norm, whereas the requirement of marriage as justification is far too narrow and does not meet today's social requirements.[5]

In fact, the concept of family in Austria is subject to constant change due to social developments as well as psychological and medical findings.[6] In the process of legal development, Austrian law has been strongly influenced by the case law of the European Court of Human Rights in recent decades.[7] Although the European Convention on Human Rights itself does not define the terms 'family' or 'family life',[8] an application in the sense of Article 8 of the European Convention on Human Rights must be independent of marriage. However, the European Court of Human Rights emphasises that the main criterion is an existing 'family life'.[9] A family in the legal sense is therefore not only the 'traditional family' of a married couple with children, but also a registered partnership or informal partnership, each with or without biological or at least legal children, as well as single mothers or fathers and alternative and modern families such as step-families.[10] It needs no special mention that – regardless of the legal form of the relationship – Austrian law treats all genders equally: same-sex spouses/partners have the same rights and obligations towards the other spouse/partner and his or her children as opposite-sex partners.[11]

As far as the concept of family may have developed, it is still restricted in certain manifestations: polygamous family forms are prohibited; therefore no one can marry or enter into a registered partnership if he or she is still living in such a relationship.[12] Austria also does not recognise a 'family-guarantee

---

[5] Inter alia, C. Kronthaler, 'Section 40 General Civil Code' in M. Schwimann and G. Kodek (eds), *ABGB: Praxiskommentar*, 5th ed., LexisNexis, Vienna 2020, marg. no. 2.

[6] P. Smutny, 'Section 44 General Civil Code' in A. Kletečka and M. Schauer (eds), *ABGB-ON*, v 1.07, Manz, Vienna 2017, marg. no. 2.

[7] Since 1958, the ECHR has been an integral part of Austrian constitutional law, Federal Law Gazette No. 210/1958.

[8] T. Schoditsch, *Gleichheit und Diversität im Familienrecht*, Manz, Vienna 2020, p. 22.

[9] C. Grabenwarter and K. Pabel, *Europäische Menschenrechtskonvention*, 7th ed., C.H. Beck, Munich 2021, s. 22 ECHR, marg. no. 16; P. Smutny, 'Section 44 General Civil Code' in A. Kletečka and M. Schauer (eds), *ABGB-ON*, v 1.07, Manz, Vienna 2017, marg. no. 2.

[10] Austrian Constitutional Court (*Verfassungsgerichtshof*, VfGH), e.g. Judgments of 28.06.2003, G 78/00 and 22.06.2009, U 1031/09.

[11] Since 2019 same-sex as well as opposite-sex partners have been allowed to enter into either a civil marriage or a registered partnership. In addition to several other rulings by the Constitutional Court, far-reaching equality of the two institutions was recently achieved. Judgment of 04.12.2017, G 258–259/2017.

[12] Bigamy or polygamy is punishable according to s. 192 of the Austrian Penal Code (*Strafgesetzbuch*, StGB), Federal Law Gazette No. 60/1974, in the version dated 31.12.2021, Federal Law Gazette I No. 242/2021; s. 5(1) para. 2 of the Registered Partnership Act (*Eingetragene-Partnerschaft-Gesetz*, EPG), Federal Law Gazette I No. 135/2009, in the version dated 14.05.2021, Federal Law Gazette I No. 86/2021.

system' as exists in the *kafala* often known in Arab countries. This is in line with the recent case law of the European Court of Justice, according to which only biological and adopted children can be considered direct descendants of citizens of the European Union and *kafala* cannot be recognised as a legal form to establish a parent–child relationship according to European and Austrian legal understanding.[13]

2.2. FAMILY'S FUNCTIONS

Representative of a broad range of family forms today, the 'traditional' family concept of marriage describes a number of functions that should be at the centre of the family: among them the mutual maintenance obligation, community of property, parenthood and the upbringing of children.[14] However, the latter is no longer an essential feature of marriage and the concept of family from the perspective of modern legislature.[15] Austrian law thus recognises several functions of the family; however, not all are applicable to every family form.

Due to the equal treatment of different family forms in the Austrian legal system, it is almost impossible to make a statement about which function is favoured under Austrian law. In the summary of any type of family, however, the mutual support obligation is quite important; both spouses[16] and registered partners[17] are obliged to fulfil this duty and a breach may be relevant in divorce proceedings or the dissolution of a registered partnership. The obligation may arise in various situations of family life, such as ensuring economic security or fulfilling welfare functions. As not all of these functions are explicitly regulated, individual interpretation is left to case law.[18]

2.3. THE ROLE OF CHILDREN IN THE FAMILY

Although children are no longer a prerequisite for starting a legal family, the family's functions naturally shift when there are children in the

---

[13] Case C-129/18, *SM v. Entry Clearance Officer, UK Visa Section*, ECLI:EU:C:2019:248.
[14] S. 44 of the General Civil Code.
[15] J. Höllwerth, 'Section 44 General Civil Code' in E. Gitschthaler and J. Höllwerth (eds), *Kommentar zum Ehe- und Partnerschaftsrecht*, Springer, Vienna 2011, marg. no. 21; S. Ferrari, 'Section 44 General Civil Code' in M. Schwimann and G. Kodek (eds), *ABGB: Praxiskommentar*, 5th ed., LexisNexis, Vienna 2020, marg. no. 1; Austrian Supreme Court (*Oberster Gerichtshof*, OGH), Judgment of 19.06.2013, 7 Ob 92/13z.
[16] Ss 44 and 90(1) of the General Civil Code.
[17] S. 8(2) of the Registered Partnership Act.
[18] E.g. see Austrian Supreme Court, Judgment of 13.09.1988, 2 Ob 83/88.

family – the most important task of parents is to care for and raise their children.[19]

The nature of parental responsibilities (*Obsorge*) implies that the primary holders should be the parents of a minor child according to section 158 of the General Civil Code; they must be recognised as the mother and father or other parent in order to be entitled to take care of the child.[20] Married parents or parents in a registered partnership are usually both entrusted with parental responsibilities, while the single mother initially bears the responsibilities alone.[21] Considering the best interests of the child, however, parental responsibilities can also be assigned to grandparents, foster parents (*Pflegeeltern*) or other persons, as well as to the Child and Youth Welfare Agency (*Kinder- und Jugendhilfeträger*).[22] Parental responsibilities include not only certain rights, such as legal representation of the child, but also duties, such as care and education.[23]

In accordance with Article 2(1) of the Federal Constitutional Law on the Rights of Children,[24] section 187 of the General Civil Code determines the right of the child and the parent who is not living in the same household as the child to regular personal and direct contact, unless this is contrary to the best interests of the child. This right to personal contact is a fundamental right that forms part of the parent–child relationship and constitutes a universally recognised human right protected by Article 8 of the European Convention on Human Rights. In this context, section 187 of the General Civil Code refers to the 'legal parents', which is why the recognition of parenthood is a prerequisite for the right to access.[25] However, another person may obtain a subsidiary visiting right (*Kontaktrecht*) under section 188 of the General Civil Code if there is an emotional bond between the child and the person which

---

[19] P. Smutny, 'Section 44 General Civil Code' in A. Kletečka and M. Schauer (eds), *ABGB-ON*, v 1.07, Manz, Vienna 2017, marg. no. 42; Austrian Supreme Court, Judgment of 19.06.2013, 7 Ob 92/13z.

[20] M. Roth, *Außerstreitverfahrensrecht*, 6th ed., Sramek, Vienna 2019, p. 122; E. Gitschthaler, 'Section 158 General Civil Code' in M. Schwimann and G. Kodek (eds), *ABGB: Praxiskommentar*, 5th ed., LexisNexis, Vienna 2018, marg. no. 2.

[21] J. Weitzenböck, 'Section 185 General Civil Code' in M. Schwimann and M. Neumayr (eds), *ABGB: Taschenkommentar*, 5th ed., LexisNexis, Vienna 2020, marg. no. 6.

[22] Ss 181(1) and 182 of the General Civil Code; M. Huber, 'Rechte und Pflichten zwischen Eltern und Kindern' in A. Deixler-Hübner (ed.), *Handbuch Familienrecht*, 2nd ed., Linde, Vienna 2020, p. 297.

[23] M. Roth, *Außerstreitverfahrensrecht*, 6th ed., Sramek, Vienna 2019, p. 113; P.A. Eschig and E. Pircher-Eschig, *Das österreichische ABGB – The Austrian Civil Code*, 2nd ed., LexisNexis, Vienna 2021, s. 158.

[24] Federal Constitutional Law on the Rights of Children (*Bundesverfassungsgesetz über die Rechte von Kindern*) of 15.02.2011, Federal Law Gazette I No. 4/2011.

[25] M. Huber, 'Rechte und Pflichten zwischen Eltern und Kindern' in A. Deixler-Hübner (ed.), *Handbuch Familienrecht*, 2nd ed., Linde, Vienna 2020, p. 333; Austrian Supreme Court, Judgment of 24.05.2007, 2 Ob 26/07y.

is significant for the psychological wellbeing of the child.[26] Consequently, protecting the best interests of the children becomes 'the' fundamental family function.[27]

In the 2013 Act Amending the Act of Children and Names (*Kindschafts- und Namensrechts-Änderungsgesetz*, KindNamRÄG 2013)[28] the legislator prioritised the best interests of the child as a radical concept of the law.[29] However, the legal situation of the child should not only relate to their protection: it is fundamental that the views of the child concerning care and education matters shall always be considered.[30] The treatment of children's rights in the Austrian legal system, of course, does not differ depending on whether it is a biological child, a child born as a result of donor-assisted reproductive technologies, an adopted child or a step-child.

3. DIVERSITY AND PLURALITY OF FAMILY FORMS

3.1. RECOGNITION OF MULTIPLE PARENTS IN THE CONTEXT OF STEP-FAMILIES

Two adults and one or more children can live together and yet not form a family in the classical sense because one of the adults is not the biological parent of at least one of the other adult's children:[31] in 2020, there were 83,000 such 'families' in Austria, which is 8.6% of all couples who have shared a household with children under the age of 18.[32] Despite the increasing importance of step-families, however, there are neither explicit definitions in the legal system nor are the rights and obligations of step-parents mapped out in a separate law.[33]

The discussions under the following headings provide an overview of the legal position of step-parents in Austria with a special focus on the extent to which and the legal basis on which a parenting role of the step-parent can be justified.

---

[26] Austrian Supreme Court, Judgment of 21.02.2018, 3 Ob 130/17i.
[27] See the 'good conduct requirement' (*Wohlverhaltensgebot*) pursuant to s. 159 of the General Civil Code.
[28] Federal Law Gazette I No. 2013/15.
[29] S. 137 et seq. of the General Civil Code.
[30] S. 160(3) of the General Civil Code.
[31] I. Théry, 'Einführung: Die Zeit der Fortsetzungsfamilien' in M. Meulders-Klein and I. Théry (eds), *Fortsetzungsfamilien, Neue familiale Lebensformen in pluridisziplinärer Betrachtung*, Universitätsverlag Konstanz, Konstanz 1993, p. 19.
[32] Statistik Austria, *2020 Survey of Family Forms*, available at https://www.statistik.at/statistiken/ bevoelkerung-und-soziales/bevoelkerung/familien-haushalte-lebensformen/lebensformen, accessed 28.02.2022.
[33] C. Kronthaler, 'Section 40 General Civil Code' in M. Schwimann and G. Kodek (eds), *ABGB: Praxiskommentar*, 5th ed., LexisNexis, Vienna 2020, marg. no. 3.

3.1.1. Step-Parents without Parental Responsibilities

3.1.1.1. Spouses and Registered Partners

In 2006, a first attempt was made to establish a provision obliging one spouse to provide reasonable assistance to the other in the exercise of parental responsibilities for his or her biological children.[34] However, it was only in the course of the 2009 Family Law Amending Act (*Familienrechtsänderungsgesetz 2009*, FamRÄG 2009)[35] that the legislator succeeded in introducing a special consideration of modern family forms and relationships.[36] Although established case law had already in the past subsumed the spouse's participation in the upbringing of the other spouse's children under the general duty to assist (*Beistandspflicht*) of section 90(1) of the General Civil Code,[37] the newly added section 90(3) of the General Civil Code is noteworthy: it provides for an explicit extension of the spouse's duty to cooperate in non-essential matters of parental responsibilities.[38] The duty to assist exists irrespective of whether the new spouse lives in a joint household with his or her step-child.[39] If a parent to whom parental responsibilities for his or her child were transferred from a previous relationship enters into a civil marriage, the new spouse must assist in the exercising of parental responsibilities.[40] It is irrelevant whether the biological parent has full or joint parental responsibilities. This power of representation is by law an essential element of marriage and does not require the consent of the spouse who holds parental responsibilities.[41]

The provision, however, covers only those areas of parental responsibilities that concern matters of daily life, namely those that occur regularly and affect the child's development only in a way that is correctable,[42] such as picking up

---

[34] P. Smutny, 'Section 44 General Civil Code' in A. Kletečka and M. Schauer (eds), *ABGB-ON*, v 1.07, Manz, Vienna 2017, marg. no. 43.
[35] Federal Law Gazette I No. 75/2009.
[36] Explanatory notes to the Individual Request (*Erläuterungen zum Individualantrag*) 673/A, XXIV. legislation period (*Gesetzgebungsperiode*, GP), p. 16.
[37] Austrian Supreme Court, Judgment of 29.03.1972, 2 Ob 293/71; S. Ferrari, 'Section 90 General Civil Code' in M. Schwimann and M. Neumayr (eds), *ABGB: Taschenkommentar*, 5th ed., LexisNexis, Vienna 2020, marg. no. 9.
[38] G. Hopf and G. Kathrein, *Eherecht*, 3rd ed., Manz, Vienna 2014, s. 49 of the Austrian Marriage Act, marg. no. 10.
[39] C. Fischer-Czermak, 'Beistandspflichten und Vertretung in Obsorgeangelegenheiten nach dem FamRÄG 2009' (2010) 2 *Zeitschrift für Familien- und Erbrecht* 4.
[40] S. 90(3) sentence 2 of the General Civil Code.
[41] M. Volgger, 'Die Hinderung eines Elternteils an der Ausübung der Obsorge' (2011) 57 *Zeitschrift für Familien- und Erbrecht* 95; Explanatory notes to the individual request 673/A, XXIV. legislation period, p. 26.
[42] P. Smutny, 'Section 90 General Civil Code' in A. Kletečka and M. Schauer (eds), *ABGB-ON*, v 1.07, Manz, Vienna 2017, marg. no. 29; S. Ferrari, 'Section 90 General Civil Code' in M. Schwimann and G. Kodek (eds), *ABGB: Praxiskommentar*, 5th ed., LexisNexis, Vienna 2020, marg. no. 13.

the step-child from kindergarten or writing an absence note for school.[43] The step-parent's power of representation results from the legal relationship of the spouses and therefore only exists vis-à-vis the other spouse, but not towards a step-child. The step-parent has no parental responsibilities of his or her own[44] and his or her representation is only necessary if the biological parent is prevented from fulfilling the responsibilities by illness or absence.[45] If the biological parents share parental responsibilities, the step-parent's right of legal representation is only relevant if both biological parents are unable to exercise their responsibilities.[46] The spouse entrusted with parental responsibilities may even – expressly or impliedly – grant power of representation for matters other than those concerning daily life and thereby go beyond the wording of the provision. On the other hand, he or she may also limit or prohibit the step-parent's authority under section 90(3) of the General Civil Code. In the event that a step-parent acts contrary to the declared intent of the spouse holding parental responsibilities, the act is nevertheless legally effective if the third party was not aware of the restriction. However, such an act may constitute marital misconduct or lead to a claim for damages by the child involved.[47] The special duty of assistance of the step-parent towards his or her spouse includes every element of parental responsibilities: the care and upbringing of the child as well as the administration of property (*Vermögensverwaltung*) and representation of the child.[48] However, section 90(3) of the General Civil Code does not oblige the step-parent to provide maintenance for his or her step-child.[49]

---

[43] G. Hopf and G. Kathrein, *Eherecht*, 3rd ed., Manz, Vienna 2014, s. 90 of the Austrian Marriage Act, marg. no. 16/1; P. Smutny, 'Section 90 General Civil Code' in A. Kletečka and M. Schauer (eds), *ABGB-ON*, v 1.07, Manz, Vienna 2017, marg. no. 29; Explanatory notes to the Individual Request 673/A, XXIV. legislation period, p. 26.

[44] M. Volgger, 'Die Hinderung eines Elternteils an der Ausübung der Obsorge' (2011) 57 *Zeitschrift für Familien- und Erbrecht* 95; Explanatory notes to the individual request 673/A, XXIV. legislation period, p. 26.

[45] P. Smutny, 'Section 90 General Civil Code' in A. Kletečka and M. Schauer (eds), *ABGB-ON*, v 1.07, Manz, Vienna 2017, marg. no. 29.

[46] C. Fischer-Czermak, 'Beistandspflichten und Vertretung in Obsorgeangelegenheiten nach dem FamRÄG 2009' (2010) 2 *Zeitschrift für Familien- und Erbrecht* 4; Explanatory notes to the individual request 673/A, XXIV. legislation period, p. 26.

[47] P. Smutny, 'Section 90 General Civil Code' in A. Kletečka and M. Schauer (eds), *ABGB-ON*, v 1.07, Manz, Vienna 2017, marg. no. 29.

[48] M. Nademleinsky, 'Das FamRÄG 2009 – die wichtigsten Änderungen' (2009)17 *Zivilrecht Aktuell* 326; Explanatory notes to the individual request 673/A, XXIV. legislation period, p. 26; C. Fischer-Czermak, 'Beistandspflichten und Vertretung in Obsorgeangelegenheiten nach dem FamRÄG 2009' (2010) 2 *Zeitschrift für Familien- und Erbrecht* 5; S. Jetzinger, 'Gesetzliches Erbrecht für Stiefkinder' (2019) 3 *Journal für Erbrecht und Vermögensnachfolge* 112.

[49] Explanatory notes to the individual request 673/A, XXIV. legislation period, p. 26.

The extension of the duty to assist under section 90(3) of the General Civil Code is only relevant if the biological parent entrusted with parental responsibilities and the step-parent are married. While a direct application or even analogy to registered partnerships cannot be derived, there is a parallel provision to section 90(1) of the General Civil Code in section 8(2) of the Registered Partnership Act. Although this duty to assist the other registered partner does not contain an explicit reference to representation in matters of parental responsibilities, the content of the provision must be understood in the same way as the provision for married couples – if only because of the case law of the Constitutional Court on the equality of marriage and registered partnership.[50]

Children in step-families also find noteworthy consideration in Austrian social insurance law: if the biological parent and the step-parent are married or have entered into a registered partnership, step-children are treated the same as biological relatives under the General Social Insurance Act (*Allgemeines Sozialversicherungsgesetz*, ASVG)[51] with regard to their step-parents.[52] This classification entitles step-children to claim under the health insurance of their step-parents.[53] Even if the spouses divorce or the registered partnership is dissolved, the step-child remains a relative of the step-parent in this connection.[54]

3.1.1.2. Informal Partners

Informal partners have had a weak position in Austrian law so far: only in a few respects does the law place their relationship on an equal footing with marital and formal partnership relationships or at least attach legal consequences to the existence of the informal partnership.[55]

For step-parents living in an informal partnership, the situation appears to be as follows: neither section 90(3) of the General Civil Code nor section 8(2) of the Registered Partnership Act can be applied by analogy to informal partnerships, as such relationships do not give rise to mutual duties

---

[50] S. Jetzinger, 'Gesetzliches Erbrecht für Stiefkinder' (2019) 3 *Journal für Erbrecht und Vermögensnachfolge* 112.
[51] Federal Law Gazette I No. 189/1955, in the version dated 30.12.2021, Federal Law Gazette I No. 238/2021.
[52] S. 123(3) General Social Insurance Law.
[53] M. Windisch-Greatz, 'Section 123 General Social Insurance Law' in R. Mosler, R. Müller and W.J. Pfeil, *Der SV-Komm*, Manz, Vienna 2016, marg. no. 22.
[54] S. 123(3) General Social Insurance Law.
[55] E.g. in the recently updated inheritance law, see ss 677(3), 745(2) and 748 of the General Civil Code.

of assistance under Austrian law.[56] Therefore, the 2013 Act Amending the Act on Children and Names separately considers step-parents living in an informal relationship: section 139(2) of the General Civil Code for the first time provides a legal basis to represent the biological parent in parental responsibility for matters of daily life. The provision enables informal partners to participate in family issues in the same way as is provided for spouses[57] and registered partners.[58] According to its wording, section 139(2) of the General Civil Code also obliges partners to safeguard the best interests of the child (*Kindeswohl*).[59] However, these rights and obligations only apply if the partner lives in the same household as the parent and the parent's minor child[60] and if there is also a family relationship with the parent.[61] The provision therefore refers to step-parents, irrespective of whether they are married/partnered[62] or live in an informal partnership,[63] and goes beyond the scope of application of section 90(3) of the General Civil Code and section 8(2) of the Registered Partnership Act; section 139(2) of the General Civil Code is not primarily about supporting a partner, but about protecting the child within a partnership. The legislature wants to ensure that every person who is in the immediate vicinity of the child does everything in his or her power to protect the best interests of the child. Although the right to represent the partner in daily matters of parental responsibilities also arises from section 139(2) of the General Civil Code, it can be restricted by the biological parent – just as is provided for in section 90(3) of the General Civil Code. These restrictions would render the respective act of representation ineffective if a third party were to become aware of it.[64]

---

[56] M. Stefula, 'Die Neuerungen zur Patchworkfamilie – Anwendungsbereich und Reichweite von §90 Abs 3 und §137 Abs 4 ABGB' (2009) 5 *Interdisziplinäre Zeitschrift für Familienrecht* 266; C. Fischer-Czermak, 'Beistandspflichten und Vertretung in Obsorgeangelegenheiten nach dem FamRÄG 2009' (2010) 2 *Zeitschrift für Familien- und Erbrecht* 4; S. Jetzinger, 'Gesetzliches Erbrecht für Stiefkinder' (2019) 3 *Journal für Erbrecht und Vermögensnachfolge* 112.

[57] S. 90(3) of the General Civil Code.

[58] S. 8(2) of the Registered Partnership Act.

[59] In addition to the constitutional anchoring in Austrian law, the best interests of the child are described based on a conclusive list of criteria under s. 138 of the General Civil Code.

[60] This additional requirement has been established by the 2013 Act Amending the Act on Children and Names to extend the duty of assistance to informal partners: see Explanatory notes to the Governmental Proposals (*Erläuterungen zur Regierungsvorlage*), 2004 of the addenda to the stenographic protocol of the national council (*Beilagen zu den stenographischen Protokollen des Nationalrats, BlgNR*), XXIV. legislation period, p. 18.

[61] P. Barth and G. Jelinek, 'Das neue Obsorgerecht' in P. Barth, A. Deixler-Hübner and G. Jelinek (eds), *Handbuch des neuen Kindschafts- und Namensrechts*, Linde, Vienna 2013, p. 140.

[62] According to s. 2 of the Registered Partnership Act.

[63] A. Deixler-Hübner, 'Obsorge' in A. Deixler-Hübner (ed.), *Scheidung, Ehe und Lebensgemeinschaft*, 13th ed., LexisNexis, Vienna 2019, p. 201; C. Fischer-Czermak, 'Section 139 General Civil Code' in A. Kletečka and M. Schauer (eds), *ABGB-ON*, v 1.05, Manz, Vienna 2017, marg. no. 6.

[64] Explanatory notes to the Governmental Proposals, 2004 of the addenda to the stenographic protocol of the national council, XXIV. legislation period, p. 18.

3.1.2. Step-Parents as Foster Parents

Under special conditions, step-parents may also be foster parents within the meaning of section 184 of the General Civil Code. Foster parents wholly or partly take care of the upbringing of a child with whom they have a relationship comparable to the parent–child relationship.[65] The following statements refer to all variants of partnership; any unequal treatment of same-sex partners has been abolished so that they too can become foster parents for their partner's child.[66] A foster care relationship (*Pflegeverhältnis*) can be implied[67] if the conditions are met,[68] which is often the case between a step-parent and a step-child.[69] However, the practical exercise of care by the step-parent does not automatically affect the parental responsibilities of other persons, that is, usually the responsibilities of one or both biological parents. Foster parents can only assume parental responsibilities if the responsibilities are assigned to them by the court upon application pursuant to section 185 of the General Civil Code.[70] The person who holds parental responsibilities at the time of the application for foster parenthood must consent to this assignment. Without consent, the court shall withdraw parental responsibilities from this person only as *ultima ratio* if the best interests of the child are endangered.[71] If parental responsibilities are transferred to a foster parent, they must always be transferred as a whole. A foster parent cannot be entrusted with joint parental responsibilities together with the other biological parent.[72] In other words, as long as the step-parent's partner is entrusted with parental responsibilities for his or her child, a step-parent – even

---

[65] See M. Roth, *Außerstreitverfahrensrecht*, 6th ed., Sramek, Vienna 2019, p. 131.
[66] Austrian Supreme Court, Judgment of 28.06.2012, 8 Ob 62/12v.
[67] Austrian Supreme Court, Judgment of 26.08.2003, 5 Ob 187; A. Deixler-Hübner, 'Section 184 General Civil Code' in A. Kletečka and M. Schauer (eds), *ABGB-ON*, v 1.06, Manz, Vienna 2017, marg. no. 5.
[68] In order to meet the definition of 'foster parent', it is sufficient if a person actually provides care and upbringing in whole or in part and at least intends to establish a personal relationship that comes close to the relationship between biological parents and children. See Austrian Supreme Court, Judgment of 14.12.2011, 3 Ob 165/11b.
[69] P. Barth and M. Neumayr, 'Section 186 General Civil Code' in A. Fenyves, F. Kerschner and A. Vonkilch (eds), *Großkommentar zum ABGB*, 3rd ed., Verlag Österreich, Vienna 2008, marg. no. 15.
[70] A. Deixler-Hübner, 'Section 185 General Civil Code' in A. Kletečka and M. Schauer (eds), *ABGB-ON*, v 1.06, Manz, Vienna 2017, marg. no. 3.
[71] S. 185(1) and (2) and s. 181 of the General Civil Code; A. Deixler-Hübner, 'Section 185 General Civil Code' in A. Kletečka and M. Schauer (eds), *ABGB-ON*, v 1.06, Manz, Vienna 2017, marg. no. 2; J. Weitzenböck, 'Section 185 General Civil Code' in M. Schwimann and M. Neumayr (eds), *ABGB: Taschenkommentar*, 5th ed., LexisNexis, Vienna 2020, marg. no. 1.
[72] A. Deixler-Hübner, 'Section 185 General Civil Code' in A. Kletečka and M. Schauer (eds), *ABGB-ON*, v 1.06, Manz, Vienna 2017, marg. no. 3; J. Weitzenböck, 'Section 185 General Civil Code' in M. Schwimann and M. Neumayr (eds), *ABGB: Taschenkommentar*, 5th ed., LexisNexis, Vienna 2020, marg. no. 3; Austrian Supreme Court, Judgment of 25.09.2002, 7 Ob 144/02f.

if he or she could be considered a foster parent according to the requirements of the law – cannot be granted parental responsibilities.[73] Thus, the rights and duties of the biological parent cannot clash with those of the step-parent. As long as the parent is entrusted with parental responsibilities in respect of his or her child, the rights and obligations arising therefrom are always superior to those of the step-parent.

As per section 184 of the General Civil Code, step-parents may be entrusted with parental responsibilities for their step-child if they fulfil the requirements as foster parents, if their partner holding sole parental responsibilities dies, if his or her place of residence has been unknown for at least six months, or if contact has been impossible or at least difficult to establish.[74] If the 'disabled' parent shares parental responsibilities with the other parent, there is no possibility of transfer to the step-parent, as the remaining biological parent is given full parental responsibilities.[75] Only if the deceased or absent parent had full parental responsibilities according to section 178 of the General Civil Code can the foster parent (i.e. the current partner of the deceased or absent parent) also be entrusted with full parental responsibilities.[76] This decision shall be taken by the court with particular regard to the best interests of the child. It is important to note that none of the persons mentioned in section 178(1) sentence 2 of the General Civil Code takes precedence over another: step-parents are therefore on an equal footing with the step-child's remaining biological parent and grandparents. The decision as to who parental responsibilities are ultimately assigned to is based on the emotional and social relationship the child has with the person in question.[77] Accordingly, if a step-parent can be considered a foster parent pursuant to section 184 of the General Civil Code and if he or she is closely associated with the child at the time of the shift of parental responsibilities, the court shall transfer parental responsibilities to him or her instead of to the other biological parent with whom the child has almost no

---

[73] Austrian Supreme Court, Judgment of 25.09.2002, 7 Ob 144/02f and Resolution of 30.11.2011, 7 Ob 124/11b.
[74] S. 178(1) of the General Civil Code; E. Gitschthaler, 'Section 178 General Civil Code' in M. Schwimann and G. Kodek (eds), *ABGB: Praxiskommentar*, 5th ed., LexisNexis, Vienna 2020, marg. no. 3.
[75] S. 178(1) sentence 1 of the General Civil Code.
[76] E. Gitschthaler, 'Section 178 General Civil Code' in M. Schwimann and G. Kodek (eds), *ABGB: Praxiskommentar*, 5th ed., LexisNexis, Vienna 2020, marg. no. 12; Regional Court of Linz (*Landesgericht Linz*, LG Linz), Judgment of 24.04.2014, 15 R 190/14p.
[77] C. Fischer-Czermak, 'Section 178 General Civil Code' in A. Kletečka and M. Schauer (eds), *ABGB-ON*, v 1.04, Manz, Vienna 2017, marg. no. 9; E. Gitschthaler, 'Section 178 General Civil Code' in M. Schwimann and G. Kodek (eds), *ABGB: Praxiskommentar*, 5th ed., LexisNexis, Vienna 2020, marg. no. 12; Vienna Higher Civil Court (*Landesgericht für Zivilrechtssachen Wien*), Judgment of 04.09.2007, 44 R 370/07y.

contact.[78] If both the remaining biological parent and the step-parent appear equally suitable to assume parental responsibilities, the court favours the biological parent.[79]

Step-parents who are considered foster parents are entitled to a childcare allowance (*Kinderbetreuungsgeld*) according to section 2(1) of the Childcare Allowance Act (*Kinderbetreuungsgeldgesetz*, KBGG).[80] However, the entitlement of the step-parent only exists if no other parent receives benefits on the same legal grounds. The 2012 Social Law Amending Act (*Sozialrechts-Änderungsgesetz*, SRÄG 2012)[81] opened up the possibility for step-parents – irrespective of whether they are spouses, registered partners or informal partners of the biological parent – to claim care leave (*Pflegefreistellung*) for their step-child[82] pursuant to section 16(1) para. 2 of the Annual Leave Act (*Urlaubsgesetz*, UrlG).[83] This, however, is only possible if the step-parent shares his or her common household with the step-child.[84]

3.1.3. Rights and Obligations of a Step-Parent and the Biological Parent Towards the Child

As outlined above, a step-parent who is married to or partnered with the biological parent and/or lives in a joint household with his or her step-child can obtain rights and obligations from section 90(3) and/or 139(2) of the General Civil Code and/or section 8(2) of the Registered Partnership Act. However, for the rights and duties of the other biological parent vis-à-vis the rights and duties of the step-parent, the decisive question is whether both biological parents have joint parental responsibilities or the biological parent with whom the child resides is entrusted with sole full parental responsibilities.

---

[78] Explanatory notes to the Governmental Proposals, 296 of the addenda to the stenographic protocol of the national council, XXI. legislation period, p. 52; M. Volgger, 'Die Hinderung eines Elternteils an der Ausübung der Obsorge' (2011) 57 *Zeitschrift für Familien- und Erbrecht* 92.

[79] C. Fischer-Czermak, 'Section 178 General Civil Code' in A. Kletečka and M. Schauer (eds), *ABGB-ON*, v 1.04, Manz, Vienna 2017, marg. no. 17; Vienna Higher Civil Court, Judgment of 01.02.2007, 45 R 18/07s.

[80] Federal Law Gazette I No. 103/2001, in the version dated 30.12.2021, Federal Law Gazette I No. 221/2021.

[81] Federal Law Gazette I No. 3/2013.

[82] The step-child in this context must be the biological child of the spouse/partner of the step-parent.

[83] Federal Law Gazette No. 390/1976, in the version dated 10.01.2013, Federal Law Gazette I No. 3/2013.

[84] M. Drs, 'Section 16 Annual Leave Act' in M. Neumayr and G.P. Reissner, *Zeller Kommentar zum Arbeitsrecht*, 3rd ed., Manz, Vienna 2018, marg. no. 14.

3.1.3.1. Joint Parental Responsibilities

If the biological parents exercise parental responsibilities jointly, the parent who does not live with the child in a shared household has the same rights as the parent who permanently lives with the child. In the case of joint parental responsibilities, the biological parent who does not live with the child nevertheless has more rights and duties than the step-parent who shares the household with his or her step-child.[85] Consequently, there can be no conflict between the rights and duties of the biological parent and the step-parent's duty of representation. It is assumed that in the case of joint parental responsibilities, the step-parent's power of representation can only be exercised if both biological parents are unable to exercise their parental responsibilities – possible conflicts between the biological parent and the step-parent are thus prevented.[86]

3.1.3.2. Sole Parental Responsibilities

If one biological parent is entrusted with full parental responsibilities, the other biological parent has certain rights and duties with regard to personal contact and the right to information, expression and representation (*Informations-, Äußerungs- und Vertretungsrecht*) according to section 189 of the General Civil Code.[87] The parent who is not entrusted with parental responsibilities may represent the parent who is fully entrusted with parental responsibilities in matters of daily life if circumstances so require and the child lawfully stays with that parent at that time.[88] This right resembles the right of step-parents pursuant to sections 90(3) and 139(2) of the General Civil Code as portrayed above. However, the rights and duties of the other biological parent and the step-parent do not contradict or compete with each other because the biological parent who has no parental responsibilities can only exercise the duty of representation if the child is currently staying with him or her. On the other hand, if the child is

---

[85] Even if parental responsibilities are shared with the other biological parent, each of them is the recipient of all rights and duties in matters of parental responsibilities under s. 158 et seq. of the General Civil Code.

[86] G. Hopf, 'Neues im Ehe- und Kindschaftsrecht – Änderungen des ABGB und des EheG durch das FamRÄG 2009' (2010) 19 *Österreichische Juristen Zeitung* 156; P. Smutny, 'Section 90 General Civil Code' in A. Kletečka and M. Schauer (eds), *ABGB-ON*, v 1.07, Manz, Vienna 2017, marg. no. 29; C. Fischer-Czermak, 'Beistandspflichten und Vertretung in Obsorgeangelegenheiten nach dem FamRÄG 2009' (2010) 2 *Zeitschrift für Familien- und Erbrecht* 6.

[87] M. Roth, *Außerstreitverfahrensrecht*, 6th ed., Sramek, Vienna 2019, p. 138; s. 186 et seq. of the General Civil Code.

[88] S. 189 of the General Civil Code; M. Roth, *Außerstreitverfahrensrecht*, 6th ed., Sramek, Vienna 2019, p. 141; Explanatory notes to the Governmental Proposals, 2004 of the addenda to the stenographic protocol of the national council, XXIV. legislation period, p. 30.

staying with the step-parent and with the biological parent who has full parental responsibilities and a situation arises in which the biological parent is unable to exercise his or her parental responsibilities, the step-parent may exercise his or her duty of representation pursuant to section 90(3) of the General Civil Code, section 8(2) of the Registered Partnership Act or section 139(2) of the General Civil Code. However, if such a situation occurs while the child is lawfully staying with the other biological parent based on the right of contact, this parent is obliged to act pursuant to section 189(1) para. 2 of the General Civil Code. This in turn means that conflicts between the other biological parent and the step-parent are de facto excluded in this scenario as well.

3.1.4. The Child's Place of Residence

Pursuant to sections 179(2) and 180(2), sentence 3 of the General Civil Code, parents have to determine in which household the child should predominantly reside, even if they share parental responsibilities. Since the 2015 ruling of the Constitutional Court[89] and its adoption by the Supreme Court,[90] the indication of the main residence should only be a nominal factor for other legal claims.[91] This leads to the applicability of the double-residence model (*Doppelresidenzmodell*), which states that children can legally live in one household with their mother and in a different one with their father.[92] The prerequisite is the equal care of the child and thus mostly joint parental responsibilities.[93] It is therefore obvious that the father's new partner and the mother's new partner can become step-parents of the child and receive rights and obligations. As long as the biological parents have joint parental responsibilities, the step-parent is only obliged to act according to section 90(3) of the General Civil Code or section 8(2) of the Registered Partnership Act and 139(2) of the General Civil Code if both biological parents are unable to exercise their parental responsibilities. In this case it is unclear which of the two step-parents is obliged to represent the biological parents. A logical solution is that the step-parent with whom the child is staying in such a situation has to fulfil the duty of representation.

---

[89] Austrian Constitutional Court, Judgment of 09.10.2015, G 152/2015.
[90] Inter alia, Austrian Supreme Court, Judgment of 24.08.2016, 3 Ob 121/16i.
[91] E.g. in registration law.
[92] C. Fischer-Czermak, 'Doppelresidenz aus obsorge- und kontaktrechtlicher Sicht' (2019) 6 *Zeitschrift für Familien- und Erbrecht* 250.
[93] It is also conceivable that the child could live with both parents, but only one parent has full parental responsibilities, as the application here is based on the parent's comprehensive right of access. As a rule, however, the double-residence model is mainly applicable when the parents have joint parental responsibility, see C. Fischer-Czermak, 'Doppelresidenz aus obsorge- und kontaktrechtlicher Sicht' (2019) 6 *Zeitschrift für Familien- und Erbrecht* 254.

3.2. RECOGNITION OF MULTIPLE PARENTS IN THE CASE OF AN ADOPTION

At the outset, it should be stressed that adoption in Austria is accessible in all types of relationships, regardless of gender or sexual orientation;[94] in particular, homosexuality may not be an impediment to adoption under Austrian law.[95] The following remarks therefore apply equally to all variants of opposite-sex and same-sex relationship constellations.

Austrian law distinguishes between adoption of a minor (*Minderjährigenadoption*)[96] and adoption of an adult (*Erwachsenenadoption*), with both variants representing a full adoption that legally replicates parenthood. The system of 'simple adoption', in which a descendency tie is added to a prior legal relationship, is not known under Austrian law.[97] Austrian law also does not recognise multiple parents in the case of adoption, which is why a mechanism such as 'open adoption', in which the biological parents can continue to participate in the life of their biological child, does not exist in the Austrian legal system. In the case of adoption by two adoptive parents, any non-property family law relationship (*familienrechtliche Beziehung*) with the biological parents ceases to exist.[98] This means that the biological parents have no right of contact pursuant to section 187 of the General Civil Code and no right of information, opinion and representation pursuant to section 189 of the General Civil Code.[99] However, biological parents can have the right of contact if they are treated as third persons in accordance

---

[94] B. Beclin, 'Gemeinsame und sukzessive Adoption nicht mehr auf Ehepaare beschränkt' (2016) 3 *Zeitschrift für Familien- und Erbrecht* 142; C. Rudolf, 'Adoption' in A. Deixler-Hübner (ed.), *Handbuch Familienrecht*, 2nd ed., Linde, Vienna 2020, p. 349; N. Kutscher and T. Wildpert, 'Section 191 General Civil Code' in N. Kutscher and T. Wildpert (eds), *Personenstandsrecht*, 2nd ed., Manz, Vienna 2019, marg. no. 6; L.K. Fuhrmann, 'Gemeinsame Adoption für alle?' (2016/2017) 10 *Juristische Ausbildung und Praxisvorbereitung* 117.

[95] *EB v. France*, no. 43546/02, 22.01.2008: the national legislator is therefore not allowed to distinguish between the sexual orientation of applicants for adoption. For detail, see C. Rudolf, 'Adoption' in A. Deixler-Hübner (ed.), *Handbuch Familienrecht*, 2nd ed., Linde, Vienna 2020, p. 349.

[96] Under Austrian law, minors are persons under the age of 18: s. 21(2) of the General Civil Code.

[97] For a detailed report on both the substantive and procedural aspects of adoption in Austria, see M. Roth, *Außerstreitverfahrensrecht*, 6th ed., Sramek, Vienna 2019, p. 73.

[98] S. 197(2) of the General Civil Code; J. Höllwerth, 'Section 197 General Civil Code' in M. Schwimann and G. Kodek (eds), *ABGB: Praxiskommentar*, 5th ed., LexisNexis, Vienna 2020, marg. no. 6; T. Schoditsch, *Gleichheit und Diversität im Familienrecht*, Manz, Vienna 2020, p. 25.

[99] Austrian Supreme Court, Judgment of 29.01.1961, 6 Ob 410/61; A. Deixler-Hübner, 'Section 197 General Civil Code' in A. Kletečka and M. Schauer (eds), *ABGB-ON*, v 1.07, Manz, Vienna 2017, marg. no. 2; C. Rudolf, 'Adoption' in A. Deixler-Hübner (ed.), *Handbuch Familienrecht*, 2nd ed., Linde, Vienna 2020, p. 363; G. Hopf and M. Weixelbraun-Mohr, 'Section 197 General Civil Code' in H. Koziol, P. Bydlinski and R. Bollenberger (eds), *Kurzkommentar zum ABGB*, 6th ed., Verlag Österreich, Vienna 2020, marg. no. 1.

with section 188(2) of the General Civil Code – but only if this is in the best interests of the child. The family law relationship with a biological parent may continue if the child is adopted by only one person (*Einzeladoption*) pursuant to section 197(3) of the General Civil Code, whereby the adoptive mother/father takes the place of the biological parent of the same sex.[100] In this case, the family law relationship between the child and this parent terminates *ex officio*, while the family law relationship with the biological parent of the opposite sex remains, unless the latter consents to the termination.[101] The court terminates the family law relationship with the biological parent who has not been replaced by the adoptive mother/father.[102] The family law relationship between a biological parent and the adopted child also continues if the new partner of the biological parent[103] adopts his or her partner's child (*Stiefkindadoption*).[104] Thus, the new partner becomes the adoptive parent of his or her partner's child and takes the place of the other biological parent. This concept also applies if a same-sex partner wishes to adopt his or her partner's child. In this case, the male same-sex partner takes the place of the biological mother, and the female same-sex partner takes the place of the child's biological father.[105]

Certain property relationships between the biological parents and the child are generally not extinguished by adoption. The biological parents are still obliged to provide maintenance[106] and equipment (*Ausstattung*),[107] but only if the adoptive parents cannot fulfil this obligation.[108] The biological parents can therefore not be obliged to provide maintenance if the adoptive parents are unwilling to provide maintenance for the adopted child.[109] Moreover, the

---

[100] N. Kutscher and T. Wildpert, 'Section 191 General Civil Code' in N. Kutscher and T. Wildpert (eds), *Personenstandsrecht*, 2nd ed., Manz, Vienna 2019, marg. no. 10.

[101] A. Deixler-Hübner, 'Section 197 General Civil Code' in A. Kletečka and M. Schauer (eds), *ABGB-ON*, v 1.07, Manz, Vienna 2017, marg. no. 3; J. Höllwerth, 'Section 197 General Civil Code' in M. Schwimann and G. Kodek (eds), *ABGB: Praxiskommentar*, 5th ed., LexisNexis, Vienna 2020, marg. no. 10.

[102] S. 197(3) of the General Civil Code.

[103] This applies to a new spouse, a registered partner or even an informal partner, see s. 197 of the General Civil Code.

[104] In this case it does not matter if the child is the biological child or already an adopted child (*Sukzessivadoption*) of the partner. For further details, see C. Rudolf, 'Adoption' in A. Deixler-Hübner (ed.), *Handbuch Familienrecht*, 2nd ed., Linde, Vienna 2020, p. 350.

[105] Austrian Constitutional Court, Judgment of 03.10.2018, G 69/2018; M. Nademleinsky, 'Section 197 General Civil Code' in M. Schwimann and M. Neumayr (eds), *ABGB: Taschenkommentar*, 5th ed., LexisNexis, Vienna 2020, marg. no. 2.

[106] S. 231 of the General Civil Code.

[107] S. 1220 et seq. of the General Civil Code.

[108] S. 198(3) of the General Civil Code; M. Roth, *Außerstreitverfahrensrecht*, 6th ed., Sramek, Vienna 2019, p. 76.

[109] Austrian Supreme Court, Judgments of 21.12.1982, 2 Ob 517/81 and 13.02.1991, 1 Ob 507/91; A. Deixler-Hübner, 'Section 198 General Civil Code' in A. Kletečka and M. Schauer (eds), *ABGB-ON*, v 1.05, Manz, Vienna 2017, marg. no. 1.

secondary maintenance obligation of the biological parents does not apply if the adoptive parents are in default, their whereabouts are unknown or there are difficulties in enforcing the maintenance obligation.[110] The inability of the adoptive parents to provide maintenance is more likely to be assumed if all efforts are insufficient to ensure the maintenance of the child.[111]

The right of inheritance between biological parents and their child is preserved despite the adoption.[112] The adopted child and his or her descendants, therefore, retain their statutory right of inheritance (*gesetzliches Erbrecht*) against their biological parents and relatives.[113] However, the legal succession (*gesetzliche Erbfolge*) in the event of the death of the adopted child presupposes that the adoptive parents and their descendants always inherit after the descendants of the adopted child, but before the biological parents of the adopted child pursuant to section 199(2) of the General Civil Code.[114]

Adoption also does not automatically result in a change of the name of the adopted child.[115] The adopted child may continue to bear the same name as his or her biological parents, but the child's name may be changed as a result of the adoption if so desired.[116]

3.3. RECOGNITION OF MULTIPLE PARENTS IN THE CASE OF MEDICALLY ASSISTED PROCREATION

3.3.1. Introduction to Austrian Reproductive Law

The original version of the Reproductive Medicine Act was implemented in Austrian law in 1992 after intense political and ethical discussions. The

---

[110] A. Deixler-Hübner, 'Section 198 General Civil Code' in A. Kletečka and M. Schauer (eds), *ABGB-ON*, v 1.05, Manz, Vienna 2017, marg. no. 1; M. Nademleinsky, 'Section 198 General Civil Code' in M. Schwimann and M. Neumayr (eds), *ABGB: Taschenkommentar*, 5th ed., LexisNexis, Vienna 2020, marg. no. 1.
[111] A. Deixler-Hübner, 'Section 198 General Civil Code' in A. Kletečka and M. Schauer (eds), *ABGB-ON*, v 1.05, Manz, Vienna 2017, marg. no. 1.
[112] S. 199(1) of the General Civil Code; F. Haunschmidt and J. Haunschmidt, 'Das gesetzliche Erbrecht' in F. Haunschmidt and J. Haunschmidt (eds), *Erbschaft und Testament*, 6th ed., LexisNexis, Vienna 2020, p. 18.
[113] C. Rudolf, 'Adoption' in A. Deixler-Hübner (ed.), *Handbuch Familienrecht*, 2nd ed., Linde, Vienna 2020, p. 366.
[114] M. Roth, *Außerstreitverfahrensrecht*, 6th ed., Sramek, Vienna 2019, p. 76; C. Rudolf, 'Adoption' in A. Deixler-Hübner (ed.), *Handbuch Familienrecht*, 2nd ed., Linde, Vienna 2020, p. 366.
[115] S. 157(2) of the General Civil Code; P. Barth and R. Fucik, 'Neuerungen im Abstammungs- und Adoptionsrecht' in P. Barth, A. Deixler-Hübner and G. Jelinek (eds), *Handbuch des neuen Kindschafts- und Namensrechts*, Linde, Vienna 2013, p. 65.
[116] Explanatory notes to the Governmental Proposals, 2004 of the addenda to the stenographic protocol of the national council, XXIV. legislation period, p. 22; N. Böhsner and E. Wagner, 'Section 157 General Civil Code' in A. Kletečka and M. Schauer (eds), *ABGB-ON*, v 1.05, Manz, Vienna 2017, marg. no. 2.

law of that time was restrictive; methods such as egg donation and in vitro fertilisation with donorsperm were completely prohibited and the use of the few permitted techniques was subject to numerous restrictive conditions (e.g. subsidiarity to biological reproduction and the exclusion of same-sex couples).[117] A 2013 ruling of the Austrian Constitutional Court[118] lifted the ban on the use of reproductive medicine by female same-sex partners[119] and at the same time initiated a general amendment of the Reproductive Medicine Act, which was finally implemented in the 2015 Reproductive Medicine Act (*Fortpflanzungsmedizingesetz*, FMedG).[120]

The methods permitted today are insemination[121] and in vitro fertilisation,[122] in each case in homologous[123] and heterologous[124] form. Both forms, but especially the heterologous one, are only available under strict conditions. Medically assisted reproduction may in general only be carried out with the gametes of the intended parents, that is, spouses, registered partners or informal partners, which is why the principle of the homologous system prevails in Austrian reproductive law.[125]

Basically, neither sperm nor egg donation is permitted:[126] as an exception, the donated sperm of a third party other than the spouse/partner may be used if the sperm of the intended father is not capable of reproduction.[127] In addition, the semen of a third party may also be used to induce a pregnancy in one of

---

[117] M. Erlebach, 'Section 1 Reproductive Medicine Act' in M. Flatscher-Thöni and C. Voithofer (eds), *FMedG und IVF-Fonds-Gesetz*, Verlag Österreich, Vienna 2019, marg. no. 2; M. Hinteregger, *Familienrecht*, 8th ed., Verlag Österreich, Vienna 2017, p. 190.

[118] Austrian Constitutional Court, Judgment of 10.12.2013, G 16/2013, G 44/2013.

[119] Male same-sex partners, however, are still excluded from reproductive medicine technologies due to the ban on surrogacy, see M. Mayrhofer, 'Section 2 Reproductive Medicine Act' in M. Neumayr, R. Resch and F. Wallner (eds), *Gmundner Kommentar zum Gesundheitsrecht*, Manz, Vienna 2016, marg. no. 6; C. Wendehorst, 'Neuerungen im österreichischen Fortpflanzungsmedizinrecht durch das FMedRÄG 2015' (2015) 1 *Interdisziplinäre Zeitschrift für Familienrecht* 4; Explanatory notes to the Governmental Proposals, 445 of the addenda to the stenographic protocol of the national council, XXV. legislation period, p. 1.

[120] Federal Law Gazette No. 275/1992, in the version dated 14.08.2018, Federal Law Gazette I No. 58/2018.

[121] Insertion of semen into the female reproductive organs; see s. 1(2) para. 1 of the Reproductive Medicine Act.

[122] Fusion of egg and sperm outside the female body; see s. 1(2) para. 2 of the Reproductive Medicine Act.

[123] Use of eggs and sperm of spouses, registered partners or informal partners; see s. 2 in conjunction with s. 3 of the Reproductive Medicine Act.

[124] Use of sperm cells from a third person; see s. 2 in conjunction with s. 3 of the Reproductive Medicine Act.

[125] M. Mayrhofer, 'Section 3 Reproductive Medicine Act' in M. Neumayr, R. Resch and F. Wallner (eds), *Gmundner Kommentar zum Gesundheitsrecht*, Manz, Vienna 2016, marg. no. 1.

[126] Explanatory notes to the Governmental Proposals, 445 of the addenda to the stenographic protocol of the national council, XXV. legislation period, p. 7.

[127] S. 3(2) of the Reproductive Medicine Act.

two women living together in a registered or an informal partnership. The eggs of a third woman shall only be used if the eggs of the woman who is to have the child, that is, the spouse, registered partner or informal partner, are not capable of reproduction.[128] The Reproductive Medicine Act does not contain an exception to the homologous system in favour of embryo donation. The donation of embryos, including surplus embryos, is therefore inadmissible.[129] The *ultima ratio* principle of medical reproduction also results in the prohibition of 'social egg-freezing', that is, the precautionary freezing of unfertilised eggs without medical reason.[130] Below, two rather 'prominent' techniques prohibited by Austrian law are discussed separately. This seems reasonable as it shows the limits of the possibility of having multiple parents in Austrian law.

3.3.2. Legal Limitations of Medically Assisted Reproduction

3.3.2.1. Surrogacy

Austrian law does not allow the procedure of surrogacy (*Leihmutterschaft*).[131] The prohibition derives not explicitly from the law, but from the synopsis of a number of provisions: according to the will of the legislator, the opening up of medically assisted reproductive technologies to same-sex couples is exclusively limited to lesbian couples.[132] For gay couples, the exclusion results from the biological necessity of having to use a surrogate mother.[133] Surrogacy also fails to comply with the provisions of section 3(1) of the Reproductive Medicine Act, which states that primarily the egg cells of the intended parents

---

[128] S. 3(3) of the Reproductive Medicine Act; for further details, see M. Erlebach, 'Zur Zulässigkeit medizinisch unterstützter Fortpflanzung aus rechtlicher Sicht' in P. Barth and M. Erlebach (eds), *Handbuch des neuen Fortpflanzungsmedizinrechts*, Linde, Vienna 2015, p. 219.

[129] C. Wendehorst, 'Neuerungen im österreichischen Fortpflanzungsmedizinrecht durch das FMedRÄG 2015' (2015) 1 *Interdisziplinäre Zeitschrift für Familienrecht* 7.

[130] Semen, ova and testicular and ovarian tissue may only be collected and stored for future medically assisted reproduction if a physical condition or its treatment in accordance with the state of medical science and experience causes a serious risk that pregnancy can no longer be induced by sexual intercourse (s. 2b of the Reproductive Medicine Act).

[131] See inter alia, M. Erlebach, 'Die Samen- und Eizellspende im FMedG' in P. Barth and M. Erlebach (eds), *Handbuch des neuen Fortpflanzungsmedizinrechts*, Linde, Vienna 2015, p. 228; B. Lurger 'International Private Law' in M. Flatscher-Thöni and C. Voithofer (eds), *FMedG und IVF-Fonds-Gesetz*, Verlag Österreich, Vienna 2019, marg. no. 26; C. Fischer-Czermak, 'Section 143 General Civil Code' in A. Kletečka and M. Schauer (eds), *ABGB-ON*, v 1.05, Manz, Vienna 2017; Explanatory notes to the Governmental Proposals, 445 of the addenda to the stenographic protocol of the national council, XXV. legislation period, p. 1; G. Hopf, 'Fortpflanzungsmedizinrecht neu' (2014) 19 *Österreichische Juristen Zeitung* 1037.

[132] Austrian Constitutional Court, Judgment of 10.12.2013, G 16/2013, G 44/2013; s. 2(1) of the Reproductive Medicine Act.

[133] M. Mayrhofer, 'Section 2 Reproductive Medicine Act' in M. Neumayr, R. Resch and F. Wallner (eds), *Gmundner Kommentar zum Gesundheitsrecht*, Manz, Vienna 2016, marg. no. 5.

are to be used and only exceptionally – in the case of reproductive incapacity of the woman for whom the pregnancy is to be induced – the egg cells of a third person.[134] However, surrogacy for gay couples would always require egg donation by a third person. Section 16(2) para. 3 of the Reproductive Medicine Act prohibits the procurement of persons who are willing to have sperm, ova or cells capable of development transferred to them.[135] Finally, the Reproductive Medicine Act contains a comprehensive prohibition of commercialisation (*Kommerzialisierungsverbot*): the provision of semen or ova for medically assisted reproduction in the context of a remunerated transaction is prohibited. The term 'remunerated' refers to an expense allowance that exceeds the proven cash expenses in connection with the medical treatment.[136] Any person who procures surrogate mothers in contravention of section 16(2) para. 3 of the Reproductive Medicine Act commits an administrative offence under section 22(1) para. 4 of the Reproductive Medicine Act and is liable to a fine of up to €50,000 and, if this fine cannot be paid, to a custodial sentence of up to 14 days. Outside the Reproductive Medicine Act, the prohibition on surrogacy can be inferred from section 143 of the General Civil Code, according to which the legal mother is always the woman who gave birth to the child. Likewise, the nullity of surrogacy contracts is implicitly stated in section 879(2) para. 1a of the General Civil Code.[137]

There are serious ethical concerns against a lifting of the ban on surrogacy, in particular the protection of the best interests of the child (e.g. the child's right to have contact with his or her birth parents), and also the protection of the physical integrity of potential surrogate mothers.

3.3.2.2. Three-Parent Child

The use of the genetic material of two women and one man instead of only one woman and one man is also not allowed in Austrian law. Even the use of a female gamete that is not the genetic material of the woman who wants to become pregnant is only permitted in exceptional cases according to section 3(3) of the Reproductive Medicine Act.[138] The process of creating a 'three-parent child'

---

[134] S. 3(3) of the Reproductive Medicine Act.
[135] M. Erlebach, 'Die Samen- und Eizellspende im FMedG' in P. Barth and M. Erlebach (eds), *Handbuch des neuen Fortpflanzungsmedizinrechts*, Linde, Vienna 2015, p. 222.
[136] S. 16(1) of the Reproductive Medicine Act.
[137] W. Kolmasch, 'Section 879 General Civil Code' in M. Schwimann and M. Neumayr (eds), *ABGB: Taschenkommentar*, 5th ed., LexisNexis, Vienna 2020, marg. no. 7.
[138] P. Barth, 'Zur Zulässigkeit der medizinisch unterstützten Fortpflanzung aus rechtlicher Sicht' in P. Barth and M. Erlebach (eds), *Handbuch des neuen Fortpflanzungsmedizinrechts*, Linde, Vienna 2015, p. 16; M. Mayrhofer, 'Section 3 Reproductive Medicine Act' in M. Neumayr, R. Resch and F. Wallner (eds), *Gmundner Kommentar zum Gesundheitsrecht*, Manz, Vienna 2016, marg. no. 7.

in the context of mitochondrial donation would require the manipulation of the human genome, which in turn is prohibited under section 9(3) of the Reproductive Medicine Act: any medical procedure involving gametes,[139] and thus the use of genetic material from three persons (mitochondrial donation), as required for a 'three-parent child', is inadmissible under Austrian law.[140]

3.3.3. Rights and Obligations of the Anonymous Donor

Within the framework of the Austrian legal system, it is basically not possible for an anonymous donor to participate in the parenthood of the biological (legal) mother and her spouse/partner. This is due not only to the lack of substantive legal regulations, but also to the fact that the data of the third-party donor (*Drittspender*) must be treated confidentially pursuant to section 20 of the Reproductive Medicine Act.[141] Furthermore, the General Civil Code stipulates that a male donor cannot be identified as the legal father of the child born through donor-assisted reproductive technology.[142] Access to a donor's data can only be granted by way of exception: at the request of the child when he or she has reached the age of 14, by his or her legal representatives in the event of a medical emergency, and by the administrative authorities of the courts when this information is indispensable for the performance of their duties.[143] Apart from these exceptions, it is not possible to obtain any information about the

---

[139] The only exception is the genetic survey of viable cells before their insertion into the female body according to s. 9(3) sentence 2 of the Reproductive Medicine Act.

[140] C. Voithofer, 'Section 9 Reproductive Medicine Act' in M. Flatscher-Thöni and C. Voithofer (eds), *FmedG und IVF-Fonds-Gesetz*, Verlag Österreich, Vienna 2019, marg. no. 47; E. Bernat, 'Das Recht der Fortpflanzungsmedizin im Spiegel der sich wandelnden Sozialmoral' in S. Arnold, E. Bernat and C. Kopetzki (eds), *Das Recht der Fortpflanzungsmedizin 2015 – Analyse und Kritik*, Manz, Vienna 2016, p. 76; A. Zwettler, 'Durchbruch oder Zwischenschritt? Eine Analyse der Neuerungen im FmedG unter Berücksichtigung weiterhin offener Aspekte' (2016) 2 *Zeitschrift für Gesundheitsrecht* 51.

[141] A. Leischner-Lenzhofer, 'Fortpflanzungsmedizin' in G. Aigner, A. Kletečka, M. Kletečka-Pulker and M. Memmer (eds), *Handbuch Medizinrecht*, Manz, Vienna 2021, chap. I.23, marg. no. 6.5.

[142] S. 148(4) of the General Civil Code; E. Bernat, 'Das Recht der Fortpflanzungsmedizin im Spiegel der sich wandelnden Sozialmoral' in S. Arnold, E. Bernat and C. Kopetzki (eds), *Das Recht der Fortpflanzungsmedizin 2015 – Analyse und Kritik*, Manz, Vienna 2016, p. 31; J. Pierer, 'Abstammung' in A. Deixler-Hübner (ed.), *Handbuch Familienrecht*, 2nd ed., Linde, Vienna 2020, p. 286.

[143] S. 20(2) and (3) of the Reproductive Medicine Act; A. Leischner-Lenzhofer, 'Fortpflanzungsmedizin' in G. Aigner, A. Kletečka, M. Kletečka-Pulker and M. Memmer (eds), *Handbuch Medizinrecht*, Manz, Vienna 2021, chap. I.23, marg. no. 6.5; K. Leitner, 'Section 15 Reproductive Medicine Act' in M. Flatscher-Thöni and C. Voithofer (eds), *FMedG und IVF-Fonds-Gesetz*, Verlag Österreich, Vienna 2019, marg. no. 8; also see E. Bernat, 'Das Recht der Fortpflanzungsmedizin im Spiegel der sich wandelnden Sozialmoral' in S. Arnold, E. Bernat and C. Kopetzki (eds), *Das Recht der Fortpflanzungsmedizin 2015 – Analyse und Kritik*, Manz, Vienna 2016, p. 32.

donor or the recipient, which is why Article 15 of the General Data Protection Regulation (*Datenschutzgrundverordnung*, DSGVO)[144] does not standardise a right of access to such information.[145] It should also be pointed out that the donor's data may only be kept by the clinic or doctor who performed the medically assisted fertilisation for a maximum period of 30 years, after which it must be destroyed in accordance with data protection law.[146] This means that the child in particular, who can only apply at the age of 14, is faced with a rather short period of 16 years in which information about the donor can be retrieved.

Donors themselves have no right to information about children born as a result of their donation; however, the legislature does not exclude the possibility of a breakthrough acknowledgement of paternity (*durchbrechendes Vaterschaftsanerkenntnis*) by the donor.[147] Of course, this is only possible if the donor is not anonymous.[148]

In contrast, a donor can never become the legal mother of a child born from an egg donation. The legal mother can only be the birth mother, according to section 143 of the General Civil Code.[149] Involvement of the donor in parenthood is therefore generally excluded. A donor and the child who is the result of medically assisted reproduction are not related to each other in terms of family and inheritance law, so that no mutual legal obligations arise.[150] This rule exists not only to make donation more attractive for reproductive medicine, but above all to protect the social family.[151]

---

[144] Regulation (EU) 2016/679 of the European Parliament and of the Council of 27 April 2016 on the protection of natural persons with regard to the processing of personal data and on the free movement of such data, and repealing Directive 95/46/EC [2016] OJ L119/1.
[145] A. Leischner-Lenzhofer, 'Fortpflanzungsmedizin' in G. Aigner, A. Kletečka, M. Kletečka-Pulker and M. Memmer (eds), *Handbuch Medizinrecht*, Manz, Vienna 2021, chap. I.23, marg. no. 6.4.
[146] S. 18(3) of the Reproductive Medicine Act.
[147] C. Wendehorst, 'Medizinisch unterstützte Fortpflanzung und Abstammungsrecht' in S. Arnold, E. Bernat and C. Kopetzki (eds), *Das Recht der Fortpflanzungsmedizin 2015 – Analyse und Kritik*, Manz, Vienna 2016, p. 111.
[148] See *infra*, section 3.3.4.
[149] Explanatory notes to the Governmental Proposals, 216 of the addenda to the stenographic protocol of the national council, XVIII. legislation period, p. 24; C. Wendehorst, 'Medizinisch unterstützte Fortpflanzung und Abstammungsrecht' in S. Arnold, E. Bernat and C. Kopetzki (eds), *Das Recht der Fortpflanzungsmedizin 2015 – Analyse und Kritik*, Manz, Vienna 2016, p. 104; J. Pierer, 'Abstammung' in A. Deixler-Hübner (ed.), *Handbuch Familienrecht*, 2nd ed., Linde, Vienna 2020, p. 253.
[150] P. Husslein and E. Bernat, 'Das durch Samenspende gezeugte Kind und die ärztliche Verschwiegenheitspflicht' (2014) 6 *Recht der Medizin* 328; E. Bernat, 'Das Recht der Fortpflanzungsmedizin im Spiegel der sich wandelnden Sozialmoral' in S. Arnold, E. Bernat and C. Kopetzki (eds), *Das Recht der Fortpflanzungsmedizin 2015 – Analyse und Kritik*, Manz, Vienna 2016, p. 32.
[151] J. Pierer, 'Abstammung' in A. Deixler-Hübner (ed.), *Handbuch Familienrecht*, 2nd ed., Linde, Vienna 2020, p. 286; T. Maier, 'Samenspende: Das Recht des Kindes auf Kenntnis seiner Abstammung' (2014) 2 *Zeitschrift für Familien- und Erbrecht* 52.

3.3.4. Rights and Obligations of the Known Donor

Third-party donors are usually anonymous, but if a donor wishes to donate to friends or family members, his or her anonymity is no longer guaranteed. Donors can even restrict the use of their donation to such special cases and therefore give their consent to the use of the donation for medically assisted reproduction only if they disclose the selected parents.[152] The same provisions apply as for anonymous third-party donors[153] and the donor has no legal rights or obligations towards the child. However, if the male donor is not an anonymous donor, he can be recognised as the legal father and thus receive parental rights and obligations. The legislature does not explicitly exclude the recognition of paternity by the sperm donor. This recognition is possible if the child or the mother agrees to it and the current other legal parent does not object[154] to the donor's application.[155] Furthermore, it might be possible for the male donor to obtain legal parenthood through the so-called father-swap (*Vätertausch*) according to section 150 of the General Civil Code. In this case, however, only the child can apply for the replacement of his or her legal father.[156]

As shown above, there are no comparable possibilities for the recognition of motherhood by the female gamete donor. The legislator justifies this 'unequal' treatment between male and female donors with the fundamental biological differences between the sexes. The legal mother should only be the woman who gave birth to the child.[157] The bond between woman and child, which develops especially during pregnancy, is much stronger than the bond between the legal father and the child. Consequently, there can be no breakthrough recognition of maternity under Austrian law.[158]

---

[152] A. Leischner-Lenzhofer, 'Fortpflanzungsmedizin' in G. Aigner, A. Kletečka, M. Kletečka-Pulker and M. Memmer (eds), *Handbuch Medizinrecht*, Manz, Vienna 2021, chap. I.23, marg. no. 4.3.7; Explanatory notes to the Governmental Proposals, 216 of the addenda to the stenographic protocol of the national council, XVIII. legislation period, p. 21.
[153] S. 11 et seq. of the Reproductive Medicine Act.
[154] S. 148(3) of the General Civil Code.
[155] Ss 146 and 147(3) of the General Civil Code; C. Wendehorst, 'Medizinisch unterstützte Fortpflanzung und Abstammungsrecht' in S. Arnold, E. Bernat and C. Kopetzki (eds), *Das Recht der Fortpflanzungsmedizin 2015 – Analyse und Kritik*, Manz, Vienna 2016, p. 111.
[156] P. Barth, D. Dokalik and M. Potyka, 'Section 150 General Civil Code' in P. Barth, D. Dokalik and M. Potyka (eds), *Das Allgemeine Bürgerliche Gesetzbuch ABGB*, 26th ed., Manz, Vienna 2018.
[157] The ancient Roman principle '*mater semper certa est*' was adopted in s. 143 of the General Civil Code in order to clarify that the position of the biological mother is to be inviolable in Austrian law.
[158] C. Wendehorst, 'Medizinisch unterstützte Fortpflanzung und Abstammungsrecht' in S. Arnold, E. Bernat and C. Kopetzki (eds), *Das Recht der Fortpflanzungsmedizin 2015 – Analyse und Kritik*, Manz, Vienna 2016, p. 115.

4. CONCLUSION

Current Austrian family law corresponds to societal needs: all family forms that are compatible with European values are legally recognised and largely equalised with regard to the parent–child relationship. However, the rights and obligations emanating from modern family forms are primarily implemented by case law following the rulings of the European Court of Human Rights and the European Court of Justice. While recent law reforms have adopted individual aspects of the complex parent–child relationship in the setting of 'multiple parents', the Austrian legislator has not yet succeeded in establishing a separate legal regime for such modern forms of family life. Despite the immense number of actual cases, Austrian politics seems to be rather cautious about enacting new family law provisions. Hence, the present government programme does not provide for major adjustments in this area.[159]

---

[159] See the 2020 to 2024 Austrian Government Programme, p. 24 ff., available at https://www.bundeskanzleramt.gv.at/bundeskanzleramt/die-bundesregierung/regierungsdokumente.html, accessed 07.03.2022; A. Zadić, 'Speech before the National Council' in Correspondence of the National Council (*Parlamentskorrespondenz*) No. 1352, 02.12.2020. In this speech the Minister of Justice underlines that every legislative initiative in the field of family law shall be preceded by an extensive survey of the current social situation and an outlook on future developments.

DIVERSITÉ ET PLURALITÉ DES FORMES ET FONCTIONS FAMILIALES EN BELGIQUE

Nicole Gallus, Yves-Henri Leleu, Géraldine Mathieu
et Frederik Swennen

1. Diversité et pluralité des formes familiales 161
   1.1. Introduction 161
   1.2. Le statut juridique du beau-parent dans les familles recomposées . . . 163
   1.3. L'adoption 165
   1.4. Parenté médicalement assistée 167
   1.5. Gestation pour autrui 171
2. Diversité et pluralité des fonctions de la famille. 172
   2.1. Fonction 1 – Épanouissement personnel des membres
       de la famille. 173
   2.2. Fonction 2 – Ancrage généalogique et identitaire des enfants. 176
   2.3. Fonction 3 – Éducation et entretien des enfants 180
   2.4. Fonction 4 – Mutualisation des charges et production
       de valeurs. 183
   2.5. Fonction 5 – Entraide en cas de vulnérabilité physique
       ou financiere 186

1. DIVERSITÉ ET PLURALITÉ DES FORMES FAMILIALES

1.1. INTRODUCTION

La présente étude concerne encore des familles « biparentales », la parenté pouvant prendre diverses formes selon le mode d'engendrement ou d'intégration dans la famille.

Le droit belge ne dispose pas de loi pour encadrer les cas d'enfants de plus de deux parents. Le contraire est même suggéré par la loi : « un enfant ne peut pas faire l'objet de plus de deux liens de filiation produisant effet » (art. 329, al. 1er, de l'ancien Code civil).[1] Il n'y a pas de projet d'une loi générale qui reconnaîtrait juridiquement la multiparentalité d'une manière générique et large, par exemple en précisant quelles personnes peuvent légalement se qualifier en tant que parent d'un enfant et prescrivant le nombre maximum de parents légaux qu'un enfant peut avoir.

En dehors du contexte de la gestation pour autrui, qui n'est pas interdite en Belgique, le législateur n'est intervenu qu'en matière d'accueil familial pour accorder aux accueillants familiaux, au lieu des parents d'origine ou adoptifs, les droits d'hébergement, de prendre les décisions quotidiennes et extrêmement urgentes et, exceptionnellement, de prendre les décisions importantes.[2] Il n'en résulte donc pas une forme de multiparentalité. Ce système peut néanmoins servir de modèle au développement d'une protection de la multiparentalité.

Le statut des beaux-parents reste légalement indéfini même si la Cour constitutionnelle[3] et le Conseil d'état[4] ont incité le législateur à intervenir. Le Sénat s'est penché sur la question d'une éventuelle loi générale en 2015, en vue de rédiger un rapport d'information. La demande d'établissement de ce rapport faisait notamment référence aux possibilités :

- … de créer un régime légal de coparentalité, et de définir pour la gestation pour autrui le cadre légal performant qui lui est intrinsèquement associé ;
- … de créer un régime légal permettant d'octroyer l'autorité parentale à plus de deux adultes.

Cet exercice n'a cependant pas abouti à une initiative législative concrète. En ce qui concerne la gestation pour autrui, le Sénat n'a rédigé que des conclusions

---

[1] Dans le cadre d'un projet législatif à long terme, les livres du Code civil de 1804 ont vocation à être remplacés par de nouveaux livres. En l'attente de l'introduction des nouveaux livres restant, le législateur a posé le choix de renommer « ancien Code civil » le reste du Code civil de 1804 (art. 2 de la loi du 13.04.2019 portant création d'un Code civil et y insérant un livre 8 « La preuve », entrée en vigueur le 01.11.2020, *M.B.*, 14.05.2019). Les dispositions qui concernent le droit de la famille citées dans la présente contribution le sont donc sous le vocable « ancien Code civil » mais sont toujours d'application.

[2] Loi du 19.03.2017 modifiant la législation en vue de l'instauration d'un statut pour les accueillants familiaux, *M.B.*, 05.04.2017, partiellement annulée par un arrêt n° 36/2019 de la Cour constitutionnelle du 28.02.2019, www.const-court.be. Voy à propos de cet arrêt : E. Adriaens et G. Loosveldt, « De bevoegdheid voor het nemen van belangrijke beslissingen m.b.t. het kind: geen rechterlijke delegatie meer aan pleegzorgers », *T. Fam.*, 2020/5, pp. 129 et s. ; M. Berghmans, « Pathos en logos in het recht », *T.J.K.*, 2019/4, pp. 454 et s. ; A. Jannone et G. Mathieu, « Compétences concurrentes des tribunaux de la jeunesse et de la famille en matière d'autorité parentale et d'accueil familial après la loi du 19 mars 2017 » in F. Mouffe et A. Quevit (coord.), *Quand le protectionnel et le civil s'(en)mêlent – Le nouvel article 7 de la loi du 8 avril 1965*, Larcier, Bruxelles 2021, p. 38, n° 47 ; G. Mathieu, « Enfant placé, parents écartés ? La Cour constitutionnelle réagit en rappelant les prérogatives des parents d'origine », *Justice en ligne*, 29.04.2019.

[3] Arrêt n° 134/2003 de la Cour constitutionnelle du 08.10.2003, www.const-court.be.

[4] Avis du Conseil d'état sur la proposition de loi complétant le Code civil par des dispositions relatives à la parenté sociale, *Doc.*, Ch., 2004–2005, n° 51-0393/002, www.lachambre.be.

synoptiques avec les points de convergence et de divergence entre les groupes politiques. En ce qui concerne la pluriparentalité, certains groupes politiques n'ont formulé qu'une amorce de questionnement.[5]

Il n'en reste pas moins qu'une pratique sociale de pluriparentalité – associée ou non à la gestation pour autrui – existe et que les adultes concernés ont recours aux conventions (notariales) qui n'offrent pas de sécurité juridique et encore moins de contrôle sur l'intérêt supérieur de l'enfant. A notre connaissance, il n'y pas de jurisprudence publiée sur cette matière mais cette pratique a bel et bien suscité l'intérêt de la doctrine (juridique).

La plupart des constats de l'étude sont indifférents au fait que les parents sont impliqués dans une relation de même sexe. Un enfant peut avoir deux parents de même sexe en droit belge. Si le droit belge autorise la co-maternité d'origine (art. 325/1 et s. de l'ancien Code civil), il ne connaît par contre pas la co-paternité d'origine dans la mesure où deux hommes ayant un désir de parenté ne peuvent le réaliser que grâce à une femme porteuse qui sera la mère légale de l'enfant (voy. ci-après 1.5). Si la procréation médicalement assistée est ouverte aux couples de même sexe, la gestation pour autrui n'est pas réglementée (voy. ci-après 1.5). L'adoption est ouverte aux couples de même sexe (art. 343 de l'ancien Code civil). La gestation pour autrui ne leur est pas interdite.

1.2. LE STATUT JURIDIQUE DU BEAU-PARENT DANS LES FAMILLES RECOMPOSÉES

D'un point de vue technique, en droit belge, aucune disposition légale n'organise un statut du beau-parent (nouveau partenaire du parent, quel que soit le statut du couple – mariage, cohabitation légale ou cohabitation de fait – ou l'orientation sexuelle du couple).

Le droit belge confie la titularité de l'autorité parentale aux seuls parents – ascendants au premier degré – de l'enfant et en fait donc un effet juridique de la filiation légale ou adoptive. Cette autorité parentale appartient conjointement aux parents (art. 373, al. 1er, de l'ancien Code civil). Si l'enfant a un seul parent, un seul parent en vie ou un seul parent capable d'exercer l'autorité parentale, ce parent est seul titulaire de l'autorité parentale (art. 375 de l'ancien Code civil).[6]

Le beau-parent qui participe en fait à l'éducation de l'enfant par le biais de la communauté de vie avec le parent ne peut revendiquer légalement aucun partage de l'autorité parentale.

---

[5] Rapport d'information concernant l'examen des possibilités de créer un régime légal de coparentalité, *Doc.*, Sén., 2015-2016, n° 6-98/002 et addendum n° 6-98/003, www.senate.be.

[6] Y.-H. Leleu, *Droit des personnes et des familles*, Larcier, Bruxelles 2020, pp. 268–69, n° 262 et pp. 721–50, n° 753–71; G. Mathieu, *Droit de la famille*, Larcier, Bruxelles 2022, pp. 458–60, n° 651–55 ; F. Swennen, *Het personen en familierecht*, Intersentia, Mortsel 2021, p. 177, n° 260–61.

Cette absence de toute prise en considération de la fonction de parentalité du partenaire non parent a été censurée par la Cour constitutionnelle. La Cour relève une différence de traitement entre, d'une part, les enfants qui n'ont qu'un seul lien de filiation établi mais vivent de manière durable au sein d'une famille composée de leur parent et d'un tiers qui les éduque – en l'espèce, la compagne de la mère –, d'autre part, les enfants qui ont une double filiation. Il appartenait néanmoins au législateur de mettre fin à cette discrimination, ce qui n'a toujours pas été fait, notamment en raison de la complexité des questions posées et de la difficulté de prévenir ou gérer les conflits susceptibles de naître si l'autorité parentale est exercée par plus de deux personnes.[7]

Le beau-parent marié avec le parent contribue néanmoins indirectement aux frais d'entretien et d'éducation des enfants non communs par le biais de son obligation de contribuer aux charges du mariage et de son obligation solidaire pour les dettes contractées pour les besoins du ménage et l'éducation « des enfants », lesquelles comprennent le coût des enfants même non communs élevés au foyer (art. 221 et 222 de l'ancien Code civil). Le beau-parent qui est en cohabitation légale avec le parent est tenu de contribuer aux charges de la vie commune et est tenu solidairement pour les dettes contractées pour les besoins de la vie commune et « des enfants qu'ils éduquent », y compris les enfants non communs élevés au foyer, même s'ils ne sont pas « éduqués » par le beau-parent (art. 1477 de l'ancien Code civil).[8]

En cas de décès du parent, le conjoint survivant ou le cohabitant légal survivant est tenu à l'entretien et l'éducation des enfants du parent prédécédé qui ne sont pas des enfants communs et ce, dans les limites de ce qu'il a recueilli dans la succession du prédécédé et des avantages que celui-ci a consenti par contrat de mariage, convention de cohabitation, donation ou testament (art. 203, §3 et 1477, §5, de l'ancien Code civil). Ces obligations alimentaires à l'égard des enfants, détachées de tout lien de filiation, n'existent que dans le mariage ou la cohabitation légale ; la cohabitation de fait n'entraîne en effet aucune obligation légale à l'égard des enfants du partenaire (à l'exception de ce qui est volontairement payé par le non-parent, qui ne peut pas être récupéré en tant qu' « obligation naturelle » exécutée volontairement).[9]

On notera aussi le droit aux relations personnelles organisé par l'article 375*bis*, al. 2 de l'ancien Code civil qui permet au beau-parent, après rupture de la recomposition familiale, de conserver un contact avec l'enfant à condition de

---

[7] C. const., n° 36/2019, 28.02.2019, *T. Fam.*, 2020, p. 125, note G. Loosveldt, E. Adriaens ; *T.J.K.*, 2019, p. 452, note M. Berghmans ; CA, n° 134/2003, 08.10.2003, *E.J.*, 2003, p. 134, note P. Senaeve ; *NjW*, 2004, p. 80, note RDC ; *Rev. trim. dr. fam.*, 2004, p. 185, note J.-L. Renchon ; *R.W.*, 2003–2004, p. 1016, note T. Robert ; *R.W.*, 2003–2004, p. 1016, note V. Verlinden ; *T.J.K.*, 2004, p. 39, note T. Robert.

[8] Y.-H. Leleu, *Droit des personnes et des familles*, Larcier, Bruxelles 2020, pp. 799–801, n° 793.

[9] Ibid., pp. 386–88, n° 379 ; J. Sosson, « L'obligation alimentaire naturelle » in *L'argent pour vivre : vers une réforme de l'obligation alimentaire*, Kluwer, Bruxelles 2000, pp. 125–53.

démontrer un lien d'affection particulier avec ce dernier et à condition également que lesdits contacts ne soient pas contraires à l'intérêt de l'enfant.[10]

Sauf hypothèse de l'adoption simple (voy. ci-après 2.2), le droit belge ne connaît pas la multiparentalité au sens de l'exercice des fonctions parentales par des personnes autres que les parents de l'enfant.

1.3. L'ADOPTION

Une certaine forme de reconnaissance de la multiplicité des parents existe dans les formes ouvertes d'adoption, celles qui ne rompent pas tous liens avec les parents biologiques.

Le droit belge connaît en effet deux formes d'adoption : l'adoption simple (art. 353-1 et s. de l'ancien Code civil) et l'adoption plénière (art. 355 et s. de l'ancien Code civil). Dans les deux cas, l'adoptant peut être une personne seule ainsi que des conjoints ou (anciens) partenaires cohabitants (art. 343-1 de l'ancien Code civil).[11]

L'adoption simple ne rompt pas les liens de filiation d'origine et, par conséquent, crée une potentielle multiplicité juridique de deux parents d'origine au maximum et de deux adoptants au maximum. Il ne s'agit toutefois pas d'une forme d'« adoption ouverte » telle qu'elle existe dans d'autres juridictions.[12]

En réalité, la titularité de l'autorité parentale est limitée à deux parents au maximum : l'adoptant, les adoptants ou, en cas d'adoption par un beau-parent, un parent d'origine et son (ex-)partenaire-adoptant. La titularité de l'autorité parentale ne peut donc être partagée par les deux parents d'origine et un (beau-parent-)adoptant, et encore moins par les deux parents d'origine et deux (beaux-parents-)adoptants.[13] En cas de décès de l'adoptant ou des adoptants, les

---

[10] S. Cap et J. Sosson, « La place juridique du tiers au lien de filiation » in *Filiation et parentalité*, Actes du XIIIème Colloque de l'Association « Famille & Droit », Bruylant, Bruxelles 2014, pp. 301–10.

[11] L. Cohen, « Actualités législatives et constitutionnelles en droit de l'adoption » in J. Sosson (dir.), *Actualités législatives en droit de la personne et de la famille*, Larcier, Bruxelles 2018, pp. 96–106, n° 6–24.

[12] Y.-H. Leleu, *Droit des personnes et des familles*, Larcier, Bruxelles 2020, pp. 655–83, n° 683–717 ; G. Mathieu, *Droit de la famille*, Larcier, Bruxelles 2022, pp. 529–32, n° 760–74 ; F. Swennen, *Het personen en familierecht*, Intersentia, Mortsel 2021, pp. 509–32, n° 772–823.

[13] La Cour constitutionnelle est actuellement saisie d'une question préjudicielle, posée par jugement du 1er avril 2022 du tribunal de la famille d'Anvers, division d'Anvers (*R.W.*, 2022–2023/1, p. 35) à cet égard (affaire inscrite sous le n°7793 du rôle de la Cour)? Voy.: F. Swennen, « Kruiselingse stiefouderadoptie: laaghangend wetgevend fruit? », *R.W.*, 2022–2023/1, p. 2. Comp. les propositions faites pour la France dans le rapport *Filiation, origines, parentalité. Le droit face aux nouvelles valeurs de responsabilité générationnelle*, https://www.vie-publique.fr/rapport/33805-filiation-origines-parentalite, accessed 29.08.2022 et les propositions faites pour les Pays-Bas dans le rapport *Kind en ouders in de 21ste eeuw*, de la *Staatscommissie Herijking Ouderschap*, https://www.rijksoverheid.nl/documenten/rapporten/2016/12/07/rapport-van-de-staatsommissie-herijking-ouderschap-kind-en-ouders-in-de-21ste-eeuw, accessed 29.08.2022.

parents d'origine, ou l'un d'eux, peuvent demander que l'enfant soit replacé sous leur autorité parentale (art. 353-10 de l'ancien Code civil).

Le maintien des liens de filiation d'origine laisse subsister dans la famille d'origine un droit aux relations personnelles avec l'adopté mineur (art. 375*bis* de l'ancien Code civil) ; droit naturel en ce qui concerne les parents d'origine.[14] Mais il est rare qu'un tel droit soit accordé aux parents d'origine. S'il est indiqué de maintenir un contact régulier entre les parents d'origine et leur enfant, l'accueil familial de l'enfant dans le cadre de l'aide à la jeunesse ou de la protection de la jeunesse apparaît comme une solution plus appropriée que l'adoption.[15]

L'obligation de fournir des aliments continue d'exister entre l'adopté et ses parents d'origine, subsidiairement à l'obligation de l'adoptant ou des adoptants (art. 353-14 de l'ancien Code civil).[16]

En cas d'adoption plénière, l'enfant « cesse d'appartenir à sa famille d'origine » et acquiert dans la famille adoptive « un statut comportant des droits et obligations identiques à ceux qu'ils auraient si l'enfant était né de l'adoptant ou des adoptants » (art. 356 de l'ancien Code civil). L'adoption par un beau-parent laisse néanmoins subsister unilatéralement les liens de filiation d'origine (art. 356-2 de l'ancien Code civil). Il n'existe donc pas de multiplicité de parents en cas d'adoption plénière, sous réserve des deux exceptions mentionnées ci-dessous.

En premier lieu, les empêchements à mariage entre proches parents subsistent dans la famille d'origine après adoption plénière (art. 356, al. 1er, de l'ancien Code civil).

En second lieu, les membres de la famille d'origine peuvent revendiquer un droit aux relations personnelles avec l'adopté mineur. La Cour de cassation a fondé cette revendication, dans un cas concernant des grands-parents d'origine, sur un « principe de droit fondé sur des relations d'affection, de respect et de dévouement, dues à la communauté du sang ».[17] Il n'est à cet égard pas nécessaire que la communauté de sang soit confirmée par des relations d'affection : un droit aux relations personnelles a même été accordé aux grands-parents d'origine qui n'avaient auparavant jamais rencontré leurs petits-enfants.[18] Le fondement pour accorder un droit aux relations personnelles s'applique d'avantage aux parents d'origine mais on ne voit pas comment l'exercice d'un tel droit servirait l'intérêt de l'enfant au cas où l'adoption plénière est prononcée.[19]

---

[14] F. Swennen, *Het personen en familierecht*, Intersentia, Mortsel 2021, p. 530, n° 813.
[15] Ibid., p. 553, n° 856.
[16] N. Gallus, « Les aliments », *Rép. Not.*, t. I, l. IV, Larcier, Bruxelles 2005, p. 290, n° 337.
[17] Cass., 04.03.1976, *Pas.*, 1976, I, p. 733.
[18] Anvers, 01.03.2010, *T. Fam.*, 2010, p. 195.
[19] F. Swennen, *Het personen en familierecht*, Intersentia, Mortsel 2021, p. 553, n° 856. Voy. également R. Heps, « Behouden de oorspronkelijke grootouders na volle adoptie hun principieel recht op persoonlijk contact ? », note sous Anvers, 01.03.2010, *T. Fam.*, 2010, p. 196.

1.4. PARENTÉ MÉDICALEMENT ASSISTÉE

Les techniques d'assistance médicale à la procréation créent de nouvelles formes de parenté. La loi belge reconnaît la parenté de la mère biologique et de son conjoint/partenaire si un enfant est né à la suite d'une technique de reproduction assistée à l'aide des gamètes dont les donneurs (homme ou femme) étaient anonymes. L'anonymat du donneur est encore protégé et sa parenté ne peut en principe pas être établie, mais cela fait débat.

La loi du 6 juillet 2007 relative à la procréation médicalement assistée et à la destination des embryons surnuméraires et des gamètes (ci-après « la loi »)[20] autorise, à titre gratuit, le don de sperme, d'ovocytes et d'embryons et dispose que les activités de fécondation in vitro et de cryoconservation d'embryons ou de gamètes ne peuvent être réalisées que dans les centres de fécondation agréés.[21]

Une demande de procréation médicalement assistée peut être formée tant par une femme seule que par un couple et, lorsque la demande émane d'un couple, aucune exigence n'est posée relativement à sa stabilité.[22] Le texte de la loi définit en effet l'auteur du projet parental comme « toute personne ayant pris la décision de devenir parent par le biais d'une procréation médicalement assistée ».[23]

Enfin, si l'anonymat du don est la règle,[24] le don non anonyme de gamètes est toutefois possible en cas d'accord entre le donneur et la receveuse ou le couple receveur.

Concernant plus précisément la question de la parentalité, les articles 27 et 56 de la loi disposent qu'aucune action relative à la filiation ou à ses effets

---

[20] *M.B.*, 17.07.2007. Voy. à propos de cette loi : G. Genicot, *Droit médical et biomédical*, Larcier, Bruxelles 2016, pp. 588 et s. ; Y.-H. Leleu, *Droit des personnes et des familles*, Larcier, Bruxelles 2020, pp. 148 et s. ; G. Mathieu, *Droit de la famille*, Larcier, Bruxelles 2022, pp. 395 et s.

[21] F. Swennen, *Het personen en familierecht*, Intersentia, Mortsel 2021, p. 457-60, n° 682 ; Y.-H. Leleu, *Droit des personnes et des familles*, Larcier, Bruxelles 2020, pp. 148-52, n° 118 ; G. Mathieu, *Droit de la famille*, Larcier, Bruxelles 2022, pp. 395-96, n° 582.

[22] G. Mathieu, *Droit de la famille*, Larcier, Bruxelles 2022, p. 396.

[23] Art. 2, f), de la loi.

[24] Pour une critique de l'anonymat du don, voy. : E. Decorte, « Een kinderrechtenconforme benadering van toegang tot afstammingsinformatie voor donorkinderen », *T.J.K.*, 2021, pp. 7 et s. ; G. Génicot, « Le secret des origines biologiques dans les procréations médicalement assistées faisant appel à un tiers : un dispositif à questionner » in N. Massager et N. Gallus (dir.), *Procréation médicalement assistée et gestation pour autrui. Regards croisés du droit et de la pratique médicale*, Anthémis, Limal 2017, pp. 75 et s. ; G. Mathieu, *Droit de la famille*, Larcier, Bruxelles 2022, pp. 402 et s. ; G. Mathieu, *Le secret des origines en droit de la filiation*, Kluwer, Waterloo 2014, pp. 317 et s. ; G. Mathieu, « L'anonymat du don dans le contexte des procréations médicalement assistées : une nécessaire réforme du droit belge à la lumière des droits humains », N. Dandoy, J. Sosson, F. Tainmont et G. Willems (coord.), *Individu, Famille, Etat : Réflexions sur le sens du droit de la personne, de la famille et de son patrimoine. Hommage au Professeur Jean-Louis Renchon*, vol. 1, Bruxelles, Larcier, 2022, pp. 1081 et s. ; F. Swennen, *Het personen- en familierecht. Een benadering in context*, 7ᵉ éd., Intersentia, Anvers 2021, p. 422. Voy. aussi : I. Boone et E. Decorte, « Hoelang nog blijft België het recht van donorkinderen op informatie over hun genetische afkomst negeren? », *R.W.*, 2021-2022/5, p. 190.

patrimoniaux n'est ouverte au donneur, ni au(x) receveur(s) ou à l'enfant issu du don à l'encontre du donneur, et qu'à compter de l'implantation des embryons ou de l'insémination des gamètes, les règles de la filiation telles qu'établies par le Code civil jouent en faveur du ou des « auteurs du projet parental ». La loi fait donc des auteurs du projet parental les seuls parents légaux de l'enfant et empêche qu'un lien de filiation soit établi à l'égard du donneur ou de la donneuse.

La mère biologique sera ainsi toujours reconnue comme la mère juridique de l'enfant. Le nom de la femme qui accouche sera en effet mentionné dans l'acte de naissance et cette mention suffira à établir la maternité.[25] Le critère de l'établissement de la maternité est donc l'accouchement et la donneuse d'ovocytes n'a aucun droit ni aucun devoir à l'égard de l'enfant issu du don.[26]

Si la mère est mariée, son époux ou son épouse sera présumé(e) être le père[27] ou la coparente[28] de l'enfant et aucune action en contestation de cette présomption ne sera possible si l'époux ou l'épouse a consenti à l'acte de procréation médicalement assistée, pour autant que la conception de l'enfant soit la conséquence de cet acte.[29]

Si la mère n'est pas mariée, son compagnon ou sa compagne pourra reconnaître l'enfant avec son accord, et ce déjà à tout moment de la grossesse.[30]

A défaut de reconnaissance volontaire, la mère pourra agir en établissement judiciaire de la paternité ou de la co-maternité.[31] L'établissement de la co-maternité ne posera pas de difficulté dès lors que la preuve de la co-maternité sera rapportée par la signature de la convention avec le centre de fécondation conformément à l'article 7 de la loi. L'établissement de la paternité est plus complexe dans la mesure où tant l'action en autorisation de reconnaissance en cas de refus de consentement de la mère que l'action en établissement judiciaire de la paternité exigent, selon les dispositions de l'ancien Code civil,[32] la preuve du lien biologique pour établir la paternité, lien qui fait précisément défaut dans le cas du recours à une procréation médicalement assistée avec donneur.

---

[25] Art. 44 et 312, §1er, de l'ancien Code civil.
[26] G. Mathieu, *Droit de la famille*, Larcier, Bruxelles 2022, p. 399.
[27] Art. 315 de l'ancien Code civil.
[28] Art. 325/2 de l'ancien Code civil.
[29] Art. 318, §4 et 325/3, §3, de l'ancien Code civil. On relèvera à cet égard que la Cour constitutionnelle est actuellement saisie d'une question préjudicielle posée par le tribunal de la famille de Liège, division de Liège (jugement du 04.02.2022), libellée comme suit : « L'article 318, §4 de l'ancien Code civil viole-t-il les articles 10, 11 et 22 de la Constitution, lu ou non en combinaison avec l'article 8 de la Convention européenne des droits de l'homme, en ce qu'il instaure une fin de non-recevoir absolue, due au consentement donné par le mari à l'insémination artificielle ou à un autre acte ayant la procréation pour but, sauf si la conception de l'enfant ne peut en être la conséquence, à l'action en contestation de la paternité du mari introduite par l'homme qui se prétend le père de l'enfant, dans l'hypothèse où cet enfant a été conçu dans le cadre d'une gestation pour autrui s'inscrivant dans un projet parental mené par lui et non par la mère de l'enfant et son mari ? » (n° de rôle 7746).
[30] Art. 328, §3, de l'ancien Code civil.
[31] Art. 322 et 325/8 de l'ancien Code civil.
[32] Art. 329*bis*, §2, al. 4, et 332*quinquies*, §3, de l'ancien Code civil.

Certains tribunaux n'ont toutefois pas hésité à s'écarter de ces dispositions et à se baser sur les articles 27 et 56 de la loi qui prévoient que les règles du Code civil doivent jouer en faveur du ou des auteurs du projet parental pour établir la paternité en l'absence de lien biologique.[33] On mentionnera à cet égard un arrêt récent de la Cour constitutionnelle[34] au terme duquel la Cour a constaté l'inconstitutionnalité de la disposition de l'ancien Code civil qui implique cette impossibilité d'établir un lien de filiation paternelle en l'absence de lien biologique dans le contexte d'une procréation médicalement assistée avec don. Dans cette affaire, il n'était pas contesté que l'homme dont la filiation était recherchée avait participé aux démarches ayant abouti à la conception et à la naissance de l'enfant et que, jusqu'à son décès inopiné, cet homme avait considéré l'enfant à naître comme le sien. La Cour a estimé qu'

> [e]n faisant obstacle à l'établissement judiciaire de la paternité du co-auteur du projet parental ayant abouti, à l'issue d'une procréation médicalement assistée exogène, à la naissance de l'enfant, l'article 332*quinquies*, §3, du Code civil porte une atteinte disproportionnée au droit au respect de la vie privée et familiale de l'enfant concerné, ainsi qu'à son droit à ce que soit pris en compte son intérêt supérieur . La disposition en cause est dépourvue de justification lorsqu'elle est appliquée dans le contexte d'une action en recherche de paternité concernant un enfant né grâce à la mise en œuvre d'une technique de procréation médicalement assistée exogène.

Cet arrêt a été prononcé à propos d'une action en établissement judiciaire de la paternité mais son enseignement pourrait être élargi à l'hypothèse où l'homme ayant participé au projet parental souhaiterait reconnaître l'enfant et se heurterait au refus de consentement de la mère.[35]

Si le don s'est réalisé de manière non anonyme, ce que la loi autorise pour le don de gamètes en cas d'accord entre le donneur et la receveuse ou le couple receveur, les seuls parents légaux de l'enfant restent le ou les auteurs du projet parental et aucune action relative à la filiation ou à ses effets patrimoniaux n'est ouverte au(x)

---

[33] Bruxelles, 29.05.2012, *T. Fam.*, 2013, p. 201, note U. Cerulus ; Civ. Dinant, 05.03.2009, *Rev. trim. dr. fam.*, 2010, p. 1095, note J. Sosson.

[34] C. const., arrêt n° 19/2019 du 07.02.2019, www.const-court.be. Voy. à propos de cet arrêt : I. Boone, « De gerechtelijke vaststelling van het vaderschap getoetst aan de Grondwet », *R.W.*, 2019-2020, pp. 1525 et s. ; I. Boone, « Recente ontwikkelingen in het afstammingsrecht en het naamrecht (2017-2019) » in I. Boone et C. Declerck (éd.), *Themis 111 – Personen- en familierecht*, die Keure, Bruges 2020, p. 21 et s. ; S. Cap, « L'insémination artificielle et la fécondation *in vitro* » in N. Dandoy et G. Willems (dir.), *Les grands arrêts du droit au respect de la vie familiale*, Larcier, Bruxelles 2022, pp. 350 et s. ; E. Decorte, « Afstamming langs vaderszijde : over de (on)mogelijkheden na medisch begeleide voortplanting met donorzaad », *T.J.K.*, 2019, pp. 266 et s. ; P. Senaeve, « Medisch begeleide voortplanting met donorsperma en onderzoek naar het vaderschap », *T. Fam.*, 2019/5, pp. 138 et s. ; G. Willems, « La filiation après PMA à l'épreuve du contrôle de constitutionnalité : vers une consécration législative de la parenté intentionnelle ? », *J.T.*, 2019, pp. 455 et s.

[35] G. Mathieu, *Droit de la famille*, Larcier, Bruxelles 2022, p. 400.

donneur(s) et ne peut être intentée à l'encontre du ou des donneur(s) par le(s) receveur(s) de gamètes ou par l'enfant né de l'insémination de gamètes.

On précisera encore que lorsque le don se réalise de manière non anonyme, l'anonymat n'est levé qu'entre le donneur et la receveuse ou le couple receveur. L'enfant né suite à un don non anonyme de gamètes n'a aucun droit d'accès aux informations relatives au(x) donneur(s). Le centre de fécondation reste par ailleurs tenu de rendre inaccessible toute donnée permettant l'identification du donneur et toute personne travaillant pour ou dans un tel centre qui prend connaissance, de quelque manière que ce soit, d'informations permettant l'identification des donneurs d'embryons ou de gamètes est tenue au secret professionnel.[36]

Les développements qui précèdent ne valent toutefois que dans le cadre d'un projet parental réalisé dans un centre de fécondation agréé conformément à la loi. Un projet « artisanal » effectué en dehors du cadre légal, ce qui peut s'envisager pour le don de sperme, n'offre en effet pas les mêmes garanties. L'homme ayant fourni ses gamètes pourrait dans ce cas voir sa paternité établie, soit via une reconnaissance volontaire, soit via une action en établissement judiciaire de la paternité, moyennant le consentement de la mère, de l'enfant s'il est âgé de 12 ans ou plus et également, dans le cadre d'un établissement judiciaire de la paternité, moyennant l'absence d'opposition du ministère public.[37] En cas de refus de consentement ou d'opposition du ministère public, le critère biologique n'emportera pas automatiquement l'établissement du lien de filiation mais sera contrebalancé par d'autres intérêts au premier rang desquels figure l'intérêt de l'enfant. L'établissement de la paternité de l'homme ayant fourni ses gamètes pourrait ainsi être refusé si cet établissement s'avère contraire à l'intérêt de l'enfant.[38]

Si la paternité de l'homme ayant fourni ses gamètes est établie, cette paternité produira tous les effets de la filiation (attribution du nom, obligation d'entretien, autorité parentale, …). On relèvera toutefois que le droit belge n'autorise pas qu'un enfant fasse l'objet de plus de deux liens de filiation produisant effet[39] de sorte que l'établissement de cette paternité implique que l'enfant n'ait pas un lien de paternité ou de co-maternité établi par ailleurs. Si la paternité ou la co-maternité était établie à l'égard d'un autre homme ou d'une femme, il faudrait au préalable la contester. L'action en contestation est ouverte à celui qui revendique la paternité s'il parvient à démontrer qu'il est le père biologique de l'enfant mais, dans ce cas également, une balance des intérêts pourrait faire échec à l'aboutissement de l'action.

Relevons enfin qu'à défaut d'établissement de la paternité de l'homme ayant fourni ses gamètes, un droit aux relations personnelles pourrait néanmoins lui être octroyé si l'exercice de ce droit n'est pas contraire à l'intérêt de l'enfant.[40]

---

[36] Ibid., p. 402.
[37] Art. 332*quinquies* de l'ancien Code civil.
[38] G. Mathieu, *Droit de la famille*, Larcier, Bruxelles 2022, p. 401.
[39] Art. 329, al. 1er, de l'ancien Code civil.
[40] Art. 375*bis* de l'ancien Code civil.

La question de savoir si le père biologique doit ou non prouver l'existence d'un lien d'affection particulier avec l'enfant reste controversée.[41]

1.5. GESTATION POUR AUTRUI

La gestation pour autrui est une quatrième configuration possible de parentalité multiple ou diversifiée. Cette pratique n'est pas explicitement réglementée en Belgique. Elle n'est toutefois pas prohibée. Elle demeure soumise au droit commun de la filiation.

Si la femme[42] porteuse accouche en Belgique, elle est la mère légale de l'enfant, la filiation maternelle étant fondée sur l'accouchement (art. 44 et 312, §1er, de l'ancien Code civil).

Lorsque la convention de gestation pour autrui est volontairement exécutée, le lien de filiation avec les parents d'intention se réalise le plus souvent comme suit :

- pour un couple hétérosexuel, le père d'intention, qui est le plus souvent le père génétique, reconnaît l'enfant et la mère d'intention procède à l'adoption ; il s'agira généralement d'une adoption plénière intra-familiale rompant ainsi le lien de filiation avec la femme porteuse ;
- pour un couple homosexuel, l'un des membres du couple reconnaît l'enfant et son partenaire procède également à une adoption.

L'établissement de la filiation vis-à-vis du père intentionnel peut être plus complexe si la femme porteuse est mariée puisque son mari est alors présumé père légal de l'enfant (article 315 de l'ancien Code civil). L'homme qui est à la fois père génétique et père d'intention doit contester la paternité du mari pour y substituer la sienne (art. 318, §5, de l'ancien Code civil).[43]

Ce mécanisme mis en œuvre lorsque la femme porteuse exécute volontairement la convention de gestation pour autrui permet de donner à l'enfant un double lien de filiation vis-à-vis des parents d'intention qui ont alors conjointement l'exercice de l'autorité parentale. Le lien de filiation avec la femme porteuse disparait par l'effet de l'adoption plénière et cette femme n'a plus aucun droit ni obligation vis-à-vis de l'enfant (seuls les empêchements à mariage subsistent). Lorsque la gestation pour autrui suppose l'intervention non seulement d'une femme porteuse mais également d'une donneuse d'ovocytes, celle-ci demeure totalement étrangère à l'enfant : les articles 27 et 56 de la loi du 6 juillet 2007 disposent en effet qu'aucune action relative à la filiation ou à ses

---

[41] Y.-H. Leleu, *Droit des personnes et des familles*, Larcier, Bruxelles 2020, p. 767, note 339.
[42] En Belgique, ce pourrait aussi être un homme porteur transgenre : art. 135/2 de l'ancien Code civil.
[43] Trib. fam. Bruxelles, 12.12.2017, *Act. dr. fam.*, 2019, p. 150.

effets patrimoniaux n'est ouverte aux donneurs, ni aux receveurs ou à l'enfant issu du don contre le donneur.

Si la mère porteuse refuse d'exécuter la convention et de confier l'enfant aux parents d'intention, il ne paraît pas possible de poursuivre judiciairement l'exécution forcée de la convention. Celle-ci apparaît en effet, en l'absence de toute disposition légale, frappée de nullité pour violation des principes d'indisponibilité du corps et de l'état des personnes ainsi que pour violation du droit inaliénable de la femme qui accouche d'établir sa maternité conformément à l'article 312 de l'ancien Code civil.

2. DIVERSITÉ ET PLURALITÉ DES FONCTIONS DE LA FAMILLE

Les familles, toutes différentes, assurent globalement les mêmes fonctions : permettre à leurs membres de s'épanouir, partager des charges et des ressources, assurer en réseau une entraide.

En différenciant cinq fonctions des familles, d'après les bénéficiaires et la nature économique ou matérielle de ces fonctions, nous pourrons distinguer, d'une part, la *reconnaissance* par le droit des fonctions familiales et, d'autre part, la *protection* que le droit accorde à ces fonctions.

Le système juridique reconnaît une fonction de la famille quand des normes permettent son accomplissement au sein de la famille. Le droit protège la fonction quand il encourage ou sanctionne cet accomplissement.

En décrivant l'intensité plus ou moins forte de la protection juridique d'une fonction familiale, il sera possible de relever l'existence ou les traces d'une politique familiale assumée ou inconsciente, dont le moyen de réalisation serait le droit des personnes et des familles, et ensuite de porter un jugement sur son efficacité dans ce cadre.

Nous centrons le propos sur les besoins et les droits des membres des familles, et plus particulièrement sur ceux des enfants et des personnes vulnérables. Les fonctions assumées par les familles sont exercées par et pour les individus.

Le droit belge reconnaît plusieurs types de familles qu'il caractérise par des statuts ou par des liens juridiques (mariage, cohabitation légale, filiation, adoption, degré de parenté éloigné, …).

Toutes les personnes et toutes les familles bénéficient d'une reconnaissance et d'une protection par la loi, la Constitution et les droits fondamentaux (art. 8 de la Convention européenne des droits de l'homme (ci-après : CEDH), art. 22 et 22*bis* de la Constitution). Mais cette protection varie souvent selon le statut des familles et le lien de parenté. Si des variations de protection apparaissent dénuées de rapport avec les fonctions que la famille doit assumer, mais résultent de choix politiques, il pourrait y avoir des différences de traitement discriminatoires à défaut de justification objective.

2.1. FONCTION 1 – ÉPANOUISSEMENT PERSONNEL DES MEMBRES DE LA FAMILLE

La famille a pour fonction principale de permettre à ses membres de s'épanouir en vue d'atteindre un degré suffisant d'autonomie et de bonheur, grâce à l'amour, l'affection, l'entraide ou le partage qui caractérisent normalement la vie en famille.

Dans notre société, le couple est un moyen pour deux personnes de s'épanouir sur le plan affectif et sexuel. Le couple n'est plus un vecteur d'intégration sociale qui serait prioritaire sur ces projets individuels. Il en résulte une plus grande fragilité des couples, laquelle appelle une protection juridique efficace contre les conséquences négatives de la rupture (fonction 4 – *infra*, 3.4).

Le même constat peut être fait à propos des enfants : la famille est le lieu de leur épanouissement individuel. Ils y sont encadrés par leurs parents tant qu'ils ne sont pas devenus des adultes autonomes.

Cette fonction épanouissante de la famille est reconnue et protégée, mais jusqu'au point où le droit ne peut plus intervenir dans la vie privée sans limiter l'autodétermination de manière disproportionnée.

Comme le droit n'a aucun moyen de garantir l'épanouissement et encore moins le bonheur, la protection juridique de cette fonction consiste à éviter au maximum les situations où la vie en famille restreint les droits et libertés individuels. Ces restrictions furent fortes et nombreuses dans notre système juridique, découlant toutes plus ou moins directement de l'ancienne organisation patriarcale de la famille et de la société.

Les exemples témoignant de la reconnaissance de cette fonction protectrice de la liberté individuelle au sein de la famille sont légion en droit belge, car notre droit est parmi les plus avancés au monde sur le terrain de l'autodétermination.

Le statut juridique du couple – mariage, cohabitation légale – ne diminue plus les droits personnels des partenaires comme dans le passé (ex. obéissance au mari et incapacité de la femme mariée). Actuellement, seul le mariage impose encore des obligations personnelles (cohabitation, assistance, fidélité – art. 213 de l'ancien Code civil), mais elles ne sont pas sanctionnées *in corpore*, et le sont exceptionnellement sous forme financière (en cas de divorce, seule une « *faute grave* » qui a causé la désunion irrémédiable du couple « *peut* » entraîner une perte d'un droit à la pension alimentaire – art. 301, §5, de l'ancien Code civil).[44]

---

[44] S. Brouwers, « De 'zware fout' als uitsluitingsgrond voor een uitkering na echtscheiding », *R.A.B.G.*, 2008, p. 732 ; G. Hiernaux, « Le divorce et la séparation de corps » in D. Carré et al. (éd.), *Droit des personnes et des familles. Chronique de jurisprudence 2011-2016*, Larcier, Bruxelles 2018, pp. 215 et s., n° 223 et s. ; G. Hiernaux, « L'adultère, la 'faute grave' et le droit du divorce », *Rev. trim. dr. fam.*, 2012, p. 319 ; A.-Ch. Van Gysel, « Quelques questions au sujet de la pension alimentaire après divorce » in Y.-H. Leleu (dir.), *Divorce et aliments*, Bruylant, Bruxelles 2013, pp. 103 et s.

Les autres statuts ne contiennent aucune mesure restrictive de l'autodétermination (les cohabitants légaux ne doivent pas cohabiter ni respecter une obligation de fidélité).

L'ouverture du mariage aux personnes de même sexe en 2003 (art. 143, al. 1er, de l'ancien Code civil) protège la liberté de se marier des personnes qui en étaient empêchées pour des raisons morales ou à cause du lien ancien entre mariage et procréation. De même, l'ouverture de l'adoption aux parents de même sexe en 2006, et de la procréation médicalement assistée en 2007, a permis aux enfants accueillis par des couples de même sexe de s'épanouir en famille quel que soit leur mode d'accueil dans celle-ci (fonction 2 – *infra*, 3.2).[45]

La prévention des mariages forcés (art. 146*ter* de l'ancien Code civil) et des violences conjugales (art. 1253*ter*/5, al. 3, du Code judiciaire) prouve à la fois que la famille peut devenir un lieu de souffrance et qu'il est nécessaire de protéger la liberté individuelle des membres de la famille.

En matière biomédicale, l'autodétermination des personnes faisant partie d'une famille est protégée dans des situations cruciales pour la vie ou l'épanouissement des personnes (euthanasie, arrêt de traitement, IVG, transgendérisme).

Le patient qui demande l'euthanasie doit donner son accord pour que les « *proches* » qu'il désigne soient informés de sa demande (art. 3, §2, 5°, de la loi du 28 mai 2002 relative à l'euthanasie). La famille peut donc être tenue à l'écart d'un projet d'euthanasie comme de sa réalisation.

Une décision d'arrêt de traitement médical, même susceptible d'entraîner la mort, est prise par le patient seul. Ni le médecin ni les membres de la famille ne peuvent s'y opposer (art. 8, §4, de la loi du 22 août 2002 relative aux droits du patient). Si un patient ne peut pas exprimer sa volonté, c'est en priorité son mandataire ou son représentant légal qui exprimera un consentement de substitution. Les membres de la famille n'interviennent qu'en l'absence de représentant et dans un ordre fondé sur leur proximité de fait (l'époux ou le partenaire passe avant les parents – art. 14 de la loi du 22 août 2002 relative aux droits du patient).[46] Au contraire, dans les systèmes juridiques où le médecin doit consulter la famille

---

[45] Sur ces deux réformes : J.-L. Renchon, « Mariage et homosexualité », *J.T.*, 2002, p. 505, « L'avènement du mariage homosexuel dans le Code civil belge », *Rev. trim. dr. fam.*, 2003, pp. 439 et s., et « Parenté sociale et adoption homosexuelle. Quel choix politique ? », *J.T.*, 2005, p. 125. Sur la question du nom : J.-L. Renchon, « Du nom de l'enfant lors de son adoption au sein d'un couple de même sexe ou d'une manière supplémentaire de gommer la différence des sexes dans l'identité de l'enfant », *Rev. trim. dr. fam.*, 2011, pp. 11 et s. Voy. également : L. Cohen, « L'adoption simple ou plénière de l'enfant issu d'une gestation pour autrui par le co-parent de même sexe », *Rev. trim. dr. fam.*, 2019, pp. 845 et s. ; M. Demaret, « L'adoption homosexuelle à l'épreuve du principe d'égalité. L'arrêt E.B. contre France », *J.T.*, 2009, pp. 145 et s.

[46] G. Genicot, *Droit médical et biomédical*, 2e éd., Larcier, Bruxelles 2016, pp. 261 et s., « Le grand âge en droit médical, entre ombres et lumière » in *Le droit des seniors. Aspects sociaux et fiscaux*, Anthemis, Louvain-la-Neuve 2010, pp. 328 et s., et « Vulnérabilité et intégrité physique en droit belge. Entre protection renforcée et autonomie encadrée », *Rev. dr. ulg.*, 2019, pp. 132 et s.

en cas d'incapacité du patient, l'intérêt de la collectivité l'emporte sur les droits du patient, ce qui lui enlève une part d'autonomie.[47]

En matière d'IVG (loi du 15 octobre 2018), les femmes ne doivent pas informer leur partenaire.[48]

A fortiori les personnes transgenres ne doivent pas obtenir l'accord de membres de la famille, malgré l'impact important de leurs décisions sur la vie familiale (art. 135/1 et 135/2 de l'ancien Code civil).[49]

La protection de l'autodétermination des personnes en famille doit être conciliée avec la protection des enfants mineurs. La famille assume aussi cette fonction, dans l'intérêt des enfants, mais sous le contrôle de l'autorité pour éviter les abus (fonction 3 – *infra*, 3.3).

Quand un mineur demande l'euthanasie, il fait sa demande à titre personnel si un pédopsychiatre atteste sa capacité de discernement ; ses parents interviennent pour donner leur accord, mais la loi ne prévoit pas de procédure en cas de désaccord (art. 3, §2, 7°, de la loi du 28 mai 2002 relative à l'euthanasie).[50]

De même, un mineur transgenre de plus de 16 ans[51] peut faire seul une demande de modification à l'état civil, mais un pédopsychiatre doit attester sa capacité de discernement et il doit être « *assisté* » par ses parents, qui ne décident pas à sa place (art. 135/1, §10, de l'ancien Code civil).[52] Pour les plus jeunes, l'emprise des parents sur le corps de leurs enfants quand ils sont intersexes fait débat. Les parents ne sont pas légitimes à décider sans garde-fou des interventions chirurgicales irréversibles dont l'issue pourrait diverger de l'identité de genre de l'enfant.[53]

---

[47] En France : G. Genicot, « Arrêt de traitement, droit à la vie, autonomie personnelle et patients vulnérables – Réflexions autour de l'affaire Vincent Lambert », *J.T.*, 2016, p. 17.

[48] Cass., 14.12.2001, *Pas.*, 2001, p. 2129, concl. J. du Jardin ; *J.L.M.B.*, 2002, p. 532, obs. Y.-H. Leleu et G. Genicot ; *J.T.*, 2002, p. 261, obs. C. Trouet (consentement du mari) ; Gand, 08.08.1992, *R.W.*, 1992–1993, p. 366, note T. Balthazar, conf. par Civ. Gand, 07.08.1992, *R.W.*, 1992–1993, p. 370 (consentement du partenaire non marié).

[49] Plus critique : J.-L. Renchon, « Le nouveau régime juridique du changement de sexe », *Rev. trim. dr. fam.*, 2018, pp. 255 et s.

[50] Pour plus de détails : E. Delbeke, « Euthanasie bij minderjarigen », *Rev. dr. santé*, 2014–2015, p. 163 ; G. Genicot, « Rejet du recours en annulation de la loi étendant l'euthanasie aux mineurs : validation d'une évaluation logique et récente », note sous C. const., n° 153/2015 du 29.10.2015, *J.L.M.B.*, 2015, pp. 1933 et s. ; M. Mallien, « L'extension de l'euthanasie aux mineurs non émancipés. Une analyse des conditions requises par les lois des 28 mai 2002 et 28 février 2014 », *J.D.J.*, 2015, n° 342, p. 17.

[51] Pour une critique du seuil d'âge retenu par le législateur : G. Mathieu, A.-C. Rasson et M. Rolain, « L'appréhension des violences subies par les personnes trans* et intersexes au prisme des droits humains : une révolution douce », S. Wattier (dir.), *Les violences de genre au prisme du droit*, Bruxelles, Larcier, 2020, pp. 54 et s.

[52] Si les parents refusent d'assister le mineur, celui-ci peut demander au tribunal de la famille de l'autoriser à poser l'acte assisté d'un tuteur *ad hoc*.

[53] M.-P. Allard, G. Mathieu et A.-C. Rasson, « L'invisibilité des enfants intersexes en droit belge : vers un changement de paradigme ? », *L'enfant et le sexe*, Paris, Dalloz, 2021, pp. 57 et s. ; P. Cannoot, « Do parents really know best ? Informed Consent to Sex Assigning and 'Normalising' Treatment of Minors with Variations of Sex Characteristics » (2021) 23(4) *Culture Health & Sexuality* 564 ; G. Willems, « Les personnes intersexes : à la croisée des genres » in *L'étranger, la veuve et l'orphelin ... Le droit protège-t-il les plus faibles ?*, Larcier, Bruxelles 2020, p. 489.

En matière d'IVG, les parents n'interviennent pas du tout car la protection de l'autodétermination doit être plus forte en raison des conséquences très graves pour l'épanouissement futur de la mère ou pour l'enfant non désiré.[54]

Grâce à ces dispositifs mesurés dans la contrainte, le système juridique donne clairement la priorité à l'autodétermination des membres de la famille sur l'intérêt du groupe (familial ou social). Les tiers habilités par la loi à intervenir dans certaines décisions individuelles (médecin, état civil, parents) ont pour mission non de décider mais de donner effet à la volonté de l'individu. La loi se borne à fixer les conditions de leur intervention au service de la personne. La protection de la société et des valeurs partagées est assurée par des contrôles *a posteriori* ou marginaux (commissions de contrôle, recours judiciaire à la demande de l'officier d'état civil).

Cette première fonction de la famille est dotée d'une reconnaissance et d'une protection fortes. Elle n'est pas liée au statut juridique de la famille (mariage, cohabitation légale, cohabitation de fait).

2.2. FONCTION 2 – ANCRAGE GÉNÉALOGIQUE ET IDENTITAIRE DES ENFANTS

Une des plus importantes fonctions des familles est la procréation ou l'accueil d'enfants qui ne seraient pas biologiquement liés à tous ses membres (double filiation biologique et légale, filiation envers un seul membre de la famille, adoption par le couple, adoption par un membre du couple, adoption de l'enfant du partenaire, parenté socioaffective, accueil temporaire d'enfants, etc.). Cette fonction conditionne l'exercice de la fonction suivante, éducative, de la famille (fonction 3 – *infra*, 3.3).

Elle est, comme la première fonction, dotée d'une reconnaissance et d'une protection fortes. Elle n'est plus liée au statut juridique de la famille (mariage, cohabitation légale, cohabitation de fait).

Les enfants ont tous besoin d'une identité et d'un ancrage généalogique, des besoins protégés par le droit fondamental au respect de la vie privée (art. 8 CEDH ; art. 22 Const.).[55] Le droit des familles reconnaît depuis toujours cette fonction

---

[54] CA, 19.12.1991, n° 39/91, *T.B.P.*, 1992, p. 341 ; *J.T.*, 1992, p. 362, note Ph. Coenraets, obs. S. Van Drooghenbroeck, in *Droit international des droits de l'homme devant le juge national*, Larcier, Bruxelles 1999, p. 61 ; D. Duval-Arnould, « Minorité et interruption volontaire de grossesse », *D.*, 1999, p. 471 ; Y.-H. Leleu et S. Delval, « Autorité parentale et actes médicaux », *J.D.J.*, 2002, n° 214, p. 29 ; M. Veys, « Abortus bij minderjarige en wilsonbekwame patiënten : de rol van de Wet Patiëntenrechten en de noodtoestand », *Rev. dr. santé*, 2006–2007, p. 153.

[55] C. const., arrêt n° 18/2016 du 03.02.2016, B.5.3, *Act. dr. fam.*, 2016, p. 52, note J. Fierens et G. Mathieu ; *J.T.*, 2016, p. 162, note J.-P. Masson ; *J.L.M.B.*, 2016, p. 404, note D. Pire ; *Rev. trim. dr. fam.*, 2016, p. 367, note G. Mathieu ; *R.W.*, 2015–2016, p. 1198, note I. Boone ; *T. Fam.*, 2016, p. 80, note F. Swennen, G. Verschelden, T. Wuyts ; G. Mathieu et G. Willems, « Origines, parentalité et parenté dans la jurisprudence de la Cour européenne des droits de l'homme » in J.-L. Renchon et J. Sosson (éd.), *Filiation et parentalité*, Bruylant, Bruxelles 2013, p. 35.

de la famille, mais élargit depuis quelques décennies sa protection à tous les enfants, sans distinctions selon le type de procréation ou la forme d'accueil dans une structure parentale.

Cette fonction est protégée par le droit de la filiation et de l'adoption qui organisent le rattachement juridique des enfants à leurs parents. Ces matières ont subi de très fortes mutations, car elles étaient à l'origine du Code civil des instruments quasi politiques au service d'une politique familiale méchamment patriarcale. Elles dépendaient aussi des faibles connaissances scientifiques en matière de procréation. Le contexte et les techniques ont bien changé. L'impératif de stabilité des filiations doit composer avec le droit à l'identité. Le droit de la filiation doit respecter les principes d'égalité et de respect de la vie privée, mais aussi une juste proportionnalité des limites juridiques opposées aux recherches d'origines et à l'établissement des filiations.[56]

Le système belge a commencé (1987) par égaliser les filiations et supprimer la plupart des avantages donnés à la procréation dans le mariage.[57] Il n'a pas autorisé l'accouchement sous X qui prive l'enfant d'une filiation.[58]

Deux réformes ultérieures (2003, 2007) ont encadré la procréation médicalement assistée pour répondre au besoin d'accueil d'enfant de tous les auteurs d'un projet parental, sans distinction selon le statut (mariage ou cohabitation), le sexe des parents (même sexe ou sexe différent) ou les auteurs du projet parental (femme seule, gestation pour autrui tolérée).[59]

L'évolution suivante a été de permettre de rattacher des enfants aux auteurs d'un projet parental sans procréation biologique ou même sans la réunion des gamètes des auteurs du projet. L'adoption était déjà une consécration de la notion de projet parental comme base d'ancrage généalogique.[60] La réglementation de la filiation co-maternelle (2014)[61] est une preuve supplémentaire que la filiation

---

[56] Sur ces évolutions, voy. not. : G. Mathieu, *Le secret des origines en droit de la filiation*, Kluwer, Malines 2014 ; G. Mathieu, *Droit de la famille*, Larcier, Bruxelles 2022, pp. 271 et s., et pp. 401 et s.

[57] *Marckx c. Belgique*, n° 6833/74, 13.06.1979, Publ. C.E.D.H., Série A n° 31.

[58] Le droit belge reconnaît néanmoins la validité d'actes de naissance sans mention d'une mère, notamment dans le cadre de la politique de reconnaissances de gestations pour autrui dans l'intérêt de l'enfant : Bruxelles, 05.12.2019, *J.L.M.B.*, 2021, p. 1394, note P. Wautelet.

[59] N. Gallus, *Le droit de la filiation – Rôle de la vérité socio-affective et de la volonté en droit belge*, Larcier, Bruxelles 2009, pp. 311 et s. ; G. Genicot, *Droit médical et biomédical*, 2ᵉ éd., Larcier, Bruxelles 2016, pp. 588 et s.

[60] Sur les réformes récentes : L. Cohen, « Actualités législatives et constitutionnelles en droit de l'adoption » in J. Sosson (éd.), *Actualités législatives en droit de la personne et de la famille*, Larcier, Bruxelles 2018, p. 93.

[61] J.-E. Beernaert et N. Massager, « Loi du 5 mai 2014 instaurant le régime de la comaternité : 'Trois femmes, un homme et un couffin' », *Act. dr. fam.*, 2015, p. 74 ; M. Demaret et E. Langenaken, « La loi portant établissement de la filiation de la coparente : bien dire et laisser faire … », *Rev. trim. dr. fam.*, 2015, pp. 455 et s. ; G. Seghers et F. Swennen, « Meemoederschap zonder adoptie – de wet van 5 mei 2014 tot vaststelling van de afstamming van de meemoeder », *R.G.D.C.*, 2014, p. 483.

peut reposer sur le projet parental, sur une intention d'assumer la fonction de parent.[62] Récemment, la jurisprudence constitutionnelle a forcé le système juridique à permettre l'établissement de la filiation paternelle envers l'homme qui recourt à la procréation médicalement assistée avec sa compagne sans fournir ses propres gamètes.[63] Et une tendance jurisprudentielle émerge pour protéger l'enfant contre une paternité « imposée » par sa mère, en observant notamment si les parents biologiques avaient eu un véritable projet parental lors de sa conception.[64] Un dernier exemple concerne la gestation pour autrui, qui n'est pas réglementée, mais dont la mise en œuvre doit respecter le cadre juridique de la procréation médicalement assistée. Les enfants issus d'une gestation pour autrui peuvent bénéficier d'une double filiation envers les parents d'accueil fondée sur leur projet parental, même dans des cas où l'opération s'est déroulée à l'étranger.[65]

Une avancée parallèle est l'émergence de la proportionnalité dans l'application par le juge de certaines normes en matière de filiation, celles qui limitent des droits fondamentaux.

La Cour constitutionnelle juge disproportionnées et contraires au droit au respect de la vie privée (art. 22 Const. ; art. 8 de la CEDH) les causes légales d'irrecevabilité des actions en matière de filiation qui empêchent le juge d'examiner tous les intérêts en présence pour accueillir ou rejeter une contestation ou une

---

[62] Pour une analyse des fondements possibles : F. Swennen, « Wat is ouderschap ? », *T.P.R.*, 2016, p. 11.

[63] C. const., arrêt n° 19/2019, 07.02. 2019, *T. Fam.*, 2019, p. 135, note P. Senaeve ; *J.T.*, 2019, p. 452, note G. Willems ; *T.J.K.*, 2019, p. 263.

[64] M. Beague, « L'intérêt de l'enfant dans le cadre d'une action en recherche de paternité introduite par la mère à l'encontre d'un homme qui ne veut pas être père », note sous C. const., n° 190/2019 du 28.11.2019 et n° 92/2020 du 18.06.2020, *Rev. trim. dr. fam.*, 2020/4, pp. 988–1010 ; M. Beague et M. Coune, « L'appréciation de l'intérêt de l'enfant face à la paternité imposée », note sous Trib. fam. Brabant wallon (23ᵉ ch.), 21.06.2021 et Liège (10ᵉ ch.), 07.07.2021, *Rev. trim. dr. fam.*, 2021/4, pp. 1147 et s. ; M. Coune, « La place du projet parental et de l'intérêt de l'enfant dans les affaires de paternité imposée », note sous Trib. fam. Namur, div. Namur (2ᵉ ch.), 06.01.2021 et Trib. fam. Namur, div. Namur (2ᵉ ch.), 20.01.2021, *Rev. trim. dr. fam.*, 2021/1, pp. 249–75.

[65] E. Dos Reis, G. Ruffieux, J. Terel et G. Willems, « La maternité de substitution » in H. Fulchiron et J. Sosson (éd.), *Parenté, Filiation, Origines. Le droit de l'engendrement à plusieurs*, Bruylant, Bruxelles 2013, pp. 188 et s. ; N. Gallus, « L'adoption par les parents intentionnels de l'enfant né d'une mère porteuse », *Act. dr. fam.*, 2013, p. 100 ; G. Mathieu et J. Mary, « Gestation pour autrui, filiation et droit international privé : vers une reconnaissance automatique de l'acte de naissance étranger ? », *Rev. trim. dr. fam.*, 2021, pp. 189 et s. ; J. Sosson et G. Mathieu, « L'enfant né d'une gestation pour autrui : quelle filiation ? Quels liens avec la mère porteuse ? » in J. Sosson et G. Schamps (éd.), *La gestation pour autrui. Vers un encadrement ?*, Bruylant, Bruxelles 2013, p. 375 ; J. Sosson et J. Mary, « Gestation pour autrui pratiquée à l'étranger : l'intérêt de l'enfant, sésame d'une reconnaissance en Belgique ? », *Rev. trim. dr. fam.*, 2014, pp. 552 et s. ; P. Wautelet, « La filiation issue d'une gestation pour autrui : quelles règles de droit international privé pour la Belgique ? » in J. Sosson et G. Schamps (éd.), *La gestation pour autrui. Vers un encadrement ?*, Bruylant, Bruxelles 2013, pp. 213 et s.

recherche de filiation.[66] Depuis 2010, dans la plupart des actions, les intérêts des parties doivent être mis en balance par le juge en accordant la prépondérance à l'intérêt de l'enfant.[67]

L'enfant voit ainsi renforcé son droit d'établir sa filiation biologique si tel est son intérêt, même s'il a été élevé par ses parents socio-affectifs, même s'il a attendu très longtemps pour agir, même s'il est issu de parents incestueux.

Par contre, quand ce sont les adultes – parents légaux, parents biologiques – qui agissent à propos de la filiation d'un enfant, pour la contester ou l'établir, la jurisprudence reste sévère et admet que des règles légales fassent obstacle à l'action, parce que ces adultes n'agissent pas nécessairement dans l'intérêt de l'enfant (prescription, veto de l'enfant majeur à sa reconnaissance paternelle, appréciation de l'intérêt de l'enfant lors de la reconnaissance ou de la recherche de paternité en cas d'opposition de la mère ou de l'enfant).

On conclura de ces évolutions que le droit protège fortement la fonction d'accueil de la famille, et spécialement l'intérêt d'un enfant à avoir une double filiation envers ses parents biologiques ou envers les auteurs d'un projet parental. On notera que cette protection est plus forte et plus individualisée que dans le passé.

Parce que les situations familiales se diversifient, le droit législatif est devenu incapable de réglementer toutes les hypothèses qui se présentent en matière de filiation. Le législateur est contraint par la Cour constitutionnelle de partager sa compétence normative avec le juge, pour rendre possibles des décisions individuelles fondées principalement sur les intérêts de l'enfant et des autres protagonistes, et beaucoup moins sur l'intérêt général. L'appréciation des intérêts individuels ne peut être prise en charge que par un juge au fait de la situation concrète d'une famille.[68] Et peu importe si des cas apparemment similaires sont traités différemment, contexte familial exposé à huis clos oblige. La société va d'ailleurs progresser bien plus avec un droit casuel sur-mesure pour tous, qu'avec des lois générales ne pouvant prendre en compte que des modèles anticipés et

---

[66] Prescription des actions, possession d'état, parenté socio-affective dans la famille légale : jurisprudence constante et notamment l'arrêt précité n° 18/2016 de la Cour constitutionnelle du 03.02.2016 (B.7.3 et B.16). Prohibition d'établissement d'une filiation incestueuse : C. const., 09.08.2012, n° 103/2012, *Act. dr. fam.*, 2012, p. 150, note A.-Ch. Van Gysel ; *J.D.J.*, 2012, liv. 319, p. 35, note G. Mathieu et A.-C. Rasson ; *J.L.M.B.*, 2012, p. 1281, note P. Martens ; *T. Fam.*, 2012, p. 219, note T. Wuyts ; *Rev. trim. dr. fam.*, 2013, p. 204, note Y.-H. Leleu et L. Sauveur. Voy. aussi : C. const., 14.07.2022, n°99/2022. *Adde* Loi du 21.12.2018. Pour plus de détails voy. Y.-H. Leleu, « Filiation 2017 : l'intérêt bien pondéré », *Rev. trim. dr. fam.*, 2017, p. 9.

[67] Pour une anticipation et une synthèse intermédiaire : N. Massager, « La prophétie de Gerlo. Réflexion à propos des derniers arrêts de la Cour constitutionnelle en matière de filiation », *Act. dr. fam.*, 2011, p. 130 ; N. Massager et J. Sosson, « Filiation et Cour constitutionnelle » in N. Massager et J. Sosson (éd.), *La Cour constitutionnelle et le droit de la famille*, Anthemis, Limal 2015, p. 33.

[68] Pour une proposition méthodologique : Y.-H. Leleu, « Filiation 2017 : l'intérêt bien pondéré », *Rev. trim. dr. fam.*, 2017, p. 9.

validés par le législateur. L'évolution récente en jurisprudence constitutionnelle et de fond prouve que la fonction d'ancrage identitaire et généalogique des enfants est devenue principalement familiale, voire parentale, et moins un enjeu de société. La société a enfin pris acte de la diversification des familles. La société et les valeurs communes sont protégées par la garantie d'un examen judiciaire des intérêts en présence.

2.3. FONCTION 3 – ÉDUCATION ET ENTRETIEN DES ENFANTS

La fonction de la famille qui découle de l'accueil des enfants (fonction 2 – *supra*, 3.2) est leur éducation et leur entretien matériel.[69] Parce que les enfants ne sont pas autonomes et que la société est intéressée au bien-être de ses membres vulnérables, cette fonction ne peut pas être abandonnée aux parents. Elle doit être contrôlée et sponsorisée (pour les personnes âgées ou malades : fonction 5 – *infra*, 3.5). La reconnaissance juridique de cette fonction implique une protection très forte, sans différence selon le statut du couple parental. Elle comprend l'articulation de l'intervention de la société en appui ou en contrôle des familles (institutions de protection de l'enfance et de la jeunesse, allocations familiales, subsides aux études).

L'autorité parentale est l'institution qui protège la fonction éducative de la famille.[70] Elle est réglementée depuis 1995 sans distinction selon le statut du couple parental ou le genre de ses membres (mariage, cohabitation, vie commune, séparation). La titularité de l'autorité parentale est liée à la parenté (filiation ou adoption), avec pour conséquence que seuls les parents sont titulaires de l'autorité parentale, à l'exclusion de tout autre tiers même s'il s'occupe de l'enfant (beau-parent, parent affectif, famille d'accueil).

Ce principe connaît des exceptions qui prouvent la nécessité d'une évolution vers une plus grande individualisation du droit de l'autorité parentale pour atteindre toutes les situations familiales dans l'intérêt de l'enfant.

Dans les familles recomposées, le beau-parent n'est pas titulaire de l'autorité parentale, et a tout au plus un droit aux relations personnelles avec l'enfant en cas de séparation, à condition qu'il prouve un lien affectif avec lui (art. 375*bis* de l'ancien Code civil).[71]

---

[69] Voy. : J.-L. Renchon, « La fonction parentale au temps du divorce », *Ann. dr. Louvain*, 1994, p. 259 ; J.-L. Renchon (éd.), *L'enfant et les relations familiales internationales*, Bruylant, Bruxelles 2003 ; J.-L. Renchon, « La nouvelle réforme législative de l'autorité parentale », *Rev. trim. dr. fam.*, 1995, p. 361.

[70] J.-L. Renchon, « Bicentenaire du Code civil (1804–2004). De l'autorité parentale. Livre I – Titre IX », *J.T.*, 2004, pp. 269 et s.

[71] S. Cap et J. Sosson, « La place juridique du tiers au lien de filiation » in J.-L. Renchon et J. Sosson (éd.), *Filiation et parentalité*, Bruylant, Bruxelles 2013, pp. 301–10 ; G. Hiernaux, « L'autorité parentale et le rôle des tiers » in N. Gallus (éd.), *Les recompositions familiales.*

Dans les familles déstructurées, l'enfant peut être placé temporairement en famille d'accueil. Les accueillants familiaux peuvent exercer certaines prérogatives de l'autorité parentale (art. 387*quater* et s. de l'ancien Code civil ; réd. L. du 19 mars 2017).[72] Cette situation est la seule où l'autorité parentale est exercée par plusieurs personnes assumant des fonctions éducatives.

Ces aménagements peuvent servir de modèle à un développement futur d'une protection de l'enfant dans un cadre de pluriparentalité. Cette dernière pourrait émerger autant des attentes des parents ou acteurs de la naissance, que de la reconnaissance du besoin de l'enfant à se déterminer lui-même par rapport à ceux-ci.[73]

La nature privée de l'éducation des enfants et les difficultés d'organiser la contrainte laissent une grande marge d'appréciation aux parents. Une caractéristique de la protection de cette fonction familiale est de privilégier l'autonomie des parents. L'autorité n'intervient qu'en cas de désaccord contraire à l'intérêt de l'enfant (art. 374, §1er, al. 2, de l'ancien Code civil – répartition de l'exercice de l'autorité parentale en cas de désaccord ; art. 374, §2, al. 1er, de l'ancien Code civil – priorité aux accords sur l'hébergement des enfants après séparation).[74]

Une autre caractéristique de la protection de la fonction éducative de la famille est son individualisation et sa proportionnalité. Les recours en matière d'autorité parentale en cas de conflits entre les parents laissent une très grande marge d'appréciation au juge (art. 387*bis* de l'ancien Code civil).

Les nouveaux enjeux de la parentalité et de la filiation, Anthemis, Limal 2015, pp. 75 et s. ; M. Mallien, « Les relations personnelles de l'enfant avec ses grands-parents ou avec un tiers qui lui est lié affectivement. Analyse de quelques décisions judiciaires récentes », *Act. dr. fam.*, 2016, pp. 149 et s. ; J.-L. Renchon, « Vers l'octroi de l'autorité parentale à des beaux-parents ? », note sous CA, 08.10.2003, *Rev. trim. dr. fam.*, 2004, pp. 190 et s.

[72] J. Fierens, « La loi du 19 mars 2017 modifiant la législation en vue de l'instauration d'un statut pour les accueillants familiaux », *Act. dr. fam.*, 2017, pp. 138-48 ; A. Jannone et G. Mathieu, « Compétences concurrentes des tribunaux de la jeunesse et de la famille en matière d'autorité parentale et d'accueil familial après la loi du 19 mars 2017 » in F. Mouffe et A. Quevit (coord.), *Quand le protectionnel et le civil s'(en)mêlent – Le nouvel article 7 de la loi du 8 avril 1965*, Larcier, Bruxelles 2021, pp. 36 et s. ; T. Vercruysse, « Burgerrechtelijk statuut voor pleegzorgers – Commentaar bij de wet van 19 maart 2017 », *T. Fam.*, 2018, pp. 6-14.

[73] Y.-H. Leleu, *Droit des personnes et des familles*, 4e éd., Larcier, Bruxelles 2020, pp. 770-71, n° 782-1 et s. La prochaine individualisation sera probablement celle du rattachement de l'enfant à une pluralité plus étendue de parents. Il s'agira de concilier la reconnaissance et la protection des besoins identitaires de l'enfant issu d'une configuration procréative élargie, avec les droits et devoirs des acteurs de sa naissance : I. Boone, *Gedeeld geluk : ouderschap in intentionele meeroudergezinnen*, Intersentia, Mortsel 2016 et « Van co-ouderschap naar intentioneel meerouderschap » in I. Boone et Ch. Declerck (éd.), *Actualia Familierecht: Co-ouderschap Vandaag en Morgen*, die Keure, 2017, p. 79 ; F. Swennen, « Wat is ouderschap ? », *T.P.R.*, 2016, p. 11.

[74] G. Hiernaux, « Difficultés actuelles en matière d'autorité parentale et d'hébergement » in A.-Ch. Van Gysel (éd.), *Filiation, autorité parentale et modalités d'hébergement*, Bruylant, Bruxelles 2011, p. 129.

Les besoins matériels de l'enfant sont aussi assumés par ses deux parents (filiation, adoption) jusqu'à la fin de sa formation (art. 203 de l'ancien Code civil). Cette fonction familiale bénéficie d'une protection juridique plus efficace qu'en matière d'autorité parentale car une contrainte financière est possible. Elle est également caractérisée par la proportionnalité aux besoins des enfants et aux ressources des parents (art 203, §1er, de l'ancien Code civil),[75] et une certaine autonomie contractuelle (art. 1321, §1er, al. 2, du Code judiciaire).

Dans plusieurs situations, d'autres personnes que les parents sont débitrices de l'obligation d'entretien. Dans un couple marié ou en cohabitation légale, l'obligation de contribuer aux charges du mariage ou du ménage inclut les frais d'éducation des enfants issus d'un seul des époux ou partenaires, quand l'autre parent fait défaut (art. 221 et 1477, §3, de l'ancien Code civil).

Si l'enfant est lui-même marié ou cohabitant légal, l'obligation d'entretien se reporte par priorité sur son conjoint si ses ressources sont suffisantes (art. 213, 221 et 1477, § 3, de l'ancien Code civil[76]), jusqu'à une éventuelle rupture du couple.[77]

En cas de décès d'un parent marié ou cohabitant légal, le survivant doit financer l'entretien de l'enfant, mais son obligation est limitée à ce qu'il a recueilli dans la succession (art. 203, §3 et 1477, §5, de l'ancien Code civil).

Enfin, le géniteur à l'égard duquel la filiation n'est pas établie peut être condamné à contribuer à l'entretien de l'enfant (art. 336 de l'ancien Code civil),[78] ou empêché de récupérer les subsides volontairement fournis (obligation naturelle).[79]

Malheureusement, l'éducation et la formation des enfants permettent le développement de pratiques genrées, qui pèsent encore actuellement plus sur les femmes que sur les hommes.[80] Il peut en résulter des préjudices financiers ou personnels (retards de carrière ou de développement personnel), qui appellent une protection juridique pour tous les couples (fonction 4 – *infra*, 3.4).

---

[75] J.-E. Beernaert, N. Dandoy, S. Louis et P.-A. Wustefeld, *Parts contributives : un jeu de hasard ?*, Anthemis, Limal 2019 ; N. Gallus, « L'obligation d'entretien des parents à l'égard des enfants » in Y.-H. Leleu (dir.), *Divorce et aliments*, Bruylant, Bruxelles 2013, pp. 69 et s. Pour une systématisation de la casuistique et des barèmes : S. Louis, « Calcul des parts contributives des père et mère au profit de leurs enfants – Analyse bisannuelle de décisions de jurisprudence », *Rev. trim. dr. fam.*, 2019, p. 159 (et les éditions précédentes).

[76] Les obligations de contribuer aux charges du mariage ou du ménage sont des obligations d'entretien indirectes.

[77] Cass., 20.04. 2007, *Rev. trim. dr. fam.*, 2008, p. 1009.

[78] Liège, 13.10.2010, *Act. dr. fam.*, 2010, p. 175 ; Mons, 28.10.2003, *R.G.D.C.*, 2004, p. 279 ; Y.-H. Leleu, *Droit des personnes et des familles*, 4e éd., Larcier, Bruxelles 2020, pp. 642 et s., n° 677-3 et s.

[79] G. Genicot, « L'obligation naturelle du père biologique de fournir des aliments à son enfant », note sous Liège, 15.06.1998, *R.G.D.C.*, 1999, p. 311, n° 14.

[80] Voy. C. Bessière et S. Gollac, *Le genre du capital. Comment la famille reproduit les inégalités*, La Découverte, Paris 2020.

2.4. FONCTION 4 – MUTUALISATION DES CHARGES ET PRODUCTION DE VALEURS

Une fonction économique des couples est de mutualiser les charges de la vie de famille et de produire de la valeur économique pour assurer la sécurité d'existence des membres de la famille. Cette fonction est assumée au profit des partenaires du couple et des enfants qu'il éduque (fonction 3 – éducation des enfants – *supra*, 3.3). Elle est fondée sur une logique de partage et pas de nécessité ou de besoins (fonction 5 – entraide familiale – *infra*, 3.5).

Au sein du couple, les partenaires assument individuellement cette fonction dans une association économique où sont mises en commun des forces et des ressources parfois différentes (financières et matérielles). Dans de nombreuses familles, la répartition de ces ressources est genrée, souvent au préjudice des femmes et des mères.[81]

La reconnaissance juridique de la solidarité économique dans le couple est nécessaire pour protéger les membres du couple contre d'éventuels déséquilibres entre l'investissement de chacun dans les tâches communes. Le partenaire qui a financé par ses revenus les biens du couple ne doit pas être privilégié en cas de rupture par rapport au partenaire qui a accompli des prestations matérielles durant la vie en couple.

La protection de cette fonction consiste à identifier avec précision à qui appartiennent les biens acquis et produits par le couple pendant la relation (solidarité patrimoniale – régime matrimonial) et comment compenser l'éventuelle perte de revenus ou de niveau de vie subie par un conjoint à la fin du partage des ressources (solidarité alimentaire – pensions alimentaires). La protection juridique de cette fonction devrait être très forte car son accomplissement peut être menacé par des comportements volontaires contraires à l'idéal de solidarité, doublés de déséquilibres dans les rapports de force.

Le droit belge accorde une protection très efficace à cette fonction du couple par le mariage en régime de communauté (art. 2.3.16 et s. du Code civil) et par la pension alimentaire après divorce (art. 301 de l'ancien Code civil).

Le régime de la communauté légale, qui est le droit commun de tous les couples mariés sans contrat de mariage, impose le partage de tous les acquêts quel que soit le niveau de revenus de chacun des époux (art. 2.3.22, §1er, et 2.3.43 du Code civil).[82]

---

[81] Sur l'aggravation de cette situation au moment de la rupture du couple par des biais de genre dans le chef des professions juridiques actrices du règlement des conflits familiaux : C. Bessière et S. Gollac, *Le genre du capital. Comment la famille reproduit les inégalités*, La Découverte, Paris 2020. Voy. aussi : A. Verbeke, E. Alofs, C. Defever et D. Mortelmans, « Gender Inequalities and Family Solidarity in Times of Crisis » in L. Cornelis (éd.), *Finance and Law: Twins in Trouble*, Intersentia, Anvers 2014, p. 57.

[82] Voy. not. Ph. De Page et I. De Stefani, « Les régimes matrimoniaux » in *Traité de droit civil belge*, Bruylant, Bruxelles 2018, pp. 261 et s. ; Y.-H. Leleu, *Droit patrimonial des couples*, 2e éd., Larcier, Bruxelles 2021, pp. 93 et s.

Les époux peuvent toutefois exclure la protection du régime de communauté et choisir un régime de séparation de biens qui n'impose aucune solidarité patrimoniale et laisse aux époux une liberté dans la répartition des biens acquis au moyen des revenus (art. 2.3.61 du Code civil). Ce choix doit être éclairé par le conseil des notaires lors du contrat de mariage.[83] Le juge ne peut pas corriger *a posteriori* les déséquilibres dans une répartition inégale des acquêts, sauf si les époux ont permis son intervention dans le contrat de mariage (correctif judiciaire en équité : art. 2.3.81 du Code civil).[84] Cela n'empêche toutefois pas la jurisprudence de mettre en œuvre des mécanismes d'équité en cas de déséquilibres injustes entre les patrimoines à la dissolution du mariage (enrichissement sans cause).[85]

Le couple non marié est toujours en séparation de biens (cohabitation légale : art. 1478 de l'ancien Code civil ; cohabitation de fait : absence de réglementation), ce qui pose un problème grave car la majorité des jeunes couples belges ne se marie plus[86] et s'engage par conséquent dans un statut sans solidarité patrimoniale sans que ce choix puisse être qualifié juridique ou contractuel.

L'obligation alimentaire après la rupture est également liée au statut du couple, donc au choix des partenaires au début de la vie commune. Seul le divorce donne droit à une pension alimentaire, limitée à la durée du mariage (art. 301 de l'ancien Code civil).[87] La pension n'est plus garantie à vie ni dépendante de la faute, mais vise à compenser une dégradation significative de la situation économique durant le mariage, ou une perte de niveau de vie dans des situations particulières (longue durée du mariage, état de santé dégradé …).[88]

---

[83] Art. 2.3.64, §3, et 2.3.81, §2, al. 2, du Code civil ; art. 9 L. de Ventôse ; Y.-H. Leleu, « La séparation de biens corrigée » in A. Gillard (éd.), *Les régimes matrimoniaux après la loi du 22 juillet 2018*, Larcier, Bruxelles 2019, pp. 82 et s.

[84] J. Sauvage, « Les créances entre époux et la clause d'équité » in M. Van Molle (éd.), *La réforme des régimes matrimoniaux en pratique*, Anthemis, Limal 2019, p. 59.

[85] Cass., 04.02.2022, *J.T.*, 2022, p. 203, note V. Makow ; Cass., 11.06.2021, *J.T.*, 2022, p. 207, note Y.-H. Leleu ; *T. Fam.*, 2021, p. 22, note A. Van Thienen ; Cass., 09.06.2017, *R.G.D.C.*, 2017, p. 502, note F. Deguel ; Cass., 23.10.2014, *R.G.D.C.*, 2015, p. 559, note J. Lambrechts ; Fr. Deguel et V. Makow, « L'enrichissement sans cause et les comptes entre époux séparés de biens : en marche vers un raisonnement jurisprudentiel abouti », *Rev. trim. dr. fam.*, 2020, pp. 363 et s. ; J.-L. Renchon, « Le sort des apports des époux à la communauté conjugale en régime de séparation de biens » in *Liber amicorum Paul Delnoy*, Larcier, Bruxelles 2005, p. 443.

[86] I. Pasteels et D. Mortelmans, « Huwen en scheiden in de levensloop » in D. Mortelmans (éd.), *Scheiding in Vlaanderen*, Acco, Leuven 2011, pp. 65–84.

[87] Pour une synthèse de la jurisprudence et des barèmes indicatifs : N. Dandoy, « Calcul des pensions alimentaires entre époux et après divorce – Analyse bisannuelle de décisions de jurisprudence (2018) », *Rev. trim. dr. fam.*, 2018, p. 761.

[88] Cass., 06.10.2017, *Rev. trim. dr. fam.*, 2018, p. 310 (somm.), note N.D. ; Cass., 03.11. 2016, *Act. dr. fam.*, 2017, p. 58, note D. Carre ; *J.L.M.B.*, 2017, p. 392 ; *R.C.J.B.*, 2018, p. 515, note N. Dandoy ; *T. Fam.*, 2017, p. 272, note C. Van Roy ; Cass., 12.10.2009, *Act. dr. fam.*, 2009, p. 199, note (critique) A.-Ch. Van Gysel ; *T. Fam.*, 2010, p. 71, note (critique) C. Van Roy ; *R.C.J.B.*, 2010, p. 470, note N. Dandoy ; *Rev. trim. dr. fam.*, 2010, p. 553, note N. Dandoy.

Les autres statuts, qui drainent actuellement la majorité des couples, n'entraînent aucune obligation alimentaire lors de la rupture, alors que des préjudices de carrière s'y produisent de la même manière que pour les couples mariés.

La protection de la fonction de solidarité économique au sein du couple apparaît discriminatoire en Belgique, car les différences de traitement entre les statuts du couple n'ont pas de justification raisonnable.[89]

Les traitements différenciés découlent en effet du choix de se marier, de ne pas se marier, ou d'exclure la protection du régime légal. Or l'autonomie des partenaires lors de ce choix est contestable, car ils sont amoureux, au seuil d'un destin qu'ils ne maîtriseront pas entièrement, mais qu'ils veulent entrevoir agréable en tous ses aspects.[90] L'autonomie des partenaires est fallacieuse quand des forces de négociation différentes sont en présence ou si une interdépendance économique s'est installée dès avant le choix.[91] En outre, un tel choix est irréversible sans commun accord sauf par séparation, ce qui s'apparente à une ingérence dans l'autodétermination. Enfin, lier la protection de cette fonction familiale au choix du statut est d'autant plus injustifiable que le besoin de protection peut découler de l'assignation genrée de tâches d'éducation des enfants, lesquelles s'imposent au couple (fonction 3 – *supra*, 3.3).

Une protection juridique forte de la solidarité économique au sein du couple pourrait être utile à tous les couples puisque c'est la vie familiale, avant le statut du couple, qui peut causer des préjudices patrimoniaux.

Une exclusion contractuelle de cette protection doit probablement rester possible, par respect pour l'autonomie de la volonté, mais le consentement des partenaires doit être éclairé par deux professionnels indépendants, avec une « *full disclosure* » des forces économiques en présence.

Tant que le législateur refuse de protéger la fonction familiale de solidarité économique au sein de *tous* les couples, le juge doit pouvoir compenser les

---

[89] Telle ne fut pas la vision du législateur lors de la réforme du 22.07.2018, considérant que le mariage pouvait encore offrir une protection supérieure aux autres statuts, et sans discrimination puisque le choix du couple serait le critère pertinent des différences jugées raisonnables. De même, pour les couples mariés en séparation de biens pure et simple, le législateur de 2018 considère que le choix d'exclure le régime légal, sous le conseil d'un notaire indépendant, est un critère objectif d'une différence de traitement raisonnable entre époux communs en biens et époux séparés de biens.

[90] Sur les motivations non juridiques et la non-pertinence juridique des choix faits par les couples quant à leurs statuts : N. Dethloff, « Contracting in family law: a European perspective » in K. Boele-Woelki, J. Miles et J. Scherpe (dir.), *The Future of Family Property in Europe*, Intersentia, Anvers 2011, pp. 88–89 ; Y.-H. Leleu, *Les collaborations économiques au sein des couples séparatistes : pour une indemnisation des dommages collaboratifs envers et contre tous choix*, Thémis, Montréal 2014.

[91] A.-L. Verbeke, « Gender-ongelijkheid bij zuivere scheiding van goederen. Pleidooi voor een gedwongen en onderhandelde aanpak », *T.E.P.*, 2010, pp. 98–117.

préjudices liés à la vie en couple d'une manière équitable et proportionnée. La jurisprudence comble de mieux en mieux cette lacune et exploite l'enrichissement sans cause avec un haut degré de sécurité juridique grâce à la jurisprudence de la Cour de cassation et la systématisation de la casuistique.[92] Comme en filiation, elle reprendra au législateur sa compétence normative s'il demeure dans l'inertie.

2.5. FONCTION 5 – ENTRAIDE EN CAS DE VULNÉRABILITÉ PHYSIQUE OU FINANCIERE

Les familles doivent protéger leurs membres vulnérables à cause de leur âge ou de leur état de santé, et ceux qui manquent de ressources financières. Cette fonction est reconnue par le droit qui organise la répartition des obligations entre la famille et les institutions de la société, et de plus en plus à charge de la société (ex. : soins de santé, maisons de repos et de soins, allocations familiales, bourses d'études, SECAL, CPAS).[93]

Dans un environnement individualiste et caractérisé par une forte diversification des familles, l'entraide a tendance à diminuer. Mais si des liens se distendent, de nouveaux liens se nouent (par exemple personne de confiance), de sorte que le « *réseau d'entraide* » n'est plus uniquement familial.

La société doit contrôler, contraindre ou compléter l'exercice de cette fonction familiale, en veillant à ne pas détruire par un contentieux induit, des liens familiaux fragilisés par le sentiment de vulnérabilité.

Par ailleurs, l'aide familiale ou sociale aux personnes vulnérables doit être individualisée et professionnalisée pour répondre à leur besoin d'autonomie. La dimension symbolique de cette fonction est double : indiquer qui dans la famille doit aider un proche en difficulté et renforcer l'appartenance d'une personne à un groupe familial et social.

La protection juridique de l'entraide familiale est organisée par les incapacités et l'administration des personnes vulnérables (art. 488/1 et s. de l'ancien Code

---

[92] L'analyse de la jurisprudence favorise la prévisibilité dans un système casuel (Y.-H. Leleu, note sous Cass., 04.06.2020, *J.T.*, 2021, p. 561, n° 9–14). Pour des analyses récentes : Y.-H. Leleu (éd.), *Les relations patrimoniales des couples. Actualités de jurisprudence*, CUP/Anthemis, Limal 2022 ; Y.-H. Leleu et J. Laruelle, « Examen de jurisprudence (2006–2017). Régimes matrimoniaux », *R.C.J.B.*, 2018, n° 154 et s., pp. 490 et s. La jurisprudence « familialise » le droit commun, faute pour le législateur de le faire, comme il l'a fait pour tous les couples aux temps révolus où tous ou presque étaient mariés (sur le concept de familialisation : G. Willems, « La séparation des couples en droit anglais et belge : contribution de droit comparé à la réflexion entre équité et sécurité juridique en droit de la famille », *Rev. dr. int. dr. comp.*, 2016, p. 565).

[93] K. De Vos, « Commentaar bij de wet van 12 mei 2014 tot wijziging van de Davo-wet met het oog op een effectieve invordering van onderhoudsschulden », *T. Fam.*, 2015, p. 202 ; P. Weber, « Service des créances alimentaires : du neuf en ce qui concerne les avances et le recouvrement des créances alimentaires », *Act. dr. fam.*, 2015, p. 3.

civil) et par l'obligation alimentaire au sein de la famille élargie (art. 205 et s. de l'ancien Code civil). Elle est fortement individualisée et proportionnée afin de préserver, d'une part, l'autonomie de la personne vulnérable et, d'autre part, les capacités des membres de la famille. Le juge y exerce une fonction centrale, la loi fournissant le cadre d'exercice de son pouvoir de décision.

Le droit des incapacités concerne les adultes car les enfants sont protégés par leurs parents (fonction 3 – *supra*, 3.3). La loi du 17 mars 2013 a réformé la matière[94] en privilégiant une détermination de l'incapacité judiciaire et limitée au strict nécessaire (art. 492, al. 1er, de l'ancien Code civil), conformément aux principes de droit international de nécessité, subsidiarité et proportionnalité.[95] La loi favorise l'implication de la famille en favorisant le mandat extrajudiciaire confié à un proche (art. 490 et 492, al. 1er et 3, de l'ancien Code civil),[96] la gestion par les parents (art. 500 de l'ancien Code civil) et la désignation de personnes de confiance (art. 501 de l'ancien Code civil). Les actes relatifs au patrimoine (par exemple gestion des revenus, vente de biens, testament, donation) font l'objet d'un contrôle judiciaire strict et de redditions de compte détaillées. Le régime des actes personnels (ex. mariage, divorce, actes médicaux, …) est plus radical par respect pour l'autodétermination. Si la personne en est déclarée incapable dans l'ordonnance initiale, ils pourront encore être accomplis par elle après autorisation du juge, mais ils ne pourront l'être par son représentant si la personne n'est plus apte (art. 497/2 de l'ancien Code civil).

L'obligation alimentaire de droit commun protège un devoir de solidarité différent de celui entre parents et enfants (fonction 3 – *supra*, 3.3) ou entre époux (fonction 4 – *supra*, 3.4). Il ne s'agit pas de partager des ressources ou des niveaux de vie, mais de fournir le minimum pour vivre en cas de besoin.[97] Elle suppose des liens familiaux légaux (filiation, adoption), une nécessité appréciée par le juge (état de besoin) et des ressources suffisantes chez le débiteur. Elle est parfois élargie à la famille par alliance (art. 206 de l'ancien) ou reportée sur la succession d'un débiteur dans les limites de celle-ci (art. 205*bis* de l'ancien Code civil).

---

[94] F. Deguel, « Les personnes majeures protégées », *Rép. not.*, t. I, Les personnes, l. 8, Larcier, Bruxelles 2021 ; F. Deguel, « Pot-pourri pour les personnes majeures protégées », *J.T.*, 2019, p. 369 ; N. Gallus, *La protection des personnes vulnérables à la lumière de la loi du 17 mars 2013* (F.R.N.B. éd.), Bruylant, Bruxelles 2014 ; N. Gallus et T. Van Halteren, *Le nouveau régime de protection des personnes majeures. Analyse de la loi du 17 mars 2013*, Bruylant, Bruxelles 2014.

[95] Convention des Nations unies du 13.12.2006 relative aux droits des personnes handicapées.

[96] E. Beguin et J. Fonteyn, « Le mandat de protection extrajudiciaire », *Rev. not. belge*, 2014, pp. 463 et s.; C. Castelein, « Enkele notariële bedenkingen inzake de redactie van de lastgevingsovereenkomst inhoudende een buitengerechtelijke bescherming » in *Liber amicorum André Michielsens*, Kluwer, Malines 2015, p. 259 ; F. Deguel, « Le nouveau mandat de protection extrajudiciaire » in B. Kohl (éd.), *Le mandat dans la pratique. Questions choisies et suggestions de clauses*, Larcier, Bruxelles 2014, p. 201.

[97] N. Gallus, « Les aliments », *Rép. not.*, t. I, l. IV, Larcier, Bruxelles 2005.

La nature familiale de cette fonction se révèle dans les règles de hiérarchie créées par la jurisprudence quand plusieurs membres de la famille sont appelés à l'aide alimentaire.[98] La proportionnalité est prescrite par la loi (art. 208 de l'ancien Code civil) et se manifeste aussi lorsque plusieurs débiteurs de même rang sont appelés : l'obligation est répartie sur chaque débiteur en proportion de ses ressources personnelles.

---

[98] Cass., 16.03.1995, *Div. Act.*, 1996, p. 28, note E. de Wilde d'Estmael ; *R.W.*, 1995–1996, p. 743, note J. Roodhoofdt ; *R. Cass.*, 1995, p. 305, note J. Gerlo.

VERS LA RECONNAISSANCE JURIDIQUE DE LA DIVERSITÉ DES FAMILLES

Portrait québécois dans le contexte canadien

Michelle GIROUX et Louise LANGEVIN

1. Le traitement des différentes formes familiales 191
   1.1. La biparenté comme fondement en droit québécois 191
        1.1.1. La recomposition familiale 191
        1.1.2. La multiparenté : hésitation au Québec et reconnaissance dans d'autres provinces. 193
   1.2. L'union du couple limitée à deux personnes. 195
   1.3. Une reconnaissance partielle de la pluralité des familles 197
        1.3.1. La filiation additive et les ententes facilitant le maintien des relations en matière d'adoption 197
        1.3.2. L'adoption coutumière autochtone 198
        1.3.3. La reconnaissance de parents non-binaires. 199
2. L'établissement de la parenté dans le contexte de la procréation assistée et de la maternité de substitution 200
   2.1. La procréation assistée. 201
   2.2. La maternité de substitution. 202
        2.2.1. Au Québec. 202
        2.2.2. En Colombie-Britannique et en Ontario 205
3. Conclusion 208

À l'image de la société, la famille évolue. Le modèle patriarcal fondé sur la biparenté hétérosexuelle et génétique ne peut être imposé par le législateur,[1] qui

---

[1] Voir notamment M. Giroux, L. Brunet, M. Gross et J. Courduriès, « La difficile conciliation entre le vécu des familles conçues avec assistance médicale à la procréation et le droit : perspectives franco-québécoise » dans M.-X. Catto et K. Martin-Chenut, *Procréations assistées et filiation : PMA et GPA au prisme du droit, des sciences sociales et de la philosophie*, Mare et Martin, Paris 2019, pp. 81–112.Voir aussi M. Giroux, C. Bensa et V. Gruben, « Les liens parentaux en droit québécois : quelle place pour la fiction biologique à l'aube d'une réforme du droit de la famille ? » (2021) 55(3) *Revue Juridique Thémis de l'Université de Montréal* 705.

ne peut discriminer entre la « bonne » famille et d'autres modèles d'organisation familiale. Les droits fondamentaux de toutes les personnes doivent être respectés. Ainsi, les territoires et provinces canadiennes ont déjà entamé un processus de révision de leur droit pour reconnaître la diversité des familles.

Dans la fédération canadienne, le droit de la famille constitue une compétence partagée. Le gouvernement fédéral peut légiférer dans le domaine du mariage (règles de fond) et du divorce. Les provinces peuvent intervenir en matière de propriété et droits privés,[2] ce qui inclut les rapports interpersonnels, par exemple le droit des contrats et de la famille. Le droit de la famille varie donc selon la province. Cependant, on y retrouve de nombreuses similarités.[3] Dans le domaine de la procréation assistée, le gouvernement fédéral interdit certaines activités[4] et règlemente l'administration et l'application de la loi.[5] Ce sont les provinces qui édictent les lois encadrant les techniques de procréation assistée,[6] le consentement aux soins médicaux et la filiation des enfants qui en sont issus.

Le Canada est un pays bijuridique, puisque deux traditions juridiques, la *common law* et le droit civil, coexistent sur son territoire. Le Québec connaît deux systèmes juridiques. Il s'agit de la seule province canadienne dans cette situation. D'origine française, le Code civil du Québec contient le droit commun, c'est-à-dire qu'il porte sur les personnes, les rapports entre les personnes et les biens.[7] Le droit de la famille, réformé en 1980, y est inclus. Bien qu'il ait subi quelques ajustements au cours des décennies, il doit être revu en profondeur pour refléter les nouvelles réalités familiales. Ce processus est déjà entrepris.[8] Quant au droit public (les relations entre l'État et les personnes), il est d'origine britannique.

---

[2] Art. 92 (13), *Loi constitutionnelle de 1867* (R.U.), 30 & 31 Vict, c 3, reproduit dans LRC 1985, annexe II, n° 5.

[3] Voir un projet d'uniformisation du droit de la famille au Canada : *Loi uniforme sur le statut de l'enfant (2010)*, Conférence pour l'harmonisation des lois au Canada.

[4] Loi sur la procréation assistée, LC 2004, c. 2, art. 5–9, selon sa compétence en matière de droit criminel, art. 91 (27) Loi constitutionnelle de 1867, 30 & 31 Victoria, ch. 3 (R.U.).

[5] Loi sur la procréation assistée, LC 2004, c. 2, art. 45–58. Plusieurs articles de cette loi ont été déclarés inconstitutionnels, car ils empiétaient sur les pouvoirs provinciaux en matière de santé. *Renvoi relatif à la Loi sur la procréation assistée*, 2010 CSC 6. Le Canada ne possède pas de législation nationale qui encadre tous les aspects de la procréation assistée.

[6] Le Québec est la seule province qui a adopté une loi dans ce domaine. Loi sur les activités cliniques et de recherche en matière de procréation assistée, RLRQ c. A-5.01.

[7] Voir Code civil du Québec, RLRQ c. CCQ-1991, disposition préliminaire (CcQ).

[8] *Projet de loi 2 – Loi portant sur la réforme du droit de la famille en matière de filiation et modifiant le Code civil en matière de droits de la personnalité et d'état civil*, 2e session, 42e législature, Québec, 2021. Une partie de ce projet de loi a été adopté au printemps 2022 : *Loi portant sur la réforme du droit de la famille en matière de filiation et modifiant le Code civil en matière de droits de la personnalité et d'état civil*, LQ 2022 c 22. Un rapport d'experts a précédé le dépôt du projet de loi : Québec, Comité consultatif sur le droit de la famille, A. Roy (prés.), *Pour un droit de la famille adapté aux nouvelles réalités conjugales et familiales*, Thémis, Montréal 2015.

Notre texte est divisé en deux grandes parties : d'abord, le traitement des différentes formes familiales ; ensuite, l'établissement de la parenté dans le contexte de la procréation assistée et de la maternité de substitution. Nous terminons en conclusion par une réflexion sur les fonctions de la famille. Comme le droit de la famille canadien varie de province en province, nous nous sommes concentrées sur le droit québécois, en soulignant les réformes dans les autres provinces.

1. LE TRAITEMENT DES DIFFÉRENTES FORMES FAMILIALES

La biparenté demeure le fondement de la famille en droit québécois, bien que d'autres provinces reconnaissent la multiparenté. L'union du couple est limitée à deux personnes, mais certains tribunaux canadiens ont admis le polyamour. Enfin, dans certains domaines, le droit québécois ouvre la porte à la pluralité des familles.

1.1. LA BIPARENTÉ COMME FONDEMENT EN DROIT QUÉBÉCOIS

À la suite d'une rupture conjugale, de nouvelles figures parentales entrent dans la vie des enfants. Se pose la question de leur reconnaissance sur le plan juridique. Au côté du modèle biparental, des adultes veulent que leur modèle de famille triparental soit reconnu.

1.1.1. La recomposition familiale

Fondé sur la biparenté, le droit québécois de la famille ne reconnaît pas le beau-parent (le-la conjoint-e du parent de l'enfant). Plusieurs experts ont demandé une reconnaissance juridique de ce dernier.[9]

Lors de la rupture conjugale, le statut juridique du beau-parent varie en fonction du type de lien conjugal qui l'unit au parent de l'enfant. Si les parties sont mariées et que l'une d'entre elles ou les deux s'adressent au tribunal pour obtenir le divorce, le principe « qui tient lieu de parent à l'enfant » introduit en 1968[10] pourrait leur être opposé. En effet, l'article 2 (2) de la Loi

---

[9] Voir notamment D. Goubau et M. Chabot, « Recomposition familiale et multiparentalité : un exemple du difficile arrimage du droit à la famille contemporaine » (2018) 59(4) *Cahiers de droit* 889 ; Comité consultatif sur le droit de la famille, A. Roy (prés.), *Pour un droit de la famille adapté aux nouvelles réalités conjugales et familiales*, Thémis, Montréal 2015, pp. 207–216, recommandations 4.1–4.6.

[10] Loi concernant le divorce, SC 1967–68, c. 24.

(fédérale) sur le divorce[11] permet au tribunal d'ordonner à l'époux du parent « qui tient lieu de parent à l'enfant » le paiement d'une pension alimentaire au profit de l'enfant à charge, selon les critères définis par la Cour suprême du Canada (la plus haute instance canadienne) dans l'arrêt *Chartier*.[12] Par ailleurs, le beau-parent « qui tient lieu de parent » pourra en revendiquer la garde ou, à tout le moins, bénéficier de droits d'accès. Le beau-parent à qui le tribunal confiera la garde de l'enfant ne deviendra pas pour autant titulaire de l'autorité parentale ; hormis les décisions courantes qui s'attachent accessoirement à la garde, les attributs de l'autorité parentale, tout comme la tutelle légale, resteront l'apanage du parent. De même, l'application du principe « qui tient lieu de parent » n'entraînera la création d'aucun droit successoral entre l'enfant et son beau-parent.[13] Tel que précisé dans l'arrêt *Chartier*, le beau-parent sera reconnu « avoir tenu lieu de parent », s'il a agi auprès de l'enfant comme un véritable parent de remplacement, témoignant ainsi de sa volonté claire d'assumer sur une base continue et permanente les responsabilités que la loi attribue normalement aux parents.[14]

Contrairement au droit privé des autres provinces, le Code civil du Québec – qui ne reconnaît pas les conjoint-e-s de fait en cas de rupture[15] – ne prévoit pas de règle équivalente à l'article 2 (2) (le principe « qui tient lieu de parent ») de la Loi (fédérale) sur le divorce. En principe, l'arrêt *Chartier* n'a donc aucune pertinence à l'égard du beau-parent qui n'est pas marié au parent de l'enfant.[16] Peu importe le rôle qu'il aura tenu auprès de ce dernier durant la vie commune, le beau-parent non marié ne pourra donc se voir imposer l'obligation de lui verser des aliments, pas plus qu'il ne pourra revendiquer de droits spécifiques en matière de garde et d'accès. Tout au plus pourra-t-il, comme tout autre tiers, invoquer le principe de l'intérêt de l'enfant dans le but de maintenir sa relation avec lui. Le fardeau de preuve lui incombera alors de repousser la présomption selon laquelle l'intérêt de l'enfant commande d'être sous la garde de ses parents, tel que la Cour suprême du Canada l'a spécifié.[17]

---

[11] LRC 1985, c. 3 (2e suppl.) (ci-après « Loi sur le divorce »).
[12] Loi sur le divorce, art. 15.1 (1); *Chartier c. Chartier* [1999] 1 RCS 242.
[13] Notons que la Loi C-78 (Loi modifiant la Loi sur le divorce, la Loi d'aide à l'exécution des ordonnances et des ententes familiales et la Loi sur la saisie-arrêt et la distraction de pensions et apportant des modifications corrélatives à une autre loi, 1re session, 42e législature, 64–65–66–67–68 Elizabeth II, 2015–2016–2017–2018–2019), sanctionnée en juin 2019 (entrée en vigueur mars 2021), permet au tribunal d'attribuer des responsabilités décisionnelles à l'égard de l'enfant non seulement aux époux (ou ex-époux) et à ses parents, mais également à une personne qui « lui en tient lieu ou a l'intention d'en tenir lieu ». Voir l'article 12 introduisant dans la Loi sur le divorce les nouveaux articles 16.1 et 16.3. La loi vient ainsi codifier les principes de l'arrêt *T.V.F. et D.F. c. G.C.* [1987] 2 RCS 244.
[14] *Chartier c. Chartier* [1999] 1 RCS 242.
[15] Les lois à caractère social et fiscal reconnaissent les conjoint-e-s de fait.
[16] *Chartier c. Chartier* [1999] 1 RCS 242.
[17] *T.V.F. et D.F. c. G.C.* [1987] 2 RCS 244. Voir aussi J. Pineau et M. Pratte, *La famille*, Thémis, Montréal 2006 ; A. Roy, « Le droit de la famille à l'heure des choix » (2019) 2 *Cours de perfectionnement du notariat* 97.

Au nom du droit à l'égalité de tous les enfants (art. 522 CcQ), les tribunaux ont appliqué le principe « qui tient lieu de parent » à des conjoint-e-s de fait lorsque le conjoint-e du parent de l'enfant tient, dans les faits, lieu de second parent pour l'enfant.[18]

Le beau parent obtient droit de citer dans le nouvel article 611 CcQ, adopté en juin 2022, dans le cadre de la réforme partielle de la filiation. S'il s'agit d'une personne « significative » et si l'intérêt de l'enfant le commande le maintien de relations personnelles sera accordé. Le consentement de l'enfant de 14 ans et plus est requis pour maintenir des relations. Il sera intéressant de voir l'interprétation qu'en feront les tribunaux; s'agit-il d'une simple codification de la jurisprudence actuelle ou davantage?

1.1.2. La multiparenté : hésitation au Québec et reconnaissance dans d'autres provinces

Le droit québécois n'admet pas, pour le moment, plus de deux parents (qui peuvent être de même sexe ou de sexes différents). La Cour d'appel a refusé de reconnaître la paternité d'un homme, qui était le géniteur, tout en s'étant impliqué comme figure paternelle auprès de l'enfant, mais cet homme et les deux mères avaient décidé dans un document écrit que les deux mères seraient déclarées comme parents à son acte de naissance. Le tribunal distingue entre la parenté (notion juridique qui reconnaît la filiation d'une personne) et la parentalité (notion sociologique qui reconnaît le rôle joué par une personne dans la vie d'un enfant, sans pour autant lui accorder un lien de filiation au sens juridique). La Cour d'appel ne se prononce pas pour ou contre la pluriparenté.[19] Dans le projet de loi réformant le droit de la famille déposé en octobre 2021,[20] le législateur québécois a décidé de ne pas admettre la pluriparenté en raison de l'absence d'études sur les effets de cette forme de parenté sur les enfants.

---

[18] *Droit de la famille – 072895*, 2007 QCCA 1640, a proposé une interprétation plus large des articles 32 CcQ et 39 Charte des droits et libertés, RLRQ c. C-12.

[19] Art. 538.2 CcQ. Voir *Droit de la famille – 191677*, 2019 QCCA 1386, conf. pour d'autres motifs *Droit de la famille – 18968*, 2018 QCCS 1900.

[20] *Projet de loi 2 – Loi portant sur la réforme du droit de la famille en matière de filiation et modifiant le Code civil en matière de droits de la personnalité et d'état civil*, 2e session, 42e législature, Québec, 2021. La partie du projet de loi portant sur la filiation n'a pas été adoptée en raison du déclenchement des élections provinciales au Québec à l'automne 2022. En revanche, le nouvel art. 611 CcQ fait partie des quelques articles adoptés et entré en vigueur en juin 2022 (projet de loi 2 ; LRQ 2022, c 22) et vient spécifier les trois conditions applicables au maintien des relations personnelles entre l'enfant et l'ex-conjoint.e de son parent : 1. Les liens entre eux doivent être significatifs ; 2. Le maintien de ces liens doit être dans l'intérêt de l'enfant ; et 3. L'enfant de 10 ans et plus consent au maintien de ces liens. Il y est également prévu que le tribunal peut trancher en cas de refus de l'enfant de moins âgé entre 10 ans et moins de 14 ans ou de désaccord entre les parties. Dans tous les cas, le consentement de l'enfant de 14 ans et plus est requis pour assurer le maintien de ces relations. Notons que les conditions 2 et 3 s'appliquent également pour le maintien des relations entre les petits enfants et leurs grands-parents.

La situation est différente au Canada anglais où soit la *common law*,[21] soit la loi[22] permettent la pluriparenté. Nous présentons ici la situation juridique dans deux provinces qui ont réformé leur droit dans ce domaine, la Colombie-Britannique et l'Ontario.

En Colombie-Britannique, la loi prévoit la possibilité de trois parents[23] lorsque l'enfant est conçu par procréation assistée[24]. Deux situations sont visées : la femme qui accouche est une mère porteuse ou elle ne l'est pas (elle porte pour elle-même). Dans un contrat de préconception, une femme porteuse qui accouchera d'un enfant décide avec un ou deux parents intentionnels (de même sexe ou de sexes différents) d'être les parents légaux de l'enfant à concevoir par procréation assistée. Il peut aussi s'agir d'une femme qui accouchera d'un enfant (elle porte pour elle-même), son ou sa conjoint-e ainsi que le donneur de gamètes qui planifient par contrat d'être les parents légaux de l'enfant à venir.[25] Si ces personnes n'ont pas changé d'idée avant la conception de l'enfant, elles seront les parents de l'enfant sans la nécessité d'obtenir une ordonnance d'un tribunal pour connaître leur lien de filiation.[26] Une procédure administrative de reconnaissance de la filiation s'applique.

Un tribunal de la Colombie-Britannique a aussi reconnu la triparenté à un enfant (né d'une relation sexuelle) dont les parents biologiques font partie d'une relation polyamoureuse (un « trouple »).[27] La seconde mère demandait l'établissement de son lien de filiation. Le tribunal a accepté en preuve que les trois adultes avaient l'intention d'être les parents légaux de l'enfant et s'en occupaient à parts égales. Même si la loi sur le droit de la famille de 2013 n'admettait pas la triparenté pour un enfant né d'une relation sexuelle, le tribunal a utilisé sa compétence *parens patriae* (qui lui accorde une discrétion pour combler les

---

[21] La Cour suprême de Terre-Neuve et Labrador (Unified Family Court) a reconnu la triparenté dans le cadre d'une relation polyamoureuse. *Reference re: Children's Law Act (Nfld. & Lab.)*, 2018 NLSC 71.

[22] En Ontario : Loi portant réforme du droit de l'enfance, LRO 1990, c. C.12. En Colombie-Britannique : Family Law Act, SBC 2011, c. 25. Au Manitoba : Loi modifiant la Loi sur l'obligation alimentaire, LM 2021, c. 63. En Saskatchewan : Loi de 2020 sur le droit de l'enfance, LS 2020, c. 2.

[23] Selon l'article 30 (1) (b), Family Law Act, SBC 2011, c. 25, lorsque l'enfant est conçu par procréation assistée, le troisième parent doit être soit la mère porteuse ou un donneur de gamètes. La situation dans laquelle un couple lesbien et un couple gai (quatre parents) conçoivent un enfant est exclue.

[24] L'exigence de la procréation assistée exclut les personnes mariées ou en relation conjugale qui conçoivent leur enfant par relation sexuelle avec une personne autre que leur conjoint-e, mais avec l'intention d'élever l'enfant avec leur conjoint-e.

[25] Family Law Act, SBC 2011, c. 25, art. 30. Voir C. Rogerson, « Determining Parenthood in Cases Involving Assisted Reproduction: An Urgent Need for Provincial Legislative Action » dans T. Lemmens et al. (dirs), *Regulating Creation, the Law, Ethics, and Policy of Assisted Human Reproduction*, University of Toronto Press, Toronto, 2017, pp. 100 et s. Il pourrait y avoir plus de trois parents, voir F. Kelly, « Multiple-Parent Families Under British Columbia's New Family Law Act: A Challenge to the Supremacy of the Nuclear Family or a Method by which to Preserve Biological Ties and Opposite-Sex Parenting? » (2014) 47 *University of British Columbia Law Review* 565.

[26] Family Law Act, SBC 2011, c. 25, art. 30 (2).

[27] *British Columbia Birth Registration No. 2018-XX-XX5815*, 2021 BCSC 767.

silences législatifs) pour reconnaître l'autre mère au nom de l'intérêt de l'enfant. Il a conclu que le législateur n'avait pas envisagé cette possibilité de triparenté pour un enfant né d'une relation sexuelle. La triparenté a aussi été reconnue dans une autre province canadienne qui n'a pas réformé son droit de la famille. Le tribunal a permis la triparenté d'un enfant issu d'une relation polyamoureuse, en raison de l'égalité entre tous les enfants, peu importe les circonstances de leur naissance, malgré le silence de la loi à ce sujet.[28]

En Ontario, quatre parents d'intention (le « substitut », c'est-à-dire la mère porteuse, est exclu[29]) peuvent être reconnus, si ceux-ci ont donné leur consentement par écrit avant la conception de l'embryon.[30] Par exemple, il peut s'agir d'un couple gai et d'un couple lesbien qui désirent un enfant. Une des femmes porte l'enfant dont le père biologique est l'un des hommes. Dans ce dernier cas, il n'y a pas de mère porteuse. Une procédure administrative de reconnaissance de la filiation s'applique. Avec l'autorisation du tribunal, plus de quatre parents peuvent être reconnus.[31]

1.2. L'UNION DU COUPLE LIMITÉE À DEUX PERSONNES

Le mariage est, sur le plan civil, l'union légitime de deux personnes, à l'exclusion de toute autre personne.[32] Les autres types d'union, tels que la polygamie ou le polyamour, ne sont pas reconnus en droit québécois.

La polygamie constitue un crime au Canada (art. 293 Code criminel canadien). La validité constitutionnelle de cet article a été maintenue par les tribunaux.[33] Les hommes et les femmes polygames peuvent donc être condamnés et emprisonnés, quoiqu'il y ait eu très peu de condamnation dans ce domaine. Les autorités de la protection de la jeunesse peuvent prendre en charge les enfants vivant dans des familles polygames et dont la sécurité est menacée.

---

[28] *Reference re: Children's Law Act (Nfld. & Lab.)*, 2018 NLSC 71.
[29] Voir définition : Loi portant réforme du droit de l'enfance, LRO 1990, c. C.12, art. 2 « parent d'intention » : partie à une convention de gestation pour autrui, à l'exclusion du substitut.
[30] Ibid., art. 10 (2).
[31] Ibid., art. 11.
[32] Loi sur le mariage civil, LC 2005, c. 33, art. 2.
[33] *Reference re: Section 293 of the Criminal Code of Canada*, 2011 BCSC 1588 (CanLII) (poursuite contre deux dirigeants de la communauté mormone de Bountiful en Colombie-Britannique pour avoir pratiqué la polygamie. Ces derniers soutenaient que les lois qui régissent la polygamie allaient à l'encontre du droit à la liberté de religion garanti par la Charte canadienne des droits et libertés, partie 1 de la Loi constitutionnelle de 1982 (annexe B de la Loi sur le Canada (1982, R.-U., c. 11))). En juillet 2017, la Cour supérieure de la Colombie-Britannique a condamné les deux hommes pour polygamie. Ils ont été condamnés à des peines avec sursis, à purger dans la collectivité. Voir M. Bailey, « Should Polygamy be a Crime ? » dans J. Bennion et L. Fishbayn Joffe (dirs), *The Polygamy Question*, Utah State University Press, Logan 2016, p. 210 ; M.-P. Robert, « La constitutionnalité de la criminalisation de la polygamie au Canada : une question d'objectif » (2014) 7 *Annuaire Droit et religions* 501.

Des hommes qui ont « épousé » des filles de moins de 16 ans pourraient être accusés d'agressions sexuelles (lorsqu'il y a plus de 5 ans entre l'homme et la personne mineure, ou une relation d'autorité entre eux, art. 153 Code criminel canadien). La question se pose à savoir si cet article du *Code criminel* s'applique aux couples non mariés vivant dans une relation polyamoureuse.[34]

Depuis 2005, la loi fédérale sur le mariage, qui prévoit les conditions de fond du mariage, permet le mariage civil entre personnes de même sexe[35]. Toutes les provinces ou territoires au Canada reconnaissent le mariage civil pour les couples de même sexe.[36] Au Québec, une autre forme d'union, l'union civile, est instituée dès 2002 pour permettre aux couples de même sexe de s'unir plus formellement.[37] Cette forme de conjugalité ouverte à tous les couples peu importe leur sexe est rarement utilisée aujourd'hui.

Les conjoint-e-s de fait de même sexe sont reconnus dans les lois à caractère social et fiscal. Dans toutes les provinces, sauf au Québec,[38] en cas de rupture

---

[34] Voir M. Lessard, « Les amoureux sur les bancs publics : Le traitement juridique du polyamour en droit québécois » (2019) 32(1) *Revue canadienne de droit familial* 1.

[35] Loi sur le mariage civil, LC 2005, c. 33, art. 2 et 4. Avant la modification de 2005, les tribunaux dans neuf provinces avaient déjà reconnu la légalité du mariage entre personnes de même sexe. Voir aussi *Renvoi relatif au mariage entre personnes de même sexe* [2004] 3 RCS 698 et Loi d'harmonisation n° 1 du droit fédéral avec le droit civil, LC 2004, c. 4. Sur la reconnaissance du mariage de conjoint-e-s de même sexe au Canada, voir R. Leckey et N. Bala, « Les trente premières années de la charte canadienne en droit de la famille » (2012) 42 *Revue de droit de l'Université de Sherbrooke* 409, 419 et s. Pour un historique de l'évolution des droits des personnes LGBTQI+ au Canada entre 1993 et 2003, voir J. Fisher, « Outlaws or In-laws? Successes and Challenges in the Struggle for LGBT Equality » (2003–2004) 49 *Revue de droit de McGill* 1183 ; M. Giroux, « Le mariage homosexuel : perspective québéco-canadienne » dans S. Navas Navarro (dir.), *Matrimonio homosexual y adopcion. Perspectiva nacional e internacional*, coll. Juridica General, Jornadas, Editorial Reus, Madrid 2006, pp. 17–44.

[36] Québec : art. 365 CcQ et Loi d'interprétation, RLRQ c. I-16 : définition de conjoint ; Ontario : Loi sur le mariage, LRO 1990, c. M.3 : on utilise l'expression neutre « personne » ; Nouveau Brunswick : Loi sur le mariage, LRN-B 2011, c. 188, art. 2 (1); Manitoba : Loi sur le mariage, CPLM, c. M50, art. 29 ; Terre-Neuve et Labrador : Marriage Act, SNL 2009, c. M-1.02, art. 2 : (l); Ile-du-Prince Édouard : Marriage Act, RSPEI 1988, c. M-3 ; Alberta : Marriage Act, RSA 2000, c. M-5, art. 22 (1); Saskatchewan : Loi de 1995 sur le mariage, LS 1995, c. M-4.1 : on utilise l'expression neutre « parties » ou « personnes » ; Yukon : Loi sur le mariage, LRY 2002, c. 146, art. 44 ; Territoires du Nord-Ouest : Marriage Act, LTN-O 2017, c. 2, art. 1 ; Nunavut : Loi sur le mariage, LRTN-O (Nu) 1988, c. M-4 : on utilise l'expression neutre « les parties », art. 1 (f) ; Nouvelle-Écosse : Solemnization of Marriage Act, RSNS 1989, c. 436 : on utilise l'expression neutre « persons » ; art. 10 (1), 22 (2), 45 (1); Colombie-Britannique : Marriage Act, RSBC 1996, c. 282 : on utilise l'expression neutre « parties ».

[37] Loi instituant l'union civile et établissant de nouvelles règles de filiation, LQ 2002, c. 6. N'ayant pas compétence sur les conditions de fond du mariage, le Québec adopte l'union civile, calquée sur le mariage, mais ouverte aux conjoint-e-s de même sexe, pour les accommoder dans l'attente de l'action du gouvernement fédéral, qui adopte le mariage pour tous en 2005.

[38] *A c. Québec (Procureur général)*, 2013 CSC 5. Dans ce jugement serré (cinq juges contre quatre), le plus haut tribunal du pays a refusé d'invalider l'article 585 CcQ au motif qu'il était discriminatoire en traitant différemment les couples mariés et non mariés lors de la rupture. Au total, cinq juges ont considéré qu'il y avait discrimination au sens de l'article 15 de la Charte canadienne des droits et libertés, partie 1 de la Loi constitutionnelle de 1982 (annexe B de la Loi sur le Canada (1982, R.-U., c. 11)), mais pour la juge en chef McLachlin,

conjugale, le conjoint-e de fait économiquement vulnérable pourra obtenir une pension alimentaire de l'autre conjoint-e, selon ses besoins et la capacité de payer de son ex-conjoint-e. Au Québec, le conjoint-e de fait défavorisé par l'union conjugale peut intenter une action en enrichissement injustifié afin d'obtenir une indemnisation pour son investissement dans la famille qui a enrichi son ex-conjoint-e (art. 1493 CcQ).[39] Partout au pays, les conjoint-e-s de même sexe peuvent adopter des enfants[40] et avoir recours aux techniques de procréation médicalement assistée. La réforme du droit de la famille de juin 2023 élargit l'application de la présomption de paternité aux conjoints de fait (art. 114 et 525 CcQ).

1.3. UNE RECONNAISSANCE PARTIELLE DE LA PLURALITÉ DES FAMILLES

L'adoption plénière s'applique au Québec, mais l'adoption coutumière autochtone a récemment été admise, maintenant la filiation d'origine dans certains cas. Ainsi le pluralisme juridique en cette matière est reconnu. Devant la lenteur du législateur à apporter des réformes au droit de la famille, des parents trans et non-binaires ont demandé au tribunal de corriger des dispositions qu'ils considéraient comme discriminatoires à leur égard.

1.3.1. *La filiation additive et les ententes facilitant le maintien des relations en matière d'adoption*

La multiplicité des parents dans le cas d'une adoption ouverte n'est pas envisagée par le droit civil québécois. L'adoption plénière prévaut et a pour effet de remplacer la filiation d'origine.[41] Des propositions de réforme recommandaient la reconnaissance d'autres modèles de filiation, incluant l'adoption ouverte et sans rupture de lien.[42] Sans retenir cette dernière option, en juin 2017, une nouvelle

---

cette discrimination se justifie dans une société libre et démocratique en vertu de l'article 1. Voir R. Leckey « Strange Bedfellows » (2014) 64(5) *University of Toronto Law Journal* 641.

[39] *Droit de la famille – 132495 (N.D. c. B.C.)*, 2013 QCCA 1586. Afin de faciliter la preuve, une présomption d'appauvrissement du conjoint-e qui a quitté le marché du travail et qui s'est occupé des enfants est appliquée. Voir aussi notamment B. Lefebvre, « Fascicule 28 : Union de fait », dans Pierre-Claude Lafond, dir, JCQ Personnes et famille.

[40] Au Canada généralement, voir entre autres L.E. Ross et al., « Policy and Practice Regarding Adoption by Sexual and Gender Minority People in Ontario » (2009) 35(4) *Canadian Public Policy* 451.

[41] Art. 577 CcQ.

[42] Voir Groupe de travail sur le régime québécois de l'adoption, C. Lavallée (prés.), *Pour une adoption québécoise à la mesure de chaque enfant*, Ministère de la Santé et des services sociaux and Ministère de la justice du Québec, Québec 2007 ; Québec, Comité consultatif sur le droit de la famille, A. Roy (prés.), *Pour un droit de la famille adapté aux nouvelles réalités conjugales et familiales*, Thémis, Montréal 2015, appuyait ces recommandations, p. 189. Des projets de loi ont aussi été déposés en ce sens, sans jamais être adoptés.

loi a été adoptée[43] et aménage une nuance. On y prévoit la reconnaissance de la filiation d'origine et la possibilité, si l'intérêt de l'enfant le commande, de rédiger par écrit « une entente visant à faciliter l'échange de renseignements ou des relations interpersonnelles entre l'adoptant et les membres de sa famille d'origine » (art. 579 CcQ). L'adoption succède à la filiation d'origine, mais les effets de la filiation d'origine prennent fin malgré tout. Ainsi, l'adoption plénière demeure la règle ; le parent d'origine n'est plus tenu par l'obligation alimentaire à l'égard de son enfant et les règles de la succession *ab intestat* cessent de s'appliquer. On permet néanmoins d'inscrire le nom des parents d'origine au côté de ceux des parents adoptifs pour permettre à l'enfant l'accès à ses origines biologiques. Le projet de loi 2 réformant le droit de la famille[44] ne fait aucune nouvelle proposition en la matière.

1.3.2. L'adoption coutumière autochtone

Il faut noter que lors de la réforme de 2017, le Québec a aussi reconnu l'adoption coutumière autochtone et par le fait même le pluralisme juridique en cette matière. En effet, la coutume prend le relais du droit étatique, car l'adoption est alors effectuée non pas par le régime étatique, mais par l'autorité compétente désignée pour la communauté ou la nation autochtone de l'enfant.[45] Une fois que cette autorité délivre un certificat d'adoption coutumière autochtone, elle doit toutefois le notifier dans les 30 jours au Directeur de l'état civil du Québec.[46] Le certificat pourra indiquer des droits et des obligations qui demeurent et qui pourraient avoir ainsi pour effet de se distancer des effets généraux de l'adoption en droit civil québécois, c'est-à-dire la rupture du lien de filiation.[47] Un autre nouveau mécanisme inspiré de la tradition autochtone est aussi adopté, celui de la tutelle supplétive.[48] Cette dernière permet au père ou à la mère de désigner une personne qui exercera le rôle de tuteur et de titulaire de l'autorité parentale lorsqu'il est impossible pour eux ou pour l'un d'eux de les exercer pleinement.

---

[43] Loi modifiant le Code civil et d'autres dispositions législatives en matière d'adoption et de communication de renseignements, LQ 2017, c. 12. Pour une étude plus approfondie de cette réforme, voir M. Giroux et L. Brunet, « Quelle place pour le droit aux origines de l'enfant adopté en France et au Québec ? » (2021) 37 *Enfances Familles Générations*, en ligne : http://journals.openedition.org/efg/11554 (10 août 2022).

[44] *Projet de loi 2 – Loi portant sur la réforme du droit de la famille en matière de filiation et modifiant le Code civil en matière de droits de la personnalité et d'état civil*, 2e session, 42e législature, Québec, 2021. Seule une partie de projet de loi a été adoptée en juin 2022 en raison du déclenchement d'élections provinciales à l'automne 2022.

[45] Art. 543.1, 152.1, 574.1 et 132.0.1 CcQ. Pour plus de détails, voir entre autres Gouvernement du Québec, Rapport du groupe de travail sur l'adoption coutumière en milieu autochtone, 2012 ; G. Otis (dir.), *L'adoption coutumière autochtone et les défis du pluralisme juridique*, Les Presses de l'Université Laval, Québec 2013.

[46] Art. 129, al. 2 CcQ.

[47] Art. 132.0.1 CcQ.

[48] Art. 199.1 CcQ.

L'intérêt de l'enfant, notion inconnue de la coutume autochtone, demeure applicable lorsque le tribunal doit prendre une décision autorisant la tutelle supplétive.[49] Reste à voir comment ces nouveaux mécanismes évolueront et s'ils permettront pleinement à la coutume autochtone de prévaloir.[50]

Quant au cas des *kafalas*, le législateur québécois n'a pas adopté de dispositions spécifiques, bien qu'il l'ait envisagé.[51] En revanche, les modifications apportées en 2017 et reconnaissant la filiation d'origine lorsqu'il est dans l'intérêt de l'enfant de le faire[52] vont peut-être favoriser les adoptions d'enfants musulmans au Québec.[53] Les noms des parents d'origine pourront dans ce cas être ajoutés à ceux des parents adoptifs sur le nouvel acte de naissance de l'enfant découlant du jugement d'adoption.

1.3.3. *La reconnaissance de parents non-binaires*

Au Québec, comme dans d'autres provinces,[54] une action a été intentée par un groupe de parents trans et non-binaires, afin que leurs réalités familiales soient reconnues dans le Code civil du Québec. Parmi leurs demandes, retenons celles qui portent sur le droit de la filiation. Ils contestaient la mention obligatoire du sexe apparaissant à l'acte de naissance de l'enfant (art. 111 CcQ). Ils demandaient que cette mention soit optionnelle pour tous les parents. Ils plaidaient aussi pour le remplacement des termes « père » et « mère » par celui de « parent » dans tout le droit québécois. Ils contestaient le refus du Directeur de l'état civil de modifier de façon rétroactive l'acte de naissance d'un enfant dont le parent a changé d'identité de genre (art. 132 CcQ). Leurs demandes étaient fondées sur leur droit à l'égalité protégé à l'article 10 de la Charte des droits et libertés de la personne du Québec[55] et à l'article 15 (1) de la Charte canadienne des droits et libertés.[56] Ils se disaient victimes de discrimination en vertu de leur identité de genre.

---

[49] Art. 199.3 CcQ.
[50] Voir à ce sujet le questionnement très pertinent de R. Leckey, « L'adoption coutumière autochtone en droit civil québécois » (2018) 59(4) *Cahiers de Droit* 973.
[51] Voir J. Tugault-Lafleur, « Analyse comparative des conceptions de l'enfant et des institutions de l'adoption dans le monde arabo- musulman et en Occident : une réconciliation est-elle possible ? » Mémoire présenté à la Faculté de droit (Université de Montréal) en vue de l'obtention du grade de L.L.M., maîtrise en droit – option recherche, février 2011.
[52] Art. 577 CcQ.
[53] Voir H. Al Dabbagh, « La réception de la kafala dans l'ordre juridique québécois : vers un renversement du paradigme conflictuel ? » (2017) 47 *Revue générale de droit* 165.
[54] D'autres actions de la même sorte ont été intentées en Colombie-Britannique. The Gender Free ID Coalition, qui a déposé huit plaintes à la Commission des droits de la personne de la province pour faire enlever la mention du sexe sur l'acte de naissance. En ligne : http://gender-freeidcoalition.ca/. (10 août 2022).
[55] Charte des droits et libertés, RLRQ c. C-12.
[56] Charte canadienne des droits et libertés, partie 1 de la Loi constitutionnelle de 1982 (annexe B de la Loi sur le Canada (1982, R.-U., c. 11)).

Le tribunal de première instance a décidé que l'obligation de déclarer le sexe du nouveau-né à l'acte de naissance (art. 111 CcQ) n'est pas discriminatoire.[57] Le gouvernement a besoin de cette mention pour identifier le-la citoyen-ne afin de lui offrir de meilleurs services. Le juge ajoute que l'identité de genre de l'enfant se précise vers l'âge de 3 ans. L'article 71 CcQ permet alors de faire modifier par voie administrative la mention de l'identité de genre de la personne dans les documents officiels.[58] Quant aux termes père et mère (art. 111, 115 et 116 CcQ), le tribunal conclut qu'il s'agit de discrimination, puisque les parents non-binaires sont exclus, ce qui porte atteinte à leur dignité. Le législateur devra utiliser une terminologie inclusive. Le projet de loi 2 adopté en partie en juin 2022[59] a ajouté le terme « parent » au côté des termes « père » et « mère » dans toute la législation québécoise. Dans le cas de la gestation pour autrui, le projet de loi 2[60] proposait comme expression « la femme ou la personne qui a accepté de donner naissance à l'enfant ». Si le parent modifie la mention de son identité de genre au registre de l'état civil (art. 71 CcQ), le Directeur de l'état civil doit modifier de façon rétroactive l'acte de naissance d'un enfant déjà né (art. 132 CcQ). Cette décision s'inscrit dans la foulée d'autres modifications législatives qui ont reconnu la diversité familiale, comme le mariage, l'adoption et l'accès à la procréation médicale assistée pour tous. Elle marque aussi un pas de plus vers la désexualisation du droit.

2. L'ÉTABLISSEMENT DE LA PARENTÉ DANS LE CONTEXTE DE LA PROCRÉATION ASSISTÉE ET DE LA MATERNITÉ DE SUBSTITUTION

Les avancées médicales dans le domaine de la procréation assistée ont mis en question le concept traditionnel de père et de mère et de la famille hétéronormée

---

[57] *Center for Gender Advocacy c. P.G. (Québec)*, 2021 QCCS 191 (en appel sur la seule question de l'article 71 CcQ, invalidé en première instance, qui impose aux mineurs de plus de 14 ans d'obtenir une lettre d'un professionnel de la santé pour demander le changement de sexe à l'acte de naissance).

[58] Précisons que toutes les provinces permettent le changement de la mention du sexe sans exiger la transition médicale. Voir M. Giroux et L. Langevin, « La reconnaissance des droits des personnes trans au Canada », dans I.C. Jaramillo et L. Carlson (dirs), *Trans Rights and Wrongs, A Comparative Study of Legal Reform Concerning Trans Persons,* Ius Comparatum – Global Studies in Comparative Law, Springer, 2021.

[59] *Loi portant sur la réforme du droit de la famille en matière de filiation et modifiant le Code civil en matière de droits de la personnalité et d'état civil*, LQ 2022 c 22.

[60] *Projet de loi 2 – Loi portant sur la réforme du droit de la famille en matière de filiation et modifiant le Code civil en matière de droits de la personnalité et d'état civil*, 2e session, 42e législature, Québec, 2021 (projet de loi partiellement mort au feuilleton lors du déclenchement des élections en août 2022).

et biocentrée. Des personnes seules ou des couples infertiles de même sexe ou de sexes différents peuvent aspirer à la parenté. Le droit doit s'adapter à cette nouvelle réalité. Nous abordons ici l'établissement du lien de filiation dans le contexte de la procréation assistée et de la maternité de substitution.

2.1. LA PROCRÉATION ASSISTÉE

Que l'enfant soit conçu par procréation assistée ou non, la femme qui accouche est la mère légale au sens de l'article 111 CcQ, qu'elle ait ou non fourni l'ovule. Son époux ou conjoint uni civilement qui a consenti au projet parental est le père de l'enfant, qu'il ait ou non fourni le matériel génétique (art. 538 et 539 CcQ). Une femme seule ou deux femmes peuvent aussi décider d'avoir recours à la procréation assistée pour avoir un enfant ; elles pourront dans ce dernier scénario toutes deux déclarer leur maternité à l'état civil (art. 115 CcQ).[61] Cette filiation fait naître les mêmes droits et obligations que la filiation par le sang (art. 538.1 CcQ). Les donneurs de matériel génétique anonymes ou non ne peuvent établir aucun lien de filiation avec l'enfant ainsi conçu. Si l'enfant est conçu par relation sexuelle directe,[62] un lien de filiation peut toutefois être établi dans l'année qui suit la naissance de l'enfant entre l'auteur de l'apport et l'enfant, mais toujours dans le respect de la biparenté. Cette possibilité écarte alors la filiation du parent de même sexe ayant formulé le projet parental, mais n'ayant pas accouché de l'enfant.

S'il le désire, le donneur de matériel génétique pourrait participer à l'éducation de l'enfant, sans être reconnu comme un parent sur le plan juridique, puisque le droit québécois ne reconnaît pas plus de deux parents jusqu'à ce jour.[63] Il pourrait toujours utiliser le droit commun pour demander du temps parental auprès de l'enfant si l'intérêt de l'enfant le commande.[64]

---

[61] Par la ROPA (Réception des Ovocytes de la Partenaire, ou maternité partagée dans les couples de lesbiennes), une des conjointes donne ses ovules à l'autre qui portera l'enfant (grâce à une fécondation in vitro). Les deux femmes auront ainsi des liens génétiques biologiques avec l'enfant. La femme qui accouche est la mère légale de l'enfant : art. 111 CcQ. La donneuse d'ovules devient la co-mère de l'enfant si les deux femmes sont mariées ou si elles ont consenti à un projet parental ensemble (avec un fournisseur de sperme) : art. 538, 538.1 CcQ. Pour plus de détails sur les règles de la filiation par procréation assistée, voir M. Giroux, « Fascicule 30 : Filiation de l'enfant né d'une procréation assistée », dans Pierre-Claude Lafond, dir, JCQ Personnes et famille.

[62] I.e. avec pénétration et sans l'utilisation de seringue.

[63] Voir *Droit de la famille – 191677*, 2019 QCCA 1386.

[64] Voir art. 605 CcQ ; *T.V.F. et D.F. c. G.C.* [1987] 2 RCS 244.

2.2. LA MATERNITÉ DE SUBSTITUTION

Au Canada, seule la pratique de la maternité de substitution à titre gratuit est permise par la loi fédérale sur la procréation assistée.[65] Toute forme de rémunération de la mère porteuse ou des intermédiaires est interdite.[66] Cependant, la mesure dans laquelle une convention de mère porteuse est juridiquement contraignante varie d'une province ou d'un territoire à l'autre. Nous analysons ici l'état du droit au Québec et dans deux provinces de *common law*, la Colombie-Britannique et l'Ontario.

2.2.1. Au Québec

Nous présentons ici l'état du droit québécois sur la maternité de substitution en 2022. Il est cependant appelé à changer de façon importante. En effet, le législateur a l'intention de reconnaître cette pratique et d'imposer une convention de gestation pour autrui dont le contenu serait strictement encadré. La femme porteuse pourrait toujours changer d'avis et garder l'enfant. Le ou les parents d'intention ne pourraient se soustraire à leurs obligations.

Au Québec, depuis 1994, l'article 541 CcQ prévoit la nullité des conventions entre des parents intentionnels et une mère porteuse, peu importe qu'il s'agisse d'une convention de gestation ou de procréation, à titre gratuit ou non. Cette nullité est fondée sur le principe de non-commercialisation du corps humain, l'indisponibilité de l'état des personnes de même que sur l'intérêt de l'enfant *a priori* ou *in abstracto*. Ainsi, toute personne ayant recours à cette technique le fait à ses propres risques. Dans l'éventualité d'un conflit concernant la convention, celle-ci n'est pas susceptible d'exécution.

La nullité de la convention a un impact sur l'établissement de la filiation de l'enfant. Pour la déterminer, plusieurs possibilités existent selon le scénario en jeu, mais dans tous les cas, on utilise d'abord les règles de la filiation par le sang pour déterminer la filiation de l'enfant ainsi conçu. En effet, conformément à la maxime de droit romain *mater semper certa est*, la femme qui accouche est la mère de l'enfant, peu importe si elle a fourni ou non ses gamètes.[67] Elle peut décider de garder l'enfant. Si elle est mariée ou unie civilement, la présomption de paternité trouvera application à l'égard de son conjoint ou de sa conjointe.[68]

---

[65] Loi sur la procréation assistée, LC 2004, c. 2, art. 6 et 12 (art. 12 entrée en vigueur le 09.06.2020).

[66] Seules les catégories de dépenses de la mère porteuse prévues au règlement peuvent être remboursées par le parent ou les parents intentionnels sur présentation des reçus. Il s'agit de dépenses de base en lien avec la grossesse et l'accouchement. Règlement sur le remboursement relatif à la procréation assistée, DORS/2019-195, La Gazette du Canada, Partie II, vol. 153, no. 13, 10.06.2019 (entrée en vigueur le 10.06.2020).

[67] Art. 111 CcQ.

[68] Conformément à l'article 525 CcQ.

Ce conjoint ou cette conjointe peut contester sa paternité.[69] Si le conjoint de la mère porteuse ne conteste pas sa paternité, le père génétique devient un donneur de sperme[70] et ne peut réclamer sa paternité. Tout se passe comme s'il n'y avait pas eu d'entente de gestation pour autrui. Les tribunaux ne sont d'aucun secours pour le père génétique ou sa conjointe. Il semble ici que la mère porteuse doive procéder rapidement pour déclarer son conjoint comme père de l'enfant, puisque le père génétique pourrait le faire avant le mari de la mère porteuse (la déclaration de naissance l'emportant sur la présomption de paternité[71]), auquel cas un tribunal devra décider qui aura la garde de l'enfant.

Par ailleurs, l'un des parents d'intention, qui est généralement le parent biologique, pourra déclarer son lien de filiation à l'égard de l'enfant au directeur de l'état civil. La présomption de paternité en cas de mariage ou d'union civile, cède le pas à la déclaration de naissance si celle-ci est faite par l'un des parents d'intention.

Pour éventuellement régler la filiation de l'enfant ainsi conçu, l'adoption est utilisée, quoique ce mécanisme n'ait pas été conçu pour ce type de scénario. Ainsi, par consentement spécial à l'adoption du parent inscrit à l'acte de naissance[72] et de la mère porteuse, le processus d'adoption par la mère d'intention (ou le co-père) pourra dès lors être enclenché par le mécanisme qui permet l'adoption intrafamiliale.[73] Cette possibilité d'adoption par l'autre parent dépend du consentement de la mère porteuse et du conjoint/parent inscrits à l'acte de naissance de l'enfant.[74] En cas de litige entre les parents intentionnels, le parent inscrit à l'acte de naissance de l'enfant pourrait refuser de consentir à la demande d'adoption de l'autre parent.

La Cour d'appel du Québec a tranché la question de l'établissement de la filiation de l'enfant conçu à la suite d'une convention de mère porteuse.[75] Le tribunal a autorisé l'adoption de l'enfant du conjoint, par l'autre parent, au nom

---

[69] Art. 539 CcQ.
[70] Art. 538.2 CcQ.
[71] Art. 523 CcQ.
[72] Art. 555 CcQ. Toutes des décisions publiées et accessibles au Québec qui portent sur la maternité de substitution sont des requêtes en matière d'adoption ou des demandes de correction au registre de l'état civil. Comme le contrat entre la mère porteuse et les futurs parents d'intention est inexécutoire, il n'est pas possible de savoir s'il y a eu des conflits entre les parties. Cependant dans l'affaire *Adoption – 1874*, 2018 QCCQ 1694, la mère porteuse américaine refuse de consentir à l'adoption par l'autre conjoint de l'enfant, qui vit déjà avec ses parents au Québec. Le nom de la mère porteuse demeure sur l'acte de naissance de l'enfant. Le nom de son autre père n'apparait pas.
[73] Pour plus de détails sur l'établissement de la filiation de l'enfant ainsi conçu, voir M. Giroux, « Le recours controversé à l'adoption pour établir la filiation de l'enfant né d'une mère porteuse : entre ordre public contractuel et intérêt de l'enfant » (2011) 70 *Revue du Barreau* 509, 521–24 ; sur les difficultés de ce mécanisme d'adoption, voir I. Coté et J.-S. Sauvé, « Homopaternité, gestation pour autrui : no man's land ? » (2016) 46 *Revue générale de droit* 27.
[74] Voir *Droit de la famille – 212386*, 2021 QCCS 5233, conf. par 2022 QCCA 1036.
[75] *Adoption – 1445*, 2014 QCCA 1162 et *Adoption – 161*, 2016 QCCA 16.

de l'intérêt de l'enfant, mettant ainsi fin au débat jurisprudentiel de droit interne qui hésitait, en première instance en Cour du Québec, entre ordre public et intérêt de l'enfant. Comme la Cour ne peut qu'interpréter le droit applicable, l'article 541 CcQ n'a toujours pas été modifié et cette situation peut paraître contradictoire.

La procréation pour autrui internationale est permise (ou tolérée), puisque les tribunaux québécois entérinent des documents étrangers reconnaissant que les parents canadiens ont fait affaire avec une agence et une mère porteuse, contre rétribution, qui a accepté de céder son droit à la filiation avec l'enfant à naître.[76]

Si la mère porteuse désire remettre l'enfant à sa naissance aux parents intentionnels et que ceux-ci n'en veulent pas, les règles de l'adoption s'appliqueront.[77] L'enfant sera pris en charge par la direction de la protection de la jeunesse. La mère porteuse n'aura aucun droit de regard sur le choix des parents adoptifs.

Malgré le caractère non exécutoire du contrat prévu à l'article 541 CcQ, il demeure néanmoins nécessaire.[78] D'abord, il sert d'élément de preuve de

---

[76] Voir *Adoption – 1631*, 2016 QCCQ 6872 (GPA en Inde); *Adoption – 16199*, 2016 QCCQ 8951 (GPA en Thaïlande); *Droit de la famille – 151172*, 2015 QCCS 2308 (GPA en Pennsylvanie). Sur certains enjeux de droit international privé concernant la transcription à l'état civil et la reconnaissance d'un jugement étranger en matière de maternité de substitution, voir M. Giroux, « Les conventions de procréation ou de gestation pour autrui au Québec : entre solution jurisprudentielle et réforme du droit » dans E. de Luze, M. Roca i Escoda et V. Boillet (dirs), *La gestation pour autrui. Approches juridiques internationales*, Limal et Bâle, Éditions Anthémis et Coédition Helbing Lichtenhahn Verlag, 2018, pp. 125–42. Le gouvernement fédéral facilite l'obtention d'un passeport pour l'enfant né à l'étranger : *Détermination de la filiation aux fins d'attribution de la citoyenneté dans les cas où interviennent des techniques de procréation assistée (PA), y compris la maternité de substitution*, en ligne : https://www.canada.ca/fr/immigration-refugies-citoyennete/organisation/publications-guides/bulletins-guides-operationnels/citoyennete-canadienne/admininistration/identite/determination-filiation-fins-attribution-cas-interviennent-techniques-procreation-assistee-compris-maternite-substitution.html. (10 août 2022).

[77] La mère porteuse dans ce cas pourra donner son consentement à la reconnaissance des liens préexistants de filiation (art. 544.1 CcQ tel que modifié par Loi modifiant le Code civil et d'autres dispositions législatives en matière d'adoption et de communication de renseignements, LQ 2017, c. 12). Les nouvelles règles permettent aussi de conclure une entente visant à faciliter l'échange de renseignements ou des relations interpersonnelles entre elle et l'enfant (art. 579 CcQ).

[78] Santé Canada mentionne le contrat de gestation pour autrui dans la Ligne directrice : Règlement sur le remboursement relatif à la procréation, 30.08.2019, p. 17. La conclusion d'un contrat est obligatoire entre autres dans le programme de GPA d'une clinique de fertilité dans un hôpital torontois : voir S. Dar et al., « Assisted Reproduction Involving Gestational Surrogacy: an Analysis of the Medical, Psychosocial and Legal Issues: Experience from a Large Surrogacy Program » (2015) 30(2) *Human Reproduction* 345 : analyse de l'expérience d'une clinique de fertilité dans un hôpital torontois de 1998 à 2012, 178 grossesses de mère porteuse. Il semble aussi que la majorité des cliniques de fertilité exigent qu'un contrat soit conclu entre la mère porteuse et les parents intentionnels. Voir K. Busby et D. Vun, « Revisiting *The Handmaid's Tale*: Feminist Theory Meets Empirical Research on Surrogate Motherhood » (2010) 13 *Canadian Journal of Family Law* 26, 27.

l'intention des parties quant à la parenté. Il vise à démontrer que le consentement des parties a été donné avant la conception de l'embryon et qu'il ne s'agit pas d'adoption privée ou de traite d'enfants.[79] Le contrat a servi à prouver le consentement de la mère porteuse dans des requêtes en adoption au Québec, même lorsque l'enfant est né dans des pays où la GPA commerciale se pratique.[80] La conclusion du contrat n'équivaut cependant pas au consentement à l'adoption de la mère porteuse, si celle-ci refuse de l'accorder.[81]

Il sert aussi d'outil de protection[82] et de négociation entre les parties, même si la mère porteuse n'est pas obligée de le respecter par les termes de l'article 541 CcQ. Elle peut refuser tout traitement médical pour elle ou le fœtus,[83] même si elle a consenti au préalable à ces traitements, ou à toute forme de contrôle de son mode de vie par les parents intentionnels. Elle peut garder l'enfant. La rédaction du contrat permet aux parties de prendre conscience de certaines situations qui peuvent se présenter et d'en discuter. Il prévoit aussi les modalités de remboursement des dépenses de la mère porteuse, en conformité avec le règlement fédéral.[84]

2.2.2. En Colombie-Britannique et en Ontario

Plusieurs provinces canadiennes ont réformé leur droit de la famille pour tenir compte des nouvelles réalités familiales, en mettant le modèle traditionnel de deux parents génétiques de côté.[85] Nous nous concentrerons sur la réforme en Colombie-Britannique et en Ontario, qui ont influencé les choix législatifs des autres provinces de *common law*.

---

[79] Pour un faux cas de mère porteuse qui cachait un projet d'adoption privée internationale et de traite d'enfant : *Protection de la jeunesse – 179444*, 2017 QCCQ 15359.

[80] Dans ces décisions, les tribunaux recherchent le consentement de la mère porteuse à l'adoption : *Adoption – 1631*, 2016 QCCQ 6872 (GPA en Inde); *Adoption – 16199*, 2016 QCCQ 8951 (GPA en Thaïlande); *Droit de la famille – 151172*, 2015 QCCS 2308 (GPA en Pennsylvanie).

[81] L'article 555 CcQ exige le consentement de la mère porteuse, si son nom apparaît à l'acte de naissance, comme dans l'affaire *Adoption – 1874*, 2018 QCCQ 1694. Dans cette affaire, la mère porteuse américaine refuse de consentir à l'adoption de l'enfant, qui vit déjà avec ses parents au Québec.

[82] Voir K. Lavoie et I. Côté, « Navigating in Murky Waters: Legal Issues Arising from a Lack of Surrogacy Regulation in Quebec » dans V. Gruben et al. (dir.), *Surrogacy in Canada: Critical Perspectives in Law and Policy*, Irwin Law, Toronto 2018, p. 81.

[83] Art. 11 CcQ ; *Office des services à l'enfant et à la famille de Winnipeg (région du Nord-Ouest) c. G (DF)* [1997] 3 RCS 925.

[84] Règlement sur le remboursement relatif à la procréation assistée, DORS/2019-193, Gazette du Canada, Partie II, vol. 153, no. 13 (10.06.2019) (entrée en vigueur le 09.06.2020).

[85] L'Ontario : Loi de 2016 sur l'égalité de toutes les familles (modifiant des lois en ce qui concerne la filiation et les enregistrements connexes), LO 2016, c. 23. La partie 3 porte sur la filiation. La Colombie-Britannique : Family Law Act, SBC 2011, c. 25. Le Manitoba : Loi modifiant la Loi sur l'obligation alimentaire, LM 2021, c. 63. La Saskatchewan : Loi de 2020 sur le droit de l'enfance, LS 2020, c. 2.

En Colombie-Britannique, les parties, future mère porteuse et futurs parents intentionnels, doivent rédiger un contrat avant la conception de l'embryon.[86] Ce contrat prévoit, entre autres, que la future mère porteuse, qui peut avoir ou non fourni le matériel génétique,[87] sera la mère de l'enfant conçu grâce à la procréation assistée. Après la naissance de l'enfant, si elle consent par écrit, elle remettra l'enfant aux parents intentionnels, renoncera à ses droits sur l'enfant et ne sera pas considérée comme le parent légal de l'enfant.[88] Aucun délai n'est prévu pour remettre l'enfant. Les parents intentionnels, qui peuvent être de même sexe ou de sexes différents (il peut aussi s'agir d'un seul parent), sont présumés être les parents légaux de l'enfant, qu'ils aient fourni ou non le matériel génétique.[89] Les parties n'ont pas l'obligation d'obtenir des avis juridiques indépendants avant la signature du contrat de préconception.[90] Si les parties n'ont pas rédigé de tel contrat, la procédure judiciaire d'adoption s'applique pour faire reconnaître le lien de filiation de l'autre parent. La loi prévoit la possibilité de trois parents[91] lorsque l'enfant est conçu par procréation assistée. Le troisième parent doit être soit la mère porteuse ou un donneur de gamètes.

En cas de conflit, le contrat entre les parties ne lie pas la mère porteuse, qui peut toujours changer d'avis et garder l'enfant.[92] Son consentement à agir comme mère porteuse n'équivaut pas à son consentement à renoncer à ses droits parentaux et à remettre l'enfant. Le contrat peut cependant servir de preuve de l'intention des parties au sujet de la filiation de l'enfant. Un tribunal prendra une décision sur la filiation de l'enfant, selon son intérêt.

Les parents intentionnels ne peuvent pas changer d'avis.[93] La loi prévoit qu'ils seront les parents légaux. Si la mère porteuse et les parents intentionnels refusent d'accueillir l'enfant, ce dernier sera pris en charge par les autorités, mais les parents intentionnels demeurent les parents légaux et sont tenus des obligations qui en découlent.[94]

---

[86] Family Law Act, SBC 2011, c. 25, art. 29 (2) (en vigueur mars 2013).
[87] Ibid., art. 20 (1).
[88] Ibid., art. 29 (2) (b).
[89] Ibid.
[90] Si les parties n'ont pas obtenu l'avis juridique obligatoire et n'ont pas rédigé l'entente de préconception, voir *Cabianca v. British Columbia (Registrar General of Vital Statistics)*, 2019 BCSC 2010.
[91] Selon l'article 30 (1) (b), Family Law Act, SBC 2011, c. 25. La situation dans laquelle un couple lesbien et un couple gai (quatre parents) conçoivent un enfant est exclue.
[92] Ibid., art. 29 (6). Pour un conflit entre la mère porteuse qui veut être reconnue comme la mère et les parents d'intention, voir *K.B. v. M.S.B.*, 2021 BCCS 1283, la décision finale doit être rendue très bientôt.
[93] Ibid., art. 29 (3) (a) et (b) (i).
[94] Selon l'analyse de S.G. Drummond, « Fruitful Diversity: Revisiting the Enforceability of Gestational Carriage Contracts » dans T. Lemmens et al. (dirs), *Regulating Creation: The Law, Ethics, and Policy of Assisted Human Reproduction*, University of Toronto Press, Toronto 2017, pp. 274–90.

Dans les 30 jours de la naissance de l'enfant, les parents de l'enfant (les parents intentionnels) doivent compléter et remettre au registraire général les renseignements nécessaires sur le formulaire prescrit.[95] Le transfert de filiation par voie administrative a été préféré à un processus judiciaire. Il n'est donc pas nécessaire de présenter une requête devant le tribunal pour faire corriger les registres de l'état civil.

Quant au droit ontarien, il impose une convention de préconception entre « le substitut », comme la loi qualifie la mère porteuse, et le ou les parents intentionnels.[96] Le contrat porte sur la question du consentement des parties : le substitut convient de ne pas être le parent de l'enfant à être conçu ; les autres personnes (jusqu'à quatre) s'engagent à être les parents légaux de l'enfant. Toutes les parties doivent avoir reçu des avis juridiques indépendants (d'un-e avocat-e autre que celui-celle qui rédigera le contrat).[97] L'enfant doit être conçu par procréation assistée (et non par relation sexuelle).[98] La loi ne distingue pas entre substitut (mère porteuse) génétique ou non génétique, ou parent d'intention génétique ou non. Les futurs parents intentionnels peuvent être de même sexe ou de sexes différents ; il peut aussi s'agir d'un seul parent.

Pendant la période de réflexion de sept jours du substitut (la mère porteuse) après l'accouchement, les parents d'intention et la mère porteuse partagent les droits et responsabilités à l'égard de l'enfant, sauf si l'entente de préconception en dispose autrement.[99] Après ce délai de réflexion, si la mère porteuse renonce à ses droits parentaux, les parents intentionnels deviennent les parents légaux de l'enfant ; le nom de la mère porteuse n'apparaît pas à l'acte de naissance.[100] Une procédure administrative est prévue pour reconnaître la filiation des parents intentionnels.[101] Aucune intervention judiciaire n'est nécessaire. Si les parties n'ont pas rédigé de contrat de préconception, la procédure judiciaire d'adoption s'applique.

L'entente entre les parties est inexécutoire.[102] La mère porteuse peut changer d'avis et garder l'enfant. Son consentement à agir comme mère porteuse n'équivaut pas à son consentement à renoncer à ses droits parentaux. L'entente

---

[95] Vital Statistics Act, RSBC 1996, c. 479, art. 3 (1.1).
[96] Loi portant réforme du droit de l'enfance, LRO 1990, c. C.12, art. 10 (2). Loi de 2016 sur l'égalité de toutes les familles (modifiant des lois en ce qui concerne la filiation et les enregistrements connexes), LO 2016, c. 23. Voir R. Leckey, « One Parent, Three Parents: Judges and Ontario's All Families Are Equal Act, 2016 » (2019) 33(3) *International Journal of Law, Policy and the Family* 298.
[97] Loi portant réforme du droit de l'enfance, LRO 1990, c. C.12, art. 10 (2).
[98] Ibid., art. 10 (2).
[99] Ibid., art. 10 (5).
[100] Ibid., art. 10 (3).
[101] Dispositions générales, RRO 1990, Règl. 1094, art. 3.1 (Loi sur les statistiques de l'état civil, LRO 1990, c. V.4).
[102] Loi portant réforme du droit de l'enfance, LRO 1990, c. C.12, art. 10 (9).

peut cependant servir de preuve de l'intention des parties.[103] Dans l'éventualité où la mère porteuse refuse de renoncer à ses droits de filiation (elle dispose de sept jours pour le faire), toute partie à la convention peut saisir le tribunal pour obtenir une déclaration de filiation à l'égard de l'enfant.[104] Il pourrait aussi s'agir de l'autre parent non génétique qui s'adresse au tribunal, s'il y a eu rupture du couple intentionnel pendant la grossesse et le parent génétique ne veut plus être parent légal. L'intérêt de l'enfant dictera la décision du tribunal.[105] On peut imaginer qu'un tribunal puisse reconnaître des droits de garde à la mère porteuse (en lui reconnaissant un lien de filiation) et aux parents intentionnels. Donc, la mère porteuse dans ces cas n'aura pas le dernier mot. On pourrait y voir une forme d'exécution du contrat.

Puisque le contrat est inexécutoire pour les deux parties,[106] les parents intentionnels peuvent changer d'avis et ne pas prendre l'enfant. Cependant, la loi les déclare parents légaux.[107] Ils sont tenus aux obligations juridiques, comme le versement d'une pension alimentaire pour l'enfant. Évidemment si aucune des parties au contrat ne veut accueillir l'enfant, ce dernier sera remis aux autorités de protection de la jeunesse. Le contrat peut servir à prouver que les futurs parents intentionnels ont consenti à être parents et qu'ils n'ont pas retiré leur consentement avant la conception par procréation assistée.

Dans les provinces n'ayant pas de législation (Ontario jusqu'en 2017,[108] et Nouveau-Brunswick), des déclarations de parenté ont été émises par le tribunal au nom de l'intérêt de l'enfant à l'égard de parents d'intention.[109]

3. CONCLUSION

Ce portrait juridique de la famille québécoise dans le contexte canadien permet une réflexion sur la diversité et la pluralité des fonctions de la famille. Le droit de la famille et les politiques familiales doivent être respectueux des droits fondamentaux des citoyen-ne-s. L'État ne peut imposer sa propre conception de

---

[103] Ibid., art. 10 (9).
[104] Ibid., art. 10 (6).
[105] Ibid., art. 10 (8).
[106] Voir la rédaction de l'article 10 (9) Loi portant réforme du droit de l'enfance, ibid.
[107] Ibid., art. 10 (3).
[108] Voir *A.A. c. B.B.*, 2007 ONCA 2 (appel à la Cour suprême refusée, 2007 3 SRC 124) : comme la loi de l'Ontario à cette époque ne permettait pas à un enfant d'avoir plus de deux parents, le tribunal avait utilisé sa compétence *parens patriae* pour ce faire.
[109] Voir notamment K. Busby, « Of Surrogate Mother Born: Parentage Determinations in Canada and Elsewhere » (2013) 25 *Canadian Journal of Women and the Law* 284. Voir aussi Québec, Comité consultatif sur le droit de la famille, A. Roy (prés.), *Pour un droit de la famille adapté aux nouvelles réalités conjugales et familiales*, Thémis, Montréal 2015, pp. 166–86, 507.

la famille (par exemple, une conception judéo-chrétienne de la famille patriarcale ou une certaine conception morale). Il doit respecter les valeurs individuelles et la diversité des expériences.[110] La très grande majorité des citoyen-ne-s s'entendent sur la fonction protectrice du droit de la famille : il doit protéger les membres vulnérables dans un contexte de recomposition familiale et d'instabilité familiale. Il doit aussi respecter le droit à l'égalité entre les conjoint-e-s. Le droit québécois de la famille comme celui des autres provinces canadiennes est marqué par la tension entre le respect des libertés individuelles et la protection des membres vulnérables. Comme l'affirme Moore, « [d]'un rôle organique, le droit de la famille est passé à un rôle individuel, l'objectif de celui-ci n'étant plus de protéger la société, mais de proposer un équilibre, pourtant difficile à atteindre, entre la protection de l'égalité des membres de la famille et le respect de leur liberté[111] ».

Le droit de la famille reconnaît indirectement que la famille a un rôle à jouer dans la procréation. Il n'impose cependant pas une obligation de procréation aux couples. À l'instar de nombreux pays occidentaux, le taux de natalité au Québec est à la baisse.[112] Presque toutes les formes de familles sont reconnues. Plus de 70 % des enfants naissent hors des liens du mariage. L'État ne peut discriminer entre les enfants selon les circonstances de leur naissance (art. 522 CcQ). Les techniques de procréation médicalement assistée sont disponibles pour toute personne ou couple infertile, peu importe leur statut matrimonial ; elles ne sont pas limitées aux couples hétérosexuels. Un programme étatique couvre une certaine partie des coûts à certaines conditions.[113] De nombreuses mesures et programmes étatiques aident les familles avec des enfants.[114]

---

[110] Le respect de la diversité des couples et des familles est aussi un des principes directeurs qui ont inspiré le Rapport du Comité consultatif sur le droit de la famille. Voir Québec, Comité consultatif sur le droit de la famille, A. Roy (prés.), *Pour un droit de la famille adapté aux nouvelles réalités conjugales et familiales*, Thémis, Montréal 2015.

[111] B. Moore, « Culture et droit de la famille : de l'institution à l'autonomie individuelle » (2009) 54 *Revue de droit de McGill* 257, 272. Sur les fonctions de la famille et l'évolution du droit de la famille, voir M. Tétrault, *Droit de la famille, Volume 1 – Le mariage, l'union civile et les conjoints de fait : Droits, obligations et conséquences de la rupture*, Yvon Blais, Cowansville 2010, paras 1.5 et s.; A. Roy, « Le droit de la famille à l'heure des choix » (2019) 2 *Cours de perfectionnement du notariat* 97 ; A. Roy, « Droit de la famille – Revue de jurisprudence sélective. Quel droit pour les familles d'aujourd'hui et de demain ? » (2019) 121 *Revue du Notariat* 1.

[112] En 2017, l'indice synthétique de fécondité au Québec a été mesuré à 1,54 enfant par femme. Voir Évolution de l'indice synthétique de fécondité, Québec, 1980 à 2017, *Statistiques de santé et de bien être selon le sexe – Tout le Québec*.

[113] Voir Loi modifiant diverses dispositions en matière de procréation assistée, LQ 2021, c. 2 (adoption le 11.03.2021 et entrée en vigueur le 15.11.2021).

[114] Par exemple, des congés de parentalité payés pour s'occuper des nouveaux nés, des allocations familiales versées à la mère des enfants, des déductions fiscales pour les parents (ou titulaires de l'autorité parentale) d'enfants de moins de 18 ans et pour ceux aux études, des déductions fiscales pour les aidant-e-s naturel-le-s, un réseau de garderies financé par l'État. Toutes ces mesures de conciliation entre la vie familiale et professionnelle n'ont pas permis d'augmenter le taux de natalité.

La famille constitue le premier lieu d'éducation des enfants. Les parents ont le devoir d'éducation de leur enfant (art. 599 CcQ). Cependant, bien qu'un petit nombre de parents choisissent de faire l'école à la maison, c'est principalement l'État qui se charge de l'éducation des enfants dès l'âge de quatre à cinq ans (ex. : obligation de fréquentation scolaire, école maternelle à quatre ans, garderies étatiques à prix réduit).

L'État prend en charge les personnes vulnérables[115]. Cependant, avec le désengagement de l'État-providence, la famille doit aussi s'en occuper en raison du vieillissement de la population.[116] Avec les séjours hospitaliers de plus en plus courts, ce sont les membres de la famille, surtout les femmes,[117] qui doivent s'occuper de leurs malades. Il en va de même pour les personnes âgées, qui ne peuvent compter sur l'État pour leur fournir tous les soins. Notons, par ailleurs, qu'un nombre grandissant de personnes vivent seules sans enfant, ni conjoint, ni famille. Elles doivent compter sur les services fournis par l'État.

Ce portrait sommaire de la famille québécoise dans le contexte canadien témoigne bien que les nombreuses transformations de la famille contemporaine et les défis qu'elles posent n'échappent pas à notre pays. Les approches en ce qui a trait aux fonctions de la famille et à la réforme du droit varient grandement d'un océan à l'autre, selon les choix de politiques publiques et économiques qui diffèrent. Elles s'expliquent également en partie par le bijuridisme qui coexiste sur son territoire.

En 2002, le droit de la famille québécois innovait en encadrant l'homoparenté. Aujourd'hui, le droit de certaines autres provinces canadiennes va beaucoup plus loin en reconnaissant la pluriparenté. Une réforme en cours au Québec propose une modernisation de certains aspects du droit de la filiation, notamment l'encadrement de la gestation pour autrui, mais la conjugalité est toujours en attente de réforme. Alors que les deux tiers des enfants québécois naissent de conjoint-e-s uni-e-s de fait, l'encadrement de cette union demeure exclu du Code civil entraînant des inégalités entre les conjoint-e-s et entre les enfants.

---

[115] Voir entre autres la Loi visant à lutter contre la maltraitance envers les aînés et toute autre personne majeure en situation de vulnérabilité, RLRQ, c. l-6.3.

[116] Selon les prévisions, en 2066, la population québécoise de 65 ans et plus devrait augmenter de près de 1,3 million, s'élevant à 2,7 millions de personnes. La part des personnes aînées dans la population totale grimperait ainsi à 25 % en 2031 et à 28 % en 2066, comparativement à 18 % en 2016. Voir Institut de la statistique du Québec, *Perspectives démographiques du Québec et des régions, 2016–2066*, Édition 2019, p 10 ; Vieillissement : réalités sociales, économiques et de santé, en ligne : https://statistique.quebec.ca/docs-ken/vitrine/vieillissement/index.html?theme=population&tab=3. (le 10 août 2022).

[117] Voir Conseil du statut de la femme, *Portrait : les proches aidants et les proches aidantes au Québec. Une analyse différenciée selon les sexes*, Gouvernement du Québec, 2018.

CROATIAN LEGISLATION'S RESPONSE TO MULTIPLE PARENTHOOD AND CHALLENGES OF DETERMINING FAMILY FUNCTIONS

Branka REŠETAR and Nataša LUCIĆ

1. Introduction 211
2. Part A. Diversity and Plurality of Family Forms 212
   2.1. Recognition of Multiple Parents in the Context of Step-Families 213
   2.2. Recognition of Multiple Parents if a Child is Raised in More than One Household. 218
   2.3. Recognition of Multiple Parents if a Child is Raised in a Polygamous Family 219
3. Part B. Diversity and Plurality of Family's Functions 221
   3.1. Legal Recognition of Various Functions of the Family............ 221
   3.2. The Functions which are Predominantly Favoured............... 224
4. Conclusion.. 225

1. INTRODUCTION

In Croatia, as in many other countries, the understanding that the family consists exclusively of spouses and children has disappeared. Consequently, changes in family forms are a reality that Croatian society has been facing in recent decades. National legislation accepts and responds to some of these social changes, extending the legal effects of marriage to other forms of family unions, such as cohabitation and same-sex partnerships. Changes in family forms have brought about an increase in the number of children born out of wedlock, growing up with one parent, in a household with one parent and a parent's cohabitant who is not the child's other parent, etc. In this regard, this report seeks to determine whether, and if so, how, family law in the Croatian jurisdiction recognises that a child can have multiple parents. In addition, since the law follows the development of modern biomedical achievements in the field of medically assisted reproduction, the report provides an answer to the question of whether medically assisted reproduction can lead to some form of multiple parenthood, and whether Croatian law recognises other family law institutions that can create multiple parenthood.

While the first part of the report deals with family forms and possible forms of multiple parenthood within them, the second part of the report is dedicated to family functions. In general, it can be said that changes in family forms are not followed by changes in family functions. Therefore, Croatian law has been focusing on the same or similar family functions for decades. The report seeks to answer the question of what the key family functions that are recognised by Croatian legislation are and whether some of them are predominantly favoured.

2. PART A. DIVERSITY AND PLURALITY OF FAMILY FORMS

The Constitution of the Republic of Croatia[1] places the family under the special protection of the State.[2] It explicitly refers to two family forms: marriage and cohabitation, which in Croatian law are exclusively unions of persons of different sexes. Although the Constitution does not explicitly mention same-sex families, they undoubtedly enjoy constitutional protection under Article 61 because national legislation defines same-sex partnerships as family unions.

The basic legal sources of family law in Croatia are the Family Act[3] (FA 2015) and the Same-Sex Life Partnerships Act[4] (LPA 2014). The FA 2015 regulates two forms of family unions, namely marriage[5] and cohabitation,[6] and the legal relations of parents and children. The LPA 2014 regulates family law relations of same-sex partners in two forms of family unions, namely life partnership[7] and

---

[1] Constitution of the Republic of Croatia (Official Gazette no. 56/90, 135/97, 08/98, 113/00, 124/00, 28/01, 41/01, 55/01, 76/10, 85/10, 05/14).
[2] Art. 61 of the Constitution.
[3] Family Act (Official Gazette no. 103/15, 98/19).
[4] Same Sex Life Partnership Act (Official Gazette no. 92/14, 98/19).
[5] Marriage is defined as a 'legally regulated life relationship between a woman and a man': Art. 12 of the FA 2015.
[6] Cohabitation is defined as 'the life relationship between an unmarried woman and an unmarried man which lasts at least three years or less if partners have a joint child born or if the relationship has been succeeded by marriage': Art. 11 para. 1 of the FA 2015.
[7] Life partnership is defined as a 'family life relationship between two persons of the same sex that was concluded before a competent body pursuant to the provisions of the LPA': Art. 2 of the LPA 2014.

informal life partnership,[8] and legal relations of a child with a life partner or informal life partner of one of his or her parents.

Of course, the diversity of family forms is not limited to the aforementioned family institutions defined by law. In practice, various other forms of family unions occur, such as a family union consisting of two sisters and a child of one of them, a family union consisting of one parent, a child, grandparents, etc. In this sense, the remainder of the report will discuss whether Croatian family law recognises multiple parents in the context of step-families, but also beyond them, if a child is raised in more than one household.

2.1. RECOGNITION OF MULTIPLE PARENTS IN THE CONTEXT OF STEP-FAMILIES

In the absence of official statistics, it is difficult to estimate how many couples live in a family union with a child who is not their joint child, but this is certainly no longer rare in Croatia.[9] Although the FA 2015 does not define the term 'step-parent', its provisions imply that a step-parent is a spouse of a parent living in a family union with a child.[10] The FA 2015 does not pay significant attention to the legal relationship between the child and the step-parent. It explicitly refers to their family law relations only in the part which regulates maintenance. It stipulates that the stepmother or stepfather is obliged to support the minor step-child if the child cannot obtain maintenance from the other parent. The stepmother or stepfather is obliged to support the minor step-child after the death of the child's parent only if the step-parent was living with the step-child at the time of the parent's death.[11]

---

[8] Informal life partnership is defined as 'a family life relationship between two persons of the same sex, who have not concluded a life partnership before a competent body, provided the relationship has lasted no less than three years and from its beginning has met the requirements prescribed for the validity of a life partnership': Art. 3 para. 1 of the LPA 2014.

[9] Statistical indicators of a steady increase in the number of divorces of marriages with minor children and an increase in the number of people entering into more than one marriage during their lifetime also point to the same conclusion: see data available at https://ec.europa.eu/eurostat/statistics-explained/index.php?title=Archive:Marriages_and_births_in_Croatia/hr&oldid=248719, accessed on 22.02.2022. In addition, some research shows that some divorced people are reluctant to remarry, i.e. that after divorce they prefer cohabitation to remarriage: see N. Lucić, *Izvanbračna zajednica i pravna sigurnost*, doctoral thesis, Faculty of Law, University of Zagreb, 2015. Therefore, there are families in which children live with one parent and the parent's cohabitant.

[10] Since marriage and cohabitation are legally equal in Croatian law, they create exactly the same legal effects. Consequently, everything that is stated in this report regarding spouses also applies to cohabitants. Therefore, a 'step-parent' should also be considered a cohabitant of a parent living in a family union with a child.

[11] Art. 288 para. 3 of the FA 2015. The maintenance obligation is mutual. The FA 2015 also stipulates that an adult step-child is obliged to maintain his or her stepmother or stepfather if

It follows, therefore, that the step-parent, at least from a legal point of view, does not play a major role in raising the child. The FA 2015 entrusts the parental responsibility exclusively to parents.[12] Only in situations where parents are prevented from adequately exercising parental responsibility (due to certain circumstances that they caused themselves or unintentionally found themselves in) can parental responsibility be entrusted to other persons,[13] where a step-parent has no legal 'precedence' over other persons.

In respect of making decisions relating to the child, the FA 2015 distinguishes between decisions that are particularly important for the child, daily decisions and emergency decisions. Although not explicitly stated, the step-parent may, in certain circumstances, make daily decisions[14] regarding the child and emergency decisions when there is an imminent danger to the child. Thus, the FA 2015 stipulates that parents, regardless of whether they exercise parental responsibility jointly or solely, have the right to make daily decisions regarding the child independently while the child is with one of them.[15] However, daily decisions may also be made by another family member living with the child, with parental consent.[16] Although this is not explicitly stated, it certainly includes the step-parent who lives with the child. In addition, the FA 2015 stipulates that in emergencies, when there is an imminent danger to the child, each parent has the right, without the consent of the other parent, to make decisions to take necessary action in accordance with the child's welfare and to inform the other parent as soon as possible. Decisions to take necessary action can be made by any other family member living with the child as well as by the step-parent.

Children and other persons have the right to personal relations if they have lived in a family with a child for a long time, have cared for the child during that time and have developed an emotional relationship with the child.[17] Thus, there

---

the stepmother or stepfather is unable to work, does not have enough means of subsistence or sufficient means of subsistence cannot be generated by the step-parent's assets and the step-parent supported or cared for the child for a longer period of time: Art. 293 of the FA 2015. The FA 2015 does not specify what is to be considered a longer period of time; the court decides on this in accordance with the principle of fairness.

[12] As a rule, both parents exercise parental responsibility together. Parental responsibility will be exercised by only one parent if the other parent died, was declared dead, is unknown or if the court so decides. A court decision may restrict the exercise of parental responsibility by one parent in full, in part, or in relation to decision-making on a particularly important issue for the child. The Croatian legal system has historically protected the right to joint parental responsibility. See D. Hrabar, 'Razvoj instituta roditeljske skrbi u hrvatskoj obiteljskopravnoj povijesti' in B. Rešetar, (ed.), *Pravna zaštita prava na (zajedničku) roditeljsku skrb*, Faculty of Law Osijek, Osijek 2012, pp. 13–30.

[13] Or social welfare institutions.

[14] E.g. these may be everyday decisions relating to a child's daily rest, play, studying, meal times, etc.

[15] Art. 110 para. 3 of the FA 2015.

[16] Art. 110 para. 4 of the FA 2015.

[17] Art. 120 para. 2 of the FA 2015.

is no doubt that this right is enjoyed by both the child and the step-parent, which is confirmed by the procedural provisions of the FA 2015.[18]

While the FA 2015 largely ignores the legal relationship between a child and a parent's spouse, that is, it does not refer to their relationship explicitly (except regarding the right to and duty of maintenance), the LPA 2014 regulates in detail the legal relationship between a child and his or her parent's life partner.[19] Pursuant to a court decision, in line with the provisions of a separate Act regulating family relations, the LPA 2014 stipulates that a life partner who is not the parent of a child has the right to exercise parental responsibility for the child (i.e. the content of parental responsibility) together with or instead of the child's parents.[20] Furthermore, the LPA 2014 stipulates that both parents jointly or a parent who solely exercises parental responsibility for a child may temporarily entrust the exercise of parental responsibility for a child partially or entirely to their life partner,[21] and if the parental responsibility for a child is entrusted for a period longer than 30 days, the entrusting statement by the parent must be certified by a notary public.[22]

Concerning maintaining personal relations after the termination of a life partnership, the LPA 2014 stipulates that both the child and the life partner have the right to maintain a personal relationship if the partner lived with the child for a long period of time and took care of the child over that time, or developed an emotional relationship with him or her, and the court shall render a decision on the motion by the former life partner, taking into account the best interests of the child.[23]

Although the right of adoption is reserved only for heterosexual couples in Croatian law, that is spouses and cohabitants, the LPA 2014, under certain conditions, through the so-called institution of partner-guardianship enables a kind of 'adoption' of a child of a same-sex partner. Partner-guardianship, under

---

[18] Art. 413 para. 2 of the FA 2015 stipulates that the court may decide on the divorce and in other cases of parental separation establish a personal relationship between the child and the stepmother or stepfather if they lived together and cared for the child at the time of divorce.

[19] Just as the FA 2015 makes the legal status of spouses and cohabitants equal, so the LPA 2014 makes the legal status of a life partner and an informal life partner equal. Moreover, in Art. 4 para. 1 it explicitly emphasises that the provisions of that law regulating the relations of life partners relating to children apply to informal life partnerships. Therefore, everything stated in this report regarding life partners also applies to informal life partners.

[20] Art. 40 para. 1 of the LPA 2014.

[21] A life partner needs to meet the prerequisites for a guardian. Art. 248 of the FA 2015 stipulates that a guardian cannot be a person: who has been deprived of the right to exercise parental responsibility; who has been deprived of legal capacity; whose interests conflict with those of the ward; who, given his or her behaviour and characteristics and his or her relationship with the ward, cannot be expected to perform the duties of a guardian properly; with whom the ward has concluded a contract about lifelong maintenance; or with whose spouse or cohabitant the ward has concluded a contract on lifelong maintenance.

[22] Art. 40 paras 2 and 3 of the LPA 2014.

[23] Art. 42 of the LPA 2014.

the requirements established by the LPA 2014, is defined as a form of care for a minor child, which may be provided by a life partner after the death of the life partner who is the parent of the child and, exceptionally, during the life of the life partner who is the parent of the child, if the other parent is unknown or has been divested of parental responsibility due to abuse of the child.[24] In the case of the death of the life partner who is the parent of the minor child, who at the time of that death was living in the family union of life partners, the surviving life partner may approach the competent court to appoint him or her as the partner-guardian of the minor child, subject to the condition that the other parent is not alive, has been declared dead, or has been divested of parental responsibility due to abuse of the child.[25] As an exception, if the other parent of the child is unknown or has been divested of parental responsibility due to abuse of the child, and in order to protect the interests and welfare of the child, the life partners may file a motion with a court to appoint the other life partner, who is not the child's parent, as partner-guardian.[26] The court shall appoint the informal life partner as the partner-guardian of the minor child if this is in the best interests of the child.[27] Pursuant to the court decision on the partner-guardianship of a minor child, the partner-guardian of the child shall acquire parental responsibility and all the rights and obligations that derive from it, and a note on the partner-guardianship shall be recorded on the child's birth certificate.[28] With the foundation of guardianship between the partner-guardian of a child on the one part, and the child and the child's descendants on the other, the permanent rights and obligations which exist under the law between parents and children and their descendants are established.[29] In this sense, partner-guardianship lasts until the child reaches the age of majority,[30] and may be terminated earlier by a court decision upon a motion of the Social Welfare Centre, if it establishes that this is required by the justified interests of the minor child; upon a mutually agreed motion by the partner-guardian of the child and the child; upon a request by the partner-guardian of the child or the child; or upon a motion by a parent whose parental responsibility has been restored by a court ruling.[31]

---

[24] Art. 44 of the LPA 2014.
[25] Art. 45 para. 1 of the LPA 2014.
[26] Art. 45 para. 2 of the LPA 2014.
[27] During the proceedings, the court shall request an expert opinion from the Social Welfare Centre and caution the Social Welfare Centre that, when drawing up its expert opinion, it must strictly respect the prohibition of discrimination on the basis of sexual orientation: Art. 46 paras 3 and 5 of the LPA 2014.
[28] Art. 47 of the LPA 2014.
[29] Art. 48 of the LPA 2014.
[30] Or by marrying before reaching the age of majority.
[31] Art. 49 para. 1 of the LPA 2014.

Conflict between Step-Parent and Parent

Since the FA 2015 does not give a significant role in the care of a child to the spouse of the child's parent, it is difficult to discuss any conflicts they might have over childcare. It is possible that certain conflicts relating to contact between the child and the former spouse of the parent may arise. As previously stated, both children and other persons have the right to personal relations if they have lived in a family with a child for a long time, have cared for the child during that time and have developed an emotional relationship with the child. Parents and other persons living with and caring for a child are obliged to enable the child to have personal relationships with persons entitled to them and to refrain from any conduct that would make it difficult to have personal relationships with the child.[32] Thus, in the event that, for example, the family union between a parent and his or her spouse is terminated, the child and the parent's ex-spouse would have a mutual right of contact even in cases where the parent opposes such contact. Only if making contact with each other would be contrary to the best interests of the child would the former spouse of the parent not be entitled to have contact with the child.[33]

The LPA 2014 stipulates that when a parent and their life partner exercise joint parental responsibility, they shall render decisions which are of importance for the child and shall give consent in relation to those decisions in mutual agreement.[34] To make decisions and resolve possible conflicts over decisions that are particularly important for the child and that may significantly affect his or her life, the LPA 2014 refers to the application of the FA provisions. In this regard, valid representation relating to changing the child's personal name, a change of residence, or choice or change of religious affiliation requires the written consent of the other holder of parental responsibility who has the right to represent the child.[35] In the case of non-consent, the court may decide which holder of parental responsibility will represent the child in the legal matter.[36] Representation of a child in relation to his or her valuable property or property rights[37] is valid if the person representing the child obtains the written consent

---

[32] Art. 120 para. 3 of the FA 2015.
[33] Art. 120 para. 4 of the FA 2015.
[34] Art. 41 para. 1 of the LPA 2014.
[35] Written consent is not required if the relocation does not significantly affect the establishment of existing personal relationships, but such relocation requires the consent of the Social Welfare Centre.
[36] Art. 100 of the FA 2015 in connection with Art. 41 para. 2 of the LPA 2014.
[37] These are representations during the alienation and encumbrance of real estate, movables that are entered in public registers or other valuable movables, disposal of shares and business interests, disposition of inheritances, acceptance of encumbered gifts or rejection of offered gifts and disposition of other valuable property rights, depending on the circumstances of the case.

of the other holder of parental responsibility and the approval of the court in out-of-court proceedings.[38]

As for possible conflicts between the parent and his or her former life partner regarding contact with the child, the same applies as in the case of conflicts between the parent and his or her ex-spouse.

It is important to emphasise that, whether it is a conflict between the parents themselves or the parents and other persons, before initiating court proceedings to resolve issues relating to parental responsibility and personal relationships with the child, it is necessary to conduct mandatory counselling. Mandatory counselling is a form of assistance to family members to make consensual decisions on family relations, taking special care to protect family relations in which the child participates and the legal consequences of not reaching an agreement and initiating court proceedings to decide on the child's personal rights.[39] It is conducted by the expert team of the Social Welfare Centre. Family members participate in person and without a proxy, and the report of the Social Welfare Centre on the mandatory counselling procedure has great weight when the court makes a decision that finally resolves the disputed issue in respect of the child.[40]

2.2. RECOGNITION OF MULTIPLE PARENTS IF A CHILD IS RAISED IN MORE THAN ONE HOUSEHOLD

Although a child may be raised in one or in more than one household and outside the context of step-families, persons living with a child in the same household do not qualify as multiple parents in terms of family law.

In certain circumstances, certain aspects of parental responsibility may be exercised by persons other than the parents themselves, but this does not create multiple parents. Thus, for example, the FA 2015 stipulates that both parents (or the parent who holds parental responsibility for the child) may temporarily entrust the daily care of the child, including accommodation, to another person, and if daily childcare is entrusted for more than 30 days, the parent's signature on the entrusting document must be notarised.[41] The persons to whom the parents

---

[38] Art. 101 of the FA in connection with Art. 41 para. 2 of the LPA 2014.
[39] See A. Čulo Margaletić, 'Obvezno savjetovanje i obiteljska medijacija kao oblici obiteljskopravne pomoći obitelji u krizi' (2021) 12 *Godišnjak Akademije pravnih znanosti Hrvatske* 67.
[40] On the role of the child in these proceedings, see B. Rešetar and N. Lucić, 'Child Participation in Family Law – Croatia' in W. Schrama, M. Freeman, N. Taylor and M. Bruning (eds), *International Handbook on Child Participation in Family Law*, Intersentia, Mortsel/Cambridge 2021, pp. 143–155.
[41] Art. 102 of the FA 2015.

may temporarily entrust the care of the child are not prescribed, but these persons must certainly meet the preconditions for a guardian prescribed by the provisions of the FA 2015.[42] Therefore, temporary childcare cannot be entrusted to a person who has been deprived of the right to have parental responsibility, has been deprived of legal capacity or whose interests conflict with those of the child. There are no other restrictions on the choice of a person to whom the parents can temporarily entrust the daily care of the child. Therefore, the person can be either someone with whom the child lives in the same household or any other person. It is important that this person has the characteristics and abilities to care for the child on a daily basis, that he or she has consented to being entrusted with the daily care of the child, and that it is for the benefit of the child.[43] In any case, the person who is temporarily entrusted with the daily care of a child does not become a multiple parent, but only temporarily cares for the child because the parent is prevented from doing so. The parent remains the holder of all rights and duties that make up the content of parental responsibility.

2.3. RECOGNITION OF MULTIPLE PARENTS IF A CHILD IS RAISED IN A POLYGAMOUS FAMILY

Croatian legislation does not recognise polygamy or multiple parents in the context of a polygamous family. *Kafala* and open adoption are institutions unknown to Croatian law. Only one form of adoption is possible, which creates a permanent and unbreakable parent–child relationship between the adopter and the child and all the rights and duties that arise from it. The biological parent loses the right to parental responsibility even before the adoption is established, as soon as 30 days have elapsed from the date of giving consent to the adoption. Therefore, it is not possible for adoption to create a multiplicity of parenthood.

Likewise, medically assisted reproduction cannot lead to multiplicity of parenthood. Although medically assisted reproduction is allowed and legally regulated in Croatia, according to the Assisted Human Reproduction Act (AHRA 2012),[44] donors do not have the right to know the identity of either the child born as a result of donor-assisted reproductive technology or the child's legal parents. Donors do not have any family rights or obligations or any other family connections with the child born as a result of donor-assisted reproductive technology.[45] Donors in Croatia are not anonymous. Therefore, the child born as a result of donor-assisted reproductive technology has a right to know the

---

[42] See section 2.1 above.
[43] Art. 247 para. 1 and Art. 248 in connection with Art. 102 para. 1 of the FA 2015.
[44] Assisted Human Reproduction Act (Official Gazette no. 86/12).
[45] Art. 19 of the AHRA 2012.

identity of the donor. The child can exercise the right to know the identity of the donor after turning 18.[46]

If the child was born as a result of donor-assisted reproductive technology using one male and one female gamete, he or she can only have legal parents (a mother and a father) and they are the only holders of parental responsibility. The right to medically assisted reproduction is granted to an adult woman with legal capacity and a man who are married or in cohabitation and who are able to exercise parental responsibility for a child, taking into consideration their age and general health status.[47] In order to avoid any disputes over the origin of the child or his or her legal parents, couples undergoing medically assisted reproduction must give their explicit consent.[48] Moreover, when cohabitants participate in a medically assisted reproduction procedure, the man is obliged to give a certified statement of acknowledgement of paternity of the child, and the woman is obliged to give a certified statement of consent to the acknowledgement of paternity of the child before the procedure takes place.[49] Therefore, when the child is born, data on the child's origin will be entered on the basis of the presumption of paternity if the child was born in wedlock, and on the basis of prior acknowledgement and consent to acknowledgement of paternity if the child was born to a couple in cohabitation. The persons registered as the child's parents are the only holders of parental responsibility and the donor has no rights or duties towards the child.

Surrogacy is strictly forbidden in Croatia. The AHRA 2012 explicitly states that it is prohibited to publicly advertise or otherwise offer the service of bearing a child for another. It is also prohibited to contract or perform medically assisted reproduction for the purpose of giving birth to a child for another person and of handing over a child born after medically assisted reproduction.

---

[46] Art. 15 of the AHRA 2012.
[47] See Art. 10 of the AHRA 2012. Women in a same-sex union are not entitled to medically assisted reproduction. However, Art. 10, para. 2 of the AHRA 2012 stipulates that the right to medically assisted reproduction is also granted to an adult, capable woman who is not married, in cohabitation or in a same-sex partnership, whose previous treatment for infertility was unsuccessful or hopeless, and who, given her age and general health, is capable of exercising parental responsibility for the child. It could happen that a single woman undergoes the procedure of medically assisted reproduction. The assumption is that this is a woman who was unsuccessfully treated for infertility. In that case, the partner of the woman who underwent the medically assisted reproduction procedure, in accordance with the provisions of the LPA 2014, could subsequently get partner-guardianship of the child conceived as a result of the medically assisted reproduction procedure. This would enable lesbian partners to become parents. However, this would only be possible in rare cases, if one of the female partners was unsuccessfully treated for infertility. N. Lucić, 'Pravno uređenje braka i drugih oblika životnih zajednica' in B. Rešetar, S. Aras Kramar, N. Lucić, I. Medić, D. Šago, I. Tucak and P. Mioč, *Suvremeno obiteljsko pravo i postupak*, Faculty of Law Osijek, Osijek 2017, p. 81.
[48] Art. 14 of the AHRA 2012.
[49] Art. 16 of the AHRA 2012.

Contracts, agreements or other legal transactions concerning bearing a child for another and the handing over of a child born after medically assisted reproduction, with or without monetary compensation, are void.[50]

3. PART B. DIVERSITY AND PLURALITY OF FAMILY'S FUNCTIONS

3.1. LEGAL RECOGNITION OF VARIOUS FUNCTIONS OF THE FAMILY

The Croatian legal system recognises many functions of a family. Some of them are mentioned in the Constitution itself. Thus, for example, the Constitution recognises childcare by the parents as a function of a family. It guarantees parents the freedom to decide independently on the upbringing of children, but also obliges them to raise, support and educate their children, and imposes on them the responsibility to protect their children's right to full and harmonious development of their personality. The Constitution emphasises that a physically and mentally disabled and socially neglected child is entitled to special care, education and welfare. On the other hand, the Constitution recognises the role of the child in protecting his or her parent in case of need. It obliges the child to care for his or her elderly and infirm parents.[51]

Family law recognises fulfilling the emotional needs of family members, producing and raising children, creating property protection, protecting the vulnerable, etc., as some of the key functions of the family. Some of these functions can be deduced from the very principles of family law, such as the principle of equality of women and men in the family,[52] the principle of solidarity, mutual respect and assistance among all family members,[53] the principle of primary protection of the welfare and rights of the child,[54] the principle of the primary right of parents to care for the child and the duty of competent bodies to provide assistance,[55] and the principle of guardianship protection.[56]

Regarding the fulfilment of emotional needs by creating close family relationships, the FA 2015 stipulates that in family relations, spouses and cohabitants should be equal, be loyal to each other, help and support each other,

---

[50] Art. 31 of the AHRA 2012. Croatian family law theory also opposes surrogacy. See e.g. D. Hrabar, 'Surogatno majčinstvo kao moderan oblik eksploatacije žena i trgovine djecom' (2020) 70 *Zbornik Pravnog fakulteta u Zagrebu* 171.
[51] Art. 65 of the Constitution.
[52] Art. 3 of the FA 2015.
[53] Art. 4 of the FA 2015.
[54] Art. 5 of the FA 2015.
[55] Art. 6 of the FA 2015.
[56] Art. 8 of the FA 2015.

respect each other and maintain harmonious marital and family relations. The FA 2015 obliges them to make consensual decisions on the birth and raising of children and on performing work in the family community.[57] Similarly, the LPA 2014 stipulates that life partners and informal life partners must mutually and jointly decide on all issues relevant to living together, have an obligation to help each other and must provide care and assistance in case of illness.[58]

Family legislation pays a lot of attention to raising children as a function of the family.[59] The protection and promotion of the child's personal and property rights is a responsibility, a duty and a right of the parents which they cannot waive.[60] Raising children is a function of the family that is emphasised in family law regardless of the personal and/or family relationships of the parents themselves. The need for both parents to provide the child with adequate care even in the event of termination of the family union between the parents makes a divorce procedure in which there are minor children more complex than one without minor children.[61] Precisely because, in families with children, raising children is recognised as one of the most important functions of the family, family legislation is aimed at ensuring that the fulfilment of this function is not jeopardised even in situations where the child does not live in a family union with both parents.[62]

Croatian family legislation does not neglect the family's functions of a property nature. In this sense, it regulates property relations in the family in detail, and from the provisions of FA 2015 it can be concluded that the system of family property regulation favours the weaker party. Even today, women are mostly considered to be the weaker party regarding property rights as well

---

[57] Art. 31 of the FA 2015.
[58] Art. 37 of the LPA 2014.
[59] Art. 91 of the FA 2015. See D. Hrabar, 'Prava djece u obiteljskom zakonodavstvu' in D. Hrabar (ed.), *Prava djece – multidisciplinarni pristup*, Faculty of Law, University of Zagreb, Zagreb 2016, pp. 63–82.
[60] Given the connection between parents and children and, as a rule, the upbringing of children in the family with their parents, the parental responsibility must be a response to the needs of children, shaped by their rights. However, it is clear that many of the rights of children contained in family law belong to children independently of their parents because they have the meaning of original human rights. D. Hrabar, 'Obiteljskopravni odnosi roditelja i djece' in D. Hrabar (ed.), *Obitelj- sko pravo*, Official Gazette, Zagreb 2021, p. 182.
[61] In the case of a divorce with minor children, the mandatory counselling procedure must be carried out before the divorce proceedings. If they do not reach an agreement on joint parental responsibility during the compulsory counselling (or family mediation) procedure, it will not be possible to divorce in non-contentious proceedings; then, they can exclusively divorce in contentious proceedings. See B. Rešetar, 'The New Divorce Legislation in the Republic of Croatia under the Influence of Psychology, Sociology, and International Law' (2018) 32 *International Journal of Law Policy and the Family* 63.
[62] In this sense, the raising of children as a function of the family is not neglected in the LPA 2014 either, which regulates in great detail how the life partner of the parent with whom the parent and child live in a family union can participate in raising the child and in childcare. See section 2.2 above.

as the standard of living in the family and after divorce or separation. Croatia emphasises the 'dominant ideology of the family' which understands the husband to be the main breadwinner and the wife to be the primary carer of the children and other dependants. This conclusion can help in determining the preferred purpose and the foundation of the matrimonial property system, that is, the regulation of protection of the weaker party.[63] However, the weaker party in a partnership is not necessarily a woman. The property management system obliges spouses to mutually support each other's property for the duration of the family union, especially in situations where one of the spouses finds himself or herself at a disadvantage. The same goes for life partners. Through the institution of maintenance, this family function can be extended for a certain period of time after the termination of their family union.

The fulfilment of the family's property function through the institution of maintenance is, of course, not limited to family partnerships. Family maintenance is both the right and duty of parents and children[64] and, as previously stated, of stepmothers and stepfathers and children,[65] of grandparents and children,[66] and of the parents of an illegitimate child.[67]

The protection and care of family members who are deprived of legal capacity and who are otherwise unable to protect their rights and interests are also the focus of family law. The very fact that the institution of guardianship is regulated by family legislation indicates that the Croatian legislator primarily recognises the family as the best place to protect persons deprived of legal capacity or persons who, due to certain circumstances, are unable to take care of themselves.[68] Although the guardian of a person deprived of legal capacity does not necessarily have to be a member of his or her family, it is certain that the guardian will be primarily sought from among the persons with whom the ward has close family ties. Moreover, if a person who is deprived of legal

---

[63] B. Rešetar, 'Matrimonial Property in Europe: A Link Between Sociology and Family Law' (2008) 12 *Electronic Journal of Comparative Law* 1.
[64] Parents are the first parties who are obliged to maintain their minor child. The maintenance obligation between parents and children is mutual. Therefore, an adult child has the duty to maintain a parent who is unable to work and does not have enough means of subsistence or who cannot generate sufficient means through his or her assets.
[65] Also mutually. See section 2.1 above.
[66] If a parent does not support a minor child, the child's grandparents are obliged to support him or her. An adult grandchild is obliged to maintain his or her grandmother or grandfather if the grandmother or grandfather is unable to work, does not have enough means of subsistence or cannot generate sufficient means through his or her assets and the grandparent supported or cared for the child for a longer period of time: Art. 294 of the FA 2015. The FA 2015 does not specify what is to be considered a longer period of time; the court decides on this in accordance with the principle of fairness.
[67] The parent of an illegitimate child is obliged to support the other parent for one year from the birth of the joint child if that parent is caring for the child and does not have sufficient means of subsistence: Art. 305 of the FA 2015.
[68] The institution of guardianship is regulated by Arts 224–280 of the FA 2015.

capacity has a parent or parents who agree and are able to take care of their adult child who is deprived of legal capacity, the Social Welfare Centre will give such parent or parents priority over other persons when deciding on the choice of guardian.[69] Therefore, there is no doubt that the family can also have and fulfil its guardianship function.

3.2. THE FUNCTIONS WHICH ARE PREDOMINANTLY FAVOURED

It is difficult to single out predominantly favoured functions of the family in the Croatian legal system. Nevertheless, it can be noted that national legislation pays special attention to the protection of vulnerable family members. All other functions of the family are in some way related to the protection of the vulnerable family members.

By 'vulnerable person' we primarily mean a child. It has already been pointed out that family legislation gives a lot of attention to raising children as a function of the family. The health, development, welfare and other personal and property rights of the child as a vulnerable person are primarily provided for within the family.

The property function, too, is closely related to the protection of the vulnerable. This is confirmed by the matrimonial property system itself, which stipulates that everything that spouses acquire through work for the duration of their union is co-owned in equal parts, regardless of the spouses' individual contributions. This legal provision is, of course, aimed precisely at protecting the weaker and thus the more vulnerable party. Likewise, the right to maintenance for the duration of the family union and after its termination is unquestionably aimed at protecting the vulnerable family member, that is, one who does not have sufficient means of subsistence, is not employed or cannot be employed because he or she suffers from certain illnesses or for other reasons.

Finally, the purpose of the institution of guardianship, which is regulated in great detail by family law, is to protect persons deprived of legal capacity or persons who, due to certain circumstances, are unable to take care of themselves, that is, vulnerable persons. Therefore, the link between guardianship protection and protection of the vulnerable family member as the family's function is obvious and clear.

Therefore, although it cannot be said that it is predominantly favoured, protecting the vulnerable family members is certainly a function of the family to which Croatian legislation pays very significant attention and which it links to most other functions of the family.

---

[69] Art. 247 para. 2 of the FA 2015.

4. CONCLUSION

The first part of the report sought to determine whether, and if so, how, family law in the Croatian jurisdiction recognises that a child can have multiple parents. The review and analysis of the relevant rules leads to the conclusion that the Croatian legislation does not contain provisions that create multiple parenthood. The starting point is that family law recognises only two legal parents (and these are only the biological parents or adoptive parents of the child), although under certain circumstances the holders of certain parental responsibilities may be other persons, and not only parents.

Concerning step-families, it can generally be said that Croatian law neglects the family law relations of the child and his or her step-parent. Moreover, given its frequency, the law almost ignores this form of family relationship. For decades, Croatian family law has explicitly mentioned the legal relationship between a child and his or her step-parent only in connection with the step-parent's obligation to maintain the child in the event that the child cannot be supported by his or her parent. However, although we do not have exact numbers, in practice it is not uncommon for a step-parent to care for a child and to protect the child's personal and property rights as his or her parent. The step-parent often does this in addition to the child's parents. In other words, a step-parent exercises many aspects of parental responsibility, not because he or she is obliged to do so by family law, but because the step-parent lives with the child in the family union and wants to take care of the child and meet the child's needs. The modern development of family law has, however, recognised the importance of regulating the family relationship of a child and his or her parent's same-sex partner, while the family relationship between a child and a spouse or cohabitant of his or her parent (and this family relationship is much more common in practice) is, for some reason, not regulated.

The second part of the report, which analyses the family's functions, points to the conclusion that Croatian legislation recognises a number of the family's functions, among which none is explicitly predominantly favoured. Nevertheless, the analysis of family law shows that the protection of vulnerable family members is the focus of many family law institutions, and in this sense the protection of vulnerable family members is in some way linked to almost all other functions of the family. Whereas family forms are changing more and more significantly, the family's functions show immutability in both social and legal contexts. Modern law does not create new functions of either an emotional or a property nature for the family; it only develops mechanisms for their effective fulfilment in all family forms.

NEW FAMILY FORMS IN DENMARK

Legal Adaptability and Rigidity

Ingrid Lund-Andersen and Frank H. Pedersen

1. Introduction 227
2. Step-Parents 228
   2.1. The Requirements and Legal Effects of Adoption 228
   2.2. Contact with an Adopted Child's Original Relatives 230
   2.3. Transfer of Parental Responsibility 231
   2.4. Indirect Duty of Support 232
   2.5. Contact and Visitation Rights 233
   2.6. Care of a Seriously Ill Child 234
3. Parentage of a Child Born as a Result of Donated Gametes 235
   3.1. A Female Donor 235
   3.2. A Male Donor 236
4. Parentage of a Child Born through Surrogacy 238
5. Various Functions of the Family 242
   5.1. Having and Raising Children 242
       5.1.1. Producing Children 242
       5.1.2. Financial Aid to Parents 243
   5.2. Providing Economic Security 243
       5.2.1. Protecting the Vulnerable in Marriage 243
       5.2.2. Protecting the Vulnerable Child 245
   5.3. New Family Forms and the Latest Debate 245
6. Closing Considerations 248

1. INTRODUCTION

In this chapter, we will describe the pluralities in Danish families and the different forms of families. The purpose of family law is to create a framework for the community in the family and to support the many caring tasks that form an important part of the family's functions, especially in families with children.

The close emotional ties in a family must be taken into account while it must at the same time be recognised that families are different and want to arrange themselves in different ways.

Denmark does not recognise polygamous families, and a child is not allowed to have more than two legal parents. Nevertheless, a kind of multiple parenthood may arise in special situations – especially in the context of step-families.

There is no general description of the relationship between a step-parent and a step-child, but there are a number of provisions that, to varying degrees, attach legal significance to this relationship. In what follows, the emphasis is on family law issues.

A number of legal issues arise from the use of reproductive technology. In this chapter, the focus is on parentage of children born as a result of donated gametes or through surrogacy. Denmark has very flexible rules concerning whether a man who has donated sperm shall be deemed to be a legal father or not. This means that in most scenarios the parties involved can reach the desired legal result. However, this only applies to donated gametes from a man, not from a woman. Denmark adheres strictly to the norm that the woman giving birth is the legal mother of the child. Partly due to this, the Danish rules concerning surrogacy are anything but flexible.

In the closing considerations it will be highlighted how new family forms are making their mark on the legal policy debate in Denmark.

2. STEP-PARENTS

A step-parent cannot be an additional legal parent to a step-child if the child has two legal parents.

However, a step-parent may obtain rights in relation to a step-child or indirect obligations can be imposed on the step-parent.

2.1. THE REQUIREMENTS AND LEGAL EFFECTS OF ADOPTION

As the most far-reaching relationship between a step-parent and a step-child, an adoption can be granted which means that the step-parent obtains the same rights and responsibilities as a biological parent. Upon adoption, a complete parent–child relationship will take effect between the adopter and the adopted child, for example in relation to parental responsibility, the maintenance obligation, and inheritance. At the same time, the legal relationship between the adopted child and the biological parent with whom the child does not live terminates.[1]

Adoption is granted by permission, which is issued by the Agency of Family Law. The adoption requirements set by sections 2–15 of the Adoption Act must be fulfilled.

It is a condition for the adoption that the adoption is for the benefit of the child. In the assessment of whether the adoption will benefit the child, emphasis is placed on whether the applicant and his or her spouse or cohabitant and the child have lived together for a continuous period of at least two-and-a-half years at the time of the application.

A cohabitation relationship must be stable and of a marriage-like nature. Marriage-like conditions usually require a common registry address immediately up to the filing of the application. Other elements may be whether the couple has held joint vacations or celebrated the holidays together, and whether they have acted as a couple, regardless of gender.[2]

An applicant must be over the age of 25 and at the same time be at least 14 years older than the child.

If the child is under the age of 18, both parents must give their consent to the adoption. A child who has reached the age of 12 must also give his or her consent.[3] Before giving consent, the child has to receive information about the legal effects of adoption. If the child is under the age of 12, information on his or her attitude towards the adoption shall be available to the extent that the child's maturity and the circumstances of the case so require. The child's opinion must be taken into account as far as possible.

In cases where a parent is not the co-holder of parental responsibility, the parent must submit a declaration of his or her opinion on the adoption.[4] If the parent objects to the adoption, the Agency of Family Law has to decide whether or not the adoption is to be permitted. If the parent's objection is due to the fact that the parent will lose contact with the child, then permission to adopt will normally be refused.

It is possible for a step-parent to adopt a step-child of a deceased spouse or cohabitant. Likewise, a step-parent may be permitted to adopt his or her step-child after a divorce or a termination of cohabitation, but then it is required that the person who is to be adopted is of legal age (18 years old). Even if the step-parent has remarried, a step-child can be adopted. Consent from the step-parent's new spouse is not required for adoption of a former spouse's child.

---

[1] S. 16 of the Adoption Act (Consolidation Act No. 775 of 07.08.2019).
[2] Guidance notes on Adoption (*Vejledning*) No. 9401 of 26.06.2020 pkt. 4.4.1.
[3] S. 6 of the Adoption Act (Consolidation Act No. 775 of 07.08.2019).
[4] S. 7 of the Adoption Act (Consolidation Act No. 775 of 07.08.2019).

In special cases, the adoption of a step-child can be revoked by a court judgment,[5] and the court can decide that the legal relationship with the biological parent and his or her family shall be re-established.[6]

To take an example from case law, after divorcing the adoptive stepfather, the mother found out that a termination of the adoption would be of significant importance to the child.[7] The now 11-year-old adopted child had lived with her biological father until she was three-and-a-half years old. Then she had lived with her stepfather for almost two years, but shortly thereafter contact between them had ceased due to a suspicion of sexual assault against the girl. With the exception of a two-year period, she had had constant contact with her biological father, whom she wanted to be her legal father again. A court annulled the adoption and the legal relationship between the child and the biological father, and his family was re-established despite the fact that it was against the wishes of the biological father. Surprisingly, he was not interested in having a formal legal relationship with his daughter again, as he did not have close contact with her, because he was seeing her only monthly. The court emphasised the reason for the revocation, the child's age and the other circumstances, including that contact between the child and the biological father had only been interrupted for a relatively short time.

In this case, the child had her legal father replaced with her mother's new partner for a period of two years, after which the biological father re-entered as the legal father. Throughout her childhood, the girl had two de facto fathers, but not two legal fathers at the same time.

2.2. CONTACT WITH AN ADOPTED CHILD'S ORIGINAL RELATIVES

At the request of the child's original relatives, contact rights may be granted to the relatives in terms of section 20 a of the Parental Responsibility Act. This may particularly be the case if the child had contact with the original relatives prior to adoption.[8] Section 20 a is primarily aimed at the adopted child's original parents, but the provision can also be invoked by other relatives, including grandparents and siblings. The purpose is to preserve the biological ties in situations where this is in the best interests of the child. The provision covers

---

[5] S. 19(1) of the Adoption Act (Consolidation Act No. 775 of 07.08.2019).
[6] S. 23(3) of the Adoption Act (Consolidation Act No. 775 of 07.08.2019).
[7] *Ugeskrift for Retsvæsen (Weekly Law Journal)* 2006.2830.
[8] S. 20 a of the Parental Responsibility Act was introduced in 2009 by Act No. 494 of 12.08.2009. In 2019, the requirement 'in very special cases' was abolished as it was unlikely that this restriction was in line with the European Convention on Human Rights.

all adoptions, including step-child adoption.[9] Thus – on a psychological level – a child can experience having more than two parents.

The contact that can be provided under section 20 a will be more limited in frequency and scope than contact in other family relations. The extent and frequency will, as a general rule, not exceed the scope and frequency of the contact which has been practised prior to the adoption. If several members of the original family ask for contact, it must be considered whether it will be in the best interests of the child to have contact with several original relatives. In this regard, attention must be paid to the child's overall situation and to the fact that contact is established for a long time to come. This may justify limiting the extent and frequency of the contact.

2.3. TRANSFER OF PARENTAL RESPONSIBILITY

In order to avoid the far-reaching legal effects of an adoption, it is possible by agreement to transfer parental responsibility to others, for example to a step-parent.[10] When the agreement is approved by the Agency of Family Law or by the Family Court, joint parental responsibility is established between one parent and his or her spouse or cohabitant. As a holder of parental responsibility, the step-parent is obliged to take care of the child and can decide on the child's personal conditions based on the child's interests and needs. This means that a step-parent can decide on where the child should live, about the child's food and clothes, which kindergarten or school the child should go to, etc. Both parents maintain a legal affiliation with the child, especially support obligations, and the child retains the right to visitation and the right of inheritance in relation to the parents.

Prior to the approval of the agreement, the parent who does not have parental responsibility has to give a statement.[11] The parent's objection will be given weight, as the legal ties between the parent and the child will be weakened.[12]

An example from case law is illustrative of this. A mother, who had sole parental responsibility, wanted joint parental responsibility with her spouse, to whom she had been married for seven years.[13] The child's father objected to this agreement. The mother referred to the fact that in everyday life she and her spouse behaved as if they had joint parental responsibility. The child had difficulty speaking and needed support for his schooling. The father had not

---

[9] See S. Krone Christensen, *Forældreansvarsloven med kommentarer*, Karnov Group, Copenhagen 2020, p. 394.
[10] S. 13(2) of the Parental Responsibility Act (Consolidation Act No. 1768 of 30.11.2020).
[11] S. 36 of the Parental Responsibility Act (Consolidation Act No. 1768 of 30.11.2020).
[12] S. Krone Christensen, *Forældreansvarsloven med kommentarer*, Karnov Group, Copenhagen 2020, pp. 240–41.
[13] *Tidsskrift for Familie- og Arveret (Journal of Family Law and Succession Law)* 2006.518/2.

wanted contact with the child for the last two years. The administrative appeal authority found that there was no particular reason to approve the agreement of the joint parental responsibility, as the legal ties between father and child would be weakened. The stepfather's ability to support the child – among other things to attend parent–teacher meetings at school – did not require that he have parental responsibility.

The case shows that when the parties involved do not agree, the authorities make a strict assessment of the need to transfer parental responsibility to a step-parent. This is probably due to both safeguarding the interests of the biological parent and to ensuring that the child does not have multiple parents.

2.4. INDIRECT DUTY OF SUPPORT

A step-parent – married or cohabiting – has no direct obligation to provide for the step-child. Regardless of this fact, some provisions on social benefits impose an indirect duty on a step-parent to support the step-child. When a parent applies for certain social benefits, the total household income is taken into consideration, which also includes the income of a step-parent who is married to or lives in a marriage-like relationship with the applicant. For example, when a low-income mother applies for a reduced payment of her child's day-care costs, the stepfather's income – as part of the household income – may result in a rejection of the mother's application. Similarly, a parent will lose the child allowance as a single parent if he or she marries a new partner or establishes a marriage-like relationship.[14] A relationship similar to marriage exists when the parties have a joint household and live together in a relationship that can lead to marriage.[15] It is not important whether they are registered in the national register as residing at the same address. There will be an assessment of the character of the parties' relationship and their housing circumstances. Even if they have different homes, they may be considered to be living in a relationship similar to marriage.

Consequently, a step-parent's contributions to the family expenses, including some of the expenses of the step-child, are often necessary. This creates an indirect duty of support towards the step-child. At the same time, the parent who does not live with the child has a duty to pay child support. The stepfather's indirect economic duty cannot be enforced, and therefore in this regard a multiplicity of obligations following from parenthood will not arise.

---

[14] S. 2(1) of the Consolidation Act on Child Allowance (Consolidation Act No. 63 of 21.01.2019).
[15] Guidance notes on child allowance (*Vejledning om børnetilskud*) No. 10177 of 11.10.2007 pkt. 13.

2.5. CONTACT AND VISITATION RIGHTS

When the relationship between a child's parent and a step-parent ends, the step-parent – one of the child's closest family members – can apply for contact rights. To decide whether a person is to be considered as next of kin, the child's social relationship to the person is the most important factor and not the child's biological connection to the person.[16]

Section 20 of the Parental Responsibility Act has a narrow scope. According to the section, a request for contact may become relevant in different situations.

Firstly, if a parent or both parents are dead or a parent is unknown, contact with the child's closest relatives may be established.[17] A person who has lived with a child's mother and served as a parent of the child (a social parent/step-parent) can apply for visitation rights if the child was born through anonymous donor sperm or if the child's mother does not know who the biological father is. The social parent and the child's mother must have been in a relationship as cohabiting, married or registered partners.[18] A female party to a same-sex couple (not being the biological mother) may also apply, if she has acted as the child's parent, but not as a co-mother who has adopted the child prior to the dissolution of the relationship.

Secondly, if there is no, or only very limited, contact with the parent with whom the child does not reside, contact can be established with the child's closest relatives.[19] In the assessment, considerable weight will be given to the reason for the very limited contact with the legal parent with whom the child does not live. Therefore, the Agency of Family Law must obtain a declaration from this parent.[20] The importance of the parent's opinion depends on the specific situation. If the child has for several years been closely related to the applicant (e.g. a former step-parent), the application could be granted despite objections from the parent.

If there has been established contact with the child and a former step-parent, and the child is reunited with the parent with whom the child does not reside, this does not mean that the child's contact with the step-parent will automatically cease. In this situation, the legal parent can request a change of the step-parent's visitation rights.

Contact with a child's former step-parent may be established in cases where a parent with whom the child does not reside is periodically absent, for example because he or she is staying abroad or is in prison. Attention must be paid to

---

[16] S. Krone Christensen, *Forældreansvarsloven med kommentarer*, Karnov Group, Copenhagen 2020, p. 387.
[17] S. 20(1) of the Parental Responsibility Act (Consolidation Act No. 1768 of 30.11.2020).
[18] Guidance notes on Parental Responsibility (*Vejledning*) No. 10064 of 20.12.2020 pkt. 5.8.
[19] S. 20(2) of the Parental Responsibility Act (Consolidation Act No. 1768 of 30.11.2020).
[20] S. 36(2) of the Parental Responsibility Act (Consolidation Act No. 1768 of 30.11.2020).

whether it would be best for the child to alternate between the other legal parent and the step-parent, or whether such a scheme would cause instability for the child.[21] The assessment must be based on the child's overall situation. It will be taken into account whether the resident parent opposes contact with anyone other than the legal parent and perhaps also opposes contact with the other legal parent. It is important that contact is stable and continuous for the child and is established for a long time to come. The duration of the other legal parent's absence will also have an impact on the assessment.

In these cases, a child may experience having contact with two different kinds of parents (the former step-parent and the biological parent with whom the child does not reside), which can be stressful for the child. It is important to be aware that all decisions under the Parental Responsibility Act must be made based on what is best for the child.[22]

In a situation where a child lives with both his or her biological parents, a step-parent who had previously lived with the child cannot obtain visitation rights under section 20 of the Parental Responsibility Act. This prevents the step-parent's contact rights from competing with the biological parent's rights when he or she lives with the child.

An example that can be mentioned is a case where a man had lived with a mother and her daughter for eight years.[23] He had acted as a father, and after the parties split up he was granted the right to have contact with the girl. Shortly afterwards, the mother moved in with a new partner who was the biological father of the girl and now registered his paternity. The mother opposed continuation of the stepfather's right to contact. The Supreme Court ruled that there was no longer a legal basis for contact rights for the stepfather, as the daughter was living with her two biological parents.

2.6. CARE OF A SERIOUSLY ILL CHILD

According to a decision from the National Social Appeals Board, a step-parent may be included in the group of persons who are entitled to unemployment benefits for the care of a seriously ill child.[24] When assessing whether a step-parent is entitled to the unemployment benefit on that basis, the authority will emphasise the step-parent's relationship with the child's biological or adoptive parent and the step-parent's relationship with the child, including how long they have lived together and have functioned as a family. Substantial weight will be given to

---

[21] Guidance notes on Parental Responsibility (*Vejledning*) No. 10064 of 20.12.2020 pkt. 5.8.
[22] S. 4 of the Parental Responsibility Act (Consolidation Act No. 1768 of 30.11.2020).
[23] *Ugeskrift for Retsvæsen (Weekly Law Journal)* 2015.957.
[24] Decision 100-113 of 30.08.2013. See the provisions of the Social Services Act on the right to compensation for lost earnings.

the question whether the step-parent usually participates in the day-to-day care of the child. If a step-parent has taken care of a seriously ill step-child and is entitled to compensation for lost earnings, he or she will receive the same financial amount as a parent would have received.

3. PARENTAGE OF A CHILD BORN AS A RESULT OF DONATED GAMETES

The Danish rules for gamete donation are highly gendered, particularly concerning the question of whether a donation entails the status of legal parent for the donor. The legal consequences here are constructed as two opposites. Oocyte donation can never create any parental rights, whereas the principal rule for sperm donation is that a sperm donor will be deemed the father of any child born as a result of his donation. However, this is merely the default rule and not the main rule in practice. That is, if a man's donation has been made to a tissue establishment or to medical staff, he will not be considered the father of any child born as a result of his donation.

Danish law and practice distinguish between an anonymous donor, a non-anonymous donor, and a known donor.[25] With an anonymous donation, the donor can never be revealed to the child or the parents. With a non-anonymous donor or open donor, the child born as a result of the donation can contact the donor after reaching 18 years of age. The donor still has no legal rights or obligations, and the contact can only take place at the initiative of the child. In addition to these two possibilities, Danish legislation has a category of donation normally referred to as 'known donation'. With a known donation, the identity of the donor is known by the recipient at the time of the donation, and the donor knows to whom she or he is donating.

3.1. A FEMALE DONOR

Section 30 of the Danish Children's Act provides that a woman who gives birth to a child conceived through assisted reproduction is deemed to be the legal mother of the child. Hence, whether or not the woman giving birth is genetically related to the child does not alter the fact that she is regarded as the legal mother. It follows, *a contrario*, that oocyte donation cannot create any parental rights. A female who makes a known donation will thus under no circumstances have any parental rights or obligations.

---

[25] Executive order on Assisted Reproduction (*Bekendtgørelse*) No. 672 of 08.05.2015, ss 11 and 16; Guidance notes for Tissue Establishments (*Vejledning om sundhedspersoners og vævscentres virksomhed og forpligtelser i forbindelse med assisteret reproduktion*) No. 9351 of 26.05.2015, s. 9.

For a child born as a result of so-called 'three-parent' medical technology – that is, where the genetic material of one male and two females is used in order to remove genetic mutations that cause serious hereditary diseases – the parentage question also follows the unconditional rule that the woman giving birth is the legal mother. Hence, in a case referred to as a three-parent case, where the woman giving birth is the intended mother and probably one of the females who has provided genetic material, no legal issues arise about her parentage. It is important to note that such a situation would only occur if the assisted reproduction treatment has happened outside Denmark, as Denmark does not allow modification of oocytes or spermatozoa.[26]

In surrogacy cases where the intended mother is also the genetic mother, Danish law maintains that the woman giving birth, that is, the surrogate, is the legal mother. The intended mother will therefore have to attain parenthood through a step-parent adoption process. In deciding whether the step-parent adoption should be granted, the Danish authorities even claim that it is not a factor of any relevance that the child was born as a result of gametes from the intended mother having been used.[27]

Double donations – the term used when both the sperm and oocyte originate from people other than the intended parents – have been legal in Denmark since 2018. However, this is allowed only when the reason for the double donation is a medical indication.[28] In addition, one of the donors must be non-anonymous.

For female same-sex couples who want to have a child together, with one of them providing an egg and the other carrying the pregnancy, this will most often not be allowed in Denmark. The reason for this is that it will be perceived as double donation: no gametes would come from the woman carrying the pregnancy, and even though the oocyte comes from her partner, it will still be perceived as double donation. Only if there is a medical reason for not achieving pregnancy through an oocyte from the woman who intends to carry the pregnancy can an oocyte from her partner be used.

3.2. A MALE DONOR

For a male donor, the question may arise whether he will be deemed to be the legal father of any child born as a result of his donation. In practice, for the large majority of cases there is no real question and it is straightforward that he will not. This is the case when the donation happens in compliance with

---

[26] S. 2 of the Act on Assisted Reproduction (Consolidation Act No. 902 of 23.08.2019).
[27] According to Principle Decision 6-21 by the Danish Board of Appeals (KEN no. 9198, 23.03.2021), the genetic link to the child has no bearing on the decision.
[28] S. 5 of the Act on Assisted Reproduction (Consolidation Act No. 902 of 23.08.2019).

the standards for donation to a tissue establishment or authorised medical staff.[29] Such donations can be either anonymous or non-anonymous.

There are two situations in which the question of whether a male donor will be deemed to be the legal father actually becomes relevant: with a known donor and with a private donation which happens outside the established health system. The extent of private donations is probably rather limited.[30] A known donor/known donation is when a donor donates sperm to a specific couple or a single woman.[31]

For a woman who has a partner, a known donor does not have to be deemed to be the legal father, and most often probably will not be. The situation can be that a heterosexual or female same-sex couple has a male friend whom they want to be the donor. However, he is not supposed to have any role or recognition as a father, and if they follow a simple formal procedure, he will not; the partner will instead be the legal father or co-mother.[32]

For a female same-sex couple, the Children's Act contains an explicit regulation for cases in which the parties involved want the known donor to be recognised as the legal father.[33] An example of this would be that one or both of the women are long-term friends with the man, and have planned to have a child with him. If they choose this option, the woman who does not give birth will not be a parent to the child, as Danish law only allows for two legal parents. The situation can be that the child primarily lives with the father – he is the resident parent. Or, as occurs more frequently, the mother can be the resident parent. One possibility is that she has shared parental responsibilities with her partner, even though the partner is not a legal parent. A consequence of such an arrangement would be that the father cannot have any part in the parental responsibilities, as only two people can take part in the parental responsibilities. Yet he can still have visitation rights.

If a single woman chooses assisted reproduction with sperm from a known donor, the donor will be the legal father of the child born as a result of his donation[34] (there is an exception where the sperm was used without the donor's knowledge or after he has passed away).[35]

---

[29] S. 28 of the Children's Act (Consolidation Act No. 1250 of 29.11.2019 and Act No. 227 of 15.02.2022).
[30] For references to private sperm donations, see e.g. Jyllands-Posten, *32-årig blev gravid med sæddonor, hun mødte i en lukket Facebook-gruppe*, 19.01.2022.
[31] See e.g. J. Waage, *Børneloven med kommentarer*, DJØF Forlag, Copenhagen 2015, s. 2 in reference to s. 27 b.
[32] S. 27 of the Children's Act (Consolidation Act No. 1250 of 29.11.2019 and Act No. 227 of 15.02.2022).
[33] S. 27 a of the Children's Act (Consolidation Act No. 1250 of 29.11.2019 and Act No. 227 of 15.02.2022).
[34] S. 27 b and c of the Children's Act (Consolidation Act No. 1250 of 29.11.2019 and Act No. 227 of 15.02.2022).
[35] S. 27 c of the Children's Act (Consolidation Act No. 1250 of 29.11.2019 and Act No. 227 of 15.02.2022).

For a donation occurring outside the established health system – a private donation and home insemination not performed by authorised health workers – the donor will, by default, be considered the legal father.[36] Until very recently, the donor in such situations would always have been considered the father. However, a statutory change has now made it possible that in the case of private home insemination too, the partner of the woman giving birth can become the legal parent of the child by complying with a simple formal procedure.[37] Home insemination has thereby become an option for a same-sex female couple, where the intention is that they both shall be the parents of the child born as a result of the insemination.[38]

For the parties involved, it is important to be aware that the parenthood attained by the partner of the woman giving birth is binding. Hence, although the partner has not contributed any gametes, the parenthood attained through having given consent to the woman receiving assisted reproduction treatment is an obligation like any other recognised form of legal parenthood. This is established in a decision from the Supreme Court.[39] The same-sex partner of the woman giving birth had consented to her receiving assisted reproduction treatment,[40] and the partner was registered as the co-mother of the child who was born as a result of the treatment. Less than two months after the child's birth, the couple split up, and the co-mother had very limited contact with the child. The former partners were in agreement that the co-mother should be granted non-recognition of her status as a legal mother to the child. However, the application for this was denied.

4. PARENTAGE OF A CHILD BORN THROUGH SURROGACY

Denmark has some very harsh rules against attempting to found a family through surrogacy. The rules are probably some of the strictest in Europe, certainly in Northern Europe.[41] However, it is important to note that surrogacy is legal in Denmark.[42] Thus, the point of departure for legal analysis is that surrogacy is not

---

[36] S. 28 of the Children's Act (Consolidation Act No. 1250 of 29.11.2019 and Act No. 227 of 15.02.2022).
[37] Act No. 227 of 15.02.2022.
[38] For an example of denial of recognition of the female same-sex partner as the co-mother under the former rules, due to the insemination being perceived as a private home insemination, see (2022) 1 *Tidsskrift for Familie- og Arveret (Journal of Family Law and Succession Law)* 77.
[39] *Ugeskrift for Retsvæsen (Weekly Law Journal)* 2020.237.
[40] In accordance with s. 27 of the Children's Act (Consolidation Act No. 1250 of 29.11.2019).
[41] See e.g. response from the Minister for Gender Equality to the Parliament's Gender Equality Committee, question 11 in concern of B72, 01.03.2022.
[42] See F.H. Pedersen, 'Forældremyndighed i forbindelse med økonomisk kompenseret surrogatmoderskab', (2017) 2 *Tidsskrift for Familie- og Arveret (Journal of Family Law and*

banned and not generally criminalised,[43] yet rules have been created to prevent surrogacy from happening. Among the rules is criminalisation of intended parents for receiving assistance to find a surrogate.[44] Indeed, domestic surrogacy is precluded almost absolutely, whereas the estimated number of children born abroad in terms of surrogacy arrangements with Danes is 100–200 children per year.[45]

The question of parentage is the regulatory tool that is applied at full strength to deter families in Denmark from having a child through surrogacy.[46] An intended father who is the genetic father of a child born through surrogacy will be recognised as the legal father. His partner, whether a woman or a man, will not. Hence, an intended mother in this situation will not be recognised as the legal mother, even if the child is born as a result of having used an egg from her and sperm from her male partner. This follows from section 30 of the Danish Children's Act, which provides that the woman giving birth is deemed to be the legal mother; thus, the surrogate will be the legal mother. This is interpreted as also being the case even if the surrogate is living abroad and in her jurisdiction is not deemed to be the legal mother of the child,[47] indeed this has even been construed as *always* the case, although questionable.[48]

Succession Law) 76 1. The Children's Act, s. 31, contains a paragraph stating that a contract requiring a surrogate to hand over the child she has given birth to is void. This paragraph is surely effective, but should not be conflated with any ban on surrogacy.

[43] After the Danish regulation of surrogacy, there are three actions which are criminalised. Firstly, it is forbidden for medical staff to assist with surrogacy arrangements: s. 13 of the Act on Assisted Reproduction (Consolidation Act No. 902 of 23.08.2019). Additionally, it is forbidden to receive or provide assistance in finding a surrogate as well as to advertise for this: s. 33 of the Adoption Act (Consolidation Act No. 775 of 07.08.2019).

[44] S. 33 of the Adoption Act (Consolidation Act No. 775 of 07.08.2019). For reference to criminal proceedings, see e.g. https://www.sn.dk/soroe-kommune/nu-skal-kvinde-straffes-hun-fik-hjaelp-til-at-finde-rugemor-i-usa/, accessed 25.05.2022.

[45] See response from the Minister for Gender Equality to the Parliament's Gender Equality Committee, question 15 in concern of B72, 01.03.2022. See also F.H. Pedersen, 'Almindelige kriterier for påberåbelse af ordre public: specielt i relation til forældremyndighed på baggrund af surrogati-arrangementer', note 30 (2019) 2 *Tidsskrift for Familie- og Arveret (Journal of Family Law and Succession Law)* 99. By comparison, 23 children came to Denmark in 2020 through adoption from abroad: https://faktalink.dk/titelliste/adoption-i-danmark, accessed 19.05.2022.

[46] For a discussion of the various regulatory tools applied in the regulation of assisted reproduction in Denmark, see F.H. Pedersen, 'Tacit Concepts of Family in Danish Legislation on Assisted Reproduction' in review.

[47] See F.H. Pedersen, 'Almindelige kriterier for påberåbelse af ordre public: specielt i relation til forældremyndighed på baggrund af surrogati-arrangementer', (2019) 2 *Tidsskrift for Familie- og Arveret (Journal of Family Law and Succession Law)* 99.

[48] That the present legal position should be that the foreign surrogate always is the legal mother of the child she has given birth to and never the intended mother or co-father, unless there has been a recognized adoption, appears misread. Two examples can illustrate that this can hardly be the current standpoint of the law. 1) A female Californian employee of the global Danish company Novo Nordisk is transferred to work at the headquarters in Denmark. She is the genetic mother of her 6-year-old daughter, whom she and her husband, who is the

Transfer of legal parenthood from the surrogate to the intended mother or a co-father requires the parties to go through a step-parent adoption process. As a rule, a person eligible to adopt the child of that person's partner is an adult who has lived with the child for two-and-a-half years. Recently, however, this requirement has been relaxed, and in some cases the waiting time can be expected to be around half a year.[49] But this is possible only if no compensation has been given to the surrogate.

Among Danish politicians and opinion makers, it is often said that commercial surrogacy is illegal under Danish law. That is not correct.[50] What is true is that if the surrogate has received compensation for carrying the pregnancy and giving birth, it should nearly always be expected that a step-parent adoption would be denied. Any reimbursement beyond expenses directly caused by the assisted reproduction and pregnancy can be cause for the step-parent adoption to be denied.[51] The consequences are that the surrogate's legal parenthood continues, at least until the child turns 18 years of age and adoption under other rules might be possible. For children living in Denmark after having come into the world through a surrogacy arrangement abroad, the attainment of parenthood by the intended mother or co-father during their childhood will thus rarely be possible. Hence, although compensated surrogacy is legal under Danish law, the granting of compensation for surrogacy has severe consequences for all the parties involved.

This interpretation of the current legal position has for years been maintained by the Danish authorities and was upheld in a 2020 Supreme Court decision

---

genetic father, had with the help of a surrogate in California. The surrogate was monetarily compensated at a standard rate in California. According to Californian law, the woman and her husband were both recognised as parents of the child. After arriving in Denmark, she goes to her new municipality citizen services to become registered and sign the girl up for school. She is the talkative type and tells the municipality officer about the girl's birth story. Does Danish law recognize the woman as the legal parent of the girl with the right to represent her? 2) Same factual circumstances as in example one, with the only difference being that the woman is a Danish citizen who has lived in California for a number of years, where the daughter was born. In both examples, the answer must be that Danish authorities are obliged to acknowledge the intended mothers as the legal parents respectively. The misreading seems to originate from the *travaux préparatoires* to s. 30 of the Danish Children's Act, which in an explanation uses the word 'always', FT 2000-01, Appendix A, 78. However, the context for the *travaux préparatoires*' use is a different one than in the above examples. There are no court cases which answer what the present legal position is, and only one published administrative decision (2014) *Tidsskrift for Familie- og Arveret (Journal of Family Law and Succession Law)* 96. In that case the intended mother had legal domicile in Denmark. The extent to which foreign judgments in the field of surrogacy should be recognized and the interplay with the public order is a question in urgent need of further analysis.

[49] Principle Decision 6-21 by the Danish Board of Appeals (KEN no. 9198, 23.03.2021); response from the Minister for Gender Equality to the Parliament's Gender Equality Committee, question 3 in concern of B72, 01.03.2022.
[50] *Betænkning no. 1350 om børns retsstilling*, 1997, Justitsministeriets Børnelovsudvalg, section 4.5.
[51] See *Folketingstidende* (Official Record of Parliamentary Proceedings) 1985–86 Appendix A, columns 4164–65.

where a child was born of a surrogate in Ukraine.[52] The surrogate was not the genetic mother and did not perceive herself to be the mother of the child, nor was she the mother according to Ukrainian law. A Danish married couple were the intended parents, and the husband was the genetic father. Shortly after the child was born in 2013, the child came to Denmark together with its father and the intended mother. The child lived with them, and since 2018 the father and the intended mother have had shared parental responsibilities. In 2017, a step-parent adoption request from the intended mother was denied based on the surrogate's having been compensated. The Supreme Court upheld this decision on the basis of the Danish law's unmitigated injunction against allowing adoption when monetary compensation has been provided to the woman giving birth. The court found this absolute rule to be contrary to the requirement under the decisions of the European Court of Human Rights to consider the best interests of the child. As a consequence, the court recommended that the legislature should consider a new statutory provision and stated that such considerations must also be taken into account at present. In the weighing of this consideration, the judges were split four to three, with a majority of judges finding that the denial was justified. A key argument for the majority of judges was that the father and intended mother had shared parental responsibilities, and according to the majority, this meant that the child's everyday life was not significantly influenced by the denial of recognition of the de facto mother as the legal mother.

A particular example of how significant parental responsibility can be is a judgment from the High Court of Eastern Denmark in another surrogacy case regarding which parent the child should live with after the couple had split up.[53] In this case, similarly, the husband and wife had shared parental responsibility, and only the father was recognised as a legal parent of the child. The court decided that the child should reside with the woman in spite of the fact that the legal father wanted the child to reside with him. Currently, it can thus be argued that it is an open question whether or to what extent the Danish authorities' general practice of denying step-parent adoptions in cases where the surrogate has been compensated constitutes a violation of Article 8(2) of the European Convention on Human Rights.[54]

As described above, in a formal sense, male same-sex couples are not treated differently from heterosexual couples – the rules are the same for an intended co-father as for an intended mother. In reality, however, in comparing the two groups, the harsh rules obviously affect male same-sex couples proportionately

---

[52] *Ugeskrift for Retsvæsen (Weekly Law Journal)* 2021.517. The case has been brought to the European Court of Human Right, where it is pending.
[53] (2013) 6 *Tidsskrift for Familie- og Arveret (Journal of Family Law and Succession Law)* 750.
[54] Cf. Advisory Opinion of 10.04.2019, Request no. P16-2018-001.

much more than heterosexual couples, since for a male same-sex couple, surrogacy much more often will be the necessary means of creating a family with children.[55]

For a same-sex female couple living in Denmark, having a child through surrogacy is even more difficult, as it is possible that neither of the partners would be recognised as a legal parent, even if one of them is genetically related to the child. The situation is similar for a single woman. Yet it is conceivable, if the child were de facto present in Denmark, that the couple could be granted temporary custody, which they could in principle exercise until the child turned 18 years old.[56]

5. VARIOUS FUNCTIONS OF THE FAMILY

5.1. HAVING AND RAISING CHILDREN

5.1.1. Producing Children

The birth rate in Denmark is around 1.7, which means that Danish women on average give birth to under two children each.[57] Thus, the Danish population is increasing only as a result of fairly significant immigration and because people are living longer.

The State has an interest in more children being born in Denmark, and for this reason, among other things, the State provides support for families with children. This includes offering a woman medical help to become pregnant as well as financial help to families while a child is growing up.

Many couples seek assistance from a doctor if they are unable to conceive within one year of trying to have a child together. Doctors may refer their patients for public health treatment for infertility. In 2019, every tenth child born in Denmark was a result of the parent(s) having received fertility treatment at either a public or a private clinic.[58]

---

[55] For a blatant example of downplaying this issue, see response from the Minister for Gender Equality to the Parliament's Gender Equality Committee, question 18 in concern of B72, 01.03.2022.

[56] See J.R. Herrmann and F.H. Pedersen, 'Barnets bedste ved omsorgsrelationer uden genetisk tilknytning – nogle kommentarer i lyset af Paradiso & Campanelli v. Italien' (2017) 15–16 *Nordisk socialrättslig tidskrift* 129.

[57] The birth rate is an expression of how many births there have been on average per woman of childbearing age.

[58] Danish Fertility Association, *Danish Report on Fertility Treatments in 2019*, available at https://fertilitetsselskab.dk/wp-content/uploads/2020/10/dfs2019-til-hjemmesiden.pdf, accessed 10.05.2022.

Treatment for infertility is free at public fertility clinics, but only a limited number of treatments are available. Couples (including lesbian couples) and single women can receive fertility treatment in the public system.

A public clinic requires that a couple does not already have a child together, or in the case of a single woman, that the woman is childless.

5.1.2. Financial Aid to Parents

It is expensive to be a family with children in Denmark and the State provides automatic financial assistance from the time when the child is born. This is called the 'child and youth benefit'.[59] No eligibility requirements apply for the benefit. How much is paid depends on the age of the child. The highest benefit is paid when the child is 0–2 years old and then the benefit is adjusted three times until the child reaches 18 years old. In addition, the amount depends on the parents' income. However, the income threshold is so high that most families with children receive the child and youth benefit. From 1 January 2022, new rules have been introduced, according to which parents who have joint parental responsibility automatically receive half of the benefit each, whether they are cohabiting or not. This is a recognition of the fact that both parents have equal responsibility for the child's support. Previously, the benefit was paid to the parent with whom the child was living mostly or where the child had his or her address.

Single parents receive an extra amount, called a 'child allowance', from the State.[60] To be single, the parent must not be married or cohabiting with another person. In the assessment of the nature of the cohabitation, the authorities take into account whether an applicant has a marriage-like relationship and shared household with a person who is not a family member.

The State is obliged to establish subsidised childcare for all children. This applies from the time that the child is 26 weeks of age until the child starts school. The parents have to pay a minor share of the cost of childcare but the parents can get this payment reduced or fully waived if the household income is low.

5.2. PROVIDING ECONOMIC SECURITY

5.2.1. Protecting the Vulnerable in Marriage

In family law, family members are granted special rights and obligations towards each other. This also applies in financial situations, where the

---

[59] Act on Child and Youth Benefit (Consolidation Act No. 609 of 03.06.2016).
[60] S. 2(1) of the Act on Child Allowance (Consolidation Act No. 63 of 21.01.2019).

financially weaker party should be ensured a financial safety net, in particular after the end of a marriage or cohabitation or the death of one of the parents. In this way, the needs of the children are also secured.

In Denmark, the legal matrimonial regime is deferred community of property as the statutory basis.[61] In the event of a legal separation, divorce or death, each spouse (or the heirs) receives half of the community property which he or she owns, while receiving half of his or her spouse's share of the community property in return. This includes both the property which the spouses own at the time of the marriage and the property acquired by them during the marriage. The rule ensures the equality of house and care work with paid work. However, there are a number of particular rights – for example ordinary pension rights and personal possession rights – which are not included in the community property. It is also possible for spouses to enter into different kinds of contracts for separate property.[62] In recent years, the protection of the weaker party has diminished, with many spouses entering into separate property agreements or receiving inheritances as separate property.

Spouses have a mutual obligation to support each other.[63] After legal separation or divorce, the spouses may reach an agreement about contributing spousal maintenance to the financially weaker party, or the spouses may refer the whole question on maintenance for decision by the Agency of Family Law.[64] Maintenance can be claimed for a maximum period of 10 years. Under special circumstances, the claim can exist for life. When fixing the period of maintenance, great importance will be attached to the length of the relationship and the overall situation of the receiving spouse. Emphasis will be placed on whether the maintenance is solely to ease the transition or to act as a safety net for a longer period of time. In addition to this, importance is attached to the age of the children living with the receiving spouse. The trend has been towards fewer spouses being granted spousal maintenance, and the maintenance is usually only granted for a period of a few years.

---

[61] S. 5 of the Act on Spouses' Financial Relations (Consolidation Act No. 774 of 07.08.2019).
[62] Ss 12–14 of the Act on Spouses' Financial Relations (Consolidation Act No. 774 of 07.08.2019). By a marriage settlement, spouses can enter into contracts for separate property covering all assets or a part thereof, or for specific assets to be held as separate property, so that the assets are held as partly separate property and partly community property. It is also possible to enter into a fixed-term contract providing for separate property, e.g. for five years. Further, spouses can make contracts for separate property which are only to become effective upon the division of the matrimonial property in both spouses' lifetime (divorce separate property).
[63] S. 4 of the Act on Spouses' Financial Relations (Consolidation Act No. 774 of 07.08.2019).
[64] S. 50 of the Marriage and Matrimonial Causes Act (Consolidation Act No. 771 of 07.08.2019).

5.2.2. Protecting the Vulnerable Child

In Denmark, there is an increased awareness that a child should be raised under the best social circumstances and that children should be protected from neglect and discomfort.

The Danish Prime Minister, Mette Frederiksen, has called herself the 'children's Prime Minister'. She has stated that more children who are mistreated by their parents must be removed and grow up outside their families under the protection of the State.

Families with children, including single parents, receive special social benefits from the State. To receive such a benefit, a parent must be a legal mother or a legal father of a child. This requirement can also be met where the child is born as a result of donor-assisted reproductive technology or surrogacy. A child who only has one parent – for example if its mother has, as a single parent, conceived the child with sperm from an anonymous donor – will receive an increased special social benefit. This does not apply to step-children unless the child is adopted by the step-partner. Denmark does not recognise 'three-parent' children.

5.3. NEW FAMILY FORMS AND THE LATEST DEBATE

In 2021, the number of so-called 'rainbow families' in Denmark was 1,623.[65] According to figures from Statistics Denmark, the number has more than doubled since 2009.[66] Statistics Denmark defines a rainbow family as a same-sex female or male couple with children living at home.[67] In practice, these rainbow families often consist of more than two parents, for example a mother, co-mother and a father, who is not recognised as a legal parent, but often acts as the father in the child's everyday life (social father).

In August 2019, a left-wing political party, the Red-Green Alliance (*Enhedslisten*), suggested in its programme on equality, gender and sexuality that, in future, a child should be able to have up to four legal parents. The Red-Green Alliance found that new rules should be introduced taking into account developments in modern, diverse family patterns. The programme highlighted

---

[65] In 2019, the number was 1,465.
[66] T. Stenholt Engmann, 'Regnbuefamilien er blevet større', 15.08.2019, available at https://www.dst.dk/da/Statistik/nyheder-analyser-publ/bagtal/2019/2019-08-14-regnbuefamilien-er-blevet-stoerre, accessed 10.05.2022.
[67] Ibid.

two situations where a child in particular had a need for more than two parents: (1) all parents of a child should be allowed to take the child to a doctor, and (2) the child should inherit from all of his or her parents.[68]

On 16 August 2019, Mogens Jensen, the Gender Equality Minister, stated in response to this proposal that he would have the relevant legislation – especially possible discriminatory legislation – reviewed before he could decide on the proposal.[69] At the same time, one of the Children's Associations (*Børns vilkår*) expressed scepticism about the proposal and emphasised that problems in divorce proceedings would be doubled.[70] In March 2022, the new Minister for Gender Equality highlighted the difficulty of having more than two parents to agree on the break-up of the family, and for that reason the government wanted to maintain the principle of two legal parents. The Minister referred to safeguarding the best interests of the child.[71]

In 2022, a new Act was introduced that amends the Children's Act so that parents who completed legal gender reassignment before the child was born are designated and registered as parents in accordance with their legal gender.[72] Further, the Act will entail amendments to the Names Act, so that transgender people who have not completed legal gender reassignment can be given a name that matches the person's gender identity. It is sufficient that the person declares that the desire to be given the name is based on an experience of belonging to the opposite sex. Thus, it will no longer be a condition for a name change that the person in question makes a declaration of being transsexual or similar.

For many years it has been debated whether a portion of those weeks which are available for maternity leave should be earmarked for the father. The current regulation has only earmarked maternity leave for the mother. A new Act, caused by EU legislation,[73] introduces a reform, with fathers being afforded the same position as mothers after the baby has been born.[74] The Act also contains some innovative changes aimed at rainbow families and a more equal position between female and male sole parents. One of these innovations is that part of

---

[68] Available at https://enhedslisten.dk/politikomraade/ligestilling-koen-og-seksualitet, accessed 10.05.2022. See a corresponding proposal of 15.08.22, available at https://enhedslisten.dk/wp-content/uploads/2022/08/Rettigheder-til-regnbuefamilier.pdf, accessed 4.09.2022.

[69] https://www.altinget.dk/artikel/minister-afviser-ikke-paa-forhaand-forslag-om-fire-juridiske-foraeldre, 16.08.2019, accessed 10.05.2022.

[70] Available at https://www.bt.dk/samfund/boerns-vilkaar-er-bange-for-forslag-om-fire-foraeldre, 16.08.2019, accessed.10.05.2022.

[71] See response from the Minister for Gender Equality to the Parliament's Gender Equality Committee, question 19 in concern of B72, 01.03.2022.

[72] Act No. 227 of 15.02.2022.

[73] Directive (EU) 2019/1158 of the European Parliament and of the Council of 20.06.2019 on work–life balance for parents and carers and repealing Council Directive 2010/18/EU, OJ L 188.

[74] Bill No. L 104 of 22.02.2022 amending the Act on Maternity Leave was adopted on 03.03.2022. The new rules concerning the father's leave entered into force on 01.07.2022: https://www.ft.dk/ripdf/samling/20211/lovforslag/l104/20211_l104_som_vedtaget.pdf, accessed 10.05.2022.

the maternity leave can be transferred from a legal parent to a so-called 'social parent'. A social parent is a spouse or cohabitant of the legal parent who is intended to have a parental relationship with the child. A social parent can also be a known donor or a spouse or cohabitant of a known donor who is intended to have a parental relationship with the child.[75] An example is a known donor to a female same-sex couple, who is not a legal father but is intended to have a parental relationship with the child.

A citizens' proposal called 'Recognise co-paternity in rainbow families' was submitted on 7 January 2022. Just four days later, more than 79,000 Danes had signed the proposal, making it Denmark's most supported citizens' proposal ever.[76] The proposal refers to the lack of legal recognition and equality between female and male parents, as well as calling for recognition of more than two parents. Although it contains some misunderstandings of the current regulation, the citizens' proposal has succeeded in sparking new political debate about family formation and gender equality. This includes focusing on the lack in Danish law of any formal term to designate a co-father. The citizens' proposal was discussed in a formal parliamentary debate on 31 March 2022.[77] The Minister for Gender Equality supported part of the proposal and announced that she would set up an expert group. The experts are expected in particular to be working on possible solutions for children who have come into the world through a surrogacy arrangement, where the surrogate has been compensated and for this reason cannot have their de facto other parent recognised as one of their legal parents.[78]

In summary, recent developments show a greater openness among politicians to expanding the concept of family, particularly in terms of equality between the mother and the father in their role as parents when the child is newly born, and in terms of securing more rights for rainbow families. On the other hand, there does not appear to be a political majority in favour of introducing rules that allow a child to have more than two legal parents.

---

[75] See Approved Bill L 104, S. 1, no. 40. The new rules concerning rainbow families' leave will enter into force on 01.12.2023.

[76] Available at https://www.elle.dk/agenda/samfund/saadan-er-danmarks-mest-stoettede-borger forslag-blevet-til, accessed 10.05.2022.

[77] Beslutningsforslag nr. B 72 submitted 25.01.2022. Parliament's decision B72 adopted on 08.06.2022 https://www.ft.dk/ripdf/samling/20211/beslutningsforslag/b72/20211_b72_som_ vedtaget.pdf.

[78] Available at https://www.ft.dk/samling/20211/beslutningsforslag/B72/BEH1-84/forhandling. htm, accessed 10.05.2022. The terms of reference for the work of the expert group can be found at https://www.trm.dk/nyheder/2022/ekspertgruppe-om-anerkendelse-af-foraeldreskab-ved-kommercielle-surrogataftaler-er-nedsat.

6. CLOSING CONSIDERATIONS

In Denmark, recent developments show that there is an openness to granting rights to new family forms. In this context, it should be remembered that Denmark was a pioneer in giving same-sex couples rights, as in 1989 Denmark was the first country in the world to introduce a registered partnership with almost the same rights as marriage.[79]

The State focuses on protecting the vulnerable parties in the family, especially children and single parents. Financial assistance is provided to families with children where there is only one breadwinner (child allowance). Likewise, financial assistance (child and youth benefit) is provided to all families with children, although the assistance is reduced or waived for families with high incomes. The State's provision of financial help thus encompasses both families where the money is needed to keep the personal finances afloat and more well-off middle-class families.

On the other hand, the protection of vulnerable adults in connection with divorce has become less prevalent, as most people who get divorced are able to support themselves through professional work. Further, individual agreements between spouses increasingly play an important role, in particular in terms of how the property is to be divided upon the termination of the marriage. This can be seen in the limited use of resolutions on spousal maintenance and the many separate ownership agreements. However, there is still a need to protect vulnerable adults so that they can have an acceptable standard of living after divorce.

In regard to step-parents, rules concerning rights and obligations have been introduced in phases, and in some special cases, for example contact rights for both the biological father and the stepfather, a situation with three parents may arise, at least on the psychological level. It would provide a more predictable legal position if a comprehensive review of the legal relationship of a step-parent to a step-child were to be carried out. Such a review could also contribute to a clarification of the possible need to consider some kind of multiplicity of parenthood or the extent to which the regulation covering the legal relationship between step-parent and step-child might be a better legal framework to develop further.

Surrogacy is a field where countries and states Denmark normally compares itself with have moved on with new legal practices, whereas the Danish rules have been at a standstill. The Danish regulation regarding surrogacy is one of the strictest in Europe. The barrier that hits hardest is the many cases of refusal of recognition of an intended mother or a co-father as a legal parent of a child born through surrogacy. This is the current rule when financial compensation has been

---

[79] Act No. 372 of 07.06.1989.

provided to the surrogate. The consequence is that most children born through surrogacy will have to grow up under circumstances where their de facto mother or second father is not formally their parent. However, this state of affairs may have created a political openness for a re-evaluation of the appropriateness of the current regulation. Another harsh rule is that it is a criminal offence to receive any help finding a surrogate. Hence, for a heterosexual woman who cannot give birth herself, the options for becoming a parent recognised by the law are few, regardless of whether she has a partner or is single. Likewise, for a male same-sex couple or a single male, family formation in compliance with Danish law is currently very difficult.

THE INCONSISTENT APPROACH TO FAMILY FORMATION IN ENGLAND AND WALES

Claire FENTON-GLYNN and Jens M. SCHERPE

1. Introduction 252
2. Legal Parenthood in England and Wales: There can Only be Two 252
   2.1. Natural Reproduction 253
   2.2. Assisted Reproduction Generally.......................... 254
       2.2.1. Motherhood...................................... 254
       2.2.2. Fatherhood or 'Other Parent' under the Human
              Fertilisation and Embryology Act 2008................ 255
       2.2.3. Legal Fatherhood According to the Common Law 256
   2.3. Surrogacy.. 256
       2.3.1. Surrogate is Married or in a Civil Partnership 257
       2.3.2. Surrogate is not Married or in a Civil Partnership......... 257
       2.3.3. Transferring Parenthood Subsequent to Birth:
              Parental Orders 257
       2.3.4. Reform Proposals 258
3. Parental Responsibility in England and Wales: Accommodating
   Multiple Parental Relationships and 'Non-Traditional' Families? 259
4. Recognising Adult Relationships and Family Functions................ 261
   4.1. Adult Relationship Recognition in General: Marriage, Civil
        Partnership, and Cohabitation 261
   4.2. Financial Remedies when Adult Relationships End through
        Separation or Death... 264
5. Conclusion.. 267

1. INTRODUCTION

The family law of England and Wales[1] is far from being a coherent and consistent body of law.[2] It consists of a multitude of different statutes and diverse case law, creating a confusing tapestry that often is difficult to navigate. Thus it is unsurprising that the underlying policy aims are not necessarily consistent or complimentary and sometimes even contradictory, as both legislation and case law often is a reaction to a specific policy change or emergence of a specific issue.

In order to give an impression – because that is all a short contribution like this one can do – on how diversity in family forms is dealt with in England and Wales, first two areas regarding parent–child relationships will be looked at: legal parenthood[3] and parental responsibility.[4] This is followed by an overview of the recognition of adult relationships[5] and of the financial consequences of such relationships coming to an end,[6] as this sheds light on one of the primary functions English law ascribes to relationships. This contribution will conclude[7] that English law in many areas still prioritises form over function, but that when it comes to many aspects of child law as well as children's financial security, English law takes a much more pragmatic – and to a great extent functional – approach.

2. LEGAL PARENTHOOD IN ENGLAND AND WALES: THERE CAN ONLY BE TWO

Unlike some other jurisdictions, English law does not recognise the legal parenthood of more than two persons – in any situation. Thus, while the legal rules on the allocation of legal parenthood differ depending on whether a child is born through natural reproduction,[8] assisted reproduction[9] or surrogacy,[10] the outcome will never be that a child has more than two parents. So when persons

---

[1] The United Kingdom consists of three separate jurisdictions: Scotland, Northern Ireland and England and Wales. This contribution only discusses the law of the jurisdiction of England and Wales, and when in the following a reference is made to 'England' or 'English law' this must be understood to refer to the whole jurisdiction. It is also worth noting that some of the statutes referred to in this contribution, such as the Human Fertilisation and Embryology Act 2008, apply to the whole of the United Kingdom.
[2] On this see e.g. J.M. Scherpe, 'Modernität, Originalität und Inkohärenzen im Familienrecht von England und Wales' in M. Gebauer and S. Huber (eds), *Gestaltungsfreiheit im Familienrecht*, Mohr Siebeck, Tübingen 2017, pp. 55–102.
[3] See section 2 below.
[4] See section 3 below.
[5] See section 4.1 below.
[6] See section 4.2 below.
[7] See section 5 below.
[8] See section 2.1 below.
[9] See section 2.2 below.
[10] See section 2.3 below.

are gaining legal parenthood (for example through a parental order in case of surrogacy, or through adoption), others will lose that legal position.

2.1. NATURAL REPRODUCTION

In England and Wales, when a child is born through natural reproduction, the child's mother will be the person who gives birth,[11] and their legal father will be their biological father.[12] This is the case whether the mother is married, in a civil partnership or single.[13]

If the child's parents marry or enter into a civil partnership with other people, who then go on to share a household with the parent, that step-parent does *not* – and cannot – gain legal parenthood except through adoption,[14] which then terminates the parental status of the other parent. Under English law, an adoption leaves no legal links with the family of birth. While contact may be maintained with the birth family,[15] no legal rights or responsibility remain.[16]

A step-parent may, however, obtain parental responsibility, as this is not restricted to two persons. If the person who wishes to obtain parental responsibility is married or in a civil partnership with the legal parent, this requires the consent of that parent, and any other parent with parental responsibility. If consent cannot be obtained, an order of the court is needed.[17]

If the new relationship is not formalised as a marriage or a civil partnership, parental responsibility for the new partner can be obtained through a court order called a 'child arrangements order' stipulating that the child (also) is to live with the person in question.[18] If the child arrangements order merely stipulates

---

[11] *Ampthill Peerage* [1977] AC 547. This is the case even where the mother is legally male – he will still legally be the 'mother', which the courts have ruled is a gender-neutral term: *R (McConnell and YY) v. Registrar General* [2020] EWCA Civ 559.
[12] See s. 55A of the Family Law Act 1986.
[13] Note that in England and Wales both marriage and civil partnership are open to couples of the same and the opposite sex. On the genesis of the opening up of civil partnership to opposite-sex couples see J.M. Scherpe, 'Family Law, Ideology and the Recognition of Relationships: R (Steinfeld and Keidan) v Secretary of State for International Development' in D. Clarry (ed.), *The UK Supreme Court Yearbook*, Vol. 9: 2017–2018 Legal Year, Appellate Press, London 2019, pp. 150–73 and J.M. Scherpe, 'A Comparative View on Registered Partnerships and Formal Family Recognition Beyond Marriage' (2019) 6 *Journal of International and Comparative Law* 273.
[14] *Kafala* is not a mechanism that is recognised under English law.
[15] Ss 51A and 51B of the Adoption and Children Act 2002. See also B. Sloan, 'Post-adoption Contact Reform: Compounding the State-ordered Termination of Parenthood?' (2014) 73(2) *Cambridge Law Journal* 378; B. Sloan and K. Hughes, 'Post-adoption Photographs: Welfare, Rights and Judicial Reasoning' (2011) 23(3) *Child and Family Law Quarterly* 393.
[16] See ss 46 and 67 of the Adoption and Children Act 2002.
[17] S. 4A of the Children Act 1989.
[18] Ss 8 and 12(2) of the Children Act 1989.

that the child is to have contact with the person in question, the court also has discretion to give parental responsibility to that person.[19] Parental responsibility obtained via a child arrangements order is subject to certain restrictions, in particular with regard to agreement or refusal of adoption and appointment of guardians.[20]

If a step-parent (or indeed, any other non-parent) obtains parental responsibility, they will, apart from the above-mentioned restrictions, have the same decision-making responsibility and authority as any other person with parental responsibility – whether they share a household with them or not. In the event of a clash of opinions, it will be for the courts to decide which will prevail.

2.2. ASSISTED REPRODUCTION GENERALLY

English law also does not permit multiplicity of legal parenthood in case of assisted reproduction. In relation to parenthood in the context of assisted reproduction, the most relevant legislation is the Human Fertilisation and Embryology Act 2008, which provides exceptions to the common law rules on parenthood.[21]

First, it is important to say that gamete donors in England cannot remain anonymous. Donor-conceived children who were conceived on or after 1 April 2005 are able to receive non-identifying information on the donor once they reach age 16, and identifying information (including last known address) at age 18.[22]

2.2.1. Motherhood

Under the Human Fertilisation and Embryology Act 2008, the person who gives birth to the child will always be the legal mother,[23] even in cases where the person giving birth is legally male.[24] Thus, legal motherhood is determined by

---

[19] Ss 8 and 12(2A) of the Children Act 1989.
[20] S. 12(3) of the Children Act 1989.
[21] This Act replaces the previous provisions in the Human Fertilisation Embryology Act 1990. See also the Surrogacy Arrangements Act 1985, and the Human Fertilisation and Embryology Act 1990, which also contain rules concerning surrogacy and artificial reproduction respectively.
[22] Human Fertilisation and Embryology Authority, https://www.hfea.gov.uk/donation/donors/rules-around-releasing-donor-information/, accessed 16.08.2022.
[23] S. 33 of the Human Fertilisation and Embryology Act 2008. As noted above, the mother does not have to be legally female. In the case of *TT and YY* [2019] EWHC 2384 (Fam), the Court found that a transgender man who gave birth should be registered as the 'mother', rather than 'father' or 'parent'.
[24] *R (McConnell and YY) v. Registrar General* [2020] EWCA Civ 559. On this case see C. Fenton-Glynn, 'Deconstructing Parenthood: What Makes a Mother?' [2020] *Cambridge Law Journal* 34.

gestation and is independent of whether there is a genetic relationship with the child or not – the only determining factor is the carrying of the child, and giving birth. As a result, the egg donor will not be recognised as a legal parent. These rules apply irrespective of where in the world the child is conceived or born – English law always applies English rules of parenthood, and will not recognise parenthood established by foreign law.

2.2.2. Fatherhood or 'Other Parent' under the Human Fertilisation and Embryology Act 2008

Section 41 of the Human Fertilisation and Embryology Act 2008 provides that the sperm donor is explicitly excluded from parenthood, if conception has occurred in a licensed clinic.[25] Thus it makes no difference whether the donor is a known donor or not.[26]

English law differentiates between a person married to (or in a civil partnership with) the mother regarding the acquisition of the status of legal father (for men) and 'other parent' for women.[27]

If the mother is married/in a civil partnership (either to a man[28] or a woman[29]), her husband/wife/civil partner will become the legal parent at birth (male: father; female: other parent), unless it is shown that they did not consent to the placing in her of the embryo, sperm and eggs, or artificial insemination.[30] This applies irrespective of whether the fertility treatment took place in a licensed clinic or not, and also in cases when the treatment took place outside of the United Kingdom.[31]

If the mother is not married or in a civil partnership, then her male partner can also gain legal parenthood if he meets the 'agreed fatherhood conditions'.[32] These are that both he and the mother consent to him being treated as the legal father (and have not withdrawn this consent), and that they are not within the prohibited degrees of relationship (and provided his sperm was not used in the procedure).[33] Moreover, the fertility treatment must take place in a licensed

---

[25] S. 41 of the Human Fertilisation and Embryology Act 2008.
[26] But see section 2.2.3 below if the sperm of the intended father is being used or when the insemination falls outside of the rules of the Human Fertilisation and Embryology Act 2008.
[27] The English legislator deliberately chose not to use terms such as 'co-mother'.
[28] S. 35(1) of the Human Fertilisation and Embryology Act 2008.
[29] S. 42 of the Human Fertilisation and Embryology Act 2008.
[30] Provided the sperm of the husband was not used in the procedure; but in that case the man becomes the father according to the common law rules, see e.g. *Re H (a minor) (blood tests: parental rights)* [1996] 3 WLR 506, CA.
[31] S. 35(2) of the Human Fertilisation and Embryology Act 2008.
[32] S. 36 of the Human Fertilisation and Embryology Act 2008.
[33] See Marriage (Prohibited Degrees of Relationship) Act 1986.

clinic in the United Kingdom. Similar provisions apply to the mother's female partner (to whom she is not married or in a civil partnership).[34]

Having said this, there does not have to be a second legal parent – if no man or woman obtains legal parenthood by virtue of the Human Fertilisation and Embryology Act 2008 (through marriage/civil partnership, or meeting the 'agreed parenthood conditions'), then the child will only have a legal mother, and no second parent.

2.2.3. Legal Fatherhood According to the Common Law

The rules of the Human Fertilisation and Embryology Act 2008 do not cover cases where the sperm of the intended father is used for the insemination. In these cases, legal fatherhood is allocated according to the common law rules, meaning that the genetic father is the legal father of the child.[35]

The same applies if for some other reason the legal requirements for allocating legal parenthood (i.e. father/'other parent') of the Human Fertilisation and Embryology Act 2008 are not met, for example if the mother is not married or in a civil partnership and the treatment happened outside of the United Kingdom or inside the United Kingdom but not in a licensed clinic. In such cases the common law also applies, and the person whose sperm was used will be the legal father on the basis of the genetic relationship.[36]

2.3. SURROGACY

The fact that the child was conceived as part of a surrogacy arrangement currently makes no difference to the establishment of legal parenthood at birth under English law. Any changes to the legal position can only be made via a parental order (or an adoption order).[37]

Hence the surrogate will be the legal mother at birth.[38] This is the case whether she has a genetic relationship with the child or not, or whether it is intended that she will raise the child.

The legal status (if any) of a second parent of the child depends on whether the surrogate mother was married/in a civil partnership or not, and whether the sperm used was donated or from the intended father.

---

[34] Ss 43 and 44 of the Human Fertilisation and Embryology Act 2008
[35] See e.g. *Re H (a minor) (blood tests: parental rights)* [1996] 3 WLR 506, CA.
[36] Ibid.
[37] However, see the proposals of the England and Wales Law Commission and Scottish Law Commission, *Building Families through Surrogacy: A New Law. A Joint Consultation Paper*, Law Commission Consultation Paper No. 244/Scottish Law Commission Discussion Paper No. 167, June 2019, available at https://www.lawcom.gov.uk/project/surrogacy/, accessed 30.05.2022.
[38] S. 33 of the Human Fertilisation and Embryology Act 2008.

2.3.1. Surrogate is Married or in a Civil Partnership

If the surrogate is married or in a civil partnership (either to a man[39] or a woman[40]), her husband/wife/civil partner will become the legal parent at birth, unless it is shown that they did not consent to the placing in her of the embryo, sperm and eggs, or artificial insemination.

2.3.2. Surrogate is not Married or in a Civil Partnership

If the surrogate is not married or in a civil partnership, then her male partner will be the child's father if he meets the 'agreed fatherhood conditions'.[41] These are that both he and the mother consent to him being treated as the legal father (and have not withdrawn this consent), and that they are not within the prohibited degrees of relationship.[42] Similar provisions apply to the mother's female partner (to whom she is not married).[43]

Of course, the surrogate would have to consent to the intended father being the legal father under the 'agreed fatherhood conditions'. There is no requirement that the mother and the man recognised under these provisions be in a sexual relationship. Equally, the surrogate could consent to the intended mother being the 'second female parent'.

If no father/other parent obtains legal parenthood through the provisions of the Human Fertilisation and Embryology Act 2008, then according to the common law the person who provided the sperm will be the legal father of the child.[44] Thus in many cases the intended father will be the legal father from birth by virtue of his genetic contribution. However, where the sperm was donated in accordance with the provisions of the Human Fertilisation and Embryology Act 2008, the child will not have a second legal parent.

2.3.3. Transferring Parenthood Subsequent to Birth: Parental Orders

English law permits the transfer of legal parenthood from the surrogate (and any other legal parent at birth) to the intended parents, through a parental order.[45] Where the requirements for a parental order are not met, the only remaining option for acquiring legal parenthood then is adoption.

---

[39] S. 35 of the Human Fertilisation and Embryology Act 2008.
[40] S. 42 of the Human Fertilisation and Embryology Act 2008.
[41] S. 36 of the Human Fertilisation and Embryology Act 2008.
[42] See Marriage (Prohibited Degrees of Relationship) Act 1986.
[43] Ss 43 and 44 of the Human Fertilisation and Embryology Act 2008.
[44] See e.g. *Re H (a minor) (blood tests: parental rights)* [1996] 3 WLR 506, CA.
[45] Ss 54 and 54A of the Human Fertilisation and Embryology Act 2008.

The key requirements for a parental order according to the statute are as follows:

- there must be a genetic relationship between (one of) the intended parent(s) and the child;
- if there are two intended parents, they must be either married, civil partners or in an enduring family relationship;
- the application must be made within six months of the child's birth;
- the child must already be living with the intended parent(s);
- the intended parent(s) must be domiciled in the United Kingdom;
- the intended parent(s) must be over 18;
- both the surrogate mother, and any other man or woman recognised as a legal parent, must have freely, unconditionally and with full understanding consented to the making of the order – unless such parent cannot be found or is incapable of giving consent;
- the consent of the surrogate mother must be given more than six weeks after birth;
- unless authorised by the court, no money other than 'expenses reasonably incurred' can be given in relation to making the surrogacy arrangement, handing over the child or consenting to the order.[46]

However, in recent years, there has been significant jurisprudence developed concerning the consequences of non-fulfilment of one, or several, of these requirements. While the courts have viewed some criteria as indispensable – for example, the consent of the surrogate,[47] or domicile in the United Kingdom[48] – others have been dispensed with on the grounds that it would not be in the child's best interests to refuse to make a parental order on such considerations – for example, the six-month time limit for bringing an application,[49] or payments in excess of reasonable expenses.[50]

2.3.4. Reform Proposals

The Law Commission of England and Wales, in conjunction with the Scottish Law Commission, has undertaken a major consultation concerning a possible

---

[46] For more information on this topic, see C. Fenton-Glynn, 'Surrogacy in England' in J.M. Scherpe, C. Fenton-Glynn and T. Kaan (eds), *Eastern and Western Perspectives on Surrogacy*, Intersentia, Cambridge 2019, pp. 115–34.
[47] *Re P (Surrogacy: Residence)* [2008] 1 FLR 177.
[48] *Re G (Surrogacy: Foreign Domicile)* [2007] EWHC 2814 (Fam).
[49] *Re X (A Child) (Surrogacy: Time Limit)* [2014] EWHC 3135 (Fam).
[50] See e.g. *Re X and Y (Foreign Surrogacy)* [2008] EWHC 3030 (Fam). For a comprehensive discussion of the interpretation of the requirements in s. 54 of the Human Fertilisation and Embryology Act 2008, see C. Fenton-Glynn, 'The Regulation and Recognition of Surrogacy in English Law' (2015) 27(1) *Child and Family Law Quarterly* 83.

amendment to the law of surrogacy in the United Kingdom.[51] One of the key proposals is that the intended parents would obtain legal parenthood from birth, provided that certain requirements are fulfilled, but that the surrogate would retain the right to object to thus become the legal mother of the child.

In their consultation paper, the Law Commissions also discussed the possibility of the adoption of a three-parent model in relation to surrogacy. Under this model, the intended parents and the surrogate would all become the legal parents at birth, and the surrogate's parenthood could then later be extinguished.[52] This was not their preferred model for reform, however, for two reasons: first, that it was not appropriate for surrogacy, as this was not the desire of the parties; and second, because this would require far-reaching reforms to the birth registration system.

However, the Law Commissions went on to say the following:

> We think that there could be much merit outside surrogacy arrangements in further exploring the possibility of permitting a child to have more than two legal parents. That would enable the legal position to reflect reality where there is genuine co-parenting of a child by three or four people. It might be that a future project could address this area.[53]

3. PARENTAL RESPONSIBILITY IN ENGLAND AND WALES: ACCOMMODATING MULTIPLE PARENTAL RELATIONSHIPS AND 'NON-TRADITIONAL' FAMILIES?

While the law of England and Wales does not, as explained above, allow for more than two persons to have legal parenthood, it arguably is able to accommodate what may be called non-traditional family structures to a certain extent by its rather unique approach to, and concept of, parental responsibility.[54] Crucially, English law allows more than two persons to hold full parental responsibility for a child, and a person does not lose parental responsibility when another

---

[51] England and Wales Law Commission and Scottish Law Commission, *Building Families through Surrogacy: A New Law. A Joint Consultation Paper*, Law Commission Consultation Paper No. 244/Scottish Law Commission Discussion Paper No. 167, June 2019, available at https://www.lawcom.gov.uk/project/surrogacy/, accessed 30.05.2022.
[52] Ibid., s. 8.88.
[53] Ibid., ss 7.85–7.90.
[54] On which see e.g. J.M. Scherpe, 'Establishing and Ending Parental Responsibility – A Comparative View' in R. Probert, S. Gilmore and J. Herring (eds), *Responsible Parents and Parental Responsibility*, Hart Publishing, Oxford 2009, pp. 43–62; J.M. Scherpe, 'Elterliche Sorge von nicht miteinander verheirateten Eltern in England und Wales' in D. Coester-Waltjen, V. Lipp, E. Schumann and B. Veit (eds), *Alles zum Wohle des Kindes? Aktuelle Probleme des Kindschaftsrechts*, Universitätsverlag Göttingen, Göttingen 2012, pp. 71–84.

acquires it.[55] Hence step-parents[56] can acquire parental responsibility by agreement with the current holders of parental responsibility, or by court order.[57] Parental responsibility will also be given to a person named in a 'child arrangements order'. These orders can name a person or persons with whom the child shall live, or have contact. In the former case, the person named will always acquire parental responsibility;[58] in the latter, the courts have discretion to allocate parental responsibility.[59]

Child arrangements orders have often been utilised for so-called 'rainbow-families', but also for grandparents, known gamete donors, etc. The allocation of parental responsibility by a court always is subject to it being in the best interest of the child.

Parental responsibility for multiple persons has been made possible by the way parental responsibility is set up in England and Wales. The general concept underlying parental responsibility is one of *individual* responsibility,[60] so unlike in most jurisdictions,[61] there is no 'joint' responsibility. This means that each holder of parental responsibility in principle can take all decisions regarding the child without needing the consent of the other holders of parental responsibility. However, there are a small number of decisions that must be taken jointly (e.g. permanently leaving the jurisdiction, or change of surname under certain circumstances), but these are the exception rather than the rule.[62]

Thus, English child law can and does recognise diverse family forms for vertical family law relationships, and arguably here takes a more functional rather than formal approach. While the acquisition of parental responsibility by persons other than those who are given it by law of course requires a formal act, this nevertheless allows the law to capture the lived social reality of the child and thus to recognise social parenthood.[63]

---

[55] S. 2(5) and (6) of the Children Act 1989.
[56] Meaning a person who is married or in a civil partnership with a legal parent of a child.
[57] S. 4A of the Children Act 1989.
[58] S. 12(2) of the Children Act 1989.
[59] S. 12(2A) of the Children Act 1989.
[60] S. 2(7) of the Children Act 1989.
[61] See J. Ferrer-Riba, 'Parental Responsibility in a European Perspective' in J.M. Scherpe (ed.), *European Family Law Vol. III – Family Law in a European Perspective*, Edward Elgar, Cheltenham 2016, pp. 284–310 and J.M. Scherpe, 'Establishing and Ending Parental Responsibility – A Comparative View' in R. Probert, S. Gilmore and J. Herring (eds), *Responsible Parents and Parental Responsibility*, Hart Publishing, Oxford 2009, pp. 43–62; J.M. Scherpe, 'Elterliche Sorge von nicht miteinander verheirateten Eltern in England und Wales' in D. Coester-Waltjen, V. Lipp, E. Schumann and B. Veit (eds), *Alles zum Wohle des Kindes? Aktuelle Probleme des Kindschaftsrechts*, Universitätsverlag Göttingen, Göttingen 2012, pp. 71–84.
[62] On this see also J.M. Scherpe, 'Parental Responsibility – To Consult or to Consent, that is the Question' in J.M. Scherpe and S. Gilmore (eds), *Family Matters – Essays in Honour of John Eekelaar*, Intersentia, Cambridge 2022, pp. 638–653.
[63] On this see also J.M. Scherpe, 'Social Parenthood in England and Wales' in C. Huntingdon, C. Joslin and C. von Bary (eds), *Social Parenthood in Comparative Perspective*, New York University Press, New York, forthcoming in 2023.

4. RECOGNISING ADULT RELATIONSHIPS AND FAMILY FUNCTIONS

English law does not have a definition of 'family' as such, and recognition of relationships as family is largely driven by interpretation of the law based on the ECHR, incorporated into English law through the Human Rights Act 1998.[64] Thus it is not surprising that English law does not explicitly identify specific 'functions' for the family. However, it is possible to discern certain principles from an examination of the laws concerning the formalisation of adult relationships, and the remedies available upon their dissolution.

When it comes to the recognition of horizontal family relationships (i.e. the relationships between adults) England and Wales maintains a very strong focus on formalised relationships, that is marriage and civil partnership – both of which are now open to couples of the same or the opposite sex.[65]

4.1. ADULT RELATIONSHIP RECOGNITION IN GENERAL: MARRIAGE, CIVIL PARTNERSHIP, AND COHABITATION

The law of marriage traditionally had a strong focus on the sexual union, and arguably following from this, the producing and raising of children. For example, the non-consummation[66] of the marriage (either due to incapacity or wilful refusal)[67] would render a marriage voidable (but not void).[68] However, in *Baxter v. Baxter*[69] the court expressly found that intercourse with a condom suffices to fulfil the consummation requirement, thus detaching this requirement from procreation. This is also supported by the earlier case of *Clarke v. Clarke*,[70]

---

[64] On this see e.g. J.M. Scherpe, C. Fenton-Glynn and K. Hughes, 'Family Forms and Parenthood in England and Wales' in A. Büchler and H. Keller (eds), *Family Forms and Parenthood – Theory and Practice on Article 8 ECHR in Europe*, Intersentia, Cambridge 2016, pp. 145–99.

[65] Issues of non-binary legal gender identities have not yet been addressed in England and Wales.

[66] There is a surprising number of cases dealing with the 'technical' details of what amounts to consummation: *D-E v. A-G* (1845) 1 Rob Eccl 279 (intercourse needs to be 'ordinary and complete, not partial and imperfect'); *R v. R* [1952] 1 All ER 1194 (no orgasm or ejaculation required); *D v. D (Nullity Statutory Bar)* [1979] Fam 70 (refusal to undergo non-dangerous surgery which would restore physical ability to consummate can be considered wilful refusal); *Brodie v. Brodie* [1917] P 271 (agreement not to consummate marriage violates public policy), but cf. *Morgan v. Morgan* [1959] P 92.

[67] S. 12(1)(a) and (b) of the Matrimonial Causes Act 1973.

[68] The distinction being that a voidable marriage is valid until annulled by a court, which is only possible at the instance of one of the parties and during the lifetime of the parties, whereas a void marriage is void *ab initio*. On the causes for a marriage being void see s. 11 of the Matrimonial Causes Act 1973.

[69] [1948] AC 274.

[70] [1943] 2 All ER 540.

in which a child was conceived but not through sexual intercourse, and the court found that procreation in itself did not suffice for the consummation requirement. Hence procreation, whether or not it originally may have been an intended policy behind the consummation requirements, can no longer be seen as an express policy ground embodied in these provisions.

It is interesting to note that when civil partnerships were introduced for same-sex couples in 2004,[71] no consummation requirements were included, leading some to argue that therefore partnerships were to be regarded as 'sexless'. But, as Jo Miles has put it, this can also be explained more prosaically:[72] consummation had been defined very precisely by the courts[73] as requiring the penile penetration of the vagina, and that therefore this concept simply could not apply to same-sex relationships. The same applies to the omission of adultery (until 6 April 2022 a possible fact on which a divorce could be based[74] and defined with equal technical rigour by the courts),[75] as a fact upon which the separation of civil partners could be based as evidence of the irretrievable breakdown of the relationship.[76]

The view that civil partnerships were not intended to be regarded as 'sexless' is also supported by the fact that when marriage was opened up to same-sex couples in 2013,[77] Parliament saw it necessary to clarify what adultery is by inserting section 1(6) into the Matrimonial Causes Act 1973. This new section stipulates that 'only conduct between the respondent and a person of the opposite sex may constitute adultery for the purposes of this section'. Thus, the adultery fact is applicable to same-sex marriages in principle, but only for the prescribed conduct. So for both consummation and adultery it arguably

---

[71] Civil Partnership Act 2004; subsequently, and following the decision in *Steinfeld and Keidan v. Secretary of State for Education* [2018] UKSC 32, civil partnerships were also made available to opposite-sex couples by the Civil Partnerships, Marriages and Deaths (Registration etc) Act 2019. On this see J.M. Scherpe, 'Family Law, Ideology and the Recognition of Relationships: R (Steinfeld and Keidan) v Secretary of State for International Development' in D. Clarry (ed.), *The UK Supreme Court Yearbook*, Vol. 9: 2017–2018 Legal Year, Appellate Press, London 2019, pp. 150–73.

[72] J. Miles, R. George and S. Harris-Short, *Family Law: Text, Cases and Materials*, 3rd ed., Oxford University Press, Oxford 2015, p. 96.

[73] See e.g. J.M. Scherpe, 'Establishing and Ending Parental Responsibility – A Comparative View' in R. Probert, S. Gilmore and J. Herring (eds), *Responsible Parents and Parental Responsibility*, Hart Publishing, Oxford 2009, pp. 43–62; J.M. Scherpe, 'Elterliche Sorge von nicht miteinander verheirateten Eltern in England und Wales' in D. Coester-Waltjen, V. Lipp, E. Schumann and B. Veit (eds), *Alles zum Wohle des Kindes? Aktuelle Probleme des Kindschaftsrechts*, Universitätsverlag Göttingen, Göttingen 2012, pp. 71–84.

[74] The Divorce, Dissolution and Separation Act 2020, which received Royal Assent on 25.06.2020, introduced proper no-fault divorce in England and Wales from 06.04.2022, and thus the ground of divorce (irretrievable breakdown) and the five facts necessary to prove such a breakdown (one of which is adultery) were abolished.

[75] *Dennis v. Dennis* [1955] 2 All ER 51.

[76] For marriages contained in s. 1(2)(a) of the Matrimonial Causes Act 1973.

[77] Marriage (Same Sex Couples) Act 2013.

is the heteronormative technical definition of these terms that prevents their application to civil partnerships and same-sex marriages, rather than a difference in the function of the relationship.[78]

Curiously, a further difference between nullity of marriages and of civil partnerships is the absence of a ground for voidability based on 'the respondent at the time of the marriage suffering from a venereal disease in a communicable form'[79] for civil partnerships, which again may be thought to point towards a supposed 'non-sexual nature' of civil partnerships. However, in parliamentary debates the omission was explained as one 'from a bygone age when, perhaps, we were less informed about sexually transmitted diseases' and that it would be 'highly questionable' that such a provision would have been included for marriage today, and therefore it should not be for civil partnerships.[80] Thus, this also cannot be seen as proof of making a distinction between marriage and civil partnership based on there being sexual activity in the relationship or not.

By contrast, the nullity ground of 'pregnant by some person other than the petitioner'[81] is available to civil partners as well.[82] This suggests, as does the adultery fact for divorce, that the law is actually more concerned with protecting lineage. Arguably, this also finds support in the case law on the permissibility of DNA testing to establish parentage; the English position, unlike that in many other jurisdictions, is that the testing should be permitted unless the welfare of the child 'clearly justified the cover up'.[83]

In any event, as far as the formalised relationships are concerned, it appears that while there traditionally may have been a focus on procreation, this potential purpose certainly has been diluted with the changing social attitudes and the diversification of adult relationships.

By contrast, and despite elaborate proposals by the Law Commission of England and Wales which sought to address the vulnerabilities of informally cohabiting families,[84] there is no comprehensive framework for informal cohabitation relationships (i.e. a couple in a de facto relationship), even though

---

[78] Though it is worth noting that when civil partnerships were opened up to opposite-sex couples, no provisions regarding adultery or consummation were inserted into the Civil Partnership Act 2004.
[79] S. 12(1)(e) of the Matrimonial Causes Act 1973.
[80] A. McGuire (Parliamentary Under-Secretary of State), Hansard, Official Report – Civil Partnership Debates, HC Standing Committee D, col. 162, 26.10.2004.
[81] S. 12(1)(f) of the Matrimonial Causes Act 1973.
[82] S. 50(1)(c) of the Civil Partnership Act 2004.
[83] *Re H (a minor) (blood tests: parental rights)* [1996] 3 WLR 506, CA.
[84] Law Commission of England and Wales, *Cohabitation: The Financial Consequences of Relationship Breakdown*, Consultation Paper No. 179, 2006, and Report No. 307, 2007. On these proposals see also the series of articles by S. Bridge, 'Cohabitation: Why Legislative Reform is Necessary' [2007] *Family Law* 911; 'Financial Relief for Cohabitants: How the Law Commission's Scheme Would Work' [2007] *Family Law* 998; and 'Financial Relief for Cohabitants: Eligibility, Opt Out and Provision on Death' [2007] *Family Law* 1076.

such couples have access to joint adoption,[85] assisted reproduction,[86] and parental orders in case of surrogacy.[87] In particular, there are no financial remedies for cohabitants in case of separation, although some limited remedies exist in case of death or when the couple had joint children (on which see below).

4.2. FINANCIAL REMEDIES WHEN ADULT RELATIONSHIPS END THROUGH SEPARATION OR DEATH

For married and civil partnership couples, there are rules on financial remedies in case of divorce/dissolution of the marriage/the civil partnership. However, unlike most jurisdictions, England and Wales does not operate with a matrimonial property regime, but the financial remedies upon divorce are expressly left to the discretion of the judge. There is no separation of the remedies for property redistribution, maintenance or pension sharing, etc.; instead the courts take a holistic view. England and Wales thus favours flexibility and fairness in individual cases over legal certainty, as this better allows to protect the vulnerable.[88] The statutes provide only limited guidance as to how this overall fairness is to be achieved, merely listing 'matters to which court is to have regard' when considering all the circumstances.[89] However, one of those factors is given particular prominence, namely that when exercising the discretion, the courts must ensure that 'first consideration [is] given to the welfare while a minor of any child of the family who has not attained the age of eighteen'.[90] It is important to note that the concept of 'child of the family' not only comprises the joint children of the couple, but can also refer to children (e.g. from previous relationships) who lived with the couple. In section 105 of the Children Act 1989, 'child of the family' of a married couple/couple in a civil partnership[91] is defined as '(a) a child of both of them, and (b) any other child, other than a child placed with them as a foster parent by a local authority or voluntary organisation, who has been treated by both of them as a child of their family'.

---

[85] Ss 50 and 144(4)(b) of the Adoption and Children Act 2002.
[86] Ss 26 and 43 of the Human Fertilisation and Embryology Act 2008.
[87] S. 54(2)(c) of the Human Fertilisation and Embryology Act 2008.
[88] For a comparative overview see J.M. Scherpe, 'Marital Agreements and Private Autonomy in Comparative Perspective' in J.M. Scherpe (ed.), *Marital Agreements and Private Autonomy in Comparative Perspective*, Hart Publishing, Oxford 2012, pp. 443–518 and J.M. Scherpe, 'Financial Consequences of Divorce in a European Perspective' in J.M. Scherpe (ed.), *European Family Law Volume III: Family Law in a European Perspective*, Edward Elgar, Cheltenham 2016, pp. 147–208.
[89] S. 25 of the Matrimonial Causes Act 1973; Schedule 5, Part 5, No. 21 of the Civil Partnership Act 2004.
[90] S. 25I(1) of the Matrimonial Causes Act 1973; Schedule 5, Part 5, Nos 20(b) and 22 of the Civil Partnership Act 2004.
[91] The concept of child of the family does not extend to cohabitants.

The seemingly unfettered discretion of the courts has been tempered somewhat by case law, especially since 2000. While space precludes a lengthy exposition,[92] it is certainly safe to say that the courts follow the seminal precedents of *White v. White*[93] and *Miller v. Miller; McFarlane v. McFarlane*[94] in reaching the overarching aim of fairness by looking at the rationales of needs, compensation and equal sharing. Of those, 'needs' is the dominant rationale, and in large parts influenced by the above-mentioned 'first consideration' of the welfare of the children of the family. In practice, only when the needs of the parties and the children have been secured do the other rationales have a role to play. It is also worth noting that in reaching their discretionary decision the courts are not limited to any concept or matrimonial/relationship property but can take any property available at the time (so include pre-marital/relationship property as well as inheritances, etc.) into account, and even assets that are likely to be generated in the future.

In case of death, the intestacy rules are rather generous towards the spouse, allocating assets to them in the first instance up to a maximum amount (currently £270,000).[95] Indeed, in many cases children will not inherit as the estate does not go beyond the portion set aside for the spouse. Where a will has been made, English law has a strong emphasis on the freedom of testation and does not, unlike many jurisdictions, recognise a mandatory portion/forced heirship.[96] However, spouses and civil partners have very strong claims against the estate should they be provided for inadequately under the will, and the yardstick for this effectively is what they would have received in case of divorce.[97] Children, however, are limited in their claims against the estate to what 'would be reasonable in all the circumstances of the case' to receive for their maintenance;[98] given the high regard which the freedom of testation enjoys in England and Wales, these claims

---

[92] But see J. Miles, 'Marital Agreements and Private Autonomy in England and Wales' in J.M. Scherpe (ed.), *Marital Agreements and Private Autonomy in Comparative Perspective*, Hart Publishing, Oxford 2012, pp. 89–121 and J.M. Scherpe, 'Towards a Matrimonial Property Regime for England and Wales?' in R. Probert and A. Barton (eds), *Fifty Years in Family Law – Essays for Stephen Cretney*, Intersentia, Cambridge 2012, pp. 129–42.

[93] [2000] UKHL 54.

[94] [2006] UKHL 24; for a comparative comment see J.M. Scherpe, 'Matrimonial Causes for Concern? – A Comparative Analysis of Miller v Miller; McFarlane v McFarlane [2006] UKHL 24' (2007) 18 *King's Law Journal* 348 and J.M. Scherpe, 'Marital Agreements and Private Autonomy in Comparative Perspective' in J.M. Scherpe (ed.), *Marital Agreements and Private Autonomy in Comparative Perspective*, Hart Publishing, Oxford 2012, pp. 443–518.

[95] The Administration of Estates Act 1925 (Fixed Net Sum) Order 2020.

[96] For a comparison and an English national report, see K. Reid, M. de Waal and R. Zimmermann (eds), *Comparative Succession Law Volume III: Mandatory Family Protection*, Oxford University Press, Oxford 2020.

[97] Ss 1(1)(a), 2(a) and 2(aa) of the Inheritance (Provision for Family Members and Dependants) Act 1975.

[98] S. 1(1)(c), (d) and (2)(b) of the Inheritance (Provision for Family Members and Dependants) Act 1975.

cannot be regarded as generous by comparison to the succession law rules in other jurisdictions.[99]

Thus, it can be said that with needs being the dominant factor, particularly in so-called 'small money cases', English law in formalised relationships in particular aims to ensure that the primary carer and the children are financially secure as far as possible under the circumstances, that is to ensure the caring function and protect the vulnerable.

However, for couples in informal cohabitation the picture is rather different. In case of death, there is the possibility for family provision for the surviving cohabitant upon death of the other. However, family provision in these circumstances – unlike that for spouses or civil partners – is limited to what is reasonable to receive for the maintenance of the surviving cohabitant, just as it is for children.[100] Hence, for cohabitants there is a much greater need to make wills to protect each other in case of death.

While in case of death there at least is some legal protection for the surviving cohabitant, there are no comparable rules in case of separation – and so the cohabitants have to rely on the rather inadequate and unsuited rules of the general law, and in particular property and trust law.[101]

However, there are some – arguably underutilised – remedies available in the Children Act 1989 to make provision in relation to financial relief for children.[102] While the primary carer may benefit from these indirectly, they are intended only for the children and thus leave the primary carer unprotected when the child reaches maturity/leaves the home.

The law of cohabitants (or rather the absence of it) in England and Wales makes clear what the preferred family forms are, and that English law arguably prefers form over function. But the need to protect the vulnerable/ensure a caring function in non-formalised relationships at least has been recognised to a limited extent in case of death through the Inheritance (Provision for Family Members and Dependants) Act 1975 and in case of separation through the remedies available in the Children Act 1989.

Finally, it is worth mentioning that child support in England and Wales is payable to the primary carer by the non-resident parent, and this solely depends

---

[99] See e.g. *Ilott v. The Blue Cross and others* [2017] UKSC 17. On this case and the surrounding law see B. Sloan, 'Ilott v The Blue Cross: Testing the Limits of Testamentary Freedom' in B. Sloan (ed.), *Landmark Cases in Succession Law*, Hart Publishing, Oxford 2019, ch. 17.

[100] S. 1(ba), (1A), (1B) and (2)(b) of the Inheritance (Provision for Family Members and Dependants) Act 1975.

[101] See the analysis by the Law Commission of England and Wales, *Cohabitation: The Financial Consequences of Relationship Breakdown*, Consultation Paper No 179, 2006, and Report No. 307, 2007.

[102] S. 15 and Schedule 1 of the Children Act 1989.

on the legal status, that is whether the child is the legal child of the parent, and not the way they were conceived/born or whether they were adopted.[103]

For those 'children of the family', that is children (usually from a previous relationship) that have 'been treated by both of them as a child of their family',[104] child maintenance claims may be available under the Children Act 1989. But it is worth repeating that the concept of 'child of the family' only applies to children in a formalised relationship, that is marriage or civil partnership, and therefore not to those who were treated like family in cohabitation relationships. This distinction may or may not be justified, but this means that, unlike in many jurisdictions, one can incur financial obligations towards children that are not one's own in England and Wales. This is yet another expression of the emphasis that English law places on caring functions and protecting the financially vulnerable, but again contingent on there having been a formalised relationship, thus arguably again preferring form over function.

What can be seen from the above by the elevation of the welfare of the children's welfare as a 'first consideration' under the Matrimonial Causes Act 1973 as well as the dominant role the needs rationale plays in the application of the law, and taking into account the remedies available under the Children Act 1989, Schedule 1, is that English law places great emphasis on the financial security of children and their primary carers.

5. CONCLUSION

This contribution has highlighted the disparate nature of English family law. There has not been a considered, wholescale consideration of family law, its structures or its policy aims in a long time – and it is unlikely that there is going to be one. In some areas English family law has reacted to societal changes (e.g. by recognising same-sex relationships first through civil partnership and then marriage,[105] and – to some extent – social parenthood through the concept of parental responsibility[106]) and scientific advances (e.g. recognition of parenthood in cases of assisted reproduction, including for same-sex couples[107]). At the same time, English family law seems stuck in 'old thinking', for example by insisting that the person giving birth under all circumstances (including surrogacy arrangements) is not only the legal parent of the child, but also the 'mother', even if the person giving birth is male.[108] Other examples

---

[103] Child Support Act 1991.
[104] S. 105 of the Children Act 1989.
[105] See section 4.1 above.
[106] See section 3 above.
[107] See section 2.2 above.
[108] See *R (McConnell and YY) v. Registrar General* [2020] EWCA Civ 559 and the text above.

discussed were the limitation of legal parents to a maximum of two[109] and that cohabitation/de facto relationships are not adequately protected by law.[110]

Another observation is that – like many family laws – English family law in many areas still very much is focused on the form of the familial relationship – legal parenthood, marriage, civil partnership. However, for child law English law at the same time allows for a very flexible regime regarding parental responsibility, which can be held by more than two persons. This allows the accommodation of many diverse family forms and especially social parenthood, albeit only in a minor form. Arguably parental responsibility in many situations will be seen by those concerned as nothing but a consolation prize.[111]

When looking at the financial consequences of relationship breakdown, the absence of remedies for cohabitants because of the insistence on formalisation of relationships is striking, particularly when contrasted with the neighbouring jurisdictions of Scotland and the Republic of Ireland, which do have specific legal regimes for such relationships. Nevertheless, where children are involved, the Children Act 1989, Schedule 1, at least in theory provides reasonably strong – but child-centred – remedies to protect children and the primary carer (at least while they are still exercising this care). Similarly, the financial remedies in case of divorce and civil partnership dissolution, while discretionary, elevate the welfare of the children involved above all others as the 'first consideration', and indeed this is applied accordingly in practice. Thus within the form-centred framework there is a strong degree of functionality.

All in all, like many family laws, English family law is struggling to keep up with societal changes and medical advances. Unsurprisingly, it does better in some areas than in others, and some well-established 'traditional' paradigms still need to be broken to reflect the diversity of modern family life.

---

[109] See section 2 above.
[110] See section 4 above.
[111] Cf. e.g. J.M. Scherpe, 'Mehrelterlichkeit statt Mehrelternschaft?' in A. Dutta, H. Guhling and F. Klinkhammer (eds), *Das Familienrecht in seiner großen Vielfalt – Festschrift für Hans-Joachim Dose*, Gieseking, Bielefeld 2022, pp. 533–44.

FAMILY FUNCTIONS AND NEW FAMILY FORMS IN GERMANY

Anne SANDERS

1. Introduction 269
2. Family Functions in Germany 271
   2.1. Family Functions and the German Constitution............... 271
   2.2. Family Functions and Family Support 272
   2.3. Family Functions and Children 273
   2.4. Three Family Functions.................................... 274
3. Diversity and Plurality of Family Forms 275
   3.1. Children in Multiple Households 275
   3.2. Recognition of Multiple Parents in the Context of Step-Families 277
   3.3. Multiple Parenthood and Open Adoptions 279
   3.4. Multiple Parenthood and Guardianship...................... 280
   3.5. Parenthood and Reproductive Technology 281
      3.5.1. Legal Motherhood.................................... 281
      3.5.2. Legal Fatherhood 282
   3.6. Same-Sex Parents 283
   3.7. Multiple Parenthood 285
   3.8. Parenthood and Surrogacy.................................. 287
4. Conclusions... 288

1. INTRODUCTION

This report discusses family forms and family functions in Germany, focusing on diverse family forms, especially children in families with more than two parents.

Germany's legal system adheres to the civil law tradition. Family law is regulated in the German Civil Code (*Bürgerliches Gesetzbuch*, BGB), which came into operation in 1900. Since then, of course, German family law has changed considerably. A major influence was and still is the Federal German Constitution (*Grundgesetz*, GG) of 1949 and its interpretation by the Federal Constitutional Court (*Bundesverfassungsgericht*, BVerfG). This court may be described as the 'engine of German family law'[1] and has initiated major changes for the equality of husband and wife,[2] children born out of wedlock,[3] joint custody,[4] transgender rights,[5] the introduction of a third gender,[6] same-sex partnerships,[7] and adoption by same-sex partners[8] and cohabitants.[9] Many times, decisions of the Federal Constitutional Court have declared legislation unconstitutional and demanded change.

There have been some developments in recent decades in favour of diverse family forms, for example the introduction of civil partnerships in 2001 with the opportunity to adopt the partner's children, more opportunities for joint custody of unmarried parents, same-sex marriage in 2017, and joint adoption for cohabitants in 2021. However, reform of family law, especially the law of parentage, has not been undertaken despite a number of research projects[10] and commissions[11] and a draft law the Federal Ministry of Justice published in 2019.[12]

---

[1] On the importance of German Constitutional Family Law, see J. Gernhuber and D. Coester-Waltjen, *Familienrecht*, 7th ed., C.H. Beck, Munich 2020, §5; A. Sanders, 'Paternidad y responsabilidad parental en el derecho constitucional familiar alemán' in N.E. Yaksic (ed.), *La responsabilidad parental en el derecho: una mirada comparada*, Suprema Corte de Justicia d al Nación, Centro de Estudios Constitucionales SCNJ Mexico, Mexico City 2021, p. 255.

[2] Bundesverfassungsgericht (BVERFG), Judgment of the First Senate of 29.07.1959 – 1 BvR 205, 332, 333, 367/58, 1 BvL 27, 100/58 – BVerfGE 10, 59; Order of the First Senate of 05.02.2002 – 1 BvR 105/95, 559/95, 457/96 – BVerfGE 105, 1.

[3] Bundesverfassungsgericht (BVERFG), Order of the First Senate of 29.01.1969 – 1 BvR 26/66 – BVerfGE 25, 167.

[4] Bundesverfassungsgericht (BVERFG), Judgment of the First Senate of 03.11.1982 – 1 BvL 25, 38, 40/80, 12/81 – BVerfGE 61, 358; Order of the First Senate of 07.05.1991 – 1 BvL 32/88 – BVerfGE 84, 168, Judgment of the First Senate of 29.01.2003 – 1 BvL 20/99 – BVerfGE 107, 150; Order of the First Senate of 21.07.2010 – 1 BvR 420/09 – BVerfGE 127, 132.

[5] Bundesverfassungsgericht (BVERFG), Order of the First Senate of 11.01.2011 – 1 BvR 3295/07 – BVerfGE 128, 109.

[6] Bundesverfassungsgericht (BVERFG), Order of the First Senate of 10.10.2017 – 1 BvR 2019/16 – BVerfGE 147, 1.

[7] Bundesverfassungsgericht (BVERFG), Order of the First Senate of 05.02.2002 – 1 BvR 105/95, 559/95, 457/96 – BVerfGE 105, 313.

[8] Bundesverfassungsgericht (BVERFG), Order of the First Senate of 19.02.2013 – BvR 3247/09 – BVerfGE 133, 59.

[9] Bundesverfassungsgericht (BVERFG), Order of the First Senate of 26.03.2019 – 1 BvR 673/17 – BVerfGE 151, 101.

[10] See in particular P.M. Reuß, *Theorie eines Elternschaftsrechts*, Duncker & Humblot, Berlin 2018; A. Sanders, *Mehrelternschaft*, Mohr Siebeck, Tübingen 2018.

[11] Conference of German Lawyers (*Deutscher Juristentag*) with Expert Opinion by Tobias Helms in 2016, a working group of the Federal Ministry of Justice and Consumer Protection, which published a final report containing proposals for reforms in 2017: BMJV Bundesministerium für Justiz und Verbraucherschutz, *Arbeitskreis Abstammungsrecht, Abschlussbericht*, Bundesanzeigerverlag, Cologne 2017.

[12] Bundesministerium für Justiz und Verbraucherschutz (Ministry of Justice and Consumer Protection), *Diskussionsteilentwurf, Entwurf eines Gesetzes zur Reform des Abstammungsrechts*, 2019, available at https://www.bmjv.de/SharedDocs/Gesetzgebungsverfahren/DE/Reform_Abstammungsrecht.html?nn=6704238, accessed 10.05.2022.

The coalition government of Social Democrats (SPD), the Green Party (Bündnis 90/DIE GRÜNEN) and the Liberal Party (FDP) has put a number of family reform projects on its agenda,[13] including a highly anticipated reform of the law of parenthood and custody. There are also reform projects mentioned on the agenda concerning the freedom in reproductive choice and expression of gender identity.

This discussion focuses on the status quo but shall mention areas where reform is possible or perhaps even expected in the near future. Hopefully, these reforms will allow diverse families to fulfil their function better. The report starts with family functions in Germany[14] before it focuses on diverse family forms, especially multi-parenthood situations, that is situations of children with more than two parents.[15]

2. FAMILY FUNCTIONS IN GERMANY

It is difficult to assign specific, official functions to the family in German law, as there is no law or official document stating such functions. Therefore, family functions shall be discussed here in a more general way, addressing different legal issues, starting with constitutional law,[16] followed by family support and solidarity,[17] and concluding with raising children.[18]

2.1. FAMILY FUNCTIONS AND THE GERMAN CONSTITUTION

It is important to note that marriage, the family, and parent–child relationships are constitutionally protected. The reason for doing this in 1949 was to provide a protected private space for self-determined life and development in the solidarity and community of the family.[19] This was particularly important at the time the German Constitution was drafted after the horrors of the Nazi regime.[20] Between 1933 and 1945, the family's function was conceptualised as producing children as future soldiers and settlers for a future of world dominance by the

---

[13] Koalitionsvereinbarung, Coalition Agreement 'Mehr Fortschritt wagen' 2021–2015, paras 3375–415, 3878–903, 4010–28.
[14] See section 2 below.
[15] See section 3 below.
[16] See section 2.1 below.
[17] See section 2.2 below.
[18] See section 2.3 below.
[19] Bundesverfassungsgericht (BVERFG), Decision of 17.01.1957 – 1 BvL 4/54 – BVerfGE 6, 55.
[20] On the debates in the German constitutional convention, see Der Parlamentarische Rat, Vol. 5/II, 617, 645, 814, 823; see also A. Sanders, *Mehrelternschaft*, Mohr Siebeck, Tübingen 2018, pp. 109–11.

'Aryan race'. At the time the German Constitution, the Basic Law, was drafted, West Germany also wanted to distance itself from Communist East Germany and the Soviet Union, where the education of children was also seen as the State's rather than the family's responsibility.[21] Following this tradition, the education of children is seen as the family's rather than the State's responsibility in Germany.

The family is constitutionally protected in Article 6 of the Basic Law. Article 6(1) of the Basic Law protects marriage[22] and the family. According to Article 6(2) of the Basic Law, the care and upbringing of children is the natural right of parents and a duty primarily incumbent upon them. The State shall watch over them in the performance of this duty. Children may be separated from their families against the will of their parents or guardians only pursuant to a law and only if the parents or guardians fail in their duties or the children are otherwise in danger of serious neglect.[23] In addition, the position of the mother is especially emphasised. According to the Basic Law, she has the right to be protected and cared for by the community.[24] Moreover, Article 6(5) of the Basic Law clarifies that children born outside of marriage shall, by legislation, be provided with the same opportunities for physical and mental development and for their position in society as are enjoyed by those born within marriage.

Thus, an important function of the family which is protected by the Constitution is providing freedom to people to create a private space of trust, for self-development and expression, for mutual support and for the education of children, for which private citizens rather than the State are responsible.[25]

2.2. FAMILY FUNCTIONS AND FAMILY SUPPORT

Moreover, the family also functions as a main source of mutual care and support for the elderly, spouses and children, including being a source of income through child, spousal, and parental support in Germany. Providing support and care is seen primarily as the responsibility of the family. However, the rights of parents to financial support from their children was significantly cut back by the legislator recently; only children earning more than €200,000 a year have to pay it in practice. Still, in Germany, the family has a particularly high standing

---

[21] See M. Coester, *Das Kindeswohl als Rechtsbegriff*, Alfred Metzner Verlag, Frankfurt am Main 1983, p. 12 ff.
[22] For a discussion in English, see A. Sanders, 'Marriage, Same-Sex Partnership, and the German Constitution' (2012) 13 *German Law Journal* 911.
[23] Art. 6(3) of the Basic Law.
[24] Art. 6(4) of the Basic Law.
[25] See F. Wapler, *Kinderrechte und Kindeswohl*, Mohr Siebeck, Tübingen 2015, p. 133 ff.

when it comes to the care of relatives. 1.86 million people are cared for at home. This is roughly 71% of all people in need of care. Of those cared for at home, 1.25 million are looked after by relatives alone.[26] Relatives are the backbone of the German system of care for the elderly.[27] There are rights to take time off from work to care not only for children but also for elderly relatives.

Another important point when it comes to support as a family function is spousal support. Spousal support is calculated according to the couple's living standard based on the value judgement that care work and paid employment have to be evaluated as of equal value.[28] Spousal support was restricted by the legislator in 2008. Before that, claims for support for decades were not uncommon. After the reform, the basic approach to the calculation of support remained the same. However, unless the marriage has lasted for many decades, support is limited to a few years and is not necessarily based on the living standard jointly enjoyed by the spouses. While the reform pursued laudable goals, the demand for spousal support must be seen in the context of slowly changing gender roles and little available childcare.

Reforms of spousal support show that legal rights to family solidarity have been cut back. Nevertheless, the law still shows that it is the function of the family to provide support, rather than the State providing support through social benefits. This idea is so strong that support is even assumed to exist when there is no legal claim to it: if a couple lives together without being married, social benefits will be significantly reduced for one of the partners without income, even though he or she has no right to such support against the partner.[29] This shows again that the family is seen as the main source of support, not the State.

2.3. FAMILY FUNCTIONS AND CHILDREN

At least one of the functions, if not the central function, of families must be seen as raising children as new members of society. In Germany, the role of the State in relation to education of children has been tainted by Nazi ideology. As a response, German constitutional law after World War 2 stressed that it is

---

[26] S. Nowossadeck, H. Egstler and D. Klaus, *Pflege und Unterstützung durch Angehörige*, Deutsches Zentrum für Altersfragen (Hrsg), report Altersdaten 1/2016, pp. 7–8, available at https://www.dza.de/fileadmin/dza/Dokumente/Report_Altersdaten/Report_Altersdaten_Heft_1_2016.pdf, accessed 11.05.2022.

[27] U. Ehrlich and N. Kelle, *Wer pflegt für wen, wo und wie?* DZA Fact Sheet 2019 p. 2, available at https://www.dza.de/fileadmin/dza/Dokumente/Fact_Sheets/FactSheet_Hilfe_und_Pfleget aetigkeiten.pdf, accessed 11.05.2022.

[28] Bundesverfassungsgericht (BVERFG), Order of the First Senate of 05.02.2002 – 1 BvR 105/95, 559/95, 457/96 – BVerfGE 105, 1.

[29] Bedarfsgemeinschaft, s. 7(3) of the Sozialgesetzbuch II (SGB II, Social Law Code II).

the function of the family rather than of the State to bring up children and to educate them to be responsible persons and citizens. Therefore, the parent–child relationship has always been at the centre of German family law, with parents being granted constitutional rights. As will be shown below, while society and family law do change, German law is still based to a large extent on the ideal of the two-parent family of married, heterosexual parents and their mutual children.

The German Constitutional Court defines a family as the community of children and their parents, or to put it differently: family is where children are.[30] In contrast to the understanding of the European Convention on Human Rights,[31] a couple without children is not a family in German law.

The family function of raising children has gained new prominence in times of demographic change. Moreover, gender equality is recognised as an important issue of assigning care work, especially childcare. While professional childcare is of increasing importance, there are not always enough places yet, because of a German tradition that childcare should be provided by the family. Traditionally, schools were closed at lunch time, assuming that mothers would provide lunch and support for homework at home. The situation is different now, however, with children having a legal right to day-care. There are special benefits for children and paid parental leave for mothers and fathers to raise very small children in the family.[32] There are also certain tax and social benefits for children. However, there are also tax benefits just for married couples, no matter whether they have children or not.

2.4. THREE FAMILY FUNCTIONS

The discussion above shows three major functions of the family in Germany:

1. raising children as future members of society (care and education);
2. supporting and caring for family members rather than seeing support as only the State's responsibility (solidarity and subsidiarity); and
3. providing a protected space for individual development in relationships with others (self-development and privacy).

All three functions overlap, of course, with for example children being cared for and supported in the family as a protected place of privacy rather than by the

---

[30] See only Bundesverfassungsgericht (BVERFG), Decision of 29.07.1959 – 1 BvR 205, 332, 333, 367/58, 27, 100/58 – BVerfGE 10, 59, 66, para. 27.
[31] *Schalk and Kopf v. Austria*, no. 30141/04, 26.06.2010, §§93–99, NJW 2011, 1421; *Oliari v. Italy*, nos. 18766/11, 36030/11, 21.05.2015.
[32] Gesetz zum Elterngeld und zur Elternzeit (BEEG) BGBl. I 33 (2015), last changed by Art. 1 of the Law of 15.02.2021, BGBl. I 239.

State. Nevertheless, distinguishing these three functions might still be helpful to understand the peculiarities of German law.

While these principles have remained relevant, the legal rules organising their fulfilment must change with time. From the founding of the German Federal Republic in 1949, family law has already changed considerably. However, the development cannot stop there. Today's families that are enjoying and providing these functions are becoming more and more diverse. So far, German law has not fully responded to these changes. This will be discussed in the next part.

3. DIVERSITY AND PLURALITY OF FAMILY FORMS

German family law is based on the principle of the two-parent family.[33] The following discussion will highlight the effects of this principle for different new family forms.

In German law, like in most civil law jurisdictions, parenthood is understood not as a natural fact, as in English and Scottish law,[34] but rather as an – in principle unchanging – legal status,[35] which can be established by descent according to the law of parentage or through adoption. Legal parenthood is assigned at birth to up to two legal parents. From legal parenthood, all other parental rights and duties follow, for example visitation rights, custody and the duty to support the child.

According to section 1591 of the BGB, a child's legal mother is the woman who gave birth to the child. According to section 1592 of the BGB, the legal father is the man who is the husband of the mother, who has acknowledged the child or whose paternity has been ascertained by a test.

3.1. CHILDREN IN MULTIPLE HOUSEHOLDS

Married legal parents have joint custody by law, while unmarried legal parents can establish joint custody by agreement or a court decision, which only denies joint custody if the child's best interests require this.[36] In general, the German law of parental responsibility/custody includes the right and the duty to take

---

[33] See A. Sanders, *Mehrelternschaft*, Mohr Siebeck, Tübingen 2018; A. Sanders, 'Multiple Parenthood: Towards a New Concept of Parenthood in German Family Law' in H. Willekens, K. Scheiwe, T. Richarz and E. Schumann (eds), *Motherhood and the Law*, Universitätsverlag Göttingen, Göttingen 2019, pp. 119–51, https://doi.org/10.17875/gup2019-1201, accessed 10.05.2022.
[34] In the matter of the *Baronetcy of Pringle of Stichill* [2016] UKPC 16; B. Häcker, 'Honour Runs in the Blood' (2017) 133 *Law Quarterly Review* 36.
[35] U. Wanitzek, *Rechtliche Elternschaft bei medizinisch unterstützter Fortpflanzung*, Gieseking E. u W., Bielefeld 2002, p. 152; A. Sanders, *Mehrelternschaft*, Mohr Siebeck, Tübingen 2018, pp. 11–16.
[36] S. 1626a of the BGB.

care of the child as a person, the child's property and the legal representation of the child.[37] The parents shall exercise their custody responsibility by mutual agreement.[38] In case of disagreement, they must try to come to an agreement.[39] If this is not possible, the family court may, at the request of one parent, grant the sole power of decision to one parent.[40] In case of imminent danger, each parent is entitled to perform all legal acts necessary for the welfare of the child; the other parent must be informed immediately.[41] In all cases, the best interests of the child should serve as the basis for all decisions. The child shall be involved in matters of parental custody to the extent appropriate to his or her stage of development.[42]

Even if parents separate, they remain the legal parents of the child and hold the rights and duties of parental responsibility. The only way to change parenthood in this situation is adoption. German family law addresses the situation of children with separated parents by regulating the parents' decision-making powers.[43] It distinguishes between parents with joint custody and parents where only one parent has sole custody. Separation, and even divorce, does not change joint custody as such. However, custody can be assigned to one parent alone in the child's best interests.[44]

In the case of separation, section 1687 of the BGB determines the decision-making powers of the parents who have joint custody. It is important to note that German law still assumes that the child stays mainly with one parent and visits the other for brief periods. Models where a child stays with both parents equally (so-called *Wechselmodell*) are becoming increasingly popular. They have been discussed in detail by German family scholars and practitioners[45] for a couple of years now and will probably – finally – be taken up by the new legislator.

Section 1687 of the BGB, which is still the basis for organising joint custody, distinguishes between three types of matters. For decisions on matters of considerable importance, mutual agreement between the parents is required.[46] This includes decisions such as the choice of school or the child's place of

---

[37] S. 1626(1) sentence 1 and 2 and s. 1629(1) sentence 1 of the BGB.
[38] S. 1627 sentence 1 of the BGB.
[39] S. 1627 sentence 2 of the BGB.
[40] S. 1628 sentence 1 of the BGB.
[41] S. 1629(1) sentence 4 of the BGB.
[42] S. 1626(2) sentence 2 of the BGB.
[43] Ss 1687 and 1687a of the BGB.
[44] S. 1671 of the BGB.
[45] See only the *Resolutions at the 72. Deutsche Juristentag*, Leipzig 2018, available at https://www.famrz.de/files/Media/dokumente/pdfs/Beschl%C3%BCsse%2072.%20DJT%20Familienrecht.pdf, accessed 10.05.2022; and with further references the expert opinion by E. Schumann, *Gutachten Teil B: Gemeinsam getragene Elternverantwortung nach Trennung und Scheidung – Reformbedarf im Sorge-, Umgangs- und Unterhaltsrecht?*, C.H. Beck, Munich 2018.
[46] S. 1687(1) sentence 1 of the BGB.

habitual residence. Matters of daily life can be decided solely by the parent with whom the child usually resides.[47] According to the legal definition in section 1687(1) sentence 3 of the BGB, matters of daily life are usually those which occur frequently and which do not have irreversible effects on the child's development. This covers, for example, participation in school trips or simple medical treatments. Finally, matters of actual care can be decided solely by the parent with whom the child is currently staying.[48] Matters of actual care are, for example, feeding children or organising their leisure time. Decision-making powers in matters of daily life and actual care can be limited or excluded by the family court if this is necessary for the child's welfare.[49] Furthermore, one parent has sole decision-making power in case of imminent danger.[50]

Section 1687a of the BGB defines the decision-making powers of the non-custodial parent. As long as the child is staying with the non-custodial parent, the parent can decide matters of actual care (e.g. what the child will have for supper) and matters in case of imminent danger.[51] The power of decision on matters of actual care can be limited by the family court.[52]

The best interests of the child usually include contact with both parents.[53] Therefore, the child has a right to contact with each parent.[54] The parents also have a duty to refrain from doing anything that might impede the child's relationship with the other parent.[55]

The genetic father who is not the legal father – for example if a wife had an affair and conceived a child but later decided to raise the child with her husband – may have information rights and visitation rights according to section 1686a of the BGB.[56]

3.2. RECOGNITION OF MULTIPLE PARENTS IN THE CONTEXT OF STEP-FAMILIES

Despite the fact that step-parents often play an important role in the emotional and economic support of their step-children,[57] in Germany they usually do not have parental rights or duties. This can be changed by adoption. However,

---

[47] S. 1687(1) sentence 2 of the BGB.
[48] S. 1687(1) sentence 4 of the BGB.
[49] S. 1687(2) of the BGB.
[50] S. 1687(1) sentence 5 in conjunction with s. 1629(1) sentence 4 of the BGB.
[51] S. 1687a in conjunction with s. 1687(1) sentence 4 and 5 of the BGB.
[52] S. 1687a in conjunction with s. 1687(2) of the BGB.
[53] S. 1626(3) sentence 1 of the BGB.
[54] S. 1684 (1) BGB.
[55] S. 1684(2) sentence 1 of the BGB.
[56] See further section 3.7 below.
[57] More than 10% of German families include step-children and their parents: see T. Helms, *Gutachten Teil F zum 71. Deutschen Juristentag Essen 2016*, C.H. Beck, Munich 2016,

since 1977, German law has stuck to the principle of two-person parenthood in case of adoption: a minor can only be adopted if all legal ties to both original parents are cut. The law does make an exception and allows spouses to adopt his or her spouse's children so that the couple become the child's two parents. A new law, which came into force in March 2020 after a decision of the Federal Constitutional Court,[58] allows such an adoption even for unmarried stepparents in a stable relationship.

For example, A and B have a child, C. A and B split up and A marries stepparent S. S can adopt C and thus form a two-parent family with A and their child, C. However, with this adoption, the legal ties between C and B are cut. B ceases to be C's legal parent. Such drastic steps are rarely taken by step-parents. Moreover, the other parent (B) will usually not give his or her consent to the adoption. This is different in the case of adoption of children who have reached majority.

Step-parents who have not adopted the child have no duty to support them but often in fact do so. Moreover, there is the so-called *kleines Sorgerecht*, 'little custody', under section 1687b of the BGB and section 9(1)–(4) of the Civil Partnership Act. It allows a step-parent to make certain everyday decisions for the child. However, this right is limited; it is not equal to the right of custody of a legal parent[59] but is only meant to legitimise and acknowledge actual care work.[60] Therefore, the right may well be described as only having symbolic meaning.[61] Moreover, this right is limited to the spouse of a parent who does not share custody with the other legal parent. Given that joint custody is becoming increasingly normal, the scope of the rule is becoming increasingly narrow. However, extending this right to both new partners of separated parents with joint custody would mean softening the two-parent principle. However, the Coalition Agreement of 2021 states that the right of parental care of step-parents shall be extended to up to two persons and be developed further.[62]

---

pp. 58–59; see for statistical data: S. Walper, *Festschrift für Gerd Brudermüller zum 65. Geburtstag*, 2014, p. 889.

[58] Bundesverfassungsgericht (BVERFG), Decision of 26.03.2019 – 1 BvR 673/17 – NJW 2019, 1793.

[59] D. Schwab, *Familienrecht*, C.H. Beck, Munich 2021, §60, 718.

[60] BT-Drucks. 14/3751, 39.

[61] T. Helms, *Gutachten Teil F zum 71. Deutschen Juristentag Essen 2016*, C.H. Beck, Munich 2016, pp. 58–59; M. Löhnig, 'Politischer Signalcharakter' in D. Schwab and L.A. Vaskovics (eds), *Pluralisierung von Elternschaft und Kindschaft*, Verlag Barbara Budrich, Leverkusen 2011, pp 157–167.

[62] Koalitionsvereinbarung, Coalition Agreement 'Mehr Fortschritt wagen' 2021–2015, paras 3375–77.

If step-parents separate, the former step-parent can ask for visitation rights[63] if such visits benefit the child and if the former partner has been responsible for the child. Outside these rules, step-parents do not have a formal position under the law.

3.3. MULTIPLE PARENTHOOD AND OPEN ADOPTIONS

As already explained, an adoption of a minor under German law requires cutting all legal ties with the old family. However, that was not always the legal situation. Until 1977, an adopted child kept his or her 'old' legal parents and gained new ones. Today, this is still the law when adults are adopted.[64] At the time of the entry into force of the Adoption Act in 1977, legislators and academics assumed that the integration of the child into the adopted family would be facilitated by the complete legal separation of the child from the family of origin.[65] Therefore, the adoption of a minor required cutting off all legal ties to the original parents, such as custody, information and visitation rights. The child's privacy was secured by a number of measures, including the prohibition on disclosure and investigation.[66] Facts which would reveal the adoption and its circumstances may not be disclosed and investigated without the consent of the adoptive parents and the child. This legal situation still exists today.

However, recent research shows that it is in the child's best interests to build and sustain a stable relationship with both step-parents and biological parents.[67] Therefore, today there is a change in the discussion and demands in academia and practice for the introduction of forms of open adoption.[68] In practice, with the help of the adoption agency, the adoptive parents and parents of origin reach agreements on the opening up of the adoption, which may include, for example, information and access rights. However, compliance with such an agreement is solely at the discretion of the adoptive parents. In the future, this may be a point of discussion as well.

---

[63] S. 1685 of the BGB.
[64] See A. Sanders, *Mehrelternschaft*, Mohr Siebeck, Tübingen 2018, pp. 54–62.
[65] Official documents of the legislator: BT-Drucks. 7/738; BT-Drucks. 7/716, 1–2; BT-Drucks. 7/3061, 15 ff.; BT-Drucks. 7/5087. On the discussion, see H. Engler, 'Die Vorschläge zur Änderung des Adoptionsrechts im Referentenentwurf eines Unehelichengesetzes' (1966) *Zeitschrift für das gesamte Familienrecht* 551; A. Lüderitz, *Adoption*, C F Müller, Karlsruhe 1972, pp. 77–78.
[66] S. 1758 of the BGB.
[67] S. Walper, C. Enleitner-Phelps and E.-V. Wendt, 'Brauchen Kinder immer (nur) zwei Eltern?' (2016) *Recht der Jugend und des Bildungswesens* 210, available at https://www.nomos-elibrary.de/10.5771/0034-1312-2016-2-210.pdf, accessed 10.05.2022.
[68] For further references, see T. Helms, *Gutachten Teil F zum 71. Deutschen Juristentag Essen 2016*, C.H. Beck, Munich 2016, F pp. 85 et seq.

3.4. MULTIPLE PARENTHOOD AND GUARDIANSHIP

Since German law is not influenced by Islamic traditions, there is no *kafala* in Germany. However, German law provides a comparable legal institution: guardianship (*Vormundschaft*). Minors are given a guardian if they are not subject to parental custody or if the parents are not entitled to represent the minor either in matters affecting the person or in matters affecting property.[69] A minor is also given a guardian if the minor's parents cannot be determined.[70]

The guardian has the right and the duty to care for the person and the property of the ward, and in particular to represent the ward.[71] If the ward is taken into the household of the guardian for a long period, the ward – just like a child in relation to his or her parents – has a duty to perform services for his or her guardian in the household and business in a manner appropriate to the child's development and position in life.[72] Otherwise, the guardian should as a rule visit the ward once per month in his or her customary environment unless shorter or longer visiting intervals or a different place is required in individual cases.[73] The guardianship is conducted for free.[74] Exceptionally, the guardian may be paid. This happens if the court finds when the guardian is appointed that the guardian is conducting the guardianship as an occupation or profession.[75] The guardian must report to the family court at least once a year on the personal circumstances of the ward.[76] The report must also contain information on the guardian's personal contact with the ward.[77] The guardian should also provide the family court with an account of the management of the ward's assets.[78] The account is examined by the family court.[79]

If there are several guardians, they conduct the guardianship jointly.[80] In the case of a difference of opinion, the family court will make the final decision, unless provided otherwise upon the appointment of the guardians.[81]

Furthermore, the family court can appoint a supervisory guardian.[82] The supervisory guardian must ensure that the guardian conducts the guardianship in accordance with his or her duty.[83]

---

[69] S. 1773(1) of the BGB.
[70] S. 1773(2) of the BGB.
[71] S. 1793(1) sentence 1 of the BGB.
[72] S. 1793(1) sentence 3 in conjunction with s. 1619 of the BGB.
[73] S. 1793(1a) of the BGB.
[74] S. 1836(1) sentence 1 of the BGB.
[75] S. 1836(1) sentence 2 of the BGB.
[76] S. 1840(1) sentence 2 of the BGB.
[77] S. 1840(1) sentence 2 of the BGB.
[78] S. 1840(2) of the BGB.
[79] S. 1843(1) of the BGB.
[80] S. 1797(1) sentence 1 of the BGB.
[81] S. 1791(1) sentence 2 of the BGB.
[82] S. 1792(1) sentence 1 of the BGB.
[83] S. 1799(1) sentence 1 of the BGB.

3.5. PARENTHOOD AND REPRODUCTIVE TECHNOLOGY

Reproductive technologies have influenced German family law in a fundamental way and continue to do so. The following sections shall discuss this in more detail. German law has taken a hesitant approach so far, with many reproductive technologies not yet available in the country.

3.5.1. Legal Motherhood

Sperm donations are legal in Germany, but surrogacy and egg donations are forbidden by the *Embryonenschutzgesetz*.[84] There is only one rather unclear exception: the donation of embryos resulting from the fertilisation of an egg for the purpose of impregnating the woman from whom the egg was derived. These embryos are the result of in vitro fertilisation, as this usually produces more embryos than are implanted.

The law which criminalises a doctor's assistance in the making of egg donations and the performance of surrogacy was reformed in 1998 when a new law of legal motherhood was simultaneously enacted. While motherhood had not been regulated in the BGB of 1900 – which assumed that everybody knew who a child's mother was (*mater semper certa est*) – the 1998 law stipulated that only the woman who gives birth is the legal mother. In this way, the legislator wanted to avoid all cases of 'split motherhood'.[85] Thus, until today, according to section 1591 of the BGB, the woman who gives birth to the child is the child's sole legal mother. Legally, it is of no consequence if the birth mother is not the child's genetic parent. The genetic mother may only adopt the child if she is not the birth mother. This was the decision of the Higher Regional Court of Cologne in a case where a woman had donated an egg which was inseminated with the sperm of a donor. The pregnancy was then carried to term by the egg donor's partner. While both women established a biological bond with their child, only one of them, the birth mother, was seen as the child's legal mother.[86] The other one had to adopt the child.

The German Federal Court of Justice – the highest court for civil and criminal law cases – reached the same result in a case where an opposite-sex couple had concluded a surrogacy agreement with a Ukrainian surrogate.[87] Both the sperm

---

[84] Law of 13.12.1990, BGBl. I 2746, last changed by Art. 1 of the Law of 21.11.2011, BGBl. I 2228.
[85] BT-Drucks. 11/4154, 7; BT-Drucks. 11/5460, 6 ff., 17; BT-Drucks. 11/8057, 12; BT-Drucks. 13/4899, 52, 82; BT-Drucks. 17/3759, 113.
[86] Oberlandesgericht (OLG, Higher Regional Court) Cologne, Decision of 26.03.2015 – II-14 UF 181/14 – juris.
[87] Bundesgerichtshof (BGH, Federal Court of Justice, FCJ), Decision of 20.03.2019 – XII ZB 530/17 – NJW 2019, 1605.

and the egg came from the German couple. Despite the fact that Ukrainian law considered the genetic mother as the legal mother, the German Federal Court of Justice, applying German law according to German private international law, decided that the Ukrainian surrogate was the legal mother. Again, adoption was the only route to legal parenthood for the genetic mother. At least there is hope that the adoption will not be denied: in another recent case, the Court of Appeal of Frankfurt[88] agreed that another genetic mother could adopt her own genetic child who was also born of a surrogate in Ukraine. The Court held that the German prohibition on surrogacy did not prevent the adoption despite a legal regulation against the adoption of children by the commissioning parents. In this case, constitutional law demanded that the child could be adopted by the genetic mother.

3.5.2. Legal Fatherhood

For legal fatherhood, genetic descent is important but not the only factor. The mother's husband or the man who acknowledges the child becomes the child's legal father even if there is no genetic connection between him and the child. However, a man who finds out that he is not the genetic father may challenge his legal fatherhood. If a child is born to a couple after artificial insemination, the mother's husband,[89] or – if the mother is not married – the man who acknowledges the child with the consent of the mother, becomes the legal father.[90] However, he cannot challenge the paternity of the donor if they have agreed to artificial insemination by sperm donation from a third party.[91]

Since the Sperm Donor Registry Act came into force on 1 July 2018, sperm donations to official sperm banks are no longer anonymous. Any person who suspects that he or she was conceived by heterodox use of semen in a medically assisted artificial insemination is entitled to information from the semen donor register from the German Institute for Medical Documentation and Information. After reaching the age of 16, the person can only assert this claim him- or herself.[92] In private sperm donations, anonymous sperm donors are not very common. In any case, the criterion of anonymity is not decisive for the rights and obligations of the birth mother, her spouse or partner and the donor.

If a man who is not married to the mother but has agreed to her insemination refuses to acknowledge the child, he cannot be forced to become the child's

---

[88] Oberlandesgericht (OLG, Higher Regional Court) Frankfurt, Decision of 28.02.2019 – 1 UF 71/18 – juris.
[89] S. 1592 no. 1 of the BGB.
[90] S. 1592 no. 2 and ss 1594–98 of the BGB.
[91] S. 1600(4) of the BGB.
[92] S. 10(1) of the Sperm Donor Registry Act.

legal parent. Only a child's genetic father can be ascertained by a family court as the child's legal parent.[93] A decision of the German Federal Court of Justice[94] provides an interesting perspective. An unmarried man had agreed to the insemination of his partner. After the birth, however, the man refused to acknowledge the child. Therefore, he was not the legal father. Despite his refusal, the court held him liable for child support based on an agreement with his former partner. The man's consent to the insemination could be understood as an 'intentional assumption of parenthood'. To this extent, it could be compared to the adoption of a child. Thus, the court assumed parental responsibility without legal and genetic fatherhood being present just because of the man's consent to the insemination.

In relation to the sperm donor, the question arises under which conditions he can be made the legal father of a child he helped conceive. As long as there is no second legal parent – whether because the birth mother is single, because she has a male partner who refuses to acknowledge the child, or because her female partner has not (yet) adopted the child – the question arises whether a man who donates sperm can be made the legal father and thus be liable for child support. Since he is the child's genetic father, this was possible for a long time according to section 1591 no 3 of the BGB, even if he just wanted to help others to become parents. Like in many other legal systems, the German legislator has realised that this is a problem. A statute now provides that a sperm donor cannot be made the legal father.[95] Moreover, an official sperm donor register makes it possible for a child to find out the identity of the genetic father later. The purpose of this law is to secure the child's right to know his or her genetic descent and to provide certainty for the sperm donor that he will not be held financially responsible for the child. However, this law covers only sperm donated to and used in official sperm banks. If a couple, as is not uncommon among same-sex couples, uses the sperm of a friend or someone found via the internet, this person can still be ascertained as the child's legal father in a family court.

3.6. SAME-SEX PARENTS

Same-sex parenthood has been possible in Germany since the Civil Partnership Act 2001 introduced the adoption of step-children. In 2013, the Federal Constitutional Court expanded step-child adoption to cases where the child had been adopted by the other partner before. In this important decision, the

---

[93] S. 1592 no. 3 of the BGB.
[94] Bundesgerichtshof (BGH, Federal Court of Justice, FCJ), Decision of 23.09.2015 – XII ZR 99/14 – NJW 2015, 68, p. 3434.
[95] S. 1600d(4) of the BGB.

Federal Constitutional Court recognised that same-sex parents were protected under Article 6(2) of the Constitution just like other parents and that they were as able to exercise parental responsibility as other parents.[96]

So far, adoption has remained the only route to joint parenthood, even if a child is born into a same-sex family. After same-sex marriage was introduced in Germany in 2017, there was a discussion on whether a mother's wife could become a parent just like a husband could.[97] While this outcome would be appropriate, the German Federal Court of Justice held that this would require a change of the law by the legislator, since section 1592 no 1 of the BGB refers only to the 'man' and the 'husband'. A woman also cannot acknowledge a child but must adopt the child.[98] Since 2019, a draft bill has been under discussion which would provide immediate co-parenthood to a child born to a lesbian couple.

Hopefully, the legislator will act now after the 2021 election. Moreover, there are a number of constitutional cases pending which claim that the legislator is obliged to regulate this case properly and to stop discrimination against children born into same-sex families.[99] According to a draft section 1592 of the BGB published by the Federal Ministry of Justice and Consumer Protection in 2019, not only the husband but also the wife of the mother would become the second parent at birth. Moreover, both male and female partners would be able to acknowledge the child after a joint decision to use donor sperm. An 'intended parent',[100] as the draft bill puts it, who later changes his or her mind and does not acknowledge a child, can also be made the second parent after a court decision, just like a genetic father who refuses to acknowledge a child can be declared the legal father in a court decision now.

Until the law is finally changed, it seems that a fiction of genetic descent from the legal father is at least one of the reasons for the legal parenthood of husbands and acknowledging men. The current legal situation is also one of the reasons why fertility clinics in Germany still hesitate to provide artificial insemination

---

[96] Bundesverfassungsgericht (BVERFG), Order of the First Senate of 19.02.2013 – BvR 3247/09 – BVerfGE 133, 59.

[97] M. Löhnig, 'Ehe für alle – Abstammung für alle?' (2017) *Neue Zeitschrift für Familienrecht* 643.

[98] See A. Sanders, 'Multiple Parenthood: Towards a New Concept of Parenthood in German Family Law' in H. Willekens, K. Scheiwe, T. Richarz and E. Schumann (eds), *Motherhood and the Law*, Universitätsverlag Göttingen, Göttingen 2019, pp. 124–25.

[99] Oberlandesgericht (OLG, Higher Regional Court) Celle, Decision of 24.03.2021 – 21 UF 146/20 – FamRZ 2021, 862 = NZFam 2021, 352 (with case comment M. Löhnig); see also P.M. Reuß, 'Das Abstammungsrecht auf dem verfassungsrechtlichen Prüfstand' (2021) *Zeitschrift für das gesamte Familienrecht* 824; A. Sanders, 'Wunschkinder, Wunscheltern und das Grundgesetz (2021) 9 *Forum Familienrecht* 341; s. Kammergericht (KG, Higher Regional Court) Berlin of 24.03.2021 – 3 UF 1122/20 – FamRZ 2021, 854 = NJOZ 2021, 840 = StAZ 2021, 142.

[100] 'Intendierter Vater', 'intendierte Mutter'.

to lesbian couples. Lesbian couples often used the sperm of private donors or sperm banks from other countries. Thus, if the mother's female partner refuses to adopt the child after birth, it is as difficult to hold her responsible for child support as a man who is unwilling to acknowledge the child. Just as in the case of the reluctant man mentioned above, courts have to construct agreements for child support between the former partners because the law does not establish immediate parental responsibility.

3.7. MULTIPLE PARENTHOOD

So far, the discussion has shown that German law sticks to the principle of two-parent family law, even in cases where, in fact, more than two persons are involved in the conception and/or upbringing of a child. This would also be the case when the biological material of more than two people is used. German family law also does not recognise multiplicity of parenthood if a child is raised in a polygamous family. In accordance with the ideal of the two-parent family, a marriage can only be concluded between two persons. A marriage cannot be concluded if one of the parties is already married.[101]

According to section 1591 of the BGB, the mother who gives birth to a child becomes the sole legal mother. The second parent is either her husband,[102] a male person who acknowledges the child[103] or a female spouse or partner who adopts the child. Legally, there can only be two parents of a child. If for example a male friend of a lesbian couple provides the sperm for a child, either he would become the legal father of the child with the birth mother as the child's mother, or the child's mother with her female partner who adopts the child with the genetic father's consent would be the two parents. Even if the three have agreed to conceive and raise the child jointly, one of the three would have no legally secure position. There has been a discussion about this point,[104] but the draft bill on the reform of parentage[105] still states that German law will stick to the principle of two parents in the future. It remains to be seen if this approach will change.[106]

---

[101] S. 1306 of the BGB.
[102] According to s. 1592 no. 1 of the BGB.
[103] According to s. 1592 no. 2 of the BGB.
[104] See A. Sanders, *Mehrelternschaft*, Mohr Siebeck, Tübingen 2018, pp. 275–78; N. Dethloff, *Gleichgeschlechtliche Paare und Familiengründung durch Reproduktionsmedizin*, Friedrich-Ebert-Stiftung, Berlin 2016, pp. 53–54, available at https://library.fes.de/pdf-files/dialog/12770.pdf, accessed 10.05.2022; R. Ernst, 'Abstammungsrecht – Die Reform ist vorbereitet!' (2018) 10 *Neue Zeitschrift für Familienrecht* 443.
[105] Draft discussion section: s. 2 of the Draft Law on the Reform of the Law of Descent of 14.03.2019.
[106] For a suggestion for regulation of multiple parenthood, see A. Sanders, 'Multiple Parenthood: Towards a New Concept of Parenthood in German Family Law' in H. Willekens, K. Scheiwe,

In the case of a child whose genetic father is not the same as the child's legal father, however, there is a legal provision, section 1686a of the BGB, which in a way recognises a three-parent situation. This shall be explained in more detail. As described above, the law of descent establishes the legal fatherhood of the husband or the man who acknowledges the child according to section 1592 no. 1 and 2 of the BGB. If the man later finds out that the child is not his biologically, he does not cease to be the father in a legal sense but he has the right to contest paternity in a family court.[107] The genetic father used to have no rights to become the child's father or even just to see the child if the child lived with his or her legal father in a family.

The effects of this legal situation can best be explained by the famous *Anayo* case. In the *Anayo* case, a married woman had an affair with Mr Anayo and became pregnant. Nevertheless, she decided to stay with her husband and raise the twins with him. Both husband and wife denied Mr Anayo any contact with the children. At that time, there was nothing Mr Anayo could do. If there is an established social and family relationship between the legal father and the child, the genetic father is barred from becoming the legal father.[108] Thus, in relation to the genetic father, German law protects the legal father who took responsibility for the child, irrespective of a genetic bond.[109]

However, the European Court of Human Rights, to which Mr Anayo applied, held that a genetic father should not be barred completely from playing a role in his child's life without a careful assessment of the individual situation, even though the court did not require that the genetic father become the legal father.[110] In section 1686a of the BGB, the German legislator introduced a compromise: a genetic father can ask for information about the child's life if providing such

---

T. Richarz and E. Schumann (eds), *Motherhood and the Law*, Universitätsverlag Göttingen, Göttingen 2019, pp. 119–51; A. Sanders, *Mehrelternschaft*, Mohr Siebeck, Tübingen 2018; I. Plettenberg, *Vater –Vater – Mutter – Kind – Ein Plädoyer für die rechtliche Mehrvaterschaft*, Mohr Siebeck, Tübingen 2016.

[107] Ss 1599(1) and 1600(1) no. 1 of the BGB.

[108] See Bundesgerichtshof (BGH, Federal Court of Justice, FCJ), Decision of 15.11.2017 – XII ZB 389/16 [2018] *Neue Zeitschrift für Familienrecht* 76, with a case note by A. Schneider; s. 1600 of the BGB. The Oberlandesgericht (OLG, Higher Regional Court) Hamm, Decision of 20.07.2016, had reached another conclusion and allowed the genetic father to contest the fatherhood of the legal father: FamRZ 2016, 2135 with a case note by P.M. Reuß.

[109] The child and the mother can contest fatherhood within two years after they have learned about the possibility that another man might be the genetic father. For the child, the limitation period does not start running before his or her 18th birthday.

[110] *Anayo v. Germany*, no. 20578/07, 21.12.2010 [2011] 1 FLR 1883; *Schneider v. Germany*, no. 17080/07, 15.12.2011; *Kautzor v. Germany*, no. 23338/09, 22.03.2012 [2012] 2 FLR 396. See also a decision by the FCJ concerning Mr Anayo, who is still fighting for the right to see his children: FCJ, Decision of 05.10.2016 – XII ZB 280/15 – NJW 2017, 160 with a case note by M. Löhnig.

information is not harmful for the child. Moreover, the father can ask for contact with the child if such contact is beneficial for the child.[111] However, the legal father is and remains legally responsible for the child; for example, he is obliged to pay child support. If the legal father dies intestate, the child inherits from him, while the death of the genetic father has no effect unless he makes a will. This distinction between a 'rightful father' and a 'father with rights (and no duties)' is an interesting invention of family law. It allows the German legislator to have its cake and eat it too: providing some legal acknowledgement of a multiple parenthood situation without formally abolishing two-person parenthood and the status of the legal father.

If the 2019 discussion draft bill of the German Federal Ministry of Justice and Consumer Protection should become law, this situation would change. Within the first six months of the child's life, the biological father would be able to contest the legal father's position. If both the biological and the legal father have formed a social connection with the child, the father with the stronger bond would prevail. The question of how section 1686a of the BGB and the new law could be reconciled will be open for discussion. However, after the 2021 election, it seems to be likely that the draft will be reworked again.

3.8. PARENTHOOD AND SURROGACY

Surrogacy is a fascinating case of multiple parenthood raising important ethical and legal questions. As was already explained above, German law prohibits surrogacy, because the legislator wants to avoid 'split motherhood'. With the same intention, the legislator of 1998 also introduced, for the first time, a definition of motherhood in the German Civil Code: only the woman who gives birth to the child is the child's mother.

However, forbidding surrogacy in terms of German law has not kept surrogacy out of Germany. Both opposite-sex and same-sex couples from Germany go abroad to countries where surrogacy is legal to fulfil their wish for parenthood. If these couples come home to Germany with the children, the question arises of who the child's parents are. German law stipulates that

---

[111] On the legislative history and the reasoning of the legislator, see Entwurf eines Gesetzes zur Stärkung der Rechte des leiblichen, nicht rechtlichen Vaters (Draft Bill of the German Parliament), BT-Drucks. 17/12163. Lower instance courts have decided a number of cases in relation to s. 1686a of the BGB. Most cases deal with the questions of the conditions in which meeting a non-legal father can benefit a child's interest and whether the legal parents can decide this question.

it is the child's birth mother, while the law of the country where the child was born might make the intended parents the child's parents. The German Federal Court of Justice has held that decisions of foreign courts assigning parenthood to the intended parents may be acknowledged in Germany and do not violate the German ordre public.[112] The situation is more complicated if there is no foreign court decision but parenthood of the intended parents is just acknowledged by other means, for example a birth certificate.[113]

According to the Coalition Agreement of the new German government, the introduction of altruistic surrogacy will be reassessed.[114] This is to be welcomed. Rather than forcing couples to go abroad, surrogacy should be possible in Germany and be adequately regulated to protect children and surrogate mothers.

4. CONCLUSIONS

As discussed in section 2 above, family functions in Germany may be described as:

1. raising children as future members of society;
2. supporting and caring for family members rather than seeing support as only the State's responsibility; and
3. providing a protected space for individual development in relationships with others.

These functions have been recognised by the legislator and enjoy constitutional protection. They are still as relevant today as they were decades ago. However, in today's society, families that enjoy these functions are becoming more and more diverse. Society and the law accept same-sex relationships, divorce, remarriage, cohabitation and gender diversity. These changes and the development of reproductive technologies facilitate more diverse families with more than two people who contribute to a child's conception and upbringing.

However, German law has been slow to recognise new family forms which perform the three family functions listed above. Reform of the law of parentage

---

[112] Bundesgerichtshof (BGH, Federal Court of Justice, FCJ), Decision of 10.12.2014 – XII ZB 463/13 – BGHZ 203, 350, see also *Mennesson v. France*, no. 65192/11, 26.06.2014, and *Labassee v. France*, no. 65941/11, 26.06.2014.

[113] See e.g. Bundesgerichtshof (BGH, Federal Court of Justice FCJ), Decision of 20.03.2019 – XII ZB 530/17 – FamRZ 2019, 892.

[114] Koalitionsvereinbarung, Coalition Agreement 'Mehr Fortschritt wagen' 2021–2015, para. 3903.

is long overdue and will hopefully be introduced soon by the new German government elected in 2021.

So far, German law has been hesitant to accept multiple parenthood situations. However, the rights of step-parents and the biological non-legal father show the first cracks in the principle of the two-parent family. It is to be expected, however, that this will change as well. The law should allow new family forms to fulfil their function.

THE NOTION AND FUNCTION OF FAMILY IN GREEK LAW

Eleni ZERVOGIANNI

1. Introduction: General Remarks on the Notion of Family in
   Greek Law 291
2. Diversity and Plurality of Family Forms 294
   2.1. Step-Families 294
   2.2. Children Raised in More than One Household 296
   2.3. Children Raised in Polygamous Families 299
   2.4. 'Open-Adoption' Families 300
   2.5. *Kafala* and Equivalent Institutions 301
   2.6. Medically Assisted Reproduction with Donated Genetic Material 302
   2.7. Medically Assisted Reproduction and 'Three-Parent Children' 305
   2.8. Surrogacy 306
   2.9. Same-Sex Parents 308
3. Diversity and Plurality of Family's Functions 309
   3.1. An Overview of Family Functions in Greek Law 309
   3.2. Family as a Refuge of Love and Companionship and as a
        Place to Raise Children 312
   3.3. Families with and without Children 314
4. Conclusions 315

1. INTRODUCTION: GENERAL REMARKS ON THE NOTION OF FAMILY IN GREEK LAW

The meaning of 'family', as a legal term, is no longer self-evident in Greek law. Certainly, two married persons of the opposite sex and their child(ren) fall within the legal notion of family. The answer is not equally straightforward when it comes to family forms that depart from this traditional model. The definition of family in a legal sense is in fact harder than it may initially appear, since the term 'family' is used throughout the law in different senses.

In Greek civil law, family is typically defined as a fundamental social unit which is comprised of persons bonded with each other through marriage, birth or adoption.[1] Thus, spouses with or without children certainly constitute a family.[2] After the introduction in Greece of the institution of the 'cohabitation agreement', which is a form of registered partnership for both couples of different and of the same sex,[3] there can be little doubt that partners who have concluded such an agreement also qualify as a family, in a legal sense. Moreover, children and each of their legal parents[4] can constitute a family, irrespective of the legal relations between the parents.

The issue is thornier when it comes to both unmarried and unregistered partners. According to the still prevailing opinion, this de facto family relationship between the partners does not qualify as family in the legal sense.[5]

---

[1] See G. Koumantos, *Oikogeneiako Dikaio I*, P.N. Sakkoulas, Athens 1988, p. 17; E. Kounougeri-Manoledaki, *Oikogeneiako Dikaio I*, 8th ed., Sakkoulas, Athens/Thessaloniki 2021, pp. 19–20; A. Georgiades, *Oikogeneiako Dikaio*, 2nd ed., Sakkoulas, Athens/Thessaloniki 2017, §2 no. 2.

[2] A family without children is sometimes characterised as an 'incomplete family'. See E. Kounougeri-Manoledaki, *Oikogeneiako Dikaio I*, 8th ed., Sakkoulas, Athens/Thessaloniki 2021, pp. 20–21. It is worth noting that according to the prevailing opinion in Greek literature the notion of 'family' in constitutional terms (Art. 21 para. 1 of the Constitution refers, inter alia, to the protection of family) pertains to parent(s) and children, so that there cannot be a family in this sense without children. See in more detail on this issue K. Chrysogonos and S. Vlachopoulos, *Atomika kai Koinika Dikaiomata*, 4th ed., Nomiki Vivliothiki, Athens 2017, p. 561, and in more detail L. Papadopoulou, 'I nomiki ennoia tis oikogeneias kai ta omofyla zevgaria' in *Timitikos Tomos gia tin Kathigitria Efi Kounougeri-Manoledaki*, Sakkoulas, Athens/Thessaloniki 2016, pp. 355 ff., pp. 362 ff.

[3] The 'cohabitation agreement' is currently regulated by Law 4356/2015. A previous form of registered partnership only for persons of the opposite sex was introduced in 2008 by Law 3719/2008, which was abolished, after the European Court of Human Rights in decision *Vallianatos and Other v. Greece*, nos 29381/09 and 32684/09, 07.11.2003, ruled that the exclusion of persons of the same sex from the field of application of Law 3719/2008 violated Art. 14, in conjunction with Art. 8, of the European Convention on Human Rights.

[4] The answer is no longer straightforward when it comes to step-parents. See in more detail section 2.1 below.

[5] See esp. A. Georgiades, *Oikogeneiako Dikaio*, 2nd ed., Sakkoulas, Athens/Thessaloniki 2017, §5 no. 9. See also Art. 6 of Law 4356/2015 with explicit reference to the inapplicability of family law provisions to the property relations of unregistered partners. See also the decisions 775/2011 and 1735/2006 of the Greek Supreme Court (Areios Pagos, AP), published in *Chronika Idiotikou Dikaiou* (*ChrID*) 2012, 181 and *ChrID* 2007, 131 respectively, which did not grant the partner of the deceased compensation for immaterial loss due to the latter's tortious death, on the basis of Art. 932 of the Greek Civil Code (GrCC), on the grounds that the claimant did not qualify as a member of the family of the deceased, although in the second case the partners had been living together for 20 years and had children together. This approach of case law has been rightfully criticised in the legal literature. See A. Georgiades, *Oikogeneiako Dikaio*, 2nd ed., Sakkoulas, Athens/Thessaloniki 2017, §23 no. 23; G. Georgiades, in A. Georgiades (ed.), *Syntomi Ermineia tou Astikou Kodika I* (*SEAK I*), P.N. Sakkoulas, Athens 2010, Art. 932 nos 26–27 with further references. Cf. also G. Koumantos, *Oikogeneiako Dikaio I*, P.N. Sakkoulas, Athens 1988, p. 20; S. Paterakis, *I chrimatiki ikanopoiisi logo ithikis vlavis*, 2nd ed., Ant. N. Sakkoulas, Athens/Komotini 2001, p. 301; I. Giarenis, 'I nolologiaki diamorfosi tis ennoias tis oikogeneias stin epidikasi chrimatikis ikanopoiisis logo psychikis odynis', *Elliniki Dikaiosyni* (*EllDni*) 2013, 318 ff., 323.

Therefore, the provisions on family law do not apply, unless the law stipulates otherwise.[6] This approach has nevertheless recently been challenged by the lower courts, which draw on the functional approach of family, in view of the case law of the European Court of Human Rights on the protection of family life, according to Article 8 of the European Convention on Human Rights.[7]

The next issue pertains to the question of how close the aforementioned bonds should be in order to assume that two persons are members of the same family. To this there is no single answer. Most provisions of Greek family law pertain to the so-called nuclear family, meaning children and their (legal) parent(s).[8] Nevertheless, there are provisions that recognise rights of and/or impose obligations on persons belonging to the extended family as well. How extended this family is also depends on the specific provision. The rules on maintenance, for instance, between ancestors and descendants,[9] and (exceptionally) between siblings, refer to blood relatives. To the contrary, the 'members of the family' of a deceased person who, in case of tortious death, may claim from the tortfeasor damages for their immaterial loss may well be relatives by marriage,[10] for example a mother-in-law or step-parent, provided that there actually existed bonds of love with the deceased.[11]

The legal guardian and the child under guardianship, as well as the foster parents and the child in foster care, are not thought to constitute a genuine family, but the legislator has modelled their relations on the pattern of family law relations. The same holds for the institution of 'judicial assistance', which is a

---

[6] The law does explicitly stipulate otherwise for example in regard to access to medically assisted reproduction (Art. 1456 of the GrCC) and protection from family violence (Art. 1 para. 2 γ of Law 3500/2006), under the condition that the partners are of the opposite sex.

[7] See decisions 1264/2018 of the Single-member Court of First Instance of Piraeus, *EllDni* 2019, 1698; 1815/2019 of the Single-member Court of First Instance of Athens, *Database Isokratis*; 2/2020 of the Single-member Court of First Instance of Thessaloniki, *EllDni* 2020, 826.

[8] See on this point A. Georgiades, *Oikogeneiako Dikaio*, 2nd ed., Sakkoulas, Athens/Thessaloniki 2017, §2 no. 3. Cf. G. Koumantos, *Oikogeneiako Dikaio I*, P.N. Sakkoulas, Athens 1988, p. 19.

[9] See Arts 1485 et seq. of the GrCC.

[10] According to Art. 1462 of the GrCC, relatives by blood of the one spouse (or registered partner) are relatives by marriage of the same degree of the other spouse (or registered partner).

[11] See Art. 932 of the GrCC, as well as decision AP (full bench) 21/2000, *Nomos Database*, which states that the actual existence of loving bonds between the person claiming compensation for non-pecuniary loss and the deceased should be assessed in each particular case. See also in more detail K. Pantelidou, 'I Ennoia tis Oikogeneias sto Arthro 932 ed. 3 AK', *Harmenopoulos* (*Harm.*) 1982, pp. 402 ff.; S. Paterakis, *I chrimatiki ikanopoiisi logo ithikis vlavis*, 2nd ed., Ant. N. Sakkoulas, Athens/Komotini 2001, pp. 292 ff.; G. Georgiades, in *SEAK I*, Art. 932 nos 25–26; I. Giarenis, 'I nolologiaki diamorfosi tis ennoias tis oikogeneias stin epidikasi chrimatikis ikanopoiisis logo psychikis odynis', *EllDni* 2003, 326, with further references to case law.

protective regime for adults who are not capable of entering into legal transactions themselves.[12] These are thus characterised as quasi-family relations.[13]

To the contrary, in Greek law there is no room in the family for donors of genetic material or surrogates. These persons are consistently treated in the law as third persons who contribute to the creation or expansion of a family but are not part of it.[14]

It is on this basis that we assess in what follows the different forms and functions that families assume according to Greek law.

2. DIVERSITY AND PLURALITY OF FAMILY FORMS

Children may be raised in a variety of settings that constitute a family in a sociological sense. Whether the persons who factually raise the children and the children qualify as members of a family in the legal sense depends largely on the rules on the establishment of kinship and on parental responsibilities. In Greek law, the attribution of parental responsibilities is basically reserved for the legal parents of the child. Thus, the rules on parental responsibilities intertwine with the rules on the establishment of kinship. According to the latter a child cannot have more than one mother and one father. Persons other than the child's legal parents may be assigned such responsibilities only exceptionally, especially if the parents are no longer in a position to exercise them properly. These main principles are further analysed below, in the framework of particular instances that raise questions of multiplicity of parenthood.

2.1. STEP-FAMILIES

Although undeniably the number of blended families is steadily increasing in Greece,[15] there is no recognition of multiplicity of parenthood in the context of step-families. The law treats step-parents in the same way as any third-person, non-family member, in regard to the child, with few exceptions.

---

[12] Art. 1666 et seq. of the GrCC. According to Art. 1682 of the GrCC, provisions on guardianship apply to 'judicial assistance' as well.
[13] See E. Kounougeri-Manoledaki, *Oikogeneiako Dikaio I*, 8th ed., Sakkoulas, Athens/Thessaloniki 2021, pp. 1–2; A. Georgiades, *Oikogeneiako Dikaio*, 2nd ed., Sakkoulas, Athens/Thessaloniki 2017, §1 no. 2 and in more detail section 2.5 below.
[14] See in more detail sections 2.6–2.8 below.
[15] According to recent statistics of the OECD (available at http://www.oecd.org/social/family/SF_3_1_Marriage_and_divorce_rates.pdf, accessed 29.05.2022), the divorce rate in Greece is steadily increasing (see Chart SF3.1.C), while more than 10% of persons who get married have been previously divorced (see Chart SF3.1.D). Moreover, in more than two-thirds of divorces there are children involved. See http://www.oecd.org/els/family/SF_3_2_Family_dissolution_children.pdf, Chart SF3.2.B 2, accessed 29.05.2022.

More precisely, the law is quite restrictive as regards the attribution of parental responsibilities and rights to step-parents. Such responsibilities are in principle reserved for the (legal) parents of the child, who have to exercise them in person. The legal parent may thus not assign to another extensive tasks pertaining to the care of the child,[16] while, if the child has two legal parents, both of whom exercise parental care jointly, the assumption of parental responsibilities by the step-parent against the will of either parent may qualify as an interference with this parent's right of parental care.[17] The step-parent therefore is not entitled to take decisions for the child, not even on daily matters or in cases of emergency.[18] Moreover, since the child and the step-parent are not related by blood, the child does not participate in the intestate succession of the step-parent (and vice versa).

In 2021 the legislator proceeded to take the first step for the protection of the relationship between the child and the step-parent, establishing a right of contact between a social parent and the child.[19] This new provision clearly draws upon the relevant case law of the European Court of Human Rights.[20] Furthermore, for the purposes of Law 3500/2006 on family violence,[21] the step-parent and the child are considered as members of the same family. Similarly, the step-parent can also be considered family in the sense of Article 932 of the Greek Civil Code and thus be awarded damages for immaterial loss in the case of tortious death of the step-child, while the same holds for the step-child in the case of death of the step-parent.[22]

The step-parent may become the legal parent of the child through adoption, if he or she is married to the child's legal parent,[23] provided that the child's other

---

[16] See also E. Kounougeri-Manoledaki, *Oikogeneiako Dikaio II*, 8th ed., Sakkoulas, Athens/Thessaloniki 2021, p. 280; A. Georgiades, *Oikogeneiako Dikaio*, 2nd ed., Sakkoulas, Athens/Thessaloniki 2017, §30 nos 3, 4. Nevertheless, it is worth noting that according to Art. 1655 of the GrCC and Arts 10 and 11 of Law 4538/2018 parents can place their child in foster care by concluding a contract with the foster parent(s). On foster care see section 2.5 below.

[17] See V. Peraki, 'Dynatotites askisis gonikis merimnas se tekna omofylon syntrofon', *Efarmoges Astikou Dikaiou (EfAD)* 2020, 567, 571–572 with further references.

[18] According to Art. 12 para. 2 of Law 3418/2015, if the child is in need of medical treatment only the persons who exercise parental care may consent to this treatment. In extremely urgent cases, the doctor may act without any consent, to prevent an eminent danger to the life of the child.

[19] According to the new provision of Art. 1520 para. 2 of the GrCC, as amended by Art. 13 of Law 4800/2021, '[t]he parents do not have the right to obstruct the contact of the child with third persons who have developed a social-emotional bond of family nature with the child, if contact serves the best interests of the child' (translation by the author).

[20] *Nazarenko v. Russia*, no. 39438/13, 16.07.2015 (challenge of paternity/contact); *Fatkhutdinov v. Russia*, no. 36335/18, 29.09.2020 (challenge of paternity/contact); and *V.D. and Others v. Russia*, no. 72931/10, 09.04.2019 (foster parents/contact).

[21] See Art. 1 para. 2 a of Law 3500/2006.

[22] See section 1 above.

[23] See Arts 1544 sentence 3 and 1562 of the GrCC.

parent also grants his or her consent.[24] Even in such cases, however, no instance of multi-parenthood arises, since the adoption of minors leads to the termination of the legal bonds between the child and his or her biological parent who is not married to the step-parent. No adoption is possible if the step-parent is not married to the child's legal parent.[25]

2.2. CHILDREN RAISED IN MORE THAN ONE HOUSEHOLD

A child may be raised in more than one household when the child's legal parents do not live together. This can be the case if the parents are factually separated or divorced or their marriage has been annulled,[26] or when the child was born out of wedlock. Irrespective of whether the parents live together or not, as a rule, they both hold parental rights (and responsibilities)[27] and exercise them jointly.[28] A parent alone can only take care of pressing or daily matters, referring either to the usual care of the child or to the ongoing administration of the child's property.[29] Apart from these matters, if the parents fail to reach a common decision, the issue is decided by the court.[30]

Deviations from the principle of joint exercise of parental care are possible when the parents have separated, divorced or their marriage has been annulled, through agreements between the parents.[31] Such an agreement is necessary if the

---

[24] See Art. 1550 of the GrCC.
[25] See Art. 1545 of the GrCC. It is worth noting that same-sex marriage is not recognised in Greece. See decision AP 1428/2017, *EfAD* 2018, 170. According to the prevailing opinion, persons who have concluded a 'cohabitation agreement' cannot proceed to adoption. See E. Kounougeri-Manoledaki, *Oikogeneiako Dikaio II*, 8th ed., Sakkoulas, Athens/Thessaloniki 2021, p. 603 with further references. Granting registered partners of the opposite sex the possibility to adopt, while depriving registered same-sex partners of the same possibility would most probably constitute a violation of Art. 14, in combination with Art. 8, of the European Convention on Human Rights. Contra A. Georgiades, *Oikogeneiako Dikaio*, 2nd ed., Sakkoulas, Athens/Thessaloniki 2017, §36 no. 41, who claims that persons of the opposite sex who have concluded a 'cohabitation agreement' are eligible to adopt.
[26] The situation is the same if the child's parents had concluded a 'cohabitation agreement', according to Law 4356/2015.
[27] According to Art. 1537 of the GrCC, a parent forfeits parental care when he or she is finally condemned to imprisonment for at least one month by reason of a fraudulent offence of vice against the child, or because of any offence against the child's life or health.
[28] See Art. 1510 of the GrCC para. 1, Art. 1513 of the GrCC as well as Art. 1515 of the GrCC (as amended by Law 4800/2021). If the child's parents had concluded a registered partnership, the joint exercise of parental care is provided by Art. 11 para. 1 of Law 4356/2015. The principle of joint exercise of parental responsibilities does not hold in cases of children born out of wedlock, if their kinship with the father has been established by means of a court ruling, against the father's will (Art. 1515 para. 2 of the GrCC).
[29] See Art. 1516 of the GrCC.
[30] See Art. 1512 of the GrCC.
[31] See Art. 1514 para. 1 of the GrCC, as amended by Art. 8 of Law 4800/2021.

parents wish to dissolve their marriage by divorce by mutual consent (which is no longer issued by a court).[32]

If the joint exercise of parental care is not possible due to persistent disagreements between the parents[33] or due to other significant reasons, such as the unwillingness of one parent to participate actively in the exercise of parental care or to comply with the agreement concluded with the other parent on the joint exercise of parental care,[34] and provided that these problems cannot be solved through mediation, the case can be brought before the court.[35]

The court may deal with the issue in a flexible way, on the basis of the particularities of the specific case. Among other options, the court may assign the exercise of parental care to one of the parents, granting the other contact rights, or distribute the exercise of parental care between the parents.[36] Such distribution may relate either to the functions of parental responsibilities or to time.[37] In the former case the judge attributes the exercise of parental responsibilities in some matters to the one parent and in others to the other parent (e.g. decisions on education and property administration to the mother and the rest to the father).[38] In such a case, each parent decides alone on the matters that fall within his or her competence. If the distribution of the exercise of parental responsibilities pertains to time, each parent has the sole right to exercise parental responsibilities over a particular specified period of time (e.g. on even months the one parent and on odd months the other parent).[39]

---

[32] According to Art. 1441 of the GrCC, as amended by Art. 22 para. 2 of Law 4509/2017 (and then again by Art. 4 of Law 4800/2021), the procedure for a divorce by mutual consent takes place before a notary, who then files the notarial act on the dissolution of marriage in the registry office. On the agreement of the parents on the exercise of parental care see however K. Fountedaki, *To neo dikaio ton skheseon goneon kai paidion*, Nomiki Vivliothiki, Athens 2021, p. 23, who points out that the agreement of the parents on the exercise of parental care just needs to regulate the child's place of residence; as to the rest, the default rule of joint exercise of parental care after divorce can apply.

[33] If the disagreements are not persistent but pertain to a specific issue, this issue may be resolved by the court according to Art. 1512 of the GrCC.

[34] In more detail on the interpretation of this provision see K. Fountedaki, *To neo dikaio ton skheseon goneon kai paidion*, Nomiki Vivliothiki, Athens 2021, pp. 50 ff.

[35] See Art. 1514 para. 2 of the GrCC, as amended by Art. 8 of Law 4800/2021.

[36] Art. 1514 para. 3 of the GrCC, as amended by Art. 8 of Law 4800/2021.

[37] See in more detail P. Agallopoulou, in A. Georgiades and M. Stathopoulos (eds), *Astikos Kodikas*, vol. 8, 2nd ed., P.N. Sakkoulas, Athens 2003, Arts 1513–1514 GrCC, no. 77; G. Ladogiannis, in A. Georgiades (ed.), *Syntomi Ermineia tou Astikoy Kodika II (SEAK II)*, P.N. Sakkoulas, Athens 2013, Arts 1513–1514 no. 9.

[38] See, inter alia, the decisions AP 616/2020, *Nomos Database*; Athens Court of Appeals 4948/2015, *Nomos Database*.

[39] This was the case in the decision 7131/2017 of the Single-member Court of First Instance of Athens, *EfAD* 2017, 951. The Areios Pagos (decision 1016/2019, *EfAD* 2020, 640) had initially expressed reservations as to whether such arrangements indeed serve the child's best interests. Nevertheless, after the reform of the law on parental responsibilities in 2021, court decisions that proceed to the distribution of the exercise of parental responsibility on the basis of time have increased. See already decisions 298/2021 of the Piraeus Court of Appeals,

Under such an arrangement, thus, the parents alternate in the exercise of responsibilities. Irrespective of the assignment of the exercise of parental care to one of the parents or the distribution of its exercise between them, decisions that have a significant effect on the child's life, pertaining to religion, health or education, are to be decided by both parents.[40] If the parents fail to reach a common decision, the issue is resolved by the court.[41]

Moreover, if the parents do not live together, the parent who does not reside with the child has the right to contact the child. The recent reform of family law has strengthened the parent's right to contact mainly in three ways. First, it is explicitly stipulated in the law that as a rule the parent has the right to contact the child for one-third of the latter's time, unless this is incompatible with the child's best interests.[42] Therefore, in this case too, the child is actually raised in two households, even when the exercise of parental care is assigned to one of the parents. Second, the law explicitly states that the hindering of this contact by the parent with whom the child resides amounts to faulty exercise of parental care, and may thus lead to adjustments to the court decision on the attribution of the exercise of parental care between the parents.[43] Third, the parent with whom the child resides may not proceed to change his or her place of residence if this would have a significant negative impact on the right of the other parent to contact the child, unless the latter agrees to the change or this is authorised by the court.[44]

All decisions (and agreements) of the parents on parental care should serve the best interests of the child, while the same holds for all relevant court decisions.[45] After its amendment in 2021, the law explicitly stipulates that the

---

Nomos Database; 915/2022 of the Single-member Court of First Instance of Thessaloniki, *Nomos Database*; 85/2021 of the Single-member Court of First Instance of Zakynthos, *Nomos Database*; 1267/2021 of the Single-member Court of First Instance of Piraeus, *Nomos Database*; 283/2021 of the Single-member Court of First Instance of Rethymno, *Nomos Database*.

[40] See new Art. 1519 para. 1 of the GrCC (as amended by Art. 12 of Law 4800/2021), which actually reflects the doctrine of the 'nucleus of parental care' that had been developed by case law (see, among many others, decisions AP 1321/1992, *EllDni* 1994, 376; AP 1005/2006, *EllDni* 2006, 1531; Athens Court of Appeals 2405/2018, *EfAD* 2018, 936) and had also found strong support in the literature (see T. Papachristou, *Oikogeneiako Dikaio*, P.N. Sakkoulas, Athens 2014, pp. 339 ff.; P. Filios, *Oikogeneiako Dikaio*, 4th ed., Sakkoulas, Athens/Thessaloniki 2011, §131 A 2; G. Lagodiannis, in *SEAK II*, Art. 1512 no. 2 and Arts 1513–1514 no. 6).

[41] See Art. 1512 of the GrCC.
[42] See Art. 1520 para. 1 of the GrCC, as amended by Art. 13 of the GrCC.
[43] See Art. 1532 para. 2 γ of the GrCC, as amended by Art. 14 of Law 4800/2021.
[44] See Art. 1519 para. 2 of the GrCC, as amended by Art. 1519 of Law 4800/2021.
[45] See Art. 1511 paras 1 and 2 of the GrCC, as amended by Art. 5 of Law 4800/2021. The pursuit of the interest of the child is a general principle which goes through the whole of Greek family law. See E. Kounougeri-Manoledaki, *Oikogeneiako Dikaio I*, 8th ed., Sakkoulas, Athens/Thessaloniki 2021, pp. 12 ff. and *Oikogeneiako Dikaio II*, 8th ed., Sakkoulas, Athens/Thessaloniki 2021, pp. 300 ff.; A. Georgiades, *Oikogeneiako Dikaio*, 2nd ed., Sakkoulas, Athens/Thessaloniki 2017, §3 no. 6–7. See also section 3.2 below.

best interests of the child are in principle best served by the essential involvement of both parents in the child's upbringing.[46] In assessing the child's best interests, the judge should also take into consideration the child's own opinion, depending on the child's maturity.[47]

2.3. CHILDREN RAISED IN POLYGAMOUS FAMILIES

The existence of a prior marriage that has not been dissolved constitutes an impediment to remarriage.[48] Bigamy also constitutes a criminal offence.[49] The prohibition of polygamy holds also for the Greek Muslim minority of Western Thrace,[50] where Islamic law may be applicable in certain matters pertaining to family and succession law.[51] Although polygyny is allowed in the Qur'an, in Greece in practice the issue is no longer relevant. The Muftis in principle do not grant permission to a man to marry a second wife before his first marriage is dissolved.[52] Within this legal framework, there are no special rules for children who may in fact be raised in polygamous family settings.

---

[46] See Art. 1511 para. 2 of the GrCC, as amended by Art. 5 of Law 4800/2021.
[47] Art. 1511 para. 4 of the GrCC as amended by Art. 5 of Law 4800/2021.
[48] See Art. 1354 of the GrCC. Thus the subsequent marriage is void (Art. 1372 para. 1 of the GrCC), but is nevertheless governed by the same rules as valid marriages, until it is annulled by a court decision. If the marriage is annulled, its consequences are lifted retroactively (see Arts 1376, 1381 of the GrCC).
[49] See Art. 356 of the Greek Penal Code.
[50] A landmark decision on this issue is the Ruling 89/1995 of the Council of the Court of Appeal, *Yperaspisi* 1998, 78, annotated by S. Pavlou. See also K. Chrysogonos and S. Vlachopoulos, *Atomika kai Koinika Dikaiomata*, 4th ed., Nomiki Vivliothiki, Athens 2017, p. 562. See however the rulings of the Council of the Court of Misdemeanours of Xanthi, no. 38/1989 (unpublished) and 14/1995, *Yperaspisi* 1996, 1335, which had decided the issue differently. See also I. Ktistakis, *Ieros Nomos tou Islam kai Mousoulmanoi Ellines polites*, Sakkoulas, Athens/Thessaloniki 2006, p. 55; A. Kotzampasi, 'To pedio efarmogis tou ierou mousoulmanikou nomou stis oikogeneiakes skheseis ton Ellinon mousoulmanon', *EllDni* 2003, 57, 66.
[51] See Art. 4 of Law 147/1914 and Art. 5 para. 2 of Law 1920/1991. For an overview of the legal framework on the application of the Sacred Islamic Law in Thrace see A. Tsaoussi and E. Zervogianni, 'Multiculturalism and Family Law: The Case of Greek Muslims' in K. Boele-Woelki and T. Sverdrup (eds), *European Challenges in Contemporary Family Law*, Intersentia, Antwerp 2008, pp. 209 ff. with further references. See also the judgment of the European Court of Human Rights in *Molla Sali v. Greece*, no. 20452/14, 19.12.2018. It is worth noting that after the enactment of Law 4511/2018 the rules of *Sharia* apply only if all involved parties file a request before the Mufti (who acts as a judge) to try their case. If not, the provisions on family and succession law of the GrCC apply.
[52] See I. Ktistakis, *Ieros Nomos tou Islam kai Mousoulmanoi Ellines polites*, Sakkoulas, Athens/Thessaloniki 2006, p. 55. See also judgment 58/1991 of the Single-member Court of First Instance of Rodope, which recognised as enforceable the decision of the Mufti of Komotini to annul the second marriage of a man because of the prohibition of bigamy. This unpublished decision is mentioned by K. Tsitselikis, 'I thesi tou moufti stin elliniki ennomi taxi' in D. Christopoulos (ed.), *Nomika zitimata thriskeftikis eterotitas stin Ellada*, Kritiki, Athens 1999, pp. 271 ff., at n. 50, available at https://www.kemo.gr/doc.php?fld=doc&doc=96.pdf, accessed 29.05.2022.

2.4. 'OPEN-ADOPTION' FAMILIES

Greek law only provides for the full adoption of minors. The adopted child is fully integrated into the family of the adoptive parents and all bonds with his or her biological family are terminated.[53] Moreover, the law adopts the principle of secrecy of adoption, until the child reaches majority.[54] Irrespective of whether or not the biological parents of the adoptee have a de facto relationship with him or her, the law treats them in principle like any other person who is not related to the child.[55] Along these lines, the law explicitly states that the biological parents have no right to contact the child.[56] Even if the adoptive parents die, or for any other reason are not able to exercise parental care properly, the adopted child does not 'return' to his or her biological family.[57] Rather, a guardian has to be appointed. It is up to the court to decide whether or not the biological parents would be suitable guardians or not.[58]

Multi-parenthood may arise in the case of adoption of adults, which is nevertheless subject to restrictions, the most important of which is that it is only possible between close relatives by blood or by marriage or between ex-foster parents and the adult that had been under their foster care as a child.[59] The adopted adult then maintains the bonds with his or her biological family.[60] The adoptive parents are primarily responsible for the maintenance of the adoptee,[61] while the adoptee is equally liable to grant maintenance to both his or her adoptive and biological parents.[62]

---

[53] See Art. 1561 of the GrCC.
[54] See Art. 1559 of the GrCC.
[55] An exception to this is the fact that, according to case law, if a biological parent dies as a result of a tort, in spite of the adoption and the consequent interruption of the legal bonds with the biological family, the child may claim compensation for immaterial damages, even if the child has been adopted. See decision 289/2007 of the Court of Appeals of Larisa, *Database Isokratis* and cf. V. Peraki, in *SEAK II*, Art. 1561 no. 8.
[56] See Art. 1566 of the GrCC. Nevertheless, after the recent amendment of Art. 1520 para. 2 by Art. 13 of Law 4800/2021, this can be questioned in cases in which there already exists a social-emotional bond between the biological parents and the child (esp. if the child had not been adopted as a baby). On the right of contact of third persons on the basis of Art. 1520 para. 2, see section 2.1 above.
[57] See Art. 1568 of the GrCC.
[58] See A. Georgiades, *Oikogeneiako Dikaio*, 2nd ed., Sakkoulas, Athens/Thessaloniki 2017, §37 no. 11.
[59] See Art. 1579 of the GrCC, as amended by Art. 51 of Law 4837/2021. According to this provision, the adoptive parents and the adoptee have to be related by blood or by marriage up to the fourth degree.
[60] See Art. 1584 sentence 2 of the GrCC.
[61] See Art. 1587 of the GrCC. The conditions of maintenance are set out in Arts 1485 et seq. of the GrCC. For a brief overview in English see E. Zervogianni, 'The Changing Concept of Family and Challenges for Family Law in Greece' in J.M. Scherpe (ed.), *European Family Law*, vol. II, Edward Elgar, Cheltenham 2016, p. 102.
[62] See A. Georgiades, *Oikogeneiako Dikaio*, 2nd ed., Sakkoulas, Athens/Thessaloniki 2017, §39 no. 8.

2.5. *KAFALA* AND EQUIVALENT INSTITUTIONS

Since *kafala* is an institution of Muslim law it does not, as such, exist in Greece. Nevertheless, it might be applicable in the Muslim minority of Western Thrace, since *kafala* is a form of guardianship,[63] and according to the relevant Greek legal framework, the Muftis' jurisdiction may extend to issues of guardianship,[64] provided that all the parties involved voluntarily bring the case before the Mufti.[65] The issue is nevertheless rather unclear,[66] while the existence of the Muftis' jurisdiction in matters of guardianship is disputed in the legal literature.[67]

The only Greek legal text where the term '*kafala*' actually comes up is Law 2101/92, which ratified the United Nations Convention on the Rights of the Children (1989), which in Article 20(3) lists *kafala* among the appropriate institutions of alternative care for a child deprived of his or her family environment. Other such appropriate institutions in Greek law are guardianship and foster care, which may thus qualify as functional equivalents of *kafala*.

More specifically, a guardian of a minor may be appointed by the court if both parents have been deprived of their right to exercise parental care, or for other reasons are not in a position to fulfil their duties towards the child.[68] Guardianship can also coexist with parental rights if only a specific part of parental responsibilities is assigned to the guardian (e.g. the administration of the child's property).[69] In any case, the responsibilities that are assigned to the guardian and those that are still exercised by the parents are neatly distinguished; therefore, in principle no clash of the responsibilities of the parents and the guardian may arise.

Foster care constitutes a supplementary institution to parental care and guardianship.[70] The foster parents, who may also be same-sex partners who have concluded a registered partnership,[71] are charged with the daily care of the

---

[63] See on this issue also case C-129/18, *SM v. Entry Clearance Officer, UK Visa Section*, ECLI:EU:C:2019:248.
[64] See Art. 5 para. 2 of Law 1920/1991.
[65] On the application of Islamic law in Greece see section 2.3 above.
[66] I. Ktistakis has performed the most significant primary research into the decisions of Greek Islamic courts. In his book *Ieros Nomos tou Islam kai Mousoulmanoi Ellines polites*, Sakkoulas, Athens/Thessaloniki 2006, Ktistakis refers to the absence of the institution of adoption in *Sharia* (p. 76) and to guardianship in the sense of *Wilaya* (p. 70) but does not refer to the institution of *kafala*. No such reference could be found in the relevant Greek legal literature.
[67] See K. Pantelidou, *I epitropeia anilikon*, Sakkoulas, Athens/Thessaloniki 2007, pp. 44 ff., with further references.
[68] See Art. 1589 of the GrCC.
[69] See, inter alia, K. Pantelidou, *I epitropeia anilikon*, Sakkoulas, Athens/Thessaloniki 2007, pp. 83–84.
[70] Foster care is regulated in Arts 1655–1665 of the GrCC. These provisions are further concretised in Law 4538/2018 on foster care and adoption.
[71] See section 2.9 below.

child and may also take care of emergencies, but the child's legal relationship with his or her parents (or guardian) remains, in principle, unaltered.[72] Thus, the fundamental decisions regarding the child's life are taken by the parents (or guardian).[73] Given the clear allocation of the functions of parental care between the parents (or guardian) and the foster parents, there is hardly room for a clash, unless the foster parents exceed their competences. The foster parents have the right to be heard before the parents take any decision regarding the child,[74] but they do not have the right to act against the stated will of the parents,[75] with a possible exception in case their act best serves the interest of the child.[76] After the termination of foster care the foster parents may have the right to contact the child, since they qualify as 'third persons who have developed a social-emotional bond with the child of family nature'.[77]

2.6. MEDICALLY ASSISTED REPRODUCTION WITH DONATED GENETIC MATERIAL

In 2002 a comprehensive regulatory framework for medically assisted reproduction was enacted, which also brought about amendments to the provisions of the Civil Code on maternal and parental descent.[78] The law provides, among other things, the possibility for married couples, partners of the opposite sex (irrespective of whether they have entered into a 'cohabitation agreement' or not) and single women[79] to use medically assisted reproduction

---

[72] See Arts 1655 and 1659 of the GrCC.
[73] See in detail G.A. Georgiadis, *Anadochi anilikou*, Sakkoulas, Athens/Thessaloniki 2019, no. 354 ff.
[74] See Art. 1659 of the GrCC.
[75] See Art. 1658 of the GrCC.
[76] See A. Georgiades, *Oikogeneiako Dikaio*, 2nd ed., Sakkoulas, Athens/Thessaloniki 2017, §45 no. 26.
[77] See Art. 1520 para. 2 of the GrCC, as amended by Art. 13 of Law 4800/2021.
[78] See Law 3089/2002, which amended the GrCC, and Law 3305/2005, which subsequently supplemented Law 3089/2002. The relevant legal framework was recently revised by Law 4958/2022.
[79] Single men would also need a surrogate to procreate. Surrogacy is comprehensively regulated in Greece (see section 2.8 below). According to the prevailing opinion in case law, single men do not have access to medically assisted reproduction (see decisions 3357/2010 of the Athens Court of Appeals, *Nomiko Vima* 2012; 1437 and 8641/2017 of the Multi-member Court of First Instance of Thessaloniki, *EfAD* 2017, 925. Contra the older decisions 2827/2008 of the Single-member Court of First Instance of Athens, *ChrID* 2009, 816; and 13707/2009 of the Single-member Court of First Instance of Thessaloniki, *ChrID* 2011, 267). The issue is vividly debated in the legal literature. In favour of the opinion that single men are also granted access to medically assisted reproduction, if they fulfil the relevant legal conditions: I. Spyridakis, *I nea rythmisi tis technitis gonimopoiiseos kai tis suggeneias*, Ant. N. Sakkoulas, Athens/Komotini 2003, p. 29; T. Papachristou, Comment on the decision 2827/2008 of the Single-member Court of First Instance of Athens, *ChrID* 2009, 818; N. Koumoutzis, in

techniques, either with their own genetic material or with the genetic material of third-party donors.

In cases of medically assisted reproduction, the establishment of kinship between the parents and the child is based on social-emotional rather than biological foundations.[80] The couple, or the single woman, who wished to have the child are the child's legal parents, no matter whether their own genetic material has been used or not.[81] That is, if they have given their consent to

---

A. Georgiades and M. Stathopoulos (ed.), *Astikos Kodikas*, vol. 7, 2nd ed., P.N. Sakkoulas, Athens 2007, Arts 1457–1458 no. 77; N. Koumoutzis, 'I techniti anaparagogi tou monou agamou antra' *ChrID* 2011, 316 ff.; N. Koumoutzis, 'I techniti anaparagogi monon prosopon kai i europaiki symvasi ton dikaiomaton tou anthropou' in *Ypovoithoumeni anaparagogi kai nees morfes oikogeneias*, Sakkoulas, Athens/Thessaloniki 2014, pp. 25 ff., esp. p. 37; E. Kounougeri-Manoledaki, *Oikogeneiako Dikaio II*, 8th ed., Sakkoulas, Athens/Thessaloniki 2021, pp. 56–57; E. Kounougeri-Manoledaki, 'Iatrika Ypovoithoumeni anaparagogi: Epanaprosdiorizontas tin ennoia tis oikogeneias' in Omilos Meletis Iatrikou Dikaiou kai Bioithikis, *Iatriki ypovoithisi stin anthropini anaparagogi. 10 chronia efarmogis tou nomou 3089/2002*, Sakkoulas, Athens/Thessaloniki 2013, pp. 47–48; T. Trokanas, *Anthropini anaparagogi. I idiotiki autonomia kai ta oria tis*, Sakkoulas, Athens/Thessaloniki 2011, p. 222; V. Peraki, in *SEAK II*, Art. 1458 no. 21; P. Agallopoulou, 'Parentheti mitrotita' in M. Kanellopoulou-Boti and F. Panagopoulou-Koutnatzi (eds), *Iatriki euthyni kai bioithiki. Sygchrones proseggiseis kai prooptikes tou mellontos*, Paschalidis, Athens 2014, p. 180; cf. Explanatory Memorandum of Law 3089/2002, available at www.hellenicparliament.gr/UserFiles/2f026f42-950c-4efc-b950-340c4fb76a24/i-human-eisig.pdf, accessed 29.05.2022, Point II 1 (p. 3); cf. also I. Androulidaki-Dimitriadi, 'I symvasi iatrikis ypovoithisis stin anthropini anaparagogi' in *Genethlion Apostolou S. Georgiadi*, vol. I, Ant. N. Sakkoulas, Athens/Komotini 2006, p. 31. Contra: D. Papadopoulou-Klamari, *I syggeneia. Themeliosi, katachorisi, prostasia*, Ant. N. Sakkoulas, Athens/Komotini 2010, pp. 220 ff., esp. p. 224; K. Pantelidou, 'Isi metaxeirisi kai iatriki ypovoithisi stin anthropini anaparagogi' in *Timitikos Tomos Pinelopis Agallopoulou*, vol. II, Ant. N. Sakkoulas, Athens/Komotini 2011, pp. 1095 ff., esp. pp. 1099–100; P. Nikolopoulos, 'Comment on the decision 3357/2010 of the Athens Court of Appeals', *Nomiko Vima* 2012, 1440; A. Koutsouradis, 'Entwicklungen des griechischen Familien- und Erbrechts' (2013–2014) *Zeitschrift für das gesamte Familienrecht* 2014, 1509 ff., 1509. On the relevant argumentation in English see in more detail E. Zervogianni, 'Surrogacy in Greece' in J.M. Scherpe, C. Fenton-Glynn and T. Kaan (eds), *Eastern and Western Perspectives on Surrogacy*, Intersentia, Cambridge 2019, pp. 145 ff., section 4.2.

[80] For the notion of 'social-emotional' kinship see already I. Deliyannis, 'Idrysi kai amfisvitisi tis syggeneias kata to elliniko dikaio', *EllDni* 1992, 1 ff. For the use of this notion in the framework of (heterologous) artificial reproduction see the Explanatory Memorandum of Law 3089/2002, Point II 1 (p. 4); G. Lekkas, 'Iatrikos ypovoithoumeni anaparagogi kai syggeneia sto elliniko dikaio. Kathierosi tis koinonikosynaisthimatikis syggeneias i tis teknopoiias choris suggeneia?' in T. Papachristou and E. Kounougeri-Manoledaki (eds), *To oikogeneiako dikaio ston 21o aiona*, Sakkoulas, Athens/Thessaloniki 2012, pp. 57 ff. See also E. Kounougeri-Manoledaki, *Oikogeneiako Dikaio I*, 8th ed., Sakkoulas, Athens/Thessaloniki 2021, pp. 14–15, who stresses that the prevalence of the 'social-emotional' kinship constitutes a general principle going through the whole of family law.

[81] According to Art. 1463 of the GrCC the woman who gives birth to the child is the child's legal mother, unless a court authorisation for surrogacy has been granted, in which case the woman who wished to have the child, and not the surrogate, is the child's legal mother. The establishment of paternity is derived either from marriage (or from the 'cohabitation agreement') of the father with the mother of the child (Art. 1465 of the GrCC and Art. 9 of Law 4356/2015 respectively) or it is based on the legal recognition of the child by the father

the use of the genetic material (sperm or ovum, or both) of third persons, the kinship between them and the child may not be contested.[82] The legislator has thus been very clear that the role of the donor of genetic material does not go any further than the donation of the sperm or ovum.

Along these lines, the Greek legislator had initially opted for the absolute anonymity of donors.[83] In cases of medical necessity, the child could have access to the medical records of the donor, but not to information regarding the latter's identity.[84] Nevertheless, in accordance with the current tendency in most Western jurisdictions against anonymity of donors, also evidenced in the recent recommendation of the Council of Europe,[85] the rule of anonymity had been challenged in legal literature.[86] In July 2022 the relevant legal framework was

---

as his own. In case (unregistered) partners proceed to medically assisted reproduction, they grant their consent to it before a notary (Art. 1456 of the GrCC). The consent of the father holds as a voluntary recognition of the child that will be born and the consent of the mother holds as her consent to this recognition by the father (Art. 1475 para. 2 of the GrCC).

[82] Contestation of maternity is possible only in the case of surrogacy, if it is proven that the ovum that has been fertilised was the ovum of the surrogate (see Art. 1464 para. 2 of the GrCC). As regards paternity, if the legal father had given his consent to heterologous assisted reproduction, no challenging of paternity is possible. See Art. 1471 para. 2 no. 2 of the GrCC, if the father is married or has concluded a 'cohabitation agreement' with the mother, and Art. 1478 para. 2 of the GrCC, if unregistered partners proceeded to medically assisted reproduction.

[83] See Art. 1460 para. 1 sentence 1 of the GrCC, before its amendment by Law 4958/2022. The revelation of the identity of the donor constitutes a criminal offence according to Art. 26 para. 11 of Law 3305/2005.

[84] See Art. 1460 para. 1 sentence 2 of the GrCC. In extreme cases of medical necessity (e.g. when the child is in need of organ donation) it is supported that the child shall be granted access to the archive of the National Authority of Assisted Reproduction, which also includes information on the identity of the donor. See A. Georgiades, *Oikogeneiako Dikaio*, 2nd ed., Sakkoulas, Athens/Thessaloniki 2017, §25 no. 41. On the archive of the National Authority of Assisted Reproduction see Art. 20 para. 2 of Law 3305/2005.

[85] Recommendation 2156 (2019) on the Anonymous Donation of Sperm and Oocytes: Balancing the Rights of Parents, Donors and Children, available at http://assembly.coe.int/nw/xml/XRef/Xref-XML2HTML-EN.asp?fileid=27680&lang=en, accessed 29.05.2022.

[86] On this issue see in English P. Agallopoulou, 'Assisted Reproduction Techniques and Anonymity under Greek Law' in B. Feuillet-Liger, K. Orfali and T. Callus (eds), *Who is My Genetic Parent?, Donor Anonymity and Assisted Reproduction: A Cross-Cultural Perspective*, Bruylant, Brussels 2011, p. 189. See C. Stampelou's opinion in P. Agallopoulou and A. Koutsouradis (eds), *Iatriki ypovoithisi stin anthropini anaparagogi. N. 3089/2002. Proparaskevastikes ergasies. Syzitisi sti Vouli*, Sakkoulas, Athens/Thessaloniki 2004, p. 59; C. Stampelou, in A. Georgiades and M. Stathopoulos (ed.), *Civil Code*, vol. 7, Art. 1460 no. 6 ff.; idem, 'I anonymia tou doti gennitikou ylikou' in *Sygchrones taseis oikogeneiakou dikaiou*, Nomiki Vivliothiki, Athens 2013, pp. 16 ff., esp. p. 31; P. Agallopoulou, 'Iatriki ypovoithisi stin anthropini anaparagogi kai anonymia triton doton gennitikou ylikou' in *Timitikos Tomos Mich. P. Stathopoulou*, vol. I, Ant. N. Sakkoulas, Athens/Komotini 2010, p. 19; cf. A. Kotzampasi, 'I anonymia tou doti spermatos stin techniti gonimopoiisi os nomiko kai ithiko zitima', *Harm*. 2000, 710 ff., 716; G. Lekkas, 'Iatrikos ypovoithoumeni anaparagogi kai syggeneia sto elliniko dikaio. Kathierosi tis koinonikosynaisthimatikis syggeneias i tis teknopoiias choris suggeneia?' in T. Papachristou and E. Kounougeri-Manoledaki (eds), *To oikogeneiako dikaio ston 21o aiona*, Sakkoulas, Athens/Thessaloniki 2012, pp. 65–66;

revised. The legislator introduced a mixed system, according to which donors of genetic material can choose if they wish to be anonymous or not, and it is then up to the persons who use medically-assisted reproduction techniques to decide if they wish to use the genetic materials of anonymous or known donors.[87] Irrespective of this, the donor does not have the right to be informed about the identity of the child and his or her legal parents.[88] The new provision is puzzling to the extent that children born through medically-assisted reproduction methods with the use of donated genetic material are divided into two groups; those who are granted the right to know their origins and those who are not. This in turn gives rise to concerns on equal treatment.

Regardless of the rules on anonymity, the donor of genetic material is confronted by the law as a third person not related to the child and thus has no right to participate in the child's upbringing.[89] There is only one possible exception to this: if a single woman (without any partner) has had recourse to medically assisted reproduction, the sperm donor may voluntarily proceed to acknowledge the child as his own, provided that the mother grants her consent to this acknowledgment.[90]

2.7. MEDICALLY ASSISTED REPRODUCTION AND 'THREE-PARENT CHILDREN'

Maternal spindle transfer is practised in Greece and it is not considered illegal, although both the National Bioethics Committee and the National Authority of Assisted Reproduction have expressed their reservations as to the safety of the

---

E. Zervogianni, 'Künstliche Fortpflanzung in Griechenland' in A. Dutta, D. Schwab, P. Gottwald, D. Henrich and M. Löhnig (eds), *Künstliche Fortpflanzung und Europäisches Familienrecht*, Gieseking Verlag, Bielefeld 2015, pp. 227–28. Contra (in favour of anonymity) K. Fountedaki, 'I pliroforisi tou paidiou pou gennithike apo eterologi texniti gonimopoiisi gia tin katagogi tou' in *Techniti gonimopoiisi kai genetiki technologia: I ithikonomiki diastasi*, Publications of the Association of Jurists of North Greece, vol. 48, Sakkoulas, Thessaloniki 2003, pp. 129 ff., esp. p. 138; E. Kounougeri-Manoledaki, *Oikogeneiako Dikaio II*, 8th ed., Sakkoulas, Athens/Thessaloniki 2021, pp. 80 ff.; T. Papachristou, *Oikogeneiako Dikaio*, P.N. Sakkoulas, Athens 2014, p. 222; cf. also T. Vidalis, *Zoi xoris prosopo*, Ant. N. Sakkoulas, Athens/Komotini 2003, pp. 153 ff., esp. p. 159.

[87] See Art. 1460 GrCC, as amended by Art. 11 of Law 4958/2022.
[88] See Art. 1460 sentence 6 of the GrCC, as amended by Art 11 of Law 4958/2022.
[89] See Art. 1460 sentence 4 of the GrCC, as amended by Art. 11 of Law 4958/2002.
[90] This is derived by Art. 1479 para. 2 of the GrCC, according to which, even if the donor's identity is revealed, judicial acknowledgment of fatherhood (which leads to the establishment of kinship between the father and the child by means of a court decision, if either the father refuses to acknowledge the child voluntarily or the mother does not grant her consent to the voluntary acknowledgment by the father) is not possible. See on this point also E. Kounougeri-Manoledaki, *Oikogeneiako Dikaio II*, 8th ed., Sakkoulas, Athens/Thessaloniki 2021, p. 204 ff.; A. Georgiades, *Oikogeneiako Dikaio*, 2nd ed., Sakkoulas, Athens/Thessaloniki 2017, §28 no. 28.

application of this method, to the extent it is still at the stage of a clinical trial, in the framework of a developing research protocol.[91] The same basically holds for pronuclear transfer.

This notwithstanding, the legal framework as regards the kinship of 'three-parent children' is clear. Namely, in Greece no child can have three legal parents. The persons who wished to have the child are legally the parents of the child. Any other person who participated in the procedure by providing genetic material is not legally related to the child in any way, and thus has no rights.[92]

2.8. SURROGACY

Gestational (but not traditional) surrogacy is permitted in Greece under specific conditions set by the law.[93] Although the issue has undoubtedly been contentious, the legislator's decision to opt for the permissibility of surrogacy has been driven by pragmatic considerations: as mentioned in the Explanatory Memorandum of the law,[94] a prohibition on surrogacy could never be enforced entirely. On this assumption, the comprehensive regulation of surrogacy, rather than its prohibition, was thought to serve the best interests of the children that would be born using this method of assisted reproduction. Along these lines, the law includes clear rules regarding the parenthood of children born from surrogates.

More specifically, if all the legal conditions for surrogacy are fulfilled and the surrogacy has been authorised by the court, as the law provides, the intended mother is the legal mother of the child already at the time of birth.[95] This is also stated on the birth certificate of the child, without any reference to the surrogate,[96]

---

[91] The joint press release is available at http://eaiya.gov.gr/%ce%b4%ce%b5%ce%bb%cf%84%ce%b9%ce%bf-%cf%84%cf%85%cf%80%ce%bf%cf%85-19-04-2019/, accessed 29.05.2022.
[92] See in more detail section 2.6 above.
[93] Surrogacy is permitted under the following conditions. First, the general conditions for access to medically assisted reproduction have to be fulfilled. These pertain to the existence of medical reasons to proceed to using medically assisted reproduction techniques in order to have a child (Art. 1455 of the GrCC), the observance of the age limit (Art. 1455 of the GrCC), which is effectively set for women at the age of 54 (Art. 4 para. 1 of Law 3305/2005, as amended by Art. 3 of Law 4958/2022), and consent of the persons who wish to have the child (Art. 1456 of the GrCC). Furthermore, the special conditions for surrogacy have to be fulfilled as well. These are the medical inability of the intended mother to bear the child herself, the conclusion of a relevant gratuitous contract between the intended parents and the surrogate (if the surrogate is married or in a registered partnership her husband or partner has to grant his consent) and the court authorisation of the procedure (Art. 1458 of the GrCC). See in more detail in English E. Zervogianni, 'Surrogacy in Greece' in J.M. Scherpe, C. Fenton-Glynn and T. Kaan (eds), *Eastern and Western Perspectives on Surrogacy*, Intersentia, Cambridge 2019, pp. 145 ff.
[94] See the Explanatory Memorandum of Law 3089/2002, Point I 4 (p. 1).
[95] See Art. 1464 para. 1 of the GrCC.
[96] See Art. 20 para. 1 of Law 344/1976 on Civil Registry Certificates, as amended.

and it holds even if the genetic material used is not that of the intended mother herself but of a third person.[97] The establishment of paternal descent, irrespective of the genetic material that has been used, is contingent upon the establishment of maternal descent.[98] In the rare but existing cases where a single man commissions surrogacy,[99] it should be accepted that the child has no legal mother, but only a legal father, whose kinship with the child is directly derived from the court decision that authorised the surrogacy.[100]

Hence, the Greek legal framework of medically assisted reproduction generally grants priority to the so-called social-emotional bond between the intended parents and the child, which prevails over biology.[101] Nevertheless, maternal descent may be contested if it is proved than the ovum that has actually been fertilised is that of the surrogate.[102] The surrogate can then bring a claim challenging the legal motherhood of the child within six months from the child's birth.[103] If the claim succeeds, the surrogate becomes the legal mother of the child.[104] This brings about changes as to the paternal descent of the child as well. Thus, if the surrogate is married or has concluded a registered partnership, the spouse or registered partner is presumed to be the father of the child,[105] unless he contests fatherhood.[106]

With the exception of the rare cases where legal motherhood is successfully contested, the surrogate has no legal relationship to the child she gave birth to and therefore also has no rights. If she does not willingly hand over the child to the legal parents, the latter may compel her to do so on the basis of the provisions of the Code of Civil Procedure on judicial execution.[107] Along the same lines,

---

[97] See section 2.6 above.
[98] Ibid.
[99] See on this controversial issue section 2.6 above.
[100] See D. Papadopoulou-Klamari, *I syggeneia. Themeliosi, katachorisi, prostasia*, Ant. N. Sakkoulas, Athens/Komotini 2010, p. 108; G. Lekkas, 'Iatrikos ypovoithoumeni anaparagogi kai syggeneia sto elliniko dikaio. Kathierosi tis koinonikosynaisthimatikis syggeneias i tis teknopoiias choris suggeneia?' in T. Papachristou and E. Kounougeri-Manoledaki (eds), *To oikogeneiako dikaio ston 21o aiona*, Sakkoulas, Athens/Thessaloniki 2012, p. 63; A. Georgiades, *Oikogeneiako Dikaio*, 2nd ed., Sakkoulas, Athens/Thessaloniki 2017, §28 no. 6. Contra: Expert Opinion 261/2010 of the Legal Council of the State (*Nomiko Symboulio tou Kratous*), available at http://www.nsk.gr/web/nsk/anazitisi-gnomodoteseon, accessed 29.05.2022, according to which in this case the surrogate should be registered on the birth certificate as the legal mother of the child.
[101] See also section 2.6 above.
[102] See Art. 1464 para. 2 of the GrCC.
[103] Ibid.
[104] See Art. 1464 para. 3 of the GrCC.
[105] See Art. 1465 para. 1 of the GrCC and Art. 9 of Law 4356/2015 on registered partnerships.
[106] See Art. 1467 of the GrCC and Art. 9 sentence 3 of Law 4356/2015, which stipulates, inter alia, that Art. 1467 of the GrCC applies by analogy in cases of registered partnership.
[107] See Art. 946 para. 1 of the Greek Code of Civil Procedure. So E. Kounougeri-Manoledaki, 'To skhedio nomou gia tin "iatrikos ypovoiithoumeni anthropini anaparagogi" kai o antilogos stis antidraseis enantion tou', *ChrID* 2002, 676 ff., 676; P. Agallopoulou, 'Chorigisi dikastikis

the surrogate has no right to contact the child.[108] Relevant agreements between the intended parents and the surrogate granting her such a right are not enforceable, since the legal parents have the sole competence to make decisions on the upbringing of their child.[109] Similarly, although the law does not provide for the anonymity of the surrogate,[110] there is no specific rule granting the child the possibility to access the relevant information.[111]

2.9. SAME-SEX PARENTS

Setting aside exceptional cases where a parent of the child subsequently changes his or her sex,[112] in Greece a child cannot have same-sex parents. Same-sex partners may not proceed as a couple to adopt a minor,[113] even if they have concluded a cohabitation agreement,[114] and they do not have access as a couple to medically assisted reproduction techniques.[115] A partner in a same-sex couple can thus only adopt on his or her own or make use of medically assisted reproduction as a single person.[116] In such a case, though, the same-sex partner of the legal parent of the child is treated like any third person and therefore does not have any parental rights or duties.[117]

---

adeias gia parentheti mitrotita', *Kritiki Epitheorisi Nomikis Theorias kai Praxis* 2003/2, 235 ff., 241; A. Georgiades, *Oikogeneiako Dikaio*, 2nd ed., Sakkoulas, Athens/Thessaloniki 2017, §25 no. 29.

[108] See also K. Rokas, 'Greece' in K. Trimmings and P. Beaumont (eds), *International Surrogacy Arrangements*, Hart Publishing, Oxford 2013, p. 151.

[109] See Art. 1510 et seq. of the GrCC on the right of parental care. On the contents of this right see in detail P. Agallopoulou, in A. Georgiades and M. Stathopoulos (eds), *Astikos Kodikas*, vol. 8, 2nd ed., P.N. Sakkoulas, Athens 2003, Art. 1510 no. 80 ff.

[110] On the anonymity of donors of genetic material see section 2.6 above.

[111] See however K. Rokas, 'Greece' in K. Trimmings and P. Beaumont (eds), K. Trimmings and P. Beaumont (eds), *International Surrogacy Arrangements*, Hart Publishing, Oxford 2013, p. 150, who bases the child's right to acquire this information on the right to know one's genetic origins, derived from the right to freely develop one's personality (Art. 5 para. 1 of the Greek Constitution).

[112] On this issue see Law 4491/2017 on the legal recognition of gender identity, which explicitly states in Art. 5 para. 2 that if the person who proceeds to the correction of his or her registered gender has children, his or her parental responsibilities are not influenced in any way.

[113] They may nevertheless proceed to adopt an adult. See section 2.4 above. On this issue see also V. Peraki, 'Dynatotites askisis gonikis merimnas se tekna omofylon syntrofon', *EfAD* 2020, 571; E. Zervogianni, 'Koinoniki goneikotita kai oikogeneiako dikaio' *EfAD* 2022, 14 ff., 17.

[114] According to the prevailing opinion in Greek law, only married persons can proceed to the adoption of a child as a couple (see section 2.4 above), while same-sex marriage is not recognised in Greece. See decision AP 1428/2017, *EfAD* 2018, 170.

[115] Only single women or opposite-sex partners have access to medically assisted reproduction techniques. See section 2.7 above.

[116] On the question whether single men have access to medically assisted reproduction see section 2.6 above.

[117] See section 2.1 above.

The floor has nevertheless opened in the debate on same-sex parenthood. Since 2018, same-sex partners who have concluded a cohabitation agreement may become foster parents.[118] Furthermore, during the discussions that preceded the enactment of Law 4356/2015 on registered partnerships, and shortly after, the assignment of at least some parental responsibilities to the same-sex registered partner of the legal parent of the child was discussed.[119] More recently, the Committee that has been assigned the task of drafting the National Strategy for the Equality of LGBTQI+ persons stressed the importance of adopting such a regime, as an interim measure, until same-sex parenthood is recognised.[120] Last but not least, in June 2022 the Opposition submitted to the Parliament a Bill for the amendment of the Greek Civil Code, based on the gender-free interpretation of all its provisions.[121] On this basis, same-sex couples would be able to marry, adopt children and make use of medically assisted reproduction as a couple. Even if the Bill does not pass, it is important that the issue is now clearly on the table.

3. DIVERSITY AND PLURALITY OF FAMILY'S FUNCTIONS

3.1. AN OVERVIEW OF FAMILY FUNCTIONS IN GREEK LAW

The legal notion of family[122] and the family forms[123] that are regulated in the law are contingent upon the functions that the family is called to serve. These functions are sensitive to social and economic change and are thus altered over time.[124]

---

[118] See Art. 8 of Law 4538/2018. On foster care in general see section 2.5 above.

[119] See the relevant Proposal of 07.12.2015 of the Greek Ombudsman (*Synigoros tou Politi*), available at https://www.synigoros.gr/?i=equality.el.files.437553, accessed 29.05.2022, as well as V. Peraki, 'Dynatotites askisis gonikis merimnas se tekna omofylon syntrofon', *EfAD* 2020, 576 ff.

[120] See the Report of the Committee, entitled 'Ethniki Stratigiki gia tin Isotita ton LOATKI+', p. 47, available at https://primeminister.gr/wp-content/uploads/2021/06/ethniki_statigiki_gia_thn_isothta_ton_loatki.pdf, accessed 29.05.2022. The Committee was set up by decision of the Prime Minister on 17.03.2021 and it submitted its report on 29.06.2021.

[121] See Bill on the Abolishment of Gender Discrimination in Family Law, Establishment of the Right to Marry for All Persons and Necessary Adjustments of the Legislation (Arsi diakriseon logo fylou sto Oikogeneiako Dikaio, katohyrosi dikaiomatos gamou gia ola ta prosopa kai anagkaies prosarmoges tis nomothesias). The Bill is available at https://www.hellenicparliament.gr/UserFiles/c8827c35-4399-4fbb-8ea6-aebdc768f4f7/11992634.pdf, accessed 12.08.2022.

[122] See section 1 above.

[123] See section 2 above.

[124] For a historical overview see F.P. Theodoropoulou, 'Nomiki kai koinoniologiki proseggisi tis ennoias tou thesmou tis oikogeneias', *EfAD* 2013, 494 ff., 515 ff.

While in the past the (extended) family was a production unit, it is nowadays a consumption unit, which is also much smaller.[125] The employment of family members is no longer within the family. Moreover, the role of the (extended) family in the entertainment of its members is restricted, as leisure activities usually take place outside family circles. Thus, most legal provisions pertain nowadays to the nuclear family, meaning parents and children.

The relaxation of the bonds between the members of the extended family has also resulted in a decline in the function of the family as a mechanism of social control of its members. Family members are more self-sufficient and do not have to seek the approval of the other family members before they act. Remnants of this controlling function of the family may however be still identified in the law. The most characteristic one is probably the provision of succession law according to which an ancestor may disinherit a descendant (and not vice versa) if the latter leads a dishonourable or immoral life against the will of the testator.[126]

Procreation is still a function within a family, albeit not a necessary one. The number of children born out of wedlock (or 'cohabitation agreement') is increasing,[127] while at the same time the number of childless families is steadily rising. This becomes particularly evident when one considers that while same-sex partners who have concluded a cohabitation agreement undoubtedly fall within the concept of family,[128] the law does not grant them access to medically assisted reproduction or adoption.[129]

Moreover, in the past the role of the family was significant for the protection of its vulnerable members, such as the elderly, disabled persons, housewives, and children. Nowadays this protective function of the family still exists, but is less prominent for a number of reasons.

The State has to a great extent assumed the protection of elderly and disabled persons through the system of social welfare, providing healthcare and pensions or other benefits to persons who are not, or are no longer, in a position to work. If, however, the State provisions do not adequately cover the needs of these persons, the family still steps in. Drawing upon the need for solidarity between generations, the Civil Code includes detailed provisions on the obligation of maintenance between ancestors and descendants (and, exceptionally, also between siblings).[130] Moreover, the law provides for a protective regime, called

---

[125] See G. Koumantos, *Oikogeneiako Dikaio I*, P.N. Sakkoulas, Athens 1988, p. 18; E. Kounougeri-Manoledaki, *Oikogeneiako Dikaio I*, 8th ed., Sakkoulas, Athens/Thessaloniki 2021, pp. 10–11; F.P. Theodoropoulou, 'Nomiki kai koinoniologiki proseggisi tis ennoias tou thesmou tis oikogeneias', *EfAD* 2013, 515.

[126] See Art. 1840 no. 5 of the GrCC.

[127] According to the statistics of Eurostat (available at https://ec.europa.eu/eurostat/web/products-eurostat-news/-/ddn-20200717-1, accessed 29.05.2022), just 4% of children were born out of wedlock in Greece in 2000, whereas in 2018 the percentage went up to 11%.

[128] See section 1 above.

[129] See section 2.9 above.

[130] See Art. 1485 et seq. of the GrCC.

'judicial assistance', for persons who suffer from a condition that does not allow them to participate safely in legal transactions.[131] In such cases, the court appoints a 'judicial assistant' who is usually, but does not have to be, a family member.[132] Depending on the specific case, the 'judicial assistant' has to grant his or her consent before the 'assisted person' enters into legal transactions or may conclude legal acts him- or herself in the name of the 'assisted person'.[133]

Women are no longer as vulnerable as they were in the past. Equality of the sexes is firmly established in the law and has also been achieved to a quite satisfactory degree in practice.[134] The great majority of women work outside the home and are (or can be) self-sufficient. The regulation of Greek family law is based on the model where both spouses work. It is in this spirit that the law explicitly states that each spouse should contribute to the family expenses in accordance with his or her means,[135] while the right to maintenance after divorce is also contingent upon the inability of one ex-spouse to cover his or her needs by his or her own means.[136] Moreover, excessive housework undertaken by any spouse or other contributions to the increase of the property of the other spouse can be rewarded after the dissolution of marriage through the institution of participation in the increments.[137] This also holds true for partners who have concluded a cohabitation agreement.[138]

Since women have entered the labour market, the State has also assumed the supervision of young children and the education of older ones. The number of State nurseries is steadily increasing and persons who cannot find a place in a State nursery can get a voucher from the State for a private one if they fulfil certain criteria, mostly financial.[139] The education of children in preschools and schools is obligatory and free of charge for children who have reached the age of four.[140]

---

[131] See Art. 1666 et seq. of the GrCC.
[132] See Art. 1669 of the GrCC.
[133] See Art. 1676 of the GrCC. For a brief overview of the institution of 'judicial assistance' in English see E. Zervogianni, 'The Changing Concept of Family and Challenges for Family Law in Greece', in J.M. Scherpe (ed.), *European Family Law*, vol. II, Edward Elgar, Cheltenham 2016, p. 101.
[134] See Art. 4 para. 2 of the Greek Constitution. Law 1329/1983 amended the Civil Code in order to ensure its compatibility with the Constitution. Equality of sexes is without any doubt a general principle that runs through the whole of Greek family law. See E. Kounougeri-Manoledaki, *Oikogeneiako Dikaio I*, 8th ed., Sakkoulas, Athens/Thessaloniki 2021, pp. 12–13; A. Georgiades, *Oikogeneiako Dikaio*, 2nd ed., Sakkoulas, Athens/Thessaloniki 2017, §3 no. 1.
[135] See Art. 1389 of the GrCC.
[136] See Art. 1442 of the GrCC. For a brief overview in English see E. Zervogianni, 'The Changing Concept of Family and Challenges for Family Law in Greece', in J.M. Scherpe (ed.), *European Family Law*, vol. II, Edward Elgar, Cheltenham 2016, p. 92.
[137] See Art. 1400 of the GrCC.
[138] See Art. 5 para. 2 of Law 4356/2015.
[139] See the Common Ministerial Decree 57382/2019, signed by the Ministers of Internal Affairs, of Economy & Development, Employment, of Social Security & Solidarity, and of Finance.
[140] See Art. 3 para. 4 of Law 1566/1985, as amended by Art. 33 of Law 4521/2018.

In addition, the family still provides economic security for its members, which goes beyond the obligation of maintenance mentioned above. Parental donations are subject to particularly beneficial taxation.[141] The same holds for succession in the estate of close relatives: the closer the relative, the lower the tax rate.[142]

The main function of family nowadays is to serve as a refuge of love and companionship between the family members.[143] It provides the necessary emotional conditions for the development of the personality of the family members. Furthermore, the law should ensure, and it does ensure, as is illustrated below, that children are raised and socialised under these conditions. This is usually listed as a separate family function,[144] but there can be little doubt that the emotional support between the family members and the raising of children actually go hand in hand.

3.2. FAMILY AS A REFUGE OF LOVE AND COMPANIONSHIP AND AS A PLACE TO RAISE CHILDREN

The predominance of the family's function as a 'refuge of companionship and love' is evidenced in the law in several provisions, the most prominent of which relates to the liberalisation of divorce and the introduction of the 'cohabitation agreement' also for same-sex couples. Moreover, the adoption of the principle of the protection of the interests of the child, which is central in all vertical family law relations, underlies the importance of raising children within a loving ambiance.

More specifically, firstly, since the entry into force of the Greek Civil Code in 1946, the provisions in respect of divorce have been subject to major reforms. It is now widely accepted that the constitutional protection of marriage does not extend to dysfunctional marriages and that the right to divorce forms an aspect of the right to free development of one's personality and is thus granted constitutional protection.[145] Along these lines, in 1983 the right to divorce was

---

[141] See Art. 44 of Law 2961/2001.
[142] See Art. 29 of Law 2961/2001.
[143] See G. Koumantos, *Oikogeneiako Dikaio I*, P.N. Sakkoulas, Athens 1988, p. 18; E. Kounougeri-Manoledaki, *Oikogeneiako Dikaio I*, 8th ed., Sakkoulas, Athens/Thessaloniki 2021, p. 20; T. Papachristou, *Oikogeneiako Dikaio*, P.N. Sakkoulas, Athens 2014, p. 2; F.P. Theodoropoulou, 'Nomiki kai koinoniologiki proseggisi tis ennoias tou thesmou tis oikogeneias', *EfAD* 2013, 516.
[144] Ibid.
[145] K. Chrysogonos and S. Vlachopoulos, *Atomika kai Koinonika Dikaiomata*, 4th ed., Nomiki Vivliothiki, Athens 2017, p. 565; A. Kotzampasi, in F. Spyropoulos, X. Kontiadis, C. Anthopoulos and G. Gerapetritis (eds), *Syntagma*, Sakkoulas, Athens/Thessaloniki 2017, Art. 21 no. 6; A. Georgiades, *Oikogeneiako Dikaio*, 2nd ed., Sakkoulas, Athens/Thessaloniki 2017, §17 no. 11.

detached from the question of fault[146] and divorce on the grounds of irretrievable breakdown of marriage was introduced.[147] In addition, separation of the spouses for a period of more than four years was recognised as an independent ground for divorce.[148] In 2008 the separation period which can lead to divorce was decreased to two years.[149] In addition, the institution of divorce by mutual consent was introduced in 1983.[150] Subsequent laws in 2012 and in 2017 simplified the relevant procedure.[151] Since the reform in 2017, divorce by mutual consent is now issued by a notary and then filed in the registry office; therefore, the parties no longer need to file for divorce before the court.[152]

Secondly, the (admittedly late) legal recognition of same-sex couples, who in 2015 were granted the right to conclude 'cohabitation agreements', also indicates the legislator's approach that the family is a refuge of love and companionship for all couples, irrespective of their sexual orientation.[153] Such cohabitation agreements may be concluded by couples of the opposite sex as well. Their easy dissolution[154] is further evidence of the dominant function of family as a way to meet the emotional needs of a person.

This prevailingly loving function of family does not change when there are children. The Civil Code explicitly states that parents and children owe to each other assistance, affection and respect.[155] Furthermore, it is a basic principle of Greek civil law that the only criterion for the regulation of the relationship between parents and children is the best interests of the child.[156] Thus, Greek law is in line with Article 3 of the United Nations Convention on the Rights of the Child of 1989, which Greece ratified in 1992.[157] There are numerous instances in family law where this becomes evident. To list only a few, every decision of

---

[146] See Art. 16 of Law 1329/1983, which fundamentally reformed the rules on divorce.
[147] See Art. 1439 of the GrCC, which was introduced into the Civil Code by Art. 16 of Law 1329/1983.
[148] See Art. 1439 para. 3 of the GrCC.
[149] See Art. 14 of Law 3719/2008.
[150] See Art. 16 of Law 1329/1983.
[151] See Art. 3 para. 2 of Law 4055/2012 and Art. 22 para. 2 of Law 4509/2017. Further amendments of smaller importance were introduced by Art. 4 of Law 4800/2021.
[152] See section 2.2 above.
[153] On the previous law on 'cohabitation agreements' only for persons of the opposite sex and the condemnation of Greece by the European Court of Human Rights, see section 1 above.
[154] See Art. 7 of Law 4356/2015.
[155] See Art. 1507 of the GrCC.
[156] See section 2.2 above.
[157] See section 2.5 above. It is worth noting that although the Greek Constitution does not contain an explicit provision on the protection of the interest of the child, there exists a constitutional regulatory framework which is beneficial for the child. Particularly significant in this respect is Art. 21 para. 1 of the Constitution that refers (inter alia) to the protection of childhood, in combination with further articles, such as Arts 2 para. 1 (protection of human dignity) and 5 para. 1 (right to the free development of a person's personality). See C. Anthopoulos, in P. Naskou-Peraki, K. Chrysogonos and C. Anthopoulos, *I diethnis symvasi gia ta dikaiomata tou paidiou kai i ethniki ennomi taxi*, Ant. N. Sakkoula Athens/Komotini 2002, Art. 3, pp. 48–49.

the parents should serve the interests of the child.[158] If the parents are not in a position to reach a decision, the judge will decide on the basis of the same criterion.[159] If the parents do not fulfil their parental responsibilities properly, they may be deprived of the right to exercise them.[160] A significant condition for the adoption of a minor is that it serves the best interests of the adoptee.[161] Even in the regulation of medically assisted reproduction, the legislator took into account the best interests of the child that will be born.[162] Quasi-family vertical relations are also governed by the same principle.[163]

3.3. FAMILIES WITH AND WITHOUT CHILDREN

With or without children, family is conceived by the legislator as a place to love and be loved. The applicable provisions of family law on marriage and on cohabitation agreements are the same, no matter whether there are children or not.[164]

If there are children in the family, no differentiation is made in the law between biological children, adopted children, children born with donated genetic material or by surrogates, children born in wedlock or by parents who have concluded a cohabitation agreement, and children born out of wedlock or cohabitation agreement. Different treatment of children based on such criteria would lead to discrimination and would thus be incompatible with Article 4 paragraph 1 of the Greek Constitution.[165]

---

[158] Art. 1511 para. 1 of the GrCC.
[159] Art. 1511 para. 2 of the GrCC.
[160] Art. 1532 of the GrCC.
[161] Arts 1542 and 1558 of the GrCC.
[162] See Art. 1 para. 2 of Law 3305/2005 and in more detail A. Koutsouradis, 'Themata parenthetis mitrotitas idios meta to N. 3305/2005' *Nomiko Vima* 2006, 337 ff., 355 ff.; T. Trokanas, 'I efarmogi ton methodon iatrikos ypovoithoumenis anaparagogis kai to symferon tou paidiou pou tha gennithei' in T. Papachristou and E. Kounougeri-Manoledaki (eds), *To oikogeneiako dikaio ston 21o aiona*, Sakkoulas, Athens/Thessaloniki 2012, pp. 135 ff.
[163] See esp. Art. 1648 of the GrCC on guardianship and Art. 1656 of the GrCC on foster care. On the notion of quasi-family relations see section 1 above.
[164] Nevertheless, according to the prevailing opinion in the Greek literature, the notion of 'family' in constitutional terms (Art. 21 para. 1 of the Constitution refers, inter alia, to the protection of family) pertains to parent(s) and children, so that there cannot be a family in this sense without children. See K. Chrysogonos and S. Vlachopoulos, *Atomika kai Koinika Dikaiomata*, 4th ed., Nomiki Vivliothiki, Athens 2017, p. 561, and in more detail L. Papadopoulou, 'I nomiki ennoia tis oikogeneias kai ta omofyla zevgaria' in *Timitikos Tomos gia tin Kathigitria Efi Kounougeri-Manoledaki*, Sakkoulas, Athens/Thessaloniki 2016, pp. 362 ff.
[165] See, explicitly, A. Kotzampasi, in F. Spyropoulos, X. Kontiadis, C. Anthopoulos and G. Gerapetritis (eds), *Syntagma*, Sakkoulas, Athens/Thessaloniki 2017, Art. 21 no. 13. Cf. also P. Dagtoglou, *Atomika dikaiomata I*, 2nd ed. Ant. N. Sakkoulas, Athens/Komotini 2005, no. 502a.

4. CONCLUSIONS

Despite the broadening of the notion of legal family in the last decades, in Greece there is still considerable divergence between the legal family and the social family. Parenthood is approached on the basis of the traditional model, according to which a child can have no more than two parents of the opposite sex. Persons other that the child's legal parents are treated with scepticism as persons who could disrupt the family peace. This approach seems to be somewhat linked to the main function of family as a refuge of love and companionship. However, this does not need to be the case.

First of all, same-sex families with children can undoubtedly fulfil this function. It is therefore a positive development that the floor has (finally) opened in the debate on same-sex parenthood. The possibility of same-sex couples becoming foster parents has been a first cautious step in this direction, hopefully to be followed, sooner rather than later, by further decisive steps.

Second, the divergence between the legal family and social family in Greece is currently considerable. Until recently, the law granted no protection to persons who factually assumed a parenting role, such as a step-parent or same-sex partner of the legal parent. Since 2021, the right to contact the child has been extended to them as well.[166] The enactment of further provisions would also encourage a more involved role of the social parent in the life of the child and would serve the interest of all parties. In more general terms, we believe that legal rules that reflect social reality serve the preservation of peace in the family better than rules aiming at the exclusion of 'third parties' from family life.

Last but not least, the exclusion of persons who have in some way contributed to the birth of the children, whether as donors of genetic material or as surrogates, from the family's life does not seem to contribute to the protection of the family. Apart from all the considerations relating to the right of a child to know his or her origins,[167] what a family needs in order to be protected is honesty and directness, whereas any rule on anonymity promotes secrecy and the potential for future conflicts.

---

[166] See section 2.1 above.
[167] See section 2.6 above.

LA LONGUE ET LENTE MARCHE DE LA PLURALISATION

Nouvelles formes familiales en Italie

Roberta Aluffi

1. Diversité et pluralité des formes familiales 317
   1.1. Les familles multiparentales 318
        1.1.1. La famille recomposée : La multiplicité de la parentalité dans le foyer 318
        1.1.2. La famille recomposée : La multiplicité de parents ne partageant pas le foyer 322
   1.2. L'enfant élevé dans plus d'un foyer. 324
   1.3. Famille polygame 325
   1.4. Adoption ouverte 326
   1.5. *Kafala* 328
   1.6. Le don des gamètes 328
   1.7. L'enfant à trois parents. 329
   1.8. Gestation pour autrui 330
   1.9. Parties impliquées dans une relation de même sexe 333
        1.9.1. Les relations de même sexe et la multiplicité de la parentalité. 333
        1.9.2. Polygamie. 334
        1.9.3. Adoption ouverte 334
        1.9.4. *Kafala* 335
        1.9.5. Procréation médicalement assistée 335
        1.9.6. Une loi sur la multiparentalité ? 339
2. Diversité et pluralité des fonctions de la famille. 339

1. DIVERSITÉ ET PLURALITÉ DES FORMES FAMILIALES

L'explosion de la famille nucléaire, hétérosexuelle et fondée sur le mariage, seul modèle familial reconnu il y a encore un demi-siècle, a donné naissance à toute une constellation de groupements familiaux différents. Cela s'est produit sous l'effet de plusieurs facteurs : transformations sociales, changements de mentalité, diversification culturelle de la société et progrès techniques.

Les nouveaux groupements familiaux, malgré leur diversité, ont en commun leur centre de gravité : non plus les adultes, mais l'enfant. Le statut de l'enfant n'est plus réglé en fonction de la relation qui lie, ou ne lie pas, ses parents. C'est plutôt l'existence de l'enfant le pivot autour duquel les relations familiales se structurent et perdurent, qu'elles soient fondées sur la relation biologique, l'intention ou les soins.[1]

Ces changements n'ont pas été conçus et préparés par le droit. Le droit les a suivis et, au plus, soutenus : il laisse les relations juridiques entre les adultes à leur propre choix ; mais pas les intérêts des enfants.

Ces transformations ont impacté en particulier l'Occident. L'Italie connaît également ces changements et l'adaptation du droit aux nouveaux défis. Mais les deux sont plus lents qu'ailleurs.

La famille nucléaire reste statistiquement prédominante et conserve son « rôle d'archétype culturel de référence ».[2] Le législateur intervient toujours tardivement, timidement et souvent de manière confuse. Le rôle principal est joué par la jurisprudence, tant de la Cour suprême que de la Cour constitutionnelle. Cette dernière fait preuve parfois de retenue et sollicite l'intervention du législateur, estimant que des changements complets du système ne peuvent qu'être basés sur des choix politiques.

1.1. LES FAMILLES MULTIPARENTALES

Le nouage et la dissolution des relations entre adultes aboutissent à la composition et recompositions de familles, ce qui impose de considérer les relations de l'enfant avec plusieurs adultes de référence et celles de ces adultes entre eux. Il convient de considérer ces deux aspects des familles recomposées séparément.

1.1.1. La famille recomposée : La multiplicité de la parentalité dans le foyer

La loi ne prévoit expressément aucune responsabilité ni droit légal du beau-parent par le seul fait de partager le foyer avec le parent de l'enfant.

---

[1] Cette révolution copernicienne de la vision de la famille est parfaitement représentée par le plus récent ouvrage italien consacré au droit de la famille : L. Lenti, *Diritto della famiglia*, Giuffrè, Milan 2021, qui fait partie du *Trattato di diritto privato* dirigé par G. Iudica et P. Zatti. L'auteur, en rupture avec une tradition séculaire, bouleverse l'ordre habituel de la matière et place les pages sur les enfants (73345) avant celles sur le couple (344–965). Cet œuvre lucide est un point d'accès très fiable à l'ensemble du droit de la famille italien, à recommander également pour la sélection de la bibliographie et sa présentation raisonnée.

[2] Ibid., p. 12.

Le rôle de parent sociale (*genitore sociale*) est parfois reconnu par la jurisprudence à la personne ayant instauré avec l'enfant une relation de famille significative et durable.

Les juges se trouvent normalement confrontés aux demandes du parent social au moment de la fin de la relation entre celui-ci et le parent de l'enfant. Elles concernent notamment son droit de visiter l'enfant et de maintenir une relation avec lui.

Il faut immédiatement préciser que le sexe du parent et du parent social n'a aucune incidence sur les décisions des juges. Leurs décisions concernent tantôt des couples de même sexe, tantôt des couples de sexe différent. Parfois le juge déclare expressément que le sexe n'a aucune importance.

Deux approches ont été envisagées pour garantir le maintien de la relation de famille entre l'enfant et le parent social : l'application de l'article 337 *ter* du code civil, qui règle le droit de l'enfant à la continuité de la relation avec ses deux parents, les ascendants et les proches, dans le cadre des procédures pour l'attribution de la garde de l'enfant né du mariage ou hors mariage ; ou bien l'application de l'article 333 du code civil, qui permet au juge d'adopter des mesures appropriées en matière de responsabilité parentale, lorsque le parent porte préjudice à l'enfant.

La première approche a été notamment adoptée par le Tribunal de Palerme (sez. I, 13 avril 2015), dans le cas de deux femmes et un couple de jumeaux. Le juge a estimé que la nécessité de garantir l'intérêt supérieur des enfants impose d'interpréter l'article 337 *ter* du code civil d'une façon évolutive, mais en même temps respectueuse de la constitution et des conventions internationales et par conséquent d'inclure le parent social dans les notions de famille et de biparentalité (*bi-genitorialità*). L'absence de qualité pour agir du parent social (qui n'est ni parent biologique, ni parent adoptif) a été compensée par la demande du Procureur de la République, qui l'a reconnu comme une ressource affective et économique importante pour les enfants. Le juge considère le maintien de la relation comme un droit des enfants, et non pas du parent social.

En appel, la Cour d'appel de Palerme soulève la question de la légitimité constitutionnelle de l'article 337 *ter* du code civil à la Cour constitutionnelle. La Cour d'appel, dans son ordonnance de renvoi, partage l'individuation des paramètres constitutionnels (articles 2 et 30 de la constitution) et conventionnels (article 8 de la Convention européenne des droits de l'homme) concernant l'intérêt supérieur de l'enfant faite par le juge 0de première instance, mais elle estime que la lettre univoque de l'article 337 *ter* du code civil, ne mentionnant pas le parent social, pose un obstacle insurmontable à une interprétation de la disposition respectueuse de ces paramètres. La Cour constitutionnelle (20 octobre 2016, n. 225) refuse de déclarer l'inconstitutionnalité de l'article 337 *ter* du code civil : le fait que cette disposition concerne exclusivement le contexte « proprement familial » (*propriamente familiare*) n'entraîne aucun vide de protection pour les relations que l'enfant entretient avec des adultes de référence qui ne sont pas ses proches. En fait, l'interruption injustifiée par le parent d'une telle relation, au cas où elle ne correspond pas à intérêt de l'enfant, constitue un préjudice pour lui, ce qui permet au juge d'adopter les mesures appropriées au cas d'espèce, en application de l'article 333 du code civil, sur l'action du Ministère Public.

La relation avec l'adulte de référence se trouve donc protégée dans le seul intérêt de l'enfant et d'une façon indirecte, par la limitation de la responsabilité parentale du parent qui l'interrompt sans justification (article 333 du code civil). Le parent social n'a pas la qualité pour agir pour défendre son intérêt personnel, mais il doit signaler le comportement du parent au Ministère Public, qui a le droit d'action dans l'intérêt de l'enfant.

La position du parent social, de ce point de vue, s'avère être moins favorable non seulement que celle du grand-parent, mais aussi que celle du conjoint ou du partenaire du grand-parent, qui n'a pas une relation « proprement familiale » avec l'enfant. Depuis 2013, la loi (article 317 *bis* du code civil) reconnait aux ascendants le droit à des relations significatives avec les petits-enfants mineurs et le droit d'agir si l'exercice de leur droit est empêché. En 2018, la Cour de cassation (Cass. 25 juillet 2018, n. 19780), en se référant aux articles 2 et 30 de la constitution, 8 de la Convention européenne des droits de l'homme et 24 alinéa 2 de la Charte européenne), reconnait ce droit aussi « à quiconque est aux côtés du grand-parent, qu'il soit son conjoint ou son partenaire, et s'est montré capable d'instaurer et maintenir une relation affective durable avec l'enfant, dont ce dernier peut tirer un avantage pour sa formation et son équilibre psychophysique ».

Revenant aux possibles approches à la protection de la relation de l'enfant avec son parent social, c'est donc la limitation de la responsabilité du parent qui l'interrompt d'une façon injustifiée (article 333 du code civil) qui est indiquée comme appropriée pour la Cour constitutionnelle et qui, par ailleurs, avait été choisie par maintes Tribunaux, à partir de la première décision en date, celle du Tribunal des mineurs de Milan du 2 novembre 2007.

Parmi les décisions les plus récentes faisant référence à l'article 333 du code civil il convient d'en mentionner deux :

1. Le Tribunal de Côme (13 mars 2019) s'est trouvé confronté à un cas de naufrage conjugal particulièrement pénible : une femme, à travers l'action de contestation de paternité, fait établir au juge l'absence de tout lien biologique entre son mari et leur fille. Le Tribunal reconnait cependant que l'homme a toujours joué le rôle de parent social pour la fille, et, en application de l'article 333 du code civil, place l'enfant chez l'homme.
2. Le Tribunal de Milan, dans une décision de 2016 (15 mars 2016), valorise les accords passés entre la mère des enfants et le père social concernant la continuité affective et la présence de ce dernier dans leur parcours d'éducation, afin d'évaluer la nécessité d'adopter les mesures appropriées pour éviter de compromettre l'intérêt des mineurs.

L'idée de régler les relations entre l'enfant et le parent social par la conclusion d'un accord était à la base de la proposition de loi visant l'introduction dans le code civil de la délégation à l'exercice de la responsabilité parentale.[3] Cette délégation aurait dû permettre au partenaire du parent biologique de l'enfant d'assumer les droits et les devoirs que le parent, ou les parents, lui attribuent expressément, sous le contrôle du juge. Le texte concernait tout couple, de sexe différent ou de même sexe, aussi bien que tout adulte de référence. Cette proposition de loi, présentée au Sénat en 2014, n'a pas eu de suite.

La loi ne règle donc pas d'une façon directe et expresse la relation du parent social avec l'enfant ; cependant, elle lui permet d'adopter le mineur, par le biais de l'adoption simple.

L'adoption simple (*adozione in casi particolari*, article 44 et s. de la loi sur l'adoption n. 184 du 1983) est prévue pour des cas particuliers où les conditions pour l'adoption plénière (*adozione piena*, auparavant *adozione legittimante*) ne sont pas réunies. En particulier, il n'est pas nécessaire que l'enfant soit déclaré en état d'abandon et que les adoptants soient mariés : l'adoption simple est ouverte aux individus, aussi bien qu'aux couples non mariés. L'âge de l'adoptant n'a pas d'importance.

Le succès de l'adoption simple réside dans le fait qu'elle ne rompt pas les liens de l'enfant avec sa famille d'origine ; donc, en cas d'une famille recomposée, avec son parent.

La loi règle expressément l'adoption de l'enfant du conjoint (article 44 point b de la loi n. 184 du 1983) et requiert le consentement des parents de l'enfant (article 46 de la loi n. 184 du 1983). En effet, l'enfant peut parfois n'avoir comme parent que le conjoint de l'adoptant. L'autre parent peut être mort ou déchu de sa responsabilité parentale ; ou encore, l'enfant peut ne pas avoir été reconnu. Mais parfois l'enfant a deux parents au moment de l'adoption : dans ce cas, qui sera traité de manière plus détaillée par la suite,[4] le consentement des deux est requis.

La responsabilité parentale exercée par le parent et son conjoint, le parent adoptif, est régie par les dispositions communes (articles 315 et s. du code civil). L'adoption simple peut être révoquée à la demande du Ministère Public pour le non-respect des devoirs incombant à l'adoptant (article 53 de la loi n. 184 du 1983). En cas de séparation et divorce, les dispositions sur le maintien de la biparentalité sont applicables.

Au cas où la séparation se produit quand l'adoption a déjà été prononcée, mais elle n'est pas encore définitive, la Cour de cassation (Cass. 19 novembre 2011, n. 21651) a déclaré que, même si en règle générale l'adoption de l'enfant du conjoint suppose la cohabitation, l'affection et l'harmonie des conjoints, et serait donc à exclure en cas de séparation, il est toujours nécessaire de considérer quel

---

[3] Dessin de loi présenté au Sénat S 1320, XVII.
[4] Voir *infra*, 1.1.2.

est l'intérêt de l'enfant (article 12 de la Convention internationale des droits de l'enfance et article 24 de la Charte Européenne).

L'adoption de l'enfant du conjoint ne concerne que le cas où le beau-parent est marié avec le parent de l'enfant. Cependant, la jurisprudence a ouvert la porte de l'adoption au partenaire qui partage le foyer avec le parent de l'enfant sans être marié avec lui, par l'application de l'article 44 point d de la loi n. 184 du 1983, prévoyant l'adoption simple pour le cas « d'impossibilité vérifiée de placer l'enfant dans une famille en vue d'une future adoption [plénière] ».

Pour ce faire, les juges ont donné de l'article 44 point d de la loi n. 184 du 1983 une interprétation évolutive et inspirée de la constitution.

Selon l'interprétation littérale qu'on en donnait originairement, cet article ne visait que les enfants qui, malgré la déclaration d'abandon, ne pouvaient pas accéder au placement familial en vue de l'adoption plénière pour des différentes raisons, comme par exemple une maladie ou la longue durée de leur séjour à l'orphelinat. Si l'adoption plénière s'avérait impossible, l'article 44 point d de la loi n. 184 du 1983 permettait de songer à une adoption simple par une personne non mariée, ou qui ne remplissait pas les conditions d'âge requises.

La jurisprudence ajoute à cette impossibilité « de fait », l'impossibilité « de droit » : l'enfant ne peut pas être placé parce qu'il se trouve inséré dans un contexte familial et il est impossible d'en déclarer l'abandon. Mieux vaut alors formaliser la relation affective instaurée entre l'enfant et la personne qui s'occupe de lui, sous la forme juridique de l'adoption simple, en garantissant ainsi la continuité de cette relation.

Ce principe, consacré par la Cour constitutionnelle dans son jugement n. 383 du 7 octobre 1999,[5] a été appliqué par le Tribunal des mineurs de Milan à un couple de sexe différent, où l'homme adoptait l'enfant de sa partenaire (n. 626 du 28 mars 2007).

En 2014, pour la première fois le Tribunal des mineurs de Rome applique l'article 44 point d de la loi n. 184 du 1983 à des partenaires de même sexe. Le juge estime que l'adoption ne pourrait pas être limitée aux partenaires de sexe différent, sans contredire la *ratio legis*, qui consiste dans la protection des intérêts de l'enfant, et le principe d'égalité, inscrit dans la constitution et la Convention européenne des droits de l'homme.[6]

1.1.2. *La famille recomposée : La multiplicité de parents ne partageant pas le foyer*

Si la loi italienne ne confère aucune responsabilité ni droit légal au beau-parent par le seul fait de partager le foyer avec le parent de l'enfant, la jurisprudence

---

[5] Ce jugement de la Cour constitutionnelle trouve son origine dans une série de cas où des oncles et des tantes qui s'occupaient de leurs neveux demandaient de les adopter.
[6] Voir *infra*, 1.6.

a toutefois permis de protéger sa relation avec l'enfant contre l'interruption injustifiée provoquée par le parent, à la suite de la fin de sa cohabitation avec le beau-parent.

Pour vérifier quelle est la position du beau-parent par rapport au parent avec qui il ne partage pas le foyer, il est nécessaire de considérer brièvement les relations des deux parents de l'enfant qui ne vivent plus ensemble, ou qui n'ont jamais vécu ensemble. Dans la grande majorité des cas, l'enfant réside avec l'un de ses parents, normalement sa mère, à l'exclusion de l'autre. La résidence alternée est rare.

Mais, même si l'enfant réside avec l'un de ses parents, l'autre n'est pas exclu de l'exercice de la responsabilité parentale. En cas de séparation et de divorce, la garde partagée (*affido condiviso*) est la règle : les deux parents exercent la responsabilité parentale ensemble et de commun accord.

Parfois le juge confie la garde exclusive au parent chez qui l'enfant réside, si ça correspond à l'intérêt de l'enfant. L'autre parent participe aux décisions les plus importantes concernant l'enfant et veille à son éducation et instruction. On parle enfin de *garde super-exclusive* lorsque le parent n'a jamais vécu avec l'enfant ; il s'agit souvent de cas de paternité établie par déclaration judiciaire. Si la garde est *super-exclusive*, le père peut uniquement veiller à l'éducation et instruction de son enfant.

Comme on l'a vu, si la relation entre l'enfant et le beau-parent est significative, elle est protégée, dans le seul intérêt de l'enfant, par le biais de l'article 333 du code civil : le juge peut adopter les mesures de limitation de la responsabilité parentale appropriées au cas d'espèce, si les parents, ou l'un d'entre eux, interrompent la relation de l'enfant avec le beau-parent sans justification.

Il est difficile d'imaginer comment, dans les cas de garde exclusive ou *super-exclusive*, le parent qui ne partage pas le foyer avec l'enfant peut provoquer l'interruption de la relation entre l'enfant et son beau-parent et, par ailleurs, il est difficile d'imaginer une limitation de sa responsabilité parentale, déjà très limitée.

En revanche, en cas de garde partagée, les frictions entre le beau-parent qui partage le foyer avec l'enfant et l'autre parent pourraient rendre nécessaire l'intervention du juge. Mais aucune décision ne peut être mentionnée à cet égard.

Comme on l'a vu, le rôle du beau-parent peut être formalisé à travers l'adoption simple de l'enfant du conjoint ou du partenaire (article 44 points b et d de la loi n. 184 du 1983). Cette adoption est possible même en présence des deux parents de l'enfant.

L'article 46 de la loi n. 184 du 1983 exige comme condition pour l'adoption le consentement des parents de l'enfant à adopter. En cas de refus du consentement par le parent qui exerce la responsabilité parentale, le juge ne peut en aucun cas prononcer l'adoption.

Il faut remarquer qu'en 1983, au moment de la sanction de la loi, en cas de divorce la responsabilité était exercée exclusivement par le parent qui avait la garde de l'enfant. Le juge pouvait donc prononcer l'adoption, s'il estimait le refus de l'autre parent injustifié ou contraire à l'intérêt de l'enfant.

Actuellement, en règle générale, après le divorce la responsabilité parentale reste partagée. La Cour de cassation (Cass. 10 mai 2011, n. 10265) a déclaré que, en vertu du principe de la garde partagée, le refus exprimé par le parent naturel de l'enfant empêche l'adoption simple, même si l'enfant n'a jamais vécu avec lui. Plus récemment, la Cour a précisé que le refus du parent exclut l'adoption, sauf si sa relation effective avec l'enfant a cessé, entrainant une situation de désintégration du contexte familial d'origine (Cass. 16 juillet 2018, ord. n. 18827).

Si les deux parents donnent leur consentement, l'adoption est prononcée. Le lien de l'enfant avec la famille d'origine et, notamment, avec le parent qui ne partage pas le foyer avec l'adoptant, n'est pas pour autant rompu. L'enfant a donc trois parents.

Evidemment le juge pourrait estimer qu'une telle solution est contraire à l'intérêt de l'enfant, en particulier si la garde est partagée entre les deux parents. Mais on n'a pas des décisions sur le point précis.

En supposant donc que l'adoption soit prononcée, il est probable que des contentieux puissent s'en suivre concernant la coordination de la responsabilité parentale des trois parents.

Une possible solution est l'affaiblissement de la responsabilité du parent qui ne partage pas le foyer avec l'enfant et les deux autres parents, en analogie avec une décision assez ancienne de la Cour de cassation (Cass. 30 janvier 1998, n. 978) en matière d'obligation alimentaire (*obbligo di mantenimento*) : l'obligation du père divorcé prend fin au moment de l'adoption. A partir de ce moment, la mère et l'adoptant doivent subvenir aux frais de l'enfant. Mais la fin de l'obligation n'est ni inconditionnelle, ni absolue. Si l'adoptant cesse d'exercer la responsabilité parentale, ou si les obligés principaux n'ont pas de moyens suffisants, l'obligation réapparait. Elle a nature subsidiaire.

Des questions similaires se poseraient en cas de séparation ou divorce de l'adoptant, ou de la fin de son rapport avec le parent de l'enfant qui était son partenaire.

1.2. L'ENFANT ÉLEVÉ DANS PLUS D'UN FOYER

La situation décrite au paragraphe précédent peut doubler lorsque l'enfant est en résidence alternée chez les deux parents qui en ont la garde partagée et chacun des parents partage le foyer avec une personne qui peut être considérée comme un adulte de référence pour l'enfant.

La loi italienne ne règle pas cette situation et il n'existe pas de décisions judiciaires sur ce point.

L'adoption simple n'offre pas la possibilité de formaliser les relations que l'enfant instaure avec les deux beaux parents, puisque l'enfant ne peut être adopté par deux personnes, sauf s'il s'agit d'un couple marié.

1.3. FAMILLE POLYGAME

Il convient d'analyser la question de la polygamie avec référence respectivement aux familles polygames traditionnelles, à structure fixe, et familles polygames ouvertes, à structure libre, ou unions polyamoureuses.

La présence en Italie de familles polygames traditionnelles est liée à l'immigration en provenance de pays qui reconnaissent la polygamie, notamment la polygynie de tradition juridique islamique : l'homme peut avoir jusqu'à quatre femmes en même temps. Il s'agit de relations conjugales juxtaposées, les femmes n'ayant aucun lien juridique entre elles.

Les règles sur le regroupement familial permettent au mari polygame de demander le regroupement d'une seule femme, alors qu'il n'y a pas de restrictions pour les enfants issus des différentes unions. Il peut donc arriver qu'un enfant partage le foyer avec son père et l'épouse de ce dernier. La situation ressemble à celle du beau-parent partageant le foyer avec le parent de l'enfant, qu'on a déjà considéré.[7]

Cependant, on ne connaît aucune décision visant la responsabilité et les droits de la femme bénéficiaire du regroupement familial par rapport à l'enfant de sa coépouse, ni les conflits entre cette femme et la mère de l'enfant restée à l'étranger.

On ne peut pas exclure l'existence de pareils conflits pour autant. Mais le modèle familial inscrit dans les droits des pays d'origine et qui modèle les mentalités rend ces conflits improbables. Le père est le titulaire de l'autorité parentale et, même là où la femme est associée à cette autorité, elle joue un rôle secondaire par rapport à ses propres enfants.

Malgré les règles restrictives sur le regroupement du conjoint, il peut arriver qu'une deuxième femme de l'homme polygame se trouve en Italie, grâce à un titre de séjour différent, ou bien à la suite de son regroupement à ses enfants mineurs, qui vivent déjà en Italie avec leur père et l'autre femme de ce dernier.

Au cas où les deux femmes partagent le même foyer avec leur mari, ce qui n'est pas la solution prônée par les droits de tradition musulmane, il peut en résulter un modèle de foyer à trois parents. Ce modèle n'est pas considéré spécifiquement par la doctrine, ni par les décisions des juges.

Les familles polygames ouvertes se trouvent au centre d'un débat animé par la doctrine juridique, qui en discute à la lumière des principes d'égalité, non-discrimination, respect de la vie familiale et privée, ainsi que de la liberté matrimoniale. L'analyse se focalise sur les relations entre partenaires, alors que le discours sur les enfants nés dans la communauté polyamoureuse est peu développé, au motif qu'il s'estompe dans le contexte plus large de la pluriparentalité.

---

[7] Voir *supra*, 1.1.1.

Par ailleurs, la jurisprudence ne s'est jamais mesurée au défi de la reconnaissance des relations parentales dans un ménage polygamique ouvert.

La seule affaire naissant d'une situation de fait qui pourrait être classée comme polygame a été traité rigoureusement selon le modèle de la biparentalité. Les allégations et les demandes des parties s'adaptent aux moules des catégories juridiques établies, alors que les rapports présentés par le psychologue et le neuropsychiatre jouant le rôle de témoins-experts renvoient à des relations plus complexes.

Le cas a été décidé par le Tribunal des mineurs de Milan et concerne deux enfants d'une femme, qui avait décidé de les avoir d'accord avec sa partenaire. Les deux enfants avaient reçu à la naissance les prénoms des deux femmes, comme deuxième et troisième prénom, dans une sorte de reconnaissance symbolique. Les enfants avaient été conçus grâce à un ami des deux femmes, qui les avait aidées à réaliser leur désir de maternité. Par la suite cet homme avait toujours été présent dans la vie des enfants, avec son partenaire à lui. Un des rapports mentionne une convention à quatre, passée entre les deux femmes avec l'aide du père biologique et du partenaire de ce dernier, pour régler le droit de visite de la mère sociale et sa contribution à l'entretien des enfants.

L'exclusion de la mère sociale des enfants a été à l'origine des procédures qui se sont déroulées devant le Tribunal des mineurs de Milan. Les deux femmes ont défini leurs positions en termes de biparentalité. La mère sociale a demandé la garde partagée des enfants ; la mère légale, afin de nier l'importance de la relation de la demanderesse avec les enfants, insistait sur le rôle joué par le « père » biologique dans leur éducation.

Le Tribunal a rejeté la demande de garde partagée de la demanderesse, qui n'était pas la mère des enfants et donc n'avait pas le droit de la demander (Tribunal des mineurs de Milan, 2 novembre 2007). Mais, en considération des circonstances, et notamment du « contexte confus » dans lequel les enfants étaient insérés, il a transmis le dossier au Ministère Public, afin qu'il demande la déchéance de la responsabilité ou sa limitation, selon l'intérêt des enfants. Cette deuxième procédure sera enfin classée (Tribunal des mineurs de Milan, 29 octobre 2009) et la mère restera la seule responsable des enfants.

1.4. ADOPTION OUVERTE

L'adoption plénière, introduite en Italie par la loi n. 184 du 1983, depuis quelques années connaît une crise importante, due principalement à sa rigidité.

L'adoption plénière se fonde sur la déclaration d'abandon (*dichiarazione di adottabilità*) de l'enfant, auquel les parents font manquer leur assistance morale ou matérielle, sauf si cette situation est due à un cas de force majeure à caractère transitoire (article 8 alinéa 1 de la loi n. 184 du 1983) : l'état d'abandon doit donc être définitif et irréversible pour qu'il y ait l'adoption.

Mais entre l'abandon définitif, qui ouvre la voie de l'adoption, et l'absence temporaire d'un milieu familial adéquat, qui permet le placement familial de l'enfant, des situations intermédiaires existent et se présentent fréquemment. L'adoption, entraînant la rupture tout lien de l'enfant avec la famille d'origine, est une solution trop radicale pour le cas où les parents ne sont pas totalement absents et ont avec l'enfant une relation affective importante, malgré leur incapacité ou discontinuité dans l'œuvre d'éducation.

Ces situations, définies par les praticiens comme des cas de « semi-abandon permanent », rendent nécessaire une solution souple, l'adoption douce (*adozione mite*).

Si la déclaration d'abandon s'avère impossible, parce que l'absence des parents n'est pas totale ni définitive, les juges font alors application des dispositions sur l'adoption simple, et en particulier de l'article 44 point d de la loi n. 184 du 1983, qui ne rompt pas les liens de l'enfant avec sa famille d'origine.

Il est possible ainsi de dépasser un des autres limites de l'adoption plénière, qui n'est ouverte qu'aux couples mariés : l'enfant en état de semi-abandon permanent peut être adopté soit par un couple, marié ou non marié, soit par un individu.

Le recours à l'adoption simple a été suivi à partir de 2003 comme pratique systématique par le Tribunal de Bari. Cette expérience a suscité un vif débat. Les critiques principales tenaient au fait que les juges avaient ainsi transformé une forme d'adoption de nature résiduelle en un instrument ordinaire pour la gestion de cas fréquents de semi-abandon des enfants. On soulignait également le grand pouvoir discrétionnaire laissé aux juges et les difficultés de coordination entre la famille adoptive et la famille d'origine.[8]

Il convient enfin de rappeler un autre cas où l'adoption n'exclut pas le maintien des relations de type familial que l'enfant a développé précédemment. La loi n. 173 du 2015, visant le droit des enfants en placement familial à la continuité affective, prévoit que l'enfant qui est adopté en adoption plénière par une famille autre que la famille qui l'avait accueilli à titre temporaire, peut garder ses relations socio-affectives avec celle-ci. Il en va de même si, après le placement familial, il rentre dans sa famille d'origine.

Des propositions de lois visant l'introduction de l'adoption ouverte ont été présentées, mais sont restées sans suite.[9]

---

[8] L'adoption simple réglée par l'article 44 point d de la loi n. 184 du 1983 est considérée favorablement par la Cour européenne des droits de l'homme (*Zhou v. Italy*, n. 33773/11, ECHR 2014-II), en raison de la possibilité qu'elle offre de garder la relation entre l'enfant et le parent en difficulté.

[9] V. les dessins de loi présentés au Sénat S 3589, XIV et S1007 XV, et à la Chambre des députés, C 5701 XIV et 5724 XIV.

1.5. KAFALA

Pour ce qui est de la *kafala*, on a longuement attendu la ratification et exécution par l'Italie de la Convention de la Haye de 1996 concernant la compétence, la loi applicable, la reconnaissance, l'exécution et la coopération en matière de responsabilité parentale et de mesures de protection des enfants.

Mais lors de la promulgation en 2015 de la loi n. 101 de ratification et exécution, les dispositions relatives spécifiquement à l'exécution de la *kafala* y ont été retirées, pour en approfondir encore l'analyse. Ces dispositions, qui définissaient la *kafala* comme l'assistance légale, morale et matérielle de l'enfant, ainsi que ses soins affectifs, ont été inscrites dans un dessin de loi,[10] qui toutefois n'a pas eu de suite.

Toutes les difficultés liées à la reconnaissance des effets de la *kafala* en Italie restent donc intacts : les juges l'ont parfois reconnue comme adoption simple (article 44 point d de la loi n. 184 du 1983),[11] parfois directement comme décision gracieuse (article 66 de la loi n. 218 du 1995 de droit international privé), ne nécessitant d'aucune mesure d'adaptation interne.[12] La Cour de cassation a reconnu une *kafala* notariale, homologuée par le juge marocain, en considération de l'intérêt de l'enfant (Cass. 24 novembre 2017, n. 28154).

Cependant, la *kafala* n'a été considérée que du point de vue du regroupement familial ou du contournement des normes sur l'adoption internationale. Les juges ne se sont jamais confrontés avec des questions liées à la possible multiparentalité.

1.6. LE DON DES GAMÈTES

A l'origine, la loi n. 40 du 2004 (Dispositions visant la procréation médicalement assistée) interdisait le don de gamètes (article 4 alinéa 3) ; la Cour constitutionnelle a toutefois déclaré cette interdiction illégitime, dans le cas où le couple est atteint d'une maladie qui provoque sa stérilité ou infertilité absolues et irréversibles (C. cost. 9 avril 2014, n. 162).

Aujourd'hui, dans de cas limités, le don de gamètes est donc admis, mais les donneurs doivent rester anonymes et aucune relation légale ne peut s'établir entre eux et les enfants (article 9 alinéa 3 de la loi n. 40 du 2004).

La maternité et la paternité sont établies selon les règles communes, tout en renforçant la protection de l'enfant et la sécurité de ses relations familiales.

Pour ce qui est de la maternité, la mère est la femme qui accouche (article 269 alinéa 3 du code civil) : la règle générale est applicable, en l'absence d'une

---

[10] Dessin de loi S 1552-BIS, XVII.
[11] Tribunal de Trente, 11.03.2002.
[12] Tribunal de Mantoue, 10.05.2018.

disposition de loi spécifique visant le cas de don de gamète femelle. Personne ne peut contester sa maternité, comme le confirme une décision du Tribunal de Rome du 8 août 2014, concernant un cas où, par erreur, l'ovule fécondé d'un couple avait été implanté à une femme différente. En considération de la relation qui s'était établie entre la femme enceinte et l'enfant, de l'idée contemporaine de famille comme lieu de l'affection et de la solidarité réciproque et encore en considération de l'intérêt supérieur de l'enfant à la sécurité de sa position et de son identité, le juge a estimé que le principe de la vérité génétique ne peut pas prévaloir sur les autres intérêts en présence.

Enfin, dans le cas spécifique de procréation médicalement assistée (article 9 alinéa 2 de la loi n. 40 du 2004), la loi interdit à la femme de demander l'anonymat au moment de l'accouchement.

Quant à la paternité, en cas de procréation médicalement assistée avec don de gamètes par un tiers, la loi interdit au mari ou au partenaire ayant donné leur consentement à ce type de procédure les actions par lesquelles le père peut normalement contester sa relation avec l'enfant, en raison de l'absence de lien génétique.

Les limitations posées par la loi à la procréation médicalement assistée avec don de gamètes sont à l'origine du phénomène du tourisme de fertilité, qui regarde les femmes, seules ou en couple. La maternité de la femme seule qui accouche à l'étranger ou en Italie est établie ou reconnue sans problèmes. Il en va différemment pour les couples des femmes.[13]

1.7. L'ENFANT À TROIS PARENTS

La loi sur la procréation médicalement assistée ne contemple pas la technique permettant d'éliminer des mutations qui causent des maladies génétiques graves à travers la correction de l'ADN d'une femme par l'ADN d'une autre femme.

La Cour constitutionnelle (C. cost. 14 mai 2015, n. 96), en déclarant l'illégitimité constitutionnelle des dispositions qui interdisaient le recours à la procréation médicalement assistée aux couple fertiles mais porteurs de maladies génétiques transmissibles, a indiqué qu'elle estimait souhaitable que le législateur identifie les pathologies admissibles.

Seulement à la suite de l'intervention du législateur, la technique pourrait donc devenir praticable en Italie.

Jusqu'à présent, aucun cas d'enfant de trois parents conçus à l'étranger n'a été porté devant les tribunaux.

---

[13] V. *infra*, 1.9.

1.8. GESTATION POUR AUTRUI

La loi italienne sur la procréation médicalement assistée (loi n. 40 du 2004) interdit la gestation pour autrui[14]. L'interdit a contribué à la croissance du tourisme de fertilité en direction de ces pays qui sont les plus libéraux dans la réglementation de cette technique.

En cas de gestation pour autrui réalisée à l'étranger, la jurisprudence reconnaît, sous certaines conditions, la parentalité des parents d'intention. Elle ne s'est pas encore confrontée avec la position de la femme porteuse ou des personnes biologiquement impliquées.

Pour ce qui est des parents d'intention, le problème se pose de l'enregistrement du certificat de naissance dressé à l'étranger, dans un pays où la gestation pour autrui est admise.

La jurisprudence, dans sa diversité, permet de déceler quelques tendances assez claires.

Il faut avant tout distinguer les différents cas de gestation pour autrui, selon que le couple y soit biologiquement impliqué ou pas. Deux sont les cas principaux : l'absence de tout lien biologique entre l'enfant et le couple et l'existence de ce lien entre l'enfant et un seul des membres du couple.

Dans le premier cas, si aucun des membres du couple n'est lié biologiquement à l'enfant, il est légitime de déclarer l'abandon du mineur en vue de son adoption plénière.

En 2014, la Cour de cassation (Cass. 11 novembre 2014, n. 24001) a considéré un tel cas. Le Tribunal des mineurs de Brescia avait entamé la procédure d'adoption d'un enfant, né en Ukraine d'une gestation pour autrui. L'enfant ne résultait lié biologiquement ni au père ni à la mère indiqués dans l'acte de naissance. La Cour confirme que le certificat de naissance était contraire à l'ordre public international, défini comme la limite fixée par l'ordre juridique national à l'entrée de dispositions ou actes étrangers, pour garantir sa propre cohérence interne. L'ordre public international ne se réduit pas aux valeurs partagées par la communauté internationale, mais inclut aussi des principes et des valeurs propres, à condition qu'ils soient fondamentaux et inaliénables. Ces principes sont individués avec référence aux principes, règles et obligations résultants de sources internationales et supranationales.

Par ailleurs, la Cour estime que l'interdiction de la gestation pour autrui n'est pas contraire à l'intérêt supérieur de l'enfant. Cet intérêt est réalisé par l'attribution de la maternité à la femme qui accouche et par le recours à l'adoption, avec les

---

[14] Avant la sanction de la loi n. 40 du 2004, les procédures de procréation médicalement assistée étaient complètement déréglementées et la gestation pour autrui était normalement pratiquée. La position des cours était incertaine, entre l'illicéité (Tribunal de Monza, 27.10.1989) et la validité du contrat de gestation pour autrui (Tribunal de Rome, 27.02.2000), à condition qu'il n'y ait pas de rémunération et que la mère porteuse s'engage à rester en relation avec l'enfant.

garanties procédurales qui lui sont propres, afin de créer une relation parentale dissociée du lien biologique.

L'affaire *Paradiso et Campanelli v. Italie* est bien connue : un couple italien a amené en Italie un enfant né en Russie, à la suite d'un accord de gestation pour autrui. Les autorités italiennes ont refusé la transcription de l'acte de naissance et, après avoir vérifié l'absence de tout lien biologique entre les adultes et l'enfant, ont ordonné le placement familial du mineur, en vue de son adoption. Sur recours du couple (requête 25358/12), la Cour européenne des droits de l'homme a conclu à la violation du droit au respect de la vie privée et familiale (article 8 de la Convention européenne des droits de l'homme).

Mais cette décision a été par la suite renversée par la Grande Chambre. En 2017 le juge, tout en excluant l'existence d'une vie familiale (en raison de l'absence de tout lien biologique entre l'enfant et les parents d'intention, de la courte durée de leur relation et de la précarité juridique des liens entre eux), a reconnu la légitimité de l'ingérence des autorités dans la vie privée des requérants. Une telle ingérence est toutefois prévue par la loi et prévisible ; les autorités ont opéré dans le but légitime de protéger l'enfant, avec la volonté légitime de réaffirmer la compétence exclusive de l'Etat pour reconnaître un lien de filiation uniquement en cas de lien biologique ou d'adoption régulière.

Dans le deuxième cas, quand l'enfant né de gestation pour autrui a un lien avec l'un des deux parents figurant dans le certificat dressé à l'étranger, la parentalité avec l'autre peut s'établir par adoption simple, selon l'article 44 point d de la loi n. 184 du 1983.

Jadis, les refus par les officiers de l'état civil de transcrire les actes dressés à l'étranger à la suite d'une gestation pour autrui recevaient des évaluations différentes par la jurisprudence. Il est intéressant de citer la décision de la Cour d'appel de Bari (13.02.2009) qui en 2009 déclare que les *parental orders* transférant la maternité légale de la mère porteuse à la mère d'intention doivent être transcrits à l'état civil, afin de garantir l'intérêt supérieur de l'enfant, qui est le paramètre pour évaluer si un acte étranger est ou non contraire à l'ordre public international.

Avec une décision de 2019, les Chambres civiles réunies de la Cour de cassation (Cass. 8 mai 2019, n. 12193) ont énoncé ce principe de droit : l'interdiction de la gestation pour autrui posée par la loi (loi n. 40 du 2004) empêche la reconnaissance de la décision étrangère établissant la relation parentale entre le parent d'intention et l'enfant né de gestation pour autrui. Cette interdiction est un principe d'ordre public, puisqu'elle protège des valeurs fondamentales, telles que la dignité humaine de la gestante et l'institution de l'adoption. Le législateur a considéré que ces valeurs priment sur l'intérêt de l'enfant et le juge ne peut pas substituer son appréciation à l'évaluation faite par le législateur. La relation parentale peut toutefois être établie à travers l'adoption simple (article 44 point d de la loi n. 184 du 1983).

A l'origine de cette décision des Chambres réunies il y avait un cas de gestation pour autrui voulue par un couple d'hommes, mais ça n'a pas d'influence.

Le principe énoncé par la Cour de cassation dans cette décision est proche de l'avis consultatif de la Cour européenne des droits de l'homme du 10 avril 2019, relatif à la reconnaissance en droit interne d'un lien de filiation entre un enfant né d'une gestation pour autrui pratiquée à l'étranger et la mère d'intention : le droit au respect de la vie privé de l'enfant (article 8 de la Convention européenne des droits de l'homme) ne requiert pas que la reconnaissance se fasse per la transcription sur les registres de l'état civil de l'acte de naissance dressé à l'étranger : elle peut se faire par une autre voie, telle que l'adoption de l'enfant par la mère d'intention, pourvu que les modalités prévues garantissent l'effectivité et la célérité de la mise en œuvre, conformément à l'intérêt supérieur de l'enfant.

La décision des Chambres réunies de la Cour de cassation et l'avis de la Cour européenne des droits de l'homme ne sont cependant pas parfaitement congruents : alors que l'adoption est préconisée par la Cour européenne des droits de l'homme comme une voie alternative et équivalente à la transcription de l'acte étranger, l'adoption simple indiquée par la Cour de cassation a des effets beaucoup plus limités que la transcription. En particulier, elle n'établit pas de relation de famille entre l'enfant et les proches de l'adoptant.

En effet l'interprétation des Chambres réunies de la Cour de cassation, en tant que droit vivant, n'a pas pleinement convaincu la Première Chambre civile de la même Cour qui, peu de temps après, saisit la Cour constitutionnelle. Encore une fois, les faits concernent un couple homosexuel, mais la Cour précise que ça n'a pas d'importance dans sa décision.

La Cour constitutionnelle (C. cost. 28 janvier 2021, n. 33) déclare qu'il est indubitable que l'enfant, pris en charge pendant des années depuis sa la naissance par le couple qui a partagé la décision de le mettre au monde, a intérêt à ce que la réalité des faits soit reconnue par le droit. Mais cet intérêt de l'enfant ne prime pas automatiquement sur tout autre intérêt. La mise en balance des différents intérêts s'impose. Dans ce cas, l'intérêt de l'enfant doit être balancé avec l'intérêt de l'État à décourager une pratique qu'il considère passible de sanction pénale.

Une solution qui niait toute possibilité pour l'enfant de voir reconnue sa relation avec les deux membres du couple ne serait pas équilibrée. Mais toute autre solution est compatible avec la constitution. Le choix de la solution incombe en premier lieu au législateur, qui jouit d'une large marge d'appréciation lui permettant de balancer tous les droits et les principes en jeu. Pour l'instant, la Cour cède le pas au législateur, sans pour autant renoncer à dénoncer comme insuffisante la protection assurée à l'intérêt de l'enfant par l'adoption simple.

A côté de ces deux cas principaux, un troisième cas existe, lorsque l'enfant né de gestation pour autrui est lié biologiquement aux deux parents d'intention, la mère d'intention étant aussi la mère biologique de l'enfant, même si elle n'accouche pas. La seule décision publiée à ce propos est celle du Tribunal de Agrigente du 6 avril 2017, qui admet la transcription de l'acte étranger même pour la part concernant la mère intentionnelle. Le principe énoncé par les Chambres réunies de la Cour de cassation de 2019 ne s'appliquerait pas, pour l'impossibilité d'adopter l'enfant biologique.

Enfin, si à la fin de la gestation pour autrui l'accouchement s'accomplit en Italie, la mère porteuse est considérée comme la mère légale de l'enfant à condition qu'elle le reconnaisse comme le sien, dans le cas où elle n'est pas mariée (article 250 du code civil). Si elle est mariée, elle peut déclarer que le mari n'est pas le père de l'enfant. Si la femme qui a accouché cède l'enfant, même sans contrepartie, elle est condamnée pour violation des règles sur l'adoption (article 71 de la loi n. 184 du 1983) (Cass. 17.01.2019, n. 2173).

En ce qui concerne le père, le père d'intention peut reconnaître l'enfant comme le sien aux conditions posées par les articles 250 et s. du code civil.

Reste ouverte à la mère d'intention l'adoption simple de l'enfant (article 44 points b ou d de la loi n. 184 du 1983).

1.9. PARTIES IMPLIQUÉES DANS UNE RELATION DE MÊME SEXE

Les règles sur les parents sociales sont indifférentes au type de relations, de même sexe ou hétérosexuelles, dans lesquelles les parties sont impliquées. Par contre, lorsque les techniques de procréation médicalement assistée (PMA) sont en jeu, la situation change, en particulier pour les couples d'hommes.

Lorsque les techniques de PMA sont en jeu, la situation change, en particulier pour les couples d'hommes pour lesquels la maternité de substitution est obligatoire – sauf dans les cas où elle recoupe des interdictions.

1.9.1. *Les relations de même sexe et la multiplicité de la parentalité*

Lorsque le beau-parent partage le foyer avec le parent de l'enfant, les solutions développées par la jurisprudence pour protéger l'intérêt de l'enfant au maintien de sa relation avec le parent social sont généralement indifférentes au sexe du couple parent/parent social.

La possibilité pour le juge d'adopter les mesures appropriées prévues par l'article 333 du code civil dans l'intérêt de l'enfant a été consacrée par la Cour constitutionnelle par rapport à un couple de femmes (C. cost. 20 octobre 2016, n. 225).

Pour ce qui est de l'adoption simple, on a vu que deux solutions sont possibles : l'adoption de l'enfant du conjoint (article 44 point b de la loi n. 184 du 1983) et l'adoption pour le cas « d'impossibilité vérifiée de placer l'enfant dans une famille en vue d'une future adoption » (article 44 point d de la loi n. 184 du 1983). Le mariage étant réservé aux couples de sexe différent, la règle sur l'adoption de l'enfant du conjoint n'est pas applicable aux parties impliquées dans une relation de même sexe. En revanche, l'autre hypothèse d'adoption simple peut être appliquée quel que soit le sexe des deux personnes qui partagent le foyer.

Il faut souligner qu'en 2016 la loi a introduit l'union civile (loi n. 76 du 2016), réservée aux couples de même sexe. L'union civile est soumise à toute disposition contenant les mots « mariage » et « conjoint/s », à quelques exceptions près : parmi les plus remarquables, les dispositions de la loi n. 184 du 1983 sur l'adoption, « sauf ce qui était déjà prévu et admis en matière d'adoption » (article 1 alinéa 20 de la loi n. 76 du 2016). Cette expression embrouillée signifie que les couples de même sexe restent exclus de l'adoption plénière, mais peuvent adopter selon l'article 44 point d de la loi n. 184 du 1983.

L'exclusion des couples de même sexe de l'adoption plénière n'est toutefois pas considérée comme un obstacle d'ordre public international qui empêche la reconnaissance des actes étrangers, selon une décision récente des Chambres réunies de la Cour de cassation (Cass. 31 mars 2021, n. 9006). La seule condition pour la reconnaissance de l'acte étranger est que l'on puisse exclure que le fondement de la filiation adoptive soit un accord de gestation pour autrui. Cette condition était remplie dans le cas d'espèce, l'acte étranger étant une *adoption order* de New York, fondé sur le consentement du *birth father* et de la *birth mother* et sur l'évaluation concrète du *best interest of the child*.

Mais revenant au thème de l'adoption simple, qui reste la seule forme d'adoption ouverte aux couples de même sexe en Italie, il convient de rappeler que ces couples, qu'ils aient ou non formalisé leur union, peuvent utiliser uniquement l'article 44 point d de la loi n. 184 du 1983 ; alors qu'une différence existe pour les couples de sexe différent, selon qu'ils soient mariés (article 44 point b de la loi n. 184 du 1983), ou qu'il n'aient pas formalisé leur union (article 44 point d de la loi n. 184 du 1983).

Pour ce qui est de la position du parent qui ne partage pas le foyer avec l'enfant, le sexe des parties impliquées dans les relations n'a aucune importance. Cela vaut également pour les cas des enfants élevés dans plus d'un foyer : l'absence totale de réglementation légale reste la même, quel que soit le sexe des parties impliquées.

1.9.2. Polygamie

La polygamie traditionnelle n'admet pas les relations de même sexe, alors que dans la polygamie ouverte ou moderne le sexe des personnes impliquées est indifférent. Rien ne peut être ajouté à ce qu'on lit *supra*, 1.3.

1.9.3. Adoption ouverte

L'adoption douce (*adozione mite*), réalisée en cas de semi-abandon permanent de l'enfant, établit la relation parentale de l'enfant avec les parents adoptifs, sans pour autant rompre sa relation avec les parents originaires (article 44 point d de la loi n. 184 du 1983). La couple de parents originaires peut bien être de même sexe.

Quant au parent/s adoptif/s, comme on l'a dit, l'adoption simple permet de dépasser la limite de l'adoption plénière, qui n'est ouverte qu'aux couples mariés :

l'enfant en état de semi-abandon permanent peut être adopté soit par un couple, marié ou non marié, soit par un individu.

Rien ne s'oppose donc à ce que l'adoptant ou le couple d'adoptants soient impliqués dans une relation de même sexe, si le juge estime que ça correspond, dans les circonstances concrètes, à l'intérêt supérieur de l'enfant et le réalise au mieux. Jusqu'à présent, aucune décision déclarant une telle adoption n'a été publiée.

On peut toutefois mentionner des cas de placement familial temporaire chez des couples de même sexe (Tribunal des mineurs de Bologne, 31 octobre 2013 ; Tribunal des mineurs de Palerme, 4 décembre 2013).

1.9.4. Kafala

Les lois de certains pays permettent le recueil légal (*kafala*) de l'enfant par un individu. Cependant, dans l'expérience italienne, on ne connaît pas de cas où le *kafil* soit impliqué dans une relation de même sexe. Le recueil légal par un couple de même sexe, quant à lui, est n'est pas prévu par les lois des pays qui réglementent la *kafala*.

1.9.5. *Procréation médicalement assistée*

La loi italienne exclut de l'accès aux procédures admises de procréation médicalement assistée les individus, aussi bien que les couples de même sexe : seules les couples de sexe différent, mariés ou non mariés, peuvent y accéder (article 5 de la loi n. 40 du 2004).

La Cour constitutionnelle (C. cost. 23 octobre 2019, n. 221) ne considère pas l'exclusion des couples de même sexe de ces procédures comme discriminatoire, puisqu'elle découle en effet des deux idées directrices à la base de la loi de 2004 : l'accès à la procréation médicalement assistée est uniquement destiné à des fins médicales et limité à la « famille naturelle », formée d'un père et d'une mère. Le choix de ces idées directrices, n'excédant pas la liberté d'appréciation du législateur, est conforme à la constitution, quoique non imposé par elle.

Les personnes impliquées dans des relations de même sexe doivent par conséquent se rendre à l'étranger pour avoir accès à ces techniques de procréation médicalement assistée, qui leur sont nécessaires pour avoir des enfants.

Il faut distinguer selon le sexe du couple. Les couples d'hommes ont recours à la gestation pour autrui. Les couples de femmes, sans exclure la gestation pour autrui, utilisent normalement le don de gamètes.

Tout ce qu'on a écrit à propos de la gestation pour autrui,[15] et plus particulièrement à propos de la reconnaissance des actes de naissance dressés à l'étranger, vaut quel que soit le sexe des parents d'intention impliqués.

---

[15] V. *supra*, 1.8.

Pour ce qui est des enfants nés grâce au don de gamètes mâles, comme on l'a vu *supra*, 1.6, la femme qui accouche est considérée la mère de l'enfant. L'autre femme du couple peut adopter l'enfant avec l'adoption simple, réglée par l'article 44 point d de la loi n. 184 du 1983.[16] La solution, adoptée par les juges romains (Tribunal des mineurs de Rome, 30 juillet 2014 et Cour d'appel de Rome, 23 décembre 2015) dans le cas d'un couple de femmes qui s'étaient rendues en Espagne pour l'insémination artificielle, a été confirmée par la Cour de cassation (Cass. 22 juin 2016, n. 12962). La Cour a, d'un côté, réitéré la possibilité d'adoption simple en cas d'absence de déclaration d'abandon, de l'autre, elle a confirmé que l'adoption simple ne pourrait être limitée aux partenaires de sexe différent, sans contredire la *ratio legis*, qui consiste dans la protection de l'intérêt supérieur de l'enfant, et les principes d'égalité et de non-discrimination inscrits dans la constitution et la Convention européenne des droits de l'homme.

Toutefois, si les circonstances de fait ne permettent pas le recours à l'adoption simple, les intérêts en jeu restent dépourvus de toute protection. C'est le cas d'un couple de femmes qui décident de commun accord le recours à la procréation médicalement assistée, de laquelle viennent au monde deux jumelles. Les deux femmes sont impliquées dans l'entretient et l'éducation des enfants pendant près de cinq ans, jusqu'à rupture, en 2017, de leur relation. A ce point, la femme qui a accouché les jumelles et les a reconnues à la naissance refuse son consentement à l'adoption simple, qui est requis par la loi, et exclut l'autre femme de toute relation avec les enfants.

Le Tribunal de Padoue, en constatant l'absence de toute protection pour l'intérêt des mineurs au maintien de leur relation avec leur mère d'intention, soulève la question auprès de la Cour constitutionnelle. La Cour constitutionnelle (C. cost. 28 janvier 2021, n. 32) reconnait que les enfants nés de la procréation médicalement assistée pratiquée par deux femmes jouissent de moins de protection que les autres enfants, uniquement en raison du sexe des personnes qui ont partagé le projet procréatif. Cependant, la Cour constitutionnelle estime ne pas pouvoir intervenir avec une déclaration d'inconstitutionnalité des dispositions de loi spécifiques, ce qui risquerait de déséquilibrer l'ensemble du système. Elle cède donc le pas au législateur, pour qu'il choisisse les moyens pour réaliser un but qui est imposé par la constitution. En même temps, elle déclare que la persistance de l'inertie législative serait intolérable, et arrive à suggérer expressément des possibles solutions (l'introduction d'un nouveau type d'adoption ou la réforme des prescriptions réglant la reconnaissance des enfants).[17]

---

[16] V. *supra*, 1.9.1.
[17] La Cour constitutionnelle avait déjà évoqué l'opportunité d'une intervention du législateur pour renforcer la protection du lien entre l'enfant et la mère d'intention dans sa décision du 04.11.2020, n. 230.

Entre-temps, en 2016, la loi (loi n. 76 du 2016) a introduit *l'union civile*, qui offre la reconnaissance légale aux couples de même sexe. Cette loi ne contient aucune disposition concernant la filiation, à l'exclusion de l'interdiction de l'adoption plénière.

Ce vide juridique en matière de filiation crée de l'incertitude dans les services de l'état civil. A partir du printemps 2018, dans un certain nombre de villes italiennes, les maires ont commencé à enregistrer systématiquement les naissances des enfants, en reconnaissant la biparentalité aux couples de même sexe, qu'il s'agisse de transcrire un acte de naissance étranger, ou d'en dresser un pour un enfant né dans la commune. Ils réclament ainsi l'intervention du législateur.

Milan est l'une des villes dont les maires adoptent une attitude d'ouverture envers l'enregistrement des enfants des couples de même sexe. Mais ces pratiques administratives ne sont pas uniformément adoptées à travers le pays, ce qui entraine plusieurs actions en justice, qui arrivent jusqu'à la Cour constitutionnelle.

Il convient de distinguer les cas où le couple de même sexe qui demande l'enregistrement de la naissance ou la reconnaissance de l'acte formé à l'étranger est formé de deux hommes ou de deux femmes.

Pour ce qui est des couples d'hommes, les incertitudes émergent en raison du recours à la gestation pour autrui, qui est dans des pareils cas fort probable.[18] Et c'est précisément le refus de l'officier de l'état civil de Milan d'enregistrer l'enfant de deux hommes qui est à l'origine de la décision des Chambres réunies de la Cour de cassation du 8 mai 2019, n. 12193.[19] Cet arrêt identifie dans la contrariété à l'ordre public de la gestation pour autrui l'obstacle incontournable à la reconnaissance de la relation entre l'enfant et le parent d'intention.

L'intérêt de l'Etat à dissuader les personnes de se rendre à l'étranger pour recourir à une pratique qu'il considère passible de sanction pénale est considéré légitime par la Cour constitutionnelle, qui toutefois invite le législateur à le balancer avec l'intérêt de l'enfant à la reconnaissance du statut d'enfant qu'il jouit à l'étranger (C. cost. 28 janvier 2021, n. 33).

Pour ce qui est des couples de femmes, en principe elles ont recours à la procréation avec don de gamètes, qui ne se heurte pas avec l'ordre public et la prohibition de gestation pour autrui. Toutefois, puisqu'en Italie la procréation avec don de gamètes n'est pas accessible aux couples de même sexe, les femmes doivent se rendre à l'étranger pour la pratiquer.

La naissance de l'enfant, au contraire, peut avoir lieu tant à l'étranger qu'en Italie. Il convient de distinguer ces deux circonstances, pour en analyser les effets.

---

[18] Il convient pourtant de rappeler l'exception constitué par l'adoption plénière à l'étranger qui a été à l'origine de la décision des Chambres réunies (Cass. 31.03.2021, n. 9006). V. *supra*, 1.9.1.
[19] V. *supra*, 1.8.

La Cour de cassation a admis la transcription de l'acte de naissance étranger de l'enfant de deux mères en 2016. Cet arrêt (Cass. 21 juin 2016, n. 19599) concerne toutefois un cas particulier : l'enfant est lié biologiquement avec une femme, qui l'a porté, et génétiquement avec l'autre, qui a donné son ovule. La Cour de cassation déclare que la règle selon laquelle la mère est la femme qui accouche (article 269 alinéa 3 du code civil) n'est pas d'ordre public, reconnaissant que la femme qui donne son ovule est, elle aussi, mère.

Par la suite, la Cour de cassation (Cass. 15 juin 2017, n. 14878) a élargi la possibilité de transcription de l'acte de naissance étranger au cas d'un enfant de deux mères, dont une seule était liée biologiquement et génétiquement à l'enfant. L'acte de naissance étranger n'est pas contraire à l'ordre public et sa reconnaissance correspond à l'intérêt de l'enfant à maintenir sa relation familiale avec les deux femmes, et au droit du couple à ne pas être discriminé quant à son droit à la vie familiale.

Si la naissance a lieu en Italie, la Cour de cassation approuve le refus des officiers de l'Etat civil de dresser des actes de naissances avec l'indication de deux mères. Contrairement que dans la reconnaissance d'actes étrangers, il n'y pas la nécessité de protéger le droit à la conservation et continuité du statut de filiation, ni de garantir la circulation internationale des actes. A la suite de la reconnaissance, l'acte ne cesse pas d'être étranger par rapport à l'ordre juridique italien ; il y produit simplement ses effets. L'acte dressé en Italie au contraire doit respecter les dispositions impératives, qui constituent l'ordre public interne.[20] Les conclusions de la Cour de cassation valent autant pour les couples en cohabitation (Cass. 3 avril 2020, n. 7668) que pour les couples en union civile (Cass. 22 avril 2020, n. 8029).

Quand la question arrive enfin à la Cour constitutionnelle (C. cost. 4 novembre 2020, n. 230), celle-ci ne déclare pas l'inconstitutionnalité des dispositions dont la Cour de cassation a fait l'application. La Cour admet que la constitution n'impose pas de reconnaître l'homoparentalité de deux femmes en union civile, mais en même temps affirme qu'elle ne l'exclut pas non plus. Le choix est remis au législateur qui, en tant qu'interprète de la volonté générale, balance les différentes valeurs en jeu, en fonctions des aspirations de la société. Le changement ne peut pas s'accomplir par une décision de la Cour.

Il est évident que, malgré l'inertie du législateur, les règles de droit applicables sont en pleine évolution. Le changement introduit par les nouvelles réalités familiales est principalement secondé par la jurisprudence. Mais les limites de l'action des juges sont mises en évidence par les plus récentes décisions de la Cour constitutionnelle, qui appelle le législateur à intervenir.

---

[20] La Cour constitutionnelle (C. cost. 237/2019 21.10.2019) a eu l'occasion de déclarer que les dispositions de loi qui empêchent la formation en Italie d'un acte de naissance avec l'indication de deux mères, malgré le fait que la loi nationale de l'enfant le permettrait, ne sont pas contraires à la constitution parce que les dispositions sur la filiation sont loi de police.

1.9.6. Une loi sur la multiparentalité ?

Le thème de la multiparentalité ne s'est pas encore imposé en tant que tel. Aucun projet de loi n'existe visant la multiparentalité au sens large et il semble peu probable qu'il soit introduit prochainement.

2. DIVERSITÉ ET PLURALITÉ DES FONCTIONS DE LA FAMILLE

Le changement qui a affecté les formes de la famille ne touche pas à ses fonctions.

La loi italienne reconnaît parmi les fonctions de la famille la procréation et l'éducation des enfants, la protection des personnes vulnérables, la sécurité économique et l'accomplissement des fonctions de soin. Mais chaque fonction peut impliquer une notion de famille différente.

Si on prend en considération la procréation, la loi italienne confie cette fonction au couple de sexe différent, alors que la jurisprudence est ouverte aux couples de même sexe aussi. Mais la dimension du couple reste incontestée.

L'éducation des enfants et les fonctions de soins sont des fonctions réglées par la loi avec référence à la famille nucléaire, avec le possible soutien des grands-parents (article 316 *bis* du code civil). Mais le parent peut être aussi isolé. Si les parents manquent complètement, la notion de famille peut s'élargir : c'est le cas de la préférence faite aux proches pour l'adoption simple de l'orphelin. D'autre part, dans l'intérêt de l'enfant, la loi reconnaît que cette famille « éducatrice » peut s'élargir jusqu'à comprendre des personnes sans aucun lien de parenté avec lui, mais avec lesquelles il a une relation affective importante.

Les fonctions de nature économique sont plus intenses dans la famille nucléaire (entretien, pension alimentaire, succession nécessaire), mais elles peuvent atteindre aussi des parents assez éloignés (obligations alimentaires, succession légitime).

La loi italienne ne donne aucune définition de famille. La plupart de ses dispositions visent la famille en tant famille nucléaire, formée du couple et des enfants mineurs ; mais il ne manque pas de dispositions sur les partenaires dans le couple, sur les familles incluant des enfants majeurs, ou des personnes âgées ou handicapées ; et enfin sur la famille au sens large, composée de plusieurs générations.

Pour ce qui est de la famille nucléaire, la constitution, à l'article 29, « reconnaît les droits de la famille en tant que société naturelle fondée sur le mariage ». Ce lien étroit famille et mariage a une valeur historique, mais il est désormais dépourvu d'une vraie force prescriptive. Les décisions de la Cour constitutionnelle reflètent l'image de la famille en tant que l'une des formations sociales où l'individu exerce sa personnalité (article 2 constitution), dans le respect de l'égalité des citoyens devant la loi (article 3 constitution). La Cour de cassation fait une référence constante à la jurisprudence de la Cour européenne des droits de l'homme, à la Charte des droits fondamentaux de l'Union Européenne et aux conceptions de famille qui y sont retenues.

Il n'en reste pas moins qu'on retrouve parfois un traitement différencié des couples, selon le sexe des partenaires et la formalisation ou absence de formalisation de l'union.

Le couple marié est le seul couple ayant accès à l'adoption plénière (loi n. 184 du 1983). Seuls les couples de sexe différent, mariés ou non mariés, sont admis par la loi aux techniques de procréation médicalement assistée, à l'exclusion des individus et des couples de même sexe.

L'union civile (loi n. 76 du 2016) ouvre aux couples de même sexe le même statut prévu pour les conjoints dans le mariage, à quelques exceptions près : si les partenaires dans l'union civile ont l'obligation d'assistance morale et matérielle, ils n'ont pas celle de collaborer dans l'intérêt de la famille, ni d'être réciproquement fidèles (v. article 1 alinéa 11 de la loi n. 76 du 2016 comparé avec l'article article 143 du code civil) ; aucune mention n'est faite à la nécessité de prendre en considération les exigences prééminentes de la famille dans la direction de la vie familiale (v. article 1 alinéa 12 de la loi n. 76 du 2016 comparé avec l'article 144 du code civil). Ces différences ont une nature idéologique et sont dépourvues de toute retombée opérationnelle.

Mais lorsqu'on considère les enfants, une fois la filiation établie, aucune différence ni discrimination n'est possible selon le type de relation qui lie, ou ne lie pas, les deux parents, quel que soit leur sexe ou la modalité de procréation. La loi italienne ne prend en considération d'une façon expresse que deux parents, même si, comme on l'a vu, par l'application des dispositions sur l'adoption simple, les parents peuvent être trois, ou parfois quatre.

L'enfant a le droit de grandir dans sa famille (article 315 bis du code civil, article 1 de la loi n. 184 du 1983) ; les parents ont le devoir, mais aussi le droit, d'élever leurs enfants, les éduquer et les assister moralement, dans le respect de leurs capacités, inclinations et aspirations (article 30 constitution ; article 315 bis du code civil). L'éducation inclut, après les toutes premières années, la fréquentation de l'école : si les parents omettent de faire fréquenter aux enfants l'école primaire, ils sont passibles d'une amende (article 731 du code pénal) et, ce qui est plus grave, ils peuvent être déchus de leur responsabilité parentale. Les parents doivent soutenir les coûts de l'éducation des enfants, ce qui n'est qu'un aspect de la plus générale obligation de les entretenir (article 30 de la constitution ; article 315 du code civil). Cette obligation ne prend sa fin qu'avec l'indépendance économique des enfants.

Les dispositions visant les obligations d'entretien des mineurs assument de l'importance réelle si l'un des parents n'a jamais vécu avec l'enfant, ou bien au moment où le couple se dissout. Avant ce moment, la vie familiale est caractérisée par la solidarité et la gratuité et par l'obligation naturelle d'entraide. Si le couple était marié ou en union civile, l'obligation d'assistance matérielle entre partenaires survit au divorce sous la forme de pension alimentaire (*assegno di divorzio*) en faveur du partenaire qui n'a pas de moyens adéquats.

Les violations les plus graves des obligations d'assistance familiales sont punies par la loi pénale (article 570 du code pénal).

Lorsque les parents ne respectent pas leurs obligations envers leurs enfants, le Tribunal peut en ordonner la déchéance de la responsabilité parentale (article 330 du code civil), ou, dans des cas moins graves, la limiter (article 333 du code civil). Si l'enfant se trouve dans un état d'abandon moral et matériel complet et irréversible, il peut être adopté (de la loi n. 184 du 1983). Toutes ces mesures n'ont pas la fonction de sanctionner les parents, mais exclusivement de protéger l'enfant.

La famille joue un rôle important comme dispensatrice de soins aux enfants, aux personnes âgées et handicapées. Sa contribution au bien-être général est d'autant plus importante que les services publics sont gravement insuffisants. Les soins aux personnes sont pourvus en grande partie par les femmes, ce qui a un impact sur leurs activités rémunérées.

Pour ce qui est spécifiquement des personnes handicapées, leur protection au moment du divorce de leurs parents est modelée sur celle prévue pour les mineurs. En cas d'absence de parents, l'assistance aux personnes handicapées est réglée par la loi n. 112 du 2016. Un soutien limité à la famille de la personne handicapée est prévu par la loi 114 du 1992, visant l'assistance, l'intégration sociale et les droits de la personne handicapée.

La loi considère parfois des relations familiales élargies, qui dépassent celles de la famille nucléaire. Avant 2012, seule la filiation légitime ou l'adoption plénière fondaient le lien entre l'enfant et ses proches ; la loi n. 219 du 2012 a aboli la discrimination à cet égard des enfants nés hors mariage.

Parmi les proches, une position particulière est celle des grands-parents. Si l'enfant a le droit de maintenir une relation significative avec tous ses proches (article 315 *bis* du code civil), les seuls proches qui aient le droit de maintenir une telle relation avec lui sont ses grands-parents (article 317 *bis* du code civil). Ce droit s'accompagne à leur implication dans l'obligation d'entretien, qui fait partie de la responsabilité parentale. Si les parents en n'ont pas les moyens, les grands-parents doivent leur fournir les ressources nécessaires pour remplir leurs obligations envers les enfants (article 316 *bis* du code civil). Il faut distinguer cette obligation de l'obligation alimentaire directement due aux descendants, même majeurs, en état de détresse.

Les obligations alimentaires sont par ailleurs l'un des aspects du droit familial qui font ressortir la pertinence de la famille élargie (articles 433 et s. du code civil) ; mais elles ne sont pas le plus important de ces aspects. Il suffit de considérer par exemple que, si l'enfant est orphelin, la présence d'un proche jusqu'au quatrième degré, disponible et capable de s'occuper de lui, exclut l'état d'abandon et donc l'adoption plénière. L'enfant pourra être donné en adoption simple à ce parent, ou lui être confié en garde, selon ce que le juge estime être l'intérêt du mineur.

La famille joue un rôle important dans la protection des sujets faibles, non seulement avec les obligations alimentaires, mais aussi en cas de nomination d'un administrateur de soutien : la loi indique comme choix préféré le conjoint, ou le partenaire, en union civile ou libre, les parents, l'enfant, les frères et sœurs et les parents jusqu'au quatrième degré (article 408 alinéa 1 du code civil). La loi ne fait que formaliser ce qu'il arrive normalement dans la réalité, avec le choix de la personne mieux en mesure d'assister le sujet à autonomie réduite. Les mêmes critères règlent le choix du tuteur en cas d'interdiction (articles 414 et s. du code civil).

Une autre fonction de la famille est enfin celle de la transmission de la richesse. Si le défunt n'a pas laissé de dispositions de dernière volonté, le conjoint ou le partenaire en union civile et les proches jusqu'au sixième degré sont les héritiers légitimes, dans l'ordre et respect des règles établis par la loi. Si le défunt rédige un testament, il doit le faire dans le respect des droits des réservataires : le conjoint ou le partenaire en union civile, les descendants et les ascendants.

Après la grande réforme de 1975, qui a aligné les dispositions réglant les relations familiales au principe d'égalité consacré par la constitution républicaine, le législateur est intervenu d'une façon fragmentaire et souvent tardive. La jurisprudence a joué un rôle important, surtout dans l'adéquation du droit interne aux principes de la Convention européenne des droits de l'homme et de la Charte des droits fondamentaux de l'Union Européenne. Mais le rôle de suppléance des cours trouve nécessairement des limites. En particulier, les juges ne peuvent pas faire de choix politiques, en décidant par exemple quelles sont les fonctions de la famille à favoriser ou à développer.

LEGAL PARENTHOOD IN DIVERSE FAMILIES IN JAPAN

A Patchwork Approach to Diversity

Maia Roots

1. Introduction 344
2. Part A. Diversity and Plurality of Family Forms 344
   2.1. Recognition of Multiple Parents if a Child is Raised in More than One Household 344
       2.1.1. Parental Authority and (Physical) Custody 345
       2.1.2. Separation of (Physical) Custody from Parental Authority 345
       2.1.3. Disagreement between Parents Concerning the Exercise of Parental Authority/(Physical) Custody 347
       2.1.4. Current Legislative Debate Concerning Joint Custody 348
       2.1.5. The Right to Contact and Child Support Obligations of Parents 348
   2.2. Open Adoption 349
       2.2.1. Brief Overview of Adoption in Japanese Law 349
       2.2.2. Legal Rights and Responsibilities of Parents in Open Adoption 350
       2.2.3. Potential Clashes between Biological and Adoptive Parents ... 351
   2.3. Step-Families 351
       2.3.1. Legal Standing of a Step-Parent who has not Adopted their Step-Child 352
       2.3.2. Where the Step-Parent has Adopted the Step-Child via Open Adoption 352
       2.3.3. The Legal Standing of the Non-Residential Biological Parent 353
   2.4. Children Born as a Result of Donor-Assisted Reproductive Technology 356
       2.4.1. Introduction 356
       2.4.2. Parenthood, Rights, and Obligations of the Birth Mother, Her Spouse/Partner, and the Donor(s) 359

    2.4.2.1. Under the 2020 ART Act 359
    2.4.2.2. Prior to the 2020 ART Act 359
    2.4.2.3. The Position of the Common-Law Partner
        of the Mother 360
   2.4.3. The Legal Standing of Donors......................... 362
  2.5. Surrogacy.. 363
   2.5.1. Parenthood of the Surrogate 364
   2.5.2. The Biological Parents 365
  2.6. Children Raised by Same-Sex Couples 366
3. Part B. Diversity and Plurality of Family Functions................... 366
  3.1. Legal Recognition of Various Family Functions 366
   3.1.1. Raising Children 366
   3.1.2. Providing Economic Security 367
   3.1.3. Protecting the Vulnerable 367
   3.1.4. Care Functions: Care for the Elderly 369
  3.2. Functions which are Predominantly Favoured 369

1. INTRODUCTION

The first part of this report gives an overview of diversity and plurality of parenthood in Japanese family law. The scenarios relevant to Japanese law are multiple parenthood following the separation/divorce of a child's parents, in the case of open adoption, in step-families, and children born as a result of artificial reproductive technologies, including surrogacy.[1] The report also touches very briefly on parenthood of same-sex couples. It should be noted at the start that Japanese law does not regulate multi-parenthood in a generic or broad manner. The second part of this report is concerned with family functions in Japan, in particular the functions recognised and enforced by family law.

2. PART A. DIVERSITY AND PLURALITY OF FAMILY FORMS

2.1. RECOGNITION OF MULTIPLE PARENTS IF A CHILD IS RAISED IN MORE THAN ONE HOUSEHOLD

This section will focus on the multiplicity of parenthood following the separation/divorce of the parents, and of non-marital children.

---

[1] Polygamous families, *kafala*, and so-called three-parent children are excluded from this report as they are not relevant in Japanese family law.

2.1.1. Parental Authority and (Physical) Custody

Parental authority (*shinken*)[2] is understood to be composed of the following two main components: (1) the rights and duties related to the day-to-day care and education of the (minor) child, also called '(physical) custody' (*kango* or *shinjou kango*);[3] and (2) the right to administer the property of the child.[4]

Japanese law only allows for joint parental authority during the (formal) marriage of the parents.[5] Divorced parents and common-law spouses cannot have joint parental authority in relation to their child(ren). After the divorce of the parents, the parents can either agree between themselves who will have sole parental authority, or, if they cannot reach an agreement, the family court will decide.[6] When the parents are separated but not yet formally divorced, they will continue to have joint parental authority. Where a child is born to a mother who is not married (including a mother living with her common-law spouse), the mother will have sole parental authority by default. Parental authority can be transferred to the man who has recognised paternity, if the parties agree that the father should have parental authority.[7] In this case, the father will have sole parental authority.

2.1.2. Separation of (Physical) Custody from Parental Authority

On the surface, Japanese law seems to have adopted a very clear-cut system, where only married couples can have joint parental authority. However, there is a kind of loophole in the law, which appears to allow for something akin to 'shared' exercise of parental responsibilities for divorced and non-marital couples. This is achieved through separating (physical) custody from the rest

---

[2] I have chosen to translate the Japanese *shinken* as 'parental authority' in this report. A direct translation of the Japanese legal term currently in use would be 'parental rights'. However, the commonly accepted understanding of the nature of *shinken* nowadays is that it comprises both the rights and responsibilities of a parent. To reflect this understanding, I have opted to use 'parental authority' to refer to *shinken*.

[3] Art. 820 of the Civil Code. If not otherwise specified, all articles in this report are articles of the Civil Code. Art 820: 'A person who exercises parental authority holds the right, and bears the duty, to care for and educate the child for the child's interests.'

[4] Art. 824. The Civil Code also mentions the following components of parental authority: (3) the right to determine the child's residence (Art. 821); (4) the right to discipline the child (Art. 822; this article is expected to be scrapped from the Civil Code in the near future); and (5) the right to give permission for the child to work (Art. 823). Furthermore, the person with parental authority can undertake the following as the legal representative of a child: (where the child is younger than 15 years old) (6) submitting a notification for the change of the child's surname (Art. 791 III), and (7) giving consent to the regular (open) adoption for the child in place of the child (Art. 797 I); (8) (in the case of a minor child) accepting or renouncing an inheritance (Art. 917), etc.

[5] Art. 818 I and III.

[6] Art. 819 I, II and V.

[7] Art. 819 IV. If the parties cannot reach an agreement, the court can make a ruling (Art. 819 V).

of parental authority and allocating (physical) custody to one parent, while the other parent is allocated the remainder of parental authority.

There is no clear statutory basis for this separation of (physical) custody and parental authority. The courts have ordered such a separation based on an interpretation of Article 766 I of the Civil Code. When the parents divorce or separate, they can agree on the above arrangement between themselves, or if they cannot reach an agreement, the family court can issue a determination. At least in theory, the same applies via analogy to unmarried parents if the father has recognised paternity.[8]

It is not necessarily clear which parent can exercise which elements of parental authority in cases where (physical) custody is separated from parental authority. It is generally thought that the parent who has been assigned (physical) custody will exercise (1) the day-to-day care of the child as well as rights and duties that are considered inextricably linked to the exercise of such care, such as (2) the rights and duties related to the education of the child, (3) the right to determine the residence of the child,[9] (4) the right to discipline the child, and so forth. The parent who has been assigned parental authority minus (physical) custody exercises the 'remaining' elements of parental authority, more particularly the right to administer the assets of the (minor) child, and the right to make applications to the court and relevant authorities to have changes made to the legal status of the child, such as the right to apply for the change of the surname of the child.[10]

In practice, the courts rarely order the separation of (physical) custody from parental authority after divorce.[11] A court might deem such an arrangement appropriate if, in light of the circumstances, one parent is more suited to exercising the day-to-day care of the child but cannot be expected to manage the child's property in an appropriate manner,[12] or this arrangement might be ordered as a means of compromise in a case where both parents appear equally suited to care for a child and neither is willing to relinquish parental authority.[13]

---

[8] Arts 766, 771 and 788. K. Akitake et al., *Ko no Shinken Kango no Jitsumu*, Seirin-Shoin, Tokyo 2015, pp. 97 ff.; Y. Maeda et al., *Minpou VI Shinzoku-Souzoku*, 5th ed., Yuhikaku, Tokyo 2019, p. 102.

[9] This also means that if the parent with parental authority retains the child against the wishes of the parent with (physical) custody, the latter can make an application to the court for the child to be handed over to them.

[10] T. Matsukawa and A. Kubota (eds), *Shin Kihonhou Kommentar*, 2nd ed., Yuhikaku, Tokyo 2019, p. 87 (Art. 766, Sue Kyo); K. Yamaguchi, 'Rikongo no Shinken to Kangoken no Bunribunzoku' (2019) 25 *Shin Hanrei Kaisetsu Watch* 115, 116; judgment of Tokyo High Court of 11.09.2006, *Kasai Geppou* 59-4-122.

[11] See e.g. S. Ninomiya, *Kazokuhou*, 5th ed., Shinsesha, Tokyo 2019, pp. 118–19; K. Akitake et al., *Ko no Shinken Kango no Jitsumu*, Seirin-Shoin, Tokyo 2015, pp. 97–99.

[12] E.g. adjudication of Yokohama Family Court of 06.01.2009, *Kasai Geppou* 62-1-105.

[13] K. Akitake et al., *Ko no Shinken Kango no Jitsumu*, Seirin-Shoin, Tokyo 2015, pp. 100 and 389; Y. Maeda et al., *Minpou VI Shinzoku-Souzoku*, 5th ed., Yuhikaku, Tokyo 2019, p. 102.

The courts are hesitant to separate (physical) custody from parental authority in the latter type of cases, as these tend to be high-conflict cases, and, so the argument goes, the parents could not be expected to cooperate in a joint exercise of parental responsibilities.[14]

(Physical) custody might also be separated from parental authority and assigned to one parent only, where the parents have separated and are living apart but are still formally married, and therefore both retain parental authority.[15] The allocation of (physical) custody to one parent during separation is justified by the need for stability for the child in high-conflict cases where it is expected that the divorce proceedings will be lengthy.[16] In practice, the allocation of (physical) custody to one parent is much more common where the parents are separated but still formally married, as compared to post-divorce arrangements.[17]

Under Japanese law, the separation of (physical) custody from parental authority in effect results in each parent exercising *different parts* of parental authority *independently of each other*. Unlike some jurisdictions, in Japan, statutory law does not identify any matters where a decision concerning the child needs to be taken *jointly* by both parents after divorce.[18] Therefore, it is questionable whether one can really speak of a '*joint*' or '*shared*' exercise of parental authority ('*separate*' or '*fractured*' might be more appropriate) in cases where one parent has been allocated (physical) custody and the other the remainder of parental authority.

2.1.3. Disagreement between Parents Concerning the Exercise of Parental Authority/(Physical) Custody

Current law in Japan does not include any clear rules as to what procedure can or should be undertaken when parents who exercise joint parental authority (or where one parent has been allocated (physical) custody and the other parent the remainder of parental authority) disagree about an aspect of the child's upbringing. With increased calls for the introduction of joint custody after divorce in recent years, many see this as a serious shortcoming of the law.[19]

---

[14] Judgment of Tokyo High Court of 06.09.1993, *Kasai Geppou* 46-12-45; judgment of Sendai High Court of 27.02.2003, *Kasai Geppou* 55-10-78, and others.
[15] Art. 766 applied by analogy.
[16] E.g. K. Akitake et al., *Ko no Shinken Kango no Jitsumu*, Seirin-Shoin, Tokyo 2015, pp. 386–87.
[17] Ibid., p. 99.
[18] Except consenting to the adoption of the child.
[19] See e.g. Shoujihoumu, *Kazokuhou Kenkyukai Houkokusho – Fubono Rikongono Ko no Youiku no Arikatawo Chuushin tosuru Shokadai nitsuite*, 2021, p. 10, available at https://www.shojihomu.or.jp/documents/10448/10304351/%E5%AE%B6%E6%97%8F%E6%B3%95%E7%A0%94%E7%A9%B6%E4%BC%9A%E5%A0%B1%E5%91%8A%E6%9B%B8.pdf/a6d0364e-96b0-47cd-8b93-96e5aed6cf0e, accessed 10.03.2022.

2.1.4. Current Legislative Debate Concerning Joint Custody

It has been increasingly argued that the option of joint parental authority after divorce (and potentially also for common-law spouses) should be introduced. Since early 2021, this question has been under discussion in the Legislative Council (Family Law Subcommittee) of the Ministry of Justice.[20] Those arguing for joint parental authority point out that it is, in general, in the best interests of a child when both parents engage in his or her care and upbringing, irrespective of whether the parents are formally married or residing in the same household. They further argue that the current system can be harmful for children as it encourages mud-slinging during parental authority hearings, as well as 'child-snatching' in order to establish oneself as the main carer.[21] On the other hand, there is also opposition to the introduction of joint parental authority, one of the main arguments being that Japan lacks sufficient legal and related infrastructure to ensure the safety of spouses who have suffered domestic violence, and of children who have witnessed it. It is argued that allowing for joint parental authority would empower the perpetrator to continue his or her control over, and endanger, the abused spouse and children.[22]

2.1.5. The Right to Contact and Child Support Obligations of Parents

A legal parent who does not reside with a child can apply for contact with the child.[23] Where the parents cannot reach an agreement about contact between themselves, an application can be made to the family court. The parties will first go through family court conciliation proceedings (the 'conciliation first principle' of Article 257 of the Domestic Relations Case Procedure Act (DRCPA)), and if conciliation fails, the case will be adjudicated by a family court judge.[24]

Irrespective of whether a (legal) parent has parental authority, parents have an obligation to support their minor children.[25] If child support is not paid, or

---

[20] See e.g. Ministry of Justice, Minutes of the First Meeting of the Family Law Subcommittee of the Legislative Council, March 2021, available at http://www.moj.go.jp/content/001350297.pdf, accessed 10.03.2022. The Legislative Council is a group of researchers, legal practitioners, experts in related fields and civil society organisations, who are tasked by the Minister of Justice with proposing outlines for legislative review.

[21] See e.g. S. Ninomiya, *Kazokuhou*, 5th ed., Shinsesha, Tokyo 2019, p. 117.

[22] See e.g. T. Kajimura et al., *Rikongono Kyoudou Shinken toha Nanika – Kodomo no Shiten kara Kangaeru*, Nihon Hyouronsha, Tokyo 2019.

[23] Art. 766. Art. 766 is applied directly in case of divorce, and by analogy where the parents are separated but not divorced (judgment of the Supreme Court of 01.04.2000, *Minshuu* 54-5-1607) and where the parents have never been formally married (Art. 788).

[24] Arts 766, 771 and Appended Table 2 of the DRCPA.

[25] Arts 877, 766, 771 and 788. See also section 2.3.3 below.

if the parties cannot agree on the amount, a party can apply to the family court. Again, the case will first go to conciliation, and if conciliation fails, a judge will decide.

2.2. OPEN ADOPTION

2.2.1. Brief Overview of Adoption in Japanese Law

Japanese law recognises two types of adoptions: (1) so-called regular adoption (simply referred to as 'adoption' in the Civil Code), which is a contract-type open adoption; and (2) special adoption, which is closed adoption. In the case of regular adoption, the legal parent–child relationship between the child and his or her birth parents (and other birth relatives) is retained, whereas in the case of special adoption, these relationships are extinguished.[26] Both minors and adults can be adopted via regular adoption, whereas, as a general rule, only minors under the age of 15 can be adopted via special adoption.[27]

Regular adoption has a long history in Japan, and is used for a variety of reasons, such as securing an heir to the family business, securing a person to care for the adoptive parents in their old age, avoiding high inheritance taxes, and so forth.[28] In such cases, the aim (or at least the sole or main aim) of the adoption is *not* to provide a minor with a loving home, but simply to achieve one or more of the legal effects that arise from establishing a legal parent–child relationship.[29]

Regular adoption takes place based on the consent of the parties (i.e. the adopting parent or parents and the adoptive child) via the submission of a notification of adoption to the family registration office.[30] In the case of adoption of a minor under the age of 15, the legal representative of that minor (such as a biological parent with parental authority) must give consent in place of the minor.[31] A minor who is 15 years or older will consent to the adoption him- or herself. In addition, in the case of minors, it is necessary to acquire the permission of the family court to adopt, before the notice for adoption can be submitted.[32]

---

[26] Art. 817-2 I. The exception to this rule is special adoption of one's spouse's child, in which case the legal parent–child relationship between the child and the spouse (the child's biological parent), as well as that spouse's family, remains intact (proviso to Art. 817-9).
[27] Art. 817-5 I.
[28] Y. Maeda et al., *Minpou VI Shinzoku-Souzoku*, 5th ed., Yuhikaku, Tokyo 2019, pp. 149–50.
[29] In contrast, special adoption was introduced in 1987 with the particular aim of furthering the welfare of the minor adoptee by providing the minor, who had no parents, with a family.
[30] Arts 799 and 739.
[31] Art. 797 I.
[32] Art. 798. Permission of the court is not needed in the case of regular adoption of a lineal descendant of the adoptive parent or the spouse of the adoptive parent (proviso to Art. 798).

The overwhelming number of adoptions in Japan are regular adoptions of adults. There are no reliable statistics concerning the breakdown of different kinds of regular adoption of minors, but it is estimated that most regular adoptions of minors are adoptions by a step-parent.[33]

2.2.2. Legal Rights and Responsibilities of Parents in Open Adoption

In the case of a regular adoption, the child will retain a legal parent–child relationship with the biological parents, with the attendant rights and obligations concerning, among others, support obligations and inheritance rights.

Parental authority over a minor adoptive child will be held by the adoptive parent(s).[34] Adoption will give rise to a mutual support obligation between the adoptive child and adoptive parents.[35] Although there is no clear provision in the Civil Code concerning the order and scope of support obligations between relatives, it is generally understood that the adoptive parents have the primary obligation to support the child, and the biological parent(s) have a secondary support obligation.[36] The secondary support obligation of the biological parents is seen as a safety net in case the adoptive parents become impoverished. An adoptive child who has reached the age of majority will have an obligation to support both the adoptive and the biological parents.[37] A child adopted through regular adoption inherits from both the adoptive and the biological parents.[38] Where an adoptive child dies without spouse and issue, both the adoptive and biological parents will be first in line to inherit on an equal standing.[39]

It is not clear whether the biological parent(s) could turn to the courts to apply for contact with their child who has been adopted via regular adoption. At least in private law, there does not seem to be a statutory basis for an application for contact from a biological parent after the regular adoption of their child (the exception here is step-child adoption, where the non-residential parent could apply for contact).[40] Based on where in the Civil Code the provision mentioning parent–child contact is situated, and the wording of the provision – Article 766 is situated under the sub-section 'Divorce' in the Civil Code, and contact is categorised as a matter regarding the custody of a child *at the time of divorce* of

---

[33] See H. Suzuki, 'Miseinenyoushiseido no seidoteki kadai' (2020) 32 *Ronkyuu Jurist* 10.
[34] Art. 818 II, in the case of adoption of a step-child, the adoptive parent and their spouse (biological parent). See also section 2.3 below.
[35] Art. 877 I.
[36] See K. Matsuhisa, 'Commentary on the judgment of Fukuoka High Court of 20.09.2017' (2019) 721 *Hanrei Hyouron* 163.
[37] Art. 877 I. See also section 2.3 below for details on support obligations in the case of regular adoption.
[38] Art. 887.
[39] Art. 889 I (1). T. Matsukawa and A. Kubota (eds), *Shin Kihonhou Kommentar*, 2nd ed., Yuhikaku, Tokyo 2019, p. 185 (Art. 809, A. Gouda).
[40] Art. 766 I.

the parents – the Civil Code appears to envision only contact applications from one parent against the other parent *after their divorce* (or, by analogy, during separation). It is not clear whether Article 766 could be applied by analogy to cases where the child has been adopted via regular adoption.

2.2.3. Potential Clashes between Biological and Adoptive Parents

Firstly, potential clashes may occur between the biological and adoptive parents concerning contact between the child and the biological parent(s). Parties may agree about contact among themselves. In the case of adoption of a *step-child*, if the parties cannot agree among themselves, the non-residential biological parent can apply to the courts.[41] The case will first go to in-court conciliation; if conciliation fails, the case will move to adjudication proceedings. As stated above, it is unclear whether in the case of regular adoption of a child who is not a step-child, an application for contact can be made to the courts.

Secondly, concerning child support obligations, Japanese law only provides very general rules concerning support obligations among family members, and as a general rule, the order of persons who are obligated to support a family member, as well as the scope of support, is to be agreed among the family members, or to be specified by the court where the family members cannot reach an agreement.[42] In the case of regular adoption, it is generally understood that the adoptive parents have a primary support obligation towards the child, and the biological parents' support obligation is secondary. Disagreements concerning support obligations towards a child who has been adopted via regular adoption are particularly frequent in the step-family scenario.[43] Where the residential parent remarries and their new spouse adopts the child, the non-residential parent not infrequently makes an application for the reduction of payable support. In such cases, first, an application for a family court conciliation must be made. If conciliation fails, the case goes on to adjudication, and the family court makes a judgment on the appropriate scope of support based on the individual circumstances of the case, taking into consideration the financial means of the parties and the number of children.[44]

2.3. STEP-FAMILIES

Japanese law recognises multiplicity of parenthood in the context of step-families only if the step-parent adopts her or his step-child via regular (open) adoption.

---

[41] Art. 766.
[42] Arts 878 and 879.
[43] See section 2.3 below.
[44] Arts 766 I, II and III, 771 and Appended Table 2 of the DRCPA.

In that case, the child will have three legal parents – the biological residential parent, the adoptive step-parent and the biological non-residential parent. Where the step-parent does not adopt, no special rights or obligations will be conferred on the step-parent vis-à-vis their step-child.

2.3.1. Legal Standing of a Step-Parent who has not Adopted their Step-Child

If a step-parent does not adopt their step-child, Japanese law does not confer any special legal responsibilities or rights on him or her. If the step-parent and the child's residential biological parent are formally married, the step-child and step-parent will be related by affinity in the first degree. This means that the step-parent and step-child have an abstract mutual obligation to 'help each other' as 'relatives who live together',[45] and if 'special circumstances' exist, the family court can impose a duty of support between a step-child and step-parent.[46] Parental authority will be exercised by the residential biological parent alone, and even if a step-parent engages in the everyday care of a step-child, there is no legal basis for such care. Furthermore, if the residential parent and the step-parent separate or divorce, the latter will be unable to apply for contact with the child, even if they had formed a close bond with the child during cohabitation.[47] Even though the Civil Code does not confer rights and obligations on a step-parent and step-child, social security law provides some recognition and protection to members of de facto step-families.

2.3.2. Where the Step-Parent has Adopted the Step-Child via Open Adoption

In theory, both regular and special adoption by a step-parent are possible; however, case law and scholarly opinion tend to deem special adoption by a step-parent inappropriate in most cases. Since regular adoption is the usual form of adoption in step-families, I will expand only on this type. The conditions for the regular adoption of a step-child under Japanese law are more relaxed, as compared to the general rules of a regular adoption of a minor. Most significantly, in the case of regular adoption by a step-parent, permission by the family court, which is required as a general rule for a regular adoption of a minor in order to verify whether the adoption is in the interests of the minor, is waived.[48] Furthermore, for children under the age of 15, their legal representative (usually the residential biological parent) will give consent on behalf of

---

[45] Art. 730.
[46] Art. 877 II.
[47] Adjudication of Tokyo Family Court of 15.11.1974, *Kasai Geppou* 27-10-55.
[48] Proviso to Art. 798.

the child,[49] and in the majority of cases the consent of the non-residential biological parent is not required.[50]

Where a step-parent adopts their step-child, the step-parent will become a legal parent and obtain all the attendant legal rights and obligations in relation to the step-child, such as parental authority (exercised jointly with the residential biological parent during their marriage),[51] the obligation to support the child, and inheritance rights. The adoptive step-parent and the residential biological parent will have the same responsibilities and rights towards the child.[52]

As with first-marriage spouses and their common children, there is no clear statutory framework for solving disputes between a residential biological parent and step-parent concerning their responsibilities and rights in relation to the child.

2.3.3. The Legal Standing of the Non-Residential Biological Parent

Although Japanese statutory law does not confer special rights or responsibilities on a step-parent unless they adopt their step-child, the existence of a step-parent (particularly one who is formally married to the residential biological parent) does in fact influence the legal standing of the non-residential parent. Furthermore, where a step-parent adopts their step-child via regular (open) adoption, the child will have three legal parents with somewhat differing rights and obligations, and this situation gives rise to various potential clashes.

First, where the step-parent has adopted the step-child via regular adoption, the non-residential biological parent will not have parental authority.[53] Second, irrespective of whether the step-parent has adopted the step-child, the non-residential biological parent may apply to the courts for contact with the child.[54]

---

[49] Art. 797 I.
[50] Indeed, it is reported that often regular adoptions of step-children are carried out without the knowledge of the non-residential parent.
[51] Circular Notice No. Min Kou 2573 of the Civil Affairs Bureau of the Ministry of Justice, etc.
[52] See also section 2.2 above.
[53] Japanese courts have further restricted the non-residential parent's chances of (re)gaining parental authority by adopting the interpretation that a non-residential parent will not be able to apply for parental authority to be transferred to her or him while the step-parent and the residential parent have joint parental authority (judgment of the Supreme Court of 14.04.2014, *Minshuu* 68-4-279).
[54] Art. 766. However, especially older case law tended to restrict or deny contact between the non-residential parent and a child living in a step-family (including in cases where the step-parent had adopted the step-child), arguing that such contact would unsettle or confuse the child, disrupt the peace of the new household, and hinder the child's integration into the new family, see M. Roots, 'Fubo no Bekkyo/Rikongo no Oyakokankei – Menkaikouryuu niokeru "Ko no Fukushi" wo Chuusinni (3)' (2013) 82(4) *Hougaku (Tohoku Daigaku)* 45.

Finally, before launching into the complex issue of support obligations in step-families, I will provide a brief overview of the approach to support obligations between family members in Japanese law. The regulation of support obligations among family members is laid down in statutory law in very general terms, and leaves many issues, such as the order of persons who are obligated to support a family member, and the scope of support, to be agreed among family members, or to be specified by the court in individual cases where the family members cannot reach an agreement.[55] The basic understanding among scholars and practitioners is that there are three categories of support obligations among family members: (1) support among spouses and support by parents of their minor children;[56] (2a) maintenance among lineal relatives by blood and siblings;[57] and (2b) (*if special circumstances exist*) between relatives within the third degree, in addition to the relatives mentioned in (2a).[58] In step-families, both of the child's biological parents, irrespective of whether they have parental authority, as well as the adoptive step-parent, have category (1) support obligations towards the child. A step-parent who has not adopted their step-child but who is formally married to the child's biological parent might have a support obligation under Article 877 II of the Civil Code (category (2b)), if a court judges that 'special circumstances' exist in a particular case.

As to the scope of the various support obligations, in the case of category (1), the obligor is understood to bear an *unlimited* special responsibility to provide support for the necessities of life, and must ensure that the standard of living of the person they are obliged to support is the same as their own. As for categories (2a) and (2b), the obligor is understood to bear a *limited* responsibility to provide support for the necessities of life. For this category, the obligor is

---

[55] Art. 878: 'In the case where there exist several persons under a duty to give support, and agreement has not or cannot be reached between the parties with respect to the order in which they are to give support, the family court shall determine the order. In the case where there exist several persons entitled to support and the financial capacity of the person under a duty to give support is insufficient to support them all, the same shall apply.'
Art. 879: 'If agreement has not, or cannot be, reached between the parties with respect to the extent and form of support, the family court shall determine such matters, considering the needs of the person entitled to support, the financial capacity of the person under a duty to give support, and any other related circumstances.'
T. Matsukawa and A. Kubota (eds), *Shin Kihonhou Kommentar*, 2nd ed., Yuhikaku, Tokyo 2019, p. 349 (Art. 877, T. Shimizu).

[56] Arts 752, 760 and Arts 877, 760, 766 and 788, respectively.

[57] Art. 877 I: 'Lineal relatives by blood and siblings have a duty to support each other.'

[58] Art. 877 II. In this case, the existence of the support obligation must be confirmed by the court. According to case law and scholarly opinion, the existence of 'special circumstances' in the sense of Art. 877 II is approved only in exceptional circumstances (T. Matsukawa and A. Kubota (eds), *Shin Kihonhou Kommentar*, 2nd ed., Yuhikaku, Tokyo 2019, pp. 350 ff. (Art. 877, T. Shimizu)).

required only to ensure a 'reasonable standard of living' for the obligee, and the extent of the obligation heavily depends on the financial resources of the obligor.

The obligation of a (legal) parent, including an adoptive parent, to support their minor child is considered an absolute support obligation. The existence of the obligation does not depend on whether the parent is a marital or non-marital parent, or whether the parent has parental authority.[59]

Where a step-parent has adopted their step-child, the following applies: both the biological parent and the adoptive step-parent will have an obligation to support the child. However, the scope of the support obligations of the different parents in this scenario is different. Namely, the biological residential parent and the adoptive step-parent have a primary obligation to support the child, and the non-residential biological parent's support obligation is secondary. That is, the non-residential biological parent will be called upon to support the child if the biological residential parent and step-parent are unable to provide sufficient support.[60]

Furthermore, the courts have judged that the remarriage of the residential spouse and the subsequent adoption of the child by the step-parent, as well as the remarriage of the *non-residential* parent (the obligor), and the birth of more children to that parent and/or the adoption by the non-residential parent of their own step-children, may qualify as a change in circumstances in the sense of Article 880,[61] and the non-residential parent may make an application for the reduction of child support.[62]

If a step-parent who is formally married to the residential biological parent does not adopt, the step-child and the step-parent will be relatives by affinity in the first degree, and therefore a support obligation will only arise if a court judges that 'special circumstances' to justify such an obligation are present. Interestingly, the courts have considered the existence and financial contribution of a step-parent who has not adopted their step-child when deciding whether an application for a reduction of child support from the non-residential parent should be approved.[63]

---

[59] T. Matsukawa and A. Kubota (eds), *Shin Kihonhou Kommentar*, 2nd ed., Yuhikaku, Tokyo 2019, pp. 350 ff. (Art. 877, T. Shimizu).
[60] Judgment of Fukuoka High Court of 20.09. 2017 (2018) 1449 *Hanrei Times* 144, etc.
[61] Art. 880: 'If an alteration in circumstances arises after an agreement or an order regarding the order of persons under a duty to support, persons entitled to support, or the extent or form of support, the family court may alter or revoke the agreement or the order.'
[62] Judgment of Tokyo High Court of 06.12.2016 (2018) 17 *Katei no Hou to Saiban* 101; judgment of Osaka High Court of 13.10.2016 (2019) 19 *Katei no Hou to Saiban* 95; etc. The amount of child support is decided based on the income of both parents and the number of children. The standard calculation table (published in (2003) 1111 *Hanrei Times* 285) is used as reference.
[63] Judgment of Tokyo High Court of 08.07.2016 (2017) 1437 *Hanrei Times* 113.

2.4. CHILDREN BORN AS A RESULT OF DONOR-ASSISTED REPRODUCTIVE TECHNOLOGY

2.4.1. Introduction

In Japan, artificial reproductive technology (ART)[64] using the couple's gametes is widely used.[65] The exception is surrogacy, which is considered controversial and is therefore rare. Despite the widespread use of ART, there was no legal regulation of any aspect of ART, including provisions concerning the legal parent–child relationships of children born as a result of ART, until December 2020, when the Act on the Providing etc. of Assisted Reproductive Technology and the Special Provisions to the Civil Code Regarding Legal Parent–Child Relationships of Children Born Through Such Technology (the 2020 ART Act) was promulgated.

Prior to the 2020 ART Act, pre-existing rules concerning legal parent–child relationships as laid out in the Japanese Civil Code were applied. This caused difficulties for the courts on numerous occasions and justices of the Supreme Court repeatedly urged the National Diet to adopt legislation.[66] In the legal vacuum, medical associations issued guidelines on ART, and various ministerial level committees have discussed the myriad issues involved and made suggestions for legislation. Below is a brief overview of the discussion on the legal regulation of ART, with a focus on the legal parent–child relationships of children born via ART.

During the prolonged legal vacuum, professional medical organisations such as the Japan Society of Obstetrics and Gynaecology (JSOG) and the Japan Society for Reproductive Medicine (JSRM) issued their own guidelines for fertility clinics and doctors on the use of ART.[67] These guidelines are not legally binding. JSOG's guidelines, which are probably the most widely recognised, state, among other things, (1) which forms of ART are permissible (surrogacy is prohibited), and (2) whether ART should be available to common-law spouses and single persons (as a general rule, the guidelines only permit ART for married couples; since 2014, ART using the couple's gametes is available to common-law heterosexual spouses).

---

[64] In this report, ART includes any form of medically assisted reproduction, including artificial insemination and in vitro fertilisation using a couple's or a donor's gametes, and surrogacy.
[65] M. Kokado, 'A New Phase in the Regulation of Assisted Reproductive Technology in Japan' (2015) 40 *Journal of Japanese Law* 211.
[66] Judgment of the Supreme Court of 23.03.2007, *Minshuu* 61-2-619; judgment of the Supreme Court of 10.12.2013, *Minshuu* 67-9-1847 (dissenting opinion of Justice Otani).
[67] JSOG's opinions: http://www.jsog.or.jp/modules/statement/index.php?content_id=3, accessed 10.03.2022; JSRM guidelines: http://www.jsrm.or.jp/guideline-statem/index.html, accessed 10.03.2022.

In December 2000 the Assessment Sub-Committee for Advanced Medical Care within the Science Council of the Ministry of Health and Welfare (MHW, now Ministry of Health, Labour and Welfare, MHLW) submitted a report on ART involving donated sperm, eggs and embryos (the 2000 MHW Report),[68] outlining basic principles for this type of treatment, and calling for the speedy enactment of relevant legislation, including statutory rules on the legal parent–child relationships of children born through ART. In April 2003, the ART Sub-Committee of the Science Council of the MHLW submitted a further report (the 2003 MHLW Report)[69] detailing which types of ART should be deemed permissible (surrogacy deemed impermissible), how donor information should be handled in conjunction with the right of the child to know his or her origins, and so forth.

In July 2003 the Legislative Council of the Ministry of Justice completed a tentative legislative proposal on special provisions of the Civil Code concerning the parent–child relationships of children born as a result of ART involving donor sperm, eggs and embryos (the 2003 Legislative Council Tentative Proposal). According to the Tentative Proposal, when a donor egg was used, the birth mother would be the legal mother. Where donor sperm was used, the husband of the mother, who consented to the use of donor sperm, would be the legal father. Furthermore, a sperm donor would not be permitted to recognise paternity of the child, and the child or mother would not be allowed to bring an action for recognition of paternity against the donor. The Tentative Proposal was compiled on the premise that surrogacy would not be permitted, and therefore the proposed rules would not be applied to surrogacy arrangements.

In April 2008, the Committee for the Deliberation of ART of the Science Council of Japan submitted a report focusing on surrogacy (the 2008 Science Council Report).[70] The report proposed prohibiting surrogacy as a general rule, but suggested that trial cases might be allowed under strict conditions. The report recognised that even if surrogacy was prohibited, children would still be born via surrogacy, either to surrogates abroad or via clandestine domestic arrangements, and therefore clear rules concerning the legal parent–child relationships of children thus born were needed. The report proposed that the birth mother should be the legal mother, but that the intended parents should be able to adopt the child.

In 2016, a private member's draft bill on ART (the 2016 draft bill) was completed. During the deliberations preceding this draft bill, the following rules were suggested for regulating the legal parent–child relationships of children

---

[68] Available at https://www.mhlw.go.jp/www1/shingi/s0012/s1228-1_18.html, accessed 10.03.2022.
[69] Available at https://www.mhlw.go.jp/shingi/2003/04/s0428-5a.html#3-4-2-3, accessed 10.03.2022.
[70] Available at http://www.scj.go.jp/ja/info/kohyo/pdf/kohyo-20-t56-1.pdf, accessed 10.03.2022.

born as a result of ART:[71] (1) if a donor egg was used, the birth mother was the legal mother; (2) a husband who had agreed to the use of donor sperm could not contest paternity of the child; (3) a sperm donor could not recognise paternity of a child conceived using his sperm, and a paternity claim could not be brought against the donor. The rules concerning the legal standing of the donor appear to have been excluded from the draft bill sometime during or after 2015.

In late 2020, the Bill on the Providing etc. of Assisted Reproductive Technology and the Special Provisions to the Civil Code Regarding Legal Parent–Child Relationships of Children Born Through Such Technology (the 2020 ART Bill) was submitted for deliberation to the National Diet, and the 2020 ART Act came into force on 11 March 2021. The third section of the Act containing special provisions to the Civil Code regarding legal parent–child relationships of children born via sperm and/or egg donation came into force on 11 December 2021.

Section 3 of the Act states that if a woman gives birth as a result of ART using a donor egg, the woman who gives birth is the legal mother.[72] Furthermore, when a wife, with her husband's consent, gestates and gives birth as a result of ART using donor sperm, the husband cannot invoke Article 774[73] of the Civil Code to deny paternity of the child (the premise being that the husband will be the legal father as per Article 772[74] of the Civil Code).[75] The 2020 ART Act does not include any regulation of the legal standing of a sperm or egg donor.

The Act specifically requires the State to take 'necessary legislative and other measures for the appropriate provision of ART'.[76] It does not specify which types of ART should be permitted or prohibited by law. This question is one of the many issues that are to be further deliberated, and legislative and other provisions are to be created 'within roughly two years' of the promulgation of the Act.[77] The permissibility of surrogacy, and the consequent regulation of legal parent–child relationships in surrogacy arrangements, are likely to be two of the more contested issues.[78] Further examples of issues to be further discussed and regulated over the 'roughly two years' are the legal standing of sperm (or egg)

---

[71] As reported by M. Kokado, 'A New Phase in the Regulation of Assisted Reproductive Technology in Japan' (2015) 40 *Journal of Japanese Law* 211, 222 ff.
[72] Art. 9 of the 2020 ART Act.
[73] Art 774: 'Under the circumstances described in Article 722, a husband may rebut the presumption of the child in wedlock.'
[74] Art. 772 I: 'A child conceived by a wife during marriage is presumed to be a child of her husband.' Art 772 II: 'A child born after 200 days from the formation of marriage or within 300 days of the day of the dissolution or rescission of marriage is presumed to have been conceived during marriage.'
[75] Art. 10 of the 2020 ART Act.
[76] Art. 8 of the 2020 ART Act.
[77] Art. 3 of the Supplementary Provisions to the 2020 ART Act.
[78] Art. 3 III (3) of the Supplementary Provisions. Further special provisions to the Civil Code concerning legal parent–child relationships are possible.

donors, and rules and policies relating to the 'right to know' of a child born as a result of ART.[79]

2.4.2. Parenthood, Rights, and Obligations of the Birth Mother, Her Spouse/Partner, and the Donor(s)

2.4.2.1. Under the 2020 ART Act

The woman who gives birth will be the legal mother.[80] The formal spouse of the mother will be the legal father.[81] Where the spouse of the mother has given consent to the use of donor sperm, he cannot invoke Article 774 to rebut the presumption that he is the father.[82] The 2020 ART Act does not regulate the legal parent–child relationship between a child conceived with donor sperm, and the (male) common-law partner of the mother. Therefore, pre-existing general rules of the Civil Code apply.[83] The same is true for the legal standing of an egg or sperm donor.

2.4.2.2. Prior to the 2020 ART Act

Prior to the 2020 ART Act, general rules concerning legal parenthood and parental rights as found in the Civil Code were applied to children born as a result of ART.

The birth mother would be the legal mother. This was based on judicial precedent, more particularly a judgment of the Japanese Supreme Court of 27 April 1962[84] concerning the legal motherhood of a mother of a non-marital child, and whether recognition of maternity by the mother was necessary to determine maternity. The Supreme Court stated that no recognition of maternity by the mother was necessary, as maternity 'occurred as a matter of course by the fact of giving birth.' Therefore, the woman who gave birth would be the legal mother. This principle was reiterated by the Supreme Court in the context of ART in 2007 in a judgment concerning surrogacy.[85] It is widely accepted that the principle that the mother is the woman who gave birth also applies in cases of donor egg conception in general. This rule is generally justified with the following arguments: (1) determining maternity by the act of giving birth

---

[79] See A. Uchida, 'Seishoku Hojo Iryouno Teikyoutou nikansuru Houseibino Jitsugento Kadai – Seishoku Hojo Iryou nikansuru Minpou Tokureihouan no Kokkaigiron' (2021) 431 *Rippou to Chousa* 210.
[80] Art. 9 of the 2020 ART Act.
[81] Art. 772 of the Civil Code.
[82] Art. 10 of the 2020 ART Act.
[83] See section 2.4.2.2 below for details.
[84] *Minshuu* 16-7-1247.
[85] Judgment of 23.03.2007, *Minshuu* 61-2-619. See also section 2.5 below.

provides an objectively clear standard for the determination; (2) this rule is in the best interests of the child, as maternity can be determined immediately at birth, and therefore there is no period of time where the child has no legal mother, or it is uncertain who the legal mother is; (3) it is thought that during pregnancy, the pregnant woman will naturally develop maternal feelings towards the baby; and (4) it is the woman who becomes pregnant rather than the egg donor who wishes to care for the child.[86]

The majority opinion before the 2020 ART Act was that where a child was conceived using donor sperm, the (formal) spouse of the mother would be presumed to be the legal father;[87] this presumption was applied with the additional condition that the husband had given his consent to the use of donor sperm.[88]

Where the birth mother and her husband are the legal parents, they will have joint parental authority.[89] If the husband has rebutted the presumption of paternity, the birth mother will be the only legal parent and have sole parental authority.

2.4.2.3. The Position of the Common-Law Partner of the Mother

The majority of the legislative proposals concerning ART envisioned that ART involving donor gametes would only be available to formally married couples, and therefore only rules concerning the legal parent–child relationships of children born to such couples were clearly outlined. Restricting the use of ART to married couples was/is at least partly due to the belief that having, from the moment of birth, two parents who are formally committed to each other will provide the most stable environment for the child.[90]

---

[86] See Supplementary Explanations to the 2003 Legislative Council Tentative Proposal, p. 8, available at https://www.moj.go.jp/content/000071865.pdf, accessed 10.03.2022. See also the 2008 Science Council Report, p. 25, available at http://www.scj.go.jp/ja/info/kohyo/pdf/kohyo-20-t56-1.pdf, accessed 10.03.2022.

[87] Art. 772 I.

[88] Judgment of Tokyo High Court of 16.09.1998, *Kasai Geppou* 51-3-165; judgment of the Supreme Court of 10.12.2013, *Minshuu* 67-9-1847; etc. The 2003 Legislative Council Tentative Proposal and the 2016 draft bill also included provisions to this effect. It was debated whether a husband could rebut the presumption of paternity (Art. 774), especially where he had given prior consent to artificial insemination by donor (AID). The Supreme Court had confirmed that the presumption of paternity in Art. 772 does not presuppose the existence of a biological link (judgment of the Supreme Court of 17.07.2014, *Minshuu* 68-6-547 (not specifically about ART)). Consequently, the majority opinion was that in a scenario where the husband had given his consent to AID, his rebuttal of paternity should be considered impermissible based on either the doctrine of abuse of one's rights or as being in violation of the principle of good faith and fair dealing (Art. 1 II). See M. Ishii, 'Kaisetsu Seishokuhojoiryou to Oyakokankei' in T. Matsukawa and A. Kubota (eds), *Shin Kihonhou Kommentar*, 2nd ed., Yuhikaku, Tokyo 2019, pp. 221–22 and 224.

[89] Art. 818 III.

[90] As background information I would like to note here that Japan has a very low percentage of non-marital children (just over 2% of all children), and that formal marriage is the only type of union between couples that receives straightforward statutory protection.

The *male* common-law partner of the mother could conceivably gain the position of legal father of a child conceived via AID by recognising paternity of the child.[91] As a general rule, once a man has recognised the paternity of a child, he cannot rescind it.[92] However, as the basis of a non-marital parent–child relationship is understood to be, at its core, the biological link between the father and the child (unlike a marital father–child relationship, which, as explained above, does *not* presuppose a biological link), a father–child relationship established through recognition of paternity, where there is no biological link, can easily be contested by any interested person,[93] as long as they can prove that there is no biological link.[94] This makes the legal father–child relationship of a child born as a result of AID to common-law partners very unstable and the child's interests extremely vulnerable.

Where the common-law (male) partner of the birth mother recognises paternity of the child, the child will be the non-marital child of the birth mother and her partner. The same rules apply as with all non-marital children. That is, at the time of birth, the birth mother will be vested with sole parental authority.[95] The parents of a non-marital child cannot hold parental authority jointly. Sole parental authority can be transferred to the non-marital father if both parents agree, or, if they cannot agree, through a court ruling.[96] If the father is not living with the child, he can make an application for contact with the child.[97] The father would also have an obligation to support the child, arising from his status as the legal father.[98]

The *female* partner of the mother would not be recognised as a parent alongside their partner, and would have no legal standing in relation to the child. Adoption of a step-child (which, in the case of a married heterosexual couple, would result in the adoptive parent and the biological parent having joint parental authority over the child) is only available to a formal spouse. Consequently, same-sex partners are excluded as same-sex marriage is not legally recognised.[99]

---

[91] Art. 779 (general provision about recognition of paternity).
[92] Art. 785. See further below for possible exceptions.
[93] Art. 786: 'A child or any other interested person may assert opposing facts against an affiliation [a recognition of paternity of a non-marital child]'.
[94] In certain situations, even the man who recognised paternity of a non-marital child while knowing of the absence of a biological link can contest the parent–child relationship (judgment of the Supreme Court of 14.01.2014, *Minshuu* 68-1-1).
[95] Art. 819 IV.
[96] Art. 819 IV and V.
[97] Arts 788 and 766 applied by analogy.
[98] Arts 788 and 766.
[99] The female partner of the birth mother could adopt the child of their partner via regular (open) adoption (adoption by a single person). However, in this case, the special rules that apply in the case of step-child adoption, such as joint parental authority with the biological parent who is married to the adoptive parent, do not apply.

2.4.3. The Legal Standing of Donors

In Japan, sperm and egg donors are in general anonymous. There are no specific rules concerning the legal standing of egg or sperm donors, anonymous or not.

It might be conceivable that a sperm donor, where he knows of the child, could try to recognise paternity of the child. However, as total anonymity has so far been one of the (semi-official) cornerstones of ART involving donated gametes in Japan,[100] excepting private sperm donation arrangements between individuals (donations from acquaintances, arrangements with donors found on social media or private matching sites), the donors will not know the identities of the children conceived using their gametes. With private arrangements, where a sperm donor knows of the child, and especially where the child has no legal father, a donor might attempt to recognise paternity. The consent of the mother (or a minor child) is not required for voluntary recognition of paternity. Conversely, it is also conceivable that a child (or the mother as the legal representative of the child) might bring an action for recognition of paternity against a sperm donor.[101] Currently there are no statutory rules to prohibit such an application.

The 2003 Legislative Council Tentative Proposal included a proposal for a clear statutory rule that prohibited a sperm donor from recognising a child born via AID using his sperm, and also prohibited the child from bringing an action of recognition of paternity against the donor.[102] Reasons given for a prohibition of recognition of paternity by (and action for recognition against) the donor were that: (1) ART was meant to be used by infertile married couples who wished to have and raise a child together, and allowing recognition of paternity by the donor would contradict this original purpose; (2) establishing paternity of the donor would be against the wishes of the donor who presumably had no interest in raising the child; (3) a potential paternity suit would discourage prospective future donors; and (4) paternity recognition by the donor would disrupt the family life of the mother and child.[103]

The 2003 Tentative Proposal, as well as most of the public debate concerning ART, is constructed on the premise that a donor would be disinterested in

---

[100] M. Kokado, 'A New Phase in the Regulation of Assisted Reproductive Technology in Japan' (2015) 40 *Journal of Japanese Law* 211, 222.

[101] Art. 787: 'A child, his/her lineal descendant, or the legal representative of either, may bring an action for affiliation [recognition of paternity]; provided that this shall not apply if three years have passed since the day of the death of the parent'.

[102] Section 3 of the Proposal. According to the Tentative Proposal, these rules were only applicable if the child was conceived in a certified clinic and inside the proposed legal framework (i.e. child born of a married woman with the consent of her husband, etc.). Therefore, children born as a result of private arrangements would have been excluded from these rules. Earlier versions of the 2016 private members draft bill also included provisions to this effect.

[103] Supplementary Explanations to the 2003 Legislative Council Tentative Proposal, p. 14, available at https://www.moj.go.jp/content/000071865.pdf, accessed 10.03.2022.

the child. It is only very recently that some scholars have suggested that this might not always be the case, and that there could be instances where it would be conceivable (and even desirable from the viewpoint of the child's interests, including the child's right to know its origins) that the donor would be involved in the child's life in some capacity.[104] At the moment, unless a donor establishes a legal father–child relationship with the child, there is no legal basis for the donor to, for instance, request contact with the child, or for the child to make maintenance claims against the donor. If a legal parent–child relationship *is* established between the sperm donor and the child via recognition of paternity, the donor will have the same rights and obligations as any non-marital father who recognises paternity of a child.[105]

According to legal precedent (and now Article 9 of the 2020 ART Act), an egg donor will not be able to establish a legal parent–child relationship with the child.

2.5. SURROGACY

The use of surrogacy is considered controversial in Japan in light of: (1) the health risks for the surrogate; (2) concerns for the best interests of the child born via surrogacy, including the uncertainties relating to his or her legal parentage and the difficulties in protecting his or her right to know his or her origins; and (3) ethical considerations such as using a woman's body as a reproductive tool and the exploitation of women from weaker socioeconomic backgrounds.[106] In light of the above, the JSOG has expressly prohibited its members from carrying out surrogacy treatments, and consequently surrogacy arrangements, especially domestic ones, are rare.[107]

---

[104] S. Ninomiya, *Kazokuhou*, 5th ed., Shinsesha, Tokyo 2019, pp. 196–97, 201; A. Hanamoto, 'Seishoku Hojo Iryou niokeru donor no houteki chii nitsuiteno Ichikousatsu' (2017) 26 *Momoyama Hougaku* 53, 78, 80; M. Ishii, 'Kaisetsu Seishokuhojoiryou to Oyakokankei' in T. Matsukawa and A. Kubota (eds), *Shin Kihonhou Kommentar*, 2nd ed., Yuhikaku, Tokyo 2019, p. 227.

[105] See also section 2.4.2.3 above.

[106] N. Mizuno, 'Parent-Child Relationship in the Japanese Civil Code – Regarding Medical Technology for Reproductive Treatment' (2009) 52 *Japanese Yearbook of International Law* 387; JSOG, *Opinion on Surrogacy*, 2003, available at http://www.jsog.or.jp/modules/statement/index.php?content_id=3, accessed 10.03.2022; 2008 Science Council Report, p. 9 ff., available at http://www.scj.go.jp/ja/info/kohyo/pdf/kohyo-20-t56-1.pdf, accessed 10.03.2022. On the other hand, some argue that due to strong societal pressure in Japan to have children, infertile married couples are likely to go on seeking surrogacy arrangements abroad (or clandestine ones in Japan) even if surrogacy is banned, and therefore banning surrogacy would simply drive it underground, causing more harm (see e.g. Y. Semba et al., 'Surrogacy: Donor Conception Regulation in Japan' (2010) 24(7) *Bioethics* 348, 356).

[107] See JSOG, *Opinion on Surrogacy*, ibid. As outlined in section 2.4.1 above, most reports and proposals so far have stated that surrogacy should be prohibited, with the exception of the

The 2020 ART Act does not include any provisions specifically concerning surrogacy. The questions of whether surrogacy should be allowed in Japan in the first place, and how parent–child relationships should be regulated in the case of surrogacy arrangements, continue to be deliberated.[108] At present, there is no law that explicitly prohibits surrogacy, and there are no rules specifically concerning the establishment of legal parent–child relationships in the case of surrogacy. Article 9 of the 2020 ART Act concerning the legal motherhood of children born using a donor egg is understood to be applicable also in surrogacy cases.[109]

2.5.1. Parenthood of the Surrogate

The surrogate is the legal mother.[110] In relation to children born prior to 11 December 2021, the surrogate is deemed the mother based on judicial precedent, namely the Supreme Court judgments of 27 April 1962[111] and 23 March 2007. In the latter case, the children (twins) were born to an American surrogate, using the egg and sperm of the intended Japanese parents. A United States court had issued an order determining the intended parents as the legal parents, and the relevant United States authorities issued a birth certificate to this effect. As the intended parents were celebrities and had made the surrogacy public, the local municipal office was aware that the twins had been born to a surrogate, and refused to accept the birth certificate which stated the intended parents as the legal parents. The intended parents sued. The courts of the different instances deliberated on whether the intended mother should be considered the legal mother. The Supreme Court stated:

> [C]onsidering that ... a natural parent–child relationship is deeply involved in the public interest as well as child welfare, and therefore it should be uniformly determined according to definite and clear criteria, there is no choice but to construe the existing Civil Code to require that a woman who has conceived and delivered a child shall be the mother of the child, and that a mother–child relationship cannot be

---

2008 Science Council Report, which, while proposing a general ban, stated that some trial cases might be permitted. Many Japanese couples look abroad for surrogates; domestic surrogates are often a family member of the intended couple: see M. Kokado, 'A New Phase in the Regulation of Assisted Reproductive Technology in Japan' (2015) 40 *Journal of Japanese Law* 211, 217; Y. Semba et al., 'Surrogacy: Donor Conception Regulation in Japan' (2010) 24(7) *Bioethics* 348, 350.

[108] As per Art. 3 of the Supplementary Provisions to the 2020 ART Act.

[109] A. Uchida, 'Seishoku Hojo Iryouno Teikyoutou nikansuru Houseibino Jitsugento Kadai – Seishoku Hojo Iryou nikansuru Minpou Tokureihouan no Kokkaigiron' (2021) 431 *Rippou to Chousa* 210, 221.

[110] Art. 9 of the 2020 ART Act; see also A. Uchida, 'Seishoku Hojo Iryouno Teikyoutou nikansuru Houseibino Jitsugento Kadai – Seishoku Hojo Iryou nikansuru Minpou Tokureihouan no Kokkaigiron' (2021) 431 *Rippou to Chousa* 210, 221.

[111] *Minshuu* 16-7-1247 and *Minshuu* 61-2-619, respectively.

deemed to be established between the child and the woman who has not conceived or delivered the child, even where the child is born using the egg donated by that woman.[112]

2.5.2. The Biological Parents

The woman whose egg was used (including cases where the intended mother provided the egg) cannot be the legal mother at birth.[113] The biological father can recognise paternity of the child.[114] However, if the surrogate is married, the presumption of paternity of the surrogate's husband would prevent the biological father from recognising paternity. If the biological father recognises paternity (e.g. where the surrogate is unmarried), the child will be a non-marital child of the surrogate and the biological father.

There is general agreement that the intended (biological) parents should be able to establish a legal parent–child relationship with the child via adoption.[115] It is reported that in the handful of clinics that carry out surrogacy treatment in Japan, the general practice is to register the surrogate (and her husband) as legal parent(s) on the child's birth certificate, followed by the intended (biological) parents adopting the child via special adoption.[116]

So far, there have been two published judgments concerning the (special) adoption of a child born to a surrogate: the judgment of Kobe Family Court of 26 December 2008 (domestic surrogate, mother of the intended mother)[117] and the judgment of Shizuoka Family Court of 14 January 2020 (foreign surrogate).[118] Both courts found, among other considerations, that the children were developing well in loving homes (both had been living with the intended parents, who were furthermore the biological parents, since birth), that the surrogates had no intention of caring for the children, and that therefore the statutory conditions for special adoption were fulfilled.[119] It is not clear how

---

[112] *Minshuu* 61-2-619, 627.
[113] See Art. 9 of the 2020 ART Act; see also section 2.4.2 above.
[114] Art. 799.
[115] 2008 Science Council Report, p. 26, available at http://www.scj.go.jp/ja/info/kohyo/pdf/kohyo-20-t56-1.pdf, accessed 10.03.2022; see also M. Tanamura, 'Dairishussan Iraisha Fuufu niyoru Dairikaitaishi no Tokubetsu Youshiengumi' (2010) 141(6) *Minshouhou Zasshi* 116, 122 ff. Even those critical of surrogacy agree that adoption by intended parents might be permissible to ensure the welfare of the child (M. Noriko, 'Dairishussan niyoru ko no ranshi oyobi seishi no teikyousha tono Tokubetsu youshiengumi no seiritsu' (2010) 41 (2010 II) *Shihou Hanrei Remarks* 70, 73.
[116] M. Tanamura, 'Dairishussan Iraisha Fuufu niyoru Dairikaitaishi no Tokubetsu Youshiengumi' (2010) 141(6) *Minshouhou Zasshi* 116, 124.
[117] *Kasai Geppou* 61-10-72.
[118] (2021) 1490 *Hanrei Times* 254.
[119] Art. 817-7: if the birth parents are 'incapable or unfit to care for the child or there are other special circumstances and it is found that adoption is especially necessary for the interests of the child.'

much importance the courts placed on the existence of a biological tie between the children and the intended parents (in both cases, the egg and sperm from the intended couple were used).

Where an adoption is undergone, the adoptive parents will have parental authority over the child.[120] In the case of special adoption, the legal parent–child relationship between the child and the birth parents will be dissolved. In the case of regular adoption, the birth parents (the surrogate alone or the surrogate and her husband) also remain legal parents, but will not have parental authority.[121]

2.6. CHILDREN RAISED BY SAME-SEX COUPLES

Japanese law does not recognise same-sex marriage. This drastically limits the legal options available for same-sex couples raising children. Such couples cannot have joint parental authority, which is only possible during marriage. Co-motherhood/fatherhood is not recognised. A male same-sex partner cannot recognise paternity of the child of his partner, as the child would already have a pre-existing legal father.[122]

3. PART B. DIVERSITY AND PLURALITY OF FAMILY FUNCTIONS

3.1. LEGAL RECOGNITION OF VARIOUS FAMILY FUNCTIONS

Japanese family law recognises that families fulfil various functions such as raising children and protecting the vulnerable. Depending on the particular function, the definition and scope of 'family', as well as which family members are expected to perform specific functions, may differ.

3.1.1. Raising Children

The law sees raising children as primarily the responsibility and right of the legal parents. Indeed, it is almost exclusively the legal parents who can be assigned legal rights and obligations concerning the care of the child.[123] Furthermore, the number of persons who can hold parental authority at a given time is

---

[120] Art. 818 II.
[121] See section 2.2 above for more details on regular adoption.
[122] See section 2.4.2.2 above about adoption by a same-sex partner of a parent.
[123] The exceptions being cases where the parents are deemed unable to care for the child and a custodian of a minor or foster parent is allocated certain rights and obligations *instead of* a parent.

restricted to a maximum of two. It is (near-)impossible for persons who are not the parents of the child, but are in fact caring for the child, such as grandparents or non-adoptive step-parents, to be allocated even (physical) custody.[124] There is no legal recognition of same-sex couples raising children together, further highlighting that only certain types of families are recognised in their child-raising function.[125]

Legal parents are assigned an array of rights and obligations related to the care and upbringing of children. Perhaps most significantly, all legal parents, irrespective of whether they have parental authority or whether they reside with the child, have an obligation to support a minor child financially. However, in reality, due in part to an insufficient enforcement mechanism, in many cases child support is not paid, or not paid in full.[126] This suggests a strong (if unarticulated) policy stance that it is the family, and particularly the legal parents, who are expected to raise and financially support the children.

3.1.2. Providing Economic Security

As outlined in section 2.3.3, in Japan a certain range of relatives have an obligation to provide financial support to each other. For certain types of close familial relationships (e.g. spouses towards each other, parents towards their minor children), this obligation arises automatically. For most other relatives up to the third degree, there is no automatic statutory support obligation, but if a family member falls on hard times, a court may establish a support obligation. The scope of a support obligation depends on the closeness of the legal familial relationship, the widest obligation being between formal spouses during their marriage and on the part of parents towards their minor children. As to the support obligation between other relatives, the scope of the obligation is relatively narrow, and the obligor is only expected to support a particular relative if they have funds to spare.

3.1.3. Protecting the Vulnerable

Japanese family law recognises that certain family members, especially minor children and women, are particularly vulnerable, and that therefore they should be entitled to protection inside and by the family. Concerning the protection

---

[124] See judgment of the Supreme Court of 29.03.2021, *Saibansho Jihou* 1765, 3 concerning grandparents; see section 2.3 above concerning step-parents.
[125] Furthermore, any person who is not a legal parent is excluded from contact with the child once they no longer reside with the child, even if they built a close relationship with the child.
[126] MHLW, *Survey of Single-Parent Households*, 2016, available at https://www.mhlw.go.jp/stf/seisakunitsuite/bunya/0000188147.html, accessed 10.03.2022. This, coupled with inadequate State support, has resulted in high poverty rates among single-parent households.

of women, Japanese family law has placed particular importance on protecting formal wives. This has been done effectively in some respects and less effectively in others. The way in which statutory law regulates the division of assets and financial support for a vulnerable spouse (wife) at divorce is an example of statutory law's failure to recognise the protective function of the family and to protect a potentially vulnerable (ex-)wife. Scholars and practitioners have consistently argued for a clear 50–50 rule (largely adopted in case law) for the division of assets at the time of divorce, but no such rule has been incorporated into statutory law, making the position of wives with lower or no earnings particularly vulnerable. In addition, a former spouse is not entitled to post-divorce maintenance. Again, this is particularly hard on women who stay at home after marrying to care for the home and children. In addition to the wide gender pay gap, in Japan it can be very difficult for a woman who has left the workforce once to find a job later on that will have similar pay and career prospects.[127] The above shortcomings of the law, combined with insufficient financial support from the State and low levels of payment of child support, have contributed to the high number of post-divorce singe-mother households living in or close to poverty.

There is no statutory recognition of common-law spouses. The courts have recognised that common-law wives are in an equally (if not more) precarious situation financially to formal spouses. Consequently, the courts have applied by analogy the provisions concerning the division of assets at the time of divorce in cases of the dissolution of (some) common-law unions.[128] Such protection does not, however, extend to the scenario where a common-law union is dissolved through the death of a common-law spouse. This could leave a common-law spouse at risk of indigence, as common-law spouses do not have inheritance rights.

Japanese inheritance law can be said to function particularly well in protecting a potentially vulnerable legal spouse, especially a wife. The statutory share of inheritance of a formal spouse is 50%. Inheritance law was amended in 2018 to provide further protection to the formal spouse. The (partial) background to this reform was the rapidly aging society and the increase in the number of elderly widows. The 2018 reform strengthened the position of the legal wife of the deceased by ensuring that the wife could continue living in the marital home.[129]

---

[127] Y. Zhuo, 'Career Interruption of Japanese Women: Why is it so hard to balance work and child care?' (2015) 12(2) *Japan Labor Review* 106. The pay gap in Japan is 23.4% (World Economic Forum *Global Gender Gap Report 2021*, March 2021, available at https://www.weforum.org/reports/ab6795a1-960c-42b2-b3d5-587eccda6023, accessed 10.03.2022).

[128] It is unclear if even this tenuous protection could be extended to same-sex couples. See briefly M. Roots, 'Bottom-Up Action and Hesitant Steps Towards Accommodating Multicultural Claims in Japanese Family Law' in N. Yassari and M.-C. Foblets (eds), *Normativity and Diversity in Family Law*, Springer, Cham 2022, pp. 120 ff.

[129] Arts 903 IV, 1037 and 1028.

3.1.4. Care Functions: Care for the Elderly

Care for elderly family members, especially parents and parents-in-law, has traditionally been seen in Japan as the responsibility of the children, and more particularly the eldest son and his wife.[130] Although the role of the State and society in caring for the elderly has increased since the 1960s, the role of and expectations towards family members are still considerable.[131]

The 2018 inheritance law reform introduced the possibility to 'reward' or 'repay' a non-relative (the legislator here primarily envisioned a daughter-in-law) who had cared for an elderly family member. The newly inserted Article 1050 of the Civil Code stipulates that if a relative who is not an heir has made a special contribution to the maintenance of the decedent through, for instance, providing unpaid nursing, their contribution is valued and they can demand payment for this from the heirs. The introduction of Article 1050 caused some controversy. While some lauded it as enabling a daughter-in-law to receive some of the inheritance in return for the care that she had provided, others feared that this provision could result in other family members forcing daughters-in-law into caring for elderly family members, since they could now expect a monetary reward.[132]

3.2. FUNCTIONS WHICH ARE PREDOMINANTLY FAVOURED

It is difficult to say which functions are predominantly favoured. The function of care for minor children is perhaps most clearly outlined in statutory law, and possibly the most consistently, if insufficiently, regulated. Protection of vulnerable women is another function that is recognisably highlighted in the law. Both functions find vastly different confirmation and backing in the law, depending on the shape and form of the family, and in particular on whether the family in question is formed around a formal marital union, and whether the persons acting as parents are in fact legal parents (and not, for example, merely social parents).

The law appears to consider families built around common-law (heterosexual) couples as 'lesser' families; those built around same-sex couples receive no recognition at all. It is the (biological or adoptive) child living in a two-parent nuclear family built around a formally married couple that enjoys the most protection and stability under Japanese law.

---

[130] According to the provisions of the Civil Code, adult children have an inherent legal obligation to provide financial support to their elderly parents if the parents are unable to care for themselves. Other relatives might also have an obligation to support an elderly relative (Art. 788 I and II).

[131] See E. Kubono and H. Ishiwata, 'Support and Care Among Family Members and State Provision for the Elderly in Japan' in J. Eekelaar and R. George (eds), *Routledge Handbook of Family Law and Policy*, 2nd ed., Routledge, Oxon and NY 2020, p. 386 ff.

[132] Ibid.

MULTIPLICITÉ DE LA PARENTALITÉ ET FONCTION(S) DE LA FAMILLE EN DROIT LUXEMBOURGEOIS

Françoise Hilger

1. Multiplicité de la parentalité 371
   1.1. La parentalité dans la famille séparée 371
   1.2. La parentalité dans la famille recomposée 371
   1.3. *Kafala* 372
   1.4. La parentalité dans la famille adoptive (adoption simple) 372
   1.5. La parentalité dans la famille « issue de trois parents » 373
   1.6. La procréation médicalement assistée. 373
   1.7. La gestation pour autrui 373
   1.8. Remarque finale 374
2. Diversité et pluralité des fonctions de la famille. 374

1. MULTIPLICITÉ DE LA PARENTALITÉ

1.1. LA PARENTALITÉ DANS LA FAMILLE SÉPARÉE

Depuis la loi du 27 juin 2018, la séparation des parents est sans incidence sur les règles de dévolution de l'exercice de l'autorité parentale. Chacun des parents doit maintenir des relations personnelles avec l'enfant et respecter les liens de celui-ci avec l'autre parent.

Donc si une résidence alternée est décidée – soit par le juge, soit par les parents – ce qui entraine donc une éducation dans deux foyers, les deux parents conservent l'autorité parentale (autorité parentale conjointe, sauf intérêt supérieur de l'enfant).

1.2. LA PARENTALITÉ DANS LA FAMILLE RECOMPOSÉE

Le principe en droit luxembourgeois en cas de famille recomposée est : il n'existe pas de multiplicité parental. L'autorité parentale est dévolue seulement si la filiation est établie. Cependant, l'adoption simple est possible par le nouveau partenaire du parent ; alors, la filiation adoptive simple coexiste avec la filiation biologique.

Depuis la nouvelle loi du 27 juin 2018 relative à la réforme du divorce, à l'autorité parentale conjointe et à l'introduction du juge aux affaires familiales, chaque parent peut, avec l'accord de l'autre parent de l'enfant, donner un mandat d'éducation quotidienne relatif à cet enfant à son conjoint ou partenaire lié par un partenariat au sens de la loi modifiée du 9 juillet 2004 relative aux effets légaux de certains partenariats avec lequel il réside de façon stable. Le mandat, rédigé par acte sous seing privé ou en forme authentique, permet d'accomplir les actes usuels de l'autorité parentale pour la durée de la vie commune.

Le mandat peut être révoqué à tout moment par le mandant. Il prend fin de plein droit en cas de rupture de la vie commune, de décès du mandant ou du mandataire ou de renonciation de ce dernier à son mandat.

1.3. *KAFALA*

Le droit luxembourgeois ne prévoit pas la *kafala* (hormis les situations de droit international privé,[1] mises entre parenthèses dans le présent ouvrage).

1.4. LA PARENTALITÉ DANS LA FAMILLE ADOPTIVE (ADOPTION SIMPLE)

Il ne sera évoqué que l'adoption simple, seule déterminant dans le discours sur la multiplicité de la parentalité.[2]

Aux termes de l'article 358 du code civil luxembourgeois, l'adopté reste dans sa famille d'origine et y conserve tous ses droits et obligations, notamment ses droits héréditaires.

Mais aux termes de l'article 360 du même code, l'adoptant est seul investi, à l'égard de l'adopté, de tous les droits de l'autorité parentale, inclus celui d'administrer les biens et de consentir au mariage de l'adopté.

Lorsque l'adoption a été faite par deux conjoints ou que l'adoptant est le conjoint de l'un des parents de l'adopté, les droits visés à l'alinéa qui précède sont exercés par le ou les adoptants suivant les dispositions des Titres IX et X du Livre Ier du code.

---

[1] À ce sujet il existe divers arrêts rendus en droit luxembourgeois.
[2] Le droit luxembourgeois connaît encore l'adoption plénière où la filiation adoptive se substitue au lien de filiation d'origine.

Lorsqu'il n'y a qu'un adoptant ou que l'un des deux adoptants décède, il y a lieu à administration sous contrôle judiciaire.

Lorsque l'adoptant ou le survivant des adoptants décède, est déclaré absent ou perd l'exercice de l'autorité parentale, il y a lieu à ouverture d'une tutelle.

Donc il n'y pas de concurrence entre les responsabilités et droits des parents.

1.5. LA PARENTALITÉ DANS LA FAMILLE « ISSUE DE TROIS PARENTS »

Le droit luxembourgeois interne ne prévoit pas la polygamie. Le droit luxembourgeois ne prévoit non plus le cas d'un « enfant de trois parents ».

1.6. LA PROCRÉATION MÉDICALEMENT ASSISTÉE

Actuellement aucun cadre légal ne réglemente les procréations médicalement assistées (PMA) effectuées au Luxembourg. Or, de facto elle est pratiquée.

Le projet de loi numéro 6568A portant réforme du droit de la filiation créera un cadre légal ensemble avec le projet de loi numéro 7674 portant organisation de l'accès à la connaissance de ses origines dans le cadre d'une adoption ou d'une procréation médicalement assistée avec tiers donneurs.

1.7. LA GESTATION POUR AUTRUI

En droit luxembourgeois, la gestation pour autrui n'est actuellement pas réglementée par la loi. Elle n'est ni explicitement prohibée, ni explicitement permise, les conventions de gestation pour autrui sont néanmoins, a priori, nulles et sans effet, et ce en vertu du principe de l'indisponibilité du corps humain et de l'état des personnes (Doc. parl. 6568, p. 37).

Mais, au vu de la réalité souvent différente des règles juridiques, il existe quelques cas de jurisprudences.

Récemment la Commission consultative des Droits de l'Homme du Grand-Duché de Luxembourg a rendu son avis sur le projet de loi en question :

> La CCDH souligne que ni le droit national, ni le droit international consacrent un véritable « droit à un enfant », dans le sens qu'il y aurait une obligation positive généralisée qui obligerait l'État à garantir à tout un chacun le droit d'avoir un enfant : « Un enfant n'est ni un bien, ni un service que l'État peut garantir ou fournir, mais un être humain titulaire de droits. » L'autorisation, voire l'interdiction, des techniques telles que la PMA ou la GPA relèvent donc principalement de choix politiques et

sociétaux, qui doivent néanmoins tenir dûment compte des différents droits humains impliqués.[3]

L'avis retient que :

> La CCDH exhorte le gouvernement à mener des réflexions et des discussions profondes, inclusives et publiques sur le sujet de la GPA, dans une perspective multidisciplinaire en tenant dûment compte des droits fondamentaux des femmes et de l'intérêt supérieur de l'enfant.[4]

1.8. REMARQUE FINALE

Le droit de la filiation connaîtra en droit luxembourgeois un toilettage assez important dans un avenir plus ou moins proche. Cette réforme sera la troisième grande réforme du droit de la famille au cours de ces dix dernières années (réforme du mariage en 2014, réforme du divorce et introduction du juge aux affaires familiales en 2018). Cette réforme traitera aussi de la procréation médicalement assistée.

2. DIVERSITÉ ET PLURALITÉ DES FONCTIONS DE LA FAMILLE

La famille n'est pas définie en tant que tel, mais l'article 213 du code civil luxembourgeois est intéressant : les conjoints concourent dans l'intérêt de la famille à en assurer la direction morale et matérielle, à pourvoir à son entretien, à élever les enfants et à préparer leur établissement.

A travers certaines obligations et devoirs légaux d'un conjoint et ou d'un parent (père, mère), la famille a une fonction de protection, d'éducation et une fonction de solidarité.

A titre d'exemples :

- devoir de contribuer aux charges du mariage des conjoints : fonction d'entraide matérielle ;[5]
- devoir d'assistance entre conjoints : fonction d'entraide morale.

---

[3] Avis 06/2021 de la Commission consultative des Droits de l'Homme du Grand-Duché de Luxembourg sur le projet de loi numéro 6568A portant réforme du droit de la filiation, rendu le 01.03.2021.
[4] Extrait du prédit avis.
[5] F. Hilger, *Droit familial luxembourgeois, Union et désunion du couple après la loi du 27 juin 2018*, Larcier, Bruxelles 2020.

Les conjoints dirigent ensemble la cellule familiale pour éduquer ensemble les enfants.

Par ailleurs, des aliments sont dus entre parents (fonction d'entraide matérielle) et des immunités en droit pénal existent entre époux, ce qui met en exergue la solidarité entre les membres d'une famille, qu'il y ait ou non des enfants.[6]

Selon qu'il y a des enfants, c'est à dire des liens de filiation établis, le couple a d'autres obligations que s'il n'est pas parents.

Les obligations existent en fonction de la situation juridique des personnes (conjoints ou non, partenaires ou non, parents ou non).

---

[6] F. Hilger et F. Mazeaud, *La solidarité familiale*, Annales du droit luxembourgeois, vol. 29, Larcier, Bruxelles 2020.

FAMILIES WITH CHILDREN IN THE POLISH LEGAL SYSTEM

Błażej Bugajski and Anna Wysocka-Bar

1. Introduction 377
2. Legal Responsibilities and Rights of a Step-Parent 378
   2.1. A Parent of the Child Being in a De Facto Union with a Non-Parental Partner 378
   2.2. A Parent Married to a Spouse who is not the Parent of the Child 379
   2.3. Adoption of a Step-Child by a Step-Parent..................... 383
   2.4. Bringing Up a Child in More than One Household 386
   2.5. Bringing Up a Child in a Polygamous Family 386
   2.6. Multiplicity of Parenthood in the Case of Open Adoption 386
   2.7. Multiplicity of Parenthood in the Case of *Kafala* 387
3. Parenthood and the Use of Assisted Reproductive Technology 387
   3.1. Parenthood if the Donor is Anonymous......................... 387
   3.2. Parenthood if the Donor is not Anonymous 389
   3.3. Three-Parent Children.. 390
   3.4. Parenthood in the Case of Surrogacy 390
   3.5. Parenthood in the Case of Surrogacy: Same-Sex Partners......... 390
   3.6. Work on Multiplicity of Parenthood 392
4. Diversity and Plurality of Family Functions 392
   4.1. Diverse Family Functions 392
   4.2. Family Function Preferred by Polish Law....................... 392
   4.3. Influence of Having Children on Family Functions 393
5. Conclusion... 394

1. INTRODUCTION

Poland – as opposed to, for example, the United States or Germany – is not a federal state. This means that all legal acts discussed below apply equally in the whole territory of the State. In Poland there are no local legal systems (local law) that could regulate matters discussed in this report differently.

The progressive moral liberalisation of Polish society that can be observed over the last decades has led to the appearance and endurance of various forms of interpersonal relations that in the past used to face clear social disapproval. Currently, the child and the parent might share a household with the parent's partner who is not the child's parent ('non-parental partner'). Such situations are not rare in contemporary Polish society and do not induce negative social reactions. Relations between such persons (for example, between a mother, her child and her partner) might be shaped by the applicable legal norms (if the mother is married to her partner) or result solely from the de facto situation existing between them without any specific legal regulation (if the mother is in a de facto union with her partner).

In Polish law, the relationship between a child and his or her parent's non-parental partner differs depending on one factor, namely whether the parent's partner is in a de facto union (meaning one without legal registration) with the parent or is the parent's spouse. Hence, under the Polish legal system, the legal analysis of family forms must always be carried out from the perspective of the existence or non-existence of a legal marriage between the parent and the parent's partner.

Polish law provides for separate legal regulation with respect to the rules on assisted reproductive technology.[1] However, this law does not contain rules which could regulate surrogacy. Surrogacy is currently discussed only within academic discourse.

In the Polish legal system, there are no general provisions which unequivocally indicate the functions that the family is supposed to fulfil. These functions are construed in legal writings based on many specific provisions included in numerous Acts.

2. LEGAL RESPONSIBILITIES AND RIGHTS OF A STEP-PARENT

2.1. A PARENT OF THE CHILD BEING IN A DE FACTO UNION WITH A NON-PARENTAL PARTNER

In general, the Polish legal system does not provide for any specific rights or duties relating to the person or the property of a child with respect to the parent's

---

[1] On the complicated historical background of this law see B. Bugajski, 'Künstliche Fortpflanzung im polnischen Recht' in A. Dutta, D. Schwab, D. Henrich, P. Gottwald and M. Löhnig (eds), *Beiträge zum europäischen Familien- und Erbrecht: Künstliche Fortpflanzung und europäisches Familienrecht*, vol. 16, Verlag Ernst und Werner Gieseking, Bielefeld 2015, p. 259 ff.; B. Bugajski, 'Das Gesetz über die Heilung der Unfruchtbarkeit und die Novellierung des polnischen Familien- und Vormundschaftsgesetzbuches' (2016) 18 *Zeitschrift für das gesamte Familienrecht* 1546 ff.

partner with whom the parent shares a common household. The sole fact of sharing a common household does not create any rights or duties resulting from the parental responsibility. Formally, such a partner with whom the child shares a household ('residential partner') is perceived as a stranger in relation to this child. In practice, this leads to substantial complications if the residential partner exercises custody over this child. In order to be able to exercise basic activities related to the functioning of the common household, the parent must make use of concepts provided for in the general provisions of the law (for example, power of attorney with respect to picking up a child from kindergarten or school). However, such concepts do not allow for a systematic and comprehensive regulation of custody over the person and the property of a child.

The child does not inherit *ab intestato* from his or her parent's residential partner, and the partner does not inherit *ab intestato* from the child. The Civil Code (CC),[2] however, provides for some temporary benefit for the child in the event of the death of the parent's partner who shares a common household with the child. If the child[3] has resided in the common household until the death of the residential partner, he or she is entitled to use the house and household appliances to the same extent as before, for a period of three months from the opening of the succession. Any disposition by the parent's partner excluding or limiting this right is invalid.[4]

There are no obstacles to prevent the partner of the child's parent, who is not a parent of the child, from designating the child as an heir in his or her will.

As the residential partner does not possess any specific rights or duties towards the person and property of the child, no question of priority between such rights and duties arises.

2.2. A PARENT MARRIED TO A SPOUSE WHO IS NOT THE PARENT OF THE CHILD

The situation is subject to certain modifications if the partner who is not the parent of the child is the parent's spouse. Pursuant to Article 61^8 §1 sentence 1 of the Family and Guardianship Code (FGC),[5] a marriage gives rise to an affinity

---

[2] The Civil Code (*Kodeks cywilny*) of 23.04.1964 (consolidated version: Dz. U. 2020, item 1740). For the English translation of the CC see E. Kucharska, *The Civil Code/Kodeks cywilny*, 4th ed., C.H. Beck, Warsaw 2019, p. 12 ff.
[3] The CC does not literally mention 'a child', but it is obvious that a child should be perceived as 'another close one' of the deceased within the meaning of Art. 923 §1 of the CC.
[4] Art. 923 §1 of the CC.
[5] The Family and Guardianship Code (*Kodeks rodzinny i opiekuńczy*) of 25.02.1964 (consolidated version: Dz. U. 2020, item 1359). For the English translation of the FGC see N. Faulkner, *The Family and Guardianship Code/Kodeks rodzinny i opiekuńczy*, 2nd ed., C.H. Beck, Warsaw 2018, p. 6 ff.

relationship between the spouse and the relatives, most importantly children, of the other spouse.

After the marriage, the parent's partner becomes the step-parent of the child of the parent. The concepts of 'stepson' and 'stepdaughter' are generally used; however, these concepts are not found in the CC or FGC. A step-child is an affine of the first degree in a straight line of the step-parent.[6]

Affinity that existed between the step-child and the step-parent due to the marriage continues to exist even after the subsequent end of the marriage between the parent and the step-parent.[7] These rules suggest that – pursuant to Article 14 §1 sentence 1 of the FGC – even after the end of the marriage of the parent, a step-parent will generally not be able to marry their step-child.[8]

The legal situation of being a stepfather or a stepmother does not mean that the spouse of the parent has vast rights and duties towards the person and property of the step-child. However, the Polish legislator provided for certain exceptions in that respect, which regulate some questions of substantive law or procedure.

The first exception concerns a question of practical importance, namely maintenance. In accordance with Article 144 §1 of the FGC, a child may claim maintenance from his or her mother's husband who is not the child's father, if this conforms with the principles of community life. The same right exists with respect to the father's wife who is not the child's mother.

Maintenance claimed by a child from the spouse of the parent will be granted only if such a claim conforms with so-called 'principles of community life'. By principles of community life, one should understand traditional norms of moral and customary character. Only those customs which deserve approval from the point of view of principles of fairness and morality may be perceived as being included in the concept of principles of community life.[9] In the light of Polish law, the maintenance obligation of a step-parent is not created solely by the fact of concluding a marriage with the parent of the child; additionally, such circumstances must exist that the claim for maintenance from the stepfather or stepmother reflects the common sense of fairness, which is grounded in moral rules and good practices within society. The existence of the obligation and its extent in each case will depend on the assessment of whether in the given circumstances a claim for maintenance from a step-parent and its amount are in conformity with the principles of community life.[10]

---

[6] See Art. 61[8] §2 of the FGC.
[7] See Art. 61[8] §1 sentence 2 of the FGC.
[8] Concluding such a marriage would only be possible exceptionally with the approval from a court, if that decision would be justified by serious reasons (Art. 14 §1 sentence 2 of the FGC).
[9] A. Zbiegień-Turzańska, 'Comment on Art. 5 CC' in K. Osajda (ed.), *Kodeks cywilny. Komentarz*, 27th ed., Legalis Online Database 2020, item 55.
[10] See judgment of the Supreme Court (*Sąd Najwyższy*) of 04.04.1968, III CZP 27/68, OSNC 1969, no. 1, item 6.

In the legal literature it is rightly submitted that all the legal and factual circumstances of the case determine whether a claim for maintenance from a step-parent is justified by the principles of community life. The following circumstances must be considered: (1) the real scheme of relations between the creditor and the debtor; (2) the duration of their relations; (3) the duration of the marriage that resulted in affinity; and (4) the actual relations between the step-child and his or her parents.[11]

It should be underlined that pursuant to Article 144 §2 of the FGC the mother's husband who is not the child's father might also claim maintenance from the child if he contributed to the upbringing and financial support of the child and the claim is in conformity with the principles of community life. The same is true with respect to the father's wife who is not the child's mother.

The second important consequence of the affinity relationship between the step-parent and the step-child concerns the child's name. If the parent of a minor marries a person who is not the child's mother or father, the spouses may make a consensual statement before the civil status registry officer or the consul that the child will be assigned the same name as would be assigned to their common child pursuant to Article 88 of the FGC.[12] To change the name of a child who is above 13 years of age, the child's consent is additionally required. The above-mentioned rules on the assignment of names of step-children do not apply if the child carries the name of his or her father or a name created by the combination of the name of the mother and the name of the father based on their consensual statement.[13]

Affinity may in exceptional circumstances lead to a situation where the step-child will inherit intestate from the step-parent. In accordance with Article 934^1 of the CC, such inheritance will take place if there is either a spouse of the step-parent or other relatives who are inheriting intestate.[14] In contrast, the step-parent does not inherit intestate from the step-child.

A step-parent may without any limitations prepare a will in which dispositions for the benefit of a step-child will be included.

There is also the temporary benefit provided for in the CC for the child in the event of the death of the step-parent who shared a common household with the child. If the child has resided in a common household with the step-parent until

---

[11] J. Pawliczak, 'Comment on Art. 144 FGC' in K. Osajda (ed.), *Kodeks rodzinny i opiekuńczy. Komentarz*, 8th ed., Legalis Online Database 2020, item 17.
[12] Pursuant to Art. 88 §1 of the FGC, a child, with respect to whom a presumption of paternity of the mother's husband exists, is assigned the common name of the parents. If the parents have different names, the child is assigned the name as indicated in their consensual statement. The spouses may indicate the name of one of them or a name created by the combination of the name of the mother and the name of the father.
[13] See Art. 90 §§1–2 in conjunction with §3 of the FGC.
[14] The estate is transferred in equal parts to these step-children, whose parents have not survived until the date of the opening of the succession.

the latter's death, the child is entitled to use the house and household appliances to the same extent as before for a period of three months from the opening of the succession. Any disposition of the step-parent excluding or limiting this right is invalid.[15]

In certain circumstances, affinity may influence the validity of testamentary dispositions stipulated for the benefit of the step-child. Pursuant to Article 957 §1 of the CC, a person for whose benefit there is any disposition in the will may not be a witness to this will. The following persons cannot serve as witnesses to a will: a spouse, his or her relatives or affines of the first and second degree, and persons in an adoption relationship. Step-children are the step-parent's affines in the first degree. Hence, if a testator provided for some dispositions in favour of a step-child, then his or her step-child may not be a witness to the will. If the step-child is a witness to the will in which a testator made a disposition in favour of that step-child, only the disposition which was made in favour of the step-child is invalid. If the wording of the will or the circumstances of the case indicate that without this invalid disposition the testator would not have drafted such a will, the whole will is invalid.[16]

The same rules apply to a testamentary disposition made by any testator in favour of the step-parent when the witness to the drafting of the will was this step-parent's step-child.[17]

Affinity has important consequences in relations between a step-parent and a step-child in court proceedings or proceedings before public administration authorities.

In civil,[18] penal,[19] and judicial administrative proceedings,[20] a judge is excluded by operation of the law (*ex lege*) from hearing a case concerning, inter alia, his or her affines in the straight line, including his or her step-children. Hence, a step-parent may not hear a case to which his or her step-child is a party. The same exclusion applies to a step-child hearing a case to which his or her step-parent is a party.

---

[15] See Art. 923 §1 of the CC.
[16] See Art. 957 §2 of the CC.
[17] Such a situation is only possible once the step-child already has full capacity to act (Art. 956 no. 1 of the CC).
[18] See Art. 48 §1 no. 2 of the Code of Civil Procedure (*Kodeks postępowania cywilnego*) of 17.11.1964 (consolidated version: Dz. U. 2020, item 1575) (CCivP). For the English translation of the CCivP see A. Rucińska, M. Świerkot and K. Tatar, *The Code of Civil Procedure/Kodeks postępowania cywilnego*, C.H. Beck, Warsaw 2016, p. 20 ff.
[19] See Art. 40 §1 no. 3 of the Code of Criminal Procedure (*Kodeks postępowania karnego*) of 06.06.1997 (consolidated version: Dz. U. 2021, item 534) (CCrimP). For the English translation of the CCrimP see J.E. Adamczyk, *The Code of Criminal Procedure/Kodeks postępowania karnego*, 2nd ed., C.H. Beck, Warsaw 2018, p. 12 ff.
[20] See Art. 18 §1 no. 2 of the Administrative Courts Proceedings Act (*Ustawa – Prawo o postępowaniu przed sądami administracyjnymi*) of 30.08.2002 (consolidated version: Dz. U. 2019 r., item 2325) (ACPA).

A step-parent, acting as an officer of the administrative authorities, is also excluded by operation of the law (*ex lege*) from administrative proceedings,[21] including tax proceedings,[22] in cases to which his or her step-child is a party. This exclusion applies equally to a step-child who acts as an officer of the administrative authorities if his or her step-parent is a party to the proceedings.

Within civil,[23] penal,[24] and administrative[25] (including tax)[26] proceedings, a step-child has the right to refuse to testify if the party to such proceedings is his or her step-parent. Similarly, a step-parent has the right to refuse to testify in proceedings to which his or her step-child is a party.

A stepfather or stepmother may not hold the position of an expert witness in civil,[27] penal,[28] and administrative[29] (including tax)[30] proceedings if the case concerns his or her step-child. This limitation applies equally to a step-child being an expert witness in proceedings concerning his or her step-parent.

2.3. ADOPTION OF A STEP-CHILD BY A STEP-PARENT

The sole fact of the conclusion of a marriage between a parent and non-parental partner does not result in automatic acquisition by the partner of parental responsibility over the child. The parent's partner may however adopt the child.[31]

Pursuant to Article 118 §1 of the FGC, adoption requires the consent of an adoptee who is over 13 years of age.[32] Adoption might exceptionally be allowed

---

[21] See Art. 24 §1 no. 2 of the Code of Administrative Procedure (*Kodeks postępowania administracyjnego*) of 14.06.1960 (consolidated version: Dz. U. 2021, item 735) (CAP). For the English translation of the CAP see M. Bińkowska, A. Chełchowski, P. Gumola, B. Kopik and R.A. Walawender, *The Code of Administrative Procedure/Kodeks postępowania administracyjnego*, 3rd ed., C.H. Beck, Warsaw 2017, p. 7 ff.

[22] See Art. 130 §1 no. 3 of the Tax Ordinance Act (*Ordynacja podatkowa*) of 29.08.1997 (consolidated version: Dz. U. 2020, item 1325) (TOA). For the English translation of the TOA see P. Jabłonowski, B. Sobieraj and K. Stępnicka, *The Tax Ordinance Act/Ordynacja podatkowa*, C.H. Beck, Warsaw 2011, p. 8 ff.

[23] See Art. 261 §1 of the CCivP. Compare Art. 261 §2 of the CCivP.

[24] See Art. 182 §1 of the CCrimP in conjunction with Art. 115 §11 of the Criminal Code (*Kodeks karny*) of 06.06.1997 (consolidated version: Dz. U. 2020, item 1444) (CCrim). For the English translation of the CCrim see N. Faulkner, *The Criminal Code/Kodeks karny*, 2nd ed., C.H. Beck, Warsaw 2012, p. 1 ff. Compare Art. 183 CCrimP in conjunction with Art. 115 §11 CCrim.

[25] See Art. 83 §1 of the CAP. Compare Art. 83 §2 of the CAP.

[26] See Art. 196 §1 of the TOA. Compare Art. 196 §2 of the TOA.

[27] See Art. 281 §1 in conjunction with Art. 48 §1 no. 2 of the CCivP.

[28] See Art. 196 §1 in conjunction with Art. 40 §1 no. 3 of the CCrimP.

[29] See Art. 84 §2 in conjunction with Art. 24 §1 no. 2 of the CAP.

[30] See Art. 197 §3 in conjunction with Art. 130 §1 no. 3 of the TOA.

[31] For details see M. Prucnal-Wójcik, 'Comment on Art. 114 et seq. FGC' in K. Osajda (ed.), *Kodeks rodzinny i opiekuńczy. Komentarz*, 8th ed., Legalis Online Database 2020, item 1 et seq.

[32] The court should hear the adoptee who has not attained 13 years of age if the adoptee understands the meaning of the concept of adoption (Art. 118 §2 F of the GC).

without the consent of the adoptee, if he or she is not capable of giving consent or it flows from the relationship between the adopter and the adoptee that the adoptee perceives him- or herself as the adopter's child and asking for the consent of or hearing the child would be contrary to the adoptee's best interests.[33]

In accordance with Article 119 §1 of the FGC, the consent of the child's parents is also usually required. However, this rule does not apply if the parents were deprived of parental responsibility or are unknown, or if contacting them would present serious obstacles. The legislator also provides that the court may, due to the specific circumstances of the case, grant an adoption even without the consent of the parents if their capacity to act is limited or their refusal is manifestly contrary to the best interests of the child.[34]

After the adoption of a child by the parent's partner who is not the child's parent the legal situation of a child changes significantly.

The FGC provides for two models of adoption: full adoption (*adoptio plena*)[35] and open adoption (*adoptio minus plena*).[36] In the case of full adoption, the adoptee becomes a child of the adopter and part of his or her family. The result of such an adoption is generally the termination of the legal relationship with the biological family of the child.[37] As regards open adoption[38] – as opposed to full adoption – it creates a legal relationship solely between the adopter and the adoptee. This means that the adoptee does not become fully included in the adopter's family. The adoptee does not become either a brother or sister of the adopter's children or a grandchild of the adopter's parents.[39]

Pursuant to Article 121 §1 of the FGC, a full adoption (*adoptio plena*) results in a relationship similar to the one between parents and their children.[40] Consequently, the adoptee acquires rights and duties resulting from consanguinity towards the relatives of the adopter.[41] The rights and duties of the adoptee towards his or her biological family terminate, as do the rights and

---

[33] Art. 118 §3 of the FGC.
[34] Art. 119 §2 of the FGC.
[35] See Arts 121–23 of the FGC. The adoption, which is indissoluble, also referred to as complete adoption (*adoptio plenissima*), is a variant of a full adoption regulated in Art. 125^1 §1 of the FGC. Based on this provision, an adoption for which the parents of the adoptee gave their consent in court without indicating the adoptive person, may not be dissolved. For details see H. Ciepła in K. Piasecki (ed.), *Kodeks rodzinny i opiekuńczy. Komentarz*, 5th ed., Lexis Nexis, Warsaw 2011, p. 897 ff.
[36] See Art. 124 §1 of the FGC.
[37] H. Ciepła in K. Piasecki (ed.), *Kodeks rodzinny i opiekuńczy. Komentarz*, 5th ed., Lexis Nexis, Warsaw 2011, p. 884.
[38] On this matter see also para. 2.6 of this report.
[39] H. Ciepła in K. Piasecki (ed.), *Kodeks rodzinny i opiekuńczy. Komentarz*, 5th ed., Lexis Nexis, Warsaw 2011, p. 895.
[40] See Art. 121 §1 of the FGC.
[41] Ibid.

duties of the adoptee's relatives towards him or her.[42] A full adoption also has consequences for intestate succession. In accordance with Article 936 §1 of the CC, the adoptee inherits intestate from the adopter and his or her relatives as if he or she were the adopter's child. The adopter and his or her relatives inherit intestate as if they were the adoptee's parents and their relatives. Consequently, the adoptee does not inherit intestate from his or her biological family and his or her biological family does not inherit from the adoptee.[43]

The rule that the rights and duties resulting from the consanguinity of the adoptee to his or her biological family and the rights and duties of the adoptee's biological family towards the adoptee terminate does not apply to the spouse (and his or her relatives) whose child has been adopted by the other spouse. This is also true with respect to adoption after the termination of the marriage because of the death of the spouse whose child has been adopted.[44] In such cases only the mutual rights and duties resulting from the consanguinity between the child who was adopted by the stepfather or stepmother and the parent of the child (and his or her relatives) who is not the spouse of the adopter are terminated. The mutual rights and duties resulting from the consanguinity between the adoptee and the adopter's spouse – that is, the adopted child's mother or father – as well as his or her relatives continue to exist.[45]

If one of the spouses adopts the other spouse's child, the rule that the adoptee does not inherit intestate from his or her biological parents and their relatives, and that these persons do not inherit intestate from the child, does not apply with respect to the spouse whose child has been adopted and his or her relatives (in accordance with Art. 936 §3 CC). Additionally, if the adoption was granted after the death of the second parent of the adoptee, this rule does not apply to the relatives of the deceased, whose rights and duties were sustained in the adoption order.

The adoption – irrespective of its mode – does not change the temporary benefit provided for in the CC in the event of the death of the step-parent who shared a common household with the child. Pursuant to Article 923 §1 of the CC, if the child has resided in a common household with the step-parent until the latter's death, the child is entitled to use the house and household appliances to the same extent as before for a period of three months from the opening of the succession. Any disposition of the step-parent excluding or limiting this right is invalid.

There is a rule that, because of the adoption, the current parental responsibility of guardianship over the child is terminated.[46] If one of the spouses adopted the

---

[42] See Art. 121 §3 of the FGC.
[43] Art. 936 §2 of the CC.
[44] See Art. 121¹ §1 of the FGC. Compare Art. 121¹ §2 of the FGC.
[45] E. Holewińska-Łapińska in T. Smyczyński (ed.), *System Prawa Prywatnego. Prawo rodzinne i opiekuńcze*, vol. 12, C.H. Beck, Warsaw 2011, item 284.
[46] Art. 123 §1 of the FGC.

child of the second spouse, parental responsibility is exercised by both spouses jointly pursuant to Article 123 §2 of the FGC.

After the adoption, the rules on parental responsibility provided for in the Family and Guardianship Code are the same as with respect to biological parents. If parental responsibility is held jointly by both parents, each of them is at the same time obliged and entitled to exercise it.[47] Making decisions on important issues concerning the child is reserved to both parents, who should decide jointly. In the case of lack of consensus between the parents, the decision may be made by the court.[48]

2.4. BRINGING UP A CHILD IN MORE THAN ONE HOUSEHOLD

If a child is brought up in more than one household (for a certain period by one parent and his or her partner and for the remaining time with another parent and his or her partner), the legal situation of the child is regulated in accordance with the same rules as described in sections 2.1–2.3 above and section 2.6 below.

2.5. BRINGING UP A CHILD IN A POLYGAMOUS FAMILY

Polish law does not provide for the existence of polygamous families. If – contrary to regulations in place in Poland – a child is raised in a de facto polygamous family, the child's legal situation should be analysed in accordance with the rules presented in sections 2.1–2.3 above and section 2.6 below.

2.6. MULTIPLICITY OF PARENTHOOD IN THE CASE OF OPEN ADOPTION

Polish law allows for an open adoption, which has legal effects only between the adopter and the adoptee. Pursuant to Article 124 §1 of the FGC, the court grants this kind of adoption on the application of the adopter, with the consent of the persons whose consent is required for adoption. When an open adoption is granted, the adoptee is not fully included in the family of the adopter. He or she does not become either the brother or sister of the adopter's children or the grandson or granddaughter of the adopter's ascendants. The effects of the adoption do extend to descendants of the adoptee.[49] Limiting the effects of the

---

[47] Art. 97 §1 of the FGC.
[48] Art. 97 §2 of the FGC.
[49] See Art. 124 §1 of the FGC.

adoption solely to the person of the adopter results in the continuation of the family relationship between the adoptee and his or her natural family.[50]

The legislator rightly decided that open adoption cannot be granted if the parents of the adoptee consented to the adoption before the court without indicating the person who is to adopt the child.[51]

Open adoption produces specific effects when it comes to intestate succession. Firstly, the adoptee inherits from the adopter in the same way as the adopter's children, and the adoptee's descendants inherit from the adopter in the same way as the adopter's more distant relatives. Secondly, the adoptee and his or her descendants do not inherit from the adopter's relatives and the adopter's relatives do not inherit from the adoptee and his or her descendants. Thirdly, the adoptee's parents do not inherit from the adoptee; instead it is the adopter who inherits.[52]

Open adoption has no influence on the possibility of disposing *mortis causa* in a will.

2.7. MULTIPLICITY OF PARENTHOOD IN THE CASE OF *KAFALA*

Polish law does not provide for the existence of an institution known in Islamic law as *kafala*. If a child is brought up in a family where the partners abide by the rules characteristic of the institution of *kafala*, the child's legal situation should be analysed in accordance with the rules outlined in sections 2.1–2.3 and section 2.6 above.

3. PARENTHOOD AND THE USE OF ASSISTED REPRODUCTIVE TECHNOLOGY

3.1. PARENTHOOD IF THE DONOR IS ANONYMOUS

Polish law does not differentiate between genetic and biological motherhood.[53] Pursuant to Article 61^9 of the FGC,[54] the mother is always the woman who gives

---

[50] H. Ciepła in K. Piasecki (ed.), *Kodeks rodzinny i opiekuńczy. Komentarz*, 5th ed., Lexis Nexis, Warsaw 2011, p. 895.
[51] See Art. 124 §1 of the FGC. Based on Art. 124 §3 of the FGC the court may – during the period of the child's adolescence – transform an open adoption into a full one. This transformation takes place on the application of the adopter and requires the consent of the persons whose consent is needed for the adoption.
[52] See Art. 937 nos 1–3 of the CC.
[53] B. Bugajski, 'Künstliche Fortpflanzung im polnischen Recht' in A. Dutta, D. Schwab, D. Henrich, P. Gottwald and M. Löhnig (eds), *Beiträge zum europäischen Familien- und*

birth to the child. Important consequences result from this rule. A woman who has donated genetic material but has not given birth to the child may not be recognised as the child's legal mother.[55]

Establishment of fatherhood depends on whether the mother – pursuant to Article 61[9] of the FGC, the woman who gave birth to the child – is married. If the mother of the child is married, the presumption of paternity applies. In accordance with Article 62 §1 of the FGC, if the child is born during the marriage or before 300 days have elapsed since its termination or annulment, there is a presumption that the child is the child of the mother's husband.

This presumption does not apply if the child is born more than 300 days after the legal separation was pronounced. If the child is born before 300 days have elapsed since the termination or annulment of the marriage but after a new marriage has been concluded by the mother, the presumption relates to the second husband of the mother. The presumption rightly does not apply if the child was born via assisted reproduction technology to which the first husband of the mother gave his consent.[56]

Rebuttal of the presumption of paternity is possible only via court proceedings on the denial of paternity.[57] Denial of paternity consists of establishing that the mother's husband is not the father of the child.[58] Article 68 of the FGC rightly provides that denial of paternity is inadmissible if the child was born via assisted reproduction technology to which the husband of the mother gave his consent. Pursuant to this rule, the mother's husband may not approach the court for denial of his paternity even if the conception took place via assisted reproduction technology with the use of another man's sperm. It is irrelevant whether the sperm donor was anonymous or his identity was known.

Pursuant to Article 72 §1 of the FGC, paternity may be established through acknowledgement of paternity or by an order of the court only if the presumption of paternity does not apply or was rebutted. Acknowledgment of paternity may be done only by the man who is the father.[59] Pursuant to Article 73 §3 of the FGC, the officer of the civil status registry should refuse to accept a statement necessary for acknowledgement of paternity if there are doubts as to

---

Erbrecht: Künstliche Fortpflanzung und europäisches Familienrecht, vol. 16, Verlag Ernst und Werner Gieseking, Bielefeld 2015, p. 271.

[54] For more details see A. Mączyński, 'Die Modernisierung des polnischen Familien- und Vormundschaftsgesetzbuches' (2009) 18 *Zeitschrift für das gesamte Familienrecht* 1556.

[55] B. Bugajski, 'Künstliche Fortpflanzung im polnischen Recht' in A. Dutta, D. Schwab, D. Henrich, P. Gottwald and M. Löhnig (eds), *Beiträge zum europäischen Familien- und Erbrecht: Künstliche Fortpflanzung und europäisches Familienrecht*, vol. 16, Verlag Ernst und Werner Gieseking, Bielefeld 2015, p. 272 and literature cited therein.

[56] See Art. 62 §2 of the FGC.
[57] See Art. 62 §3 of the FGC.
[58] See Art. 67 of the FGC.
[59] Art. 73 §1 of the FGC.

the child's origins.[60] Pursuant to Article 75 §1 of the FGC, acknowledgement of paternity after the child has been conceived but before the child is born is also admissible.

Polish law also provides for so-called 'prenatal acknowledgement of paternity'.[61] This allows for the regulation of the legal situation of a child born via a procedure of assisted reproduction technology from the moment of the child's birth. Prenatal presumption of paternity becomes effective on the day of the child's birth provided that the man makes a statement in front of the officer of the civil status registry that he will be the father of the child before the transfer into the woman of a reproductive cell from an anonymous donor or an embryo developed from the reproductive cells of an anonymous donor or a donated embryo. For the effective prenatal acknowledgement of paternity, confirmation from the mother is needed that this man will be the father of the child. This confirmation should be made simultaneously with the man's statement or within three months from that day.[62]

Prenatal acknowledgement of paternity will be effective only if the child is born after assisted reproduction technology within two years from the man's statement.[63] The prenatal acknowledgment of paternity constitutes an exception to the rule that acknowledgment of paternity is possible only in the case of the man who is the father of the child, as the genetic material transferred into the woman is not derived from the man who acknowledges his paternity.

Polish law also provides for the institution of establishment of the invalidity of the acknowledgment of paternity,[64] which is designed to correct the paternity details when the child was acknowledged by a man who is not the father. In the case of prenatal acknowledgment of paternity, establishment of its invalidity is admissible only if the child has been born but this birth was not the result of assisted reproduction technology in relation to which the man made a prenatal acknowledgment of paternity.[65]

3.2. PARENTHOOD IF THE DONOR IS NOT ANONYMOUS

The revealing of the identity of the donors of the genetic material and their intention to participate in the upbringing of the child has no influence on the

---

[60] B. Bugajski, 'Künstliche Fortpflanzung im polnischen Recht' in A. Dutta, D. Schwab, D. Henrich, P. Gottwald and M. Löhnig (eds), *Beiträge zum europäischen Familien- und Erbrecht: Künstliche Fortpflanzung und europäisches Familienrecht*, vol. 16, Verlag Ernst und Werner Gieseking, Bielefeld 2015, p. 275.
[61] J. Ignatowicz and M. Nazar, *Prawo rodzinne*, 5th ed., Wolters Kluwer, Warsaw 2016, p. 438.
[62] Art. 75¹ §1 of the FGC.
[63] Art. 75¹ §2 of the FGC.
[64] See Art. 78 et seq. FGC.
[65] Art. 81¹ of the FGC. See J. Ignatowicz and M. Nazar, *Prawo rodzinne*, 5th ed., Wolters Kluwer, Warsaw 2016, p. 457.

operation of the rules on establishment of motherhood and fatherhood as described in section 3.1 above.

3.3. THREE-PARENT CHILDREN

Polish law does not provide for the possibility of assisted reproduction technology where the DNA of one woman is 'corrected' by the DNA of another woman. If – contrary to the law in place in Poland – a 'correction' of one woman's DNA with another woman's DNA were to be carried out via assisted reproduction technology, the motherhood and fatherhood would be established in accordance with the same rules as described in sections 3.1–3.2 above. The mother – pursuant to Article 61^9 of the FGC – is only the woman who gave birth to the child. In Poland there is no such legal concept as a 'three-parent child'.

3.4. PARENTHOOD IN THE CASE OF SURROGACY

Polish law does not specifically regulate the institution of surrogacy. In the legal literature a standpoint is presented that any arrangements aimed at regulating the 'use of the womb' of one woman by another woman, from whom the genetic material comes, should be perceived as against the law and, therefore, invalid.[66]

The lack of differentiation in Polish law between biological and genetic motherhood forces the conclusion that, in accordance with Article 61^9 of the FGC, the surrogate mother, as the woman who gave birth to the child, is the child's mother. There is no normative ground allowing for recognising the woman from whom the genetic material comes but who has not given birth to the child as the mother.[67]

When it comes to fatherhood, this should be established in accordance with the same rules as described in sections 3.1–3.2 above.

3.5. PARENTHOOD IN THE CASE OF SURROGACY: SAME-SEX PARTNERS

Pursuant to Article 1 §1 of the FGC, marriage may only be concluded between persons of the opposite sex (a woman and a man). A marriage concluded between

---

[66] B. Bugajski, 'Künstliche Fortpflanzung im polnischen Recht' in A. Dutta, D. Schwab, D. Henrich, P. Gottwald and M. Löhnig (eds), *Beiträge zum europäischen Familien- und Erbrecht: Künstliche Fortpflanzung und europäisches Familienrecht*, vol. 16, Verlag Ernst und Werner Gieseking, Bielefeld 2015, p. 272 and the literature cited therein.
[67] Ibid.

persons of the same sex is perceived as non-existent (*matrimonium non existens*) by operation of the law (*ex lege*). It does not create any of the legal consequences which result from the conclusion of a marriage.[68]

The restriction of marriage solely to persons of the opposite sex results from the wording of Article 18 of the Constitution,[69] in which a marriage is defined as a union between a woman and a man. Legal scholarship discusses the issue of whether introducing same-sex marriage or registered partnership into the Polish legal system would be acceptable under the Constitution.[70]

The analysis of Article 18 of the Constitution, in particular its *travaux préparatoires*, which suggests that the aim of the drafters was to exclude unions other than a marriage of one woman and one man,[71] leads to the conclusion that the introduction of same-sex marriages would be possible only after a suitable amendment to Article 18 of the Constitution.

The question whether introduction of an institution of registered partnership for persons of the same sex who share a common life is possible remains open. It seems that this institution could not be fully equal to marriage as this would constitute evasion of the definition of marriage as stated in Article 18 of the Constitution.

In Poland there is no law providing for the possibility of formalising a same-sex union in any way. Consequently, there are no rules concerning parenthood with respect to children brought up in such unions.

If a child is conceived in a union created by persons of the same sex, motherhood and fatherhood would be established in accordance with the same rules as described in sections 3.1–3.4 above.

---

[68] B. Bugajski, 'Stand des Scheidungsrechts in Polen' in A. Dutta, D. Schwab, D. Henrich, P. Gottwald and M. Löhnig (eds), *Beiträge zum europäischen Familien- und Erbrecht: Scheidung ohne Gericht? Neue Entwicklungen im europäischen Scheidungsrecht*, vol. 18, Verlag Ernst und Werner Gieseking, Bielefeld 2017, pp. 241–42; B. Bugajski, 'Familienrecht und Religion – Länderbericht Polen' in C. Mayer, D. Schwab, P. Gottwald and D. Henrich (eds), *Beiträge zum europäischen Familien- und Erbrecht: Familienrecht und Religion. Europäische Perspektiven*, vol. 21, Verlag Ernst und Werner Gieseking, Bielefeld 2019, pp. 291–92.

[69] The Constitution of the Republic of Poland (*Konstytucja Rzeczypospolitej Polskiej*) of 02.04.1997 (Constitution) (Dz. U. 1997, no. 78, item 483). For the English translation of the Constitution see A. Pol and A. Caldwell, *The Constitution of the Republic of Poland*, Wydawnictwo Sejmowe, Warsaw 2018, p. 115 ff. Art. 18 of the Constitution reads as follows: 'Marriage, being a union of a man and a woman, as well as the family, motherhood and parenthood, shall be placed under the protection and care of the Republic of Poland'.

[70] B. Bugajski, 'Familienrecht und Religion – Länderbericht Polen' in C. Mayer, D. Schwab, P. Gottwald and D. Henrich (eds), *Beiträge zum europäischen Familien- und Erbrecht: Familienrecht und Religion. Europäische Perspektiven*, vol. 21, Verlag Ernst und Werner Gieseking, Bielefeld 2019, pp. 291–92 and literature cited therein.

[71] See W. Borysiak, 'Comment on Art. 18 Constitution' in M. Safjan and M. Bosek (eds), *Konstytucja RP. Komentarz. art. 1-86*, vol. 1, C.H. Beck, Warsaw 2016, items 38–39.

3.6. WORK ON MULTIPLICITY OF PARENTHOOD

Currently in Poland there are no legislative projects which would have as their object the concept of multiplicity of parenthood in any form.

4. DIVERSITY AND PLURALITY OF FAMILY FUNCTIONS

4.1. DIVERSE FAMILY FUNCTIONS

In legal writings, a family[72] is described as the smallest natural social unit, whose functioning serves a unique role both for individuals and for the whole of society. The adequate functioning of a family allows for all the needs, both material and immaterial, of its members to be met.[73]

In the Polish legal system there is no general provision which would unequivocally indicate the functions that a family should serve. These functions are however construed in legal scholarship based on numerous specific regulations included in different Acts.

Among the most important functions of the family, the following are often mentioned: (1) reproduction, which fulfils the individual need of parenthood of the mother and the father and the societal interest in demographic growth; (2) providing security for family members by meeting their needs (physiological, cultural and for security); (3) bringing up children (preparation for their fulfilment of social roles); (4) control of the members of the family; and (5) meeting the emotional needs of the family members (for example, acceptance, love, sense of security).[74]

4.2. FAMILY FUNCTION PREFERRED BY POLISH LAW

The analysis of the Polish legal system, in particular the norms of the Constitution, reveals that the Polish legislator clearly favours the procreative function of the family. This conclusion is supported by the wording of Article 18

---

[72] On the scope of the concept of 'family' in Polish law see T. Smyczyński in T. Smyczyński (ed.), *System Prawa Prywatnego. Prawo rodzinne i opiekuńcze*, vol. 11, 2nd ed., C.H. Beck, Warsaw 2014, items 1–6; J. Ignatowicz and M. Nazar, *Prawo rodzinne*, 5th ed., Wolters Kluwer, Warsaw 2016, pp. 29–34.
[73] J. Ignatowicz and M. Nazar, *Prawo rodzinne*, 5th ed., Wolters Kluwer, Warsaw 2016, p. 34.
[74] Ibid. Compare T. Smyczyński in T. Smyczyński (ed.), *System Prawa Prywatnego. Prawo rodzinne i opiekuńcze*, vol. 11, 2nd ed., C.H. Beck, Warsaw 2014, items 7–8.

of the Constitution, in which 'parenthood' and 'motherhood' are objects not only of 'protection', but also of 'custody' of the State. In order to correctly assess the importance of the constitutional protection and guardianship of parenthood and motherhood, it must be noted that Article 18 is located in the first chapter of the Constitution, in which fundamental principles of the legal system of the Republic of Poland are listed. The second chapter of the Constitution[75] – entitled 'Freedoms, rights and duties of a human and a citizen' – also contains provisions devoted to family law, but they constitute only an extension of the regulation provided for in Article 18 of the Constitution. This provision may be perceived as the 'constitutional fundamental rule', as it is of general character (*lex generalis*) when compared to specific questions of family law regulated in other provisions of the Constitution.[76]

Underlying the role of parenthood and motherhood – namely, the procreative function of the family – in the Constitution, which has been in force since 1997, is a manifestation of the concern for adequate demographic growth, which, in turn, will allow for the stable existence of society in the future. Such a foundation does not surprise the authors and deserves approval.

Unfortunately, the practical realisation of the procreative function of the family – despite it being made a fundamental constitutional rule – has not been successful in Poland. This is clearly proved by demographic data. The population of Poland has been constantly shrinking since 2012.[77] In Poland the rate of natural increase has remained negative since 2013.[78] Solutions created on the constitutional level and at the level of ordinary legislation, which were supposed to support the realisation of the procreative function of the family, do not constitute an adequate incentive for citizens to decide to have children.

4.3. INFLUENCE OF HAVING CHILDREN ON FAMILY FUNCTIONS

Polish law designates procreation as an important function of the family. Obviously, the realisation of this function assumes having children. Once children are born, bringing them up appropriately becomes an important factor, as it is aimed at preparing children for the fulfilment of different social roles and at securing their material and immaterial needs.

---

[75] See Arts 47, 48, 71, 72 of the Constitution.
[76] W. Borysiak, 'Comment on Art. 18 Constitution' in M. Safjan and M. Bosek (eds), *Konstytucja RP. Komentarz. art. 1-86*, vol. 1, C.H. Beck, Warsaw 2016, item 3.
[77] An almost unnoticeable increase in the population – by 1,000 – was recorded in 2017.
[78] M. Cierniak-Piotrowska, A. Dąbrowska, K. Stelmach and D. Szałtys (supervisor), *Ludność. Stan i struktura oraz ruch naturalny w przekroju terytorialnym w 2020 r. Stan w dniu 31 XII/Population. Size and structure and vital statistics in Poland by territorial division in 2020. As of 31 December*, Główny Urząd Statystyczny/Statistics Poland, Warsaw 2021, pp. 11–12.

If there are no children, the procreative function of the family is not realised. Then the function of bringing up children and securing their needs also becomes irrelevant. There are no obstacles, however, to the spouses mutually providing support for each other's material and physiological needs, controlling each other's behaviour and mutually securing each other's emotional needs (for acceptance, love and a sense of security).

In Polish law there is no normative ground which would allow a distinction between family functions depending on whether children are biological children, step-children, children born using medically assisted reproductive procedures, children born by a surrogate mother or children of 'multiple parents'. These functions are realised by a family, the composition of which may be assessed only in accordance with the legal norms in force concerning the establishment of motherhood and fatherhood.

5. CONCLUSION

Dynamic changes to the social environment require reaction on the part of the legislator in each legal system. Unfortunately, the Polish legislator often takes no action when it comes to certain of the questions discussed in this report. The lack of action on the part of the legislator may be caused by the fact that these matters are often confronted with a public discussion of a very emotional nature. Lack of legal regulation of certain questions does not result in the disappearance of such non-regulated situations; it only leads to complications when it comes to deciding on the outcomes that these non-regulated situations create.

There are two questions relating to the topic of this report that need to be answered in the Polish legal system. Firstly, surrogacy requires clear regulation in Poland. The decision of the legislator should clearly forbid it or clearly allow it. If the decision were made to permit surrogacy, it would be necessary to precisely regulate its modalities (for example, the admissibility of remuneration of the surrogate mother). Secondly, a decision on the potential institutionalisation of same-sex marriages in Polish law, which would require an amendment to the Constitution, should be made.

Considering the emotions that are caused by the discussions on the above-mentioned topics and the fact that the concept of marriage is regulated in the Constitution, it seems justified that the decisions on these matters should be taken in the form of a general referendum. Each citizen should have a voice on these matters, which could permanently influence the shape of family law.

THE DIVERSIFICATION OF FAMILY FORMS AND FUNCTIONS IN SOUTH AFRICA

Anne Louw

1. Introduction 395
2. Part A. Diversity and Plurality of Family Forms 396
   2.1. Recognition of Multiple Parents in the Context of Step-Families 396
   2.2. Recognition of Multiple Parents if a Child is Raised in More than One Household. 398
   2.3. Recognition of Multiple Parents if a Child is Raised in a Polygamous Family. 402
   2.4. Recognition of Multiple Parents in the Case of Open Adoption.... 404
   2.5. Recognition of Multiple Parents in the Case of *Kafala* 405
   2.6. Recognition of Multiple Parents in the Case of Donor-Assisted Reproduction without Surrogacy. 406
   2.7. Recognition of Multiple Parents in the Case of a 'Three-Parent Child' 408
   2.8. Recognition of Multiple Parents in the Case of Surrogacy. 409
   2.9. Recognition of Same-Sex Parents 411
   2.10. General Recognition of Multi-Parenthood 412
3. Part B. Diversity and Plurality of Family's Functions 413
   3.1. Legal Recognition of Various Functions of the Family. 413
   3.2. The Functions which are Predominantly Favoured. 414
   3.3. The Role of Children in the Legal View on the Functions of the Family 415

1. INTRODUCTION

Even though the Constitution of the Republic of South Africa, 1996 (the Constitution) does not expressly entrench the right to family life, the court in *Dawood and Another v. Minister of Home Affairs and Others; Shalabi and Another v. Minister of Home Affairs and Others; Thomas and Another v. Minister of Home Affairs and Others*[1] (*Dawood*) held that the right to dignity in section 10

---

[1] 2000 (3) SA 936 (CC), para. 36.

of the Constitution is wide enough to include the protection of such a right. The equality clauses in the Constitution, in particular the right to equality on the ground of marital status and sexual orientation, have played a major role in increasing the protection and recognition of the many different shapes and sizes of families found in South Africa.[2] Since becoming a constitutional democracy, family law has become increasingly tolerant of the many different family forms found in South Africa. Family law principles are now applicable to same-sex families as well as polygynous families. The general scope of family law in South Africa has thus expanded beyond recognition over the past three decades. The courts have also been very alert to the danger of entrenching particular forms of family at the expense of other forms.[3] In the given context of the transformation of family law that has taken place, this report provides an overview of the diversity of family forms and family functions recognised in South Africa.

2. PART A. DIVERSITY AND PLURALITY OF FAMILY FORMS

2.1. RECOGNITION OF MULTIPLE PARENTS IN THE CONTEXT OF STEP-FAMILIES

Generally speaking, South Africa does not recognise multiplicity of parenthood in the context of step-families. A step-parent is not deemed a parent for purposes of the law and does not automatically acquire parental responsibilities and rights in respect of a spouse or partner's child. To acquire such rights, a step-parent may apply for the adoption of the child – provided the parent with whom he or she does not share a household consents to the adoption.[4] A step-parent may also acquire parental responsibilities and rights[5] by means of a parental responsibilities and rights agreement and an order of court. The parent with whom the step-parent shares a household may enter into an agreement with the step-parent conferring any or all parental responsibilities and rights on

---

[2] *Dawood* 2000 (3) SA 936 (CC), para. 31.
[3] Ibid., para. 31.
[4] S. 233(1)(a) of the Children's Act 38 of 2005. All further references to the Children's Act will have this Act in mind unless expressly stated otherwise.
[5] Parental responsibilities and rights for purposes of SA law includes the incidences of care, contact and guardianship, as well as the responsibility and the right to contribute to the maintenance of a child (s. 18(2) of the Children's Act). Guardianship and contact in terms of the Act have largely retained their common law meaning as the responsibility and right to assist the child in legal actions and protect the child's property interests (s. 18(3)) and maintaining a personal relationship with the child (s. 1(1) s.v. 'contact'), respectively. Care, however, is defined (in s. 1(1) s.v. 'care') in far broader terms than the common law concept of 'custody'. See also the discussion in section 3.3 below.

the step-parent.[6] To become effective, the agreement must be registered with the Office of the Family Advocate or be made an order of court,[7] but only after having been found in the best interests of the child.[8] A court may also confer responsibilities and rights on a step-parent if the court is satisfied that it is in the child's best interests to do so.[9] The acquisition of parental responsibilities and rights by means of an agreement or court order will lapse upon the child attaining majority[10] – either by attaining the age of 18 or concluding a valid marriage.[11]

While the law has been clear on excluding step-parents from being considered parents without more, the courts have had less compunction to treat step-parents as parents for purposes of deciding the extent of their duty to contribute to the maintenance of their step-child. Some of the more questionable justifications for imposing such a duty on the step-parent include a presumed shared responsibility which arises from a marriage in community of property[12] and the fact that the step-parent acted *in loco parentis*.[13] More convincing is the argument that the child's constitutional right to parental care imposes a duty of support on a step-parent.[14] Whether or not the common law has been or should be developed to impose a general duty of support on a step-parent has as yet not been judicially considered.

Despite not formally having any parental responsibilities and rights, a step-parent who shares care of his or her spouse/partner's child (like any other person who voluntarily cares for a child) is obliged to safeguard the child's health, wellbeing and development and must also protect the child from maltreatment, abuse, neglect and other harmful and exploitative actions.[15] The Children's Act

---

[6] Parental responsibilities and rights agreements are regulated by s. 22 of the Children's Act.
[7] Because the High Court has exclusive jurisdiction in matters relating to the guardianship of children, the agreement will have to be sanctioned by the High Court if it intends to confer guardianship on the step-parent.
[8] S. 22(5).
[9] In addition to the express jurisdiction to make such orders in terms of ss 23 and 24 of the Children's Act, the High Court retains its common law jurisdiction as upper guardian of all minors to make any order it deems fit in this regard.
[10] A parental responsibilities and rights agreement can only be entered into in respect of a child, defined as a person under the age of 18 years. Since marriage confers majority status on a child, a parental responsibilities and rights agreement will no longer be possible after the child has concluded a marriage.
[11] In terms of the Marriage Act 25 of 1961 or the Recognition of Customary Marriages Act 120 of 1998. The latter Act makes provision for marriages to be concluded in terms of customary law, defined as 'the customs and usages traditionally observed among the indigenous African peoples of South Africa and which forms part of the culture of those peoples'. Customary law allows for polygynous marriages to be concluded.
[12] See *Heystek v. Heystek* 2002 (2) SA 754 (T), 757A.
[13] *MB v. NB* 2010 (3) SA 220 (GSJ), para. 20.
[14] In terms of s. 28(1)(b) of the Constitution: See *Heystek v. Heystek* 2002 (2) SA 754 (T), 757B–C and *MB v. NB* 2010 (3) SA 220 (GSJ), paras 20–21.
[15] S. 32(1).

expressly clothes de facto caregivers with the minimum power necessary to provide for the day-to-day care of the child.[16]

Without formally being vested with parental responsibilities and rights by means of an agreement, court order or adoption order, a step-parent would not be considered a so-called 'co-holder of parental responsibilities and rights' for purposes of sections 30 and 31 of the Children's Act.[17] As such, the step-parent would not need to be consulted about decisions and the child's parents are therefore at liberty to make decisions concerning their child without consulting the step-parent. However, if the step-parent is of the opinion that the decision taken by the parent(s) in respect of the child is not in the child's best interests, the step-parent may approach a court to review the decision based on the child's constitutional right to the paramountcy of his or her best interests.[18] The Children's Act empowers Children's Courts[19] to adjudicate a wide variety of matters[20] and to grant a wide range of orders, including an alternative care order, a partial care order and a shared care order.[21] Anyone acting in the interests of the child may approach the Children's Court for this purpose.[22] A step-parent would also be able to approach the High Court in terms of its common law jurisdiction as the upper guardian of all minors to review the decision.

2.2. RECOGNITION OF MULTIPLE PARENTS IF A CHILD IS RAISED IN MORE THAN ONE HOUSEHOLD

South African law recognises multiplicity of caregiving in general, if not parenthood per se, by expressly allowing more than one person or parent to hold (the same) parental responsibilities and rights in respect of the same child.[23] Multiplicity of parenthood is common in the case of divorce or the termination of a life partnership, where it is usual for parents to continue exercising guardianship despite no longer living in the same household. Joint care has also now become the norm in the case of divorce, with one of the parents being awarded the primary care or residency of the child. While mothers were traditionally favoured as the primary caregiver, maternal preference as a rule has been rejected in a number of cases as a violation of gender equality.[24]

---

[16] S. 32(2).
[17] See discussion in section 2.2 below.
[18] Encapsulated in s. 28(2) of the Constitution.
[19] Specialised Magistrates' Courts on the lowest tier of the hierarchy of SA courts.
[20] S. 45.
[21] S. 46(1)(a), (d), and (e), respectively.
[22] S. 53(2)(b).
[23] S. 30(1).
[24] *Van der Linde v. Van der Linde* 1996 (3) SA 509 (O); *Ex parte Critchfield* 1999 (3) SA 132 (W); *K v. M* [2007] 4 All SA 883 (E), 893.

Parents may share the same responsibilities and rights without ever having cohabitated.[25] Parental responsibilities and rights may be shared by persons other than the parents of a child or a parent and an interested third party. A parent or person with parental responsibilities and rights may confer some or all of those responsibilities and rights on a person who is interested in the wellbeing of the child by means of a parental responsibilities and rights agreement.[26] A court may also assign parental responsibilities and rights to non-parents to share these with parents or other persons.[27] The guiding principle in deciding the sharing of parental responsibilities and rights is always the paramountcy of the child's best interests.[28]

Many children in South Africa do not consistently live in the same household as their biological parents. According to the *South African Child Gauge 2019*,[29] this is a long-established feature of childhood in South Africa and international studies have shown that the country is unique in the extent to which parents are absent from children's daily lives. Parental absence is attributed to many factors, including labour migration, inadequate housing opportunities, low marriage and cohabitation rates, as well as customary care arrangements.[30] Many children experience a sequence of different caregivers, are raised without fathers, or live in different households to their biological siblings.[31] According to the *Child Gauge*,[32] parental absence does not necessarily mean parental abandonment and virtually all children in South Africa live in households where there are two or more co-resident adults.[33] These adults are aunts, uncles and grandparents who may contribute to the care of the children.[34]

Once a person becomes a co-holder of parental responsibilities and rights, he or she may not surrender or transfer his or her responsibilities and rights

---

[25] S. 21(1)(b) of the Children's Act allows an unmarried father to share parenthood with the birth mother of the child regardless of whether he was in a relationship with her. It is possible for him to acquire parenthood by showing a commitment only to the child, that is by acknowledging paternity and contributing to the maintenance and upbringing of the child.
[26] Such agreements are regulated by s. 22 of the Children's Act as discussed in section 2.1 above.
[27] While the Children's Courts will have jurisdiction with regard to care, contact and maintenance awards, only the High Court and the Divorce Courts have jurisdiction to make awards relating to guardianship (s. 45(3)).
[28] This principle is entrenched generally in the Constitution, and in the Children's Act in s. 9 (general principles), s. 22 (parental responsibilities and rights agreements), and ss 23 and 24 (assignment of care, contact and guardianship). The Divorce Act 70 of 1979 (s. 6) has made the best interests standard the deciding factor in the making of orders relating to children at divorce. The High Court as upper guardian uses this standard when exercising its discretion as upper guardian of all minors.
[29] K. Hall, 'Demography of South Africa's Children' in *South African Child Gauge 2019*, Children's Institute, University of Cape Town 2019, p. 216.
[30] Ibid.
[31] Ibid.
[32] Ibid.
[33] Ibid.
[34] Ibid.

to another co-holder or any other person.[35] A co-holder may, however, by agreement allow another co-holder or person to exercise any or all of his or her responsibilities and rights on his or her behalf.[36] Such an informal agreement does not divest a co-holder of his or her parental responsibilities and rights, and that co-holder remains competent and liable to exercise those responsibilities and rights.[37] The general rule in such cases is that each co-holder may exercise the shared parental responsibilities and rights without the consent of the other co-holders.[38] This rule is made subject to the provisions in the Children's Act and any other law or a court order not providing otherwise.[39] The first exception to the general rule made in the Children's Act relates to the exercise of guardianship. Where there is more than one parent or person who holds guardianship, the consent of all the guardians is required in respect of the child's marriage, adoption, departure from South Africa, application for a passport and the alienation or encumbrance of any immovable property of the child.[40]

Before a co-holder of parental responsibilities and rights makes any major decision involving a child,[41] that person must give due consideration to any views and wishes expressed by the child, bearing in mind the child's age, maturity and stage of development.[42] Any co-holder who intends to make a decision that is likely to change significantly, or to have a significant adverse effect on another co-holder's exercise of parental responsibilities and rights, must give due consideration to any views and wishes expressed by any other co-holder of parental responsibilities and rights.[43]

Any person having care or custody of a child who refuses to allow another person to exercise, or prevents that person from exercising, his or her parental responsibilities and rights is in terms of the Children's Act guilty of an offence and liable on conviction to a fine or to imprisonment for a period not exceeding

---

[35] S. 30(3) of the Children's Act.
[36] Ibid.
[37] S. 30(4).
[38] S. 30(2).
[39] Ibid.
[40] S. 18(3)(c).
[41] That is a decision that relates to a matter requiring the consent of all the guardians as outlined above; a decision affecting contact between the child and a co-holder of parental responsibilities and rights; a decision regarding the assignment of guardianship or care to another person after the death of a parent; or a decision which is likely to significantly change, or to have an adverse effect on, the child's living conditions, education, health, personal relations with a parent or family member or, generally, the child's wellbeing (s. 31(1)(b)).
[42] S. 31(1)(a).
[43] S. 31(2). According to J v. J 2008 (6) SA 30 (C), para. 33, the first case in which the court had to interpret this provision, 'due consideration' does not mean that the decision-making party (in this case the mother to whom custody was awarded at divorce) is bound to give effect to the wishes and views of the other co-holder. The court held that once she has given such consideration, she may act independently.

one year.[44] However, it is important to note that the offence can only be committed in contravention of a court order or a parental responsibilities and rights agreement that has become effective.

A co-holder who frustrates or impedes the exercise of the rights enjoyed by other co-holders may in terms of the common law seek redress from the courts in the form of an interdict, a *mandamus* reinstating the *status quo ante* in cases where interference has already occurred or an order directing compliance.[45]

Parenting plans may be agreed upon to help persons who already hold parental responsibilities and rights to exercise those responsibilities and rights.[46] Parenting plans are not obligatory in all cases. The Children's Act opens up the possibility for co-holders of parental responsibilities and rights to agree on a parenting plan. Where, however, the co-holders are having difficulties in exercising their responsibilities and rights, those persons *must* first seek to agree on a parenting plan before seeking the intervention of a court. A parenting plan may determine any matter in connection with parental responsibilities and rights, including where and with whom the child is to live, the maintenance of the child, contact between the child and any of the parties or any other person, and the schooling and religious upbringing of the child.[47] A parenting plan must comply with the best interests of the child standard as set out in section 7.[48] A parenting plan must be in writing and signed by the parties to the agreement and may be registered with a family advocate or made an order of court.[49] The Act also prescribes the way in which parenting plans may be amended or terminated.[50]

A co-holder of parental responsibilities and rights or the child affected by the conflict between the co-holders may approach the High Court, a Divorce Court or a Children's Court for an order suspending, terminating, extending or circumscribing the exercise of a co-holder's parental responsibilities and rights. This statutory remedy in terms of section 28 of the Children's Act affords the courts a wide discretion to resolve the conflict between the co-holders.[51] When considering an application in terms of this section, the court must consider the best interests of the child, the relationship between the child and the person

---

[44] S. 35.
[45] See T. Boezaart, 'The Position of Minor Dependent Children of Divorcing and Divorced Spouses or Civil Union Partners' in J. Heaton (ed.), *The Law of Divorce and Dissolution of Life Partnerships in South Africa*, Juta, Cape Town 2014, pp. 216–18.
[46] Parenting plans are regulated in ss 33 and 34 of the Children's Act. Regs 9 and 10 to the Children's Act (published under GN R261 in *GG* 33076 dd. 01.04.2010 as amended by GN R497 in *GG* 35476 dd. 29.06.2012) regulate the preparation and registration of parenting plans. The regulations (reg. 11) also specifically provide for the participation of the child in the preparation of parenting plans.
[47] S. 33(3).
[48] S. 33(4).
[49] S. 34(1).
[50] S. 34(4) and (5).
[51] A similar provision is found in s. 8 of the Divorce Act 70 of 1979 but only applies to orders made upon divorce in terms of this Act.

whose parental responsibilities and rights are being challenged, the degree of commitment the person has shown towards the child and any other fact that should, in the opinion of the court, be taken into account.[52] The court may for purposes of the hearing, inter alia, order that a report and recommendations of a family advocate, a social worker or other suitably qualified person be submitted to the court.[53] The court may also appoint a legal representative for the child at the court proceedings and order one or both of the parties to pay the costs of such representation if substantial injustice would otherwise result.[54]

In high-conflict cases, the court may appoint a parenting coordinator to facilitate the implementation of a parenting plan. The court in *TC v. SC*[55] held that a parenting coordinator could be appointed even against the wishes of one of the parents, provided, amongst other considerations, there is already an agreed parenting plan in existence and the role of the parenting coordinator is expressly limited to supervising the implementation of, and compliance with, the court order.

2.3. RECOGNITION OF MULTIPLE PARENTS IF A CHILD IS RAISED IN A POLYGAMOUS FAMILY

Polygamous families in South Africa can be found amongst the indigenous African peoples living according to their customary law and families living according to Muslim, Jewish or Hindu religious law in terms of which polygyny (but not polyandry) is possible.

Formally, in terms of the Children's Act, the allocation of parenthood should not be influenced by the fact that the child is being raised in a polygamous family. The Children's Act allocates by default parenthood to the biological mother/ birth mother of the child, regardless of her marital status and the fact that she may be one of her husband's several wives.[56] Legal paternity, on the other hand, is determined by the biological father's commitment to the birth mother or his child.[57] The commitment to the mother can take the form of a marriage to the birth mother or cohabitation at the time of the birth of the child.[58] Marriage for purposes of the Children's Act is defined in broad terms and includes both customary marriages and marriages concluded in accordance with a system of religious law.[59] While polygyny is already formally recognised and regulated in

---

[52] S. 28(4).
[53] S. 29(5).
[54] S. 29(6).
[55] 2018 (4) SA 530 (WCC), para. 71.
[56] S. 19 of the Children's Act.
[57] S. 21(1)(b) of the Children's Act.
[58] Ss 20 and 21(1)(a) of the Children's Act.
[59] S. 1(1) s.v. 'marriage'.

terms of the Recognition of Customary Marriages Act,[60] religious marriages are not yet formally recognised. The broad definition of marriage in the Children's Act is therefore significant in so far as it treats children born from religious marriages the same as children born from unions that are formally recognised in South Africa.[61] If the biological father is not married to the birth mother, he may still become the other legal parent, provided he has lived or is living with the mother in a permanent life-partnership at the time of the birth of the child.[62] Regardless of a marriage or cohabitation with the birth mother, section 21 bestows parenthood on a biological father who has shown the necessary commitment to the child himself. The commitment required includes the following:

The biological father must:

1. consent or successfully apply to be identified as the child's father or have paid damages in terms of customary law;[63]
2. in good faith contribute or have attempted to contribute to the child's upbringing for a reasonable period; and
3. in good faith contribute or have attempted to contribute towards expenses in connection with the maintenance of the child for a reasonable period.

It is generally assumed that the requirements included in 1–3 apply cumulatively. It is not yet certain if, or to what extent, these provisions determining parenthood by default in terms of the civil law will override any conflicting designation of parenthood in terms of customary law or any system of religious law.

Other interested caregivers may formally be assigned incidences or full parental responsibilities and rights by means of a registered parental

---

[60] 120 of 1998. The Children's Act (s. 1 (4)), however, prohibits any proceedings arising out of the application of inter alia the Divorce Act and the Recognition of Customary Marriages Act, in so far as these Acts relate to children, to be dealt with in a Children's Court. This means that such issues can only be heard in the High Court, which may hamper accessibility to justice for such children.
[61] With the added advantage that the Children's Courts may be approached to resolve disputes in this regard.
[62] S. 21(1)(a).
[63] There is some uncertainty regarding the effect of the payment of damages in terms of customary law. There is some evidence to support the argument that the payment of such damages, without more, vests parenthood in the biological father in terms of customary law: see T.W. Bennett, *Customary Law in South Africa*, Juta, Cape Town 2004, p. 310; R.L. Karabo and Z.M. Hansungule, 'Upholding the Best Interests of the Child in South African Customary Law' in T. Boezaart (ed.), *Child Law in South Africa*, Juta, Cape Town 2017, pp. 299–300; E. Moore and C. Himonga, 'Living Customary Law and Families' in K. Hall, L. Richter, Z. Mokomane and L. Lake (eds), *South African Child Gauge 2018. Children, Families and the State: Collaboration and Contestation*, Children's Institute, University of Cape Town 2018, p. 62.

responsibilities and rights agreement or by order of court.[64] The exercise of the parental responsibilities and rights that are shared by these co-holders is regulated as indicated in section 2.1 above. Any conflict between the co-holders of parental responsibilities and rights must be resolved in the best interests of the child, which includes the consideration, inter alia, of the need for the child to remain in the care of his or her parent, family and extended family, to maintain a connection with his or her family, extended family, culture or tradition and the child's physical and emotional security and his or her intellectual, emotional, social and cultural development.[65] Without a formal designation, informal caregivers still have the responsibility to protect the children in their care, as already discussed in section 2.1 above.

It is interesting to note that the Children's Act expressly allows 'persons sharing a common household and forming a permanent family unit' to adopt a child jointly.[66] Creating the possibility for a child to be adopted by more than two persons is rather revolutionary. In a polygynous customary setting it could make sense, for example, to allow a husband (as the head of the *kraal*) and his three or four wives to adopt a child jointly.[67] In such a case, the husband and the wives will simultaneously be vested with legal parenthood in respect of the adopted child. The husband and the wives will equally share parental responsibilities and rights as co-holders and be subject to the same duties, for example to consult each other and the child concerning major decisions.[68]

2.4. RECOGNITION OF MULTIPLE PARENTS IN THE CASE OF OPEN ADOPTION

According to the Children's Act, an adoption order terminates all parental responsibilities and rights any person, including a parent, step-parent or partner in a domestic life partnership, had in respect of the child immediately before the adoption.[69] South African law therefore does not in general recognise open adoptions. There is, however, one very important qualification in this regard: a post-adoption agreement may provide an opportunity for the parent or guardian of a child to preserve contact with the child after the child has been adopted.

In terms of section 234 of the Children's Act, the parent or guardian of a child may enter into a post-adoption agreement with a prospective adoptive

---

[64] In terms of ss 22, 23 and 24 of the Children's Act or the common law jurisdiction of the High Court as upper guardian of all minors.
[65] S. 7(1)(f) and (h) of the Children's Act.
[66] S. 231(1)(a)(iii).
[67] South African Law Commission (now called the South African Law Reform Commission), Discussion Paper 103 on the *Review of the Child Care Act*, Project 110, 2001, p. 136.
[68] For other possibilities to address conflict between the parties, see section 2.2 above.
[69] S. 242(1)(a) of the Children's Act.

parent to provide for communication[70] and information about the child[71] after the adoption order is granted. If the prospective adoptive parent(s) is/are willing to enter into a post-adoption agreement, it must be done *before* an application for the adoption of a child is made.[72] The Children's Court will confirm the post-adoption agreement only if it is in the best interests of the child.[73] The confirmation will occur at the time of the granting of the adoption order.[74] A post-adoption agreement will take effect only if made an order of court.[75] The agreement must be supported by the consent of the child unless the child is not sufficiently mature or of an age or stage of development to understand the implications of the agreement.[76] Conflict between the adoptive parents and the biological parents will have to be resolved by the Children's Court. Once the agreement takes effect, it may only be amended or terminated by an order of court.[77] As is the case with the approval of the agreement, the decision of the court to amend or terminate the agreement will depend on what the court deems to be in the best interests of the adopted child.

2.5. RECOGNITION OF MULTIPLE PARENTS IN THE CASE OF *KAFALA*

South African law does not expressly recognise *kafala*. The Children's Act, however, defines an adopted child and an adoptive parent, respectively, as a child who has been adopted and a person who has adopted a child, in terms of 'any' law.[78] It is not certain whether, or to what extent, the legislator contemplated the possible parallel recognition of extrajudicial care arrangements akin to an adoption[79] in terms of any 'other' legal system, such as customary law or Islamic law.[80]

---

[70] Communication may include visitation between the child and the parent or guardian and even another person as stipulated in the agreement: s. 234(1)(a).
[71] The information includes medical information: s. 234(1)(b).
[72] S. 234(1). The agreement must be drafted in the prescribed format: s. 234(5) read with reg. 103 containing Form 66.
[73] S. 234(4). The social worker facilitating the adoption must assist the parties in preparing the agreement and counsel them on the implications of such an agreement: s. 234(3).
[74] S. 234(4).
[75] S. 234(6)(a).
[76] S. 234(2). See also guidelines in reg. 7 of the Consolidated Regulations pertaining to the Children's Act.
[77] Only a party to the agreement or the adopted child may apply for the amendment or termination of the agreement: s. 234(6)(b).
[78] S. 1(1) s.v. 'adopted child' and 'adoptive parent'.
[79] According to U.M. Assim and J. Sloth-Nielsen, 'Islamic Kafalah as an Alternative Care Option for Children Deprived of a Family Environment' (2014) 14 *African Human Rights Law Journal* 322, 329–30, *kafala* is distinguishable from adoption in so far as *kafala* almost never results in the severing of links between the child and his or her biological parents.
[80] As far as could be ascertained, the recognition of *kafala* has not been the subject of court proceedings in SA.

Notwithstanding the possible uncertainty created by these definitions, the chapter regulating adoption in the Children's Act seems to envisage only one type of adoption, which is where the child has been placed in the permanent care of a person in terms of a court order that has the effects contemplated in section 242. A child will thus generally only acquire the status of an adopted child in South Africa if formally adopted in terms of the procedure outlined in the Children's Act.[81]

If a child is cared for in terms of *kafala*, the caregiver's position will possibly be comparable to the position of a step-parent, discussed above.

2.6. RECOGNITION OF MULTIPLE PARENTS IN THE CASE OF DONOR-ASSISTED REPRODUCTION WITHOUT SURROGACY

Except in the case of a surrogacy arrangement,[82] the woman who gives birth to an artificially conceived child will be regarded as the legal mother of the child in South Africa, regardless of her marital status or whether the child was conceived with donor gametes.[83] Whether or not she will be regarded as the sole legal parent, however, is made dependent on her marital status and the consent of her spouse. If she is married[84] and she and her spouse both consented to the artificial fertilisation,[85] the resultant child will for all purposes be considered the child of

---

[81] The order made by the court in *Maneli v. Maneli* 2010 (7) BCLR 703 (GSJ), para. 45 to have the child registered as the adopted child of the applicant and the respondent, however, effectively equated the status of a child adopted in terms of Xhosa law with a child adopted in terms of the Children's Act. The order is significant because it is wholly unprecedented in our law. While customary law adoptions have been recognised for purposes of creating a legally enforceable duty of support in the past, such adoptions have never before been recognised in express terms as having the same legal effect as formal adoptions. For further information regarding the recognition of de facto adoptions in SA, see A.S. Louw, 'A de Facto Adoption Doctrine for South Africa?' (2017) 38 *Obiter* 457.
[82] See discussion in section 2.8 below.
[83] S. 40(2) of the Children's Act.
[84] Marriage for purposes of the interpretation of this provision includes not only a formally recognised union (i.e. a heterosexual monogamous marriage in terms of the Marriage Act 25 of 1961, a monogamous heterosexual or same-sex civil union in terms of the Civil Union Act 17 of 2006 and a polygynous customary marriage in terms of the Recognition of Customary Marriages Act 120 of 1998) but also a religious marriage such as a Muslim or Hindu marriage not yet formally recognised in South Africa. Because of the restricted application of s. 40(1) to 'spouses', a life partner (of the same or opposite sex) of the birth mother will not be recognised as the other legal parent of the child. However, based on the Constitutional Court's judgment in *J v. Director-General, Department of Home Affairs* 2003 (5) SA 621 (CC), paras 13–16, the limited application of s. 40 could arguably amount to unfair discrimination on grounds of marital status and probably sexual orientation.
[85] Consent is presumed until the contrary is proved (s. 40(1)(b)). The Children's Act, however, does not prescribe the form of consent, which means oral or tacit consent will suffice.

the mother who gives birth and her spouse 'as if the gamete or gametes of those spouses had been used for such artificial fertilisation'.[86] In terms of this so-called 'deeming provision',[87] the birth mother and her spouse are to be regarded as the biological parents of the child. The gamete donor's biological contribution is thus disregarded and the donor is denied any legal rights to the child.[88] Section 40(1) clearly provides certainty regarding the legal position of the woman who is artificially fertilised, her spouse, the donor(s) of the gametes and the child when the woman who gives birth to the child is married. Section 40(2), on the other hand, simply states in general that if donor gametes are used for the artificial fertilisation of a woman, 'the child born of that woman as a result of such artificial fertilisation must for all purposes be regarded to be the child of that woman'. It has been suggested that the absence of the deeming provision in this provision could be interpreted as an indication that the donor's contribution in the case where the woman is unmarried can be taken into consideration when determining the artificially conceived child's parentage.[89] This possibility has, however, been rejected on the basis that it would result in an unjustifiable infringement of the right to equality between the position of gamete donors in the case of an unmarried woman and their position in the case of a married woman.[90]

According to the interpretation of section 40 as outlined above, the presence of known donors could not affect the legal parentage of an artificially conceived child – even one born to an unmarried mother. The donor will nevertheless still be able to acquire parental responsibilities and rights by assignment – either in terms of a parental responsibilities and rights agreement (section 22) or a court order in terms of section 23 (contact or care) or section 24 (guardianship), provided it is considered to be in the best interests of the child.[91]

Despite donors being excluded from parenthood, it is reasonable to assume that the courts will resolve disputes involving donors based on the best interests of the child.[92] This could mean that if the child already has two married (legal) parents, a donor may find it difficult to convince the court to share parenthood with the existing parents – unless of course the child has already also bonded with the known donor, in which case the court may be willing to grant the donor

---

[86] S. 40(1)(a).
[87] See *J v. Director-General, Department of Home Affairs* 2003 (5) SA 621 (CC), para. 17; J. Heaton, 'Parental Responsibilities and Rights' in C.J. Davel and A.M. Skelton (eds), *Commentary on the Children's Act*, Juta, Cape Town Revision Service 9 2018, pp. 3–8.
[88] Except if the donor is the mother who was artificially fertilised or her spouse: s. 40(3).
[89] See J. Heaton, 'Parental Responsibilities and Rights' in C.J. Davel and A.M. Skelton (eds), *Commentary on the Children's Act*, Juta, Cape Town Revision Service 9 2018, p. 3–8.
[90] Ibid., pp. 3–9; A. Louw, 'Lesbian Parentage and Known Donors: Where in the World are We?' (2016) 133 *South African Law Journal* 1, 10.
[91] See *CM v. NG* 2012 (4) SA 452 (WCC), paras 59 and 60.
[92] See discussion of the paramountcy of the child's best interests in section 3.3 below.

at least a right of contact with the child. In the case of an unmarried mother who gave birth to a child that was artificially conceived with the gametes of a known donor, it is likely that the courts will consider imposing a duty of support on the gamete donor, as a blood relative, since the child may otherwise be deprived of a source of support. Whether or not the court would be willing to recognise such a donor as a parent with full responsibilities and rights will probably depend on the particular circumstances of the case, as all determinations of the best interests of the child are made on a case-by-case basis.

2.7. RECOGNITION OF MULTIPLE PARENTS IN THE CASE OF A 'THREE-PARENT CHILD'

In terms of section 57(1) of the South African National Health Act,[93] a person may not:

(a) manipulate any genetic material, including genetic material of human gametes, zygotes or embryo; or
(b) engage in any activity, including nuclear transfer or embryo splitting, for the purpose of the reproductive cloning of a human being.

For the purpose of this section, 'reproductive cloning of a human being' is defined as 'the manipulation of genetic material in order to achieve the reproduction of a human being and includes nuclear transfer or embryo splitting for such purpose'.[94] The National Health Act does not mention alteration of germline genetics or reproductive embryo cloning. Transfer of DNA even in the form of blastomere nuclei (the technique which has been scrutinised the most by ethicists) is not 'reproductive cloning of a human being'.[95] The Act also does not specify that genetic material may not be manipulated for any other reasons. It is therefore uncertain whether mitochondrial transfer is prohibited in South Africa. Even if it is not prohibited, it seems likely that ministerial authorisation will be required for such a procedure to take place.[96]

While it is evident that the Children's Act envisaged more than one person holding the same parental responsibilities and rights in respect of the same child,[97] it is uncertain whether the Act envisaged the possibility of more than

---

[93] 61 of 2003.
[94] S. 57(6).
[95] A.S. Reznichenko, C. Huyser and M.S. Pepper, 'Mitochondrial Transfer: Ethical, Legal and Social Implications in Assisted Reproduction' (2015) 8 *South African Journal of Bioethics and Law* 32, 34.
[96] Ibid., 35.
[97] S. 30(1) and (2).

two parents acquiring parental status automatically at the birth of a child. Sections 19–21 only refer to a biological mother and father, while section 40 confers parental status on the married person who is artificially fertilised together with her spouse, to the exclusion of any gamete donor.[98]

The fact that the Children's Act has omitted to define 'biological mother' may nevertheless inadvertently have opened up the possibility of a child having two biological mothers. However, the section in the Children's Act regulating the status of artificially conceived children does not refer to biological mothers at all. Section 40 only refers to the 'married person', 'spouse', or 'woman'. In the highly unlikely event that the woman whose DNA is corrected is in a formally recognised civil union with the woman whose DNA is used for the correction, both women will be regarded as the parents of the resultant child. In such a case, however, section 40(1) would prohibit the sperm donor from being recognised as a parent.[99] Without parenting intentions, the woman who acts as the mitochondrial donor will be excluded as a parent by the definition of 'parent' contained in the Children's Act – provided, of course, she is not married to the mother who gives birth. In terms of this definition, a parent for purposes of the Act excludes 'any person who is biologically related to a child by reason only of being a gamete donor for purposes of artificial fertilisation'.

2.8. RECOGNITION OF MULTIPLE PARENTS IN THE CASE OF SURROGACY

Surrogacy is strictly regulated in South Africa in chapter 19 of the Children's Act.[100] South Africa recognises the parenthood of the intended parents in the case of surrogacy, provided the surrogate motherhood agreement was approved and confirmed by the High Court before the artificial fertilisation of the surrogate mother.[101]

The confirmation is predicated on the court finding that the commissioning parents are suitable to accept the parenthood of the child that is to be conceived and the surrogate mother is physically and mentally suitable to act as such.[102] In general, however, the court must be satisfied, having regard to the interests

---

[98] In the case of adoption there is no similar restriction. S. 231(1)(d) of the Children's Act allows 'other persons sharing a common household and forming a permanent family unit' to adopt a child jointly.
[99] In the case of spouses, donors, whether or not known, will not acquire any rights: s. 40(3).
[100] Ss 292–303 of the Children's Act.
[101] The court in *Ex parte MS and Others* 2014 (3) SA 415 (GP) was willing to relax this requirement by confirming an agreement after the surrogate mother's artificial fertilisation because of the exceptional circumstances in the case.
[102] S. 295(b) and (c).

of the child to be born above all, that the agreement should be confirmed.[103] In an attempt to protect the interests of the commissioned child, the Children's Act further requires at least one of the commissioning parents to be genetically related to the child contemplated in the agreement.[104] If only one of the commissioning parents (or the single commissioning parent) is genetically related to the child, the surrogate mother could contribute her ovum and become the other genetic parent to the child born as a result of the agreement. South Africa therefore allows for the enforcement of partial (as opposed to gestational) surrogate motherhood agreements as well.

The effect of a confirmed and valid surrogate motherhood agreement on the status of the child depends on whether or not the surrogate mother is herself related to the child she bears. If the surrogate mother is *not* genetically related to the child, the child is for all purposes in law deemed the child of the commissioning parent(s) from the moment of birth.[105] The surrogate mother or her husband/spouse/partner or relatives have no rights of parenthood and the child will have no claim for maintenance or of succession against the surrogate mother or her husband/spouse/partner or relatives.[106] However, if the surrogate mother is genetically related to the child, the surrogate mother may, without incurring any liability,[107] terminate the surrogate motherhood agreement within a period of 60 days after the child's birth.[108] If the surrogate mother terminates the agreement *before* the birth of the child, the commissioning parents will have no rights of parenthood because the surrogate mother will be considered the child's legal parent at birth together with 'her husband or partner, if any, or if none, the commissioning father'.[109] If the agreement is terminated *after* the birth of the child, the parental rights acquired by the commissioning parent(s) at birth will be terminated and vested in the surrogate mother and her husband or partner or the commissioning father.[110]

The idea was possibly to ensure that the child grows up with his or her genetic parents. However, the argument does not hold sway if the surrogate mother does

---

[103] S. 295(e).
[104] This requirement has been retained despite a constitutional challenge claiming the requirement unfairly discriminates against conception-infertile persons: *AB v. Minister of Social Development* 2017 (3) SA 570 (CC).
[105] S. 297. A surrogate mother who is not genetically related to the child may therefore not terminate a validly confirmed surrogate motherhood agreement and is obliged to hand over the child as soon as is reasonably possible after birth. Regardless of whether she is related to the child she is carrying, a surrogate mother, however, retains the exclusive right to decide to terminate her pregnancy in terms of the Choice on Termination of Pregnancy Act 92 of 1996.
[106] S. 297(1)(b), (c), (d), and (f).
[107] Excluding certain payments expressly provided for in s. 301, such as payments relating to the artificial fertilisation and pregnancy of the surrogate mother, the birth of the child and the confirmation of the agreement.
[108] S. 298(1).
[109] S. 299(b).
[110] S. 299(a).

have a spouse or partner – in that case, the unrelated spouse or partner of the surrogate mother is given preference over the genetically related commissioning father. Moreover, the practicality of simultaneously vesting parental rights in the surrogate mother and the commissioning father seems questionable at best. It is less than clear how the surrogate mother and commissioning father would co-exercise their respective rights. Would a parenting plan be the appropriate solution to delineate the exercise of their rights? The provision allowing the genetically related surrogate mother to terminate the agreement could possibly be utilised by the court to overcome these problems. In terms of section 298, the court must terminate the confirmation of the surrogate motherhood agreement after finding, inter alia, that the surrogate terminated the agreement voluntarily with full knowledge of the effects of the termination and the court 'may issue any other appropriate order if it is in the best interests of the child'. The discretion conferred on the court may be used to override the statutory provisions regulating the effect of the termination of the surrogate motherhood agreement. Generally speaking, it could be argued that the differentiation between the rights of a genetically related surrogate mother and a gestational surrogate amounts to an infringement of the constitutional right to equality.

A surrogate motherhood agreement that does not comply with the provisions outlined in the Children's Act is invalid and any child born as a result of any action taken in execution of such an arrangement is for all purposes deemed to be the child of the woman that gave birth to the child in accordance with the common law adage *mater semper certa est*.[111]

While the courts in South Africa have taken pains to provide guidance to parties wishing to apply for the confirmation of a surrogate motherhood agreement,[112] they have not had the opportunity to interpret and clarify the provisions relating to the effect and termination of such an agreement. The speculative nature of the commentary in this regard is thus the result of a lack of judicial precedent in South Africa.

2.9. RECOGNITION OF SAME-SEX PARENTS

The South African Constitution is one of the very few constitutions that protect citizens against unfair discrimination based on their sexual orientation.[113] In line with this constitutional imperative, the Civil Union Act[114] has created an equal opportunity for parties involved in a same-sex relationship in South Africa to

---

[111] S. 297(2).
[112] See e.g. *Ex parte WH* 2011 (6) SA 514 (GNP); *Ex parte MS and Others* 2014 (3) SA 415 (GP); *Ex parte HP and Others* 2017 (4) SA 528 (GP); *Ex parte CJD and Others* 2018 (3) SA 197 (GP); and *Ex parte KF and Others* 2019 (2) SA 510 (GJ).
[113] S. 9(3) of the Constitution.
[114] 17 of 2006.

formalise their union. Since this Act came into operation on 30 November 2006, any reference to marriage in any other law, including the common law, includes, with such changes as may be required by the context, a civil union, and husband, wife or spouse in any other law, including the common law, includes a civil union partner.[115] South African law thus places a same-sex spouse in the same position as a heterosexual spouse. Except for the designation of parenthood at birth to the biological mother and father of a child, the South African law of parent and child freely and equally accommodates same-sex parents.[116] This approach is evidenced by the non-gender-specific language used in the Children's Act.[117]

The Divorce Court in *Ex parte Critchfield*[118] argued that in the case of both care and contact orders the court should not be too concerned with the sexual preferences of the divorcing parents. Homosexual encounters should in the opinion of this court not be seen in a more serious light than adulterous flirtations. However, when the sexual preferences of a parent pose an actual or potential threat to the welfare (psychological or physical) of the minor, the court should consider the impact thereof on the children. The court held in such a case the best interests of the minor children should take precedence over the right of the parent not to be discriminated against based on his or her sexual orientation.

2.10. GENERAL RECOGNITION OF MULTI-PARENTHOOD

There are no plans to change or revise the law of parent and child to provide for general recognition of multi-parenthood. The Children's Act defines 'parent' in fairly specific terms but is more concerned with who does not qualify as a child's parent than who does. 'Parent', for purposes of this Act is defined as:

> The adoptive parent of a child, but excludes –
>
> (a) the biological father of a child conceived through the rape of or incest with the child's mother;

---

[115] S. 13(2).
[116] For examples supporting this trend, see e.g. *Ex parte WH* 2011 (6) SA 514 (GNP) (surrogacy) and *CM v. NG* 2012 (4) SA 452 (WCC) (IVF).
[117] E.g. in ch. 3 dealing with parental responsibilities and rights, the Act provides for a 'person' to have parental responsibilities and rights (s. 18), and for any 'person' who has an interest in the care, wellbeing and development of the child to enter into a parental responsibilities and rights agreement (s. 22) or apply for care, contact or guardianship (ss 23 and 24). In the case of an artificially conceived child, the 'spouses' will be considered the parents of the child (s. 40(1)). A child may be adopted by spouses (s. 231(a)(i) as interpreted in the light of s. 13(2) of the Civil Union Act 17 of 2006) or 'partners' in a permanent domestic life-partnership (s. 231(a)(ii)) and commissioning 'parents', regardless of whether they are formally married or in a permanent relationship, may enter into a surrogate motherhood agreement with a surrogate mother and her spouse or partner (s. 292(1) as interpreted in the light of s. 13(2) of the Civil Union Act 17 of 2006).
[118] 1999 (3) SA 132 (W), 139B–F.

(b) any person who is biologically related to a child by reason only of being a gamete donor for purposes of artificial fertilisation; and
(c) a parent whose parental responsibilities and rights in respect of a child have been terminated.

Although the Children's Act makes provision for multiple persons to acquire and exercise parental responsibilities and rights in respect of the same child, it is not quite clear whether all these persons would, technically speaking, qualify as the 'legal parents' of the child. To be considered a parent for all purposes in law, the parent would have to be a biological mother, a father who qualifies because he is married to the mother or falls within the scope of section 19,[119] the woman who gives birth to an artificially conceived child or her spouse, an adoptive parent, or a commissioning parent in terms of a confirmed surrogacy agreement. Any other person vested with parental responsibilities and rights – even full parental responsibilities and rights – will only hold such rights until the child reaches majority (whether by reaching the age of majority, which is 18 years, or by concluding a valid marriage). The assignment of parental responsibilities and rights will also not give these persons or the child a right to intestate succession or a reciprocal right and duty of support past the age of majority.

The Children's Act gives no indication of the maximum number of legal parents a child may have. The omission could be regarded as intentional considering the multiple parenting scheme envisaged in the Act and the fact that any number of persons who share a common household and form a permanent family unit may adopt a child,[120] thereby all becoming the legal parents of the child.

3. PART B. DIVERSITY AND PLURALITY OF FAMILY'S FUNCTIONS

3.1. LEGAL RECOGNITION OF VARIOUS FUNCTIONS OF THE FAMILY

The diversity of family forms found in South Africa means that marriage and the family can fulfil a multitude of functions. The Constitutional Court in *Dawood*[121] considered the institutions of marriage and the family as important

---

[119] This qualification is not evident from the definition of 'parent' quoted above. According to the definition, all biological fathers qualify as parents.
[120] S. 231(1)(a)(iii).
[121] 2000 (3) SA 936 (CC), para. 31.

social institutions 'that provide for the security, support and companionship of members of our society and bear an important role in the rearing of children'.[122]

As far as care of children is concerned, the Constitutional Court in *Freedom of Religion South Africa v. Minister of Justice and Others*[123] recently abolished the defence of reasonable chastisement that exempted a parent from prosecution for what otherwise would constitute assault. In so doing, the court removed one of the last vestiges of parents' 'power' over their children and underscored the need expressed in the preamble of the Children's Act to ensure that the child grows up in 'a family environment and in an atmosphere of happiness, love and understanding'.

3.2. THE FUNCTIONS WHICH ARE PREDOMINANTLY FAVOURED

The South African courts are increasingly favouring the social function of families to create a community of life (*consortium omnis vitae*) and to form a family unit by living together.[124]

The judiciary has also on a number of occasions been willing to develop the common law and legislation to protect the physical support function in a diversity of family contexts. For example, in a dependant's claim for damages against the Road Accident Fund, the court in *Road Accident Fund v. Mohohlo*[125] granted damages to the aunt of the deceased. The court held that the legal convictions of the community called for the recognition of a reciprocal duty of support between an aunt and her nephew where the aunt had de facto adopted the nephew and brought him up as her own child.[126] In assessing the legal convictions of the community, the court had regard to the values underlying the

---

[122] See also *National Coalition for Gay and Lesbian Equality and Others v. Minister of Home Affairs* 2000 (2) SA 1 (CC), para. 46; *Fourie and Another v. Minister of Home Affairs and Others* 2005 (3) SA 429 (SCA), para. 13; *Du Toit and Another v. Minister of Welfare and Population Development and Others (Lesbian and Gay Equality Project as Amicus Curiae)* 2003 (2) SA 198 (CC), para. 19.

[123] 2020 (1) SA 1 (CC), para. 72.

[124] *Dawood* 2000 (3) SA 936 (CC), para. 37; *Fourie and Another v. Minister of Home Affairs and Others* 2005 (3) SA 429 (SCA), para. 51. Another example of the importance of this function was highlighted in the recently reported case of *Ex parte CJD and Others* 2018 (3) SA 197 (GP), para. 24, where the court had to determine whether the applicants – one of whom did not want to admit that he was gay – would be suitable to act as commissioning parents; the court found the fact that the applicants were living apart incompatible with the idea of raising a child in a family unit.

[125] 2018 (2) SA 65 (SCA).

[126] Ibid., paras 14, 17 and 19.

Constitution, in particular *ubuntu*,[127] and (as required by the Constitution)[128] applicable customary law, which recognises a duty of support where a de facto relationship between mother and child exists.[129]

3.3. THE ROLE OF CHILDREN IN THE LEGAL VIEW ON THE FUNCTIONS OF THE FAMILY

Where children are present in a family, the care of those children becomes the primary responsibility of the family. 'Care' is defined in the Children's Act in broad terms and includes providing the child with a suitable place to live, living conditions that are conducive to the child's wellbeing and the necessary financial support; safeguarding and promoting the wellbeing of the child; protecting the child from abuse; guarding against any infringement of the child's constitutional rights; guiding and directing the child's education and upbringing; maintaining a sound relationship with the child; and ensuring that the best interests of the child is the paramount concern in all matters affecting the child. Section 28(2) of the Constitution elevates the best interests standard to 'the' 'paramount' consideration in 'all' matters concerning children. As far as the operational thrust of the paramountcy principle is concerned, the Constitutional Court in *S v. M*[130] held that the paramountcy of the child's best interests is not an absolute principle and does not mean that the best interests of children override all other considerations. Formulation of the 'best interests of children' standard must also have regard to the best interests of family relationships in particular, society generally and constitutional principles.[131]

In addition to the paramountcy principle, section 28(1)(b) of the Constitution specifically entrenches a child's right to 'family care or parental care, or to appropriate alternative care when removed from the family environment'. According to Skweyiya AJ in *Du Toit*,[132] the child's constitutional right to 'family care or parental care' gives recognition to the fact that many children are not brought up by their biological parents, that family care 'includes care by the

---

[127] 'The spirit of *ubuntu*' is described (in para. 12) as 'part of the deep cultural heritage of the majority of the population, [that] suffuses the whole constitutional order. It combines individual rights with a communitarian philosophy. It is a unifying motif of the Bill of Rights, which is nothing if not a structured, institutionalised and operational declaration in our evolving new society of the need for human interdependence, respect and concern'.
[128] S. 211(3).
[129] *Road Accident Fund v. Mohohlo* 2018 (2) SA 65 (SCA), paras 13–15.
[130] 2008 (3) SA 232 (CC).
[131] *LW v. DB* 2020 (1) SA 169 (GJ), paras 68 and 69.
[132] *Du Toit and Another v. Minister of Welfare and Population Development and Others (Lesbian and Gay Equality Project as Amicus Curiae)* 2003 (2) SA 198 (CC).

extended family of a child, which is an important feature of South African family life',[133] and that section 28(1)(b) clearly gives constitutional recognition to the importance of family life for the wellbeing of all children.[134] It is also significant that the rights are couched in the alternative, meaning that they can be satisfied in different ways. The fact that children's constitutional right to parental care may be fulfilled in different ways is significant considering the fact that almost a quarter of all African children do not live with either parent and a further 46% live with their mothers but not their fathers.[135]

In order to determine the best interests of a child, section 7 of the Children's Act provides a closed list of factors to consider, including the need for the child to remain in the care of his or her parent(s), family and extended family, to maintain a connection with his or her family, extended family, culture or tradition, and to be brought up within a stable family environment and, where this is not possible, in an environment resembling as closely as possible a caring family environment. While the 'best interests' standard is applied to all children, not all the factors mentioned in section 7 will be relevant in each case. The application of this general approach is necessarily dependent on the facts of each case.[136]

---

[133] Ibid., para. 18.
[134] Ibid. The importance of the family and the community is also reflected in the preamble to the Children's Act.
[135] Statistics South Africa, *General Household Survey 2018*, available at http://www.statssa.gov.za/publications/P0318/P03182018.pdf, accessed 29.05.2022.
[136] LW v. DB 2020 (1) SA 169 (GJ), para. 14.

DIVERSITY OF FAMILY FORMS AND FAMILY FUNCTIONS IN THE NETHERLANDS

Wendy Schrama

1. Introduction 417
2. Part A. Diversity and Plurality of Family Forms 418
   2.1. Recognition of Multiple Parents in the Context of Step-Families 418
        2.1.1. Legal Ties with Step-Family............................ 418
        2.1.2. Conflict between Step-Parent and Parent 421
   2.2. Recognition of Multiple Parents if a Child is Raised in More than One Household.. 422
        2.2.1. Intended Multi-Parent Families 422
        2.2.2. Surrogacy.. 424
        2.2.3. Recent Developments.................................. 427
   2.3. Polygamous Families 429
3. Part B. Diversity and Plurality of Family's Functions 430
   3.1. Legal Recognition of Various Functions of the Family........... 430
   3.2. The Functions which are Predominantly Favoured.............. 432
4. Conclusion.. 433

1. INTRODUCTION

This report gives an overview of Dutch law on the theme 'Diversity and Plurality in the Law: Family Forms and Family's Functions'. Dutch family law has been reformed in a number of respects to accommodate new family forms. More change is expected for some of these groups. As a general remark before delving into the various situations in which plurality issues might arise, an interesting observation is that the principle of equality and inclusion for same-sex couples and parents has been the driver for change; lobby groups with a substantial political influence have managed to push for inclusion, first in terms of equality at partner level (registered partnership, same-sex marriage), and subsequently regarding the parent–child relationship.¹ This is in contrast to more restrictive policy regarding families with a religious/Islamic background, where State recognition is more difficult and less tolerant because of the idea of inequality between men and women, but perhaps also because of the link with migration, which is politically a complex theme. Recent policy aims are to ban polygamous marriages, to reduce the negative effects of marital captivity, and to curtail forced marriages and child marriages.² The law does not recognise children born in informal marriages.³ Plurality and recognition of various types of families therefore largely depends on underlying values and political interests.

2. PART A. DIVERSITY AND PLURALITY OF FAMILY FORMS

2.1. RECOGNITION OF MULTIPLE PARENTS IN THE CONTEXT OF STEP-FAMILIES

2.1.1. Legal Ties with Step-Family

Of all minor children, 19% have experienced parental divorce, parental re-partnering, the addition of step-siblings to their family, and/or the birth of half-siblings.⁴ Even though there are many step-families, family law reform has not so much been aimed at step-families, but primarily at same-sex families, who have a strong political lobby for legal reform.⁵ However, as a result of

---

[1] W.M. Schrama, 'Marriage and Alternative Status Relationships in the Netherlands' in J. Eekelaar and R. George (eds), *Routledge Handbook of Family Law and Policy*, Routledge, Oxon 2020, pp. 15–28 and W. Schrama, J. Tigchelaar and Y. Yildiz, 'De Rol van de Staat in het Relatierecht' in W.M. Schrama and S. Burri (eds), *Verantwoordelijkheden in het Familierecht: de Rol van de Staat, Familie en Individu*, Boom Juridische Uitgevers, The Hague 2020, pp. 11–89.

[2] S. Rutten, *Gegeven de Betekenis van Islamitisch Familierecht, Samenloop van Europese en Islamitische Familierechtsordes; Nederland als Voorbeeld*, Inaugural lecture, University of Maastricht, 2017; P. Kruiniger, G. van Maanen, S. Rutten and B. Deogratias (eds), *Marital Captivity: Divorce, Religion and Human Rights*, Eleven International Publishing, The Hague 2019; S.W.E. Rutten et al., *Gewoon Getrouwd. Een Onderzoek naar Kindhuwelijken en Religieuze Huwelijken in Nederland*, Maastricht University, Maastricht 2015; S.W.E. Rutten et al., *Onderzoek naar de Werking van de Wet tegengaan Huwelijksdwang in de Praktijk*, WODC, The Hague 2019.

[3] See section 2.1 below.

[4] R. de Graaf, 'Kinderen in Complexe Gezinsverbanden', Statistics Netherlands (Centraal Bureau voor de Statistiek), 02.10.2020 available at https://www.cbs.nl/nl-nl/longread/statistische-trends/2020/kinderen-in-complexe-gezinsverbanden, accessed 30.05.2022.

[5] See on multi-parent families, both intentional and non-intentional, including empirical data for both groups: M.V. Antokolskaia, W.M. Schrama, K.R.S.D. Boele-Woelki, C.C.J.H. Bijleveld, C.G. Jeppesen de Boer and G. van Rossum, *Meerouderegezag: Een Oplossing voor Kinderen met meer dan Twee Ouders? Een Empirisch en Rechtsvergelijkend Onderzoek*, Boom Juridische Uitgevers, The Hague 2014.

some of these changes for same-sex families, step-parents benefit from newly introduced legal provisions, such as Article 1:253t of the Dutch Civil Code (DCC).[6] In general, Dutch family law does not recognise a multiplicity of parenthood; this also applies to situations in which a child has a step-parent. A child can only have two legal parents.[7] The parents' legal relationship at the time of the birth of the child determines who the child's legal parent is. When the parents are married, the child has two legal parents by operation of law.[8] There is no room for a step-parent then. When parents are not married (or in a registered partnership), only the mother will be a legal parent by operation of law. When the father does not recognise the child, there is a position vacant for the step-parent. The step-parent can recognise the child – with the consent of the mother, and if the child is aged 12 or older, with his or her consent – and thus become a legal parent.[9]

In scenarios where the child already has two legal parents, which is usually the case, the DCC provides for the option of step-parent adoption as is explained below under this heading. The conditions are strict and not easily met.[10] The result is that the step-parent becomes a legal parent instead of the original legal parent. All ties with the parent are severed.[11] This type of step-parent adoption is extremely rare in the Netherlands.

Outside family law, some provisions apply which take into account formal step-children[12] and treat them the same as one's own legal children, such as in some provisions on income tax and succession tax law, where the definition of a child includes a step-child.[13]

In general, step-parents have no legal ties with their step-children under family law. There are three exceptions.

Firstly, there is a *maintenance duty* for some step-parents towards the step-child. This only applies to formal step-parents, that is to say step-parents who are married or registered partners of one of the legal parents and where the child is part of their family.[14] Informal step-parents, who are not married to/a registered partner of one of the parents are under no such duty.

---

[6] See the discussion below.
[7] Parenthood is regulated in Arts 1:198–1:212 of the DCC.
[8] Art. 1:198 (1) sub. a of the DCC for the mother and Art. 1:199 sub. a of the DCC for the father.
[9] Arts 1:203–204 of the DCC.
[10] Arts 1:227–228 of the DCC.
[11] Art. 1:229 of the DCC.
[12] Formal step-children as opposed to informal step-children, where the step-parent has not concluded a marriage or registered partnership with the child's legal parent.
[13] Art. 2 s. 1 sub. c and Art. 4 of the Algemene Wet Inkomensafhankelijke Regelingen; Art. 2 sub. 3 sub. i of the Algemene Wet Rijksbelastingen; Art. 19 sub. b Successiewet 1956, Art. 304 of the Wetboek van Strafrecht.
[14] Art. 1:395 of the DCC.

The second exception relates to *parental responsibilities*. Parental responsibilities of the child's parents will not be affected by a divorce or separation.[15] This means that the child's parents will jointly exercise the parental responsibilities over their children after divorce or separation. Dutch family law only recognises parental responsibilities for a maximum of two adults, so if the step-parent were to play a legally recognised role in the child's life, this is only possible if one of the legal parents never had parental responsibilities or no longer has them. The first scenario is typically relevant for legal parents who have never been married to/registered partners of each other. The child's father in an informal relationship needs to apply with the mother for parental responsibilities,[16] and not all parents do so. The other scenario is one where a parent files an application at the court to be granted sole parental responsibilities. This is granted only exceptionally; the threshold to meet is high, since the underlying principle is that parents will continue to exercise parental responsibilities together after a breakdown of the relationship. Only in one of these two scenarios is it possible for a step-parent to file for joint parental responsibilities. Such a request needs to meet a number of conditions and always requires a court order. According to Article 1:253t of the DCC, the district court may, on the joint application of the legal parent with parental responsibilities and the step-parent who has a close personal relationship with the child, vest them with joint parental responsibilities. The application must be rejected by the court if, taking into account the interest of the other parent, there is a well-founded fear that the best interests of the child would be neglected.[17] Furthermore, if the child has another legal parent, the application will only be granted if prior to the application the parent and the other person have jointly cared for the child continuously for at least one year, and the parent who makes the application has been vested with sole parental responsibilities for at least three continuous years.

The third exception is that the step-parent can become *a full legal parent* of the child. The only way to achieve this is by means of partner-adoption of the child.[18] Adoption will result in severing the ties with the other legal parent and is therefore a potential infringement of the family life of the other legal parent. For that reason, very strict conditions apply. The adoption needs to serve the best interests of the child and the court needs to assess whether the child has anything to expect from the other legal parent as a parent. An essential element is that the consent of the mature child is required. Moreover, the other legal

---

[15] Art. 1:251 (2) of the DCC for married parents and Art. 1:253n of the DCC for parents in an informal relationship.
[16] Art. 1:252 of the DCC.
[17] K. Boele-Woelki, W.M. Schrama and M. Vonk, 'National Report: The Netherlands, Parental Responsibilities, Commission on European Family Law, 2004' in K. Boele-Woelki, B. Braat and I. Curry-Sumner (eds), *European Family Law in Action, Volume III: Parental Responsibilities*, Intersentia, Antwerp 2005.
[18] Arts 1:227 and 228 of the DCC.

parent needs to consent to the adoption. If he[19] does not consent, the court can only order the adoption in very limited situations. The legal parent and step-parent must live together for at least three years and must have cared for the child together. Parental responsibilities must have been vested in the legal parent who will apply for the adoption order with the step-parent. These conditions imply that in most cases step-parent adoption will not be feasible.

The second and third options which create legal ties of some kind between a step-parent and step-child seem to be used very little. This has been shown by an empirical-legal study including 302 (step-)parents, where only in 2% of the sample did legal ties exist (parental responsibilities or legal parenthood) between the step-parent and the step-child. The study demonstrated that in the sample step-parents played a crucial role in the children's life. The fact that this factual situation was not mirrored in the legal situation did not, however, according to these families, result in many problems.[20]

In the legal doctrine, some suggestions have been made in order to improve the legal framework for step-parents and step-children.[21]

2.1.2. Conflict between Step-Parent and Parent

Regarding the *maintenance duty* of formal step-parents, the following applies. Both the step-parent and the legal parent(s) have a duty to maintain the child. There is no ranking of duties; they are both responsible. Informal step-parents have no legal maintenance duty towards step-children. There is case law of the Supreme Court on the topic, resulting in quite complicated ways of assessing which of the (step-)parents need to pay what amount.[22] In the legal doctrine, it has been argued that the step-parent's duty should be subsidiary in nature to the legal parent's duty.[23]

---

[19] The other parent can also be a co-mother, but for the sake of simplicity I use the most often occurring situation.

[20] M.V. Antokolskaia, W.M. Schrama, K.R.S.D. Boele-Woelki, C.C.J.H. Bijleveld, C.G. Jeppesen de Boer and G. van Rossum, *Meerouderschap: Een Oplossing voor Kinderen met meer dan Twee Ouders? Een Empirisch en Rechtsvergelijkend Onderzoek*, Boom Juridische Uitgevers, The Hague 2014. English summary of the research available at https://repository.wodc.nl/bitstream/handle/20.500.12832/2062/2348-summary_tcm28-73104.pdf?sequence=4&isAllowed=y, accessed 20.08.2022.

[21] P. Vlaardingerbroek, 'Stiefkinderen hebben Weinig te Kiezen' (2014) *Tijdschrift voor Familie- en Jeugdrecht* 38; M.V. Antokolskaia, W.M. Schrama, K.R.S.D. Boele-Woelki, C.C.J.H. Bijleveld, C.G. Jeppesen de Boer and G. van Rossum, *Meerouderschap: Een Oplossing voor Kinderen met meer dan Twee Ouders? Een Empirisch en Rechtsvergelijkend Onderzoek*, Boom Juridische Uitgevers, The Hague 2014; M. Draaisma, *De Stiefouder: Stiefkind van het Recht*, VU Uitgever, Amsterdam 2001.

[22] Supreme Court (Hoge Raad) 22.04.2005, ECLI:NL:HR:2005:AS3643, *Nederlandse Jurisprudentie* 2005/379, annotated by S.F.W. Wortmann.

[23] P.A.J.Th. van Teeffelen, 'De Onderhoudsplicht van de Stiefouder, bezien in Nationaal en Internationaal Perspectief' (2012) *Tijdschrift voor Familie- en Jeugdrecht* 46; M. Jonker,

Regarding the exercise of *parental responsibilities*, there is no competition between the non-resident parent and the step-parent, since parental responsibilities are only vested in a maximum of two persons, usually the legal parents. If the step-parent wishes to have parental responsibilities and the proceedings for joint parental responsibilities have been successful, the non-resident parent will not/no longer have parental responsibilities. It is then up to the resident legal parent and the step-parent to make decisions, after consulting with and informing the non-resident parent.[24]

The third legal relationship of a step-parent as a *legal parent* through step-parent adoption will result in the step-parent having parental responsibilities; the non-resident parent will in this scenario never have parental responsibilities. So there is no competition either. As stated before, the second and third options are rare; the general policy is that legal parents are responsible and entitled to be responsible, during and after the relationship.

2.2. RECOGNITION OF MULTIPLE PARENTS IF A CHILD IS RAISED IN MORE THAN ONE HOUSEHOLD

2.2.1. Intended Multi-Parent Families

Leaving step-parent families aside, there is another category of multi-parent families where the child has been raised from the start by parents who do not share one household. These intentional multi-parent families often make pre-conception agreements on who has what legal rights and duties towards the child and how the care and upbringing will be organised.[25] Dutch family law is built on the traditional two-parent family and leaves little room to create legal ties with more than two adults at the same time. Currently, it is at best possible to split parenthood and parental responsibilities, which would give three adults legal rights (and duties) towards the child. The situation is quite complex. Whether this division of rights between three parents is possible depends very much on the factual situation. The birth mother is always a legal parent with parental responsibilities, which leaves room for at most one other legal parent without parental responsibilities and one non-legal parent with

---

J. Wijngaard and N.D. van Foreest, 'Proportioneel Verdelen van Draagkracht bij Kinderalimentatie in Samengestelde Gezinnen' (2020) *Tijdschrift voor Scheidingsrecht* 63.

[24] Art. 1:377b of the DCC.

[25] M.V. Antokolskaia, W.M. Schrama, K.R.S.D. Boele-Woelki, C.C.J.H. Bijleveld, C.G. Jeppesen de Boer and G. van Rossum, *Meerouderschap: Een Oplossing voor Kinderen met meer dan Twee Ouders? Een Empirisch en Rechtsvergelijkend Onderzoek*, Boom Juridische Uitgevers, The Hague 2014, p. 139. The research included a survey of 270 respondents, indicating that 51% concluded a written agreement, 37% concluded a verbal agreement and 7% concluded no agreement at all.

parental responsibilities. The other legal parent can be either the partner of the birth mother, or another adult in the second household, but this person will have no parental responsibilities (because otherwise the third person cannot have parental responsibilities). The third person will not have the option to become a legal parent but can get parental responsibilities. This construction is available only in a very specific situation.[26] The fact that parenthood and parental responsibilities for the second and third parents can only be distributed results in a clash of rights, since what one parent gets will not be available to the other. Moreover, in most situations this is even not possible.

One should bear in mind that parenthood creates lifelong bonds, has extensive legal effects in other areas of law (such as inheritance law, tax law and name law), whereas parental responsibilities only give the right and duty to take care of and raise a minor child; once the child turns 18, legal ties no longer exist.

One type of three-parent family is where a donor is used by a couple. If the donor is known to the parents, which is the case predominantly for lesbian couples (as opposed to heterosexual couples who tend not to opt for a known donor), parties tend to make agreements on their respective roles. When a known donor is used by the mothers, the co-mother will not become a legal parent by operation of law. The co-mother has to recognise the child, which can take place before the child's birth. The donor will not have a chance to become a legal parent.[27] If only the birth mother is a legal parent at birth, recognition by the social parent or donor is possible. It will depend on the agreement the parties made. The birth mother has to consent to recognition in both situations. If she withholds consent, both the social parent and the donor can request the court to make an order replacing consent to the recognition. Different tests have to applied in both cases. A donor with family life is in a more favourable position than a co-mother with family life. Admissibility of the request depends for the donor on whether he has family life with the child.[28] This is assessed on the specific facts of each case. Once the request is deemed admissible, the court will have to give consent, if the recognition would not prejudice the interests of the mother in an undisturbed relationship with the child or the interests of the child and the donor. The social parent may also request the court to make an order replacing consent to the child's recognition when she as the life companion of

---

[26] When the birth mother has concluded a marriage or registered partnership with another woman. The spouse/registered partner will automatically be vested with parental responsibilities, ex Art. 1:253sa of the DCC, but will not automatically be a legal parent. The donor/father/third mother can recognise the child with the consent of the birth mother. If the birth mother does not give consent for the recognition, the donor/third parent can apply to the court for replacement consent. If the birth mother is in an informal relationship with the co-mother, it is not possible to apply for parental responsibilities for the co-mother if the third person will be a legal parent.
[27] Art. 1:204 read with Art. 1:2 of the DCC.
[28] Art. 1:204 (3) of the DCC.

the birth mother consented to an act which could have resulted in the pregnancy and birth of the child.[29] She does not have to show family life with the child as an admissibility condition, but in general there will be, since she has to be the life partner of the co-mother (implying that there is a family). The yardstick the court has to apply is a more stringent one than the one applicable to the donor with family life. The replacement consent will be given if this is in the interest of the child. There is some case law interpreting this test, showing so far that the assessment depends on the specific facts of the case.[30] There are no published cases where there was an actual clash between the co-mother and the donor with family life. Clashes occur between one of these parties and the birth mother who does not want the child to gain a second legal parent.

Government-commissioned empirical-legal research on intentional and non-intentional multi-parent families in the Netherlands reported a number of interesting conclusions. In 71% of a sample of 270 planned lesbian families in which a child was born with the help of a known donor, both the biological and social mother were the child's legal parents, whereas in 20% the biological mother was the only legal parent and in 7% the biological mother and the known donor were the legal parents. In 88% of the respondents' families, both mothers exercised parental responsibility. In the doctrine, opposing views have been expressed on how to deal with this type of multi-parent families.[31]

2.2.2. Surrogacy

The following is applicable to surrogacy within the Netherlands. In relation to surrogacy constructions outside the Netherlands by intending parents having residence in the Netherlands, different rules (including private international law) apply, which will not be dealt with here.

Dutch family law does not (yet) contain a specific legal framework for surrogacy cases. As a result, pursuant to the rule that the woman who gives birth

---

[29] Art. 1:204 (4) of the DCC.
[30] District Court Rotterdam 29.06.2016, ECLI:NL:RBROT:2016:5327: consent granted, in the interest of child and co-mother; Court of Appeal The Hague 12.07.2017, ECLI:NL:GHDHA:2017:2462: the co-mother gets the replacement consent because the court deems this in the best interests of the child: two parents (and extended families) are better than one; both the child and co-mother have a right to have their family life recognised; Court of Appeal The Hague 17.07.2019, ECLI:NL:GHDHA:2019:2031: co-mother did not consent to the act leading to the pregnancy and her request is therefore not admissible; District Court Noord-Nederland 30.07.2019, ECLI:NL:RBNNE:2019:3359: not the final decision, so not clear how the requirement of the interest of the child has been interpreted.
[31] M.J. Vonk, 'Zijn alle Gezinnen Gelijk?, Een nadere Analyse van de Voorstellen van de Staatscommissie Herijking Ouderschap over de juridische verankering van het meerouderschap' (2017) *Ars Aequi* 790; M.J. Vonk, *Hoeveel Ouders mag, kan en wil je Hebben?*, Inaugural Lecture, University of Antwerp, 2021; I. Weijers, 'Meerouderschap en Meeroudergezag in het Belang van Kind?' (2017/1) *Tijdschrift voor Jeugdrecht* 52.

is the legal parent who is vested with parental responsibilities, the surrogate mother is always the child's legal mother. Transferring the legal status of a parent to the intending parents is difficult, uncertain and depends on the consent of all the parties involved. Surrogate parents and intending parents draw up an agreement, which is not binding but will be relevant in the subsequent adoption proceedings, which are necessary to transfer parenthood to the intending parents. The surrogate mother has to put her child up for adoption, and the child will subsequently be adopted (if the court allows the adoption). This applies regardless of whether both, one or none of the intending parents is the biological parent. The Child Care and Protection Board is involved. Taking a child under the age of six months into the family of the intending parents requires the Board's consent. When the surrogate mother is married or in a registered partnership, her spouse is the legal parent, vested with parental responsibilities. Parental responsibilities need to be taken away from the parents (surrogate mother and her spouse/registered partner). A child protection measure has to be initiated by the Child Care and Protection Board; the Board will have to apply to the court for a termination of parental responsibilities of one or both parents. The intending parents may be attributed joint guardianship (which resembles parental responsibilities). After one year of being a family and taking care of the child, an application for adoption may be filed by the intending parents. The court has to assess whether the adoption is in the child's best interests and has to check whether the general conditions for adoption are met. The surrogate mother and spouse/registered partner should not object to the adoption; if they do, the court may only disregard their objections under specific conditions. When the surrogate mother is not married or in a registered partnership at the time of the birth of the child, the transfer of parental status is less complex. One of the intended parents may recognise the child (with the consent of the surrogate mother) and acquire sole parental responsibilities through a court ruling, and the other parent may subsequently adopt the child.

Rights and duties might clash if all parents wish to have full parental status: if the surrogate mother does not wish to transfer her status as a parent to the intending parents. There is to my knowledge no case law regarding domestic surrogacy where courts have had to decide between the surrogate mother and the intended parents.

The government intends to introduce a bill on the regulation of surrogacy cases within the Netherlands. A pre-conception agreement will be tested by the family court, resulting in an easier transfer of parenthood to the commissioning parents.[32]

Multi-parenthood will also not be recognised if a child is born as a result of donor-assisted reproductive technology using anonymous male and one female

---

[32] Available at https://www.internetconsultatie.nl/kinddraagmoederschapenafstamming, accessed 30.05.2022.

gamete donors. The *birth mother* is always – by operation of law – the legal parent of the child, even if a female gamete has been used for the conception of the child.[33] She will also be vested with parental responsibilities by operation of law (meaning she does not have to take steps to acquire them).[34] Whether another woman's gamete has been used is not considered relevant by the DCC.

The *partner of the birth mother* might become the child's legal parent. This depends on whether he is married to or in a registered partnership with the birth mother or not. When the male partner and the birth mother are married/registered partners and the child is born during the formal relationship, he will become a legal parent automatically.[35] It is not relevant whether the couple used male gametes to conceive the child.

When the female partner and the birth mother are married/registered partners, she will not become a legal mother by operation of law. Although this has, since 2014, been an option available to the second mother, the couple would not meet the condition of Dutch parentage law that they need to submit a declaration to the Donor Registration Association that the child has been conceived with a male donor who is unknown to the mothers, but who is identifiable to the child once he or she is aged 16 and older.[36] In the scenario of anonymous donation (understood as absolute anonymity), the Donor Registration Association cannot register the identity and a declaration will not be given. Automatic parenthood is not an option. Still, the second mother can become a legal parent through recognition of the child.[37] Whether or not the child has been conceived with third-party material is not relevant. The birth mother has to give consent to the recognition.

In the scenario where the partners are not married/registered partners, the second parent – be this a man or a woman – can become a legal parent by recognition of the child. The consent of the birth mother is required, but may be replaced by a consent order of the court.[38] Whether or not third-party gametes have been used is irrelevant.

The *donor's* position depends on the legal status of the others. As said, the birth mother will always be a legal parent. This leaves only one space available for, potentially, two interested parties: the social parent and the donor. If the donor is anonymous, the issue of who will become a legal parent will generally not rise.

Parentage law makes a distinction not only between opposite-sex and same-sex couples, but also between female couples and male couples. For same-sex

---

[33] Art. 1:198 (1) sub. a of the DCC.
[34] Art. 1:253b of the DCC.
[35] Art. 1:199 sub. a of the DCC.
[36] Art. 1:198 (1) sub. b of the DCC.
[37] Art. 1:204 of the DCC.
[38] Ibid.

relationships of two women, almost the same rules apply as for partners of the opposite sex. Since new legislation was enacted in 2014,[39] the co-mother can become a legal parent if she is in a marriage/registered partnership with the birth mother at the time of the child's birth. There is an important condition which does not apply to opposite-sex couples in regard to the position of the donor. If the mothers have made use of an identifiable donor (who is not known to the mothers but whose identity is registered at the Donor Registration Association and will eventually be accessible to the child) the co-mother will become a legal parent by operation of law, just like a male spouse of the birth mother does. The other option available to become a legal parent is via recognition before or after the child's birth, which is the same for the male partner of the birth mother. There are differences in adoption law in favour of two-mother families over other couples, stemming from the period before 2014, when the law on parenthood had not been reformed yet, with a faster and less stringent procedure for adoption of a child born to one of the mothers.

For two-father families, the law is different, since there is always a legal mother involved. In two-mother families, one of the mothers is automatically a legal parent and the father/donor involved is not. This implies that at least one of the two fathers needs to use adoption to create a parent–child relationship; possibly, both fathers need to adopt. This depends on whether the mother is married at the time of the birth of the child: if she is, her spouse will be the second legal parent. For two-father families, it is therefore more complicated and takes longer before they both can become legal parents.

2.2.3. Recent Developments

The Dutch government has been concerned with the issue of how to integrate new families and new developments into family law for many years. Lobby groups continue to press for changes and more equality. In 2014, research by a multidisciplinary committee was commissioned on multi-parent families. In 2016, this State Committee on the Reassessment of Parenthood (*Staatscommissie Herijking Ouderschap*) published its report, titled 'Child and Parents in the 21st Century'. The report is detailed and encompasses many topics, including child participation, stronger recognition of the right of children to know their origins, the position of children born in unmarried families, and much more. One of its revolutionary ideas was to introduce legal multi-parenthood for a maximum of four parents (in two households) and multi-parent responsibilities.[40] In reaction

---

[39] M. Antokolskaia, 'Legal Embedding Planned Lesbian Parentage. Pouring new Wine into old Wineskins?' (February 2014) *Family and Law*, DOI: 10.5553/FenR/.000015.

[40] I. Boone, 'Co-parenting before Conception. The Low Countries' Approach to Intentional Multi-parent Families' (February 2018) *Family & Law*, DOI: 10.5553/FenR/.000034;

to the recommendations, the government commissioned further research on the legal and practical implications of multi-parenthood in other relevant areas of law, such as inheritance law, tax law, child maintenance, private international law, and residence law.[41] Subsequently, the government decided not to proceed with the idea of multi-parenthood, mostly because of the expected increase in conflicts between more parents.[42] The government also referred to the complexity of a four-parent system. Instead of opting for a multi-parenthood system, the government indicated that a system of partial parental responsibilities is the way forward to solve problems experienced by social parents.[43] A draft bill has been published for consultation.[44] The bill hardly resolves the fundamental problem experienced by multi-parent families: the lack of legal recognition of their family as a publicly acknowledged family, deserving the same protection as other families do. Partial parental responsibilities do not recognise this status, and hardly provide any solution at all. At the same time, this new instrument will result in further complexity of the law. Taking into account how equality for same-sex couples influenced the law on marriage and registered partnership on a step-by-step basis, resulting in the opening up of marriage, my prediction is that this is a step in the direction of the further reform of the law, resulting in more equality for multi-parent families. In 2021, a new government started to work on their political agenda for the next four years. During the summer of 2021, 10 political parties signed a 'Rainbow Agreement' stating that they will strive to introduce new legislation on multi-parenthood and multi-parental responsibilities in the next four years.[45] No bill has been published yet and it might take some time, not only given the complex nature of such bill(s), but also taking into account other topics requiring attention. It is likely that the proposed bill on partial parental responsibilities will be withdrawn.

Another recommendation of the Committee was to introduce a legal framework for domestic altruistic surrogacy. Recently, a draft bill was published.[46] This is less controversial, since there is consensus that the current situation is poorly dealt with. The Council of State produced an advice, but this has so far not been made public.

N. Cammu, '"Legal Multi-parenthood" in Context: Experiences of Parents in Light of the Dutch Proposed Family Law Reforms' (July 2019) *Family & Law*, DOI: 10.5553/FenR/.000042.
[41] Parliamentary Papers II 2018/19, no. 33 836, 42 (appendices).
[42] Parliamentary Papers II 2018/19, no. 33 836, 45, p. 11.
[43] Ibid.
[44] Available at https://www.internetconsultatie.nl/deelgezag, accessed 30.05.2022.
[45] Available at https://www.coc.nl/wp-content/uploads/2021/03/COC-Regenboog-Stembusakkoord-2021.pdf, accessed 30.05.2022.
[46] Available at https://www.internetconsultatie.nl/kinddraagmoederschapenafstamming, accessed 30.05.2022.

2.3. POLYGAMOUS FAMILIES

There is an increasing tendency in family law policy to act against what, according to the Dutch view, is perceived as undesirable, such as child marriage, polygamy and forced marriages.[47] Where Dutch family law seems to be tolerant and open to new family forms such as two-mother families or two-household families, this is less the case for family forms originating in other religions and cultures. It is noticeable that the political climate has recently had more impact on what Dutch law allows and does not allow, and that, in particular, family law forms and relationships related to Islam are more susceptible to being found contrary to public policy than before.[48]

Polygamy is one of these family forms which will not be recognised, leaving all parties, but in particular the wife and children, in a legal limbo. A report conducted in 2009 concluded that reform of Dutch law was not necessary.[49] However, in recent years, legislation allowing for the recognition of the second marriage has become stricter. It depends on where the second marriage was concluded and whether it has been included in the population registry of the Netherlands that the marriage is a polygamous one. Once the polygamous nature of the second marriage is ended because the first marriage has itself ended, the second marriage can be recognised.

There is no multiplicity of parenthood in the context of open adoption. The reason is simple: Dutch family law only recognises strong adoption, and so the legal ties with the original parents will always be severed. There is some thought of introducing open adoption for foster parents and the government commissioned research.[50] The results of this legal, comparative and empirical

---

[47] New laws have been enacted, both criminalising forced marriages and polygamy, and family law legislation aimed at the prevention of child marriage, forced marriages and polygamy: Wet van 7 maart 2013 tot wijziging van het Wetboek van Strafrecht, het Wetboek van Strafvordering en het Wetboek van Strafrecht BES met het oog op de verruiming van de mogelijkheden tot strafrechtelijke aanpak van huwelijksdwang, polygamie en vrouwelijke genitale verminking; Wet van 7 oktober 2015 tot wijziging van Boek 1 en Boek 10 van het Burgerlijk Wetboek betreffende de huwelijksleeftijd, de huwelijksbeletselen, de nietigverklaring van een huwelijk en de erkenning van in het buitenland gesloten huwelijken (Wet tegengaan huwelijksdwang).

[48] S. Rutten, *Gegeven de Betekenis van Islamitisch Familierecht, Samenloop van Europese en Islamitische Familierechtsordes; Nederland als Voorbeeld*, Inaugural lecture, Maastricht University, 2017, p. 8.

[49] K. Boele-Woelki, I. Curry-Sumner and W.M. Schrama, *De Juridische Status van Polygame Huwelijken in Rechtsvergelijkend Perspectief*, WODC/Boom Juridische Uitgevers, The Hague 2010. English summary available at https://repository.wodc.nl/bitstream/handle/20.500.12832/1801/1815_summary_tcm28-70832.pdf?sequence=3&isAllowed=y, accessed 20.08.2022.

[50] M.J. Vonk, W.D. de Haan, C.G. Jeppesen de Boer and G.C.A.M. Ruitenberg, *Simple Adoption of Foster Children*, WODC, The Hague 2020, available at https://repository.wodc.nl/bitstream/handle/20.500.12832/2437/2989_summary_tcm28-426701.pdf?sequence=3&isAllowed=y, accessed 20.08.2022.

study indicate that introducing simple adoption is worth considering because it meets the needs and interests of a group of foster parents and children. The government responded that it is not considering doing so, as this would result in the introduction of recognising multi-parent families.[51]

There will also not be a multiplicity of parenthood in the case of *kafala*. *Kafala* might be recognised under Dutch private international law but that does not mean that multiple parenthood relationships are recognised. However, it might have to be recognised in other respects: the Court of Justice of the European Union ruled in 2019 that the right to free movement and residence does not include a child who has been placed in the permanent legal guardianship of a citizen of the European Union under the Algerian *kafala* system, because that placement does not create any parent–child relationship, but that it might – under specific conditions – have the implication that the child be granted a right of entry and residence in order to enable the child to live with his or her guardian in the host Member State.[52]

3. PART B. DIVERSITY AND PLURALITY OF FAMILY'S FUNCTIONS

3.1. LEGAL RECOGNITION OF VARIOUS FUNCTIONS OF THE FAMILY

It is difficult to state the extent to which the law in the Netherlands recognises that the family may have various functions since Dutch policy-makers do not explicitly deal with family (law) policy as such. It is up to academics to distil the functions recognised by the law, but this has received little attention in the Dutch scholarly context so far. An important aspect is that it is not only family law that is relevant, but other fields of law also demonstrate how families are perceived by the legislature. In income tax and inheritance tax law, inheritance law and social security law, as well as in criminal law, social security law and adult protection law, families (partners and children) often are granted a special position compared to persons who are not relatives. From the legal consequences attached to being a family in these Acts, one might deduce some underlying notions of what families are and what family members are supposed to do and not do. In general, the law recognises at least these functions of families:[53] (1) a financial role within families regarding children and economically weaker

---

[51] Letter of the Minister to the Second Chamber, 17.12.2020, no. 3117868, p. 9.
[52] Case C-129/18, *SM v. Entry Clearance Officer, UK Visa Section*, ECLI:EU:C:2019:248.
[53] W.M. Schrama, *De Niet-huwelijkse Samenleving in het Nederlandse en Duitse Recht*, Kluwer, Deventer 2004, p. 264.

partners, in the Netherlands often part-time working mothers; and (2) a special emotional bond between people which needs to be recognised by the State and which results in specific rights and duties, such as a preferential position for being appointed as a guardian or curator in adult protection law, a right not to testify against partners and relatives in criminal proceedings, and a special duty of care. In this respect, how families are perceived is directly related to what is perceived as the role of the State in respect of financial support and care towards citizens. Family law regulates and protects partners and children, at least those families who qualify according to the law.

In this respect, it is questionable whether Dutch family law is currently effective in achieving these goals, since various types of families are excluded from access to the status of a family. This is despite the fact that family law over the last three decades has been steered and reformed with equality in mind. Families nowadays are in this sense sometimes more a private project of citizens who demand recognition by the State.[54] The status of parents and children has been profoundly changed, as has the role of the State in regard to families and family law. Where a century ago family law was aimed at dividing responsibilities between the State and the family in relation to weaker, dependent members, currently, in an era where having children is often a choice (due to birth control and medical-technological advancements), the status of being a parent is a wanted or even demanded one, instead of one which is forced upon parents by the State. The welfare state, individualisation, and globalisation have had a serious impact on families. The right to become a legal parent has become part of the equality debate. However, not all families take the same position.[55]

A recent trend is that financial protection of weaker parties within families has been reduced step by step. Family law reform has reduced the legal family protection by limiting community of property and by a reduced maintenance right after divorce (from a maximum of 12 years to five years, with some exceptions). The ongoing individualisation appears to play an important role: every person is responsible for his or her own life, regardless of relationship status and care for children and vulnerable relatives. This might imply a gradual shift of responsibilities and risks from families to individuals. That is, to my

---

[54] W.M. Schrama, 'Marriage and Alternative Status Relationships in the Netherlands' in J. Eekelaar and R. George (eds), *Routledge Handbook of Family Law and Policy*, Routledge, Oxon 2020, pp. 15–28; W.M. Schrama, 'The Dutch Approach to Informal Lifestyles: Family Function over Family Form?' (2008) 22 *International Journal of Law, Policy and the Family* 311; W.M. Schrama, 'Verschil moet er Zijn: Over Gelijkheid in het Familierecht' (2016) 22 *Tijdschrift voor Familie- en Jeugdrecht* 89; W.M. Schrama, 'Een vierde Trede in het Familierecht? Een Blik in het Verleden en op de Toekomst van het Nederlandse Familierecht' in K. Boele-Woelki (ed.), *Actuele Ontwikkelingen in het Familierecht*, UCERF reeks 3, Ars Aequi, Nijmegen 2009, pp. 69–91.

[55] See section 4 below.

mind, not something to be happy about, given the strong gendered dimension of care work within families, resulting in more financial risks for women on divorce or the death of their spouse/partner.[56]

There is no policy to encourage families to have children, but there are financial benefits for families with children.

3.2. THE FUNCTIONS WHICH ARE PREDOMINANTLY FAVOURED

Determining which functions are predominantly favoured depends on how one 'measures' predominance. It is clear that families, in particular formal ones based on marriage and registered partnership, have a special status protected by law. It is not only the relation between the partners in a marriage or registered partnership that is perceived as a special one; parents and children also have a protected status. This special status of partners and of parents and children is demonstrated by a protected legal position in various areas of law, which has both advantages and disadvantages. These advantages and disadvantages show an underlying notion of what families are supposed to do: they need to care for one another in emotional and financial respects. They are subject to a higher standard of moral and legal obligations than other types of relationships between people. This applies in family law, inheritance law, tax law, social security law, income and inheritance tax law, criminal (procedural) law, etc. For other types of family relationships than the core family, the expectations of what this relationship, according to the legislature, entails are lower, but still present, such as for siblings and grandparents and their grandchildren.[57]

There is no direct policy indicating the relevance of whether children are present in the family. Within family law, there is one exception regarding spousal maintenance law. Having cared for children during the marriage and taking care of them after divorce is one of the factors that is relevant for the right to and duration of spousal maintenance.[58] How the child has been conceived is not

---

[56] W. Schrama, J. Tigchelaar and Y. Yildiz, 'De Rol van de Staat in het Relatierecht' in W.M. Schrama and S. Burri (eds), *Verantwoordelijkheden in het Familierecht: de Rol van de Staat, Familie en Individu*, Boom Juridische Uitgevers, The Hague 2000, pp. 66–77; W.M. Schrama, 'Marriage and Alternative Status Relationships in the Netherlands' in J. Eekelaar and R. George (eds), *Routledge Handbook of Family Law and Policy*, Routledge, Oxon 2020.

[57] In some legal provisions a broader definition of relatives is taken into account, such as Art. 165 s. 2 sub. (a) Dutch Civil Procedural Code; Art. 217 Code of Criminal Procedural Law.

[58] Art. 1:156–158 of the DCC.

relevant, nor whether the child is a three-parent child, as long as the child is the legal child of these parents. There is no case law yet on these relatively new provisions in maintenance law.

A more important difference seems to be whether or not the family has opted for the formal structure of marriage or registered partnership. If not, there are safety nets for the person who undertakes most of the care of the children and elderly; Dutch law has no *lex specialis* for informal unions, but more and more families are not opting for marriage.[59] Once in a formal structure, it does not matter whether this is a family of two mothers or one consisting of a mother and a father. However, to become a two-father family is very difficult, so there is a difference. The argument here is that where two men have a child, there is always a mother involved who carried the child for nine months.

4. CONCLUSION

In a relatively short period of time, important legal reforms took place to accommodate new family forms. However, to my mind, for some families the law is more apt to adapt than for others. In the legal literature, attention has been drawn to informal families where legal steps need to be taken to become the second legal parent and to acquire parental responsibilities. This results in unnecessary conflicts at relationship breakdown, when the father discovers he does not have the same rights as the mother has. If the mother does not consent to him recognising the child and does not want to jointly apply for joint parental responsibilities, the father has to petition the court to replace consent orders. Most of the time, the consent is ordered, but by that time, the post-relationship phase has started on the basis of a legal conflict between the parents who will have to take care of raising the child together.[60] Secondly, in literature it has been argued that informal religious families should be treated better by family law.[61]

---

[59] W. Schrama, J. Tigchelaar and Y. Yildiz, 'De Rol van de Staat in het Relatierecht' in W.M. Schrama and S. Burri (eds), *Verantwoordelijkheden in het Familierecht: de Rol van de Staat, Familie en Individu*, Boom Juridische Uitgevers, The Hague 2000, pp. 11–89.

[60] W.M. Schrama, 'Marriage and Alternative Status Relationships in the Netherlands' in J. Eekelaar and R. George (eds), *Routledge Handbook of Family Law and Policy*, Routledge, Oxon 2020, pp. 15–28; W.M. Schrama, 'The Dutch Approach to Informal Lifestyles: Family Function over Family Form?' (2008) 22 *International Journal of Law, Policy and the Family* 311; W.M. Schrama, 'Verschil moet er Zijn: Over Gelijkheid in het Familierecht' (2016) 22 *Tijdschrift voor Familie- en Jeugdrecht* 89; W.M. Schrama, 'Een Vierde Trede in het Familierecht? Een Blik in het Verleden en op de Toekomst van het Nederlandse Familierecht' in K. Boele-Woelki (ed.), *Actuele Ontwikkelingen in het Familierecht*, UCERF reeks 3, Ars Aequi, Nijmegen 2009, pp. 69–91.

[61] S.W.E. Rutten, 'Hernieuwde Bezinning op Informele Religieuze Huwelijken' (2016) *Nederlands Juristenblad* 592.

The couple often is not aware that their religious status does not correspond to a formal legal status, thus creating unnecessary problems. As stated before, lobby groups for equal rights have been successful in getting attention for their poor legal status, but this has influenced the attention given to other different types of families. Hopefully, the balance will eventually be restored. Family law should, to my mind, include all these types of families, not just some.

TURKISH LAW IN AN AGE OF CHANGING FORMS AND FUNCTIONS OF THE FAMILY

Meliha Sermin Paksoy

1. Introduction 435
2. Multiplicity of Parenthood in the Context of Step-Families............ 436
   2.1. Legal Responsibilities and Rights of a Step-Parent who Shares a Household with the Child's Parent 436
   2.2. Duty of Support 439
   2.3. Representation of the Minor by the Step-Parent 439
   2.4. Household Rules... 440
3. Multiplicity of Parenthood if a Child is Raised in More than One Household.. 440
4. Prohibition of Polygamy and De Facto Polygamous Families 441
5. Multiplicity of Parenthood in the Case of an Open Adoption.......... 442
6. Multiplicity of Parenthood in the Case of Foster Families 444
7. 'Parenthood of the Birth Mother' Rule and Donor-Assisted Reproductive Technologies 445
   7.1. General Comments 445
   7.2. The Case of 'Three-Parent Children' 446
   7.3. Parenthood in the Case of Surrogacy 446
8. Parenthood in a Same-Sex Relationship 446
9. Family's Functions 447
   9.1. General Comments 447
   9.2. Family's Functions if Children are Present in the Family.......... 449
10. Conclusion.. 450

1. INTRODUCTION

The Turkish lawmaker attributes great importance to the family even at the constitutional level.[1] The family is seen as the central unit of society and as a

---

[1] For relevant articles see section 9.1 below.

secure nest for children. However, the Turkish lawmaker is very conservative with the recognition of new forms of family, surrogacy, and gamete cell and embryo donations.

Although the Turkish Civil Code (TCC) underwent a major revision in 2002, many legal issues related to surrogacy, gamete cell and embryo donation, same-sex couples, unmarried couples and joint custody remain unregulated. In the case of surrogacy, gamete cell and embryo donation and same-sex couples, the silence of the lawmaker in the TCC means intentional rejection. Consequently, surrogacy, gamete cell donation and embryo donation are explicitly prohibited in other laws.[2] However, rejection by the lawmaker does not mean that these relationships do not exist. For instance, many couples travel abroad for surrogacy and gamete cell or embryo donations.

Given this background, the author will provide information about family forms and family's functions in Turkey.

2. MULTIPLICITY OF PARENTHOOD IN THE CONTEXT OF STEP-FAMILIES

2.1. LEGAL RESPONSIBILITIES AND RIGHTS OF A STEP-PARENT WHO SHARES A HOUSEHOLD WITH THE CHILD'S PARENT

Step-families are families where children from one or both spouses/partners are raised in the same household.

Turkish law recognises multiplicity of parenthood in the context of step-families and confers limited legal responsibilities and rights on a step-parent who shares a household with the child's parent. On this issue, there is a specific article in the TCC, namely Article 338. According to this article, titled 'Step-Children', spouses are obliged to show the necessary due care and attention to their step-children who are still minors. Each spouse must give the other reasonable support in exercising parental responsibility over the latter's children and must represent the other spouse as circumstances require.

Pursuant to the lawmaker's official reasoning in Article 338, this rule turns a moral obligation into a legal one.[3] Step-parents are expected to show the

---

[2] In addition, Art. 1 of the Law on the Harvesting, Storage, Grafting, and Transplantation of Organs and Tissues prohibits surrogacy, gamete cell donation and embryo donation. Art. 15 of the same Law envisages criminal sanctions for gamete cell and embryo donors and intermediaries.

[3] T. Uyar, A. Uyar and C. Uyar, *Türk Medeni Kanunu Aile Hukuku*, Bilge, Istanbul 2016, p. 5485.

necessary due care and attention to their step-children as if they were their own children.[4] The step-parent should help and support the parent in raising his or her child. Financial aspects of the obligations of the step-parent arise from the obligation to contribute to family expenses.[5]

According to Article 338 of the TCC, this duty of a step-parent seems to be limited to minor step-children. However, the obligations of the parents do not cease as the minor reaches maturity. In Turkish law, parents are obliged to take care of their children for as long as the child continues with his or her expected studies.[6] This also includes higher education. Thus, parents must continue to support their child if he or she decides to go to university. The Turkish Court of Cassation is also of the opinion that parents should continue to support a child who, after graduating from university, enrols in a preparatory course to be able to succeed in the exam for public servant recruitment.[7] The parents must continue to support the child during this period.[8] Therefore, parallel to the duty of the parent, in the author's opinion, a step-parent's duty to support should also continue until his or her step-child completes his or her expected studies. Traditionally, Turkish children stay in the family home until they get married or start work in another city, but after they have completed their higher or vocational education, the parents' duty of financial support essentially ceases.

The step-parent's rights and obligations relating to the step-child derive from marriage and depend on the custodial/parental rights of the parent with whom the step-parent shares a household. Therefore, these rights and obligations are accepted to be irrevocable as long as the marriage and custodial/parental rights of the parent remain in force. Naturally, the rights and duties of the step-parent end if the marriage ends. However, if the marriage ends due to the death of the parent, the step-parent may be appointed as a guardian of the child. Even if

---

[4] A. Kılıçoğlu, *Aile Hukuku*, Turhan, Ankara 2020, p. 338; Ö.U. Gençcan, *Türk Medeni Kanunu Yorumu*, Yetkin, Ankara 2021, p. 2210.
[5] B. Öztan, *Aile Hukuku*, Turhan, Ankara 2015, p. 1050.
[6] Art. 328 II of the TCC.
[7] Yargıtay 3. HD, 04.05.2017, E. 2016/15392, K. 2017/654; Yargıtay 3. HD, 09.03.2015, E. 2014/16809, K. 2015/3688, available at www.hukukturk.com, accessed 03.03.2022.
[8] The nature of this alimony after the minor has reached the age of majority is disputed. Most authors think that this is a continuation of the duty of maintenance based on Art. 328 II: T. Birinci Uzun, 'Eğitimine Devam Eden Ergin Çocuğa Ödenen Nafakanin Bazi Yargıtay Kararlarinda Yardim Nafakasi Olarak Nitelendirilmesi' (2018) 20(2) *Dokuz Eylül Üniversitesi Hukuk Fakültesi Dergisi* 93. However, some authors and the Turkish Court of Cassation state that this duty of support arises from Art. 364 of the TCC: Yargıtay 2. HD, 22.09.2011, E. 12022 K. 2011/13809, available at www.hukukturk.com, accessed 03.03.2022; I. Catalbas, *Velayet ve Ortak Velayet*, Seckin, Ankara 2021, p. 70; F. Erlüle, 'Boşanmadan Sonra Birlikte (Ortak) Velayete İlişkin Güncel Gelişmeler' (2020) 45(114) *Bursa Barosu Dergisi* 71; H. Özdemir, 'Yargıtay Kararları Işığında Türk Medeni Hukukunda Yardım Nafakası' (2014) 9(100) *Terazi Hukuk Dergisi* 66.

somebody else is appointed as the guardian of the step-child, the step-parent may ask the court to grant him or her visitation rights.[9]

If the step-parent does not fulfil his or her obligations relating to his or her step-child, this can constitute a ground for divorce or a reason to strip the parent of his or her custodial rights.[10] The step-child has no right to compel the step-parent to support him or her financially.[11] However, Article 195 of the TCC[12] enables the parent to seek the intervention of the Family Court on the ground that the other spouse is not fulfilling his or her duties to his or her step-child and in this case the court will remind the spouses of their duties and try to settle their differences. If this does not work, the court can, upon the request of the parent, take the steps envisaged by the law, such as determining the amount of the contribution of the step-parent to the expenses of the step-child.

As stated in Article 327 of the TCC, parents are obliged to cover the expenses relating to the care, protection and education of the children. According to one view, the children mentioned in this article include step-children too.[13] However, most authors argue that the obligations of the step-parent are secondary and complementary to the parents' rights and obligations.[14] Therefore, as a rule, the responsibilities of the parent and the step-parent do not clash or compete with one another.

The parent who does not share a household with the child may be under an obligation to pay child support. At the same time, the step-parent is obliged to make the necessary contribution to the basic expenses of the child who is living in the same household as the step-parent. This duty of the step-parent

---

[9] B. Öztan, *Aile Hukuku*, Turhan, Ankara 2015, p. 794; İ.Z. Suata, *Çocuk Hukuku*, Yetkin, Ankara 2021, p. 69; A. Tokuş, *Birlikte Velayet*, Seckin, Ankara 2021, p.105; M. Dural, T. Öğüz and A. Gümüş, *Aile Hukuku*, Filiz, Istanbul 2018, p. 145.

[10] M. Dural, T. Öğüz and A. Gümüş, *Aile Hukuku*, Filiz, Istanbul 2018, p. 353; A. Kılıçoğlu, *Aile Hukuku*, Turhan, Ankara 2020, p. 507; Ö.U. Gençcan, *Türk Medeni Kanunu Yorumu*, Yetkin, Ankara 2021, p. 2211; Ö.U. Gençcan, *Velayet Hukuku*, Yetkin, Ankara 2015, pp. 116–17; Yargıtay 2. HD, 07.12.2005, E. 2005/13362, K. 2005/17110; Yargıtay 2. HD, 08.04.2004, E. 2004/3628, K. 2004/4542, available at www.hukukturk.com, accessed 03.03.2022.

[11] B. Öztan, *Aile Hukuku*, Turhan, Ankara 2015, p. 204.

[12] Art. 195 E reads: 'Protection of the marital union

1. In general

If a spouse fails to fulfil his/her duties to the family or if the spouses disagree on matters of importance to the marital union, they may apply jointly or separately to the court for mediation.

The court reminds the spouses of their duties and attempts to settle their differences; if the spouses consent, experts may be consulted or they may be referred to a marriage guidance or family counselling agency.

If necessary, at the request of one spouse the court will take the steps envisaged by law.'

[13] R. Serozan, *Çocuk Hukuku*, Vedat, Istanbul 2005, n. 92.

[14] Ö.U. Gençcan, *Türk Medeni Kanunu Yorumu*, Yetkin, Ankara 2021, p. 1638; Ö.U. Gençcan, *Velayet Hukuku*, Yetkin, Ankara 2015, pp. 116–17.

arises from marriage and exists independently of the parental/custodial duties of the parent with whom the step-parent does not share a household. Therefore the step-parent cannot abstain from fulfilling his or her duty on the ground that the other parent is not paying child support. In a similar way, the existence of an affluent step-parent does not remove or change the financial obligations of the parent who does not live with the child. A judge should not take the financial situation of the step-parent into consideration when determining the amount of child support to be paid by the parent.[15]

In Turkish law, a step-parent does not have the same legal responsibilities and rights as the parent with whom he or she does not share a household. As explained above, the step-parent has almost no parental rights. In contrast, the other parent may have custodial rights if the parents have been granted joint custody. Therefore, the rights of the step-parent and the other parent do not clash.

The step-parent may adopt the child of his or her spouse/partner. If this happens, the step-parent will enjoy custodial and parental rights.

2.2. DUTY OF SUPPORT

According to Article 364 of the TCC, every individual has an obligation to provide support to his or her ascendants, descendants and siblings who would fall into poverty without such help. Therefore, parents are obliged to support their children who are in need, even if the children are no longer minors. This obligation falls solely on parents. A step-parent is not under such an obligation. Similarly, parents who are facing poverty may ask their child to support them, but step-parents cannot do so.

2.3. REPRESENTATION OF THE MINOR BY THE STEP-PARENT

Only if a parent cannot do so and the circumstances require it can a step-parent represent his or her step-child, and this representation cannot be continuous.[16] Moreover, if the law explicitly requires the consent of the parents, the step-parent has no right to represent the child.[17] For example, the TCC requires the consent of the legal representative (parents or guardian) if the child wants to get married at the age of 17. In this case, the step-parent cannot represent the parent in consenting to the marriage.

---

[15] B. Öztan, *Aile Hukuku*, Turhan, Ankara 2015, p. 1050.
[16] Ibid., p. 1079.
[17] Ibid., p. 1078.

2.4. HOUSEHOLD RULES

The step-parent, together with the parent with whom he or she shares a household, may set up household rules. According to Article 339 II of the TCC,[18] the child is obliged to follow these rules.

3. MULTIPLICITY OF PARENTHOOD IF A CHILD IS RAISED IN MORE THAN ONE HOUSEHOLD

Turkish law recognises multiplicity of parenthood if the child is raised in more than one household. Especially if parents are granted joint custody, it is possible that the child can be raised in more than one household. In this case, there might be two step-parents and both of them would have rights and responsibilities in terms of Article 338 of the TCC. Since the rights of the step-parents are very limited and complementary to the parental rights, no clashes are expected.

Due to the wording of Article 336(3) of the TCC,[19] it was disputed for a long time whether joint custody is possible under Turkish family law.[20] Now the prevailing opinion[21] in the doctrine and court decisions is that a judge can grant joint custody to divorced parents,[22] The Turkish Constitutional Court has held

---

[18] Art. 339 II: 'The child owes his/her parents obedience'.
[19] Art. 336 III: 'In the event of the death of one of the parents, custody belongs to the survivor, and in divorce, to the party to whom the child is left'.
[20] P. Kahraman, *Türk Milletlerarası Aile Hukukunda Ortak Velayet*, Onikilevha, Istanbul 2019, pp. 60–65; L.M. Kurt, 'Boşanma Durumunda Birlikte (Ortak) Velâyet' (2018) 9(2) *İnönü Üniversitesi Hukuk Fakültesi Dergisi* 157, 166; E. Apaydın, 'Ortak Hayata Son Verilmesi Sonrasi Ortak Velâyet Hususunda Yasal Düzenleme Gereği' (2018) 9(1) *Inonu University Law Review* 448.
[21] M. Erdem, *Aile Hukuku*, Seckin, Ankara 2020, p. 173; K. Guven, 'Türk Hukukunda Evliliğin Sona Ermesi Halinde ve Evlilik Dışı İlişkide Velayet Hakkının Geldiği Son Nokta: Ortak Velayet' (2018) 4(1) *Başkent Üniversitesi Hukuk Fakültesi Dergisi* 62; B. Oztan and F. Oztan, 'Boşanmada Birlikte Velâyet ve Birlikte Velâyetin Uygulanmasına İlişkin Modeller' (2020) 5(1) *Çankaya Üniversitesi Hukuk Fakültesi Dergisi* 2582; İ.Z. Suata, *Çocuk Hukuku*, Yetkin, Ankara 2021, p. 127; I. Catalbas, *Velayet ve Ortak Velayet*, Seckin, Ankara 2021, p. 70; F. Erlüle, 'Boşanmadan Sonra Birlikte (Ortak) Velayete İlişkin Güncel Gelişmeler' (2020) 45 114 *Bursa Barosu Dergisi* 67; İstanbul BAM 10. HD, 26.04.2017, E. 2017/578 K. 2017/386; Ankara BAM 1. HD, 10.05.2017, E. 2017/121 K. 2017/601; Ankara BAM 2. HD, 05.12.2017, E. 2017/1132, K. 2017/1471 (in E. Apaydın, 'Ortak Hayata Son Verilmesi Sonrasi Ortak Velâyet Hususunda Yasal Düzenleme Gereği' (2018) 9(1) *Inonu University Law Review* 463).
[22] Two major changes triggered this change of opinion in the doctrine. In 2016, in Law No. 6684 Turkey ratified Protocol No. 7, which is the Annex of Protocol No. 11 to the Convention for the Protection of Human Rights and Fundamental Freedoms. According to Art. 5 of this Protocol, spouses are equal in terms of rights and responsibilities in private law in respect of marriage, during marriage and in the event of termination of the marriage, in their relations with each other and with their children. Moreover, Art. 90 V of the Turkish Constitution states that '[i]n the case of a conflict between international agreements, duly put into effect, concerning fundamental rights and freedoms and the laws due to differences in provisions on the same matter, the provisions of international agreements shall prevail'.

that within the scope of the TCC and the relevant case law, joint custody best serves the right to respect for family life, unless joint custody would violate the child's best interests.[23]

Regarding the parents, it is important to determine which parent has custody, because custodial rights grant the parent many determinative powers.[24] The parent who has custody decides which school the child will attend and how the child will be treated and what religious upbringing he or she will receive. This parent is able to change the residence of the child unless the parent moves to a place far away and this change is unfavourable to the child.[25] In this case, the parent without custody only has visitation rights.[26] If the parents have joint custody, they should agree on these issues (i.e. issues such as religious upbringing).

4. PROHIBITION OF POLYGAMY AND DE FACTO POLYGAMOUS FAMILIES

Polygamous families are families where children are raised in a household where one party has more than one wife/husband/partner.

In Turkey, polygamy has been legally forbidden since 1926. Therefore, multiplicity of parenthood is not recognised if a child is raised in a polygamous family. However, even though polygamy is forbidden, de facto polygamous families do exist, although the exact number of such unions is unknown. Parental responsibility clashes in these de facto families have not been the subject of legal dispute or legal analysis.

Since polygamy is forbidden in Turkey, the children of the second or third wives/mistresses are legally born out of wedlock. For many, this is an unwanted label. In addition, children born out of wedlock used to be disadvantaged in inheritance law.[27] Therefore, if the second wife gave birth at home, it used to be

---

After the ratification of this Protocol, the Turkish Court of Cassation changed its opinion and ruled that joint parental custody does not violate either Turkish public order or the basic structure and basic interests of Turkish society. Yargıtay 2. HD, 20.01.2017, E. 2016/15771, K. 2017/1737, available at www.hukukturk.com, accessed 10.03.2022.

[23] Anayasa Mahkemesi, 30.11.2021, available at https://www.anayasa.gov.tr/tr/haberler/bireysel-basvuru-basin-duyurulari/musterek-cocugun-velayetinin-ebeveynin-ortak-kullanimina-karar-verilmesi-nedeniyle-aile-hayatina-saygi-hakkinin-ihlal-edilmesi/, accessed 29.05.2022.

[24] L.M. Kurt, 'Boşanma Durumunda Birlikte (Ortak) Velâyet' (2018) 9(2) İnönü Üniversitesi Hukuk Fakültesi Dergisi 159.

[25] H.V. Velidedeoglu, *Medeni Hukuk Aile Hukuku*, Nurgök Matbaası, Istanbul 1965, p. 276.

[26] P. Kahraman, *Türk Milletlerarası Aile Hukukunda Ortak Velayet*, Onikilevha, Istanbul 2019, p. 58.

[27] N. Inal, *Nüfus, Babalık, Evlat Edinme, Yabancı Kararların Tenfizi, Velayet, Vesayet Davaları*, Adalet, Ankara 2001, pp. 201–02; C. Baygın, *Soybağı Hukuku*, Onikilevha, Istanbul 2010, pp. 19–20.

the practice to register this child as the child of the first and legal wife. Under these circumstances, the legal wife became the official mother of the child. This practice created many inheritance law problems. After the death of the first wife or the falsely registered child, lawsuits would be filed to abolish the false lineage link to prevent the falsely registered mother or child from inheriting. Nowadays, since most woman give birth in hospital, it is usually not possible to make false declarations of motherhood.

5. MULTIPLICITY OF PARENTHOOD IN THE CASE OF AN OPEN ADOPTION

Open-adoption families are families where children have been adopted but maintain links (legal or de facto) with their biological families.

In Turkish law, an open-adoption system is in force because the lineage links of the biological parents (if known) are maintained when a child is adopted. Thus, the child can learn the identity of his or her biological parents and inherit from them. Therefore, Turkish law recognises multiplicity of parenthood in the case of an open adoption. However, in the case of adoption, the rights of the biological parents are limited to financial rights. For example, if the child dies, only biological parents have legal inheritance rights.[28]

At the latest at the time of the child's adoption, the custodial rights of the biological parents cease. The rights and obligations of the parents pass to the adoptive parents.[29] After adoption, the adoptive parents have custody of the child. They may administer and use the assets of the child.[30] They have sole decision-making power as to the child's education, upbringing, representation, professional education and religious education.[31] However, of course, they should get the opinion of the child on these matters and take his or her opinion into consideration. Adoptive parents may set rules which have to be obeyed by the child.[32] The adopted child receives the surname of the adoptive parents and the adoptive parents can name the child.[33] The adopted child has a right to get citizenship through his or her Turkish adoptive parents.

It is a disputed topic whether biological parents have visitation rights or not. The TCC is silent on this issue. Some authors and the Turkish Court of Cassation are of the opinion that since the child's lineage links are maintained,

---

[28] Adopted parents are not legal heirs of the adopted child, but an adopted child can designate his or her adopted parents as appointed heirs in a will.
[29] Art. 314 I of the TCC.
[30] Arts 352–54 of the TCC.
[31] Art. 339 I of the TCC.
[32] Art. 339 II of the TCC.
[33] Art. 314 II of the TCC.

biological parents have visitation rights which are embedded in their right of personality.[34] According to this view, biological parents cannot give up this right. Some authors argue that biological parents can ask the court to grant them visitation rights according to Article 325[35] or to give up their right of visitation at the time of the adoption.[36] According to another opinion, by consenting to the adoption, biological parents automatically give up their visitation rights.[37] If biological parents are abusing their visitation rights as a bargaining chip against the adoptive parents, the court should reject/terminate their visitation request/right.[38]

After the adoption, the adoptive parents become the caretakers of the child. Therefore, the maintenance obligation of the biological parents is only secondary to the maintenance obligation of the adoptive parents.[39] For example, if the adoptive parents cannot finance the needs of the child, it is theoretically possible to ask the biological parents to cover these expenses.[40] However, some authors and the Turkish Court of Cassation are of the opinion that the maintenance obligation of the biological parents ceases at the time of the adoption.[41] These authors argue that if it were otherwise, the biological parents would have a chance of interfering with the adoptive parents' child-raising.

According to Article 364 of the TCC,[42] an adopted child is obliged to support his or her adoptive and biological parents.[43] The adopted child may ask both his

---

[34] B. Köprülü and P. Kaneti, *Aile Hukuku*, Filiz, Istanbul, 1989, p. 236; A.C. Ruhi and C. Ruhi, *Nafaka Hukuku*, Seckin, Ankara 2021, p. 28; T. Akıntürk and D. Ateş, *Aile Hukuku*, Beta, Istanbul 2019, p. 398; İ.Z. Suata, *Çocuk Hukuku*, Yetkin, Ankara 2021, p. 104; I. Catalbas, *Velayet ve Ortak Velayet*, Seckin, Ankara 2021, p. 70; F. Erlüle, 'Boşanmadan Sonra Birlikte (Ortak) Velayete İlişkin Güncel Gelişmeler' (2020) 45 (114) *Bursa Barosu Dergisi* 76; Yargıtay İBK, 18.11.1959, E. 1959/12, K. 1959/29; Yargıtay 2. HD, 13.05.1991, E. 1991/4151, K. 1991/7800, available at www.hukukturk.com, accessed 03.04.2022.
[35] C. Baygın, *Soybağı Hukuku*, Onikilevha, Istanbul 2010, p. 233.
[36] H. Özdemir and A.C. Ruhi, *Çocuk Hukuku*, Onikilevha, Istanbul 2016, p. 863.
[37] B. Öztan, *Aile Hukuku*, Turhan, Ankara 2015, p. 996.
[38] E. Akyüz, *Çocuk Hukuku*, Pegem, Istanbul, 2016, p. 181.
[39] M. Dural, T. Öğüz and A. Gümüş, *Aile Hukuku*, Filiz, Istanbul 2018, p. 503; B. Öztan, *Aile Hukuku*, Turhan, Ankara 2015, p. 999; A.C. Ruhi and C. Ruhi, *Nafaka Hukuku*, Seckin, Ankara 2021, p. 29; O.P. Aydos, 'Yeni Medenî Kanuna Göre Evlât Edinme' (2000) 4(2) *Gazi Üniversitesi Hukuk Fakültesi Dergisi* 17.
[40] E. Akyüz, *Çocuk Hukuku*, Pegem, Istanbul, 2016, p. 180; H. Özdemir and A.C. Ruhi, *Çocuk Hukuku*, Onikilevha, Istanbul 2016, p. 863; A.C. Ruhi and C. Ruhi, *Nafaka Hukuku*, Seckin, Ankara 2021 p. 29.
[41] Yargıtay HGK. 27.12.1972, 2-269/1524; HGK. 15.06.1968, 2-1117/462; E. Akyüz, *Çocuk Hukuku*, Pegem, Istanbul, 2016, p. 149; M. Kizir, 'Türk Hukukunda Evlât Edinme' (2009) 17(1) *Selçuk Üniversitesi Hukuk Fakültesi Dergisi* 168.
[42] For this article see section 2.2 above.
[43] H. Ozdemir, 'Yargıtay Kararları Işığında Türk Medeni Hukukunda Yardım Nafakası' (2014) 9(100) *Terazi Hukuk Dergisi* 66; B. Köprülü and P. Kaneti, *Aile Hukuku*, Filiz, Istanbul 1989, p. 1989; B. Öztan, *Aile Hukuku*, Turhan, Ankara 2015, p. 458; A.C. Ruhi and C. Ruhi, *Nafaka Hukuku*, Seckin, Ankara 2021, p. 88. A dissenting opinion is that the duty to provide support

or her adoptive and biological parents to support him or her if he or she would fall into poverty if they did not do so. However, in this case, the obligation of the biological parents is secondary to that of the adoptive parents.[44]

6. MULTIPLICITY OF PARENTHOOD IN THE CASE OF FOSTER FAMILIES

Although Turkey is a Muslim country, adoption as explained above is possible. At the same time, in Turkish law it is also possible to not adopt a child but to take care of him or her. Under this system, the person/family taking care of the child is called the foster parent/family. However, this system is considered to be temporary. The desire is to unite the child with his or her biological parents when the conditions requiring the child's removal from his or her biological parents change in favour of reunion. The foster parent/family does not have custody of the child, or any rights connected with custody. Therefore, the child does not become entitled to bear the family name of, or automatically to inherit from, the foster parent/family. The foster parent/family must take care of the child under the continuous supervision and monitoring of the Ministry of Family and Social Policy. According to Article 15 of the Foster Family Regulation, foster families must provide the conditions necessary for the healthy development of the child and undertake to maintain, educate, protect and care for the child like a biological parent would. On application, foster parents/families may receive a certain amount of financial support from the Ministry to cover the expenses of the child. The foster parent/family must get permission from the relevant authorities to take the child abroad or to take him or her to another city, even if only temporarily.[45]

Foster parents/families can, together with the child's social worker, make important decisions on the issues that affect and change the life of the child, such as which school or vocational course he or she will attend or whether the child will be circumcised. In the foster system, the child's links to his or her biological parents are maintained. The biological parents and certain other relatives are supposed to have contact and spend time with the child. These contact times

---

should be in line with inheritance rights and, since adoptive parents are not the legal heirs of the adopted child, they should not be able to ask for financial support if they live in poverty. O.P. Aydos, 'Yeni Medenî Kanuna Göre Evlât Edinme' (2000) 4(2) *Gazi Üniversitesi Hukuk Fakültesi Dergisi* 17.

[44] B. Öztan, *Aile Hukuku*, Turhan, Ankara 2015, p. 1000; A.C. Ruhi and C. Ruhi, *Nafaka Hukuku*, Seckin, Ankara 2021, p. 88; H. Ozdemir, 'Yargıtay Kararları Işığında Türk Medeni Hukukunda Yardım Nafakası' (2014) 9(100) *Terazi Hukuk Dergisi* 67.

[45] Türkiye Cumhuriyeti Aile ve Sosyal Hizmetler Bakanlığı (Ministry of Family and Social Policy), available at https://www.aile.gov.tr/koruyucuaile/koruyucu-aile, accessed 10.03.2022.

are arranged and monitored by the social workers. Foster parents/families are obliged to avoid attitudes, behaviours and any rhetoric that will harm the child's relationship with his or her biological family. If the foster parent/family violates this obligation, the child may be taken away. The foster parent/family should not have any direct contact with the biological parents of the child.

The foster parent/family has no inheritance rights unless the child appoints the foster parent/family members as his or her heirs in a will after he or she has reached the age of 15. Biological parents continue to have inheritance rights unless there is a reason to deprive them of their inheritance rights.

7. 'PARENTHOOD OF THE BIRTH MOTHER' RULE AND DONOR-ASSISTED REPRODUCTIVE TECHNOLOGIES

7.1. GENERAL COMMENTS

In Turkey, surrogacy, gamete cell donation and embryo donation are forbidden by the Law on the Harvesting, Storage, Grafting, and Transplantation of Organs and Tissues.

In Turkish law, the woman who gives birth to the child is the child's mother. This is explicitly regulated in Article 282 of the TCC. Thus, in Turkey only the parenthood of the birth mother is recognised. The biological/intended mother is not recognised as a parent. Only with the consent of the birth mother and by fulfilling other conditions can this woman adopt the child and then enjoy parenthood. Anonymity of the donor does not make any difference. If the birth mother is married, there is a legal presumption that her husband is the father of the child.[46] In this case, unless the husband renounces his fatherhood by filing a lawsuit, the biological/intended father cannot recognise the child. If the birth mother is single, the biological father may recognise the child.

Normally, if a baby is born because of an illegal gamete cell or embryo donation, the donor/donors will not have any rights or duties. However, the male gamete cell donor or father of the embryo may recognise the child and establish the link of lineage with the child if the birth mother is single. If this is the case, then he will enjoy the rights of a father. Without recognition of the child, the donor may not participate in raising the child, unless the birth mother/family allows him to do so. Therefore, no clashes are expected.

Similarly, if a male gamete cell donor is not anonymous, the birth mother, the appointed representative of the child or the child, once he or she reaches the age of 18, may bring a lawsuit against the donor for recognition of the link of lineage.

---

[46] Art. 285 of the TCC.

7.2. THE CASE OF 'THREE-PARENT CHILDREN'

'Three-parent' medical technology is like in vitro fertilisation but uses the genetic material of two females and one male, instead of only one female and one male. As a rule, the DNA of one female is used to 'correct' the DNA of the other female to remove genetic mutations that cause serious hereditary diseases.

Three-parent technology is not explicitly regulated in Turkey. However, only the gamete cells of the couple may be used for in vitro fertilisation. Genetic selection is only allowed in case of gender-related hereditary diseases or the need to have a baby who could be a bone marrow donor for his or her sibling. Genetic modification of gamete cells is not permitted. Only after fertilisation may the healthiest embryos be chosen for implantation in the uterus. However, very recently, a few in vitro fertilisation clinics have started offering mitochondrial transplantation, which is, in this author's opinion, illegal for the reasons set out above. These clinics are relying on the lack of explicit prohibition of three-parent technology. The author expects that the lawmaker will explicitly forbid three-parent technologies soon in line with its assisted reproduction policies.

7.3. PARENTHOOD IN THE CASE OF SURROGACY

In Turkish law, surrogacy is forbidden. However, if this method were to be used unlawfully, the surrogate mother would be the legal mother of the child. The biological/intended mother would have no rights unless she adopted the child. If the surrogate mother were married, the husband of the surrogate mother would be the father of the child, because in Article 285 I of the TCC fatherhood of the husband is regulated as a presumption. In this case, the biological father or intended father cannot recognise the baby unless the husband of the birth mother terminates the link of lineage by filing a lawsuit called a 'rejection of the lineage'. If the birth mother is single, the biological/intended father may recognise the child as his and establish the link of lineage and then enjoy the rights of a father.

8. PARENTHOOD IN A SAME-SEX RELATIONSHIP

In Turkey, only married couples may use in vitro fertilisation. Gamete cell donation and surrogacy are forbidden. Same-sex couples cannot get married and accordingly cannot use in vitro fertilisation. If a same-sex couple were to use this method abroad, the male gamete cell owner may recognise the child and enjoy the rights of a father.

9. FAMILY'S FUNCTIONS

9.1. GENERAL COMMENTS

Turkish law considers the family to be the basic unit of society and confers special importance on it.[47] For example, there is a specific article in the Turkish Constitution on protection of the family and children:

> ART. 41 – Family is the foundation of the Turkish society and based on the equality between the spouses.
>
> The State shall take the necessary measures and establish the necessary organization to protect peace and welfare of the family, especially mother and children, and to ensure the instruction of family planning and its practice.

There are several other articles in the Constitution that emphasise the importance of the family and protect family unity, respect for family life and privacy of family life. The Turkish Constitution also states that a citizen has several duties and responsibilities to his or her family.[48]

In this context, Turkish law recognises that the family may have various functions.

First, the family has a function of producing and raising children.[49] Some writers phrase this function as the natural function of the family.[50] The family enables the human race to continue by legally unifying a couple and creating a stable nest for their offspring. At this point, it is important to point out again that in Turkey only heterosexual couples can get married. According to Article 322 of the TCC, parents and children owe each other support, consideration and respect. Parents are also obliged to show the necessary due care for their children's maintenance, education and supervision.[51] If the family is not fulfilling its function in raising children, sanctions can be imposed. Article 347 of the TCC states that if the physical and intellectual development of the child is in danger or if the child is emotionally abandoned, then the child can be removed from his or her family and be placed in the care of another family or institution.

---

[47] H. Hatemi and B. Kalkan Oğuztürk, *Aile Hukuku*, Onikilevha, Istanbul 2016, p. 3; T. Akıntürk and D. Ateş, *Aile Hukuku*, Beta, Istanbul 2019, p. 398; İ.Z. Suata, *Çocuk Hukuku*, Yetkin, Ankara 2021, p. 3.

[48] Art. 20: 'Everyone has the right to demand respect for his/her private and family life. Privacy of private or family life shall not be violated'. Art. 62: 'The State shall take the necessary measures to ensure family unity, the education of the children, the cultural needs, and the social security of Turkish citizens working abroad, and to safeguard their ties with the home country and to help them on their return home'.

[49] H. Hatemi and R. Serozan, *Aile Hukuku*, Filiz, Istanbul 1993, p. 4.

[50] N. Feyzioğlu, *Aile Hukuku*, Filiz, Istanbul 1979, p. 2.

[51] Art. 185 II of the TCC.

Similarly, in Turkish law, the family is seen as a unit of protection especially for women and children. As quoted above, Article 41 of the Turkish Constitution places special emphasis on protection of women and children. To grant women more rights and protection during and after the marriage, the Turkish lawmaker in 1926 opted for civil marriage instead of Islamic marriage. According to Article 143 of the TCC, a religious marriage ceremony cannot be performed between a couple without showing documentation of their prior civil marriage. Until 2015, it was a criminal offence to enter into a religious marriage before the same parties entered into a civil marriage.

For the protection of women who are victims of domestic violence, a special law (the Law on Protection of Family and Prevention of Violence Against Women) was enacted in 2012. There is a special section in the TCC on the protection of children. If children are abused or neglected within the family, the court can intervene and take several measures to protect the child.

The family is also supposed to provide economic security for its members.[52] Spouses are under an obligation of continuous support and this continuity creates a stable economic union to meet their basic human needs. There are many articles in the TCC that point to this function of the family. For example, according to Article 194, '[a] spouse may terminate a tenancy agreement, alienate the family home or limit the rights in respect of the family home by other transactions only with the express consent of the other'. The family home is the shelter of the family. Therefore, even if only one spouse has the right of ownership, the fate of the family home should be determined by a unanimous decision of the couple. Similarly, according to Article 199 of the TCC, 'to the extent required to ensure the family's financial security or fulfilment of a financial obligation arising from the marital union, at the request of one spouse the court may make the power to dispose of certain assets conditional on its consent'. In the same vein, Article 196 states that both spouses are legally obliged to contribute to the maintenance of the family. Even after children reach maturity, parents must provide financial support to them until they complete their reasonable studies. Moreover, every individual has an obligation to support his or her ascendants, descendants and siblings who would fall into poverty without such help.[53]

In Turkish law, the family also fulfils some caring functions. The Turkish word for 'family' is *aile*, which etymologically means 'unit in which people are looked after'.[54] According to Article 185 of the TCC, spouses owe each other loyalty and support and they should combine their forces to ensure the happiness of the marital union. They should show the necessary due care for their children's maintenance, education and supervision. The family also has a caring function

---

[52] N. Feyzioğlu, *Aile Hukuku*, Filiz, Istanbul 1979, p. 3.
[53] Art. 364 of the TCC.
[54] H. Hatemi and R. Serozan, *Aile Hukuku*, Filiz, Istanbul 1993, p. 4.

for elderly and other close relatives. For example, if the parents of one of the spouses are in financial and physical need, that spouse may host them in the family home. This does not constitute a ground for divorce for the other spouse.

In Turkish law, protecting the vulnerable and fulfilling a caring function is a more dominant function of the marital union. According to the decisions of the Turkish Court of Cassation, even close relatives of one spouse should be taken care of in the family if they are in need.[55] Similarly, during the marriage spouses should support each other. Sometimes this obligation continues even after the termination of the marriage. According to Article 175 of the TCC, a party who will suffer poverty after the divorce may ask for alimony for his or her living expenses provided that his or her fault was not the more influential cause of the divorce. Thus, even after divorce one partner may be obliged to pay poverty alimony to the other.

9.2. FAMILY'S FUNCTIONS IF CHILDREN ARE PRESENT IN THE FAMILY

If children are present in the family, the importance of the function of caring and protecting the vulnerable members of the family increases. The couple must take care of the child and, as mentioned above, the State has a right to interfere if parents neglect their mission in child-raising. For the wellbeing of the child, the continuation of the marriage is desirable. Therefore, when a child is present in the family, divorce is not an easy process. There are more issues on which parents should agree and which the court should approve. If it is a disputed divorce and there is a benefit to the children in continuation of the marriage, then the divorce request might be rejected.[56] Similarly, it is desirable that children have a stable family, which is why adoption of step-children is encouraged in the TCC.[57]

Donor-assisted reproductive technology, 'three-parent' technology and surrogacy are forbidden in Turkey. However, if a woman gives birth by using donor-assisted reproductive technology or 'three-parent' technology unlawfully, the child will enjoy equal rights with other children.

In adoption, it is accepted that a child can have two families. However, this is not the case for children who are conceived because of a legally forbidden assisted reproduction technique. If the intended or biological parents were granted more rights, this would better serve the wellbeing of the child.

---

[55] Yargıtay 2. HD, 02.11.1995, E. 1995/10539, K. 1995/11507, available at www.hukukturk.com, accessed 10.03.2022.
[56] Art. 166 II of the TCC.
[57] Art. 306 III of the TCC.

10. CONCLUSION

The Turkish lawmaker has no plan to introduce a general law that recognises multi-parenthood. On the contrary, in 2018, the Law on the Harvesting, Storage, Grafting, and Transplantation of Organs and Tissues was amended to explicitly outlaw and criminally sanction surrogacy/donation practices. Only in the case of open adoption is multi-parenthood legally recognised. Additionally, step-parents have very limited rights in raising their step-children, but step-parents are obliged to take care of their step-children. The Turkish lawmaker plans to ease the conditions of adoption and to promote foster families. However, there is no intention to grant the right of marriage or adoption to same-sex couples.

In Turkish law, the family is seen as the basic social unit and functions as a secure nest for the children. Spouses are expected to support each other. If these functions are not fulfilled, legal intervention is possible.

AN OVERVIEW OF THE DIVERSITY IN FAMILY FORMS AND FAMILY'S FUNCTIONS FROM THE PERSPECTIVE OF VIETNAMESE LAW

Thi Anh Van Ngo

1. Introduction 452
2. Diversity and Plurality of Family Forms 452
   2.1. Recognition of Multiple Parents in the Context of
        Step-Families 452
        2.1.1. Rights and Obligations of Step-Parents in Respect
               of Step-Children 452
        2.1.2. Comparison of the Rights and Obligations of
               Step-Parents and Biological Parents 456
   2.2. Recognition of Multiple Parents if a Child is Raised
        in More than One Household 457
   2.3. Recognition of Multiple Parents if a Child is Raised
        in a Polygamous Family 458
   2.4. Recognition of Multiple Parents in an Open-Adoption
        Family 459
   2.5. The Family Relationships Formed by the Application
        of Assisted Reproductive Technology 462
   2.6. A Family with Same-Sex Parents 465
   2.7. Other Forms of Family and a General Law that Recognises
        Multi-Parenthood in a Generic Way 465
3. Diversity and Plurality of Family's Functions 466
   3.1. Legal Recognition of Various Functions of the Family 466
   3.2. Predominantly Favoured Functions 469
   3.3. The Family's Function in Different Family Models 470

1. INTRODUCTION

According to Vietnamese tradition, the family is a miniature organisation, a cell of society. It is normally where multiple generations live under the same roof.[1] Through years of economic, political and social development, the family has played a crucial role in preserving traditional culture and forming and developing the character of family members.[2] From the perspective of the law, the family is defined under Article 3 of the Marriage and Family Law 2014 as a group of persons closely bound together by marriage, blood ties or nurturing relations. A family is formed in many ways, such as through marriage, childbirth and adoption. In its simplest form, a family is established by marriage between a man and a woman. After childbirth, the family is extended because of the increased number of members. In this case, family members usually have a biological relationship. However, in other circumstances, the parent–child relationship may be more complicated. It may be confusing in the case of assisted reproductive technology, where the child does not share the same blood as either his or her father or mother. Or in some instances, the child may belong to the previous marital or de facto relationship, which means the creation of relationships between stepfathers, stepmothers and step-children. An adoption situation is also a form of parent–child relationship that is not based on a biological relationship. The current legislation confirms the existence of each aforementioned family model and even all of the above models in the same family. In other words, a family may have children who were born naturally, children conceived via assisted reproductive technology, step-children and adopted children. The diversity of family models leads to the diversity and variation of rights and obligations of the children to their parents. However, regardless of the differences, the functions of the models of families have remained unchanged through the decades and play a significant part in maintaining the role of nurturing, caring and educating children, and providing economic security.

2. DIVERSITY AND PLURALITY OF FAMILY FORMS

2.1. RECOGNITION OF MULTIPLE PARENTS IN THE CONTEXT OF STEP-FAMILIES

2.1.1. Rights and Obligations of Step-Parents in Respect of Step-Children

A 'step-family' is a family with a stepfather or a stepmother. Instead of officially using this term, Vietnamese law uses 'stepfather' or 'stepmother'.

---

[1] T. Van Nguyen (ed.), *Giáo trình Luật Hôn nhân và gia đình*, Hong Duc, Ho Chi Minh 2016, p. 32.
[2] P.M. Thi Dinh (ed.), *Bình luận khoa học Luật hôn nhân và gia đình Việt Nam năm 2000*, National Politics, Ha Noi 2004, p. 7.

One's stepfather is the husband in a later marriage of one's mother. Similarly, one's stepmother is the wife in a later marriage of one's father. Children are considered to have stepfathers or stepmothers if their mothers or fathers build a family after the children were born in a prior marriage or were born out of wedlock. Though there are no clear definitions in legislation, everybody understands the meaning of these terms in daily usage. It should be noted that there are also cases when a child is born before the marriage and is legally recognised as a common child and not as a step-child by the acknowledgment of both the wife and the husband.[3]

The current law acknowledges the legal status of step-parents. Specifically, Article 3 of the Marriage and Family Law 2014 recognises stepfathers or stepmothers as family members. In addition, Article 79 on the obligations and rights of step-parents and step-children sets out the rights and obligations of a step-parent of looking after, raising, caring for and educating step-children who live with them according to Articles 69, 71 and 72 of the Law. The Law shows the two main aspects of the relationship between step-parents and step-children, which are: (1) the condition that results in the step-parents' and step-children's rights and obligations and (2) the content of these rights and obligations.

First, the condition that results in the step-parents' and step-children's rights and obligations is living together in the same family. The relationship between step-parents and step-children has long been considered as 'a complex and delicate matter in family life'.[4] The Law does not require step-parents to take responsibility for their step-children under all circumstances. This is reasonable because these persons are not blood relations and do not have the intention of adopting the children from the start. Naturally, the relationship between step-parents and step-children results from the marriage between the step-parent and a party who had the children before getting married.[5] The relationship between step-parents and step-children clearly occurs only if the parties live together. It is necessary for individuals who are not related by blood but live in a same household to care for each other, as such acts strengthen their familial bond. A tight-knit relationship between spouses would be difficult to achieve if one

---

[3] Art. 88 of the Marriage and Family Law 2014.

'Article 88. Identification of parents:

1. ...

A child who is born before the date of marriage registration and recognized by his or her parents is the common child of the husband and wife.'

The English versions of Vietnamese laws in this chapter were referred from vbpl.vn and thuvienphapluat.vn.

[4] P.M. Thi Dinh (ed.), *Bình luận khoa học Luật hôn nhân và gia đình Việt Nam năm 2000*, National Politics, Ha Noi 2004, p. 248.

[5] Except for the cases mentioned in Art. 88 of the Marriage and Family Law 2014.

side neglected the duty he or she owed to his or her step-children – which duty he or she should have foreseen and accepted prior to entering into the marriage. Raising the step-children is a vital sign manifesting the responsibility and the sharing of material and spiritual burdens with the party who had the children before the marriage. The Law aims to protect the rights of the step-children and limit emotional or financial disagreement between spouses.

The Marriage and Family Law 2014 uses the term 'living together' but does not explain the term. According to Nguyen Phuong Lan, the concept of 'not living together' can be understood as the family members being unable to directly take care of or help each other due to physical distance.[6] As this concept is used in the context of the parental support obligation, it is not appropriate to apply it directly to the case of step-families, but it is still valuable as a point of reference. In practice, there are indirect ways to determine whether step-parents and step-children live together, such as being a member of the household registration book,[7] or the step-child living with his or her father/mother who remarried. There are cases where the child does not live under the same roof as the parent, for example because the child is at boarding school, but the level of intimacy and cohesion with the parent is acknowledged. To a degree, as the child still lives together with his or her father/mother, he or she is considered to be living with his or her stepfather or stepmother.

Under Vietnamese law, the interpretation of 'living together' is very important. Usually, when living with the child, the parent is obliged to nurture the child, otherwise the parent is obliged to support the child. Nurturing includes providing for the child's material needs and caring for and educating the child. In contrast, the support obligation focuses solely on financial matters.[8] Step-parents are only obliged to nurture step-children when they live together in the same family. Otherwise, step-parents bear no obligations to their step-children, including the duty of child support.

Secondly, in terms of Articles 69, 71 and 72 of the Marriage and Family Law 2014, step-parents have the rights and obligations to take care of, nurture and educate the other party's children who are living together with the step-parents. In other words, when living together, certain rights and obligations arise between step-parents and step-children. Specifically, step-parents are

---

[6] C. Van Nguyen (ed.), *Giáo trình Luật Hôn nhân và gia đình Việt Nam*, People's Public Security, Ha Noi 2012, p. 216.

[7] This proof was often used in the past. From 2023 Vietnam will no longer use household registration books.

[8] Art. 3 s. 24 of the Marriage and Family Law 2014 reads:

> '*Support* means an act whereby a person has the obligation to contribute money or other kinds of property to meet the essential needs of another person who does not live together with but has marriage, blood or raising relation with the former and is a minor or an adult who has no working capacity and no property to support himself or herself, or meets with financial difficulties as prescribed by this Law'.

required to love their step-children, respect the opinions of their step-children, and attend to the education of their step-children.[9] Step-parents' responsibilities can be divided into three groups: (1) the responsibility for raising their step-children; (2) the responsibility for educating their step-children; and (3) other legal responsibilities.

Under the first group of responsibilities, step-parents have the duties to care for, nurture and protect the lawful rights and interests of their minor step-children or their adult step-children who are legally incapacitated or have no ability to work and no property to support themselves.[10] This rule is applied to both parents and step-parents who live together with the children. Under the second group of responsibilities, that is education, step-parents have the obligations and rights to educate their step-children, and to attend to and create conditions for their step-children's studies. Step-parents are encouraged to create conditions for step-children to live in a harmonious family, and they must closely collaborate with schools regarding the children's education.[11] More specifically, step-parents shall mentor and respect their step-children's right to choose a career.[12] The implementation of this responsibility plays an important role in the development and maturation of the children. Under the last group, that is other legal responsibilities, step-parents are required not to (1) discriminate against children due to their gender or the marital status of their parents, (2) abuse the labour of their minor step-children, and (3) incite or force their step-children to violate the law or social ethics.[13]

When living together with step-parents, mature step-children have obligations and rights to care for their step-parents, especially when their step-parents lack legal capacity, are aged and infirm, or have disabilities.[14] From the statements above, it can be seen that the relationship between step-parents and step-children is a two-way one. This helps to build a bond between the parties in both moral and legal terms.

Besides the Marriage and Family Law 2014, the rights and obligations of the step-parents and the step-children are also described in Article 654 of the Civil Code 2015. Specifically, the law provides that if a step-child and his or her step-parent care for and nurture each other as if they were biologically related, they may inherit each other's estates and may also inherit under Articles 652 and 653 of this Code. It should be noted that the determination of caring for and nurturing each other as family members is not merely based on the fact of living together. In fact, the court shall consider factors such as whether the period of

---

[9] Arts 79 and 69 of the Marriage and Family Law 2014.
[10] Arts 79, 69 s. 2, and 71 s. 1 of the Marriage and Family Law 2014.
[11] Art. 79 and Art. 72 s. 1 para. 2 of the Marriage and Family Law 2014.
[12] Art. 79 and Art. 72 ss 1 and 2 of the Marriage and Family Law 2014.
[13] Art. 79 and Art. 69 s. 4 of the Marriage and Family Law 2014.
[14] Art. 79 and Art. 71 s. 2 of the Marriage and Family Law 2014.

living is continuous,[15] or whether there is evidence of the parties considering and nurturing each other as family members.[16] Depending on the specific case, current regulations, the economic conditions of the parties, and the dependence of the step-parents and step-children, the court shall determine whether a parent–child relationship exists.[17]

2.1.2. Comparison of the Rights and Obligations of Step-Parents and Biological Parents

As analysed above, the rights and obligations between step-parents and step-children arise only if they live together. When they live under different roofs,[18] there is no legal relationship between these persons. The law does not set out a support obligation between step-parents and step-children. In contrast, the children's biological parents are always obliged to nurture (care for and raise) the children when living together or to provide them with financial support when living apart. In other words, the stepmother or stepfather and his wife or her husband are obliged to nurture the children, while the other party to the past marriage who does not live together with the children is obliged to support them.

Moreover, even when step-parents live with their step-children, their rights and obligations are limited by the law.[19] Step-parents do not have the responsibility and rights to pay compensation for damage caused by the children, manage the children's assets, or dispose of property of minor children or adult children who are legally incapacitated. In contrast, the law recognises these rights and obligations of both biological parents, regardless of whether

---

[15] Case No. 114/2006/DSPT dated 19.05.2006 of the People's Court of Hanoi City. In the case, H1 (who passed away in 1976) and C (who passed away in 1946) had two children: G (born in 1939) and H2 (born in 1941). After C passed away, H1 married H3 in 1948. G and H2 were H3's step-children. In 1950, G and H2 lived together with H3. Before getting married, G and H2 spent time living at their uncle's house. In 1958, G got married and in 1960 H2 got married. The period of taking care of H3 did not last long. For this reason, the Court rejected G and H2's request to inherit H3's assets.

[16] Decision No. 32/2010/DS-DT dated 22.01.2010 of the Supreme People's Court. In this case, D was the child of X's husband. X comprehensively took care of D. When D got married, X was the organiser of the wedding. D considered and treated X as her mother. Therefore, the Court accepted the request to inherit X's assets.

Decision No. 289/2009/DS-DT dated 16.07.2009 of the Supreme People's Court. In this case, the Court stated that 'to consider the inherited relationship, it is important to determine whether or not the stepfather has taken care and nurtured the two children until they have grown up'.

[17] D. Van Do, *Luật thừa kế Việt Nam – Bản án và bình luận bản án*, Hong Duc, Ho Chi Minh 2016, p. 262.

[18] E.g. the children are assigned to their other parent to take care of and nurture them.

[19] Arts. 79, 69, 71 and 72 of the Marriage and Family Law 2014.

they are living with the children or not. In particular, regardless of whether the parents are living together or not, they must share the responsibility of paying compensation for damage caused by their children.[20]

In short, the rights of step-parents and step-children are not automatically established but are dependent on consideration of evidence of actually living together or caring for and nurturing each other. This position is different from the parent–child relationship. The forming of a parent–child relationship is always accompanied by the corresponding rights and obligations of nurturing, support, and inheritance, without any other conditions having to be met. These are not only the legal rights and obligations but also the moral responsibilities of parents. The implementation of step-parents' obligations and rights does not create a conflict with the rights and obligations of the child's biological parents. Similar to those of biological parents, the purpose of the rights and obligations of step-parents is to complement and facilitate better care and nurturing of the children.

2.2. RECOGNITION OF MULTIPLE PARENTS IF A CHILD IS RAISED IN MORE THAN ONE HOUSEHOLD

The law of Vietnam does not recognise the raising of a child by many families. As mentioned, the Marriage and Family Law 2014 has a clear-cut explanation of the nurture and support obligations. The child can only live with and be raised by one family at the same time.[21] For example, when parents divorce, a child, by agreement or at the discretion of the court, will live with and be raised by his or her father or his or her mother; the other parent who does not live with the child must fulfil the obligation of providing financial support. As the current law does not acknowledge the status of separation, the child is still raised in a family having both a mother and a father, regardless of the fact that the spouses may not be living together and the child is only living with his or her mother or his or her father.

Aside from the Marriage and Family Law, the Civil Code also designates the wardship of a minor in the following cases:

1. the minor has lost his or her mother and father;
2. the parents are unidentifiable;

---

[20] Judgment No. 19/2012/DSST dated 12.06.2012 of the Cum'gar People's Court District, Daklak Province. In practice, there are cases where parents are divorced and the party who does not live with the child still has to share the responsibility of compensating for damage caused by the common child with the party who is living with the child.
[21] Except for an exception that rarely occurs, which the author will mention in section 2.4 on adoption below.

3. the parents are both legally incapacitated persons;
4. the parents have limited cognition or behaviour control;
5. the parents have limited legal capacity;
6. the parents have had their parental rights restricted by a court;
7. or the parents do not have the means to care for or educate their children and request that the minor should be a ward.

The duty of a guardian to a minor has many similarities to parental responsibilities for a child. The Civil Code provides that a minor may only be protected by one guardian, except where the guardians are grandparents in charge of one grandchild.[22] This rule allegedly aims to emphasise the responsibilities of a guardian, as well as to provide a clear distinction between the responsibilities of all parties relating to an underage person.[23] Similarly, even if a child can be nurtured by many families in practice, from the legal perspective, it is necessary to identify a particular family that has the rights and duties to care for and nurture the child. This is an important basis not only for resolving but also for limiting custody disputes.

In practice, children can live with both parents even when parents are not legally recognised as husband and wife. Vietnamese law does not prohibit couples from living together as husband and wife. However, the couple in this context does not form a family since they do not meet the requirements of Article 3 section 2 and section 16 of the Marriage and Family Law. From this perspective, a child may be considered to be raised by two families. There is no conflict or competition when the couple nurtures their children.

2.3. RECOGNITION OF MULTIPLE PARENTS IF A CHILD IS RAISED IN A POLYGAMOUS FAMILY

Vietnamese law no longer recognises the polygamous family. Currently, the State has policies and measures for the protection of marriage and the family and to ensure that a man and a woman establish a voluntary marriage which assures equal rights between husband and wife.[24] The law also prohibits a married person from 'getting married to or cohabitating as husband and wife with another person, or an unmarried person getting married to or cohabitating as husband and wife with a married person'.[25]

---

[22] Art. 47 s. 2 of the Civil Code 2015.
[23] C. Van Nguyen (ed.), *Bình luận khoa học Bộ luật Dân sự năm 2015*, People's Public Security, Ha Noi 2012, p. 121.
[24] Art. 4 of the Marriage and Family Law 2014.
[25] Art. 5 of the Marriage and Family Law 2014.

However, the law still recognises the existence of polygamy in two cases: (1) if the family was formed before the prohibition on polygamy came into operation; and (2) for marriages of officers or soldiers from the South who entered the North to work, lost contact with their families due to the war, and married another wife.[26] In these cases, the wife in the polygamous family is considered as a stepmother of the children born of other wives in the family. There are no conflicts between the rights and obligations of caring and nurturing among the stepmothers who live with their own children. The only issue that arises in these cases is whether the children are considered as the stepmother's heirs or not.[27]

2.4. RECOGNITION OF MULTIPLE PARENTS IN AN OPEN-ADOPTION FAMILY

In the past, adoption was carried out for many purposes, such as ensuring ancestor worship in families without children, paying off debts, etc.[28] Nowadays, adoption is a meaningful alternative way to create a family. Article 2 of the Adoption Law 2010 emphasises that the aims of adoption are to: (1) establish a permanent relationship between parent and child for the best interests of adopted persons; and (2) ensure the nurturing, care and education of adopted persons.

For an adoption to be recognised, the parties must comply with the adoption procedure set out in Article 22 of the Adoption Law. However, Vietnamese law recognises de facto adoption. In particular, adoption that occurred before the enactment of the Marriage and Family Law 1986 is still recognised, unless the adoption goes against social purposes, such as the adoption having taken place for labor exploitation or for illegal activities. If the adoption was not previously recorded in the civil status books but is known to many people and the parents have performed their adoption obligations, the adoption is recognised by the law.[29] Before the Marriage and Family Law 1986 came into force, some part of the population's level of awareness of the law was not high.[30] Adoption sometimes

---

[26] S. 4 Decree No. 2/1990/HDTP and Circular No. 60/1978/TATC.
[27] In Case No. 20/2009/DS-PT dated 12.02.2019, T1 (who passed away in 1961) had two wives named T2 (who passed away in 1995) and T3 (who passed away in 1994). They lived together as a family. When dividing the inheritance of T2, there was a conflict between the children: T4, T2's child, did not consent to share his mother's inheritance with T5, T3's child. The court then determined that there was no basis for determining that T2 considered T5 (the child of T3) as her child. Thus, the children of T2 and those of T3 separately inherited their mothers' assets.
[28] P.M. Thi Dinh (ed.), *Commentary on the Vietnam Marriage and Family Law 2000*, National Politics, Ha Noi 2004, p. 356.
[29] S. 6 of Decree No. 01/1988/HDTP.
[30] S. III.A(1) Circular No. 81/1981/TANDTC.

occurred by custom or by agreement, neglecting the registration procedure. If the adoption occurred after the date on which the Marriage and Family Law 1986 took effect, registration is required.[31]

In de facto adoption (without registration), the nature of the parent–child relationship is reflected through the implementation of the rights and responsibilities between parties. The most important manifestation of this is that the adoptive parents and the child live together for a long time and take care of each other. The result is that the parties are acknowledged to have the rights and obligations of parents and children. There are many cases where the court has held that the adopted children are entitled to be their adoptive parents' heirs.[32]

Pursuant to Article 24 of the Adoption Law 2010, from the date on which an adoptive child is under his or her adoptive parents' custody, the adoptive parents and adopted child will have all the rights and obligations between parents and child.

Unless otherwise agreed upon between the biological and adoptive parents, the biological parents of an adopted child no longer have the rights and obligations to nurture the child, provide financial support to the child, be the child's legal representative, pay compensation for damage caused by the child, or manage and dispose the property of the child.[33] As can be seen from the above-mentioned regulations, the legislation draws a clear distinction between the rights and obligations of the biological parents and of the adoptive parents. Specifically, on the one hand, after the adoption, there is almost no relationship between the biological parents and their children. On the other hand, the biological parents' rights and obligations are transferred to the adoptive parents.

It should be noted that the relationship between the original family and the child still exists in two cases. Firstly, if the biological parents and the adoptive parents have arrived at an agreement that differs from the provisions of Article 24 section 4 of the Adoption Law. Such an agreement can permit the maintenance of some of or all of the rights and obligations of the biological parents after the adoption. However, the more expansive this agreement is, the more likely it is that conflicts will arise between the adoptive parents and the biological parents in caring for and nurturing the children. Furthermore, if the biological parents have many rights and obligations, the relationship between the adoptive parents and the adopted children may lack cohesion. As a result, such agreements seldom occur in practice.

Secondly, Article 24 section 4 of the Adoption Law lists the rights and obligations which shall cease between the biological parents and their children

---

[31] There is an exception to this rule. An adoption could still be considered legal if it was performed by a person of ethnic minority before 01.01.2001. See Decree No. 32/2002/ND-CP dated 27.03.2002.
[32] Judgment No. 182/2012/DS-GDT dated 20.04.2012 of the Supreme People's Courts.
[33] Art. 24 s. 4 of the Adoption Law 2010.

after the adoption. Therefore, the biological parents still have the rights and obligations which are not listed, such as the right to inherit from the child. Article 653 of the Civil Code 2015 provides that 'an adopted child and his or her adoptive parents may inherit each other's estates and may also inherit in accordance with Articles 651 and 652 of this Code'. In addition, Article 651 states that legal heirs are specified in the following order of priority:

(1) The first level of heirs comprises husband, wife, biological father, biological mother, adoptive father, adoptive mother, offspring, and adopted children of the deceased; (2) the second level of heirs comprises paternal grandfather, paternal grandmother, maternal grandfather, maternal grandmother, brother, sister of the deceased; and biological grandchildren of the deceased; (3) the third level of heirs comprises paternal great-grandparents of the deceased, maternal great-grandparents of the deceased; biological uncles, aunts of the deceased; biological nephew, niece of the deceased; and biological great-grandchild of the deceased.

Thus, the inheritance relationship between children and their biological parents and their relatives still exists, even after the adoption.[34]

Further, biological parents retain the right to supervise their children. Though the adoption may sever the legal rights and obligations of biological parents, caring for their children is the instinct of every parent. Therefore, the Adoption Law allows biological parents to request the termination of the adoption.[35] There are even cases where adoptions were registered but the adopted children still lived with their biological parents because of life in the adopted family being too unfamiliar. As a result, the adoptive parents agreed with the biological parents to terminate the adoption relationship. In recent years, the court has tended to accept this type of agreement, although it falls outside the grounds for termination of an adoption, which are stated in Article 25 of the Adoption Law.[36]

---

[34] L. The Hoang (ed.), *Bình luận khoa học Bộ luật dân sự năm 2005*, National Politics – The Truth, Ha Noi 2013, p. 116.
[35] Art 26 of the Adoption Law 2010.
[36] Judgment No. 01 dated 15.09.2017 of the Kon Tum People's Court, Kon Tum Province.

Article 25 of the Adoption Law 2010 reads: 'Grounds for termination of adoption:

An adoption may be terminated in the following cases:

1. The adult adopted child and the adoptive parents agree to terminate;
2. The adopted child is convicted of any of the following crimes: intentionally infringing upon the lives, health, dignity and honor of the adoptive parents; maltreating and persecuting the adoptive parents and dissipating the adoptive parents' property;
3. The adoptive parents are convicted of intentionally infringing upon the lives, health, dignity and honor of the adopted child; or maltreating and persecuting the adopted child;
4. Violating the provisions of Article 13 of this Law'.

Adoption registration has a significant role in establishing the legal rights and obligations between adoptive parents and adoptive children. However, establishing an adoption relationship does not mean that the biological parent–child relationship is completely terminated. Moreover, there are instances in which de facto adoption (unregistered adoption) can be legal if the adoption satisfies specific legal requirements. These rules accommodate the ever-changing social landscape of Vietnam throughout different historical phases; and they also guarantee better protection for individuals who are adopted.

2.5. THE FAMILY RELATIONSHIPS FORMED BY THE APPLICATION OF ASSISTED REPRODUCTIVE TECHNOLOGY

The development of modern medicine has changed the way that infertile spouses and single persons have children. The giving and receiving of ova, sperm and embryos and altruistic gestational surrogacy take place in accordance with the principles of voluntary consent and anonymity between the donor and the recipient. In addition, the ovum, sperm or embryo must be given a code to ensure confidentiality, but the donor's characteristics, especially his or her race, must be specified.[37]

According to Article 93 of the Marriage and Family Law, the identification of parents who have a child as a result of ART is done in terms of particular principles. If a married woman gives birth to an ART-conceived child, the parent is determined in terms of Article 88.[38] Article 88 stipulates that a woman is considered the mother of the child to whom she gave birth and her husband is considered the child's father. If the birth mother is single, she is the ART-conceived child's mother. The birth of an ART-conceived child does not give rise to a paternal relationship between the donor and the child.

In Vietnam, the principle of anonymity is applied thoroughly in the process of ART. To reduce the risk of a subsequent marriage with a close relative, the sperm or ovum of the donor shall be used for only one person and may be used for another person only if childbirth fails. If childbirth is successful, all unused

---

[37] Art. 3 of Decree No. 10/2015/ND-CP.
[38] Art. 88 reads: 'Identification of parents:

1. A child who is born or conceived by the wife during the marriage period is the common child of the husband and wife.

A child who is born within 300 days from the time of termination of a marriage shall be regarded as a child conceived by the wife during the marriage period.

A child who is born before the date of marriage registration and recognized by his or her parents is the common child of the husband and wife'.

sperm or ova must be destroyed or donated for research purposes. The law does not have a mechanism for designating the donor and recipient by name. 'If the recipient and donor go to a medical institution together, they are not allowed to use the donor's sperm immediately. Instead, the sperm sample is changed and replaced with random sperm'.[39]

The consequence of the principle of anonymity is that children are born without knowing who their biological parents are, and donors also do not know their children. A parent–child relationship cannot be established between the donor and the child despite the fact that they are blood relations. The donation occurs to provide reproductive support rather than to establish a parent–child relationship. However, no one can choose how they are born. The application of the principle of anonymity does affect the child's chance to determine his or her origin.[40]

At the moment, Vietnamese law does not have the concept of a 'three-parent' child. The receipt of sperm, ova and embryos is regulated by Article 5 of Decree No. 10/2015/ND-CP as follows:

1. the sperm recipient must be either a wife whose husband is infertile or a single woman whose ova qualify for impregnation;
2. an ovum recipient must be the wife in a couple who has no ova or whose ova do not qualify for impregnation; and
3. an embryo recipient must be either the wife in an infertile couple or a single woman who has no ova or whose ova do not qualify for impregnation.

The term 'father' is understood as a man, and similarly the term 'mother' as a woman. As the technique which uses the genetic material of two females and one male is relatively new in Vietnam, the law currently does not regulate this case.

Reproductive support relates not only to the application of modern medical techniques or the donation of ova or sperm to provide material for a pregnancy, but also to a woman agreeing to become a surrogate. In Vietnam, surrogacy has been officially permitted since the Marriage and Family Law 2014 came into operation. Article 3 section 22 and section 23 of the Marriage and Family Law 2014 state that altruistic gestational surrogacy refers to the voluntary pregnancy of a woman for non-commercial purposes for a couple of whom the wife is unable to give birth even with the aid of ART, by transferring embryos

---

[39] 'Nỗi lo sợ của những người xin tinh trùng để có con', available at https://news.zing.vn/noi-lo-so-cua-nguoi-xin-tinh-trung-de-co-con-post761875.html, accessed 20.10.2019.

[40] See further V.A. Thi Ngo, 'Quyền xác định nguồn gốc của con được sinh ra bằng kỹ thuật hỗ trợ sinh sản' (2018) 9 *Journal of Legal Science*.

produced by the wife's ovum and the husband's sperm into the surrogate mother's uterus.[41] In contrast, commercial gestational surrogacy means an act of pregnancy for another person by using assisted reproductive technology for financial gain or benefit.[42] Commercial gestational surrogacy is strictly prohibited.[43]

It should be noted that surrogacy in Vietnam is allowed in very limited circumstances. In the case of people who are permitted to use ART, only infertile spouses may use surrogacy. Spouses have the right to request surrogacy when they meet the following conditions:

1. the wife has not been able to get pregnant and give birth even by using ART;
2. the spouses have no common child; and
3. the spouses have received health, psychological and legal counselling before the surrogacy process starts.[44]

In addition, a surrogate mother must fully satisfy the following conditions:

1. she is next of kin in the same line as the wife or husband who is infertile;[45]
2. she has given birth before;
3. she is only allowed to become a surrogate mother once;
4. she is at a suitable age and eligible for gestational surrogacy;
5. she has obtained her husband's consent if she is married; and
6. she has received health, legal and psychological counselling.[46]

These regulations reflect strict rules on surrogate mothers and the persons requesting gestational surrogacy.

In principle, under the Marriage and Family Law 2014, if the ovum or sperm do not qualify, gestational surrogacy is impossible, because according to Article 3 section 22, gestational surrogacy can only be performed using the ovum and sperm from the infertile married couple. The consequence of gestational surrogacy is that the child and the infertile couple are deemed to be related by blood. In most cases, there is no mother–child relationship between the child and the surrogate mother. The only exception is that if both intended parents

---

[41] Art. 3 s. 22 of the Marriage and Family Law 2014.
[42] Art. 3 s. 23 of the Marriage and Family Law 2014.
[43] Art. 5 s. 2 (g) of the Marriage and Family Law 2014.
[44] Art. 95 of the Marriage and Family Law 2014.
[45] Art. 2 s. 7 of Decree No. 10/2015/ND-CP: 'Next of kin of the same line of a spouse who asks for gestational surrogacy includes his or her full sisters; half-sisters; female cousins; and sisters-in-law'.
[46] Art. 95 s. 3 of the Marriage and Family Law 2014.

die or become legally incapacitated before the child is handed over to them, the surrogate mother has the right to adopt the child. If she refuses to do so, the guardianship and support of the child must be determined in accordance with the Civil Code and the Marriage and Family Law.[47]

In a nutshell, the family model formed with the help of ART may create a situation where biological parents and legal parents are present at the same time. The purpose of using ART determines the legal parent–child relationship. Accordingly, the ovum donor, sperm donor or surrogate mother is not identified as the child's parent, and therefore they have no legal obligations to the child. Conversely, people who use ART may not be related to their children by blood but they are nevertheless the child's legal parents.

2.6. A FAMILY WITH SAME-SEX PARENTS

In Vietnam, the law does not recognise marriage between persons of the same sex.[48] Though same-sex marriage is no longer prohibited as it was in the past,[49] it has not yet been specifically regulated. If two people of the same sex live together as spouses, this unit does not legally constitute a family. Although Vietnam acknowledged the right to have sex reassignment in Article 37 of the Civil Code 2015, the specific conditions and consequences of the reassignment are still under consideration by the legislators, as the Sex Reassignment Law is still in the drafting phase. It will only be when this law comes into operation that the question of the rights and obligations of a family with same-sex parents may be answered.

In addition, the law only acknowledges the use of ART by infertile spouses or single women. Therefore, gay and lesbian couples cannot jointly use ART and be identified as parents.

Similarly, Article 8 section 3 of the Adoption Law only allows adoption by a single person or two spouses. As a result, two people of the same sex who are not recognised as spouses cannot adopt children together.[50]

2.7. OTHER FORMS OF FAMILY AND A GENERAL LAW THAT RECOGNISES MULTI-PARENTHOOD IN A GENERIC WAY

In addition to the above-mentioned cases, Vietnamese law also has provisions to protect multi-generational families. The most typical model is a family with

---

[47] Art. 99 s. 2 of the Marriage and Family Law 2014.
[48] Art. 8 s. 2 of the Marriage and Family Law 2014.
[49] Art. 10 s. 5 of the Marriage and Family Law 2000.
[50] See further P. Quynh Pham (ed.), *Người đồng tính, song tính và chuyển giới ở Việt Nam*, Institute of Social Science, Ho Chi Minh 2013, p. 227.

three generations, including grandparents, parents and children living together. In addition, the law regulates the rights and obligations of daughters-in-law, sons-in-law and parents-in-law. Specifically, if a daughter- or son-in-law lives with her or his parents-in-law, they all have the rights and obligations to respect, care for and assist one another according to Articles 69, 70, 71 and 72 of the Marriage and Family Law 2014.[51] These rules are relatively new in Vietnamese law. The relationship between daughters-in-law, sons-in-law and parents-in-law is not as comprehensive as the parent–child relationship. The rights and obligations between these subjects operate only if they live together. When they do not live under the same roof, they do not bear the burden of supporting each other. This addition to the Marriage and Family Law is essential for family members to be able to live together cohesively and in harmony.

In Vietnam, parental relations are regulated in the Marriage and Family Law and the Adoption Law. In addition to the general provisions regulating the parent–child relationship, the law also governs the relationship between parent and child based on the characteristics of each specific case. Therefore, the Marriage and Family Law and the Adoption Law have separate provisions in respect of step-parents and step-children, adoptive parents and adopted children, and ART-conceived children and their biological parents or legal parents. For example, Article 14 of the Adoption Law specifies the requirements for being adoptive parents.[52] These requirements are completely different from those that apply in other family models. It will be challenging to set a general requirement for all cases. Therefore, the need to have a general law that recognises multi-parenthood in a generic, broad manner seems unnecessary in Vietnam.

3. DIVERSITY AND PLURALITY OF FAMILY'S FUNCTIONS

3.1. LEGAL RECOGNITION OF VARIOUS FUNCTIONS OF THE FAMILY

Different family models will be formed or weakened in each of the different phases of society. For instance, in a modern society, the family model can be developed by using ART, the concept of the parent–child relationship is no longer limited to people who are blood relations, and new models of the family with

---

[51] Art. 80 of the Marriage and Family Law 2014.
[52] Art. 14 of the Adoption Law 2010.

three parents or same-sex parents may be recognised in the future. The existence of traditional families with three or four generations living together may wither away. However, regardless of the differences between the family models, the family's functions have not changed. In Vietnamese society, a family has three main functions, namely: (1) maintaining the human race; (2) providing care and education; and (3) creating assets.

The family's function of maintaining the human race exists sustainably in every period of society. Besides, giving birth is accompanied with the responsibility of nurturing and educating. The family is also known as every person's first school. Family education has a significant influence on a person's morality, life skills and personality. Through the parent's life experience, children are taught and equipped with practical lessons. In addition, the family economy occupies a certain proportion of social economics.[53] Family members jointly conduct common economic activities to satisfy their physical and spiritual needs. At the same time, they also contribute to the wealth of society.

The family's functions are not explicitly listed by regulations and categorised in an area of law. By protecting family members' personal and property rights, the law has indirectly recognised the family's above-mentioned functions. First, the recognition is stated in the Constitution and the Civil Code. These legal documents assert the family's responsibility to protect the interests of the wife, children, and the elderly in the family. Secondly, through the specific provisions of the Marriage and Family Law and the Adoption Law, the rights and obligations of the family members are expressly stated to ensure the family's functions in maintaining the human race, caring and education, and economic development.

To begin with, the law has general provisions that regulate the role of the family. The Constitution provides that children shall be protected, nurtured, and educated by the State, society and the family. Abandonment, harassment, persecution, mistreatment, and abuse of children, as well as exploitation of child labour and other violations of children's rights, are strictly prohibited. Similarly, the elderly are respected and taken care of.[54] Last but not least, society and the family have the duty to create conditions for women to develop their abilities in all aspects.[55] In addition, Article 2 of the Marriage and Family Law affirms that 'the State, society, and families shall protect and support children, elderly people and persons with disabilities in exercising their rights; assist mothers in properly fulfilling their lofty motherhood functions; and implement family planning'.

---

[53] C. Van Nguyen (ed.), *Giáo trình Luật Hôn nhân và gia đình Việt Nam*, People's Public Security, Ha Noi 2012, p. 23.
[54] Art. 37 ss 1 and 3 of the Constitution 2013.
[55] Art. 26 of the Constitution 2013.

Secondly, specific areas of the law have provisions to implement the functions of the family. For example, through the age of marriage regulations, legislation impacts the family's function of producing children, its economic function, and its educational function. To be more specific, the age of marriage is one of the critical factors affecting the family's function of maintaining lineage. Getting married at an excessively low age severely affects the health of mothers and their children. Children who are forced to marry early tend to stop studying and eliminate their chances of accessing new knowledge. In addition, getting married early reduces the ability to make a living or economic contribution, resulting in an increased likelihood of ending up in poverty.[56] Therefore, child marriage is prohibited by the law.[57]

A male must be at least 20 and a female must be at least 18 to get married.[58] When they reach a certain age, people are physiologically developed and are also more knowledgeable. By getting married, a person may become the parent of a child. To take on that responsibility, they must have a stable financial capacity and a good character. In this regard, Nguyen Minh Hang and Nguyen Thanh Danh state that the regulation of the age of marriage is based on the scientific grounds of the psychophysiological development of the male and the female and the economic conditions of society in Vietnam. The marriage age ensures that men and women are ready to take responsibility for their own families. It also ensures that they have fully developed mature thinking in order to decide to marry. In addition, the marriage age helps children to be born in healthy conditions.[59] In short, although not directly referring to the function of the family, the above-mentioned regulations help to bring about better conditions for the family to perform its roles.

The Marriage and Family Law regulates the main contents of marriage and family relationships. Corresponding to the relationship between family members, the lawmakers indirectly acknowledge one or more of the family's functions. The provisions on marriage that include the requirements for marriage and termination of a marriage reflect the function of maintaining the human race, the economic function, and the function of protecting women and children. Property relationships between spouses correspond to the economic function.

---

[56] Bien phong, 'Hệ lụy từ nạn tảo hôn và hôn nhân cận huyết thống ở vùng đồng bào dân tộc thiểu số', *bienphong.com.vn*, 14.12.2021, available at https://www.bienphong.com.vn/he-luy-tu-nan-tao-hon-va-hon-nhan-can-huyet-thong-o-vung-dong-bao-dan-toc-thieu-so-post446303.html, accessed 12.08.2022.

[57] Art. 3 s. 8 of the Marriage and Family Law 2014 reads:

'Underage marriage means getting married when one or both partners has or have not reached the marriage age prescribed at Point a, Clause 1, Article 8 of this Law'.

[58] Art. 8 of the Marriage and Family Law 2014.

[59] H. Minh Nguyen and D. Thanh Nguyen, 'Xác định thời kỳ hôn nhân trong pháp luật Hôn nhân và gia đình Việt Nam' (2012) 10 *People's Court Journal* 28, 29.

The provisions on the relationships between parents, children and other family members represent the role of nurturing, educating, and protecting vulnerable subjects.

The acknowledgment of the family's functions is also reflected in the sanctions provided for by the law when subjects fail to fulfil their responsibilities. For example, the Criminal Code has provisions on organising child marriage;[60] incest;[61] maltreatment or abuse of a parent, child, grandparent, grandchild or spouse;[62] and shirking of the obligation to provide support.[63] Through administrative and criminal sanctions, improper behaviour is terminated and the family's functions are fulfilled.

3.2. PREDOMINANTLY FAVOURED FUNCTIONS

Each family function has a different significance for society. In Vietnam, it is difficult to choose the most essential function. However, whether it is a feudal society or a modern society, the functions of producing and caring for children still play important roles. The above functions cannot be performed or are inefficiently performed without a family. In other words, the family's role in these areas cannot be substituted.

The reproductive function is mainly performed by the family. Besides this role, the law always links the family to the caring and education function. In respect of the resources for childcare and protection, the family is always what the law on children refers to.[64] This is reasonable since the family is where children are born and nurtured. In addition, family members are the closest to the children and are most favourably placed to take care of them.

Nurturing relates not only to material provision but also to education. The Education Law affirms the importance of the family in the development of education.[65] At the same time, the responsibilities of the family are not only to nurture, educate and enable children to study, but also to create a favourable environment for the comprehensive physical, intellectual and moral development of children. In addition, parents and other family members are required to educate and set an example for children, and to cooperate with schools to improve educational efficiency.[66]

---

[60] Art. 183 of the Criminal Code 2015 (amended in 2017).
[61] Art. 184 of the Criminal Code 2015 (amended in 2017).
[62] Art. 185 of the Criminal Code 2015 (amended in 2017).
[63] Art. 186 of the Criminal Code 2015 (amended in 2017).
[64] Arts 7, 9 and 42 of the Children Law 2016.
[65] Art. 16 of the Education Law 2019.
[66] Art. 90 of the Education Law 2019.

3.3. THE FAMILY'S FUNCTION IN DIFFERENT FAMILY MODELS

The family's functions can relate to the interests of one or several family members. For instance, the economic function serves the interests of all members. In contrast, producing children is directly related to the husband-and-wife relationship. Depending on the particular case, all the functions of the family may or may not be fulfilled. If a family does not have any children, the function of producing children cannot be performed. As a result, there are no responsibilities of nurturing or educating children. In some cases, the function of maintaining the lineage is not present, for instance in the adoptive family or the family using ART (with donated sperm and ovum). However, the nurturing and educational functions of those families are not different from those of a conventional family. The law recognises equality between children, whether they are in a biological relationship or not. In other words, although different forms of the family have their own characteristics, the family's function in protecting the interests of its members, especially vulnerable subjects, seems to remain unchanged.

In short, Vietnamese family law recognises many different forms of family, such as step-parent families, open-adoption families, families formed using ART, etc. Depending on the level of cohesion of the members, the rights and obligations may be slightly different for each type of family. The variability of social values and the development of medical technology have led to the extension of the family's forms, especially those involving ART. Despite the diversity and plurality of family forms, the law aims to protect the interests of family members. Family types can give rise to complicated relationships involving children. However, the provisions always equitably regulate the rights of children in all family forms.

APPENDIX

QUESTIONNAIRE

Guidelines for special rapporteurs

Part A of the questionnaire that follows below investigates diversity and plurality of family forms, while Part B relates to the family's functions. With respect to each question in each of the parts, please discuss your national law; that is, consider your specific country's constitution (where applicable), legislation and case law. Where international and regional laws have resulted in changes to, or development of, your national law, please consider such changes and developments too.

You need *not* elaborate on the following topics:

- private international law;
- medical law;
- cultural, indigenous and religious rights;
- legal pluralism.

As multicultural challenges in family law were the focus of the 20th Congress of the International Academy which took place in Fukuoka, Japan in 2018, Part A of the questionnaire does not seek to consider the multiplicity/plurality of civil, cultural, indigenous and religious unions. Instead, it deals with diversity and plurality in respect of families involving children, specifically families where children have multiple parents.

For the sake of comparability, we need to depart from a common understanding of the topic at issue. For this purpose, the multiple-parent families that are covered in Part A are limited to:

- step-families where children from one or both spouses/partners are raised in the same household;
- families where children are raised in more than one household, for example because their parents are jointly exercising custody/care after separation or have never shared a household but share parenting responsibilities;
- polygamous families where children are raised in a household where one party has more than one wife/husband/partner;

- open-adoption families, that is families where children have been adopted but maintain links (legal or de facto) with their biological families;
- families where children have not been adopted but live in a household in terms of a *kafala*. (Islamic law does not permit adoption. The Islamic concept that is closest to the notion of 'adoption' is *kafala/kafalah*. By way of *kafala*, a person other than the child's biological parent undertakes, in terms of Islamic law, to maintain, educate, protect and care for a child like a biological parent would, but the child does not become entitled to bear the family name of, or automatically to inherit from, the person who has assumed responsibility for the child.);
- families where a child was born as a result of donor-assisted reproductive technology using one male and one female gamete (i.e. sperm and an egg/ovum);
- families where a child was born as a result of so-called 'three-parent' medical technology. (This technology is similar to in vitro fertilisation, but uses the genetic material of two females and one male, instead of only one female and one male. As a rule, the DNA of the one female is used to 'correct' the DNA of the other female in order to remove genetic mutations that cause serious hereditary diseases.);[1]
- families where a child was born as a result of surrogacy.

QUESTIONNAIRE

PART A. DIVERSITY AND PLURALITY OF FAMILY FORMS

1. Does your country's law recognise multiplicity of parenthood in the context of step-families?
    (i) Specifically, does your country's law confer legal responsibilities and rights on a step-parent who shares a household with the child's parent? If so, does the step-parent have the same legal responsibilities and rights as the parent with whom the step-parent shares a household? Briefly explain your answer. Also explain the position if the responsibilities and rights of the parent and step-parent clash or compete with one another.

---

[1] The technique has been used in, inter alia, Mexico, Ukraine, and the United Kingdom: see S. Reardon 'Reports of "three-parent babies" multiply', *Nature*, 19.10.2016; E. Callaway 'Historic decision allows UK researchers to trial "three person" babies', *Nature*, 15.12.2016; S. Reardon 'Genetic details of controversial "three-parent baby" revealed', *Nature*, 03.04.2017.

(ii) If your country's law confers legal responsibilities and rights on a step-parent, does the step-parent have the same legal responsibilities and rights as the parent with whom he or she does not share a household? (In other words, does the step-parent have the same legal responsibilities and rights as the child's other parent?) Briefly explain your answer. Also explain the position if the responsibilities and rights of the parent and step-parent clash or compete with one another.

2. Does your country's law recognise multiplicity of parenthood if a child is raised in more than one household? If so, briefly explain your answer with specific reference to the legal responsibilities and rights conferred on each of the parents. Also explain the position if the various parents' responsibilities and rights clash or compete with one another.

3. Does your country's law recognise multiplicity of parenthood if a child is raised in a polygamous family? If so, briefly explain your answer with specific reference to the legal responsibilities and rights conferred on each of the parents. Also explain the position if the various parents' responsibilities and rights clash or compete with one another.

4. Does your country's law recognise multiplicity of parenthood in the case of an open adoption (as defined under the guidelines for special national rapporteurs)? If so, briefly explain your answer with specific reference to the legal responsibilities and rights conferred on each of the parents. Also explain the position if the various parents' responsibilities and rights clash or compete with one another.

5. Does your country's law recognise multiplicity of parenthood in the case of *kafala* (as defined under the guidelines for special national rapporteurs)? If so, briefly explain your answer with specific reference to the legal responsibilities and rights conferred on each of the parties. Also explain the position if the various parties' responsibilities and rights clash or compete with one another.

6. (i) Does your country's law recognise the parenthood of the birth mother, her spouse/partner and the donor if a child was born as a result of donor-assisted reproductive technology using one male and one female gamete and the donor was/donors were anonymous? If so, briefly explain your answer with specific reference to the legal responsibilities and rights conferred on each of the parties. Also explain the position if the various parties' responsibilities and rights clash or compete with one another.

(ii) Would your answer to Question 6(i) have been different if one (or both) of the donors was not anonymous and wanted to participate in raising the child? If so, briefly explain your answer. Also explain the position if the various parties' responsibilities and rights clash or compete with one another.

7. Does your country's law recognise all three parents in the case of a 'three-parent child' (as defined under the guidelines for special national rapporteurs)? If so, briefly explain your answer with specific reference to the legal responsibilities and rights conferred on each of the parents. Also explain the position if the various parents' responsibilities and rights clash or compete with one another.
8. Does your country's law recognise the parenthood of the surrogate, the biological parents and the intended parents in the case of surrogacy? If so, briefly explain your answer with specific reference to the legal responsibilities and rights conferred on each of the parents. Also explain the position if the various parties' responsibilities and rights clash or compete with one another.
9. Would your answers to any of the above questions have been different if the parties were involved in a same-sex relationship? Briefly explain your answer.
10. Does your country have, or plan to introduce, a general law that recognises multi-parenthood in a generic, broad manner, for example by stating which people can legally qualify as a child's parent and prescribing the maximum number of legal parents a child may have? If so, briefly explain the main provisions of the law or planned law.
11. Please provide any additional comments and information you consider important in respect of the diversity and plurality of family forms in your country.

PART B. DIVERSITY AND PLURALITY OF FAMILY'S FUNCTIONS

1. To which extent does your country's law recognise that the family may have various functions, including producing and raising children, protecting the vulnerable (i.e. women and children), providing economic security, and fulfilling caring functions?
2. Which of the functions is predominantly favoured by your country's law? Briefly explain your answer.
3. Does your country's law view the family's functions differently depending on whether children are present in the family? If so, does the view of your country's law as regards the family's functions differ depending on whether or not the children are step-children, biological children, children born as a result of donor-assisted reproductive technology, 'three-parent' children, or children born as a result of surrogacy? Briefly explain your answer.
4. Please provide any additional comments and information you consider important in respect of the diversity and plurality of the family's functions in your country.

QUESTIONNAIRE

Lignes directrices pour les rapporteurs spéciaux

La partie A du questionnaire qui suit examine la diversité et la pluralité des formes familiales, tandis que la partie B se rapporte aux fonctions de la famille. Veuillez mentionner votre droit national pour chaque question de chacune des parties en tenant compte de la constitution de votre pays (le cas échéant), de la législation et de la jurisprudence. Lorsque les lois internationales et régionales ont entraîné des changements ou des développements de votre droit national, merci de les indiquer.

Vous *n'avez pas* besoin d'aborder les sujets suivants:

- droit international privé ;
- droit médical ;
- droits culturels, religieux et des peuples originaux, etc. ;
- pluralisme juridique.

Comme les défis multiculturels en droit de la famille ont été au centre du 20ème Congrès de l'Académie internationale qui a eu lieu à Fukuoka (Japon, 2018), la partie A du questionnaire ne cherche pas à traiter de la multiplicité/pluralité des unions civils, culturels, indigènes et religieux. Elle se concentre sur la diversité et la pluralité des familles impliquant des enfants, en particulier les familles où les enfants ont plusieurs parents.

Pour mieux comparer, il nous faut, comme point de départ, une compréhension commune du sujet. À cette fin, les familles multi-parentales traitées par la partie A sont entendues comme :

- des familles recomposées où les enfants d'un ou de deux conjoints/partenaires sont élevés dans le même foyer ;
- des familles où les enfants sont élevés dans plus d'un foyer, par exemple parce que leurs parents exercent conjointement l'autorité parentale après la séparation ou n'ont jamais partagé un foyer mais partagent des responsabilités parentales ;
- des familles polygames où les enfants sont élevés dans un foyer où une partie a plus d'une femme/partenaire ;
- des familles d'adoption ouverte, c'est-à-dire des familles où des enfants ont été adoptés, mais qui conservent des liens (légaux ou de facto) avec leurs familles biologiques ;

- des familles où les enfants n'ont pas été adoptés mais vivent dans un foyer en termes de *kafala*. (La loi islamique ne permet pas l'adoption. Le concept islamique qui est le plus proche de la notion d'« adoption » est *kafala/kafalah*. Par le biais de *kafala*, une personne autre que le parent biologique de l'enfant s'engage, au terme de la loi islamique, à maintenir, éduquer, protéger et soigner un enfant comme un parent biologique, mais l'enfant n'est pas habilité à porter le nom de famille et ne devient pas automatiquement hériter de la personne qui a assumé la responsabilité de l'enfant) ;
- des familles où un enfant est né à la suite d'une technique de reproduction assistée à l'aide d'un donneur de gamètes, masculin ou féminin (c'est-à-dire, le sperme ou l'œuf/ovule) ;
- des familles où un enfant est né à la suite d'une technologie médicale dite « à trois parents ». (Cette technologie est similaire à la fécondation in vitro, mais utilise le matériel génétique de deux femmes et d'un homme, au lieu d'une seule femme et d'un homme. En règle générale, l'ADN de l'une des femmes est utilisé pour « corriger » l'ADN de l'autre femme afin d'éliminer les mutations génétiques qui causent des maladies héréditaires graves)[2] ;
- des familles où un enfant est né à la suite d'une gestation pour autrui.

QUESTIONNAIRE

PARTIE A. DIVERSITÉ ET PLURALITÉ DES FORMES FAMILIALES

1. La loi de votre pays reconnaît-elle la multiplicité de la parentalité dans le contexte de la famille recomposée ?
   (i) En particulier, la loi de votre pays confère-t-elle des responsabilités et des droits légaux à un beau-parent qui partage un foyer avec le parent de l'enfant ? Dans l'affirmative, le beau-parent a-t-il les mêmes responsabilités juridiques et les mêmes droits que le parent avec lequel le beau-parent partage un foyer ? Expliquez brièvement votre réponse. Expliquez également la situation si les responsabilités et les droits du parent et du beau parent s'affrontent ou se concurrencent les uns avec les autres.
   (ii) Si la loi de votre pays confère des responsabilités et des droits légaux à un beau-parent, le beau-parent a-t-il les mêmes responsabilités

---

[2] La technique a été utilisée, dans le Mexique, l'Ukraine, et le Royaume-Uni, et autres pays. Voir S. Reardon 'Reports of "three-parent babies" multiply', *Nature*, 19 octobre 2016; E. Callaway 'Historic decision allows UK researchers to trial "three person" babies', *Nature*, 15 décembre 2016; S. Reardon 'Genetic details of controversial "three-parent baby" revealed', *Nature*, 3 avril 2017.

juridiques et les mêmes droits que le parent avec lequel il *ne* partage pas un foyer ? (En d'autres termes, le beau-parent a-t-il les mêmes responsabilités juridiques et les mêmes droits que l'autre parent de l'enfant ?) Expliquez brièvement votre réponse. Expliquez également la situation si les responsabilités et les droits du parent et du beau parent s'affrontent ou se concurrencent les uns avec les autres.

2. La loi de votre pays, reconnaît-elle la multiplicité des parents si un enfant est élevé dans plus d'un foyer ? Le cas échéant, expliquez brièvement votre réponse en vous référant spécifiquement aux responsabilités et droits légaux conférés à chacun des parents. Expliquez également la situation si les responsabilités et les droits des différents parents se heurtent ou se concurrencent entre eux.

3. La loi de votre pays reconnaît-elle la multiplicité de la parentalité si un enfant est élevé dans une famille polygame ? Le cas échéant, expliquez brièvement votre réponse en vous référant spécifiquement aux responsabilités et droits légaux conférés à chacun des parents. Expliquez également la situation si les responsabilités et les droits des différents parents se heurtent ou se concurrencent entre eux.

4. La loi de votre pays reconnaît-elle la multiplicité des parents dans le cas d'une adoption ouverte (telle que définie dans les lignes directrices pour les rapporteurs spéciaux) ? Le cas échéant, expliquez brièvement votre réponse en vous référant spécifiquement aux responsabilités et droits légaux conférés à chacun des parents. Expliquez également la situation si les responsabilités et les droits des différents parents se heurtent ou se concurrencent entre eux.

5. La loi de votre pays reconnaît-elle la multiplicité de la parentalité dans le cas de la *kafala* (telle que définie dans les lignes directrices pour les rapporteurs spéciaux) ? Le cas échéant, expliquez brièvement votre réponse en faisant spécifiquement référence aux responsabilités et droits légaux conférés à chacune des parties. Expliquez également la situation si les responsabilités et les droits des différentes parties se heurtent ou se concurrencent entre eux.

6. (i) La loi de votre pays reconnaît-elle la parentalité de la mère biologique, de son conjoint/partenaire et du donneur si un enfant est né à la suite d'une technique de reproduction assistée à l'aide des gamètes dont les donneurs (homme ou femme) étaient anonymes ? Le cas échéant, expliquez brièvement votre réponse en faisant spécifiquement référence aux responsabilités et droits légaux conférés à chacune des parties. Expliquez également la situation si les responsabilités et les droits des différentes parties se heurtent ou se concurrencent entre eux.

   (ii) Votre réponse à la question 6(i) aurait-elle été différente si l'un (ou les deux) des donneurs n'étaient pas anonyme et voulait participer à

l'éducation de l'enfant ? Si oui, brièvement, expliquez votre réponse. Expliquez également la situation si les responsabilités et les droits des différentes parties se heurtent ou se concurrencent entre eux.
7. La loi de votre pays reconnaît-elle les trois parents dans le cas d'un « enfant de trois parents » (tel que défini dans les lignes directrices pour les rapporteurs spéciaux) ? Le cas échéant, expliquez brièvement votre réponse en vous référant spécifiquement aux responsabilités et droits légaux conférés à chacun des parents. Expliquez également la situation si les responsabilités et les droits des différents parents se heurtent ou se concurrencent entre eux.
8. La loi de votre pays reconnaît-elle la parentalité de la femme porteuse, des personnes biologiquement impliquées et les parents d'intention dans le cas de la gestation pour autrui ? Le cas échéant, expliquez brièvement votre réponse en vous référant spécifiquement aux responsabilités et droits légaux conférés à chacun des personnes. Expliquez également la situation si les responsabilités et les droits des différentes parties se heurtent ou se concurrencent entre eux.
9. Vos réponses à l'une des questions ci-dessus ont-elles été différentes si les parties étaient impliquées dans une relation de même sexe ? Expliquez brièvement votre réponse.
10. Votre pays a-t-il, ou envisage-t-il d'introduire une loi générale qui reconnaît la multiparentalité d'une manière générique et large, par exemple en précisant quelles personnes peuvent légalement se qualifier en tant que parent d'un enfant et prescrire le nombre maximum de parents légaux qu'un enfant peut avoir ? Le cas échéant, expliquez brièvement les principales dispositions de la loi ou de la loi prévue.
11. Veuillez fournir des commentaires et des informations supplémentaires que vous considérez importants en ce qui concerne la diversité et la pluralité des formes familiales dans votre pays.

PARTIE B. DIVERSITÉ ET PLURALITÉ DES FONCTIONS DE LA FAMILLE

1. Dans quelle mesure la loi de votre pays reconnaît-elle que la famille peut avoir diverses fonctions, y compris la procréation et l'éducation des enfants, la protection des personnes vulnérables (c'est-à-dire les femmes et les enfants), la sécurité économique et l'accomplissement des fonctions de soins.
2. Quelles fonctions sont principalement favorisées par la loi de votre pays ? Expliquez brièvement votre réponse.
3. La loi de votre pays considère-t-elle les fonctions de la famille différemment selon qu'il y a ou non des enfants ? Dans l'affirmative, la loi de votre pays,

en ce qui concerne les fonctions de la famille, diffère-t-elle selon que les enfants sont ou non des enfants biologiques, des enfants d'une famille recomposée, des enfants nés à la suite de la technologie reproductive assistée par donneur, des enfants issus de « trois parents » ou enfants nés à la suite de la gestation pour autrui ? Expliquez brièvement votre réponse.

4. Veuillez fournir les commentaires et les informations supplémentaires que vous estimez importants en ce qui concerne la diversité et la pluralité des fonctions de la famille dans votre pays.

INDEX

A

abortion/IVG   175
accords passés entre la mère des enfants et le père   320, *see also* agreement
accouchement sous anonymat   177, *see also* childbirth under anonymity
adoption (FR)   165, 203, *see also* adoption
   adoption coutumière autochtone   198–199
   adoption de l'enfant du conjoint   321
   adoption ouverte   326–327, 334–335, *see also* adoption, open
   adoption plénière   165, 197, 321
   adoption simple   165, 321, 327
adoption (ENG)   2, 4, 16–21, 30–32, 42, 104–106, 114–116, 119–122, 129, 132, 150–152, 165–166, 197–198, 203, 219, 228–234, 236, 240–241, 245, 253, 257, 276–279, 281–283, 295–296, 300, 308, 314, 321, 323, 326–327, 349–353, 355, 357, 361, 365–366, 383–387, 396, 404–405, 419–422, 425, 427, 429–430, 442–444, 446, 449–450, 459–466
   assistance after   166
   by intended parent   30–32, 203, 236, 240, 257, 357, 365–366
   by polygamous family   16, 404
   by same-sex couple   121–122, 150–151, 427, 465
   by step-parent   4, 17–18, 42, 114–116, 129, 151, 228, 236, 240–241, 245, 253, 277–278, 283–286, 295–296, 321, 350–353, 355, 361, 383, 396, 419–422
   contact after   17–20, 42, 104–105, 121, 150, 230–231, 253, 300, 350–351, 404, 442–443
   customary, *see* adoption, indigenous
   full   20, 42, 104–105, 150, 165, 197, 300, 321, 384–385
   indigenous   19, 35, 64, 197–199
   inheritance after   17–18, 105–106, 152, 350, 385, 387, 442, 461
   open   2, 17–21, 104–106, 119–122, 129, 132, 150, 219, 279, 300, 326, 349–351, 384, 386–387, 404–405, 429, 442–444, 450, 460
      definition   2, 17, 442
   plan   19, 120–121
   regular   18, 20, 349–352
   secondary duty of support   17–18, 20, 42, 104–105, 151–152, 350–351, 443–444
   sharing information after   120
   simple   4, 17, 104–106, 150, 165, 323, 327, 430
   special   349, 352, 365–366
   surname after   104, 121, 152
adoptive parent
   conflict with original parent   121, 351
agreed fatherhood conditions   25–26, 255, 257
agreement   171, 204
agreement between mother and step-parent   320
alternative dispute resolution   128
anonymat du donneur   167, *see also* assisted reproduction, anonymous donor
assisted reproduction   22–28, 41, 106, 113, 122–126, 130, 152–158, 167, 169, 194, 200–201, 204, 219–220, 228, 235–238, 242–243, 245, 247, 254–255, 260, 281–285, 294, 302–305, 308, 314–315, 328, 335, 356–363, 378, 387–392, 406–408, 423–426, 445–446, 449, 462–465
   anonymous donor   22, 24, 122–123, 156–157, 167, 235–237, 245, 255, 282, 304–305, 315, 362, 387–389, 425–426, 462–463
   donor   201, 328
   known donor   22–28, 122–124, 158, 219, 235, 237–238, 247, 254–255, 260, 282–283, 305, 362, 389–390, 407, 423–424, 445
   non-anonymous donor   24, 169, 235–237
   prohibition on   153
autodétermination   86, 173–176, 185, 187, *see also* autonomy
autonomy   39, 112, 173, 175

B

beau-parent   162, 191
best interest of the child   9, 12–13, 16–20, 26, 41, 95, 99, 104–105, 107, 114–118, 120–123, 126–127, 129, 132, 136, 139–140, 144–146, 151, 155, 175, 215–217, 230–231, 241, 246, 258, 260, 275–277, 279, 298–299, 306, 313–314, 329, 334, 336, 348, 360, 363, 384, 397–399, 401, 404–405, 407–408, 411–412, 415–416, 420, 425, 441, 459
biomedical matters/matière biomédicale   174
biological origin, *see* child, right to know origin
biological parents favoured   11, 117–118, 147
birth mother is legal mother/parent   23, 30–31, 41, 106, 108, 122–123, 125, 129–130, 155, 157–158, 168, 171, 201–202, 235–236, 239, 253–256, 267, 275, 281–282, 285, 287–288, 336, 357–359, 364, 388, 390, 402, 406, 411, 422, 425–426, 445–446, 462

Index

C

certificat de naissance/birth certificate 199, 330
child
  acknowledgement of 13, 24–25, 27, 30, 32, 41, 105, 158, 275, 282–286, 305, 362, 389, 419, 423, 426–427, 433, 445–446
  recognition of 446, *see also* child, acknowledgement of
  right to know origin 106, 123, 220, 283, 305, 315, 357, 359, 363, 463
child arrangements order 253–254, 260
childbirth under anonymity/l'anonymat au moment de l'accouchement 177, 329
child raised in more than one household 12–15, 101–104, 106–108, 116–119, 139, 144–149, 218–219, 275–277, 296–299, 322, 324, 386, 398–402, 422–428, 440–441, 457–458
conciliation 351
contrat 204
Convention 115, 127, 137, 139, 241, 274, 293, 313
  European 241, 274, 293
    on Human Rights 137, 139, 241, 274, 293, 320, 342
  on the Rights of the Child 115, 127, 313
Convention européenne des droits de l'homme 320, 342, *see also* Convention, European, on Human Rights
counselling 15, 218, 222
couples de même sexe 163, 319, 333, *see also* same-sex couples
Cour constitutionnelle/Constitutional Court 164, 169, 318, 332
Cour européenne des droits de l'homme 332, *see also* European Court of Human Rights
criminal law 341
culture 16, 18–19, 118–121, 130, 132, 402, 404, 429, 452

D

declaration of abandonment/déclaration d'abandon 326
deux parents au maximum 165, *see also* parent(s), maximum number
dignité humaine 331, *see also* human dignity
doivent être mis en balance 179
le don s'est réalisé de manière non anonyme 169, *see also* non-anonymous donor
les donneurs 201
droit de visiter 319, *see also* step-parent, contact with child

E

educational mandate/mandat d'éducation 372
education et entretien des enfants 180–182
l'enfant à trois parents 161, 329, *see also* three-parent child
l'enfant eleve dans plus d'un foyer 324, *see also* child raised in more than one household

equality
  principle/principe d'égalité 322
État prend en charge les personnes vulnérables 210
European Court of Human Rights 36, 137, 159, 241, 293, 295
European Court of Justice 138, 159
European Human Rights Convention, *see* Convention, European, on Human Rights
euthanasia/l'euthanasie 174
exercice de l'autorité parentale 371

F

familiar reunification/regroupement familial 325
famille polygame 325–326, *see also* family, polygamous
famille recomposée 163–165, 371–372, *see also* step-family
familles multiparentales 318–324, *see also* multiple-parent family
family 15–16, 36, 94, 109, 112–113, 119, 121, 130–131, 133, 137, 145, 212, 215, 219, 228, 233, 236–238, 241–242, 245–248, 262–263, 267, 283–285, 293, 299, 301, 308–310, 312–313, 315, 361, 366–367, 369, 386, 390–391, 394–396, 402–404, 411–412, 417–418, 420, 423–424, 426, 429–430, 435, 441–442, 444–447, 450, 458–459, 465
  branches of law protecting 36, 109–111, 430
  constitutional protection 212, 435, 447
  foster 444–445
  life 137, 293, 395, 420, 423–424, 447
  polygamous 15–16, 112, 119, 137, 219, 228, 285, 299, 386, 396, 402–404, 418, 429–430, 441–442, 458–459
  same-sex 94, 113, 121, 130–131, 133, 137, 145, 212, 215, 233, 236–238, 241–242, 245–248, 262–263, 267, 283–285, 301, 308–310, 312–313, 315, 361, 366–367, 369, 390–391, 394, 396, 411–412, 417–418, 426, 446, 450, 465
family function 35–40, 42–43, 111–112, 126–133, 138, 172–173, 176, 180, 183, 186, 210, 221–225, 242–248, 261–267, 271–275, 309–314, 339, 341–342, 366–369, 375, 378, 392–394, 413–416, 430–433, 447–449, 452, 466–470
  assistance after divorce 184
  caring 38–39, 43, 126–128, 222, 272–274, 369, 432–433, 448–449
  dominant 39–40, 43, 111–112, 126, 138, 224, 312, 369, 392–393, 414–415, 432–433, 469
  economic security 36–37, 40, 43, 111–112, 126, 128–129, 138, 183, 221–224, 243–245, 264–267, 272–274, 312, 339, 392, 414, 430–432, 448, 452, 467–468

Index

love and companionship   39–40, 43, 131, 221, 312–314, 392, 414
producing and raising children   37–40, 43, 111–112, 126–127, 129–131, 138, 180, 210–222, 242–243, 261–263, 271–274, 310, 339, 366–369, 392–394, 414, 447, 449, 452, 467–469
protecting vulnerable members   36–37, 43, 126, 186, 210, 221–225, 243–245, 248, 266–267, 272, 310–311, 341, 366–369, 431–432, 448–449, 467–469
role of children   40, 43, 129, 138–140, 274, 313–314, 375, 393–394, 415–416, 432, 449
sexual   261–263
father-swap   28, 158
filiation   179
fonctions de la famille   172–188, 339–342, 374–375, *see also* family function
protection des membres vulnérables   186, 341, *see also* family function, protecting vulnerable members
produire et élever des enfants   176, 210, 339, *see also* family function, producing and raising children
les fonctions de nature économique   339, *see also* family function, economic security
fonction économique des couples   183, *see also* family function, economic security
foreign birth certificate/acte de naissance étranger   338
foreign country   331
frais d'entretien   164

G
gender reassignment   131–133, 246, 465
genetic truth/vérité génétique   329
gestation pour autrui   162, 171–172, 178, 330–333, *see also* surrogacy
réalisée à l'étranger   330
interdit la gestation pour autrui   330, *see also* surrogacy, prohibited
a garde   192

H
human dignity   112, 395

I
identity/identité   176, 329
Indigenous kinship   132, *see also* culture
in loco parentis principle   6, 10, 51, 54, 191–193, 397
intention d'être les parents   194
intérêt de l'enfant/interest of the child   180, 192, 198, 320, 324, *see also* best interest of the child
intérêt supérieur de l'enfant   192, 198, 324, 329, 336, *see also* best interest of the child
international public policy   330
issue de trois parents   373, *see also* three-parent child

K
Kafala   3, 21, 42, 121, 138, 199, 219, 280, 301–302, 328, 335, 372, 387, 405–406, 430
definition   3

L
legal parenthood   14, 253, 259, 366, 422–423
distinguished from parental responsibility   253, 259, 366
split from parental responsibility   14, 422–423
loi pénale   341

M
mariage aux personnes de même sexe   174, 196, 333, *see also* same-sex marriage
la maternite de substitution   202–208
mediation   15, 103, 222, 297
la mère biologique est la mère légale   168, 201, 336, *see also* birth mother is legal mother
la mère légale de l'enfant/legal mother of the child   171
mother
intended/mère d'intention   336, *see also* parent, intended
multiparentalité   162, 339, *see also* multi-parent family
multiple-parent family   2, 34–35, 42, 106, 122, 162, 181, 193–194, 318, 339, 392, 412–413, 427–428, 450, 466
definition   2
general law recognising   34–35, 42, 106, 122, 392, 412–413, 450, 466
la multiparenté   193–195, *see also* multiple-parent family

N
nuclear family/famille nucléaire   318

O
obligation alimentaire après la rupture   184, 192, *see also* step-parent, duty of support
obligation de fournir des aliments   166, *see also* family function, economic security
ordre public international   330

P
parent(s)   4, 14, 27, 30–34, 37, 40–41, 95, 106, 108, 111, 124–126, 130, 153, 155, 161, 165, 171, 194, 225, 228, 236–237, 239–240, 243, 245–248, 252–260, 268, 274–275, 278, 284–285, 288, 294, 306–308, 315, 319, 330, 357, 364–367, 409–411, 413, 419–420, 422–425, 432, 445–446, 449, 465
intended   27, 30–33, 41, 108, 124–126, 130, 153, 155, 171, 194, 236, 240, 256–259, 284, 288, 306–308, 319, 330, 357, 364–366, 409–411, 413, 422–425, 445–446, 449, 465

Intersentia

483

Index

maximum number of   14, 27, 34, 41, 95, 106, 165, 225, 228, 237, 245–247, 252–260, 268, 275, 278, 285, 294, 315, 367, 413, 419–420, 422
social welfare benefits   37, 40, 111–112, 234–235, 243, 245, 248, 274, 432
parental order   32, 256–258
parental responsibilities   4–5, 7–8, 11–17, 26–27, 29–35, 37, 42, 97, 139, 141–149, 225, 237, 241, 294–297, 301, 308–309, 314, 345, 347, 396–404, 407–408, 413, 420–423, 425–426, 428, 433, 458
parental responsibilities after divorce   371
parental responsibilities and rights agreement   13, 206, 396–397, 399, 404, 407
parenté médicalement assistée   167–171, *see also* assisted reproduction
parenting order   31, 114, 117–118, 122–123, 126, 130
parenting plan   12, 15, 401–402
parent related by marriage   4, 94
   definition   94
parents d'intention   171, 206, 319, 330, *see also* parent, intended
parents ne partageant pas le foyer   322–324, *see also* child raised in more than one household
parent sociale   319
partenaires de même sexe   322, *see also* adoption, by same-sex couple
partner-guardianship   215–216
paternity   23–24, 28, 33, 41, 157, 168, 171, 203, 220, 307, 345–346, 357–363, 365–366, 388–389, 445–446
   acknowledgement of   28, 157, 220, 345–346, 357–358, 361–363, 365–366, 388–389
   presumption of   23–24, 33, 41, 168, 171, 203, 220, 307, 359–360, 365, 388–389, 445–446
personal development/développement personnel   173
pluriparentalité   181, 193, *see also* multiple-parent family
polygamy/polygamie   195, 334, *see also* family, polygamous
présomption de paternité   171, 203, *see also* paternity, presumption of
prévoit la nullité   202, *see also* surrogacy, prohibited
procréation assistée   194, 200, 328, 373, *see also* assisted reproduction
la protection des enfants   175
proportionality principle   179

R
responsabilité parentale   320, *see also* parental responsibilities

S
same-sex couple   163, 319, 333
same-sex marriage   174, 196, 333
shared custody/garde partagée   323

sole custody/garde exclusive   323
son épouse sera présumé(e) être le père   168, *see also* paternity, presumption of
step-child   10, 94, 295, 379, 381–382, 455
   inheritance rights   10, 94, 295, 379, 381–382, 455
step-family   163–165
step-parent   4–12, 42, 93–104, 114–116, 140–149, 162, 164, 191–192, 213–218, 225, 228–234, 248, 253–254, 260, 277–279, 294–296, 315, 319, 351–355, 378–387, 396–398, 418–422, 436–440, 450, 452–457
   as foster parent   145–147
   assists spouse/partner   8, 11, 93, 96, 141–144, 225, 436–437
   conflict with parent   11–12, 93, 95–96, 142, 146, 148–149, 217–218, 351, 353, 379, 398, 421–422, 438–439, 457
   contact with child   9–10, 42, 214–215, 217, 233–234, 248, 279, 295, 319, 352, 438
   decision-making power of   8–9, 95–97, 192, 214, 217, 231, 278, 295
   definition   114, 213, 452
   duty of support   6–7, 11, 42, 93, 98–101, 115, 142, 164, 192, 213, 225, 232, 278, 352, 354–355, 380–381, 397, 419, 421, 439
   house rules   8, 440
   inheritance rights of   10, 94, 295, 379, 381, 455
   liability for step-child's act   11, 101, 456
   parental responsibilities   420
   presiding or testifying in case involving step-child   9, 382–383
   rights conferred by   42
   social welfare benefits   147, 232, 234, 352
super sole custody/garde super-exclusive   323
Supreme Court/Cour suprême   318
surrogacy   26, 29–34, 41, 108–109, 125–126, 130, 132, 154–155, 162, 171, 178, 202, 220–221, 228, 236, 238–242, 245, 247–249, 256–259, 281–282, 287–288, 294, 306–308, 315, 330–331, 356–359, 363–366, 378, 390–391, 394, 409–411, 424–428, 436, 445–446, 450, 462–465
   altruistic   30, 32, 202, 288, 462–463
   commercial   32, 125–126, 132, 240–241, 248, 464
   intended parent   410
   not regulated   31, 33, 108, 378, 390, 424
   permitted   32, 126, 238, 306, 409, 462–463
   prohibited   26, 29, 154–155, 202, 220, 281–282, 287, 330, 356–357, 363, 436, 445–446, 450
   projects   162

T
three-parent child   3, 28–29, 41, 124–125, 132, 155–156, 161, 236, 245, 305–306, 329, 390, 408–409, 446, 449, 463
   definition   3
transmission de la richesse   342

ABOUT THE EDITORS

JACQUELINE HEATON is a professor who lectures Family Law at the University of South Africa. She is a former editor of the South African Law Journal and the Annual Survey of South African Law. She was also guest editor of Speculum Juris – Special Issue on Family Law: 2009 (2), published in 2010. She is the author/co-author of more than 30 books (some of which are in their 6th edition) and many articles in law journals, as well as editor/co-editor of three books.

AIDA KEMELMAJER is a former judge of the Supreme Court of Mendoza, Argentina and a former professor of the Universidad Nacional de Cuyo, Argentina. She is an author/co-author of more than 30 books and was a member of the commission that prepared the draft of the Civil and Commercial Code of the Argentinian Republic. She is *doctor honoris causa* of various universities in France, Argentina, and Peru, as well as Professor in many Law and Judiciary Schools of Latin America.

ABOUT THE SERIES

As globalisation proceeds, the significance of the comparative approach in legal scholarship increases. The IACL / AIDC with almost 800 members is the major universal organisation promoting comparative research in law and organising congresses with hundreds of participants in all parts of the world. The results of those congresses should be disseminated and be available for legal scholars in a single book series which would make both the Academy and its contribution to comparative law more visible. The series aims to publish the scholarship emerging from the congresses of IACL / AIDC, including: 1. of the General Congresses of Comparative Law, which take place every 4 years (Brisbane 2002, Utrecht 2006, Washington 2010, Vienna 2014, Fukuoka 2018 etc.) and which generate (a) one volume of General Reports edited by the local organisers of the Congress; (b) up to 30 volumes of selected thematic reports dealing with the topics of the single sections of the congress and containing the General Report as well as the Special Reports (national and non-national) of that section; these volumes would be edited by the General Rapporteurs of the respective sections; 2. the volumes containing selected contributions to the smaller (2-3 days) thematic congresses which take place between the International Congresses (Mexico 2008, Taipei 2012, Montevideo 2016 etc.); these congresses have a general theme such as "Codification" or "The Enforcement of Law" and will be edited by the local organisers of the respective Congress. All publications may contain contributions in English and French, the official languages of the Academy.

More information about this series at: https://intersentia.com/en/product/series/show/id/53076/

Académie Internationale de Droit Comparé
International Academy of Comparative Law

Printed in the USA
CPSIA information can be obtained
at www.ICGtesting.com
LVHW070537060224
770970LV00003B/52